Foundations of
Comparative Politics

To our most important students: Meaghan, Brian, Liam, Cameron, and Sean.

Sara Miller McCune founded SAGE Publishing in 1965 to support the dissemination of usable knowledge and educate a global community. SAGE publishes more than 1000 journals and over 800 new books each year, spanning a wide range of subject areas. Our growing selection of library products includes archives, data, case studies and video. SAGE remains majority owned by our founder and after her lifetime will become owned by a charitable trust that secures the company's continued independence.

Los Angeles | London | New Delhi | Singapore | Washington DC | Melbourne

Foundations of Comparative Politics

William Roberts Clark

Texas A&M University

Matt Golder

Pennsylvania State University

Sona Nadenichek Golder

Pennsylvania State University

FOR INFORMATION:

CQ Press

An Imprint of SAGE Publications, Inc.

2455 Teller Road

Thousand Oaks, California 91320

E-mail: order@sagepub.com

SAGE Publications Ltd.

1 Oliver's Yard

55 City Road

London, EC1Y 1SP

United Kingdom

SAGE Publications India Pvt. Ltd.

B 1/I 1 Mohan Cooperative Industrial Area

Mathura Road, New Delhi 110 044

India

SAGE Publications Asia-Pacific Pte. Ltd.

3 Church Street

#10–04 Samsung Hub

Singapore 049483

Library of Congress Cataloging-in-Publication Data

Names: Clark, William Roberts, 1962- author. | Golder, Matt, author. | Golder, Sona Nadenichek, author.

Title: Foundations of comparative politics / William Roberts Clark, Matt Golder, Sona Nadenichek Golder.

Description: Thousand Oaks, California : CQ Press/SAGE, [2018] | Includes bibliographical references and index.

Identifiers: LCCN 2018019762 | ISBN 9781506360737 (paperback)

Subjects: LCSH: Comparative government. | Democracy.

Classification: LCC JF51 .C52 2018 | DDC 320.3–dc23 LC record available at https://lccn.loc.gov/2018019762

Acquisitions Editor: Scott Greenan

Content Development Editor: Scott Harris

Editorial Assistant: Sarah Christensen

Marketing Manager: Erica DeLuca

Production Editor: Veronica Stapleton Hooper

Copy Editor: Gretchen Treadwell

Typesetter: Hurix Digital

Proofreader: Dennis W. Webb

Indexer: Joan Shapiro

Cover Designer: Candice Harman

18 19 20 21 22 10 9 8 7 6 5 4 3 2 1

BRIEF CONTENTS

PART IV • VARIETIES OF DEMOCRACY AND POLITICAL OUTCOMES

DETAILED CONTENTS

PART III • VARIETIES OF DEMOCRACY AND DICTATORSHIP

PART IV • VARIETIES OF DEMOCRACY AND POLITICAL OUTCOMES

PREFACE

In 2009, we published the first edition of *Principles of Comparative Politics*. Our goal was to (1) introduce students to the major questions in comparative politics, (2) acquaint them with the field's best answers to those questions, and (3) give them the tools to think critically about the answers. At the time, our book marked quite a radical departure from the typical comparative politics textbook. Most introductory texts were organized around a sequence of individual country studies that usually included some combination of Britain, France, Germany, Russia, Japan, India, Brazil, Nigeria, China, and Mexico. In our opinion, the country-focused approach to teaching comparative politics had some obvious limitations if the goal of an introductory class was to teach something other than descriptive information about a tiny fraction of the world's countries. *Principles* took a very different approach and instead focused on the research questions that comparative scholars have historically considered to be vitally important. It's undeniable that the causes and consequences of democracy and dictatorship have been, and continue to be, foundational to the study of comparative politics. It's for this reason that questions related to democracy and dictatorship were front and center in our book.

In the last decade, the comparative politics textbook market has changed quite a bit, and in ways we're pleased to see. While there continue to be books that teach comparative politics through a sequence of independent country studies, many others have followed our lead and adopted a more thematic approach to comparative politics. Indeed, several books have adopted a very similar thematic structure to that found in *Principles*. *Principles* remains unique, though, in its focus on the scientific approach to studying politics and its emphasis on giving students the methodological tools with which to critically evaluate competing claims in the existing literature. In the course of addressing various political phenomena, for example, the latest edition of *Principles* (2017) shows students how to solve a variety of game-theoretic models, how to evaluate one-dimensional and two-dimensional spatial models, how to think through principal-agent models, how to interpret simple statistical results, and much more. Compared to other texts, *Principles* is also unique in the level of detail it provides about different political regimes and institutions. Regimes and institutions, like dictatorships and electoral rules, differ along multiple dimensions, and *Principles* seeks to illustrate this diversity and show how these differences can influence real-world outcomes.

While we believe that *Principles* is an important contribution to the comparative politics textbook market, we recognize that not all students and faculty desire, or even need, the level of detail and emphasis on methods found in that book. This is why we've written *Foundations of Comparative Politics*. Like *Principles*, the new book introduces students to the major questions in comparative politics and acquaints students with the field's best answers to those questions. Where *Foundations* is different is that it discusses this substantive content without relying on, or introducing students to, specific methodological techniques such as game theory and statistical analysis. Rather than discuss in detail the myriad different ways in which political systems vary from one another, *Foundations* concentrates on describing the core features of regimes and institutions and on analysing how these fundamental attributes drive variation in the economic and political outcomes we care about most. By grappling with these essential characteristics of regimes and institutions, students develop a deep understanding of the foundational principles of comparative politics. A consequence of these changes is that *Foundations* is considerably shorter than its "parent" book, making it easier for students to cover all of the material, whether they're on a semester system or a quarter system.

Despite these changes, *Foundations* remains quite different from its competitors. Although the emphasis on methodological tools is gone, the book retains its focus on the scientific approach to studying politics. We still devote a chapter to discussing science and the scientific method. The lessons learned in this chapter reappear throughout the book as we survey the latest research in comparative politics and examine competing theoretical claims for their logical consistency and empirical accuracy. Most books that adopt a thematic approach to comparative politics content themselves with summarizing the main findings from comparative scholars with regard to particular topics. While *Foundations* also seeks to convey the main findings in the comparative politics literature, it also devotes considerable time to explaining exactly *why* these findings hold and examining the extent to which a scholarly consensus exists in support of these findings. Rather than treat the different "themes" or "topics" in the book as completely independent, *Foundations* also seeks to highlight the inherent interdependencies that exist between them. Thus, the theories and empirical results presented in one chapter are often used in later chapters to examine and explain other political phenomena. In this way, there's a steady accumulation of theoretical and empirical knowledge through the book.

Foundations of Comparative Politics is organized around a set of questions related to democracy and dictatorship that scholars have been asking repeatedly for many years:

- What is the state, and where did it come from?

- Why are some states democratic and others authoritarian?

- Are some cultures incompatible with democracy?

- Do natural resources and foreign aid help or hinder democracy?

- How can we explain democratic transitions?

- What explains the different types of dictatorships we observe in the world?

- Are people materially better off in democracies or dictatorships?

- Is the decision-making process in democracies normatively superior to that in dictatorships?

- How do institutions influence who gets to rule and with what consequences?

- Why do some countries have many parties whereas others have only a few?

- Are there institutional solutions to ethnic conflict?

- How do political institutions influence the quality of political representation?

- Do parliamentary or presidential democracies last longer and why?

The types of research questions we're interested in addressing in *Foundations* can't be answered by examining individual countries. Very few countries exhibit sufficient variation across time with their experiences of democracy to allow questions about democracy's causes and consequences to be answered by a single country study. Similarly, very few countries have experienced sufficient variation in their institutions across time to give us much leverage in gaining an understanding of their causes and consequences. This is one of the reasons why we adopt an explicitly cross-national approach to comparative politics in *Foundations*. It's only by making comparisons across countries that we can obtain the necessary variation to address the types of research questions that motivate our book. We believe that this general cross-national approach at the introductory level provides students with a useful foundation for taking upper-level courses that focus on a particular country or region. This is because it provides an overarching theoretical and empirical framework within which students can seek to situate and better understand specific cases.

Although our book differs in content and approach from other comparative politics text-books, we do appreciate the usefulness of textbook features that genuinely assist the reader in digesting and applying the ideas presented. To that end, we present overviews at the beginning of every chapter that help orient the reader toward each chapter's main goals. To establish a common understanding of the most important concepts we discuss, we provide a list of key terms along with their definitions at the end of each chapter. We have schematized a great deal of our data and information in tables, charts, and maps, thereby allowing students to better visualize the issues and arguments at hand. In this regard, we'd like to thank Charles Crabtree for his help and patience in producing many of our maps.

A set of online resources for students and instructors accompanies this book. A free student companion website at **edge.sagepub.com/foundationscp1e** features quiz questions, flashcards, and links to important data for further research. Finally, to help instructors "tool up," we offer a set of downloadable resources, materials we've developed for our own classes over the years. These include test bank questions, lecture slides, downloadable graphics from the book and more.

ACKNOWLEDGMENTS

We gratefully acknowledge the suggestions we've received from the many reviewers of this project:

Moises Arce, *University of Missouri*

Carolina De Miguel, *University of Toronto*

Suzanne L. Disheroon, *Cedar Valley College*

Olufunmbi Elemo, *James Madison College, Michigan State University*

Clay R. Fuller, *American Enterprise Institute*

Christopher Muste, *University of Montana*

Saul Newman, *American University*

J. Alejandro Tirado-Alcaraz, *Rhode Island School of Design*

Before closing, we'd like to thank the entire team at CQ Press working with us on this book. Scott Greenan, Veronica Stapleton Hooper, and Elise Frasier were all one could hope for in editors: insightful, patient, critical, encouraging, and honest coaches. We appreciate their efforts to keep the book moving forward. Gretchen Treadwell did a wonderful job of copyediting the manuscript. Sarah Christensen served as editorial assistant and did a terrific job helping us find photographs and maps.

ABOUT THE AUTHORS

William Roberts Clark is the Charles Puryear Professor of Liberal Arts in the department of political science at Texas A&M University. He is the author of *Capitalism, Not Globalism,* and his articles have appeared in the *American Political Science Review,* the *British Journal of Political Science, Comparative Political Studies, Political Analysis, International Organization,* and *European Union Politics,* among other journals. He has taught at a wide variety of public and private schools, including William Paterson College, Rutgers University, Georgia Tech, Princeton, New York University, the University of Essex, the University of Michigan, and Texas A&M University.

Matt Golder is Professor of Political Science at Pennsylvania State University. His articles have appeared in the *American Journal of Political Science,* the *Journal of Politics,* the *British Journal of Political Science,* the *Annual Review of Political Science, Political Analysis, Comparative Political Studies,* and *Electoral Studies,* among other journals. He has taught classes on comparative politics, quantitative methods, game theory, and European politics at the University of Iowa, Florida State University, the University of Essex, and Pennsylvania State University.

Sona Nadenichek Golder is Professor of Political Science at Pennsylvania State University. She is the author of *The Logic of Pre-Electoral Coalition Formation* and *Multi-Level Electoral Politics: Beyond the Second-Order Election Model.* Her articles have appeared in the *American Journal of Political Science,* the *Journal of Politics, Comparative Political Studies, Political Analysis, Politics & Gender,* and the *British Journal of Political Science,* among other journals. She has taught courses on game theory, political institutions, comparative politics, and quantitative analysis at Florida State University, the University of Essex, and Pennsylvania State University.

INTRODUCTION

My purpose is to consider if, in political society, there can be any legitimate and sure principle of government, taking men as they are, and laws as they might be. I shall try always to bring together what right permits with what interest prescribes so that justice and utility are in no way divided.

Jean-Jacques Rousseau, *The Social Contract*

OVERVIEW

1. Political science is the study of politics in a scientific manner. Whereas international politics is the study of politics predominantly between countries, comparative politics is the study of politics predominantly within countries.

2. In this chapter, we outline the central questions in comparative politics that form the focus of this book. These questions are all related to the causes and consequences of democracy and dictatorship, as well as to the tremendous variety of democratic and dictatorial institutions we observe in the world.

3. We also discuss why we adopt an explicitly cross-national approach to introduce students to the study of comparative politics.

On December 17, 2010, twenty-six-year-old Mohamed Bouazizi set fire to himself to protest his treatment by local officials who had confiscated the produce he had gone into debt to sell on the streets of Sidi Bouzid, Tunisia. While permits are not needed to sell produce on the streets of Sidi Bouzid, police and local officials had been harassing Bouazizi—apparently in attempts to extract bribes—ever since he left high school as a teenager to help feed his extended family. On this day, the police also confiscated the electronic scales that Bouazizi used to weigh the fruit he sold and, by some accounts, beat him and made slurs against his deceased father. Bouazizi appealed to the local governor's office and, when ignored, stood in traffic outside the governor's office, doused himself with gasoline, and lit himself on fire. He died—having survived eighteen days in a coma—on January 5, 2011. In the weeks that followed Bouazizi's self-immolation, mass protests, in which scores of demonstrators were killed, spread from his hometown to the capital city, Tunis. On January 15, after controlling the country for almost a quarter of a century, President Zine al-Abidine Ben Ali was forced to flee to Saudi Arabia, making him the first Arab leader in generations to leave office in response to public protests.

Over the next few months, expressions of discontent spread across the Middle East and North Africa (MENA) region. The first signs of contagion came in mid-January in the form of self-immolations in Egypt and Algeria, but in the following weeks mass protests would be held in more than a dozen countries across the region. For example, on January 23, protests spread to Yemen where thousands took to the streets in support of Tawakul Karman, an activist who was jailed after she called for an end to President Ali Abdullah's thirty-two-year control of the country. Organized protests, coordinated through social networking sites such as Facebook and Twitter, occurred across Egypt on January 25. In the weeks that followed, the Egyptian military showed a marked reluctance to open fire on protesters. Despite this, many protesters were injured or killed, frequently in clashes with bands of pro-regime thugs. Protesters were not placated when President Hosni Mubarak, who had ruled Egypt longer than any modern Egyptian leader, first fired his cabinet and then promised to step down before elections in the fall. Mubarak eventually resigned on February 11 and was tried and found guilty of corruption. On February 16, protests erupted in Libya—a month after Libyan leader Muammar al-Qaddafi had gone on television to bemoan the ouster of Tunisian president Zine al-Abidine Ben Ali. Within a few weeks, mass protests had turned into a full-scale insurrection that was aided by North Atlantic Treaty Organization (NATO) air strikes. On February 25, protests referred to as a "day of rage" occurred throughout the MENA region. In March government crackdowns on protesters in both Saudi Arabia and Syria followed these protests. By the end of March 2011, significant protests, frequently accompanied by violent government crackdowns, had occurred in seventeen countries throughout the Middle East and North Africa.

The fact that at least some of these popular movements led to the removal of long-standing dictators raised the prospect that we might be observing the beginning of a wave of liberalization, perhaps even a new wave of democratization, in a region that has long been dominated by resilient authoritarian regimes. A brief look at history, though, suggests that such optimism may have been unwarranted.

Beginning with a revolt in Palermo, Sicily, in January 1848, a wave of nearly fifty revolts spread across Europe, challenging dynasties that had ruled for decades in France, Austria, Prussia, and almost all of the lesser known states in Germany and Italy. This revolutionary period is known as the Spring of Nations. As with the 2011 Arab Spring, some of Europe's leaders were forcibly removed from power, some went into exile when their armies refused to fire on protesting citizens, and some used the coercive power of the state to put down rebellions. In many ways, the rebellions of 1848 shared a common set of causes with the revolts of 2011. For example, rapid changes in social structure brought about by the Industrial Revolution gave middle-class groups new power, often in coalition with working-class groups who were newly mobilized by economic crises. In many countries, rulers attempted to placate the masses by firing unpopular ministers, promising constitutional reforms, and adopting universal male suffrage. Although the rebellions often had local antecedents, they tended to share the goal of wresting power from the nobility and vesting authority in constitutional republics dedicated to the protection of individual liberties. In Frankfurt, for instance, a parliament known as the Frankfurt National Assembly wrote a constitution for what it declared to be the German Empire—a constitutional monarchy founded on eloquently expressed nineteenth-century liberal ideals including democracy and national unity.

Such changes brought about a wave of euphoria expressing the hope that government was finally going to be put under the control of the people. Tyrants were to be sent packing, and rational self-rule was to replace tradition and prejudice. National self-determination movements would produce self-rule for oppressed groups long under the thumb of monarchies such as the Habsburg Empire. In nearly all instances, though, the hope the 1848 Spring of Nations produced had turned to disappointment and recrimination by the autumn. A chilling example can be found in Austria, where the emperor's military forces, which had been cooperating with the "constituent assembly" formed in Vienna, put down the "October Rising" (the third wave of radical insurrection that year) by bombarding and then occupying the city. The constituent assembly was exiled, and many radical leaders were executed on the spot. Although Emperor Ferdinand I was convinced to step down, ceding his throne to his nephew Francis Joseph I, little else had changed. In the words of the historian Charles Breunig (1971, 1012), "to all intents and purposes the revolution in Vienna had been defeated by October, 1848."

The reversal reformers in Vienna suffered was not unusual. By April 1849, the answer to the question that Tsar Nicholas I had posed to Queen Victoria—"What remains standing in Europe?"—was not, as he had suggested a year earlier, "Great Britain and Russia" but, instead, "almost everything." Revolution had swiftly been followed by reaction. Political reforms that seemed promising turned out, in practice, to change little (at least in the short term). Power remained vested in largely the same hands as before the revolutions of the previous spring.

In the immediate aftermath of the Arab Spring, some of us emphasized that the optimism expressed by many observers at the time should be tempered by an understanding that "democratic" revolutions, like those in the 1848 Spring of Nations, are often followed by reaction and repression. We argued that regime change and political reform are difficult to predict, but that an understanding of such political change can be enhanced by the knowledge of the economic and cultural determinants of democracy, the strategic interaction between autocratic rulers and reform-minded opposition groups, the institutional determinants of policy outcomes in autocracies and democracies, and the effect of constitutional design on democratic consolidation, party competition, fiscal policy, and ethnic conflict.

Since 2012, comparative politics scholars have attempted to explain why the Arab Spring has not blossomed into a new wave of democracy. Of the fourteen countries that experienced widespread uprisings in 2011, only three—Egypt, Tunisia, and Yemen—have seen an incumbent autocrat removed as a result of domestic political pressure.[1] And of the three countries that saw an incumbent autocrat removed, only Tunisia has made progress toward becoming a democracy. Brownlee, Masoud, and Reynolds (2015) argue that the authoritarian regimes in the MENA region were, for the most part, able to withstand widespread uprisings because so many of them had significant oil wealth and systems of hereditary rule. They claim that oil wealth and hereditary rule "were each individually sufficient for authoritarian continuity—unless external powers intervened

---

[1]The removal of Muammar al-Qaddafi from his position as leader of Libya in 2011 was heavily reliant on foreign intervention. It was only thanks to the sustained aerial bombing campaign conducted by NATO forces as part of Operation Unified Protector that Libyan rebels were able to topple Gaddafi.

Christopher Furlong/Getty Images

Tunisian protesters demand the removal from office of government ministers associated with the ousted president in front of the ruling party's headquarters in Tunis on January 20, 2011.

on behalf of the opposition" (p. 61). Importantly, the reasons why oil wealth and hereditary rule might help dictatorial leaders fend off challenges from below have been well understood by comparative politics scholars for some time, as evidenced by the discussion of the "resource curse" in Chapter 5 and the consequences of monarchy in Chapter 8 of this book.

Every generation seems to have its own motivation for studying comparative politics. The unfortunate truth is that each generation seems beset by a problem that is both devastatingly complex and extraordinarily urgent. For example, the Great Depression and the rise of fascism in Europe compelled comparative politics scholars in the middle of the last century to address two important topics. The first was what governments can and should do to encourage stable economic growth. In other words, what, if anything, can governments do to protect their citizens from the devastating consequences of market instability? The second was how to design electoral institutions in such a way as to reduce the likelihood that political extremists who oppose democracy, like the Nazi Party in Germany's Weimar Republic, might be elected. Both of these topics remain central to the field of comparative politics today.

In the aftermath of World War II, decolonization and the onset of the Cold War combined to drive many comparative politics scholars to focus on the question of "political development." What, if anything, could be done to reduce political and economic instability in poor and underdeveloped countries? Research conducted at that time frequently focused on the proper relationship between the government and the market, with the central concerns of the day perhaps being best summarized in the title of Joseph Schumpeter's 1942 classic *Capitalism, Socialism, and Democracy*. The Cold War between the United States and the Soviet Union only heightened the urgency with

BOX 1.1 WHAT IS COMPARATIVE POLITICS?

Traditionally, the field of comparative politics has been characterized by many related, but distinct, endeavors. An influential comparative politics textbook by Joseph LaPalombara (1974) is titled *Politics within Nations*. LaPalombara's title distinguishes **comparative politics** from **international politics**, which Hans Morgenthau (1948) famously calls *Politics among Nations*. This definition of comparative politics, with its complementary definition of international politics, has one of the desirable features of all good scientific typologies in that it's logically exhaustive. By defining comparative and international politics in this way, these scholars have exhausted the logical possibilities involved in the study of politics—political phenomena occur either within countries or between countries.

Still, all good scientific typologies should also be mutually exclusive. Whereas logical exhaustion implies that we have a place to categorize every entity that's observed, mutual exclusivity requires that it not be possible to assign any single observation to more than one category. Unfortunately, the typology just presented doesn't satisfy mutual exclusivity. A quick glance at today's newspapers clearly reveals that many contemporary political issues contain healthy doses of both "within country" and "between country" factors. As a consequence, the line between comparative and international politics is often blurred. This is particularly the case when it comes to studying how politics and economics interact. For example, ask yourself whether it's possible to fully understand American trade policy, say, toward China, without taking account of US domestic politics or to fully understand the ongoing crisis in the Euro zone without taking into account the domestic political situation in Greece. Similarly, many environmental issues involve factors both within and across a country's borders. In addition, because many violent antistate movements receive support from abroad, it's hard to categorize the study of revolutions, terrorism, and civil war as being solely in the domain of either comparative or international

politics. Indeed, many insurgency movements have a separatist component that raises the very question of where the boundary between the "domestic" and "international" should lie.

Nonetheless, it's possible to retain the basic insights of LaPalombara and Morgenthau by simply saying that comparative politics is the study of political phenomena that are predominantly within country relationships, and that international politics is the study of political phenomena that are predominantly between country relationships. This view of comparative politics, and political science more generally, is illustrated in Figure 1.1. As you can see, international politics addresses things like conflict, foreign policy, and international organizations that shape the relationships between countries. In contrast, comparative politics focuses on issues such as party systems, elections, identity politics, and interest group relations within countries like Brazil, China, France, and Nigeria. Scholars interested in political economy issues, such as migration, trade, central bank independence, and exchange rate policy, cross the divide between international and comparative politics.

Students in the United States may wonder where American politics fits into this description. In most political science departments in the United States, American politics is considered a separate subfield. Does the fact that American politics focuses predominantly on politics within the United States mean that it should be considered part of comparative politics? This is a question that, for some reason, generates quite heated debate among political scientists. Historically, a second traditional definition of comparative politics has been that it is the study of politics in every country except the one in which the student resides. Thus, according to this definition, comparative politics is the study of what economists often like to call "the rest of the world." This definition, however, seems rather silly to us because it means that the study of Nigerian politics is part of comparative politics unless one happens to be

(Continued)

(Continued)

FIGURE 1.1   ■   **One View of Political Science**

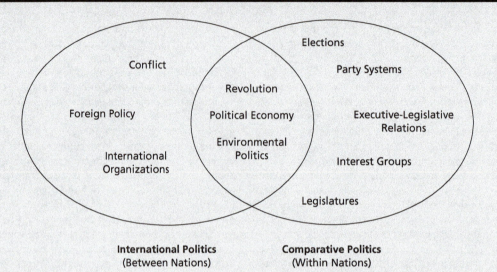

Conflict

Foreign Policy

International
Organizations

Revolution

Political Economy

Environmental
Politics

Elections

Party Systems

Executive-Legislative
Relations

Interest Groups

Legislatures

International Politics
(Between Nations)

Comparative Politics
(Within Nations)

studying it in Nigeria, in which case it's simply "Nigerian politics." We leave it up to you to decide whether you think American politics should be considered part of comparative politics or not.

In addition to the two definitions just outlined, comparative politics has sometimes been defined as the study of politics using the method of comparison. This tradition, which dates back at least as far as Aristotle's attempt to classify constitutional forms, seeks to answer questions about politics by comparing and contrasting attributes of different polities (predominantly city-states in Aristotle's day but nation-states today). Although this third definition is, to some extent, descriptively accurate, it's not particularly useful. As we show in Chapter 2, comparison is central to any and all scientific endeavors. As a result, defining comparative politics in terms of a "comparative" method would make it synonymous with political science itself. If this is the case, it makes one wonder why there are two phrases—*comparative politics* and *political science*—to describe the same thing.

We believe that comparative politics is best understood as the study of politics occurring predominantly within countries. As such, it's a rather vast field of research. For reasons we explain later in this chapter, we choose not to focus on the politics of a single nation or a particular collection of nations in this book. Instead, we try to understand political behavior through the explicit comparison of important national-level attributes. In other words, we compare domestic political behavior from a cross-national perspective. As an example of our approach, we prefer to ask why some countries have two parties (like the United States) but others have many (like the Netherlands) rather than examine the party systems in the United States and the Netherlands separately. By taking this approach, we don't mean to suggest that the study of politics within individual countries should be excluded from the field of comparative politics. Nor do we mean to imply that cross-national comparison is a more worthy endeavor than studying a single country. Having said that, we believe that a comparison of national-level attributes is a reasonable introduction to comparative politics and one that will set a broad framework for the closer study of politics within individual polities at an advanced level.

which scholars struggled to understand the causes and consequences of communist revolutions like those in China and Cuba, as well as the political turmoil that existed in places like Vietnam and Chile.

By the 1970s, economic instability, brought on by the Middle East oil crisis, returned to wealthy industrial countries. As a result, many comparative politics scholars revisited questions raised during the interwar years on their home turf of Western Europe. By now, however, the discussion had been narrowed somewhat because many scholars had come to accept the "postwar settlement" or "class compromise" that had essentially seen workers accept a capitalist economy and free trade in return for the expansion of the welfare state and other benefits. With the widespread acceptance of capitalist economies across Western Europe, researchers now turned their attention to how the specific variety of capitalism that existed in a particular country might influence that country's capacity to weather economic storms created elsewhere.

In the waning days of the twentieth century, attention turned to the fallout created by the end of the Cold War. Suddenly, dozens of countries in Eastern and Central Europe were negotiating the twin transitions from centrally planned economies to market-based ones and from one-party dictatorships to democracy. Now, in the twenty-first century, attention appears to be turning to the question of state authority. The Islamic State in Iraq and the Levant (ISIL), alternatively known as the Islamic State in Iraq and Syria (ISIS), proclaimed a worldwide caliphate in June 2014. In effect, ISIL now claims religious, political, and military authority over Muslims wherever they live in the world. Such a claim is a direct challenge to the primary organizing principle of the international system—sovereign states—that has been operative since the Peace of Westphalia in 1648. At the time of writing, ISIL controls portions of Iraq and Syria, and has imposed Sharia law on the millions of people who live in these regions. The ensuing persecution, chaos, and violence, in combination with the fallout from the Syrian Civil War, have led many to flee the region, causing an immigration crisis in Europe.

As we discuss in Chapter 4, the "modern state" is understood as an organization that uses coercion and the threat of force to control the inhabitants in a given territory. ISIL's declaration of a worldwide caliphate, and, indeed, the behavior of violent insurgency groups around the world, constitutes a direct challenge to this conception of the modern state. It remains to be seen whether such developments constitute a lasting threat to the idea that a state is an entity that can successfully control the inhabitants in a well-defined territory. Recent developments suggest, though, that we should not take political order for granted. Research by anthropologists and archaeologists reminds us that the vast majority of our experience as a species has occurred within relatively small groups of hunter-gatherers and that violence within and between these groups was commonplace (Gat 2006). Societal order in large groups is something that needs to be explained, rather than assumed.

OVERVIEW OF THE BOOK

Political science is the study of politics in a scientific manner. It's easy to see that, as it stands, this definition of political science isn't particularly informative. For example, what's politics? What's science? We explicitly address these questions in Chapters 2 and 3 of Part I. With these preliminaries out of the way, we begin to examine the substantive questions relating to the causes and consequences of democracy and dictatorship that are the book's central focus. In

Part II we contrast democracies and dictatorships. Specifically, we explore the origins of the modern state and ask why it is that some countries are democracies and others are dictatorships. In Part III we turn our attention to the different types of democracies and dictatorships that exist around the world. In particular, we examine the sometimes dizzying array of institutional forms that countries can adopt. Finally, in Part IV, we investigate how different types of democracy affect government performance and the survival of democracy itself.

Our goal in writing this book is to provide answers that are relevant to the problems motivating the study of comparative politics today and that are reliable—that is, built on the best practices of contemporary political scientists. In what follows, we highlight some of the questions and issues that we address in the upcoming chapters. These issues have been of long-standing interest to comparative political scientists and remain vitally important for understanding the contemporary world.

State Failure

Although state failure has long been recognized as one of the key sources of political and economic instability around the globe, the horrific events of September 11, 2001, have lent a new urgency to the need for understanding the conditions under which states fail and the conditions under which such power vacuums might foster international terrorism. The reason for this is that the September 11 terrorist attacks were planned from Afghanistan—a failed state in which the Taliban provided sanctuary for al-Qaida to train terrorists and plan attacks against various targets around the world. In Chapter 4 we define what political scientists mean when they speak of the "state" and describe what life is like in a failed state by looking at contemporary Syria. To understand how one might fill the power vacuum that exists in failed states, it's necessary to understand the historical development of the modern state. What distinguishes the modern state from other forms of political organization? What led to its development? The rest of Chapter 4 focuses on addressing these types of questions.

Economic Determinants of Democracy

In October 2001 the United States responded to the September 11 terrorist attacks by invading Afghanistan to overthrow the Taliban. In addition to trying to capture Osama bin Laden and destroy al-Qaida's terrorist infrastructure, one of the stated goals of this attack was to replace the Taliban with a more democratic form of government. In order to establish democracy intentionally and successfully in countries like Afghanistan and Iraq, however, it's important that we first understand the factors that encourage or discourage the emergence and survival of democracy. Similarly, to comprehend the prospects for democracy in the MENA region, we must take account of both the specific political background of the countries in this part of the world and the considerable body of theoretical and empirical evidence that comparative political scientists have compiled on the determinants of democracy.

In Chapter 5 we examine how economic development and the structure of the economy influence the likelihood that a country will be democratic. Some scholars have argued that countries are more likely to democratize as their economies become more modern—that is, less reliant on natural resource exports, more productive, more industrial, more highly educated, and so on. Other scholars have argued that such modernization may only affect the survival of democracy. In other words, they argue that modernization helps democracies stay democratic but doesn't help dictatorships become democratic. Although debate continues over the precise relationship between economic modernization and democracy, the fact that most of the countries affected by the Arab Spring don't fulfill many of the basic requirements of "modernization" means that comparative politics scholars on both sides of the debate would reach essentially the same conclusion regarding the prospects for democracy in the MENA region—they're poor. On a related note, many political scientists have argued that democracy is unlikely to arise in countries whose economies are dependent on natural resource extraction. If you find such arguments persuasive after reading Chapter 5, then the vast reservoirs of oil found in countries like Iraq and Libya should be viewed as a cause for concern, rather than hope, when it comes to trying to build democracy in these countries.

Cultural Determinants of Democracy

Over the years, many scholars have argued that democracy is incompatible with particular cultures. Exactly which cultures are thought to be bad for democracy tend to change from one time period to the next, depending on which countries in the world are democratic at a particular point in time. For example, Catholicism was seen as a hindrance to democracy during the 1950s and 1960s when few Catholic countries were democratic. As Catholic countries in southern Europe and Latin America became democratic in the 1970s and 1980s, this view began to wane. Today, of course, the culture deemed most antithetical to democracy is Islam. Again, the basic reason why people commonly view Islam as bad for democracy tends to be that they don't see many contemporary Islamic democracies. In fact, this is one of the reasons why the rapid rise in mass movements in many Muslim majority countries during the Arab Spring caught many observers by surprise. In Chapter 6 we examine the theoretical and empirical evidence behind arguments that some cultures are more suited for dictatorship than democracy. In doing so, we suggest that the type of after-the-fact theorizing that leads people to conclude, for example, that there must be something about Islam that discourages democracy because there aren't many Muslim democracies in the contemporary world should be treated with considerable skepticism.

If, after reading Chapters 5 and 6, you believe that the economic and cultural factors in countries like Iraq and Libya make democratization feasible, you might begin to wonder whether military force is the best way to bring it about. We don't examine the attempts of foreign countries to impose democracy by force in any great detail, but we do examine the process by which countries transition from dictatorship to democracy in Chapter 7. In particular, we look at bottom-up transitions to democracy, in which the people rise up as part of a popular revolution to overthrow the dictator, and top-down transitions, in which authoritarian elites introduce liberalization policies that ultimately lead to democracy. Our discussion in this chapter offers an explanation for why dictatorships frequently appear so stable, why popular revolutions are so rare, and why revolutions, when they do occur, nearly always come as a surprise even though they often appear so inevitable in hindsight. By focusing on the strategic interaction of elites and masses involved in top-down transitions, we also emphasize the important role that information, beliefs, and uncertainty can play in these types of democratic transitions.

What's So Good about Democracy Anyway?

Our time has been referred to as the "age of democracy." Even dictatorships spend a fair amount of time and energy paying lip service to the wonders of democracy. The benefits of democracy that many people speak of may be real, but political scientists like to reach conclusions on the basis of logic and evidence rather than conventional wisdom and ideology. As a result, we devote considerable effort in Chapters 8 and 9 to examining whether or not there is a sound basis for pursuing democracy in the first place.

In Chapter 8 we examine whether regime type makes a material difference in people's lives. As we demonstrate, the picture that emerges from this literature is significantly more nuanced than the rhetoric that politicians around the world typically employ. Although democracies seldom perform poorly in regard to the level of material well-being they provide their citizens, they frequently fail to outperform a substantial number of dictatorships. One of the reasons why it's difficult to compare democracies and dictatorships and come up with clear-cut answers as to which perform better has to do with the fact that dictatorships come in many different forms. For example, personalist dictatorships, such as the one in North Korea under Kim Jong-un, function quite differently from, say, the hereditary monarchies of the Gulf states or the military juntas found in countries like Thailand. Accordingly, we also devote time in Chapter 8 to discussing the institutional variation that exists among dictatorships, and how this affects things like economic performance, regime stability, and the likelihood of democratic transitions.

In Chapter 9 we take a slightly different tack and examine whether the actual *process* of democracy has some inherently attractive properties that make it morally or normatively appealing over and above any material benefits it might produce. The picture that emerges from the comparative politics literature on this matter may surprise you. The bottom line is that there's no support for the idea that there's an ideal form of political organization—and this includes democracy.

Institutional Design

If one were convinced that democracy was the best alternative for a country like Iraq, Egypt, or Libya, then the next logical question is how one should design such a democracy. Designing a democracy presumes that we know both how various democratic institutions work and what their consequences will be. In the remainder of this book, we examine what the comparative politics literature has to say in these regards.

In Chapter 10 we explore the significant differences that exist between parliamentary, presidential, and semi-presidential types of democracy. We pay particular attention to how governments form and survive in parliamentary and presidential democracies. In Chapter 11 we look at the different electoral systems employed around the world and attempt to understand each of their strengths and weaknesses with respect to things like proportionality, ethnic accommodation, accountability, and minority representation. In Chapter 12 we examine party systems. In particular, we focus on the types of parties that exist in different countries and on how the choice of electoral system in a country combines with attributes of that country's social structure to determine the number of parties that are likely to exist. In Chapter 13 we briefly examine other institutional ways in which democracies vary. Democracies can be federal or unitary, bicameral or unicameral, and they can differ in the extent to which they exhibit judicial independence. Federalism, bicameralism, and judicial independence can all be thought of as forms of checks and balances that create institutional veto players in a political system. As such, their causes and consequences are closely related, and it's for this reason that we consider them in the same chapter.

As Chapters 10 through 13 indicate, democracies around the world exhibit many different institutional forms. But do these various institutional forms produce different outcomes? This is what we examine in Chapter 14 in Part IV of the book. We begin by looking at the normative and material consequences associated with different types of democracies. Are the governments in some types of democracy more accountable and representative than the governments in other types of democracy? What are the expected economic consequences associated with different types of democracy? We then review what the comparative politics literature has to say about how the institutions a country adopts affect the survival of democracy. Many scholars have argued that the kind of ethnic and religious diversity observed in countries like Iraq is a destabilizing force in democracies. But do these types of divisions make democratic stability impossible, or are there institutional mechanisms that can be put in place that might mitigate the effects of ethnic and religious differences? In addition to examining how institutions might mitigate the effects of ethnic and religious diversity, we also look at whether a country's choice of democratic regime—parliamentary or presidential—influences the prospects for democratic survival. There's considerable evidence that parliamentary democracies survive significantly longer than presidential democracies. But if this is true, one might wonder what explains the persistence of democracy in the United States? Comparative politics scholars have an answer to this question, but to appreciate it, we must be willing to travel through both time and space.

THE APPROACH TAKEN IN THIS BOOK

Many introductory comparative politics texts are organized around a sequence of individual country studies. Typically, one starts with Britain, before moving on to France and Germany. Next it's on to Russia, Japan, India, Brazil, and, nearly always, Nigeria. Occasionally, China and Mexico might make an appearance somewhere along the line. We believe that this approach has some limitations if the goal of an introductory class is to teach something other than descriptive information about a tiny fraction of the world's countries. The eight countries that make up the domain of a typical comparative politics textbook constitute little more than 4 percent of the world's 193 widely recognized independent states. Why should we focus on these countries and not others? The response from the authors of these textbooks might be that these countries are, in some sense, either the most important or the most representative countries in the world. We find the first of these claims—that they're the most important countries—to be displeasing and the second—that they're the most representative countries—to be questionable.

An introductory class in comparative politics has many goals. We believe that it should stimulate students' interest in the particular subject matter and introduce them to the principal concerns and findings of the field. It should also give students an insight into the extent to which there's consensus or ongoing debate concerning those findings. Consequently, we have tried to focus our attention on the questions that comparative politics scholars have historically considered vitally important and those on which there's some growing consensus. It's undeniable that the causes and consequences of democracy and dictatorship are a central issue in comparative politics. It's for this reason that they're a central concern of our book. Less obvious perhaps is a growing consensus regarding the causes and consequences of particular sets of autocratic and democratic institutions. We endeavor to make this emerging consensus clearer.

In light of the types of research questions we want to address here, the traditional series of country studies found in most textbooks wouldn't provide the most useful approach. First, very few countries exhibit sufficient variation across time with their experience of democracy to allow questions about democracy's causes and consequences to be answered by a single country study. Similarly, very few countries experience sufficient variation in their institutions across time to give us much leverage in gaining an understanding of their causes and consequences. For example, countries that adopt presidentialism or a particular set of electoral laws tend to retain these choices for long periods of time. In fact, when forced to choose those institutions again (for example, at the end of an authoritarian interruption), countries frequently make the same choice. It's for these reasons that comparisons across countries are important for understanding the research questions that are at the heart of this book—they provide the much-needed variation not often found in any one country.

Second, we—personally—do not possess the required memory and attentiveness to remember the relevant details of particular countries' institutions and cultures across many weeks, and we, perhaps incorrectly, don't expect our students to either. Overall, we're not hopeful that we, or our students, can be expected in week ten of the semester when studying the intricacies of the Russian Duma to make comparisons with the Japanese Diet or the British House of Commons studied weeks earlier. Even if we could retain the relevant information across the course of a semester, it isn't obvious that eight or ten countries would produce a sufficiently large variety of socioeconomic and institutional experiences to allow us to adequately evaluate the hypotheses that are central to the comparative politics subfield and this book. Given that our primary concern in this textbook surrounds institutional, social, economic, and cultural factors that remain fairly constant across time within countries, the most a comparison of a relatively small number of countries could accomplish is to provide a collection of confirming cases. In Chapter 2 we discuss why such a practice is problematic from the standpoint of the scientific method.

We also believe that the traditional approach most textbooks adopt has the unfortunate consequence of creating a significant disjuncture between what comparative political scientists teach students and what these scholars actually do for a living. Comparative politics scholars do sometimes engage in descriptive exercises such as detailing how laws are made, how institutions function, or who has power in various countries. This is the traditional subject matter of most textbooks. However, it's much more common for comparative scholars to spend their time constructing and testing theories about political phenomena in the world. In reality, they're primarily interested in explaining, rather than describing, why politics is organized along ethnic lines in some countries but class lines in others, or why some countries are democracies but others dictatorships. Some textbook authors seem reluctant to present this sort of material to students because they believe it to be too complicated. However, we strongly believe that comparative political science is not rocket science. The fact that it's only relatively recently that the scientific method has begun to be applied to the study of political phenomena suggests to us that students should be able to engage the political science literature with relative ease. Indeed, we believe that, compared with other disciplines such as physics or mathematics, there's unusual room for students to actually make significant contributions to the accumulation of knowledge in comparative political science. As a result, one of the goals of our book is to introduce you to what comparative political scientists spend most of their time doing and to begin to give you the knowledge to evaluate the debates in our discipline.[2]

Key Concepts

comparative politics—the study of political phenomena that occur predominantly within countries

international politics—the study of political phenomena that occur predominantly between countries

---

[2]Brambor, Clark, and Golder (2006, 2007); Clark and Reichert (1998); Uzonyi, Souva, and Golder (2012); Golder and Lloyd (2014); and Golder and Thomas (2014) are examples of original research published in scientific journals in which our own undergraduate students have played significant roles.

WHAT IS SCIENCE?

The wrong view of science betrays itself in the craving to be right; for it is not his possession of knowledge, of irrefutable truth, that makes the man of science, but his persistent and recklessly critical quest for truth.

Sir Karl Popper, *The Logic of Scientific Discovery*

So I left him, saying to myself, as I went away: Well, although I do not suppose that either of us knows anything really beautiful and good, I am better off than he is—for he knows nothing, and thinks that he knows. I neither know nor think that I know. In this latter particular, then, I seem to have slightly the advantage of him.

Socrates, in *Plato's Apology*

Test everything. Keep what is good.

Saint Paul, *First Letter to the Thessalonians*

OVERVIEW

1. In this chapter, we define and examine the nature of science. Science is a strategy for understanding and explaining the social and natural world that emphasizes the use of statements that can be examined to see whether they're wrong.

2. Scientific explanations should explain previously puzzling facts, be logically consistent, and produce (many) potentially falsifiable predictions.

3. All scientific explanations are tentative. We accept some explanations as provisionally true when they've withstood vigorous attempts at refutation more successfully than competing explanations.

Consider the following five statements. What do they all have in common?

1. Science is a collection of facts that tell us what we know about the world.

2. A scientific theory is one that's been proven.

3. "The sun revolves around the earth" is not a **scientific statement**.

4. If my theory is correct, then I should observe that rich countries are more likely to be democracies. I do observe that rich countries are more likely to be democracies. Therefore, my theory is correct.

5. Politics can't be studied in a scientific manner.

The common element in these statements is that they're all wrong. Science is not a collection of facts that tell us what we know about the world. Scientific theories can't be proven. The statement that the sun revolves around the earth is a scientific statement (even though it's false). The argument outlined in statement 4 is logically invalid and therefore I can't conclude that my theory is correct. And finally, politics can be studied in a scientific manner. We suspect that many of you will have thought that at least some of these statements were correct. To know why all of these statements about science are wrong, you'll need to continue reading this chapter.

Science certainly has its detractors, largely because of what was experienced in the twentieth century. Some horrendous things were either done in the name of science or "justified" on scientific grounds or, at a minimum, made possible by science. Although we should never close our eyes to the harm that is sometimes done with science, we believe that it's as much a mistake to blame science for what some scientists have done in its name as it is to blame religion for what some believers have done in its name.

But what is science? First and foremost, science is a method; however, it's also a culture. The epigraphs at the start of this chapter are meant to capture what we might call the "culture" of science. Some of the negative views of science come from what people perceive the culture of science to be—cold, calculating, self-assured, arrogant, and, perhaps, even offensive. We believe, however, that at its best, the culture of science displays the characteristics encouraged by the otherwise very different thinkers who are quoted above. The scientific method is at its very core a critical method, and those reflective individuals who use it are much more likely to be humbled than emboldened. Sir Karl Popper ([1959] 2003) reminds us that science is not a static set of beliefs to be conserved and that all knowledge is tentative. Socrates reminds us that an acute awareness of our own ignorance is always the first step toward knowledge. Saint Paul offers hope that our willingness to test our ideas will leave us something good to hang on to. As we'll demonstrate in this chapter, science isn't about certainty, it isn't merely about the orderly collection of facts, and it isn't about invoking authority to protect our ideas from uncomfortable evidence. Instead, science is about asking tough questions and providing answers that invite criticism. Science is about recognizing the limits of our knowledge without lapsing into irresponsible cynicism. And science is about using the best logic, methods, and evidence available to provide answers today, even though we recognize they may be overturned tomorrow.

Comparative politics is a subfield of political science. But what exactly is political science? Well, it's the study of politics in a scientific way. How's that for a tautology? It's easy to see that as it stands this definition is not particularly informative. For example, what's politics? And what's science? In the next chapter we answer the first of these questions by distinguishing politics from other forms of social phenomena. In this chapter, though, we focus on the second question—what is science?

WHAT IS SCIENCE?

Is science simply a body of knowledge or a collection of facts, as many of us learn in high school? While there was a time when many scientists may have defined science this way, this definition is fundamentally unsatisfactory. If this definition of science were accurate, many of the claims about how the universe works, such as those developed through Newtonian physics, would now have to be called unscientific, because they have been replaced by claims based on more recent theories, such as Einstein's theory of relativity. Moreover, if science were simply a collection of statements about how the world works, then we would not be able to appeal to science to justify our knowledge of the world without falling into the following circular reasoning:

"Science is a collection of statements about how the world works."

"How do we know if these statements are accurate?"

"Well, of course they're accurate! They're scientific!"

The body of knowledge we call "scientific" may well be a product of science, but it's not science itself. Rather, science is a method for provisionally understanding the world. The reason for saying "provisionally" will become clear shortly. Science is one answer to the central question in epistemology (the study of knowledge): "How do we know what we know?" The scientist's answer to this question is, "Because we have subjected our ideas to the scientific method." Science, as Karl Popper indicates in one of the epigraphs at the start of this chapter, is the quest for knowledge. At this point, you might say that there are many ways to seek knowledge. Does this mean that meditation, reading scripture, and gazing at sunsets are all scientific activities? Although we agree that these are all ways of seeking knowledge, none of them is scientific. Science is a particular quest for knowledge. To use Popper's phrase, it's the "recklessly critical" pursuit of knowledge, in which the scientist continually subjects her ideas to the cold light of logic and evidence.

Although science is not the only route to knowledge, it may be unique in its emphasis on self-criticism. Scientists, like other scholars, can derive their propositions from an infinite number of sources. For example, Gregory Derry (1999) tells the story of how August Kekulé made an extremely important scientific breakthrough while hallucinating—half asleep—in front of the fireplace in his laboratory one night. He had spent days struggling to understand the spatial arrangement of atoms in a benzene molecule. In a state of mental and physical exhaustion, his answer appeared to him as he "saw" swirls of atoms joined in a particular formation dancing among the embers of his fireplace. In a flash of inspiration, he saw how the pieces of the puzzle with which he had been struggling fit together. This inspired understanding of the physical properties of organic compounds did not become a part of science that night, though. It did so only after the implications of his vision had withstood the critical and sober onslaught that came with the light of day. Thus, although flashes of insight can come from a variety of sources, science begins only when one asks, "If that's true, what else ought to be true?" And it ends—if ever—when researchers are satisfied they've taken every reasonable pain to show that the implications of the insight are false and have failed to do so. Even then, however, the best answer is not the final answer—it's just the best "so far."

So, science is the quest for knowledge that relies on criticism. The thing that allows for criticism is the possibility that our claims, theories, hypotheses, ideas, and the like could be wrong. Thus, what distinguishes science from "nonscience" is that scientific statements must be **falsifiable**—there must be some imaginable observation or set of observations that could falsify or refute them. This doesn't mean that a scientific statement will ever be falsified, just that there must be a possibility that it could be falsified if the "right" observation came along. Only if a statement is potentially testable is it scientific. We deliberately say "potentially testable" because a statement doesn't have to have been tested to be scientific; all that's required is that we can conceive of a way to test it.[1]

What sorts of statements are not falsifiable? Tautologies are not falsifiable because they are true by definition. For example, the statement "Triangles have three sides" is a **tautology**. It's simply not possible to ever observe a triangle that doesn't have three sides because *by definition* if an object doesn't have three sides, it's not a triangle. It's easy to see that this statement is not testable and hence unscientific. Tautologies, though, aren't always so easy to spot. Consider the following statement: "All good students get high grades." Is this a tautology? This statement may be true, but unless we can think of a way to identify good students without referring to their grades, then it's just a definition and is, therefore, unscientific. In other words, whether this particular statement is scientific depends on how we define good students.

Other statements or hypotheses are not falsifiable, not because they're tautological, but because they refer to inherently unobservable phenomena. For example, the claims "God exists" and "God created the world" are not falsifiable because they can't be tested; as a result, they're unscientific. Note that these claims may well be true, but it's important to recognize that science has nothing to do with the truth or falsity of statements. All that's required for a statement to be scientific is that it be falsifiable. It should be clear from this that we're not claiming that "nonscience" is nonsense or that it lacks meaning—this would clearly be a mistake. Nonfalsifiable statements like "God exists" may very well be true and have important and meaningful consequences—our claim is simply that they don't form a part of science.

Having defined science as a critical method for learning about the world, we can now evaluate the basic elements of the scientific method in more detail.

THE SCIENTIFIC METHOD

Although there's no **scientific method** clearly written down that all scientists follow, it is possible to characterize the basic features of the scientific method in the following manner.

Step 1: Question

The first step in the scientific process is to observe the world and come up with a question or puzzle. The very need for a theory or explanation begins when we observe something that's so unexpected or surprising that we ask, "Why did that occur?" Note that the surprise that greets such an observation, and that makes the observation a puzzle worth exploring, implies that the observation doesn't match some prior expectation or theory we held about how the world works. This suggests that we always have a preexisting theory or expectation when we observe the world; if we didn't have one, we could never be surprised, and there would be no puzzles.

---

[1]Indeed, a statement can be scientific even if we don't currently have the data or the technical equipment to test it. Our upcoming discussion of Einstein's special theory of relativity illustrates this point quite clearly.

Step 2: Theory or Model

Once we've observed something puzzling, the next step is to come up with a theory or model to explain it. In what follows, we'll talk of theories, models, and explanations interchangeably. Scientists use the word **theory** to describe a set of logically consistent statements that tell us why the things we observe occur. It's important that these statements be logically consistent; otherwise we have no way of determining what their empirical predictions will be and, hence, no way to test them. Put differently, theories that are logically inconsistent should not, indeed cannot, be tested, because we have no way of knowing what observations would truly falsify them.

What should theories or models look like? It's useful to think of our starting puzzle or observation as the end result of some previously unknown process (Lave and March 1975). We can then speculate about what (hidden) processes might have produced such a result. In effect, we try to imagine a prior world that, if it had existed, would have produced the otherwise puzzling observation before us. This prior world then becomes our model explaining the observation.

Notice that this process of imagining prior worlds is one place—but surely not the only one—where imagination and creativity enter the scientific process. What scientists do to stimulate this creative process is itself not part of the scientific method. Essentially, anything goes. Nobel Prize–winning physicist Richard Feynman, who himself spent a lot of time hanging out in bars, painting, and playing Brazilian hand drums, describes science as "imagination in a straightjacket"—it's imagination constrained by what we already know about the world (Feynman 1967). Whatever means we use to stimulate speculation about a prior world, if we can show through logical deduction that *if* that prior world existed, it would have produced the puzzling observation we started with, then we have a theory, or model. Note that we have only *a* theory; we don't necessarily have *the* theory. This is why we continually test the implications of our theory.

The model we end up with will necessarily be a simplified picture of the world. It's impossible to have a descriptively accurate model of the world as an infinite number of details would have to be captured in such a model. Pure description is impossible—models are always going to leave many things out. As with all arts, much of the skill of modeling is in deciding what to leave out and what to leave in. A good model contains only what's needed to explain the phenomenon that puzzles us and nothing else. If we made our models too complex, we'd have no way of knowing which elements were crucial for explaining our puzzling observation and which were superfluous. The purpose of a model is not to describe the world but to explain it, so descriptive accuracy isn't a core value in model building. Details are important only to the extent that they're crucial to what we're trying to explain. For example, if we're interested in explaining an aircraft's response to turbulence, it's not important whether our model of the aircraft includes LCD screens on the back of the passengers' seats. In fact, such inconsequential details can easily distract our attention from the question at hand. Another benefit of simple models is that they invite falsification because they make it very clear what we should not observe. The more amendments and conditions placed on an explanation, the easier it is for scholars to dismiss apparently contradictory evidence.

It's important to remember that models are always developed with a specific goal in mind. This means that we should evaluate models in terms of how useful they are for achieving that goal. As the late Dutch economist Henri Theil (1971) once said, "Models should be used, not believed." To emphasize this point, it can be helpful to think of models as being similar to maps. Like models, maps are simplified pictures of the world designed for a specific purpose.

Consider the subway map of any city. The subway map is always a simplification of the city and, indeed, an inaccurate simplification in the sense that it provides inaccurate information about the relative distances between, and geographic positions of, particular locations. Despite this, the map is incredibly useful if one's goal is to move efficiently around the city using the subway system—the purpose for which the map was designed. Of course, this map would be less useful if one's goal was to walk above ground from one location to another. As with a map, one must not judge the value of a model in some abstract sense but in terms of how well it helps us understand some particular aspect of the world and explain it to others.

Step 3: Implications (Hypotheses)

Once we have a model, the third step in the scientific process is to deduce implications from the model other than those we initially set out to explain. Why do we say "other than those we initially set out to explain"? Well, presumably the model we construct will provide a logical explanation for the puzzling observation that we started with; after all, that's what it was designed to do! In other words, there's no way a model can ever be falsified if only the observations that were employed to develop the model in the first place are used to test it. To actually test the model and allow for the possibility that it will be falsified, we'll have to find other implications that can be deduced from it. We must ask ourselves, "If the prior world we created to explain the phenomena we originally found puzzling really did exist, what else ought to exist? What else should we be able to observe?" As before, there's often room for incredible imagination here, because the complete list of logical implications of a model is seldom self-evident.

Good models are those that produce many different implications. This is so because each prediction represents another opportunity for the model to fail and, therefore, makes the model easier to falsify. This is good because if the model fails to be falsified, we gain more confidence in its usefulness. Fertile models—models with many implications—are also desirable because they encourage the synthesis of knowledge by encouraging us to see connections between ostensibly disparate events. Good models also produce surprising implications—they tell us something we wouldn't know in the absence of the model. Models are not particularly useful if they tell us only what we already know. Surprise, however, is best appreciated in small doses. If every implication of a model is surprising, either everything we thought about the world is wrong, or the model is.

Step 4: Observe the World (Test Hypotheses)

The fourth step is to examine whether the implications of the model are consistent with observation. Remember that the goal is not to dogmatically uphold the implications of our model or defend them in order to prove how right they are. On the contrary, we should try our best to falsify them, because it's only after an explanation has withstood these attempts to overthrow it that we can reasonably start to have confidence in it. While one should test as many implications of an explanation as possible, testing those that are most likely to be falsified is particularly important. Always subject your explanation to the harshest test you can devise.

It is standard practice to stop and ask if other models—models that describe altogether different processes—might also explain the phenomena of interest. When this is the case (and it almost always is), it's incumbent upon the scientist to compare the implications of those other models with the implications of her own model. Although it's always the case that competing models have some of the same implications (otherwise they couldn't explain the same observations to begin with), it's typically the case that they'll differ in some of their implications (otherwise they're not different models). The trick for a researcher is to identify these points of conflict between the different models and identify the relevant observations in the real world that would help her decide between them. This is what scientists refer to as a **critical test**. Ultimately, if a critical test is possible, observation will prove decisive in choosing between the models. This is because we know that there's only one world and the creative scientist has managed to get competing theories to say contradictory things about it—only one of the models can be consistent with the real world.

Step 5: Evaluation

If we observe the implications deduced from our theory, we say that our theory has been corroborated. Note that we can't say that our theory has been verified or proven. This important point is one we'll return to in more detail in the next section.[2] That we can never prove a scientific explanation is why we earlier called science a method for "provisionally" understanding the world. Our theory may or may not be true. All we can conclude, if observations are consistent with our theoretical implications, is that our theory has not yet been falsified; we can't rule out that it won't be falsified the next time it's tested. As you can see, the scientific method is an inherently critical method when it's "successful" (when a theory's predictions seem to be borne out), because it's precisely under these circumstances that it's most cautious in the claims it makes.

Although we can't ever prove our theories, we can claim that some theories are better corroborated than others. As a result, we can have more confidence in their conclusions. One might think that a theory that's been subjected to multiple tests is better corroborated than one that's not been subjected to many tests at all. However, this isn't always the case. If we keep testing the same implication over and over again, it's not clear how much an additional test actually adds to the degree to which the theory is corroborated. What really matters is not so much how many times a theory has been corroborated, but the severity and variety of the tests to which it has been subjected. This, in turn, will depend on the degree to which the theory is falsifiable. Again, this is why we like our models to be simple and have multiple implications. In general, we'll have more confidence in a theory that's survived a few harsh tests than a theory that's survived many easy ones. This is why scientists often talk about the world as if it were black-and-white rather than gray. Bold statements should be interpreted not as scientific hubris but rather as attempts to invite criticism—they're easier to falsify.

What happens if we don't observe the implications deduced from our theory? Can we conclude that our theory is incorrect based on one falsifying observation? The answer is "probably not." It's entirely possible that we've not observed and measured the world without error. Moreover, if we believe that human behavior is inherently probabilistic, we might not want to reject theories on the basis of a single observation. In a world in which our tests are potentially fallible, we shouldn't relegate a theory to the dustbin of intellectual history the minute one of its implications is shown to be false. Instead, we must weigh the number, severity, and quality of the tests that the theory's implications are subjected to and make a judgment. And most

---

[2]Many scientists, however, slip into the language of verification when reporting their results. Instead of simply saying that their test has failed to falsify their hypotheses or is consistent with their theory, they'll claim that the test has shown their theory is correct. For example, they might claim that their test shows that wealth causes democracies to live longer when, in fact, all they can conclude is that they were unable to falsify the claim that wealth causes democracies to live longer.

BOX 2.1 AN EXAMPLE OF THE SCIENTIFIC PROCESS
THE CASE OF SMART FEMALE ATHLETES

Because student athletes often miss classes to compete out of state, they frequently submit a letter from the athletic director asking for cooperation from their professors. Over the years, a certain professor has noticed through casual observation that women engaged in athletic competition frequently perform better academically than the average student. It's puzzling why female athletes would perform better in spite of missing classes. Can you think of a model—a process—that might produce such a puzzling observation?

You might start with the following conjecture:

- Female athletes are smart.

This is an explanation, but it's not a particularly good one. For example, it comes very close to simply restating the observation to be explained. One thing that could improve the explanation is to make it more general. This might lead you to a new explanation:

- Athletes are smart.

This model is certainly more general (but not necessarily more correct). Still, there are at least two problems with this model as things stand. First, it has no sense of process; it basically says that athletes share some inherent quality of smartness that leads them to perform better academically. In effect, this only pushes the phenomenon to be explained back one step; that is, we now need to know why athletes are smart. Second, the model comes close to being a tautology. It essentially says that athletes perform better academically because they're defined as being smart. This is problematic, as we saw earlier, because tautologies are not falsifiable—they can't be tested; hence, they're not part of the scientific endeavor.

This might lead you to look for a new explanation or model that includes some sort of process that makes female athletes appear smart. You might come up with the following model:

- Being a good athlete requires a lot of hard work; performing well academically in college requires a lot of work. Students who develop a strong work ethic in athletics are able to translate this to their studies.

This is a much more satisfying model because it provides a process or mechanism explaining why female athletes might be more academically successful than other students. An appealing feature of the model is that the logic of the argument applies not only to female athletes but to any athlete. Indeed, it applies to any person involved in an activity that rewards hard work. Thus, we might generalize this model by removing the specific reference to athletes:

- **Work ethic theory:** Some activities provide a clear, immediate, and tangible reward for hard work—in fact, they may provide an external stimulus to work hard (coaches shouting through bullhorns, manipulating rewards and punishments based on effort, and so on). Individuals who engage in these activities develop a habit of working hard and so will be successful in other areas of life as well.

At this point, you should stop and ask yourself whether there are any alternative explanations for why female athletes are successful. Can you think of any? One alternative explanation is the following:

- **Excellence theory:** Everyone wants to feel successful, but some people go long periods without success and become discouraged. Those individuals who experience success in one area of their life (perhaps based on talent, rather than hard work) develop a "taste" for it and devise strategies to be successful in other parts of their life. Anyone who achieves success in nonacademic areas, such as athletics, will be more motivated to succeed in class.

Another alternative explanation is the following:

- **Gender theory:** In many social and academic settings, women are treated differently from men. This differential treatment often leads women to draw inferences that certain activities are "not for them." Because many athletic endeavors are gender specific, they provide an environment for women to develop their potential free from the stultifying effects of gender bias. The resulting sense of efficacy and autonomy encourages success when these women return to gendered environments like the classroom.

We now have three different or competing models, all of which explain the puzzling observation that we started with. But how can we evaluate which model is best? One way is to test some of the implications that can be derived from these theories. In particular, we'd like to find some new question(s) to which the three models give different answers. In other words, we'd like to conduct a critical test that would allow us to choose among the alternative models.

We might start by wondering whether being an athlete helps the academic performance of women more than men. Whereas the work ethic theory and the excellence theory both predict that being an athlete will help men and women equally, the gender theory predicts that female athletes will perform better than nonathletic women but that male athletes will have no advantage over nonathletic men. Thus, collecting information on how well male and female athletes perform in class relative to male and female nonathletes would allow us to distinguish between the gender theory and the other theories.

But how can we distinguish between the excellence theory and the work ethic theory? One difficulty frequently encountered when trying to devise critical tests is that alternative theories don't always produce clearly differentiated predictions. For example, we just saw that the excellence theory and the work ethic theory both predict that athletics will help men and women academically. It turns out that these two theories have other predictions in common as well. The excellence theory clearly suggests that success in any nonacademic area of life is likely to encourage academic success. In other words, the excellence theory predicts that academic success will be associated with success in other areas of life. The problem is that success in many of these nonacademic areas may require hard work. As a result, if we observe, for instance, accomplished musicians performing well in our political science classes, it will be difficult to discern whether this is because they learned the value of hard work in music and transferred it to political science (work ethic theory) or because they developed a "taste" for success as musicians that then inspired success in political science (excellence theory). In effect, the excellence theory and the work ethic theory both predict that academic success will be associated with success in other areas of life.

If we want to distinguish between the work ethic theory and the excellence theory, we need to imagine observations in which they produce different expectations. Sometimes, this requires further development of a theory. For example, we might expand the excellence theory to say that those people who develop a taste for excellence also develop a more competitive spirit. If this is true, then the excellence theory would predict that student athletes are likely to be more competitive and will perform better than other students even when playing relatively frivolous board games. Since even the most driven athletes are not likely to devote time to training for board games, the work ethic theory predicts that athletes will perform the same as nonathletes in such trivial pursuits. Thus, we could look at the performance of athletes and nonathletes at board games to distinguish between the excellence theory and the work ethic theory.

The three critical tests we've come up with and their predictions are listed in Table 2.1. All that's required now is to collect the appropriate data and decide which model, if any, is best.

(Continued)

(Continued)

It's worth noting that there's considerable overlap between the predictions of our three theories. This is often the case in political science settings as well. The crucial point is not that each theory should yield a complete set of unique predictions, but that our theories should have sufficiently many distinct predictions that we can use observation to help us make decisions about which theories to embrace, however tentatively. Table 2.1 lists just some of the predictions that might help us to distinguish between the three theories outlined above. Can you think of any more?

TABLE 2.1 ■ Three Critical Tests			
		Theory	
Question	**Gender**	**Excellence**	**Work ethic**
Will athletics help women more than men?	Yes	No	No
Is academic success associated with success in other areas of life?	No	Yes	Yes
Are female athletes more successful at board games than women who are not athletes?	Yes	Yes	No

important, this judgment should be made with an eye toward what would replace the theory should we decide to discard it. This is why some scientists say that it takes a theory to kill a theory. Further, if we do embrace a new theory and disregard an alternative, it should be because the new theory is more consistent with all of the implications of both theories. Developing a new theory that explains the facts that the old theory found inconvenient without also explaining the many facts that the old theory accurately predicted is called *ad hoc* explanation. Because this practice doesn't expose the new theory to falsification as strenuously as it does the old theory, it's not consistent with sound scientific practice.

AN INTRODUCTION TO LOGIC

In the previous section, we talked in a rather casual way about constructing and testing scientific explanations. In order to better appreciate the important connection between theory construction and theory testing, it's useful to devote some time to the study of logic. The study of logic is first and foremost about learning to be careful about how we construct and evaluate arguments.

Throughout our lives, we're confronted by people trying to convince us of certain things through arguments. Politicians make arguments as to why we should vote for their party rather than the party of their opponents. National leaders provide arguments for why certain policies should be implemented or abandoned. Lawyers make arguments as to why certain individuals should be found guilty or innocent. Professors make arguments as to why students should spend more time in the library and in class rather than at parties. It's important for you to know when these arguments are logically valid and when they're not. If you can't distinguish between a valid argument and an invalid one, other people will be able to manipulate and exploit you. You'll be one of life's suckers. In this section, we give you some tools to determine whether an argument is valid or not.

Valid and Invalid Arguments

An **argument** is a set of logically connected statements, typically in the form of a set of **premises** and a **conclusion**. An argument is **valid** when accepting its premises compels us to accept its conclusions. An argument is **invalid** if, when we accept the premises of an argument, we're free to accept or reject its conclusions. One way to represent an argument is in the form of a **categorical syllogism** that consists of a major premise, a minor premise, and a conclusion. The major premise is typically presented as a conditional statement, such as "If P, then Q." The "if" part of the conditional statement (in this case "If P") is called the *antecedent*, whereas the "then" part of it (in this case "then Q") is called the *consequent*. An example of a conditional statement is "If a country is wealthy [antecedent], then it will be a democracy [consequent]." The minor premise consists of a claim about either the antecedent or the consequent in the conditional statement (major premise). The conclusion is a claim that's thought to be supported by the premises.

Four types of conditional argument can be represented with a syllogism—arguments that affirm or deny the antecedent and those that affirm or deny the consequent. Which of these four types of argument are valid? Recall that a valid argument is one such that if you accept that the premises are true, then you're compelled to accept the conclusion as true. Let's start by considering what happens when we affirm the antecedent. An example is shown in Table 2.2.

The major premise states, "If P is true, then Q must be true." The minor premise says that "P is true." Together, these premises compel us to accept that the conclusion is true. As a result, the argument is valid. In other words, the major premise states, "If a country is wealthy [antecedent], then it will be a democracy [consequent]." The minor premise says, "The observed country is wealthy." It logically follows from this that the observed country must be a democracy. To see why this type of argument is valid, consider the general form of this argument in set-theoretic form. This is shown in Figure 2.1. As Figure 2.1 indicates, the major premise indicates that the set of cases where P occurs is a subset of the cases where Q occurs. The minor premise maintains that P does occur. Figure 2.1 clearly shows that if the case in question is in P, as the minor premise affirms, then the case must also be in Q. Thus, the argument is valid—we're compelled to conclude Q.

Now let's consider what happens when we deny the antecedent. An example is shown in Table 2.3. Once again, the major premise can be represented in set-theoretic terms by

TABLE 2.2 ■ Affirming the Antecedent: A Valid Argument		
	General form	**Specific example**
Major premise	If P, then Q	If a country is wealthy, then it will be a democracy.
Minor premise	P	The country is wealthy.
Conclusion	Therefore, Q	Therefore, the country will be a democracy.

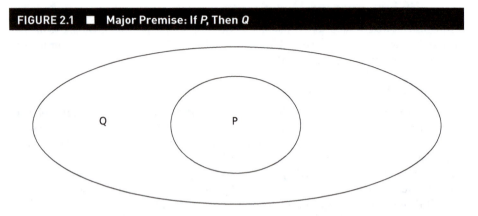

FIGURE 2.1 ■ Major Premise: If *P*, Then *Q*

	General form	Specific example
Major premise	If *P*, then *Q*	If a country is wealthy, then it will be a democracy.
Minor premise	Not *P*	The country is not wealthy.
Conclusion	Therefore, not *Q*	Therefore, the country will not be a democracy.

TABLE 2.3 ■ Denying the Antecedent: An Invalid Argument

Figure 2.1. The difference from the previous example is that the minor premise now asserts that *P* is not the case; that is, it denies the antecedent. If we accept this, does it necessarily follow that *Q* is not the case, as the conclusion maintains? Figure 2.1 clearly illustrates that even if our case is not in *P*, it could still be in *Q*. As a result, it doesn't logically follow from observing "not *P*" that *Q* is not the case. Therefore, this is an invalid argument. This is because we can contradict the conclusion (not *Q*) without running into a contradiction with either the major premise or the minor premise. Since a valid argument compels us to accept its conclusion given that its premises are true, this is sufficient to demonstrate that arguments that deny the antecedent are invalid.

In the context of our running example, does it follow from the fact that the observed country is not wealthy that it will not be a democracy? Intuitively, we can imagine that there may be other reasons why a country is a democracy even though it's not wealthy. Indeed, one example of a nonwealthy democracy is India. An important point here, though, is that the argument is invalid, not because we can come up with an example of a real democracy that's not wealthy (India), but rather because we're not compelled to accept the conclusion based on the truthfulness of the major and minor premises. It may be confusing for readers that there's no direct connection between the factual accuracy of an argument's conclusion and the validity of the argument itself—a valid argument can have a conclusion that's factually false, and an invalid argument can have a conclusion that's factually true. If we restrict our attention only to whether the argument is valid as it applies to our democracy example, we must ask, "Does the major premise claim that wealth is the only reason why a country will be a democracy?" The answer is clearly no. The major premise states only what will happen if a country is wealthy. It makes no claim as to what might happen if a country isn't wealthy. It's for this reason, and this reason alone, that the argument is invalid.

TABLE 2.4 ■ Affirming the Consequent: An Invalid Argument I		
	General form	Specific example
Major premise	If P, then Q	If a country is wealthy, then it will be a democracy.
Minor premise	Q	The country is a democracy.
Conclusion	Therefore, P	Therefore, the country is wealthy.

Now let's consider what happens when we affirm the consequent. An example is shown in Table 2.4. As before, the major premise can be represented in set-theoretic terms by Figure 2.1. The difference this time is that the minor premise now asserts that Q is the case; that is, it affirms the consequent. If we accept that the premises are true, are we compelled to accept the conclusion that P is the case? Figure 2.1 clearly illustrates that the fact that our case is in Q doesn't necessarily mean that it's also in P. As a result, the argument is invalid—we're not compelled to accept the conclusion based on the premises.

In the context of our running example, an argument that affirms the consequent confuses necessity and sufficiency. Although the major premise states that wealth is sufficient for democracy—wealthy countries will be democracies—it doesn't assert that wealth is necessary for democracy. In other words, the major premise doesn't state that wealth is the only cause of a country's democracy. Consequently, we can't make a valid inference from the fact that a country is a democracy to the claim that the country must be wealthy—it may be wealthy, or it may not be. Recall that to show that an argument is invalid, it's not necessary to show that its conclusion is false; we have to show only that it doesn't have to be true.

Finally, let's consider what happens when we deny the consequent. An example is shown in Table 2.5. As always, the major premise can be represented in set-theoretic terms by Figure 2.1. The difference this time is that the minor premise now denies that Q is the case; that is, it denies the consequent. If we accept that the premises are true, are we compelled to accept the conclusion that "not P" is the case? Figure 2.1 clearly shows that the fact that our case is not in Q necessarily means that it's not in P. As a result, the argument is valid—we're compelled to accept the conclusion based on the premises. In the context of our running example, the major premise indicates that all wealthy countries are democracies and the minor premise states that the country is not a democratic one. If these premises are both true, then it logically follows that our country can't be wealthy.

Our brief foray into the study of logic indicates that if complex arguments can be broken down into categorical syllogisms, then it's possible to classify all arguments into one of four types according to whether they affirm or deny the consequent or antecedent. Two of these arguments are valid, but the other two are invalid. Specifically, affirming the antecedent and

TABLE 2.5 ■ Denying the Consequent: A Valid Argument I		
	General form	Specific example
Major premise	If P, then Q	If a country is wealthy, then it will be a democracy.
Minor premise	Not Q	The country is not a democracy.
Conclusion	Therefore, not P	Therefore, the country is not wealthy.

TABLE 2.6 ■ What Types of Conditional Arguments Are Valid?		
	Antecedent	Consequent
Affirm	Valid	Invalid
Deny	Invalid	Valid

denying the consequent are valid arguments—if you accept the major and minor premises, you're compelled to accept the conclusion. In contrast, denying the antecedent and affirming the consequent are invalid arguments—if you accept the major and minor premises, you're not compelled to accept the conclusion. These results are summarized in Table 2.6.

Testing Theories

We obviously think that it's important for you to be able to distinguish between valid and invalid arguments so that you're not manipulated or exploited by others. However, this brief introduction to logic is also important because it tells us something about the way that scientists test their theories and explanations. Suppose we want to explain why rich countries are more likely to be democracies than poor countries. One possible explanation for why this might be the case is given in the following statements:[3]

1. Living in a dictatorship is risky—if you're one of the dictator's friends, you'll do extremely well; but if you're not, you'll do extremely poorly.

2. Living in a democracy is less risky—because more people are involved in choosing them, democratic leaders have to spread the goodies (and the pain) around more evenly. This means that you're less likely to do extremely well or extremely poorly in a democracy.

3. Rich people are less likely to take risks than poor people because they have more to lose. This means that countries with lots of rich people are more likely to be democracies than dictatorships.

This short explanation provides reasons why rich countries might be more likely to be democracies than poor countries. How good is this explanation, though? Does this argument have any testable implications? One implication is that rich democracies should live longer than poor democracies. This is because people in rich democracies should be less likely to take the "risk" of becoming a dictatorship; in contrast, people in poor democracies might wonder what they have to lose.

How can we use observations of the real world to evaluate our proposed explanation? It's often the case that the implications of an explanation are more readily observable than the elements of the explanation itself. Consider the example we're using. Although it may be possible to compare the distribution of good and bad outcomes in dictatorships and democracies, the claims that people differ in their propensity to take risks and that this propensity is

---

[3]This is a simplified version of an argument presented by Przeworski (2001). It will be discussed more fully in Chapter 5.

TABLE 2.7 ■ Affirming the Consequent: An Invalid Argument II		
General form	**Example**	**Specific example**
If *P*, then *Q*	If our theory *T* is correct, then we should observe some implication *I*.	If our theory is correct, then we should observe that rich democracies live longer than poor democracies.
Q	We observe implication *I*.	Rich democracies live longer than poor democracies.
Therefore, *P*	Therefore, our theory *T* is correct.	Therefore, our theory is correct.

related to their level of income are difficult to observe. This is because the propensity to take risks is an internal and psychological attribute of individuals. For similar reasons, scholars typically evaluate their explanations by observing the real world to see if the implications of their explanations appear to be true based on the assumption that "If my theory is true, then its implications will be true." If we take this to be our major premise and the truth or falsity of the theory's implications as the minor premise, then we might be able to use observations to draw inferences about our theory or explanation.

Suppose our theory's implications were borne out by our observation that rich democracies live longer than poor democracies. Can we conclude that our theory is true? Note that if we were to do so, we'd be engaging in reasoning that affirmed the consequent. This fact is shown more clearly in Table 2.7. As you know by now, affirming the consequent is an invalid form of argument. The major premise says only that if the theory is correct, then the implications should be observed. It never says that the only way for these implications to be produced is if the theory is correct. In other words, processes other than those described in our theory may produce the observation that rich countries live longer than poor countries. Put differently, the mere fact of observing the predicted implication doesn't allow us to categorically accept or reject our theory.

Suppose now that our observations didn't bear out our theory's implications; that is, we didn't observe that rich democracies live longer than poor democracies. Can we conclude that our theory is incorrect? Note that if we were to do so, we'd be engaging in reasoning that denies the consequent. This fact is shown more clearly in Table 2.8. As you know by now, denying the consequent is a valid form of argument. In other words, by accepting the premises, we're compelled to accept the conclusion that our theory is not correct.

If we compare the two previous examples, we can see an important asymmetry related to the logical claims that can be made on the basis of "confirming" and "disconfirming" observations. When an implication of our theory is confirmed, the most we can say is that the theory may be correct. This is because neither of the two possible conclusions—our theory is correct or our theory is not correct—contradicts our major and minor premises. In other words, we can't say that our theory is correct or verified. In contrast, if we find that an implication of our theory is inconsistent with observation, then we're compelled by logic to accept that the theory is false—this is the only conclusion that's consistent with our observation. Thus, although we can know that a theory must be incorrect in light of a disconfirming case, all we can say in light of a confirming case is that a theory may be correct (it may also be wrong). What does this mean? It means that we're logically justified in having more confidence when we reject a theory than when we don't. This, in turn, implies that the knowledge

General form	Example	Specific example
If P, then Q	If our theory T is correct, then we should observe some implication I.	If our theory is correct, then we should observe that rich democracies live longer than poor democracies.
Not Q	We do not observe implication I.	Rich democracies do not live longer than poor democracies.
Therefore, not P	Therefore, our theory T is incorrect.	Therefore, our theory is incorrect.

TABLE 2.8   ■   Denying the Consequent: A Valid Argument II

encapsulated in theories that have not been rejected remains tentative and can never be proven for sure—scientific theories can never be proven. Even if we're utterly convinced that our major and minor premises are true, all that we can logically conclude from a confirming instance is that the theory has not yet been falsified.

This asymmetry between confirming and disconfirming cases led the philosopher of science Sir Karl Popper ([1959] 2003, 280–81) to conclude:

> The old scientific ideal of *episteme*—of absolutely certain, demonstrable knowledge—has proved to be an idol. The demand for scientific objectivity makes it inevitable that every scientific statement must remain *tentative for ever.* . . . With the idol of certainty . . . there falls one of the defenses of obscurantism which bar the way to scientific advance. For the worship of this idol hampers not only the boldness of our questions, but also the rigor and integrity of our tests. The wrong view of science betrays itself in the craving to be right; for it is not his *possession* of knowledge, of irrefutable truth, that makes the man of science, but his persistent and recklessly critical *quest* for truth.

If confirming observations don't prove that our theory is correct, does this mean that they're of no use whatsoever? The answer is no. Imagine that we start with a set of implications derived from a theory and then observe some facts. In other words, let's start with the theory and then observe the world. If we do this, then it's possible that our observations will contradict our theory. If it turns out that our observations are consistent with our theory, then we can have a greater measure of confidence in our theory because it withstood the very real chance of being falsified. We can't say that our theory is verified or confirmed, just that we have more confidence in it. If our observations are inconsistent with our theory, then we can draw valid inferences about the truthfulness of our theory—we can conclude that it's wrong. This approach to doing science, which forms the basis of the scientific method described earlier, is called falsificationism. **Falsificationism** is an approach to science in which scientists generate or "deduce" testable hypotheses from theories designed to explain phenomena of interest. It emphasizes that scientific theories are constantly called into question and that their merit lies only in how well they stand up to rigorous testing. Falsificationism forms the basis for the view of science employed in this book.

The approach to science that we've described here takes a clear stance in the debate between "deductive" and "inductive" approaches to learning. The **deductive approach to learning** formulates an expectation about what we ought to observe in light of a particular theory about the world and then sets out to see if our observations are consistent with that theory. The **inductive approach to learning**, on the other hand, starts with a set of observations and then tries to ascertain a pattern in the observations that can be used to generate an explanation for the observations. Induction is problematic because in order to be successful it must rest at some point on the fallacy of affirming the consequent—the fact that observation precedes theory construction means that the theory is never exposed to potential falsification! Popper ([1959] 2003) suggests that, in fact, the biggest problem with induction is not so much that it's wrong but that it's impossible. Observational facts don't just present themselves to observers—we always decide which facts to pay attention to and which to ignore. As we noted earlier, the hunch that tells us what to observe and what to ignore, that is, what constitutes a puzzle worth explaining, constitutes a theory. In this respect, scholars who claim to be engaged in an inductive inquiry are actually engaged in an implicit deductive endeavor. If it's true that we're "all deductivists" as Popper claims, then the argument for deduction amounts to a claim that it's better to use theory explicitly than to use it implicitly.

Having described the scientific method, we'd like to briefly dispel certain myths that have developed about science. Some of these myths have been promoted by opponents of the scientific project, but others, unfortunately, have been sustained by scientists themselves.

MYTHS ABOUT SCIENCE

The first myth is that science proves things and leads to certain and verifiable truth. This is not the best way to think about science. It should be clear by now from our discussion that the best science can hope to offer are tentative statements about what seems reasonable in light of the best available logic and evidence. It may be frustrating for students to realize this, but science can speak with more confidence about what we don't know than what we do know. In this sense, the process of scientific accumulation can be thought of as the evolution of our ignorance. We use the scientific method because it's the best tool available to interrogate our beliefs about the (political) world. If we hold on to any beliefs about the (political) world, it's because, after we have subjected them to the most stringent tests we can come up with, they remain the most plausible explanations for the phenomena that concern us.

The second myth is that science can be done only when experimental manipulation is possible. This is clearly false. For theories to be scientific, they need only be falsifiable. There's no claim that the tests of these theories need to be carried out in an experimental setting. Many of the natural sciences engage in research that's not susceptible to experimental manipulation. For example, all research on extinct animals, such as dinosaurs, must be conducted without the aid of experimental manipulation because the subjects are long dead. In fact, there's also no claim that a theory must be tested before it can be called scientific. Einstein presented a special theory of relativity in 1905 that stated, among other things, that space had to be curved, or warped. It took fourteen years before his theory was tested with the help of a solar eclipse. No scientist would claim that Einstein's theory was unscientific until it was tested. Put simply, scientific theories must be potentially testable, but this doesn't mean that they stop being scientific if they're yet to be actually tested.

The third myth is that scientists are value neutral. It's necessary here to distinguish between the method of science and the individuals—the scientists—who engage in science. The scientific method itself is value neutral. As we've indicated in this chapter, science is simply a method that involves generating and evaluating logically consistent sets of falsifiable statements about the world. Scientists, though, may not be value neutral (Longino 1987;

Haraway 1988). It's important to remember that the pursuit of knowledge about the world is closely entangled with people's attempts to change the world. As a result, the types of research questions asked and the interpretation of scientific results are likely to be infused with the specific values and biases held by individual scientists and those who use their research. The lack of diversity in most scientific disciplines, whether in terms of gender, race, income, class, sexuality, religion, ethnicity, and so on, along with the power structure that exists in many societies, means that some research areas are less studied than others and that certain viewpoints are excluded or less privileged than others when it comes to interpreting scientific evidence (Smith 1974; Collins 1986, 1989; Carroll and Zerilli 1993). In effect, the knowledge science produces is socially constructed. This is one of the many reasons for trying to promote the diversity of those involved in the scientific endeavor. The fact that scientists may not be value neutral means that we should be very clear about the limits of our knowledge and not encourage others to act upon knowledge that's not highly corroborated. Moreover, we should try to conduct our studies in such a way that someone who doesn't share our biases can determine if our arguments and evidence are reasonable.

It's been argued that science is predicated on two rules (Rauch 1993). First, no one gets the final say on any issue—all knowledge claims are, for the reasons outlined in this chapter, open to criticism. Second, no individual has a personal claim of authority about whether scientific statements are true or not. Taken together, these two rules create a social system that makes it possible that even though individual scientists will have biased perspectives, others, who hold different biases, will have incentives to check their work. As a community, scientists with many different biases will use the scientific method to check the claims that are being made in an attempt to reach a consensus that's independent of the biases held by individual scholars. This is yet another reason why having a diverse group of scientists is valuable.

The fourth myth, that politics can't be studied in a scientific manner, can easily be dispelled by now. Our description of the scientific method clearly shows that this myth is false. The study of politics generates falsifiable claims and hence generates scientific statements. These theories of politics can be tested just like any other scientific theory. We'll further demonstrate that politics can be studied in a scientific manner in the remaining chapters of this book. The fact, though, that our subjects can read our work and change their behavior makes our job quite a bit harder than if we were working in one of the natural sciences.

CONCLUSION

In this chapter we've argued that it's useful to think about politics in a scientific manner. We've also tried to offer a clear view of what most practicing scientists have in mind when they use the word *science*. It's a fairly minimalist view. What unites all scientists is the idea that one ought to present one's ideas in a way that invites refutation (Popper 1962). It's incumbent upon the scientist to answer the question "What ought I observe if what I claim to be true about the world is false?" This view of science recognizes that scientific knowledge is tentative and should be objective. Although it's certainly likely that our prejudices and biases motivate our work and will creep into our conclusions, the goal of science is to present our conclusions in a way that'll make it easy for people who don't share our prejudices and biases to determine if our conclusions as reasonable.

Key Concepts

scientific statement—a statement that is falsifiable

falsifiable—potentially testable

tautology—a statement that is true by definition

scientific method—the process by which scientists learn about the world

theory—a set of logically consistent statements that tell us why the things we observe occur, sometimes referred to as a model or an explanation

critical test—a test that allows the analyst to use observation to distinguish between two or more competing explanations of the same phenomenon

argument—a set of logically connected statements, typically in the form of a set of premises and a conclusion

premise—a statement that's presumed to be true within the context of an argument leading to a conclusion

conclusion—a claim that's thought to be supported by an argument's premises

valid argument—an argument in which, if you accept the premises, you're compelled to accept the conclusion

invalid argument—an argument in which, if you accept the premises, you're free to accept or reject the conclusion

categorical syllogism—a specific type of argument that consists of a major premise, a minor premise, and a conclusion

falsificationism—an approach to science in which scientists generate testable hypotheses from theories designed to explain phenomena of interest; emphasizes that scientific theories are constantly called into question and that their merit lies only in how well they stand up to rigorous testing

deductive approach to learning—an approach that involves formulating an expectation about what we ought to observe in light of a particular theory about the world and then sets out to see if observation is consistent with that theory

inductive approach to learning—an approach that starts with a set of observations and then tries to ascertain a pattern in the observations that can be used to generate an explanation for the observations

WHAT IS POLITICS?

Being powerful is like being a lady. If you have to tell people you are, you aren't.

British Prime Minister Margaret Thatcher

OVERVIEW

1. In this chapter, we define and examine the nature of politics. Politics comprises the subset of human behavior that involves the use of power.

2. Power is involved whenever individuals can't accomplish their goals without either trying to influence the behavior of others or trying to wrestle free from the influence exerted by others.

3. We introduce an exit, voice, and loyalty (EVL) theory to help us think about the role of power in politics. The theory throws light on who has power, when and why they have it, and how they use it.

Political science is the study of politics in a scientific manner. In the previous chapter we described what we mean by science and examined the various components that constitute the scientific process. In this chapter we define what we mean by politics. What makes one situation political and another not? What is politics? Although many answers have been given to these questions over the years, most share the intuition that **politics** comprises the subset of human behavior that involves the use of power. Broadly speaking, power is involved whenever individuals can't accomplish their goals without either trying to influence the behavior of others or trying to wrestle free from the influence exerted by others. According to this definition, politics is not just about the "government." All forms of social interaction, whether at home, at work, or at play, typically involve some person or group trying to influence or avoid the influence of others. As such, politics is a key aspect of our everyday lives and relationships.

In this chapter, we introduce a simple theory to capture what we think are the key elements of many political situations.[1] Our theory represents a reformulation and extension of

---

[1]This chapter draws heavily on the ideas presented in Clark, Golder, and Golder (2017).

an argument put forth in Albert Hirschman's (1970) famous book, *Exit, Voice, and Loyalty: Responses to Decline in Firms, Organizations, and States.* Whereas Hirschman primarily addresses the power relationship between consumers and firms, we focus here on the power relationship between citizens and governments. The theory helps us understand when citizens will take direct action against the government, when governments will respond positively to citizen demands, and when governments will ignore their citizens. More generally, the theory throws light on who has power, when and why they have it, and how they use it. In other words, it helps us think about what politics is and how politics works.

THE EXIT, VOICE, AND LOYALTY (EVL) THEORY OF POLITICS

Throughout our lives we'll all experience changes to our environment we don't like. Below are examples of what some people might consider negative changes to their environment:

- The government increases taxes.

- The state imposes a ban on handguns.

- The Supreme Court rules that prayer in public schools is unconstitutional.

- The national currency drops in value.

- Fuel-efficient cars are imported from a foreign country.

- The quality of peaches at your local fruit stand declines.

Note that although some people will not like these changes and will see them as bad, others will see them as improvements. For example, those people who have to pay higher taxes will be unhappy when the government raises the tax rate, but recipients of government benefits might be better off. Although consumers in the domestic market are likely to suffer when the national currency drops in value because imports are now more expensive, exporters are likely to benefit because their goods are more competitive. The importation of fuel-efficient cars may well have negative consequences for domestic car manufacturers who can no longer compete, but it provides benefits for consumers who are struggling with high gas prices. Similarly, the Supreme Court decision that prayer in schools is unconstitutional would obviously upset some people, but it would just as likely make others happy. On the whole, political situations nearly always involve some individuals or groups benefiting at the expense of other individuals and groups. As we'll see, politics is frequently about winners and losers.

When bad things happen, though, who has the power to reverse them? Who has the power to stop bad things happening to them in the first place? To begin answering these types of questions, let's start by thinking about the options available to you when there's a negative change in your environment. Broadly speaking, you have three possible options—you can **exit**, use **voice**, or demonstrate **loyalty**.

Choosing to exit means that you accept the negative change in your environment and alter your behavior to achieve the best outcome possible given your new environment. For example, if you don't like the fact that your state has introduced a ban on handguns, you could accept the policy change as inevitable and simply move to another state where handguns are allowed. Similarly, if you don't like a decline in the quality of peaches at your local fruit stand, you could accept the decline in peach quality and either go to a different fruit stand to buy peaches or start buying mangoes instead.

Choosing to use voice means complaining, protesting, lobbying, or taking other forms of direct action to try to change your environment back to its original condition. For example, if the government increases your tax rate, you might join an antitax protest to pressure the government to reverse its tax hike. Similarly, if the importation of fuel-efficient cars is having negative effects on your automobile firm, you could consider lobbying the government to place import restrictions or tariffs on these cars.

Choosing to demonstrate loyalty means you accept the negative change in your environment and make no change to your preexisting behavior. For example, if the Supreme Court rules that prayer in public schools is unconstitutional, you could accept the situation and keep your children in the public school system. In Table 3.1, we illustrate what it means to use exit, voice, or loyalty in response to several potentially negative changes in your environment.

To put some specifics on things, let's consider the situation in which the government introduces a policy that negatively affects the environment of one of its citizens. How should the citizen respond? When should the citizen choose to exit, use voice, or remain loyal? The citizen's choice will depend on what she expects to happen when she chooses one of these options. In order for the citizen to know what to do, she needs to know what the government would do if she used voice. On the one hand, the fact that the citizen complains or protests might cause the government to respond positively to the citizen. This would lead to the restoration of the citizen's original environment. On the other hand, the government might simply ignore the citizen's use of voice. If the government ignores her, the citizen would have to decide what to do next. After all, even though the citizen's use of voice failed, she'd still have the option to exit or remain loyal. What should the citizen do? What should the government do? As you've probably noticed, the problem facing the citizen and government is complicated because the

TABLE 3.1 ■ Examples of Exit, Voice, and Loyalty			
Stimulus	**Exit**	**Voice**	**Loyalty**
The government increases taxes.	Reallocate portfolio to avoid tax increase.	Organize tax revolt.	Continue to pay taxes, and keep your mouth shut.
There is a decline in the quality of peaches at the local fruit stand.	Buy mangoes, or buy peaches somewhere else.	Complain to the store owner.	Continue to eat peaches, and keep your mouth shut.
The Supreme Court rules that prayer in public schools is unconstitutional.	Homeschool your children.	Lobby the government to change the Constitution.	Keep your children in the public school system, and keep your mouth shut.
Your state outlaws handguns.	Move to a different state.	Join the NRA or a militia group to put pressure on the state to allow handguns.	Turn in your handguns, and keep your mouth shut.

citizen's choice of what to do depends on what she thinks the government will do, and the government's choice of what to do depends on what it thinks the citizen will do. This strategic aspect of social interactions is the essence of politics.

It can be useful when thinking about a **strategic situation** like this one to map out the sequence of choices available to the actors involved. This is what we've done with the help of a decision tree in Figure 3.1. A **decision tree** is a map of the possible outcomes of a series of related choices. Recall that the government has introduced a policy the citizen doesn't like—perhaps a tax hike that increases the government's revenue but reduces the citizen's income. We can think of this more generally as the government taking something of value from the citizen. We're now at the top of the decision tree in Figure 3.1, with the citizen deciding whether to exit, use voice, or remain loyal. If the citizen decides to exit, the government gets to keep the benefit it seized from the citizen, and the citizen opts for some substitute. This is Outcome 1 (O1). If the citizen chooses to remain loyal, the government gets to keep the benefit it seized, and the citizen just suffers the loss in silence. This is Outcome 2 (O2). If the citizen chooses to use voice, the government must decide whether to respond positively to the citizen or ignore her. If the government responds positively, the government returns to the citizen the benefit it had previously taken. This is Outcome 3 (O3). If the government ignores the citizen's use of voice, the citizen must decide whether to remain loyal or exit.[2] If the citizen chooses to exit, the government gets to keep the benefit that it took, and the citizen opts for

FIGURE 3.1 ■ The Decision Tree for the EVL Theory

---

[2]You might be wondering why the citizen can't choose to use her voice again at this point. Well, obviously, she could. But ask yourself whether the government would behave any differently this time around if nothing else has changed. If the government ignored the citizen's voice before, it will do so again. Thus, allowing the citizen to use her voice at this point in the decision tree doesn't add anything substantively new. This is why we allow the citizen to choose only between exiting and remaining loyal if the government decides to ignore her use of voice.

some substitute. This is Outcome 4 (O4). If the citizen remains loyal, the government gets to keep the benefit that it took, and the citizen suffers the loss. This is Outcome 5 (O5).

What choices do you expect the citizen and government to make? To answer this question, we must first think about how the citizen and government value the possible outcomes in our decision tree. We show how our actors value each of the five possible outcomes in Table 3.2. We can think of the values in Table 3.2 as the "payoffs" that each of the actors receives from reaching a particular outcome. But where do these payoffs come from? Well, they come from the theoretical story we're telling.

If the citizen ever chooses to exit, she gets what we call her "exit payoff." We arbitrarily set the value of the citizen's exit payoff at E. The precise value of E in any specific situation will depend on the attractiveness of the citizen's exit option. Some citizens will have attractive exit options (E will be high), whereas others will not (E will be low). If the citizen ever chooses to remain loyal, she accepts her loss and gets nothing, 0. We assume that the use of voice is costly for the citizen, because protesting, complaining, lobbying, or taking direct action all require effort that could be put to an alternative use. Depending on the country in which she lives, voice might be costly in other respects as well. For example, one's involvement in a protest might be met by imprisonment, loss of employment, or even death. In other words, the degree of government repression will likely affect the citizen's cost of using voice. For these reasons, the citizen will suffer a positive cost, c, whenever she uses her voice.

Recall that the government took something of value from the citizen. If the government ever gets to keep this benefit, then it gets a payoff of 1.[3] We could have chosen any positive number to represent this payoff, but 1 is the easiest for presentational purposes. Whenever the citizen chooses to remain loyal, the government also receives a positive loyalty payoff, L. This additional loyalty payoff captures the notion that governments value having a loyal citizenry and can be thought of in at least a couple of ways. One is that loyal citizens can make life easier for government officials by providing them with support to help them stay in power or by providing them with what could be thought of as "legitimacy." The other is that loyal citizens

TABLE 3.2 ■ Turning Outcomes into Payoffs

Outcome	Description	Citizen	Government
O1	The government keeps the benefit but loses the support of the citizen. The citizen opts for some substitute.	E	1
O2	The government keeps both the benefit and the support of the citizen. The citizen suffers her loss in silence.	0	$1 + L$
O3	The government returns the benefit to the citizen and keeps her support.	$1 - c$	L
O4	The government keeps the benefit but loses the support of the citizen. Having used her voice, the citizen opts for some substitute.	$E - c$	1
O5	The government keeps both the benefit and the support of the citizen. Having used her voice, the citizen suffers her loss.	$0 - c$	$1 + L$

Note: E = citizen's exit payoff; 1 = value of benefit taken from the citizen by the government; L = government's value from having a loyal citizen who does not exit; c = cost of using voice.

---

[3]In effect, the citizen used to have a payoff of 1 but the government took it from her, leaving her with nothing. This is why the citizen receives a payoff of 0 when she chooses to remain loyal.

continue to invest in the economy or other activities that provide meaningful resources and support to the government. Whatever the precise source of this additional loyalty payoff, its size will obviously vary across governments and citizens. Some governments desire or require more support from their citizenry than others, and some citizens are more important to government officials than others.

We can now put these payoffs together to see how the citizen and government each value the five possible outcomes in our decision tree. Recall that these are the payoffs shown in Table 3.2. In Outcome 1 (O1), the citizen's payoff is E, because she exits; the government's payoff is 1, because it gets to keep the benefit it took from the citizen. In Outcome 2 (O2), the citizen's payoff is 0, because she remains loyal; the government's payoff is $1 + L$, because it gets to keep the benefit it took from the citizen and it retains a loyal citizen. In Outcome 3 (O3), the citizen's payoff is $1 - c$, because the government returns the benefit to the citizen, but the citizen had to use her voice to get it; the government's payoff is L, because the government retains a loyal citizen. In Outcome 4 (O4), the citizen's payoff is $E - c$, because she exits but only after using her voice; the government's payoff is 1, because it gets to keep the benefit that it took from the citizen. In Outcome 5 (O5), the citizen's payoff is $0 - c$, because the citizen chooses to remain loyal but only after using her voice; the government's payoff is $1 + L$, because it gets to keep the benefit it took from the citizen as well as retain a loyal citizen. We can now add these payoffs to the decision tree we constructed in Figure 3.1. The new decision tree with the payoffs is shown in Figure 3.2. The citizen's payoffs are shown first because she makes the first choice in the decision tree; the government's payoffs are shown second. A comma separates the payoffs for the two actors.

FIGURE 3.2 ■ The Decision Tree for the EVL Theory with Payoffs

Note: E = citizen's exit payoff; 1 = value of benefit taken from the citizen by the government; *L* = government's value from having a loyal citizen who does not exit; *c* = cost of using voice. It is assumed that *c, L* > 0, and that *E* < 1 – *c*. The citizen's payoffs are shown first because she is the first actor to make a choice; the government's payoffs are shown second. A comma separates the payoffs for the two actors.

We're almost ready to think about the choices the citizen and government will make. Before we do this, though, we make one final assumption. Specifically, we assume that $E < 1 - c$. Why do we assume this? Well, think about what this assumption means for a moment. This assumption states that the value the citizen gets from exiting (O1) is less than the value she gets from successfully using her voice and regaining the benefit the government has taken (O3). This assumption simply says we're considering only the set of social situations in which exit is sufficiently unattractive that the value of having the government respond positively minus the cost of using voice is greater than the value offered by exit. If we didn't make this assumption, the citizen would always exit irrespective of how the government would respond to her use of voice. We believe this assumption makes the situation we're examining more interesting from a political point of view, as there's now at least the possibility the citizen might try to exert influence over the government by choosing to use her voice.

WHAT HAPPENS IN THE EVL THEORY?

Our goal now is to say something about what we expect the citizen and government to do. What choices do you think the citizen and government will make? Actors in a strategic situation like the one shown in Figure 3.2 typically don't make choices at random. Instead, they think about the consequences of their choices and therefore think ahead. They try to think about and anticipate how the other actors they're interacting with will respond to their choices. For example, an actor might ask herself how some other actor would respond if she chooses Action A and how that same actor would respond if she chooses Action B. The actor then chooses the action, A or B, that's expected, in light of the anticipated reaction of other actors, to give her the highest payoff. This process is quite familiar to players of strategic games. Before making a move in a chess or checkers game, for example, a player takes into consideration what she thinks the other player will do if she takes each of the possible moves open to her. Based on how she thinks the other player will respond to each of these possible moves, she then chooses the move that she thinks will be the best. The logical extension of this thought process leads players to begin at the end of the game and reason backward. This process is called **backward induction** and is probably something that most of us do unconsciously when making decisions in our everyday lives.

In the context of our particular strategic situation in Figure 3.2, backward induction requires starting at the bottom of the decision tree and working our way to the top. The last choice in the decision tree sees the citizen deciding whether to exit or remain loyal. What should she do? Well, if she exits, we can see that she receives a payoff of $E - c$. If the citizen remains loyal, we can see that she receives a payoff of $0 - c$. The decision whether to exit or remain loyal therefore depends on whether $0 - c$ is larger (more valuable) than $E - c$. For now, let's assume that $E > 0$; that is, let's assume that the citizen's exit payoff is greater than her loyalty payoff. We can think that the citizen has a credible exit threat in this scenario as she prefers to exit rather than remain loyal. Once we make this assumption, it becomes clear that $E - c > 0 - c$, and, as a result the citizen will exit rather than remain loyal. We indicate this choice by making the exit option at the bottom choice in the decision tree bold. This is shown in Figure 3.3.[4]

Now we move backward, up the decision tree, to the previous choice, which is made by the government. At this point, the government has to decide whether to respond positively

---

[4]We have removed the descriptions of the five possible outcomes from our decision tree so that we can concentrate on the payoffs.

FIGURE 3.3   ■   The EVL Theory When the Citizen Has a Credible Exit Threat (E > 0): Step 1 of Backward Induction

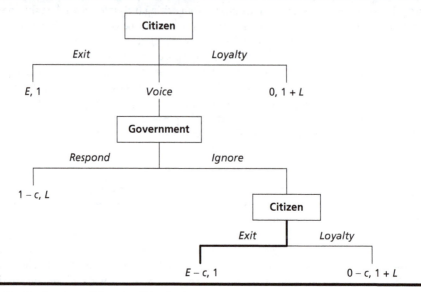

Note: E = citizen's exit payoff; 1 = value of benefit taken from the citizen by the government; *L* = government's value from having a loyal citizen who does not exit; *c* = cost of using voice. It is assumed that *c*, *L* > 0; *E* < 1 – *c*; *E* > 0. The citizen's payoffs are shown first because she is the first actor to make a choice; the government's payoffs are shown second.

to the citizen or ignore her. If the government responds positively, it receives a payoff of *L*. If the government ignores the citizen, it can look down the decision tree (follow the bold line) and anticipate that the citizen will exit and that its payoff will be 1. The decision whether to respond positively to the citizen or ignore her will obviously depend on whether *L* is larger or smaller than 1. For now, let's assume that *L* > 1. We can think that the government is *dependent* on the citizen in this scenario as it values the citizen's loyalty (*L*) more than the benefit (1) it took from her. Once we make this assumption, it becomes clear the government will respond positively to the citizen's use of voice. We indicate this choice by making the respond choice at this point in the decision tree bold. This is shown in Figure 3.4.

Now we move backward to the very top of the decision tree. Here the citizen has to decide whether to exit, remain loyal, or use her voice. If the citizen chooses to exit, she receives a payoff of *E*. If the citizen chooses to remain loyal, she receives a payoff of 0. And if the citizen chooses to use her voice, she can look down the decision tree (follow the bold lines) and anticipate that the government will respond positively and that her payoff will be 1 – *c*. As always, the citizen will choose the action that provides her with the highest payoff. Remember we've assumed in this particular scenario that the citizen has a credible exit threat (*E* > 0) and that *E* < 1 – *c*. Given these assumptions, it's easy to see that the citizen will choose to use voice to get a payoff of 1 – *c* instead of *E* or 0. Again, we indicate this choice by making the voice option at the top of the decision tree bold. This is shown in Figure 3.5.

We can now see the choices the citizen and government will make in this particular scenario of our EVL theory. Thanks to our use of backward induction, each of the choices shown in bold are the best available to the actor making the choice (citizen or government) given how

FIGURE 3.4 ■ The EVL Theory When the Citizen Has a Credible Exit Threat ($E > 0$) and the Government Is Dependent ($L > 1$): Step 2 of Backward Induction

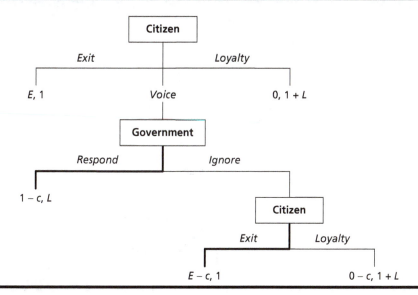

Note: E = citizen's exit payoff; 1 = value of benefit taken from the citizen by the government; L = government's value from having a loyal citizen who does not exit; c = cost of using voice. It is assumed that c, $L > 0$; $E < 1 - c$; $E > 0$; $L > 1$. The citizen's payoffs are shown first because she is the first actor to make a choice; the government's payoffs are shown second.

that actor anticipates the other actor will respond further down the decision tree. In the scenario we've examined where the citizen has a credible exit threat ($E > 0$) and the government is dependent ($L > 1$), the bold lines on our decision tree in Figure 3.5 indicate that the citizen will use her voice and the government will respond positively. The bold lines also indicate that the citizen would have exited if the government had ignored her use of voice. In this particular scenario, therefore, the citizen is able to exert power over the government and force it to retract the policy she doesn't like.

It's worth spending a moment to think through exactly why the government is responsive to the citizen in this scenario. Ask yourself why the government chooses to respond positively to the citizen's use of voice rather than ignore it? The answer is that the government responds positively because it *anticipates* the citizen will exit further down the decision tree if it ignores her, an outcome it wishes to avoid. In other words, knowledge about what the citizen will choose further down the decision tree if this point were ever reached is crucial in determining what happens. An important insight to take away from this, more generally, is that the choices not taken are often as important to understanding the outcomes of strategic interactions as the choices we actually observe. As we'll see later in the chapter, power is often most effective when it's least observable. One of the benefits of examining strategic situations like the one we have here is that it forces the analyst to consider the influence of anticipated events. These anticipated events can have a tremendous impact on people's behavior even though they might never actually occur; they never occur precisely because people anticipate them and change their behavior to avoid them.

FIGURE 3.5 ■ The EVL Theory When the Citizen Has a Credible Exit Threat ($E > 0$) and the Government Is Dependent ($L > 1$): Step 3 of Backward Induction

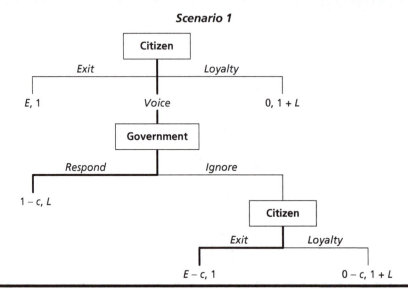

Note: E = citizen's exit payoff; 1 = value of benefit taken from the citizen by the government; L = government's value from having a loyal citizen who does not exit; c = cost of using voice. It is assumed that c, $L > 0$; $E < 1 - c$; $E > 0$; $L > 1$. The citizen's payoffs are shown first because she is the first actor to make a choice; the government's payoffs are shown second.

Our analysis of the EVL theory so far has focused on the scenario where the citizen has a credible exit threat ($E > 0$) and the government is dependent ($L > 1$). What happens if we change the scenario? What happens, for example, if we retain the assumption that the government is dependent ($L > 1$), but now assume that the citizen lacks a credible exit threat ($E < 0$)? In other words, let's assume that, as unhappy as the citizen may be with the policy that the government has introduced, remaining loyal is preferred to exiting. The decision tree for this particular scenario is shown in Figure 3.6. As before, the bold lines indicate the optimal choices for the citizen and government. As you can see, the citizen chooses to remain loyal from the very beginning. Why? Well, we know the citizen will remain loyal at the bottom of the decision tree as she doesn't have a credible exit threat. Knowing this, the government, even though it's dependent on the citizen, is free to ignore the citizen's use of voice. Because the government is going to ignore her use of voice and she lacks a credible exit threat, the citizen's best option is to remain loyal from the beginning. Thus, in the scenario where the citizen lacks a credible exit threat ($E < 0$) and the government is dependent ($L > 1$), the citizen is powerless and must simply live with the government policy she doesn't like.

Let's now look at a third scenario where we assume that the citizen has a credible exit threat ($E > 0$) but the government is autonomous and doesn't depend on the citizen ($L < 1$). An autonomous government is one that values what it took from the citizen (1) more than the citizen's loyalty (L). The decision tree for this particular scenario is shown in Figure 3.7. The bold lines again indicate the optimal choices for the citizen and government. As you can see, the citizen chooses to exit at the very beginning. Why? We know the citizen will exit at the bottom of the decision tree as she has a credible exit threat. The government, though, doesn't care if the citizen

FIGURE 3.6 ■ The EVL Theory When the Citizen Does Not Have a Credible Exit Threat ($E < 0$) and the Government Is Dependent ($L > 1$)

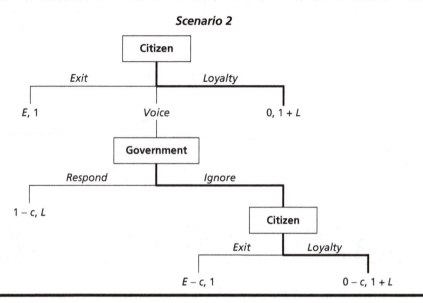

Scenario 2

Note: E = citizen's exit payoff; 1 = value of benefit taken from the citizen by the government; L = government's value from having a loyal citizen who does not exit; c = cost of using voice. It is assumed that $c, L > 0$; $E < 1 - c$; $E < 0$; $L > 1$.

FIGURE 3.7 ■ The EVL Theory When the Citizen Has a Credible Exit Threat ($E > 0$) and the Government Is Autonomous ($L < 1$)

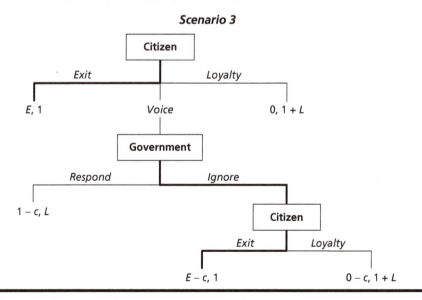

Scenario 3

Note: E = citizen's exit payoff; 1 = value of benefit taken from the citizen by the government; L = government's value from having a loyal citizen who does not exit; c = cost of using voice. It is assumed that $c, L > 0$; $E < 1 - c$; $E > 0$; $L < 1$.

exits as it's autonomous. As a result, the government will ignore any use of voice on the part of the citizen. Knowing this, the best the citizen can do in the beginning is to exit. Thus, in the scenario where the citizen has a credible exit threat ($E < 0$) and the government is autonomous ($L < 1$), the citizen is powerless and can't get the government to retract the policy she doesn't like.

Let's look at the last possible scenario. What happens if we assume the citizen lacks a credible exit threat ($E < 0$) and the government is autonomous ($L > 1$)? The decision tree for this fourth scenario is shown in Figure 3.8. As always, the bold lines indicate the optimal choices for the citizen and government. As you can see, the citizen chooses to remain loyal from the very beginning. Why? Well, we know the citizen will remain loyal at the bottom of the decision tree as she doesn't have a credible exit threat. The government doesn't really care what the citizen does at the bottom of the decision tree as it's autonomous. As a result, the government will ignore any use of voice on the part of the citizen. Because the government is going to ignore her use of voice and she lacks a credible exit threat, the citizen's best option at the beginning is to remain loyal. Thus, in the scenario where the citizen lacks a credible exit threat ($E < 0$) and the government is autonomous ($L < 1$), the citizen is powerless and must simply live with the government policy she doesn't like.

FIGURE 3.8 ■ The EVL Theory When the Citizen Does Not Have a Credible Exit Threat ($E < 0$) and the Government Is Autonomous ($L < 1$)

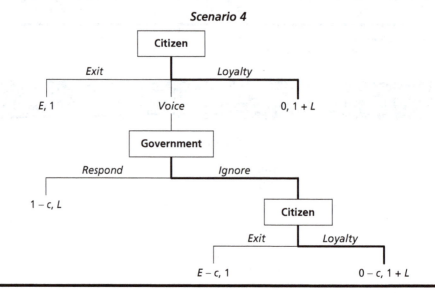

Note: E = citizen's exit payoff; 1 = value of benefit taken from the citizen by the government; L = government's value from having a loyal citizen who does not exit; c = cost of using voice. It is assumed that $c, L > 0$; $E < 1 - c$; $E < 0$; $L < 1$.

INSIGHTS FROM THE EVL THEORY

What can we learn from the EVL theory about the balance of power between citizens and the government? The outcomes associated with each of the four scenarios we've examined are summarized in Table 3.3. As we've already seen, what happens in the EVL theory depends

TABLE 3.3 ■ A Summary of the Expected Outcomes in the Four Scenarios of the EVL Theory		
	The government	
The citizen	Is autonomous ($L < 1$)	Is dependent ($L > 1$)
Has a credible exit threat ($E > 0$)	O1: The citizen exits.	O3: The citizen uses her voice and the government responds positively.
Has no credible exit threat ($E < 0$)	O2: The citizen remains loyal.	O2: The citizen remains loyal.

Note: Only in the shaded cell, where the citizen has a credible exit threat and the government is dependent, can the citizen exert power over the government.

on whether the citizen has a credible exit threat or not (rows) and whether the government is autonomous or dependent (columns).

The EVL theory offers several important insights regarding the power relationship between citizens and governments. The first is that the citizen is able to exert power over the government only when two conditions are met: (1) the citizen must have a credible exit threat ($E > 0$) *and* (2) the government must be dependent on the citizen ($L > 1$). Only in the shaded cell in Table 3.3 does the citizen use her voice and the government respond positively. You might have thought that a citizen could exert influence over the government whenever she has a credible exit threat. But this is clearly not the case. The government must also be dependent for the citizen with a credible exit threat to be able to influence it. A citizen with a credible exit threat does have an advantage in relation to one without such a threat, because the citizen with a credible exit threat has the realistic option of exiting, whereas the other citizen does not. Our point here, though, is that having a credible exit option is not sufficient in and of itself for the citizen to exert influence over the government. Put differently, an autonomous government will never respond positively even if the citizen has a credible exit threat.

Think about what this means for your life more generally. If you want to be able to influence others (say, for example, you want your employer to give you a pay raise), then you should try to make sure that you have a credible exit threat (there are other jobs you could do or other firms that would hire you) and that the person you are interacting with depends on you in some way (perhaps you are the only one who knows how the firm's accounts work). If other firms are willing to hire you but your employer doesn't depend on you, then your employer will feel free to ignore you. Similarly, if your employer depends on you but other firms are not willing to hire you, then your employer will again feel free to ignore you. The only way to have power and be able to influence others is if you have a credible exit threat and the person or group you want to influence depends on you. Think about how this applies to other relationships in your life. What about the relationship between you and your parents, you and your professors, you and your friends, or you and your significant other? Do you have a credible exit threat in these relationships? Do the actors on the other side of these relationships depend on you? Your answers to these questions will indicate whether you have power and influence in these relationships.

The second important insight is that in the absence of a credible exit option ($E < 0$) the citizen is a sitting duck. Under these conditions, the government can take away the citizen's benefits, and there is nothing the citizen can do about it but accept the new state of affairs. How can we see this insight at work in the real world? Well, some have argued that the Democratic

Party in the United States has not done enough to address the concerns of African American voters. If this is true—and we don't wish to enter that particular debate here—then our EVL theory throws some light on why this might be the case. Clearly, Democrats depend on African American voters. Without their vote, Democrats have little chance of winning national office as things stand. But ask yourself whether African American voters have a credible exit threat. In other words, is there another party that African Americans could credibly threaten to vote for instead of the Democrats? Some might argue that the fact that African Americans rarely vote for the Republican Party sends a signal to the Democratic Party that African Americans don't have a credible exit threat. Think about it this way. If the Republican Party were a credible option for African Americans, wouldn't more of them vote for it? Observing this signal, the Democratic Party can, to some extent, ignore (and exploit) African Americans even though it depends heavily on this particular constituency for its electoral success. The bottom line is that we should always strive to make sure that we have credible exit threats in our life because they're a necessary, though not sufficient, condition to make sure we're not exploited. Going back to our example, this suggests, perhaps somewhat counterintuitively, that African Americans who want the Democratic Party to pay more attention to their concerns and to treat them better should start voting for the Republican Party as a way of signaling that they have a credible exit threat. Only then will the Democratic Party feel that it has to take African Americans seriously.

On the other side of the political spectrum, conservative religious voters in the United States are often dissatisfied with the policies the Republican Party supports. However, they are even less satisfied with the policies the Democratic Party promotes. What are their options? If we follow the same logic as before, these conservative religious voters should start voting for the Democratic Party to signal to the Republican Party that they have a credible exit option. In both of these cases, though, you might argue that voting for a different party is not the only available exit option for voters who are dissatisfied with the policies offered by their political party. Eligible voters could simply refuse to vote, or they could temporarily withhold their vote as a signal to their party that its candidates need to take their concerns more seriously. These potential voters need to ask themselves if it would be worth having their less-preferred party be in office for now, if this meant that their preferred party would be more responsive to them later. The answer to that question will obviously depend on how much the voters value present-day policy versus future policy.

We have argued that the government is free to take away the citizen's benefits whenever the citizen lacks a credible exit threat. Note, though, that we can think of the "benefits" the government takes away in many ways. It could be that the government has denied the citizen some of her civil rights or liberties. Alternatively, it could be that the government has taken property away from the citizen through either taxation or appropriation. In our discussion to this point, it has implicitly been assumed that the government has taken something away from the citizen that in some sense rightfully belonged to her. That need not be the case for the EVL theory to be useful in understanding the power relationship between citizens and governments. For example, it could be the case that the government has taken away the citizen's ability to seize an unfair advantage over other citizens—say, through a licensing agreement that grants the holder of the license a market advantage. Thus, there's nothing inherently good about the government's being responsive to the citizen's use of voice; nor is it necessarily loathsome for the government to turn a deaf ear to citizen demands. In fact, we often refer to the demands that some people make on the government as "special interests," and government officials are as likely to be applauded as lambasted for ignoring them.

A third insight from our EVL theory is that it's often difficult to learn very much from observing real-world political situations. Consider the following. It's always possible to infer whether a citizen has a credible exit threat from observing her action. This is because the decision to exit or use voice requires a credible exit threat, whereas the decision to demonstrate loyalty implies the lack of such a threat. It's not so easy to learn whether a government is dependent or autonomous when the citizen has no credible exit threat, however, because both types of government will respond to the use of voice by this type of citizen in exactly the same way—they'll simply ignore her. It's precisely because she expects to be ignored in these circumstances that the citizen without a credible exit threat always chooses to remain loyal in the first place. This is an important point. It means that we shouldn't make the mistake of inferring that governments that experience little use of voice or public opposition, such as those in contemporary China, Iran, and North Korea, are autonomous or that they don't rely on the support of their citizenry. These governments may be very dependent yet feel entirely free to ignore their citizens because their citizens lack credible exit threats.

The history of the collapse of the Communist regime in East Germany is consistent with this logic. For example, one can argue that, with the exception of the Berlin Uprising in 1953, the East German population was very loyal prior to 1989 because it lacked a credible exit threat. To many outsiders (and insiders), it appeared that the Communist regime was very stable and relatively autonomous from its citizens (Kuran 1991). The opening of the Hungarian border to Austria and hence the West in May 1989, however, provided East Germans with a credible exit option for the first time since the construction of the Berlin Wall in 1961.[5] The seemingly "loyal" and rather docile East German population was transformed into enthusiastic protesters who used voice in large numbers on the streets of Leipzig and East Berlin (Garton Ash 1999). One can argue that it was precisely because the East German Communist Party did depend on its citizens, despite all evidence to the contrary for almost three decades, that the Communist regime eventually responded by opening the Berlin Wall. This particular historical example should make us wary of inferring that a government is autonomous when its citizens have no credible exit threat—it might be, but it also might not be.

Similarly, the EVL theory suggests that it's also inappropriate to use political mobilization (voting, lobbying, campaign contributions, and so on), or the lack thereof, as a straightforward revelation of citizen preferences. Citizens may remain silent on particular issues either because they're satisfied with the status quo or because they don't expect their use of voice to be effective.

The EVL theory raises a fourth important point. If the government is responsive to those citizens on whom it depends for loyalty whenever those citizens possess credible exit threats, why would the government ever take a benefit away from these citizens in the first place? This question can't be answered with the EVL theory as it stands. It's relatively easy to extend it, though, by adding a choice at the beginning of our decision trees in which the government decides whether or not to take the benefit away from the citizen. We can think of this as a decision by the government about whether to exploit the citizen by taking away some of her resources or not. If the government chooses to seize the citizen's resource, then the version of the EVL theory we've just examined begins. If the government chooses not to exploit the citizen, the citizen gets to keep her resource, and she remains loyal. What you would find if you were to investigate this "extended" EVL theory is that the government won't exploit the citizen if it depends on her and she has a credible exit threat. This in turn means that the citizen will never have to use her voice. Why? Well, put yourself in the shoes of the dependent government. You can see that if you attempt to exploit a citizen with a credible exit option,

---

[5]By 1961 the East German government had come to recognize that it relied on its citizens to keep the economy afloat and itself in power. By building the Berlin Wall and removing the one credible exit option available to its citizens, the Communist regime was able to deprive its citizens of any influence that they had over it.

the citizen will use her voice, and because you depend on her, you'll respond positively to her demands. Because you know that you'll eventually have to respond positively, you'll choose not to seize the citizen's resources in the first place. As a result, the citizen will never have to use her voice (Clark, Golder, and Golder, 2017).

The important point to note here is that those citizens who have credible exit options wield considerable power without ever needing to open their mouths (use voice) whenever the government depends on them. Consider the epigraph attributed to the former British prime minister Margaret Thatcher at the beginning of this chapter: "Being powerful is like being a lady. If you have to tell people you are, you aren't." Thatcher's major insight was that sufficiently powerful people never need to use their voice because they're already getting other people to do what they want. This insight corresponds exactly to the results we've just discussed from the extended version of the EVL theory.

There are striking similarities between the argument we've just presented and the so-called structural Marxist view of the state (Althusser 1969; Poulantzas 1975, 1980). According to this view, capitalists exercise tremendous power over the government despite speaking in a soft voice because they possess credible exit threats and the government is dependent on them for the deployment of investment that fosters job creation, economic growth, and tax revenues (Przeworski and Wallerstein 1988). It's precisely because capital is generally more mobile than labor (has more credible exit options) that capitalists typically have significantly more influence over the government than workers. This is the case even if the government depends equally on both labor and capital.

This central insight—that powerful people never need to use their voice—poses a particularly troubling problem for political scientists and other scholars who wish to empirically evaluate who has power in a given society. In many cases, the most powerful actors are precisely those citizens who are least likely to take action or use their voice—in other words, the political scientist will never be able to observe them using their power. Our EVL theory suggests that it might be misleading to infer that citizens who don't engage in protests, strikes, lobbying, advertising, and so forth have no significant influence over government policy. To provide a specific example, the EVL theory indicates that it would be wrong to infer that presidents lack power because they rarely use their right to veto legislation. The possibility that presidents will veto legislation is enough to ensure that legislatures send presidents only the bills the president wants. In effect, the president gets what she wants without having to use her veto power (Cameron 2000). The basic point here is that it's difficult to determine who has power and who doesn't simply by observing the world.

Finally, the EVL theory of politics is as noteworthy for what it doesn't explain as for what it does. Notice that in the theory as it stands, citizens use voice only when they expect it to be effective. This means that the theory can't explain why we sometimes see governments being unresponsive to the demands of their citizens. One reason governments might ignore their citizens is that the citizens may not view the use of voice as costly. It's not altogether hard to imagine that some citizens might derive intrinsic benefits from the use of voice. For example, some citizens might welcome the opportunity simply to express themselves. Alternatively, they might use protest rallies as an opportunity to network with other like-minded individuals. Or they might feel a certain pride in the fact that they're living up to their civic responsibilities. If citizens do indeed derive such "consumption" benefits from the use of voice, we could capture this in our model by relaxing the assumption that voice is costly ($c > 0$). In effect, we could assume that $c < 0$ and treat these "negative costs" as benefits. If we do this, it's relatively easy to see that the citizen will always get a higher payoff from using voice than

BOX 3.1 A COMPARISON OF BAILOUTS IN THE US FINANCIAL AND AUTO SECTORS

Many observers were surprised that the US government moved quickly and enthusiastically to bail out "rich" New York banks during the 2008 global financial crisis while moving more slowly and with greater reluctance to come to the aid of troubled car manufacturers. While a full assessment of the prudence of the US policy response to the financial crisis is beyond the scope of our discussion, it should be noted that our EVL theory can help explain why governments might respond differently to different sectors of the economy.

On Monday, September 15, 2008, Lehman Brothers, the fourth largest bank on Wall Street, declared bankruptcy. On the same day, in a deal engineered by Treasury Secretary Henry Paulson Jr., it was announced that Merrill Lynch, the troubled Wall Street financial giant, would be purchased by the Bank of America. Secretary Paulson's attempt to stem financial contagion and calm financial markets failed. The Dow Jones Industrial Average experienced its biggest decline since the aftermath of 9/11. The very next day Paulson and Chairman of the Federal Reserve Ben Bernanke informed members of Congress that the Federal Reserve intended to bail out the troubled insurance giant American International Group with an $85 billion loan. Lawmakers from both parties expressed support for the rescue plan. By the end of the week, Paulson and Bernanke briefed congressional leaders on a much broader plan to support the financial industry. The Troubled Asset Relief Program, or TARP, which authorized the Treasury to spend up to $700 billion to help financial firms get "toxic assets" off their books, was signed into law by President George W. Bush two weeks later on October 3.

In contrast, on Wednesday, September 17, two months after an ailing economy and a rise in gas prices brought car sales to a ten-year low, the chief executive officers of the "Big Three" auto manufacturers (General Motors, Ford, and Chrysler) met with House Speaker Nancy Pelosi to ask for loan guarantees to help the industry through the deepening economic crisis. They emerged from their talks with the promise that aid would be forthcoming, but with few concrete commitments from the government. By the end of the month, the situation had grown worse for the automakers as the credit crunch made it more difficult for the few consumers interested in buying new cars during a recession to find easy finance. By early October, a week after TARP came into law, Chrysler and GM were exploring a merger, something that many saw as an alternative to bankruptcy. At this point, aid was still "forthcoming."

On Tuesday, November 18, the heads of the Big Three returned to Washington to plead with lawmakers for a $25 billion piece of the $700 billion TARP funds; they received a chilly reception. Treasury Secretary Paulson urged lawmakers to resist the temptation to use any of the TARP funds to bail out the auto industry. Congress, doubtful that the $25 billion would be anything more than a lifeline tossed to a dying industry, gave the auto executives twelve days to develop a convincing plan showing how the money could be used to turn the Big Three firms into viable enterprises.

On December 4, the auto executives returned to Washington with a request for $34 billion in TARP funds and a plan for how the funds would be used to turn the firms around. Once again, they were not treated warmly. The Bush administration eventually announced that $13.4 billion of what little of the TARP funds had not already been promised to financial firms would be made available. Many observers at the time believed that this amount was just enough to delay bankruptcy until Bush left office in January 2009.

Clearly, there are striking differences in the way the US government responded to the 2008 crises in the financial and auto sectors of the economy. Most obvious is the magnitude of the

(Continued)

(Continued)

dollar amounts involved. The size of the financial sector bailout dwarfed that of the auto industry bailout, despite the fact that, in the words of GM CEO Rick Wagoner, "The societal costs [of auto industry collapse] would be catastrophic—three million jobs lost within the first year, US personal income reduced by $150 billion and a government tax loss of more than $156 billion over three years" (Vlasic and Herszenshorn 2008, para. 11). Furthermore, the auto industry's call for support came from an industry concentrated in battleground states like Michigan and Ohio just weeks before a presidential election.

Somewhat less obvious, perhaps, was the way in which the leaders of the two sectors were treated by government officials. The heads of the auto industry were publicly chastised for flying in corporate jets to Washington to ask for taxpayer money. They were rebuffed, and when they returned twelve days later to once again beg Congress, they first performed an

act of contrition by carpooling from Detroit to Washington. In contrast, when it became clear that Lehman Brothers was in trouble, Treasury Secretary Paulson flew in a private jet to New York when summoned by New York's Federal Reserve Bank President Timothy Geithner. A few weeks later, when Paulson decided the United States should inject capital into the banks, he summoned the heads of the country's biggest banks to Washington the next day; there was no discussion about how they would get there. Once assembled, the bank chiefs were told "you won't leave this room until you agree to take this money." Notice that the auto industry executives went to Washington to ask for money. In contrast, Washington first went to New York to solve the financial sector's problems and then invited the leaders of the financial sector to Washington to accept the funds the government had proactively decided to bestow upon them. The auto industry repeatedly and publicly asked for funds

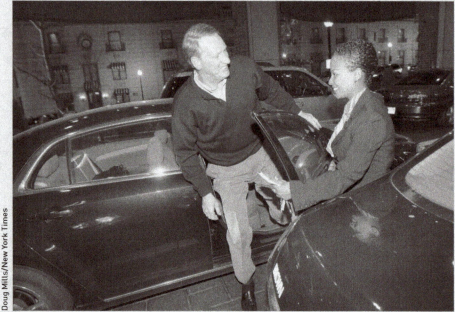

Doug Mills/New York Times

Rick Wagoner, chief executive of General Motors (left), returns to Washington in an electric car, two weeks after being chastised, along with the heads of Ford and Chrysler, for flying to Washington in corporate jets to ask for access to federal bailout funds.

from Congress. Financial industry leaders were summoned to a private meeting where Bush administration officials insisted on loaning them billions of dollars—in much the way a generous dinner host might insist on picking up the tab.

While it's difficult to establish whether the government was equally dependent on the automobile and financial sectors of the economy, there's little doubt that a collapse of either sector would have been extremely costly for the incumbent government. The EVL theory suggests that the difference in the bargaining relationship between the government and firms in both sectors can be attributed to the credibility of exit threats. The aftermath of the Lehman Brothers bankruptcy demonstrated the speed and magnitude with which liquid asset holders could respond to negative changes in their environment. Millions of stockholders suffered serious losses when the value of the stocks they held

declined during the sell-off that occurred after the bankruptcy announcement. No one had to tell the government that it was in their interest to prevent a reoccurrence of this event. In fact, the government had already engaged in dramatic activity to try to prevent the Lehman Brothers bankruptcy in the first place. In contrast, while the Big Three automakers have gradually moved production offshore and can threaten to do so more in the future, the relatively fixed nature of the assets they own makes it hard to do this in a time frame that is relevant to the calculations of survival-maximizing politicians who generally focus on short-term interests such as getting reelected. The comparison illustrates that the government will anticipate the needs of liquid asset holders upon whom it depends, but it will be relatively unresponsive when actors with less credible exit threats are similarly imperiled. This is an issue we'll return to in more detail in Chapter 5.

from exiting or remaining loyal regardless of what the government does. In other words, the citizen will always use her voice even when she knows it won't be successful.[6]

Another reason for sometimes seeing a government ignore its citizens has to do with information. In the current version of the EVL theory, we've assumed that the actors know enough about each other's preferences that they can predict each other's responses perfectly. We could easily relax this assumption, though. Perhaps the government doesn't know whether the citizen has a credible exit threat or not. Or perhaps the citizen doesn't know whether the government is dependent or not. A citizen with a credible exit option might overestimate the value of her loyalty to the government and might find out the hard way that the government is perfectly happy to let her exit. Conversely, a government may believe that a citizen who uses voice is bluffing—that the citizen doesn't intend to make good on her threat to exit.

CONCLUSION

We spend a fair amount of time in later chapters critically evaluating some of the claims we've just made. Our goal in this chapter, though, was to demonstrate that the EVL theory can be used to reveal something about what politics is and how politics works. Human interactions are considered political whenever actors can't accomplish their goals without considering the behavior of other actors. Under such circumstances, the attempt to influence—or to avoid

---

[6]Of course, this only leaves us with a different puzzle, namely, why citizens sometimes choose not to use voice when the government negatively affects their environment.

the influence of—others becomes relevant. It's here that power can, and will, be exercised. Attempts to influence, or break free of the influence of, others involve three basic strategies. Political actors can, as in the primordial response of "fight or flight," attempt to change their environment by using voice or change their position by using exit. *Voice* and *exit* are to be understood metaphorically here. A citizen's use of exit in response to a government policy need not involve emigration. Instead, a citizen might change industries, production processes, or political parties. Similarly, a citizen's use of voice might come as one of a host of behaviors, ranging from a ballot to a bullet. Finally, a citizen's best response to government policy might be to "keep on keepin' on." That is, throughout most of human history, the vast majority of humanity has often found itself between a rock and a hard place. Under such circumstances, it's possible that neither voice nor exit is a feasible or palatable option. It should be clear that here, too, the term *loyalty* is being used metaphorically—indeed, euphemistically.

Key Concepts

politics—the subset of human behavior that involves the use of power or influence

exit—you accept that there's been a negative change in your environment, and you alter your behavior to achieve the best outcome possible given your new environment

voice—you use your "voice" (complain, protest, lobby, or take direct action) to try to change your environment back to its original condition

loyalty—you accept the fact that your environment has changed and make no change to your preexisting behavior

strategic situation—a situation in which the choices of one actor depend on the choices made by other actors

decision tree—a map of the possible outcomes of a series of related choices

backward induction—the process of reasoning backward, from the end of a strategic situation to the beginning, in order to determine an optimal course of action

THE ORIGINS OF THE MODERN STATE

In framing a government which is to be administered by men over men, the great difficulty lies in this: you must first enable the government to control the governed; and in the next place oblige it to control itself.

James Madison, *The Federalist Papers,* No. 51

OVERVIEW

1. A state is an entity that relies on coercion and the threat of force to rule in a given territory. A failed state is a state-like entity that can't coerce and is unable to successfully control the inhabitants of a given territory.

2. We present two views of the state: a contractarian view and a predatory view. According to the contractarian view, the creation of the state helps to resolve political disputes that citizens might have with one another. Although the emergence of the state helps to solve these sorts of problems, it creates a potential new problem between the citizens and the state itself: if the state has sufficient power to prevent conflict between its citizens, what's to stop it from using this power against its citizens?

3. The predatory view of the state focuses on the potential conflicts of interest that exist between citizens and the state. According to the predatory view, states emerge as an unintended consequence of the strategies employed by actors like lords and kings to seize and maintain their hold on power. In many respects, a state can be viewed as an "extortion racket" that threatens the well-being of its citizens and then sells them protection from itself.

In the previous chapter, we defined the domain of politics as the subset of human behavior that involves the use of power. This includes any situation in which individuals can't accomplish their goals without either trying to influence the behavior of others or trying to wrestle free from the influence exerted by others. As anyone who's tried to get her roommate to wash the dishes or her professor to change a grade knows, political behavior is ubiquitous. Politics affects virtually every aspect of our lives. Despite this, the study of comparative politics typically focuses on political behavior that occurs at the level of the state. In this chapter, we focus on the state. We explain what it is, where it comes from, and what its function is. To do this, we concentrate on two common views of the state—the contractarian view of the state and the predatory view of the state. According to the contractarian view, the state emerges to help individuals in cases where decentralized cooperation is likely to be difficult. Although those who subscribe to this view see the creation of the state as a solution to conflicts of interest between citizens, it leads to a new problem—a conflict of interest between citizens and the state itself. The predatory view of the state looks squarely at this new conflict of interest. We'll use the predatory view of the state as a lens through which to study the historical origins of the state in early modern Europe. We begin, though, by examining standard definitions of the state.

WHAT IS A STATE?

The most famous definition of a **state** comes from the German sociologist Max Weber ([1918] 1958, 78). A state, he said, "is a human community that (successfully) claims the *monopoly of the legitimate use of physical force* within a given territory" (p. 78, italics original). Weber's definition has several different components. One is that a state requires a "given territory." In some sense, this component of Weber's definition distinguishes states from nations. At a basic level, a **nation** is a group of people who share some sort of common identity like a language, a religion, or an ethnicity—there's no obvious requirement that the nation be geographically located in a particular place, as a state must. For example, many Jews believed they belonged to a nation long before the current state of Israel was established. Of course, the gradual emergence of the **nation-state** since the eighteenth century has led many to associate nations with states and, hence, with a given territory. It's important to recognize, however, that although the nation-state has become by far the most predominant political entity in the world, there are still "stateless nations," like the Kurds in Iraq, and "diasporic nations" without a clearly identified homeland, such as the Roma. As a result, nations and states remain distinct concepts even if there are historical periods when they seem to occur together. On the whole, all definitions of a state since Weber's have retained his assertion that some kind of "given territory" is a required characteristic for a state.

A second component of Weber's definition is that the state must have a "monopoly on the *legitimate* use of physical force." This focus on "legitimacy" has troubled many scholars because it's not always easy to determine what is, and isn't, a legitimate use of force. In fact, we can all probably think of situations in which the use of force by the state lacks legitimacy. For example, many of you will think that the violence state officials perpetrated on the civil rights protesters of the 1960s in the United States was illegitimate. Martin Luther King Jr. clearly considered certain actions by the US state to be illegitimate when he criticized it for being "the greatest purveyor of violence in the world" during an anti-Vietnam War speech in New York City in 1967. These examples suggest that a state's use of force need not always be legitimate, at least in the minds of some of its citizens. It's because of this that subsequent scholars have largely dropped any reference to legitimacy in their definitions of the state.

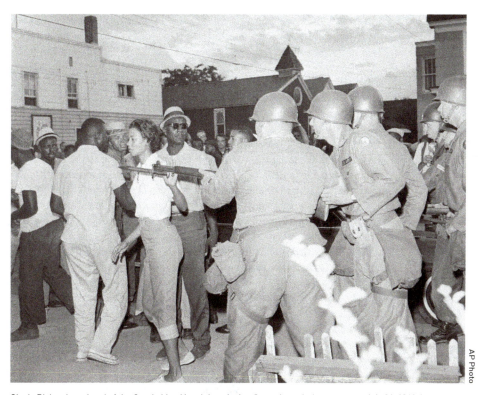

Gloria Richardson, head of the Cambridge Nonviolent Action Committee, led a protest on July 21, 1963, in Cambridge, Maryland, in the presence of the National Guard.

A third component of Weber's definition is that a state must have a "*monopoly* on the legitimate use of physical force." This focus on "monopoly" has also troubled many scholars. The primary reason for this is that it's relatively easy to think of examples in which nonstate actors have the ability to use physical force and in which this use of force might be considered legitimate. For instance, many people believe the use of force by groups such as the Irish Republican Army in Northern Ireland, Hamas and Islamic Jihad in the Palestinian territories, or al-Qaida in Iraq and Afghanistan is a legitimate response to foreign occupation and repression. Similarly, many believe that the violent resistance by the Islamic mujahideen to Soviet control in Afghanistan during the 1980s was legitimate. Of course, one man's freedom fighter is another man's terrorist, and whether you agree that the violent actions of these nonstate groups are legitimate or not will probably depend on which side of the conflict you're on. Thus, it's not obvious that a state always has a "monopoly" on the legitimate use of force. It's for this reason that subsequent scholars have tended to shy away from using the term *monopoly* when defining the state's use of physical force.

Below are two more recent definitions of a state. The first is by a sociologist named Charles Tilly, and the second is by the Nobel-laureate economist Douglass North.

[States are] relatively centralized, differentiated organizations, the officials of which, more or less, successfully claim control over the chief concentrated means of violence within a population inhabiting a large contiguous territory. (Tilly 1985, 170)

> A state is an organization with a comparative advantage in violence, extending over a geographic area whose boundaries are determined by its power to tax constituents. (North 1981, 21)

Although these definitions differ from that provided by Weber in that they no longer refer to legitimacy or a monopoly over the use of force, they share his belief that all states must have a given territory and that they inherently rely on the threat of force to rule. That states rely on the threat of forceful coercion can't be overemphasized. The economic historian Frederick Lane (1958) even refers to a state as a violence-producing enterprise. All states use at least the threat of force to organize public life. This is true whether we're referring to the harshest of dictatorships or the most laudable of democracies. The more obvious use of force by dictatorships shouldn't hide the fact that state rule in democracies is also based on the threat of force (and often the use of force). To see this, think about how many of us would actually pay our taxes in full if the threat of imprisonment from the state for tax avoidance was not implicit. Even if the state uses force in the best interests of society and is authorized to use force by its citizens, we should never forget that it still rules by coercion.

That states rule through the use of force doesn't mean they're all-powerful. As we noted earlier, states never perfectly monopolize force in any country. This explains why North claims only that states must have a "comparative advantage in violence" and Tilly that they have control "over the chief concentrated means of violence." Nor does the state's ability to use force necessarily mean that it can always enforce its will. All states tolerate some noncompliance. For example, the state doesn't punish every driver who runs a red light or every underage student who drinks alcohol. At some point, the marginal cost of enforcing laws becomes so great for any state that it prefers to allow some degree of noncompliance rather than spend more resources on improving law enforcement. The bottom line is that although various states justify coercion in different ways (through elections, through birthright, through religion, and so on), although they may use coercion for different purposes (to improve social welfare or to enrich themselves, and so on), and although their use of coercion may have different effects (higher levels of investment and economic growth or increased poverty and conflict, and so on), all states rely on, and use, coercion to rule.

States that can't coerce and are unable to use force to successfully control the inhabitants of a given territory are often described as **failed states** (King and Zeng 2001; Milliken 2003; Rotberg 2002). For example, contemporary observers frequently refer to countries such as Afghanistan, the Central African Republic, Iraq, Syria, Somalia, Sudan, and Yemen as failed states. These states aren't "failing" because they're unable to meet some policy objective; they're "failing" because they're unable to provide the functions that define them as states— they're unable to coerce or successfully control the inhabitants in their territory. In effect, states in these countries fail to exist.

SYRIA: A FAILED STATE

But what does a failed state look like exactly? In what follows, we briefly describe the history of a failed state in Syria. The collapse of the Syrian state has its roots in the 2011 Arab Spring. Syria, like the other countries in the Middle East and North Africa region that experienced pro-democracy protests, had long been a dictatorship. The president of Syria Bashar al-Assad came to power in 2000, following the death of his father, Hafez al-Assad, who had previously ruled Syria for thirty years. In March 2011, protests broke out in response to the arrest and torture of some teenagers who, inspired by events taking place in Tunisia and Egypt, had sprayed anti-regime slogans on a wall (Fahim and Saad 2013). The protests were met by gunfire from the regime's security forces, and several protesters were killed. This incident led to more demonstrations, which were met by further violence and repression, which in turn prompted larger protests. By July, hundreds of thousands of Syrians were out on the streets protesting. It wasn't long before some of the protesters began to take up arms.

Violent confrontations between protesters and regime forces soon transformed into an open civil war between rebel groups and the Syrian government. According to a 2012 UN Report, the conflict has a sectarian element, with Syria's minority Allawite community and other Shia groups on the government side fighting against the majority Sunni community on the rebels' side (United Nations High Commissioner for Human Rights [UNHCR] 2013). Numerous foreign countries have been drawn into the conflict. The Syrian government has received support from Russia, Iran, Iraq, and the Lebanese group Hezbollah, while the rebels have received support from the United States, Turkey, Saudi Arabia, and a variety of other Arab nations. Some have claimed that the conflict between the Syrian government and the rebels is a proxy war between regional Sunni and Shia powers, especially Saudi Arabia and Iran (Gerges 2013).

The conflict took on a second dimension when the Islamic terrorist group, the Islamic State in Iraq and the Levant (ISIL), sought to expand its influence beyond Iraq into Syria.[1] The United States is particularly concerned with the rise of ISIL. Indeed, US air strikes in Syria are primarily targeted at ISIL forces rather than forces controlled by the Syrian government. The United States has been joined in its fight against ISIL by Turkey, Australia, France, Canada, the

People walk over the rubble following an air strike on a rebel-held neighborhood in Aleppo, Syria, on April 28, 2016.

AMEER ALHALBI/AFP/Getty Images

---

[1]People use many different names to refer to this particular terrorist group. Some, like us, refer to it as the Islamic State in Iraq and the Levant (ISIL). However, others refer to it as the Islamic State in Iraq and al-Sham or the Islamic State in Iraq and Syria (ISIS). After it announced the restoration of a caliphate in the Middle East in June 2014, the group itself started using the name Islamic State (IS). More recently, a few countries have begun referring to the terrorist group as Daesh, an acronym derived from the group's original Arabic name.

United Kingdom, and a variety of Arab countries that believe ISIL is a threat to their own security. Kurdish ground forces have been America's main ally in the fight against ISIL. With the help of US air strikes, Kurdish forces have gained control of territory along the Turkish border in the north of Syria. This, though, has created tension between the United States and Turkey, which has been fighting a Kurdish separatist movement for several decades. Although Russia claims to also be concerned about ISIL, its bombing raids have mainly targeted areas held by antigovernment rebels instead of ISIL. Some commentators have claimed that "what started as a popular uprising against the Syrian government . . . has become a proto-world war with nearly a dozen countries embroiled in two overlapping conflicts" (Peçanha, Almukhtar, and Lai 2015).

The collapse of the Syrian state has been devastating for all Syrians. Since the violence began, more than 465,000 Syrians have been killed and another million injured. ("Syria's civil war explained from the beginning" 2017). Despite the Syrian government's claims to the contrary, international observers believe that the Syrian government has used chemical weapons against its opponents. In addition to the deaths it's caused, the Syrian civil war has left about 12 million people displaced—half of the country's pre-war population. Of the displaced persons, more than 5 million are in poorly resourced refugee camps in bordering countries, such as Egypt, Iraq, Jordan, Lebanon, and Turkey (UNHCR 2017). Others have managed to travel to Europe, where their presence has become a major political issue and contributed to the European refugee crisis ("Migrant Crisis" 2016). Between 2011 and 2017, European countries received nearly a million asylum applications from Syrian refugees alone (UNHCR 2018). The topic of Syrian refugees has even become a political issue in the United States, despite the fact that relatively few refugees have attempted to go there. In November 2015, over half of US state governors opposed letting Syrian refugees into their states (Fantz and Brumfield 2015). Between 2011 and 2017, the United States accepted just 21,000 Syrian refugees (Zong and Batalova 2017). Of the citizens who remain in Syria, it's estimated that 80 percent live in poverty and 70 percent lack satisfactory drinking water. The establishment of a functioning Syrian state seems a long way off.

How Unusual Is Syria?

We've described the failed state that currently exists in Syria in some detail. But how typical is the situation in Syria? Although Syria stands out as a particularly disturbing case of state failure, it is, unfortunately, not unique. According to the 2018 Fragile States Index, calculated by the think tank The Fund for Peace, South Sudan, Somalia, Yemen, Syria, the Central African Republic, the Democratic Republic of Congo, Sudan, Chad, Afghanistan, and Zimbabwe have the ten most fragile states in the world.[2] Each year the Fragile States Index classifies countries into one of four categories—Alert, Warning, Stable, Sustainable—based on the scores they get on twelve conflict risk indicators. The scores for each indicator run from 0 to 10, with higher numbers indicating greater state fragility. The conflict risk indicators are grouped into four distinct categories: social, economic, political, and cohesion. Social risk indicators take account of demographic pressures, refugees, and external intervention. Economic risk indicators look at economic development, poverty, and human flight. Political risk indicators focus on state legitimacy, public services, human rights, and the rule of law. Cohesion risk indicators address the security apparatus, factionalized elites, and group grievances. In 2018, Syria had a score of 111.4 out of 120 on the Fragile States Index.

In Map 4.1 we provide a look at state fragility around the world and how it's changed over the last decade. The top panel shows the geographic distribution of state fragility for 178

---

[2]For more information on the Fragile States Index, go to the website for the Fund for Peace at http://fundfor-peace.org/fsi/.

MAP 4.1

a. State Fragility in 2018

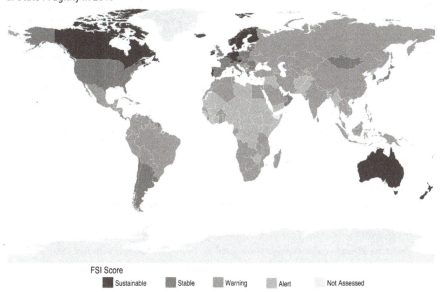

FSI Score
Sustainable Stable Warning Alert Not Assessed

b. Significant Change in State Fragility, 2008–2018

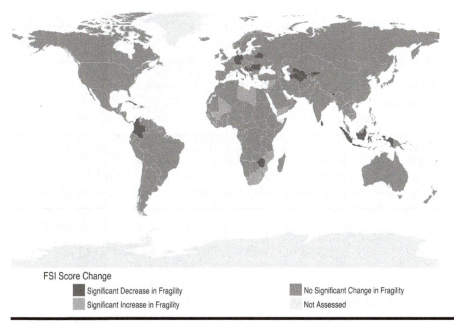

FSI Score Change
Significant Decrease in Fragility No Significant Change in Fragility
Significant Increase in Fragility Not Assessed

Note: We code a significant change in state fragility as occurring when a state's fragility score changes by more than 10 points in either direction. Data come from the Fragile States Index 2018, which is provided by the Fund for Peace at http://fundforpeace.org/fsi/excel/.

countries in 2018. The darker the shade of gray, the less fragile the state. As you can see, "sustainable" states are quite rare (16) and "stable" states are not much more common (40). Much of the world, and the vast majority of the world's population, comes under the jurisdiction of a state that has either an "alert" (32) or "warning" (90) designation. The good news is that states have, on average, become less fragile over the last decade. Indeed, 119 states exhibit less fragility in 2018 than they did in 2008 and only 58 states exhibit more fragility. The bottom panel of Map 4.1 shows those states that have experienced a *significant* change (more than 10 points in either direction) in their state fragility score over the last ten years. While 22 countries have experienced a significant decrease in their state fragility, only 7 countries have experienced a significant increase. The 22 states that have become significantly less fragile include the Bahamas, Barbados, Belarus, Bhutan, Bosnia and Herzegovina, Cape Verde, Colombia, Croatia, Cuba, Germany, Indonesia, Kyrgyzstan, Malta, Moldova, Romania, Serbia, the Seychelles, Sri Lanka, Trinidad and Tobago, Turkmenistan, Uzbekistan, and Zimbabwe. The seven countries that have become significantly more fragile include The Gambia, Libya, Mali, Mozambique, South Africa, Syria, and Yemen.

The State Fragility Index reminds us that although we often talk about "states" and "failed states," there is, in reality, a continuum of "stateness." At one end of this continuum are countries like Somalia, Syria, and Chad, which are almost completely stateless and whose weak or nonexistent central governments are ineffective at controlling inhabitants throughout their territory. At the other end of the continuum are countries like Finland, Norway, and Sweden, which have strong and effective central governments that rule in an effectively unchallenged manner. In between are countries like Colombia, Russia, and Turkey, which have somewhat effective central governments that nonetheless fail to fully control all parts of their territory and that frequently leave specific areas ungoverned. When comparing countries around the world, a famous political scientist, Samuel P. Huntington (1968, 1), once wrote that "the most important political distinction among countries concerns not their form of government but their *degree of government*" (italics added). In many ways, it's hard to disagree with this claim.

The brief history of Syria that we've presented should illustrate what life is like without a state. It should also underline the importance of understanding where the "state" actually comes from. This is a question that has drawn the attention of political theorists and political scientists for centuries. In what follows, we examine the **contractarian view of the state** and the predatory view of the state.

THE CONTRACTARIAN VIEW OF THE STATE

Early modern political thinkers like Hobbes ([1651] 1994), Locke ([1690] 1980), and Rousseau (1762) engaged in thought experiments to help them think more clearly about the role of the state in contemporary life. What, they asked, would social relationships among people be like in a world without states or governments? How would people behave if they didn't have to fear being punished by authorities if they stole things or engaged in opportunistic behavior at the expense of their neighbors? In effect, they asked what life would be like in a "state of nature" in which there was no government.

The State of Nature

Thomas Hobbes famously described life in the state of nature as a "war of every man against every man" in which life was "solitary, poor, nasty, brutish, and short" (Hobbes

[1651] 1994, chap. 13).[3] He believed that individuals in the **state of nature** faced a dilemma. Given a certain degree of equality between individuals, each person recognized she could gain by attacking her neighbor in a moment of vulnerability (say, while her neighbor slept). Each person knew, however, that her neighbors were probably thinking exactly the same thing about her. Hobbes believed that even the weakest individual in the state of nature had enough power to overcome the strongest, either by trickery or by joining forces, if she chose. In this type of situation, it's clear that the individuals in the state of nature would all be better off if they abstained from taking advantage of their neighbors than they would be in a "war of all against all." Still, if an act of violence or theft were to take place, it would obviously be better to be the attacker or thief than the victim. Without a "common power to keep them all in awe," this was the dilemma that faced individuals in the state of nature (chap. 13).

You might think this discussion is really about barbarous individuals and that it's therefore quite remote from the concerns of elevated individuals such as ourselves. It's important to recognize, though, that social contract theorists like Hobbes, Locke, and Rousseau didn't claim that life in the state of nature was problematic because of any particular moral failing on the part of the individuals involved. In fact, Jean-Jacques Rousseau worried about "modern" man and had quite romantic notions about the "noble savages" we might expect to find in the state of nature. Social contract theorists argue that there's something fundamental about the very structure of the state of nature that makes it difficult for people to behave themselves.

To see why social contract theorists think this, we begin by describing a stylized interaction between two individuals in the state of nature using Hobbes's own language. Imagine that there are two individuals who both desire "the same thing [say, a plot of land], which nevertheless they cannot both enjoy." In the absence of protection from a third-party enforcer, an "invader hath no more to fear than another man's single power" (Hobbes [1651] 1994, chap. 13). Consequently, "if one plants, sows, builds, or possesses a convenient seat, others may probably be expected to come prepared with forces united, to dispossess and deprive him, not only of the fruit of his labour, but also of his life or liberty. And the invader again is in the like danger of another" (chap. 13). Under these conditions, "there is no place for industry" because the industrious have no confidence that they'll be able to control the fruit of their labor (chap. 13).

What's Hobbes really saying here? Well, both individuals in our stylized interaction, we'll call them Individual A and Individual B, have essentially two actions they can take: they can "steal" or they can "refrain" from stealing.[4] If an individual refrains from stealing, she's essentially choosing to earn a living by doing something productive rather than by stealing. How

---

[3]Hobbes's notion of the "state of nature" is remarkably similar to the notion of "anarchy" that realist international relations scholars use today. Just as Hobbes referred to the condition in which individuals lived in the absence of government as the state of nature, realist international relations scholars refer to the international environment in which individual states live in the absence of a world government as anarchy (Waltz 1979). Like Hobbes, realist international relations scholars believe that anarchy is characterized by a security dilemma in which states are constantly engaged in conflict as they seek to increase their power.

[4]To the extent that stealing presupposes the concept of property, this choice in the state of nature is slightly inaccurate. This is because Hobbes explicitly denies that the concept of property can exist in the state of nature. A more accurate term, therefore, might be *dispossess*.

should the two individuals act? The choice facing each individual is complicated because they're in a strategic situation in which one individual's choice of what to do depends on what she thinks the other individual will do.

The two individuals in the state of nature value possessions. As a result, an individual's best outcome occurs when she steals the possessions of the other person and the other person refrains from stealing hers. The worst outcome is the exact opposite; that is, she refrains and the other person steals her possessions. Between these two fates are the outcomes in which both individuals refrain and both steal. It seems clear from Hobbes's description of the state of nature that individuals would prefer the former (both refrain) to the latter (both steal). They'd prefer this outcome because when both people "steal" they live in a state of war, which prevents them from engaging in productive activities and makes them reluctant to invest in things that would make their lives better.

Given this, how should the two individuals behave in the state of nature? Consider individual A first. If she knew for sure that B was going to refrain, A would steal to get B's possessions, safe in the knowledge that her own possessions were safe. If A knew for sure that B was going to try to steal her possessions, the best thing she could do is try to steal B's possessions. The thing to notice here is that it doesn't really matter what A expects B to do; A is always better off stealing. The same is also true for B as B is in a similar position to A and the same logic applies. If B knew for sure that A was going to refrain, she'd want to steal, and if B knew for sure that A was going to steal, she'd want to steal. Both individuals steal (because they're better off doing so) no matter what the other person does. As a result, we can expect that theft will be endemic in the state of nature. This is precisely why Hobbes described life in the state of nature as a "war of every man against every man" in which life was "solitary, poor, nasty, brutish, and short."

Keep in mind that we've simplified the state of nature a lot here in order to isolate only the most important aspects of the environment in which individual A and individual B find themselves. For example, it's hard to imagine a world in which theft and mutual predation are constantly occurring. In the real world, even the weak are able to fend off attack some of the time. When both actors are equal in strength, attacks will be successful only in moments of temporary vulnerability. Nevertheless, in the absence of someone to keep the actors in a permanent state of "awe," attacks will come when the opportunity arises. As a result, people will live in a persistent state of fear that can be debilitating, even in moments of relative calm.

Although this "abstract" state of nature probably seems remote from many of our own experiences, recall the troubled recent history of Syria. Many commentators have described the environment in Syria as a modern-day version of Hobbes's state of nature. Similar descriptions might be given of other situations in which no single actor is able to "awe" everyone in society, such as Iraq during the US occupation, the Darfur region and the "Two Areas" (South Kordofan and Blue Nile) in Sudan today, south central Los Angeles and New York City in the 1980s, or New Orleans directly after Hurricane Katrina in 2005. In fact, according to the economic historian and Nobel laureate Robert Fogel (2004), the world Hobbes described as absent of invention, trade, arts, and letters fairly accurately describes most of human history. Similarly, Azar Gat (2006) argues that humans have spent almost their entire evolutionary history in small bands of hunter-gatherers where looting and violent death were about as commonplace as the Hobbesian state of nature would suggest.

When we concluded that A and B would both steal in the state of nature, you may have been slightly puzzled by this. After all, if you looked back to where we discussed how the two individuals valued the four possible outcomes of their interaction, you'll see that such behavior leads to the second-worst outcome for both individuals. Indeed, both people could be made better off if they chose to refrain—they'd get their second-best outcome from both refraining instead of the second-worst outcome they get from both stealing. For this reason, the absence of cooperation represents a dilemma—behavior that's rational for each individual leads A and B to an outcome they both agree is inferior to some other outcome. The class of problems in which individual rationality produces outcomes that everyone in society recognizes as inferior has fascinated political thinkers since at least the time of Hobbes. One of the many ways in which it's interesting is that it doesn't seem to be enough for the players to recognize their mutually destructive behavior for cooperation to occur. Ask yourself, for example, what would happen if A and B met one sunny afternoon and promised not to steal from each other because this would make them both better off. Do you think they'd feel comforted by such promises as they lay down to sleep at night?

Part of the problem is that each person may come to feel that she's being taken advantage of. What if you're the only one who's sticking to your promise of good behavior? If your opponent breaks her promise and starts to steal, your best response is to stop refraining and start stealing as well—you'll get your second-worst outcome instead of your worst outcome by doing this. But part of the problem is that you also have an incentive to steal even if you think your opponent is going to keep her promise. Say you knew for sure your opponent was going to refrain and that, under these circumstances, you could benefit. What would you do? You would choose to break your promise to refrain and start stealing, because this would lead to your best outcome rather than your second-best outcome. Thus, promising to stop stealing because it's mutually destructive is not sufficient to prevent people in the state of nature from stealing. As Garrett Hardin (1968) points out, relying on promises of good behavior or moral suasion may actually have perverse evolutionary consequences. If the world is truly set up as in the Hobbesian state of nature, then individuals who are swayed by entreaties to "behave" and to "do unto others as you would have them do unto you" are not likely to survive long enough to pass such ideas on to their progeny (whether one thinks that the mechanism of transmission is genetics or socialization). In effect, Hardin suggests that to rely on moral suasion is to run the risk that moral people will be eliminated from society.

Civil Society and the Social Contract

Hobbes's solution to the problems individuals experience in the state of nature was to create someone or something—the "Sovereign"—that had sufficient physical force that people would stand in awe of it. Like us, Hobbes realized that simply promising not to steal would be insufficient to prevent people from stealing. Instead, he believed that "there must be some coercive power to compel men equally to the performance of their covenants, by the terror of some punishment greater than the benefit they expect by breach of their covenant" (Hobbes [1651] 1994, chap. 15). In other words, Hobbes wanted a sovereign that could "force" people to refrain—for their own good, of course. The sovereign was to be created by an implicit **social contract** between individuals in the state of nature. Individuals would "contract" with each other to give up their **natural rights** (rights given to them by nature) in exchange for **civil rights** (rights given to them by laws) that would be protected by the sovereign. In effect, individuals would give up what they had to the sovereign in return for protection, and in doing so they would move out of the state of nature into what social contract theorists refer to as civil society.

Hobbes believed that life in the state of nature was sufficiently bad that individuals would, and should, be willing to transfer everything they had to the sovereign in exchange for protection. In many ways, Hobbes's pessimistic view of the state of nature helps to explain why so many Afghans and Somalis were quick to welcome the "law and order" brought by the Taliban and al-Shabab in their respective countries even though they may have strongly disagreed with the ideologies of these particular movements. Other social contract theorists, like Jean-Jacques Rousseau and John Locke, were more hopeful that individuals in the state of nature could find ways to achieve limited degrees of cooperation. As a result, these latter theorists believed that the extent to which individuals in the state of nature should delegate authority to a "third-party enforcer" such as the sovereign should always be evaluated in light of the particular conditions in which they found themselves.

Although there are important differences between them, social contract theorists all view the state as a third-party enforcer who can dole out punishments to individuals who engage in socially destructive behavior that violates the social contract. These punishments were to be structured in such a way that "steal" would no longer be the automatic choice for individuals in society. In effect, the punishment imposed by the state for stealing would be sufficiently large that each individual in civil society would prefer to refrain rather than steal.

By creating a third-party enforcer, the state, that dutifully doles out punishments for bad behavior, we can get people to give up the sorts of behavior that made life in the state of nature "solitary, poor, nasty, brutish, and short." Problem solved, right? Well, as you might suspect, the fact that we're still studying politics some three hundred and sixty years after Hobbes wrote suggests there are some problems with his solution. Start by asking yourself why anyone would want to be the sovereign and why she'd be willing to do us all a favor by acting as our police.

One common answer to this question portrays members of civil society as being engaged in an exchange relationship with the sovereign. In effect, the sovereign agrees to police us in exchange for taxes that citizens pay. Most obviously, we can think of these "taxes" as money citizens give to the state in return for security. It's possible, however, to conceptualize these taxes more broadly. For example, we might think of required behavioral patterns—such as regularly attending religious institutions or following dress codes, such as wearing a burqa—as a kind of taxation that citizens give in exchange for state-provided security. One of the uses of this taxation will be to build up the state's "comparative advantage in violence" (North 1981) and its "control over the chief concentrated means of violence" (Tilly 1985) so that it can keep the citizens in awe and carry out its duties as a state. Given that a sovereign will demand tax revenue to carry out her job, it's not immediately obvious that the citizens will choose to leave the state of nature for civil society. Much will depend on the level of taxation imposed by the state. If the taxation rate imposed by the state is "too high," individuals may prefer to remain in the state of nature. In other words, citizens won't always choose to create a state.

Thus, for the state to be a solution to the state of nature as social contract theorists claim, it must be the case that (1) the punishment imposed by the state for stealing is sufficiently large that individuals prefer to refrain rather than steal *and* (2) the tax rate charged by the state for acting as the policeman is not so large that individuals prefer the state of nature to civil society. This comparison between the responsibilities the state imposes on its citizens (here thought of in terms of a level of taxation) and the benefits the citizen can obtain from living in civil society is central to the very nature of politics. Thinkers who see the state of nature as dire are going to expect citizens to accept a draconian set of responsibilities in exchange for the "protection" the state provides. In contrast, those who see civil society as a mere convenience over a workable, if inefficient, state of nature are going to place much greater restrictions on what the state can ask of its citizens. It is, perhaps, not an accident that Hobbes was writing at the end of a long period of religious conflict in Europe and civil war in his home country. It was because he had had a first-hand glimpse of what the "war of every man against every man" looked like that he believed the difference between civil society and the state of nature was effectively infinite. For Hobbes, almost any level of taxation the state might choose to levy on its citizens in exchange for protection looked like a good deal. You might think that many of the people living in Syria today share a similar view of the world. In contrast, Thomas Jefferson—borrowing from social contract theorists like John Locke—believed, from the relative calm of Monticello, that we had a natural right (that is, the possibility of obtaining in the state of nature) to "life, liberty, and the pursuit of happiness" and that our commitment to the state was so conditional we should probably engage in revolution, or at least the rewriting of the Constitution, every couple of decades.

The reader is likely to have noticed that contemporary disputes in the United States and elsewhere over whether we should reduce civil liberties by giving more power to the state in an attempt to better protect ourselves against terrorist threats directly echo this historical debate between scholars such as Hobbes and Jefferson. Those politicians who argue that the threat of terrorism warrants a reduction in our civil liberties on the grounds that freedom means little without security are taking a distinctly Hobbesian view of the world.

Whether you ultimately agree more with Hobbes or Jefferson, it seems clear that although the creation of the state may solve the political problem we have with each other, it may also create a potential new problem between us and the state. Put simply, if we surrender control over the means of violence to the state, what's to prevent it from using this power against us? As some have put it, "Who will guard the guardian?" At the very least, once the state has developed a "comparative advantage" in the use of violence, we'd expect a renegotiation of the social contract that, at a minimum, would set the tax rate so high as to leave the citizen indifferent between living in the state of nature and living in civil society. It's the fear that this might occur that drives civil libertarians around the world to challenge ongoing attempts to locate ever-increasing amounts of power in the hands of the state.

THE PREDATORY VIEW OF THE STATE

Whereas the contractarian view of the state focuses on the conflicts of interest that exist between individuals, the **predatory view of the state** focuses more on the potential conflicts of interest that exist between individuals and the state. Scholars who employ a predatory view of the state seek to understand the conditions under which the state can be expected to enforce rules and foster cooperation rather than use its "comparative advantage in violence" to prey upon the citizenry. According to the predatory view of the state, rulers can be viewed as similar to individuals in the state of nature. This is because rulers face their own sort of security dilemma in that they have potential rivals constantly vying to take their place. The concern for security on the part of rulers leads them to use their power to extract resources from others, both because these resources can be used to help ensure their continued existence and because leaving these resources in the hands of rivals is potentially dangerous.

The sociologist Charles Tilly (1985) went so far as to say that states resemble a form of organized crime and should be viewed as extortion rackets. Why? Like the contractarian theory of the state, the predatory approach to the state sees the state as an organization that trades security for revenue. The difference, though, is that the seller of security in the predatory view of the state happens to represent a key threat to the buyer's continued security. In other words, the state resembles an extortion racket in that it demands tribute (taxes and obedience) from citizens within its jurisdiction in return for protection from, among other things, itself. Proponents of the predatory theory of the state are essentially pointing out that if we don't think that individuals are trustworthy and public-spirited (if they were, there'd be no need for a state in the first place), why would we imagine that representatives of the state, who wield a near monopoly on the use of force, would be? In this regard, those who take a predatory view of the state are arguing that Rousseau's (1762) admonition to "take men as they are and laws as they might be" applies at least as much to rulers as to the ruled.

Tilly (1985) argues that the level of predation rulers inflicted on their subjects in early modern Europe varied from place to place because rulers faced a complex set of cross-pressures. To some extent, these rulers emerged out of what would look to us like a period of lawlessness during the Middle Ages. After the decline of the Roman Empire, Europe comprised a hodge-podge of local lords who offered protection to peasants in exchange for rents paid either in kind or in service on the lord's land. Like the heads of organized crime syndicates, feudal lords were constantly trying to put rivals down. These rivals included external competitors, such as other lords seeking to expand their territory, as well as internal challengers from within their own ranks. In part because of changes in military technology, lords who could seize control over larger numbers of peasants and more extensive areas of land were able to gain competitive advantages over their rivals. In time, feudal lands were consolidated into larger holdings under the control of feudal kings. For some time, feudal kings coexisted somewhat uneasily with local lords; although the kings controlled some lands themselves, they often relied on local lords to control other territories on their behalf. As time went on, however, the balance of power tended to tilt toward feudal kings, and local lords eventually became their subjects. The lands these kings controlled gradually began to look like the territories we'd recognize as the political geography of contemporary Europe.

This change in the balance of power between local lords and feudal kings in early modern Europe was aided by a change in the "economies of scale" in the use of violence. A production process is said to exhibit "economies of scale" if unit costs decline as the number of units produced increases. When economies of scale exist, big producers of, say, violence are advantaged over small producers. Holding the amount of agricultural land constant, population growth in the "high middle ages" (from the tenth to the thirteenth century) led to a decline in the marginal productivity of labor. In other words, it was not as profitable as it once was for a lord to simply increase the number of serfs working on his land. At the same time, changes in military technology (armored cavalry, crossbows, better fortification, and siege weapons) raised the fixed costs of providing protection (Bartlett 1993). Together, these factors increased the "economies of scale" of protection and violence. Feudal lords could restore profitability by expanding the amount of land they controlled. In effect, the decreasing marginal productivity of labor caused by population growth could be mitigated if new lands could be cultivated. In addition, investments made in the tools to protect one manor could be profitably redeployed to protect other holdings when they came under attack.

Bargaining between lords and serfs also led to a dynamic that encouraged larger protection organizations. If a serf thought his lord's demands were unreasonable, the only alternative was to flee to a neighboring lord's manor and hope for better treatment. Although lords tried to cooperate in the return of serfs, they were often tempted to keep runaway serfs for use on their own land. This implicit competition for the services of serfs could erode the lord's bargaining power in a way that advantaged serfs. This would be more difficult, however, if a particular lord could centralize coercive authority over a wide range of local manors (North and Thomas 1971). The desire to exploit the "economies of scale in protection" created incentives for entrepreneurial rulers to conquer neighboring rulers, and the availability of underutilized arable land created incentives for them to settle new lands. Because competition was fierce and the fighting was costly, it was also important for rulers to become efficient in the administration of their territories and the extraction of revenues from their subjects. Viewed in this way, the political geography of modern Europe is essentially an unintended consequence of the strategies lords and kings employed to keep a grasp on power (Tilly 1985). To remain in power, lords and kings engaged in four primary activities:

1. *War making:* Eliminating or neutralizing their own rivals outside the territories in which they had clear and continuous priority as wielders of force.

2. *State making:* Eliminating or neutralizing their rivals inside those territories.

3. *Protection:* Eliminating or neutralizing the enemies of their clients.

4. *Extraction:* Acquiring the means of carrying out the first three activities.

As Tilly (1985, 172) notes,

> Power holders' pursuit of war involved them [the state] willy-nilly in the extraction of resources for war making from the populations over which they had control and in the promotion of capital accumulation by those who could help them borrow and buy. War making, extraction, and capital accumulation interacted to shape European state making. Power holders did not undertake those three momentous tasks with the intention of creating national states—centralized, differentiated, autonomous, extensive political organizations. Nor did they ordinarily foresee that national states would emerge from war making, extraction, and capital accumulation. Instead, the people who controlled European states and states in the making warred in order to check or overcome their competitors and thus to enjoy the advantages of power within a secure or expanding territory. To make more effective war, they attempted to locate more capital. In the short run, they might acquire that capital by conquest, by selling off their assets, or by coercing or dispossessing accumulators of capital. In the long run, the quest inevitably involved them in establishing regular access to capitalists who could supply and arrange credit and in imposing one form of regular taxation or another on the people and activities within their spheres of control.

In this sense, the modern state arose as a by-product of leaders' attempts to survive. External geopolitical pressures and changes in military technology meant that lords needed to increase their war-making capacity to protect themselves and their subjects from the attack of external rivals. At the same time, this greater war-making capacity could be turned against their own subjects in order to increase their capacity to extract more resources—which, in turn, were needed to put their rivals down. The act of extraction

> entailed the elimination, neutralization, or cooptation of the great lord's [internal] rivals; thus it led to state making. As a by-product, it created organization in the form of tax-collection agencies, police forces, courts, exchequers, account keepers; thus it again led to state making. To a lesser extent, war making likewise led to state making through the expansion of military organization itself, as a standing army, war industries, supporting bureaucracies, and (rather later) schools grew up within the state apparatus. All of these structures checked potential rivals and opponents. (Tilly 1985, 183)

In effect, "war makes states" (Tilly 1985, 170). The "kill or be killed" dynamic that, to a large extent, underpins the predatory view of the state makes it abundantly clear that those states that exist today do so only because they managed to outcompete their rivals who are now gone.

The need to extract resources from their subjects placed constraints on the predation of some early modern leaders (Levi 1988; North 1981). Rulers could extract the resources they needed to respond to geopolitical pressures in one of two ways. On the one hand, they could simply seize the assets of their subjects outright. We can think of this as the strategy that a predatory state would adopt. On the other hand, rulers could try to extract the resources they needed through "quasi-voluntary compliance" (Levi 1988, 52), which refers to a situation in which the subject feels that she's getting something—maybe policy concessions or limits on future state behavior—in return for the tax dollars the state is extracting. We can think of this as the strategy a limited state would adopt. As you might expect, quasi-voluntary compliance has several positive advantages over outright predation. For example, rulers would need to use fewer resources to coerce their subjects if their subjects voluntarily complied with their demands. Moreover, subjects might feel freer to invest and innovate in ways that expanded the tax base if the state limited its level of predation. In this way, leaders who managed to build quasi-voluntary compliance could succeed in extracting the resources they needed to meet external challenges without "killing the goose that laid the golden egg." By taming their predatory instincts, rulers could opt, in effect, to increase their net extractive capacity by reducing the costs of conducting business and by taking a smaller portion of a larger pie. As it turned out, not all states were successful in limiting their predation in this way, and as a result, the character and consequences of rule exhibited quite a variety across early modern Europe. We return to the question of why some leaders chose to limit their predation more than others in Chapter 5.

Inspired by Tilly's work, Jeffrey Herbst (2000) argues that the modern state has developed later and less completely in sub-Saharan Africa because the return from agricultural activity was modest, and the rough physical geography of the region makes the administration of large holdings difficult. In effect, the payoff to effective state protection has not always been worth the cost. In addition, the large distances between populated areas and interference from outside actors has limited geopolitical competition between independent units. As a result, there are large portions of sub-Saharan Africa which, although nominally under the control of states that were established at the end of the colonial period, appear "stateless." State failure, in other words, may occur when the nominal size of states exceeds, for historical reasons such as the process of colonization and decolonization, the "economy of scale" of protection otherwise implied by political, economic, and geographic conditions.

CONCLUSION

In this chapter, we've examined different definitions of the state, as well as two conceptions of where the state comes from. The contractarian theory of the state explains how the creation of the state can help resolve conflict between members of society. Although the contractarian theory of the state identifies key functions played by the state, it has little to say about the conflicts of interest that are likely to arise between rulers and the ruled. The predatory theory of the state, on the other hand, assumes that such conflicts exist and attempts to explain why states don't always exploit their monopoly on the use of force to run roughshod over the citizens they came into being to protect.

Because the predatory view of the state both recognizes the possibility of exchange between rulers and the ruled and explains the nature and character of that exchange relationship, philosophers of science would call it a "progressive problem shift." That is, it seems to explain all of what the contractarian theory of the state explains while also answering at least some of the questions that the contractarian theory of the state raises. It should be noted, however, that the predatory theory of the state is almost exclusively "positive" in its orientation—that is, it seeks to explain the way that states and citizens behave without necessarily answering questions about what rulers or their citizens ought to do. In contrast, the contractarian theory of the state arose largely as a way of exploring the moral responsibilities of citizens to the state.

The predatory approach to the state has several other advantages over the contractarian theory of the state. First, it views rulers as egoistic, maximizing, rational actors. Consequently, we can imagine integrating explanations of leaders' behavior with other models of human behavior that have a similar view of humans. Political leaders aren't qualitatively different from the rest of us—they're concerned about their survival, their livelihood, and so on. Second, it shows how goal-oriented behavior leads to changes in the institutional environment in which political actors operate and, in addition, how changes in the institutional environment alter leader behavior. For example, it can explain why political units grew large over time: so that they might benefit from economies of scale in the production of violence. Finally, it has the potential to explain why some rulers share power or limit their extractive activity whereas others do not. This is an issue we return to in Chapter 5 when we examine economic explanations for why some states are democracies and others are not.

Key Concepts

state—an entity that uses coercion and the threat of force to rule in a given territory

nation—a group of people who share some sort of common identity like a language, a religion, an ethnicity, or a shared history

nation-state—a state in which a single nation predominates and the legal, social, demographic, and geographic boundaries of the state are connected in important ways to that nation

failed state—a state-like entity that can't coerce and is unable to successfully control the inhabitants of a given territory

contractarian view of the state—the creation of the state results from a social contract between individuals in the state of nature in which the state provides security in exchange for obedience from the citizen

state of nature—a term used to describe situations in which there is no state

social contract—an implicit agreement among individuals in the state of nature to create and empower the state; it outlines the rights and responsibilities of the state and the citizens in regard to each other

natural right—a universal right that is inherent in the nature of living beings; a natural right can exist even in the state of nature

civil right—a right that does not arise naturally but is instead created by the state through laws; a civil right can't exist in the state of nature

predatory view of the state—the view that states exercising an effective control over the use of violence are in a position to threaten the security of citizens; states can exploit the citizens who, according to the contractarian view of the state, they have a duty to protect

THE ECONOMIC DETERMINANTS OF DEMOCRACY AND DICTATORSHIP

Democracy endures only if it is self-enforcing. It is not a contract because there are no third parties to enforce it. To survive, democracy must be an equilibrium at least for those political forces which can overthrow it.

Przeworski (2006, 312)

The capacity for strategic calculations by maximizing monarchs results in the owners of *mobile* factors, which the monarch seeks to tax, being . . . given greater voice over the policy choices of governments.

Bates and Lien (1985, 61)

OVERVIEW

1. We briefly examine how the meaning and appeal of democracy has changed over time. Although a strong consensus exists today that democracy is the most desirable form of political regime, this hasn't always been the case.

2. We then turn to economic explanations for democracy. We start with classic modernization theory, which argues that countries are more likely to become democratic and stay democratic as they develop economically.

3. One criticism of classic modernization theory is that it lacks a strong causal mechanism linking economic development with democracy. A more recent variant of modernization

theory offers a potential solution to this criticism. The theory posits that changes in the socioeconomic structure of a country that accompany economic development promote the democratization process.

4. This variant of modernization theory explains why high-income countries tend to be democracies and why countries dependent on natural resource revenue tend to be dictatorships. It also has important insights for the role that foreign aid, inequality, and economic performance play in the democratization process.

In this chapter, we focus on so-called economic explanations for democracy. In particular, we investigate how economic development and the structure of a country's economy influence the emergence and survival of democracy. In doing so, we illustrate how the predatory view of the state discussed in Chapter 4 can help to explain why some states are democratic and others dictatorial. We begin, though, by briefly examining how the meaning and appeal of democracy has changed over time.

DEMOCRACY IN HISTORICAL PERSPECTIVE

We live in a world in which there's strong agreement concerning the importance and desirability of democracy. Even countries widely considered dictatorships have professed their support for democracy and simply adjusted their definition of democracy so it can be applied to their regime (see Box 5.1, "States, Regimes, and Governments"). Indeed, many acknowledged dictatorships make reference to "people" or "democracy" in their very name—the Democratic People's Republic of Korea, the Democratic Republic of Congo, and the Lao People's Democratic Republic—as if this somehow makes them democratic. China even speaks of its own unique form of "Chinese democracy."

Until the middle of the nineteenth century, though, democracy was commonly viewed as an obsolete and ancient political system that was both dangerous and unstable. Plato and Aristotle were arguably the first to think systematically about different forms of regimes. In *The Republic,* Plato ([360 BCE] 1991) argues that political decision making should be based on expertise and that "mob rule" would result if democracy was introduced (427e–29a). In effect, Plato thought that just as only trained pilots should fly airplanes, only trained statesmen should guide the ship of state. The Greek word *demokratia* often gets translated as "rule by the people" with no mention about who these people are. In Plato and Aristotle's time, though, the *demos* referred specifically to the "common people"—those with little or no economic independence who were politically uneducated (Hanson 1989, 71). Plato believed that democracy wouldn't be rule by the people but would instead be rule by the poor and uneducated against the rich and educated. In addition, he worried that the uneducated mass would be open to demagoguery, leading to short-lived democracies in which the people quickly surrender power to a tyrant (Baradat 2006, 63).

Aristotle ([350 BCE] 1996) disagreed with Plato to the extent that he believed there were some conditions under which the will of the many could be equal to or wiser than the will of the few (1281b). This isn't to say, however, that he thought highly of democracy. In his *Politics,* Aristotle ([350 BCE] 1996) classified regimes in regard to the number of rulers they had, stating that government "must be in the hands of one, or of a few, or of the many" (1279a.27–28). His classification is shown in Table 5.1. He believed that regimes came in good and bad forms. In the good forms the rulers govern for the good of all, whereas in the bad forms they govern

BOX 5.1 STATES, REGIMES, AND GOVERNMENTS

What's the difference between a state, a regime, and a government? Although it's common to see people use these terms interchangeably, they do in fact refer to distinct things. As we saw in the last chapter, the **state** is an entity that uses coercion and the threat of force to rule in a given territory. One can talk, for example, of the French state, the Iranian state, the Indian state, and so on. With the exception of relatively rare cases in which states merge (United Arab Emirates in 1971) or break up (South Sudan in 2011), the states that comprise the contemporary world system are generally quite stable.

In a very general sense, the **government** is the set of people who run the state or have the authority to act on behalf of the state at a particular point in time. That is, governments are the means through which state power is exercised. As examples, the governments of Argentina,

Saudi Arabia, and Japan in 2018 were headed by President Mauricio Macri, King Salman of the Saud family, and Prime Minister Shinzō Abe. While states are generally stable over time, governments come and go.

A **regime** is the set of rules, norms, or institutions that determine how the government is constituted, how it's organized, and how major decisions are made. Regimes are generally classified as being either democratic or dictatorial. As we'll see in later chapters, these regimes actually come in different types. For example, democracies are often classified in terms of whether they're presidential, parliamentary, or semi-presidential (Chapter 10), and dictatorships are frequently classified in terms of whether they are run by the military, a monarchy, or civilians (Chapter 8).

only for the good of themselves. The good forms of regime were monarchy, aristocracy, and *politeia*; the bad forms were tyranny, oligarchy, and democracy.

The concern for Aristotle was that each of the good forms of regime could be corrupted such that the common good would be replaced by the good of the rulers. For example, a corrupted monarchy might become a tyranny, a corrupted aristocracy might become an oligarchy, and a corrupted politeia might become a democracy. Aristotle suggests that we should choose the type of regime that had the least dangerous corrupt form. For Aristotle, this was aristocracy. Like Plato, Aristotle believed that democracy would be the most dangerous form of regime because it produced class rule in which the poor and uneducated govern for themselves rather than the commonweal. Some of the same fears about democracy—that it would result in class warfare, attempts by the poor to expropriate the rich, and so forth—were just as strong in the eighteenth and nineteenth centuries, when people were debating whether to extend the suffrage (Offe 1983; Roemer 1998). Marx ([1850] 1952, 62), for example, believed that universal suffrage and democracy would inevitably "unchain the class struggle."

TABLE 5.1 ■ Aristotle's Classification of Regimes		
Number of rulers	**Good form "For the good of all"**	**Bad form "For the good of the rulers"**
One	Monarchy	Tyranny
Few	Aristocracy	Oligarchy
Many	Politeia	Democracy

It should be noted that democracy at the time of Plato and Aristotle looked very different from what we understand it to be today. The biggest difference is that democracy had nothing to do with elections when they wrote. In fact, leaders were chosen by elections in aristocratic regimes, whereas they were decided by lot (that is, by drawing names from a hat) in democracies. The notion that democracy was a system in which political offices were determined by lot continued all the way into the eighteenth century. Those people who were arguing for representative government in the eighteenth century didn't see themselves as proponents of democracy. For them, democracy was associated with direct legislation by the people and, hence, was possible only in the city-states of the ancient world. In effect, democracy was seen as obsolete (Rosanvallon 1995, 141).

Only with the establishment of a major fault line between democracy and aristocracy in the age of revolution—French and American—did representative government and democracy come to be synonymous with each other (Hanson 1989; Rosanvallon 1995). Until this time, moves away from absolutism were motivated by attempts to get rid of unjust rulers rather than a desire to shift power to the people (Rhodes 2003, 28). In fact, lords and other members of the nobility would often side with commoners to get rid of unjust rulers. In this sense, corrupt monarchs, rather than the monarchy per se, were the target of opposition groups. This situation began to change during the French Revolution (1789) as the two opposing forces in the conflict solidified around the distinction between the aristocracy and the people. From this point on in time, the contemporary notion of democracy took on many of the characteristics that are familiar to us today. It was also at this point that Aristotle's three-way distinction of government by one, a few, and many was replaced by a simple dichotomy between democracy (many) and autocracy/dictatorship (one or a few).

The central idea underlying our contemporary concept of democracy is that "the people" rather than some subset of the people should rule. Exactly how this abstract concept is translated into a practical set of criteria for classifying political regimes varies enormously in political science. In a highly influential book, Robert Dahl (1971) identified two dimensions as being particularly important for classifying regimes—**contestation** and **inclusion**. Contestation captures the extent to which citizens are free to organize themselves into competing blocs in order to press for the policies and outcomes they desire. Aspects of contestation include the freedom to form political parties, freedom of speech and assembly, and the extent to which leaders are chosen in free and fair elections. Contestation is, therefore, largely concerned with the procedures of democratic competition. Inclusion has to do with who gets to participate in the democratic process. Political regimes in which all adult citizens are permitted to vote rank high on inclusion. In contrast, countries that have property requirements or that deny the effective right to vote based on place of birth, ethnicity, or gender are considered less inclusive. According to Dahl, countries with high levels of contestation and inclusion are more democratic.

Most contemporary measures of democracy build in some way on Dahl's conceptualization of democracy. For example, Polity IV, which provides an annual measure of democracy and dictatorship for countries around the world, explicitly takes account of both the level of contestation and inclusion in a country (Marshall, Gurr, and Jaggers 2017). Map 5.1 shows how Polity IV classified countries as democratic, mixed, or dictatorial in 2016. Mixed regimes are those countries where the level of democracy is neither very high nor very low.[1] As Map 5.1 indicates, there's considerable variation in regime type across the globe. Of the 165 countries coded by Polity IV in 2016, 97 were democratic, 21 were dictatorial, and 47 were mixed. Why are some countries democratic and others dictatorial? In the rest of the chapter, we examine various economic explanations for democracy.

MAP 5.1 ■ Democracy and Dictatorship around the World in 2016

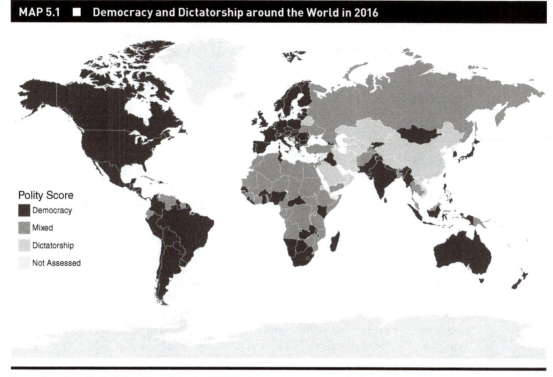

Polity Score

■ Democracy
■ Mixed
▨ Dictatorship
□ Not Assessed

Source: Data from Cheibub, Gandhi, and Vreeland (2010); Marshall, Gurr, and Jaggers (2017).

MODERNIZATION THEORY AND DEMOCRACY

Most economic explanations for democracy can be linked to a paradigm—a family of explanations—called "modernization theory." Modernization theory argues that all societies pass through the same historical stages of economic development. The claim in the aftermath of post–World War II decolonization was that contemporary underdeveloped countries were merely at an earlier stage in this linear historical process of development than more developed countries. For example, economic historians, such as Rostow (1960) and Gerschenkron (1962), believed that countries in Africa, Asia, and Latin America in the 1950s and 1960s were just "primitive" versions of European nations that would eventually "develop" and come to look like Western Europe and the United States.[2] These primitive or immature societies were characterized by large agricultural sectors and small industrial and service sectors. Eventually, these countries would "grow up" and become mature societies characterized by small

---

[1]To be precise, Polity IV provides an annual "polity score" from –10 (as dictatorial as possible) to +10 (as democratic as possible) for each country. Countries are typically coded as democracies if their score is +6 to +10, as dictatorships if their score is –6 to –10, and as mixed if their score is between –5 and 5.

[2]Modernization scholars eventually came to believe that countries could jump stages by copying and learning from countries further ahead of them. This was important because it helped to explain how the Soviet Union could advance so quickly during the middle of the twentieth century.

agricultural sectors, large industrial and service sectors, rising urbanization, higher educational attainment, and increasing societal "complexity."

Although modernization theory was originally developed by economists and economic historians, it was later taken up by political scientists. Modernization theorists in political science claim that as a society moves from being immature or "traditional" to being mature or "modern," it needs to change to a more appropriate type of government. Dictatorships might be sustainable in immature societies, but this is no longer the case in mature societies once they develop economically. Przeworski and colleagues (2000, 88) summarize modernization theory in the following way:

> As a country develops, its social structure becomes complex, new groups emerge and organize, labor processes require the active cooperation of employees, and, as a result, the system can no longer be effectively run by command: The society is too complex, technological change endows the direct producers with autonomy and private information, civil society emerges, and dictatorial forms of control lose their effectiveness. Various groups, whether the bourgeoisie, workers, or just the amorphous "civil society," rise against the dictatorial regime, and it falls.

Although this summary of modernization theory focuses on the idea that countries will become democratic as they develop economically, Lipset (1959, 75) argues that modernization theory also implies that democracy is more stable in economically developed countries. In sum, modernization theory predicts that economic development encourages both the emergence and survival of democracy. The basic features of modernization theory are shown in Figure 5.1.

For many people, the terminology modernization theory uses, and its implications, are unsettling. After all, the theory suggests that all countries, once they mature, will eventually come to look like the United States and Western Europe. In effect, countries just need to grow up—rather like a baby growing up into a responsible adult. Attempts have since been made to change the terminology used to describe these "primitive" countries. These countries used to be called primitive, but scholars started to refer to them as "backward." As this new terminology took on negative connotations of its own, "backward" countries soon became "third world" countries. With the collapse of the Berlin Wall (see Box 7.2, "A Brief History of East Germany, 1945–1990"), this new term began to seem outmoded because the "second world" countries—the command economies behind the "iron curtain"—were no longer set apart from the rest of the world in the way they once were. In addition, "third world" began to be viewed negatively because the term *third* implied that these countries were somehow behind the "first" and "second" worlds. As a result, scholars started referring to these countries as "underdeveloped."

FIGURE 5.1 ■ Classic Modernization Theory

"Traditional" society		"Modern" society
Large agriculture	⟶	Small agriculture
Small industry	⟶	Large industry
Small service	⟶	Large service
Dictatorship	⟶	Democracy

This too has recently changed to "developing" countries. Although scholars have changed the terminology of modernization theory and felt disturbed by the implication that all countries will eventually come to look like the United States and Western Europe, we shouldn't let this stop us from asking whether this theory receives empirical support. Just because we don't like some of the implications of our theory is not a good reason to reject it—we have to ask what the evidence says. Is modernization theory falsified or not?

One of the central implications of modernization theory is that there should be a strong positive relationship between economic development and democracy. In Figure 5.2, we plot the proportion of countries that are democratic at different levels of income. Income is measured here by **GDP per capita**. Figure 5.2 clearly indicates that a country is much more likely to be a democracy if its average income is high rather than low. Virtually all countries with a GDP per capita above $8,000 are democratic. In contrast, only 12 percent of the countries with a GDP per capita of less than $1,500 are democracies.

Clearly, there seems to be a strong positive relationship between income and democracy. But does this necessarily mean that modernization theory is correct? According to modernization theory, there'll be a positive relationship between income and democracy because increased income promotes both the emergence and survival of democracy. The data in Figure 5.2 are certainly consistent with these claims. However, the data are also consistent with a slightly different story, which we'll call the "survival story." According to the survival story, which is associated with the well-known political scientist Adam Przeworski, income has no effect on the emergence of democracy and the positive relationship between income and democracy observed in Figure 5.2 is entirely due to the fact that increased income helps democracies survive. The distinction between modernization theory and the survival story is an important one because it speaks to whether we can expect democracy to spread around the world as countries develop and become richer.

Before we look at the empirical evidence, let's take a closer look at the survival story. Why might increased income help democracies survive? Imagine you're a *wealthy* person living in

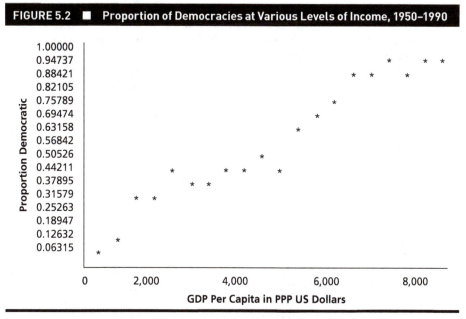

FIGURE 5.2 ■ Proportion of Democracies at Various Levels of Income, 1950–1990

Source: Data from Przeworski and colleagues (2000, 80). GDP per capita is calculated in 1985 purchasing power parity US dollars.

a democracy. What would life be like for you in a dictatorship? There's a small probability you'd be in the dictator's circle and you might become even richer. But there's a very large probability you'd not make it into the dictator's circle and you'd lose everything and become significantly poorer. Thus, switching from a democracy to a dictatorship is very much a gamble if you're wealthy. According to Przeworski, this is why most wealthy people prefer to stay in democracies and, hence, why countries where the average person has a high income tend to remain democratic. Now imagine you're a *poor* person living in a democracy. What would life be like for you in a dictatorship? There's a high probability you'd remain poor. There is, however, a small probability you could become very rich if you made it into the dictator's group. Given that you're already poor and really have nothing to lose, you might want to take a gamble and switch political regimes to a dictatorship. According to Przeworski, this is why poor people are more willing to take a chance with dictatorship and, hence, why democracy is unstable in poor countries.

Przeworski points out that if rich democracies do in fact survive longer than poor ones, then we'll observe a long-run positive relationship between increased income and democracy even if the emergence of democracy is entirely unrelated to a country's level of income. Why is this? Well, imagine that a country flips between dictatorship and democracy at random. Sometimes a country will flip to democracy when it has a high income. Even though a high level of income didn't cause the country to become democratic, it will help it stay democratic. Sometimes a country will flip to democracy when it's poor. Because the country's poor, it will likely collapse back into dictatorship. If this story is correct, we'll end up with a world in which nearly all the rich countries are democratic but in which the poor countries continue to alternate between democratic and dictatorial episodes. Unless countries for some unknown reason flip more frequently to democracy than they flip to dictatorship, democracies will—on average—be richer than dictatorships.

As you can see, the evidence presented in Figure 5.2 showing a positive relationship between income and democracy is consistent with both **modernization theory** and the **survival story**. The reason is that both of these arguments predict that democracy is more likely in high-income countries than in poor ones. This means that we can't simply look to see if high levels of income and democracy go together as we did in Figure 5.2 to determine whether modernization theory is consistent with the observed world. Instead, we need to look at how income affects the probability of democratic emergence and the probability of democratic survival.

In Figure 5.3, we use data from countries around the world to plot the probability that a country will transition from dictatorship to democracy (solid black line) and the probability that a country will transition from democracy to dictatorship (dashed gray line) at different levels of income. The numbers in Figure 5.3 indicate how many times more likely it is for a country to transition one way rather than the other. The numbers are gray whenever a country is more likely to transition to dictatorship than democracy, and black whenever a country is more likely to transition to democracy than dictatorship. Recall that both modernization theory and the survival story predict that increased income promotes democratic survival and hence that the probability of a transition to dictatorship should decline with income. The key distinction between the two stories is that modernization theory predicts that increased income makes transitions to democracy more likely whereas the survival story predicts that there'll be no relationship between income and democratic transitions.

Figure 5.3 clearly indicates that the kind of regime transition countries experience is a function of income. As predicted by both the survival story and modernization theory, the dashed gray line sloping downwards indicates that the probability of transitioning to dictatorship declines as income increases. In other words, high levels of income encourage democratic survival. In direct contradiction to the survival story but consistent with modernization theory, the solid black line sloping upwards indicates that the probability of a democratic

FIGURE 5.3 ■ Probability of Transitions to Democracy and Dictatorship at Different Levels of Income, 1950–1990

——— Transitions to democracy   ------ Transitions to dictatorship

Source: Data from Przeworski and colleagues (2000).

Note: The numbers in the figure indicate how many times more likely it is for a country to transition one way or another. The numbers are gray whenever a country is more likely to transition to dictatorship than democracy and black whenever a country is more likely to transition to democracy than dictatorship. As an example, the gray "2x" indicates that a country is twice as likely to transition to dictatorship as transition to democracy when its GDP per capita is $4,000.

transition increases with income. In other words, countries are more likely to become democratic as income increases. Indeed, the probability of a transition to democracy is about three times greater when a country has a GDP per capita of $6,000 than when it has a GDP per capita of $2,000. Moreover, the likelihood that a country transitions to democracy rather than dictatorship also increases with income. In rich countries, transitions to democracy are much more likely to occur than transitions to dictatorship. For example, the probability of becoming democratic is six times larger than the probability of becoming dictatorial when GDP per capita is greater than $6,000.

In sum, the empirical evidence we've just presented suggests that the observed world looks more like the one envisioned by modernization theory than the one envisioned by the survival story. The bottom line is that additional income is positively associated with both the emergence and survival of democracy.[3] This suggests that we can expect democracy to spread around the world as countries develop and become richer.

A VARIANT OF MODERNIZATION THEORY

A common criticism of modernization theory is that it doesn't really provide a strong explanation as to *why* economic development might produce democracy. The evidence we've just presented shows an empirical correlation between income and the emergence of democracy,

---

[3]Evidence in support of the theoretical predictions of modernization theory has been provided by a whole host of empirical analyses in recent years (Ansell and Samuels 2014; Barro 1999; Boix 2003, 2011; Boix and Stokes 2003; Epstein et al. 2006; Inglehart and Welzel 2005; Londregan and Poole 1996; Ross 2001).

but why does this correlation exist? In what follows, we examine a variant of modernization theory that explicitly proposes a causal mechanism linking economic development and democracy.[4] This variant of modernization theory says that it's not income per se that encourages democracy but rather changes in the socioeconomic structure of a country that accompany economic development. This variant of modernization theory incorporates a predatory view of the state and helps to show why some rulers share power or limit their extractive activity (democracy) whereas others do not (dictatorship). As such it helps to answer one of the puzzles we were confronted with at the end of Chapter 4 when we examined the origins of the modern state.

Not only does our variant of modernization theory explain why democracies are more likely in rich countries, but it also helps to explain why countries dependent on revenue from natural resources, such as oil, diamonds, and minerals, tend to be dictatorships rather than democracies. Additionally, the theory has important insights for the role that foreign aid, economic inequality, and economic performance play in the democratization process. Specifically, it offers an explanation for why foreign aid tends to be detrimental to democratization efforts but can sometimes promote limited democratic reforms, why economic inequality doesn't necessarily impede democracy, and why economic performance is much more varied in dictatorships than in democracies.

Economic Development and Democracy

As we mentioned earlier, one of the central features of modernization theory is the idea that all societies proceed through a similar series of economic and political stages. As a society proceeds through these stages, it undergoes structural changes. A key structural change has to do with the relative size of the "sectors" in the economy. According to this view, and illustrated in Figure 5.1, all economies can be divided into the same set of sectors—agricultural (the "traditional" sector) and manufacturing and services (the "modern" sector). Just as the relative sizes of a human's body parts change as they mature, so too do the relative sizes of a society's economic sectors. Specifically, countries tend to have large agricultural sectors but relatively small manufacturing and service sectors in the early stages of development. As the modernization process brings about efficiencies in the agricultural sector, resources are freed up for use in manufacturing and service sectors. Over time, and as countries continue to develop and mature, the manufacturing and service sectors become larger and larger relative to the agricultural sector. A consequence of these changes is that the economy increasingly comprises actors with mobile assets.

Many scholars have argued that this is precisely what started to happen in early modern Europe. As agriculture became more efficient, fewer peasants were needed to work the land, and traditional feudal bonds that tied peasants to the land were torn apart. This eventually led to a population shift from rural areas to urban ones. This shift occurred at both the top and bottom of the social spectrum. Peasants found themselves dispossessed of lands to which they had had traditional claims, and members of the landed gentry found themselves drawn into the commercial activities of the towns. A key feature of the commercialization of the agricultural gentry in England at this time was the shift from grain production to the grazing of sheep to feed the growing demand of wool producers (Moore [1966] 1999). As Bates and Lien (1985) have argued, this change in the composition of the British economy played a crucial role in creating representative government in England.

---

[4]The remaining material in this chapter draws on Clark, Golder, and Golder (2017).

By the seventeenth century, the modernization process in England had brought about a shift in economic power from a relatively small number of traditional agricultural elites, who controlled large domains producing easily quantifiable agricultural products, to a rising class of wool producers, merchants, and financial intermediaries, who controlled assets that were much more difficult for the state to count—and, hence, more difficult for the state to tax. In contrast to the traditional agricultural elites, who were unable to hide their fields from the Crown's tax collectors, wool producers and the new commercialized gentry could better hide their sheep (by moving them around) and their business profits. According to Bates and Lien (1985), the ability of the gentry to hide their assets from taxation or arbitrary seizure by the state changed the balance of power between modernizing social groups and the traditional seats of power—specifically, the Crown.

Suddenly, the kings and queens of England, who needed money to keep hold of power at home and to wage their wars abroad, found themselves in a position in which predation no longer worked; instead, they had to negotiate with economic elites in order to extract revenues. Because the growth of towns and the rise of the wool trade had also led to an increase in the number of economic decision makers whose actions determined the share of revenues available to the Crown, it was, perhaps, natural for these actors to use their newfound bargaining power to increase the strength of institutions such as the Parliament that helped aggregate their interests. The result was the supremacy of Parliament and the withering away of old avenues of representation, such as the Star Chamber, that had formerly served the traditional elites. Note that the increased mobility of assets—the ability to move and hide sheep or the ability to invest money in the Netherlands rather than in England, for example—can be thought of as equivalent to an increase in the value of the "exit option" possessed by economic elites in the exit, voice, and loyalty theory examined in Chapter 3. We return to this shortly.

North and Weingast (1989) present a similar argument, in which they claim that the development of economic actors who could hide their assets led the Crown to look for ways to credibly commit to honoring its financial obligations to the emerging financial class from whom it wished to borrow money to fund its external wars. One way to do this was by strengthening the power of Parliament in relation to the king. To see how this argument works, imagine a king who has a temporary need to raise resources above and beyond what existing tax revenues can cover. Perhaps the king is conducting an expensive foreign war against a rival power. Although the king might like to simply exploit his citizens and take the money he needs by force as he did in the past, this option is less realistic now that the new gentry can hide their assets. Instead, it's likely that the king must borrow the money he needs from the gentry and promise to pay it back with interest at a later date. The problem is that the king controls the use of violence within his territory. As a result, private capital holders always have to worry that the king will default on his debts after the war is over and that they won't get their money back. In contrast to a student who takes on large amounts of debt while in college, there is no authority over the king who can threaten to forcefully collect the debt once the smoke has cleared and the battles have been fought. In other words, sovereign debt—debt accrued by the sovereign, or Crown—creates what's known as a **credible commitment problem** (see Box 5.2, "Credible Commitment Problems"). Although the king would like to credibly commit, or promise, to pay back the money he borrows from the gentry, he can't do this because there's nothing the gentry can do to force the king to pay the debt back once the money has been borrowed. Knowing they can't force the king to pay the debt back, the lenders are unwilling to lend the king any money in the first place. As North and Weingast (1989) suggest, one solution to this problem is to make the Crown's potential financial backers more powerful by strengthening the role and importance of the Parliament vis-à-vis the king. If the king reneges on his debts now, he'll suffer punishment at the hands of the Parliament. This

BOX 5.2 CREDIBLE COMMITMENT PROBLEMS

North and Weingast (1989) suggest that kings who wish to borrow money from economic elites may have difficulty credibly committing or promising to repay any loans they obtain. The basic reason is that although the king may promise today to repay the loans in the future, the king might use his power to renege on his promise when the loans actually come due. Credible commitment problems like the one outlined here have (at least) two basic characteristics. One is that they always involve a temporal dimension: what is in your interest to promise today may not be in your interest to promise in the future. Some people refer to credible commitment problems as "time-inconsistency problems" for this very reason. The second is that they always involve situations in which power is in the hands of those who make the promise and not in the hands of those who expect to benefit from the promise. For instance, it's the king who has the power and not the economic elites in North and Weingast's example.

Credible commitment problems are not confined to politics; in fact, they occur in many areas of our lives. For example, consider an employer who promises to pay a worker at the end of the month for the work that she does. The worker must do her work before she actually gets paid. A commitment problem arises if the employer promises to pay the worker at the end of the month, but when payday comes, it's no longer in the interests of the employer to make the payment. You should immediately be able to see why the employer might have an incentive to not pay the worker once the work is done.

Society has developed at least three ways to deal with credible commitment problems like this: (1) contracts, (2) repeated interactions, and (3) institutions that alter the distribution of power (Acemoglu and Robinson 2006, 134).

1. *Enforceable contracts*: One of the most common ways to deal with a credible commitment problem like the one in our employer–worker example is with an enforceable contract.

In effect, the worker and the employer could sign a contract in which the employer promises to pay the worker for her work. If the employer reneges, the worker can file a complaint with an outside agency such as a court of law that can force the employer to pay up. Although contracts can help in the economic sphere, they're not always useful in more political settings. This is primarily because the outside agency that typically enforces the contract in a political setting (the state or the king perhaps) may well be one of the actors involved. For instance, it should be obvious that the economic elites and the king in North and Weingast's example can't write a contract to solve their credible commitment problem for the simple reason that it would be the king—who has an incentive to renege—who would have to enforce it.

2. *Repeated interactions*: Another solution to potential credible commitment problems occurs when the two sets of actors are involved in repeated interactions. For example, employers may be deterred from reneging on their promise to pay workers at the end of the month if they need those workers (or others) to work the following month. In effect, employers don't want to develop a bad reputation because they need people to be willing to work for them in the future. Note that this solution to the credible commitment problem assumes that the actors making the promise care enough about the future that they're willing to forgo the benefits they could get today from reneging on their promise. This assumption helps to explain why the repeated interactions solution to potential credible commitment problems is often not very useful in political settings. For example, the king's promise to repay his loans in the North and Weingast story is not particularly credible even though the king and the economic elites are likely to be involved in repeated interactions. The reason has to do with the fact that the king is often under financial stress, and hence in need of loans, precisely when foreign wars threaten his continued

survival. In these circumstances, the king may not be particularly forward looking. In other words, he may come to discount the future so steeply that he's relatively unconcerned with the implications of his behavior on his future reputation. After all, we're only really concerned with our future reputation when we're reasonably confident we'll have a future.

3. *Institutions that alter the distribution of power*: Recall that one of the reasons why certain promises suffer from a credibility problem is that the actor making the promise has power and the beneficiary of the promise doesn't. It's this asymmetric distribution of power that allows the promiser to renege. Given this, one solution to potential credible commitment problems is to create institutions that transfer power from the actor making the promise to the beneficiary of the promise. In our employer–worker example, one could create a trade union that would give workers the power to punish employers who renege on their promises through things like strikes. It's this ability to punish the employer that (a) encourages the employer to stick to her promise to pay the worker at the end of the month and (b) makes the worker believe that the employer will follow through with her promise and thus provide labor in the first place. This solution to potential credible commitment problems is quite common in political settings and is precisely the solution that the king of England employs in North and Weingast's example to make his promise to repay the loans from the economic elites credible. By transferring power to Parliament, which represents the interests of the economic elites and which could realistically punish the king if he reneges, the king is able to solve his credible commitment problem.

Despite these potential solutions, the difficulty in solving credible commitment problems should not be underestimated in politics. To see this, imagine you're a member of the white minority that controlled South Africa during the apartheid era. Apartheid was a system of racial segregation that was enforced from 1948 to 1994 to ensure the economic and political dominance of whites over the indigenous African population. Suppose you have come to believe that apartheid is unsustainable and you think full democracy should be introduced in South Africa. The problem is that in a democratic South Africa, the indigenous African population would represent a clear majority of the electorate and could pass policies to redistribute income and assets from the rich white minority to the poor black majority. This is likely to make you reluctant to introduce democracy. Imagine that the indigenous Africans, led by the African National Congress (ANC), promise that they'll not redistribute too much if you allow democracy. Is this promise credible? Not really. Once democracy is established, what's to stop the ANC from reneging on its promise and using its large majority to redistribute wealth away from the white minority? This credible commitment problem may well help to explain why the apartheid system lasted so long. Note that the inability of the ANC to credibly promise not to redistribute too much may have prolonged the life of the apartheid system even if both the white minority and the black majority preferred to live in a low-redistributive democracy.

You may be wondering why the apartheid regime finally came to an end in 1994. One answer is that the credible commitment problem the ANC faced was solved by structural changes in the South African economy (Wood 2000). These changes included the increased mobility of the economic assets of the white minority resulting from the globalization of the South African economy during the 1980s and early 1990s. In effect, this change in the mobility of the assets controlled by the white minority altered the power relationship between the white minority and the ANC. Now, if the ANC reneged on any promise not to redistribute too much, members of the white minority had the ability to simply remove their assets from South Africa and take them somewhere else. Because the economic performance of the South African economy depended heavily on these assets, the ANC's promise not to redistribute them became credible. This helps to explain why the transition to democracy in South Africa occurred when it did.

is precisely the explanation many scholars propose to explain the institutional reforms that led to the establishment of modern parliamentary democracy in Britain during the Glorious Revolution of 1688 (Acemoglu and Robinson 2000, 2006; Stasavage 2002).

Bates and Lien (1985) argue that the introduction of this more limited state occurred earlier and more definitively in England than it did in France because of the unique structure of the economy that early modernization had produced in England. To see why this is the case, it's useful to think in terms of the exit, voice, and loyalty (EVL) theory we analyzed in Chapter 3. Under the exigencies of war, the Crown has confiscated or taxed the assets of a segment of the elite represented by parliament. We'll refer to these people as the Parliamentarians. At this point, the Crown is still behaving in its usual predatory fashion as though the economic development sweeping through English society doesn't concern it directly. However, the Parliamentarians are operating from a newfound position of strength vis-à-vis the Crown. The Parliamentarians have three options. The first option is to take what assets remain and do everything they can to shield them from further confiscation—in part by taking their assets out of production or by consuming them (exit). If the Parliamentarians no longer invest their assets, the economy is likely to stagnate, and there'll be less for the Crown to tax or confiscate in the future. The second option is to petition the Crown for protections against future confiscations in exchange for a promise to continue investing their assets in the economy (voice). We'll assume that the petition calls for the Crown to accept limits on future predatory behavior, say, by granting Parliament the right to veto all future increases in taxation or by constructing an independent judiciary capable of policing the Crown's behavior. The third option is for the Parliamentarians to continue investing their assets as they did before the confiscation (loyalty).

If the Parliamentarians decide to use voice and petition the Crown, the Crown can respond in one of two ways. First, it can accept the new limits on its power to tax (respond). In this case, we assume the Parliamentarians will happily continue to invest their assets and the economy will grow. Second, it can reject the new limits (reject). If the Crown rejects the limits, the Parliamentarians must choose whether to continue investing as before (loyalty) or withdraw substantial portions of their assets from the market (exit). Depending on whether the Parliamentarians continue investing their assets, the economy will either stagnate or grow. The decision tree for the Parliamentarians and the Crown is shown in Figure 5.4.

According to the story we've been telling, the Crown is dependent on the Parliamentarians—the Crown needs access to their money. For now, let's assume the Parliamentarians have a credible exit threat. In other words, the Parliamentarians have mobile assets and the value they get from their assets when they hide them from the Crown is higher than it is when they continue to invest them in a confiscatory environment. The outcome in this scenario is a limited government and a growing economy (O3).[5] Why? The Crown will decide to accept limits on its predatory behavior because it knows that it's dependent on the Parliamentarians for their money and because it knows that the Parliamentarians have a credible exit threat and will therefore exit and disinvest if it rejects the limits. Knowing that their petition will be effective, the Parliamentarians use voice and demand limits from the Crown. This particular scenario helps to explain why the Crown in England, which was dependent on a social group with a credible exit threat (mobile assets), agreed to accept limits on its power.

Bates and Lien (1985) argue that, in contrast to England, the agricultural sector in France had undergone considerably less modernization and, as a result, the engine of the economy continued to be a traditional oligarchy that derived its wealth from agricultural production based on quasi-feudal processes that were easy to observe and therefore easy to tax.

---

[5]This particular scenario is equivalent to Scenario 1 in Figure 3.5 when we first examined the EVL theory in Chapter 3.

FIGURE 5.4 ■ The Decision Tree for the Parliamentarians and the Crown

In the terminology of our EVL theory, the relevant elites in France didn't possess credible exit threats. The French Crown, though, was as dependent on its economic elites as the English Crown. The outcome in this scenario is an unlimited government with a growing economy (O2). Why? The Crown will reject any demands to limit its predatory behavior. This is because it knows that although it's dependent on the Parliamentarians for money, the Parliamentarians will continue to invest and pay their taxes no matter what due to the fact that they don't have a credible exit threat. Knowing the Crown will ignore their petitions, the Parliamentarians simply continue to invest and pay their taxes from the beginning. This particular scenario helps to explain why the French Crown remained absolutist at a time when the English monarchy was accepting limits on its predatory behavior. For example, the Estates General, the chief French representative body at the time, didn't meet between 1614 and May 1789, by which point financial crises had reached such proportions that the French Revolution may have been unavoidable. For nearly two centuries, then, French elites had little choice but to try to influence the Crown's behavior through the intricacies of court politics rather than through a parliament.

Up to this point, we've assumed that the Crown depends on the Parliamentarians for money and other resources. What happens, though, if the Crown is autonomous—it has other sources of money—and doesn't depend on the Parliamentarians? There are two scenarios to consider—one in which the Parliamentarians don't have a credible exit threat and one in which they do. If the Parliamentarians don't have a credible exit threat (they have immobile assets), they'll respond to state predation by continuing to invest and paying their taxes. They'll do this because they know the Crown doesn't depend on them and so will ignore their petitions. In this scenario, the fact that the Parliamentarians continue to invest their assets means the economy will grow. However, if the Parliamentarians do have a credible exit threat (they have mobile assets), they'll choose to exit and disinvest in the economy—they realize there's no point in petitioning the Crown to limit its predatory behavior because the Crown doesn't depend on them. In this scenario, the fact that the Parliamentarians disinvest means the economy stagnates.

The outcomes of the four different scenarios are shown in Table 5.2. Note that we expect democracy (limited government) to emerge and survive only when the state (Crown) depends on economic elites (Parliamentarians) who have credible exit threats (mobile assets). This was the case during the Glorious Revolution in England. The English Crown found itself dependent on a set of societal elites with whom it was forced to bargain. It had to bargain with them because a sufficient number of these elites possessed assets that were mobile and, hence, difficult to tax. It was as a result of this that the Crown ultimately accepted serious limitations on its power, thereby bringing limited and representative government into being in England. This argument can be stated more broadly: representative government (of which democracy is an example) is more likely to emerge and survive when the rulers of a country depend on a segment of society that comprises a relatively large number of people holding mobile assets.[6] Barrington Moore Jr. ([1966] 1999, 418) essentially stated the same argument quite succinctly in his famous book about the social origins of democracy and dictatorship when he wrote, "No bourgeoisie, no democracy."

The argument we've just made helps alleviate some of the concern that political theorists, such as Locke, had with Hobbes's solution to the state of nature. Recall from our discussion in Chapter 4 that Hobbes saw the creation of a powerful state that would hold its citizens in "awe" as the solution to the "war of all against all" and the "solitary, poor, nasty, brutish, and short" life that characterizes the state of nature. Although theorists such as Locke recognized that the creation of the state might solve the problem citizens have with each other, they thought it created a potentially more troubling problem between the citizens and the state. By surrendering control over the means of violence to the state, what was to prevent the state from using its power against its citizens? The argument we've just presented illustrates that there are some conditions under which the state will *voluntarily agree* to accept limits on its predatory behavior: when the state depends on a segment of society with mobile assets. Under these conditions, the citizens needn't fear state predation.

TABLE 5.2 ■ Summary of Possible Outcomes in the Exit, Voice, and Loyalty Theory		
	Crown	
Parliamentarians	**Is autonomous**	**Is dependent**
Have a credible exit threat (mobile assets)	O1: Poor dictatorship (unlimited government, stagnant economy)	O3: Rich democracy (limited government, growing economy)
Have no credible exit threat (fixed assets)	O2: Rich dictatorship (unlimited government, growing economy)	O2: Rich dictatorship (unlimited government, growing economy)

[6]Governments that are dependent on actors with mobile assets won't necessarily be democratic in the sense that they respond to the preferences of the majority. Our argument indicates only that they'll be responsive to those citizens with credible exit threats. However, the fact that the number of people with credible exit threats typically increases with development means that dependent governments are likely to become responsive to larger and larger sections of their society over time.

Natural Resources and Democracy

In addition to providing a causal mechanism linking the process of modernization to the emergence of representative government, our variant of modernization theory also provides an explanation for something called the **political resource curse** (Barro 1999; Ross 2001, 2012). According to the political resource curse, countries that depend on revenue from **natural resources**, such as oil, diamonds, and minerals, will find it difficult to democratize. You might think that having natural resources would be a blessing as these resources provide access to "free" or "unearned" income that can be used to build democracy and improve the material well-being of citizens. The empirical evidence, though, shows that leaders in countries with natural resources don't use their "unearned" income in this way. Not only are countries that rely on natural resources more likely to be dictatorships than democracies, but they're also more prone to corruption, poor governance, and civil war (P. Collier and Hoeffler 2002, 2005; Dunning 2005; Fearon 2005; Humphreys 2005; Karl 1997; Ross 1999; Shafer 1994). Far from being a blessing, natural resources appear to be a curse.

But why? Political scientists have proposed demand-side and supply-side explanations for the political resource curse (Uhlfelder 2007). Demand-side explanations emphasize how resource revenue reduces both citizen demand for democratic reform and government responsiveness to that demand. Governments with access to natural resources don't need to raise revenue by taxing their citizenry—they can simply dig it out of the ground (Beblawi 1987; Karl 1997; Mahdavy 1970; Ross 2001). As our discussion of the emergence of representative institutions in early modern Europe indicates, there's often a close connection between taxation and representation (Bates and Lien 1985; Levi 1988; North and Weingast 1989). Citizens often demand greater representation and accountability when their leaders want to raise taxes. The fact that governments with access to natural resources have a stream of unearned income means they can afford to keep taxes low. A consequence is that citizen demand for greater representation is lower than it otherwise would be.

Governments with access to natural resources are unlikely to respond positively to demands for greater representation even if citizens were to make them. The fact that governments can simply dig revenue out of the ground means they're *autonomous* from the citizens and don't need to accept institutional limits on their political power in exchange for revenue. Does it matter if the natural resources are "controlled" or "owned" by private actors rather than the state? Not really. Natural resources are your quintessential immobile asset. Oil rigs and diamond mines, for example, are not movable. Governments are free to predate on this sector of the economy safe in the knowledge that private actors don't have a credible exit option and thus can't exert much influence over them. As you can see, the underlying logic of demand-side explanations is evident in our EVL theory. By increasing the autonomy of the government in a context where assets are immobile, resource revenue undermines a government-citizen bargaining dynamic that might otherwise culminate in democratic reforms (Wiens, Poast, and Clark 2014).

Supply-side explanations, in contrast, focus on how resource revenue enables dictators to resist pressure to democratize and helps them consolidate their hold on power. These explanations highlight how resource revenue can be distributed as patronage to preempt or co-opt opposition groups, or used to repress them (Al-Ubaydli 2012; Bueno de Mesquita and Smith 2009; Dunning 2008; Jensen and Wantchekon 2004; Morrison 2007, 2009; Paler 2013; Ross 2004; Smith 2006; Wantchekon 2001). For example, oil-funded leaders like those in the Middle East are able to placate opposition groups "by offering new handouts, lowering taxes, or both—and this usually works" (Ross 2011, 3). In response to the Arab Spring in

2011, "Algeria announced plans to invest $156 billion in new infrastructure and to cut taxes on sugar; Saudi Arabia directed $130 billion toward increasing wages in the public sector, unemployment benefits, and housing subsidies; Kuwait offered each of its citizens a cash gift of 1,000 dinars (about $3,600) and free food staples for fourteen months" (Ross 2011, 3–4). Revenue from natural resources is particularly helpful for buying the loyalty of the armed forces. For example, "Iranian president Mahmoud Ahmadinejad . . . has given billions of dollars in no-bid contracts to businesses associated with the elite Revolutionary Guards. . . . Some of the world's biggest oil producers, including Oman, Saudi Arabia, and the United Arab Emirates, are also some of the biggest military spenders. When the citizens of Oman and Saudi Arabia took to the streets [in 2011], their armies proved relatively willing and able to suppress the protests" (Ross 2011, 4).

We can see the importance of natural resource revenue for maintaining the loyalty of the military by comparing what happened in Libya and Egypt during the Arab Spring. In Libya, Muammar al-Qaddafi was able to use oil revenue to hire mercenaries from countries like Chad, Niger, Mali, and Sudan to fight rebel groups. It's widely believed that without the intervention of NATO forces in March 2011, these mercenaries, along with the rest of the Libyan military, would have easily defeated the rebels. The per capita revenue generated by oil and gas was considerably lower in Egypt compared to in Libya. As a result, it was much harder for the longtime dictatorial leader in Egypt, Hosni Mubarak, to keep the support of his military. Mubarak had historically relied on two mechanisms to ensure the loyalty of his military. One mechanism involved transferring vast amounts of aid provided by the United States to the military. Since 1979, the United States had provided Egypt about $2 billion a year, much of it in the form of military aid. The other mechanism was to allow the military to take over large parts of the Egyptian economy. The Egyptian military owns companies that sell everything from fire extinguishers and medical equipment to laptops, televisions, bottled water, and olive oil. Exactly how much of the economy is controlled by the military is unclear, with estimates varying from a low of 5 percent to a high of 45 percent (Fadel 2011). With the United States threatening to reconsider its military aid to Egypt and the military viewing the people camped out in Tahrir Square more as "customers" than "protesters," it's perhaps unsurprising the military was reluctant to fire on the people and began to distance itself from Mubarak. Without the support of the Egyptian military, it wasn't long before Mubarak was forced to step down.

The existence of dictatorships that are rich due to the presence of natural resource revenue is inconsistent with the claim that increased income leads to democracy. Although the existence of a few wealthy dictatorships, such as Saudi Arabia or Oman, is anomalous in the context of our original description of modernization theory, it should be easy to see that it's entirely compatible with the political resource curse and the variant of modernization theory that we've just presented.

Two things are worth noting about the political resource curse. First, the political resource curse doesn't say that having an *abundance* of natural resources is necessarily bad for democratization. What matters is the extent to which the government depends on natural resources for its revenue. Recall that the relative bargaining power of the actors in our EVL theory is based on whether the government depends on actors with mobile assets. If a sizable proportion of the government's revenue comes from citizens with mobile assets, then the government needs to commit to policies that favor these citizens if it wants to ensure their continued investment. However, if the government's revenue comes primarily from natural resource extraction, then its incentive to make credible commitments to its citizens by establishing representative institutions declines. This implies that it's a country's *dependence* on natural resource revenue that affects its regime type, not simply whether there's an *abundance* of natural resources. In other words, a country with an abundance of natural resources can still have a good chance at democratizing if the income the government earns from this sector of the economy is small relative to what it earns from other sectors of the economy with more mobile assets.

Second, the political resource curse is about the *emergence* of democracy, not the *survival* of democracy. In our EVL theory, one of the ways that resource revenue reduces the likelihood of democratization is by making governments autonomous from citizen demands. Although resource revenue hurts the emergence of democracy, it doesn't have to harm democratic stability. There are two reasons for this. The first is that the discovery of natural resources in a democracy occurs after the emergence of institutions capable of holding the government accountable. The second is that the popular oversight that occurs in democracy will help to prevent governments from spending natural resource revenue on patronage and coercion. This helps to explain why natural resource revenue hasn't been a "curse" in countries like Canada, Norway, the United Kingdom, or the United States. In these countries, the flow of resource revenue began only after democratic institutions were already well established.

Foreign Aid and Democracy

How does **foreign aid** affect democratization? Scholars who examine the effect of foreign aid on the democratization process can be divided into "aid optimists," who think that foreign aid can spur democratization efforts, and "aid pessimists," who think that foreign aid has a negative effect on democratization reforms (Wright and Winters 2010). The EVL theory highlights one way in which foreign aid hinders democratization. However, it also suggests there may be conditions under which foreign aid can encourage limited democratic reforms.

As the possible outcomes in our EVL theory in Table 5.2 indicate, democracy is unlikely to emerge when governments are autonomous from their citizens. By freeing governments from the need to raise taxes and providing them with access to "slack resources" that can be strategically used to reward supporters and co-opt opposition groups, foreign aid increases the autonomy of recipient governments from citizen demands (Ahmed 2012; Bueno de Mesquita and Smith 2009; Kono and Montinola 2009; Smith 2008). In addition, the low taxes and increased spending that foreign aid makes possible reduces the citizenry's demand for democratic reforms (Remmer 2004; Morrison 2007, 2009). In these ways, foreign aid hinders the emergence of democracy. Although it may be hard to see citizens living in destitution under harsh dictatorial rule, attempting to ease their pain by providing foreign aid to their governments may simply result in their prolonged suffering. The argument here is consistent with many studies showing that foreign aid to dictatorships harms the welfare of the average citizen and helps dictators stay in office through corruption and exploitation rather than through the production of effective public policy (Bräutigam and Knack 2004; Knack 2004; Djankov, Montalvo, and Reynal-Querol 2008; Moyo 2009).

If the argument here reminds you of the reasoning behind the political resource curse, you're not alone. Many scholars claim that income from foreign aid is essentially the same as income from natural resources—both represent forms of unearned income that increase the autonomy of governments relative to their citizens (Bueno de Mesquita and Smith 2009; Morrison 2007, 2009; Smith 2008). Indeed, some people speak of a foreign aid curse, similar to a political resource curse (Djankov, Montalvo and Reynal-Querol 2008). This line of reasoning, though, overlooks some important differences between natural resources and foreign aid (Altincekic and Bearce 2014; Bermeo 2016; Wright and Winters 2010). Significantly, these differences suggest that a foreign aid curse, while likely, is not inevitable.

The key thing to note is that while natural resource revenue makes governments more autonomous in a general sense, this isn't the case with foreign aid revenue. While foreign aid makes governments less dependent on their citizens, it makes them more dependent on their foreign aid donors. As we know from the EVL theory, aid donors will be able to exert

On March 27, 2009, US president Barack Obama announces a new strategy of increasing foreign aid to Pakistan in hopes of weakening al-Qaeda.

influence on these dependent recipient countries whenever the donors can credibly threaten to withdraw their aid. But what exactly do donor countries want when they give aid? And when can they credibly threaten to withdraw their aid?

Donor countries often value achieving strategic goals with their foreign aid at least as much as they value obtaining democratic reforms in recipient countries (Bearce and Tirone 2010). For example, donor countries might use foreign aid to encourage recipient countries to attack terrorist groups, such as ISIL and the Taliban, to prop up "friendly" regimes in hostile regions of the world, or to obtain privileged access to economic markets for their domestic companies. If aid is driven by strategic concerns, then we shouldn't expect it to promote democratization (Wright and Winters 2010). However, many donor countries do demand democratic and other political reforms as a condition for continued foreign aid. Empirical evidence, though, suggests that these types of conditions are rarely enforced by the donor country (Svensson 2003).[7] This has led some scholars to claim that foreign aid is effectively "unconditional" in practice (Morrison 2012). If this is true, then there's again no reason to think that foreign aid would promote democratization.

The extent to which aid donors can enforce their conditions for democratic reform depends on whether they have credible exit threats. When the aid donor has a strategic interest in the recipient country, threats to withhold aid are not credible (Bearce and Tirone 2010; Bermeo 2016). It's hard to imagine, for example, that the United States would withdraw significant amounts of aid from countries such as Iraq and Afghanistan if they fail to democratize. This is because the governments in these countries are strategically important to the United

---

[7]One reason for this is that donor countries, while publicly stating that they desire democratization, often have little actual interest in recipient countries becoming democratic. This is because it's typically cheaper to get a dictatorship rather than a democracy to adopt "friendly" policies.

States in terms of fighting international terrorism and achieving stability in the Middle East. Recipient countries that are strategically important are often aware of this fact and feel they can safely ignore any demands for political reform. All of this suggests that foreign aid will be effective at promoting democracy only when the donor country has no strategic interests in the "dependent" recipient country. Our argument here is supported by studies showing that foreign aid is more associated with democratic reforms in the post–Cold War period than during the Cold War period when alliance politics was more strategically important (Dunning 2005; Wright 2009).

What we can see, then, is that foreign aid can promote democratization, but only under extremely demanding conditions. Specifically, foreign aid will promote democratization only when (1) the recipient country is dependent on the foreign aid, (2) the aid donor wants to promote democratic reform in the recipient country, and (3) the aid donor can credibly threaten to withdraw aid if its demands for reform are not met. If any of these conditions fail to hold, then we can expect foreign aid to hinder democratization efforts. Moreover, if political reforms do actually occur in the recipient country, they're likely to be limited in scope. Most dictatorial leaders in recipient countries will try to avoid introducing meaningful reforms that put their authority in jeopardy. Instead, they'll try to implement superficial reforms that are sufficient to satisfy their foreign aid donors (it seems like they're responding to donor demands) but don't actually threaten their hold on power. Dietrich and Wright (2014) present evidence consistent with this expectation. They find that foreign aid tends to increase de jure political competition in the recipient country but not de facto political competition. In effect, there's more competition on paper but not so much in practice. For example, they find that while foreign aid might encourage the emergence of multiparty politics, the resulting multi-party politics are characterized by weak opposition parties and the continued dominance of incumbent leaders.

Inequality and Democracy

It's commonly argued that economic inequality undermines democracy (Acemoglu and Robinson 2000, 2001, 2006; Boix 2003; Houle 2009; Huntington 1991; Reenock, Bernhard, and Sobek 2007). The claim that inequality is bad for democracy actually goes back at least as far as Tocqueville ([1835] 1988, 49–55, 128–136), who argued that economic equality was important for the introduction and persistence of democratic institutions. The basic argument is that inequality produces political competition between the rich and the poor. This is because it provides incentives for the poor to redistribute wealth from the rich. The ability of the poor to take wealth away from the rich simply by voting makes democracy appealing to the poor but costly to the rich. As a result, the expectation is that economic elites will step in to block attempts at democratization or to conduct coups to reverse democratization in highly unequal societies.

Although the argument sounds compelling, it lacks strong empirical support. Some studies find a negative relationship between inequality and democracy, but most find no relationship at all (Barro 1997; Bollen and Jackman 1985, 1995; Przeworski et al. 2000). In terms of the causal story itself, there's little evidence that the demand for redistribution increases with inequality or that democracies redistribute more than dictatorships (Przeworski 1985; Roemer 1998; Scheve and Stasavage 2009; Shelton 2007). Moreover, Haggard and Kaufman (2012) find that redistributive conflict between the rich and the poor is evident in only about half of the recent transitions to democracy. The key actor in most democratic transitions is not the poor, but the middle class (bourgeoisie). That is, the key actor is a group whose income is higher than that of the average income earner and who would therefore be a net contributor, not beneficiary, from any tax and redistribution system (Ansell and Samuels 2014).

The logic inherent in our variant of modernization theory provides one explanation for why existing studies fail to find a consistent negative relationship between inequality and democracy. We saw earlier that economic elites who have credible exit options (mobile assets) can force a dependent state to accept limits on its predatory behavior. That these economic elites have credible exit options and can realistically withdraw their much-needed investment in the economy also helps to explain why the poor won't vote to expropriate them. In effect, the poor "depend" on the economic elites for the economy to grow. If this is true, then existing empirical studies examining the link between economic inequality and democracy need to be modified. Economic inequality should be bad for democracy only in countries where the economic elites have immobile assets and therefore lack credible exit threats. In countries where they have mobile assets, the elites should be willing to accept democracy safe in the knowledge that the poor will have incentives to curb their demands for redistribution.

Evidence in support of this line of reasoning comes from Freeman and Quinn (2010), who find that unequal dictatorships that are financially integrated into the global economy are much more likely to experience transitions to democracy than unequal dictatorships that are financially closed. Additional support comes from Ansell and Samuels (2014), who find that *income* inequality promotes democratization but that *land* inequality hinders it. The reason is that income inequality generally increases along with the creation of a large middle class, whereas land inequality usually goes hand in hand with a large landed aristocracy. A large middle class is a group that tends to have mobile assets, but the landed aristocracy primarily holds immobile assets. Landed elites have more to fear from democratization due to the immobile nature of their assets. As Box 5.2, "Credible Commitment Problems," indicates,

People queuing outside the polling station in the black township of Soweto, in the southwest suburbs of Johannesburg, South Africa, on Wednesday, April 27, 1994, during South Africa's first all-race elections.

Wood's (2000) account of the democratic transition in South Africa in 1994 also fits with our variant of modernization theory. As the South African economy globalized in the 1980s and early 1990s, the economic assets of the white minority became more mobile. She argues that it was the increased mobility of the white South Africans' assets that made them willing to accept a democratic transition despite the high levels of inequality in the country.

Economic Performance

In addition to providing predictions about whether countries are likely to be democratic or dictatorial, our EVL theory also offers predictions about whether they'll have growing or stagnant economies. The possible outcomes of our EVL theory shown in Table 5.2 indicate that the economic performance of democracies will be good, whereas that of dictatorships will be much more varied. Countries in which the government is dependent on citizens with a credible exit threat are likely to be democratic and have a strong and growing economy. The economy grows because the citizens freely invest their assets safe in the knowledge the government won't predate on them. Countries in which citizens lack credible exit threats are likely to be dictatorial and have a weak but growing economy. The economy grows because citizens have little option but to continue investing, making the best of what they have and hoping the government doesn't exploit them too much. Countries in which the government is autonomous and the citizens have a credible exit threat are likely to be dictatorial with a stagnant economy. The economy is stagnant because the citizens will use their assets elsewhere to avoid government predation. The prediction that dictatorships will exhibit more variation in economic performance than democracies is consistent with several theoretical and empirical studies (Alesina and Perotti 1994; Bueno de Mesquita et al. 2003).

CONCLUSION

There is considerable evidence to support modernization theory's claim that countries are more likely to become democratic and remain democratic as their economies become more "modern." Higher levels of income encourage both the emergence and survival of democracy. Changes in economic structure that accompany changes in income also matter. We've shown that limited government in early modern Europe was more likely to arise in polities in which the Crown was dependent on elites with mobile assets. This argument can be generalized to account for the emergence and survival of democracy in more contemporary periods. States that are more dependent on revenue from immobile assets are less likely to democratize. In support of this claim, we cited considerable evidence that democracy is less likely to arise in countries that are heavily dependent on revenue from natural resources. In a more detailed study than the one presented here, Ross (2001) shows that increased income affects democratization by bringing about additional changes such as increased occupational differentiation, improved education, and the growth of the service economy. All of these changes can be thought of as parts of a broader process of modernization. Moreover, all of these changes can be expected to increase the "exit options" available to citizens.

Arguments linking the prospects for democracy to the structure of a nation's economy are not popular with democratic activists. If democracy arose in Great Britain as a result of a gradual change in the British economy that took centuries to unfold, then what hope is there for people living under authoritarian regimes today? When the Arab Spring took place in 2011, many people were optimistic that a wave of democracy was washing over the Middle East and North Africa. We were less optimistic. Many, though certainly not all, of the regimes in this region of the world were dependent on oil revenue. In an age of Twitter and the Internet, we recognized that protest could spread quickly, but it wasn't clear to us that the process of democratization could be sped up appreciably. In an opinion piece written at the time, Michael Ross (2011, 5) reminded us that "no country with more oil wealth than Venezuela had in 1958" when it transitioned to democracy "has ever successfully democratized." Our knowledge of the political resource curse led us to believe there was little hope that many of the regimes that had faced widespread opposition during the Arab Spring would transition into stable democracies.

In Table 5.3, we show estimates of per capita oil and gas production in several countries in the Middle East and North Africa (Ross 2012). If the structure of a nation's economy places constraints on the propensity to democratize, then, all other things being equal, we would expect countries near the top of this list to be much less likely to democratize than countries near the bottom of this list. Removing autocrats from office is a necessary, but not sufficient, condition for democratization. We were not surprised that it was the rulers of Tunisia and Egypt—countries with the lowest levels of per capita oil and gas production in Table 5.3— who were the first leaders to lose their grip on power during the Arab Spring. Unfortunately, the events of the past half decade since the Arab Spring have seen our expectations borne out.

TABLE 5.3 ■ Estimated Value of Oil and Gas Produced Per Capita in 2009 in Current Dollars	
Country	Oil income per capita (2009 dollars)
Qatar	$24,940
Kuwait	$19,500
United Arab Emirates	$14,100
Oman	$ 7,950
Saudi Arabia	$ 7,800
Libya	$ 6,420
Bahrain	$ 3,720
Algeria	$ 1,930
Iraq	$ 1,780
Iran	$ 1,600
Syria	$ 450
Yemen	$ 270
Egypt	$ 260
Tunisia	$ 250

Source: Ross (2012). *The Oil Curse.* Princeton, N.J.: Princeton University Press.

As we mentioned in the previous chapter, only Tunisia out of the countries listed in Table 5.3 can be considered a democracy today.

If changes to the structure of the economy are prerequisites for democratization, change is likely to come slowly—even in today's fast-paced world. In the next chapter, we move away from economic arguments about democracy to consider whether cultural traits influence the emergence and survival of democracy. Unfortunately, for those who would like to speed the pace of democratization, culture too changes slowly.

Key Concepts

state—an entity that uses coercion and the threat of force to rule in a given territory

government—the set of people who run the state or have the authority to act on behalf of the state at a particular point in time

regime—the set of rules, norms, or institutions that determine how the government is constituted, how it's organized, and how major decisions are made

contestation—the extent to which citizens are free to organize themselves into competing blocs in order to press for the policies and outcomes they desire

inclusion—the extent to which citizens get to participate in the political process

GDP per capita—gross domestic product per capita. GDP measures the value of all goods and services produced in a country during a specified period, usually one year; GDP per capita is a country's gross domestic product divided by the size of the population

modernization theory—a theory that predicts that democracy is more likely to emerge and survive as countries develop and become richer

survival story—a theory that predicts that democracy is more likely to survive as countries develop and become richer, but that it's not more likely to emerge

credible commitment problem—also known as a time-inconsistency problem, occurs when (1) an actor who makes a promise today may have an incentive to renege on that promise in the future and (2) power is in the hands of the actor who makes the promise and not in the hands of those expected to benefit from the promise

political resource curse—a theory that predicts that countries dependent on revenue from natural resources are unlikely to democratize and are prone to corruption, poor governance, and civil war

natural resources—naturally occurring substances that are usually considered valuable, such as oil, diamonds, and minerals

foreign aid—aid in the form of money, food, technical assistance, military weapons, and the like, that people in one country give to another; can come from national governments, intergovernmental organizations, or private donations

6

THE CULTURAL DETERMINANTS OF DEMOCRACY AND DICTATORSHIP

There was a time when many said that the cultures of Japan and Germany were incapable of sustaining democratic values. Well, they were wrong.

George W. Bush, in a speech to the American Enterprise Institute,
Washington Hilton Hotel, February 26, 2003

I am a democrat only on principle, not by instinct—nobody is that. Doubtless some people say they are, but this world is grievously given to lying.

Mark Twain, Notebook, entry for February–March 1898

OVERVIEW

1. In this chapter, we examine various cultural explanations for democracy. According to cultural modernization theory, economic development produces certain cultural changes that lead to democracy. A key cultural change is the emergence of a "civic culture."

2. We investigate recent claims that particular religions such as Islam are incompatible with democracy. All religions have some doctrinal elements that can be seen as compatible with democracy and others that can be seen as incompatible. Overall, there's little reason to believe that certain religions are incompatible with democracy.

3. We look at evidence from a series of experiments conducted around the world that throws light on why culture may be important for democracy.

In the previous chapter, we examined economic arguments for democracy. We now turn to cultural arguments for democracy. The notion that cultural differences drive significant elements of political and economic life is commonplace and has a long history. But does democracy really require a "democratic culture"? Are certain cultures incompatible with democracy? The claim that culture plays any role with respect to democracy obviously has important implications for those wishing to spread democracy to regions of the world such as the Middle East, Africa, and Asia.

Cultural arguments for democracy typically fall into two categories: primordialist and constructivist (Laitin 1983, 1986; Przeworski, Cheibub, and Limongi 1998). **Primordialist arguments** treat culture as something that is objective and inherited—something that's been fixed since "primordial" times. According to primordialists, culture exists prior to politics—it provides the ideological guidelines that shape political behavior. As a result, political institutions, such as democracy, may not be compatible with all cultures. In effect, primordialist arguments imply that democracy is not for everyone. **Constructivist arguments** treat culture as something that is constructed or invented rather than inherited. Like primordialist arguments, constructivist arguments claim that culture has a causal effect and that a democratic culture is required for democracy to emerge and prosper. Constructivists recognize, however, that cultures are malleable and are not given once and for all—cultures can change in response to social, economic, and political actors. As a result, cultures do not necessarily represent impenetrable barriers to democracy.

CLASSICAL CULTURAL ARGUMENTS: MILL AND MONTESQUIEU

The notion that political institutions, such as democracy and dictatorship, are more suited to some cultures than others is not new (Przeworski, Cheibub, and Limongi 1998). As long ago as 472 BCE, Aeschylus contrasted the authoritarianism associated with the people of Asia with the democracy found in Athenian Greece in his play *The Persians* (Emmerson, 1995). The views of Aeschylus would later be echoed in what would become known as the Asian values debate in the 1990s. Although vague references to the compatibility of certain cultures with democracy have been around for some time, the first person to write in any great detail about the importance of culture to political institutions was Montesquieu in the eighteenth century. He claimed that monarchy was most suited to European states, that despotism was most suited to the Orient, and that democracy was most suited to the ancient world. He believed the best government for a given country was that which "leads men by following their propensities and inclinations" (Montesquieu [1721] 1899, Persian Letter 81) and which "best agrees with the humor and disposition of the people in whose favor it is established" (Montesquieu [1752] 1914, 1:3). What did this entail exactly? Montesquieu stated that political institutions "should be in relation to the climate of each country, to the quality of its soil, to its situation and extent, to the principal occupation of the natives, whether husbandmen, huntsmen, or shepherds: they should have relation to the degree of liberty which the constitution will bear; to the religion of the inhabitants, to their inclinations, riches, numbers, commerce, manners, and customs" (Montesquieu [1752] 1914, 1:3). He goes on to claim that it can be only by chance that the political institutions of one country can successfully be exported to another.

In his discussion "To What Extent Forms of Government Are a Matter of Choice," John Stuart Mill also argued that different cultures were suited to different political institutions.

He stated, "No one believes that every people is capable of working every sort of institutions" (Mill [1861] 2001, 7). To illustrate this, he claimed, "Nothing but foreign force would induce a tribe of North American Indians to submit to the restraints of a regular and civilized government" (Mill [1861] 2001, 8). Mill believed that even those people who recognized the benefits of a civilized government might still have to live under authoritarianism if they didn't have the required characteristics to support a better system of government. These necessary characteristics included "moral" or "mental habits," such as the willingness to "co-operate actively with the law and the public authorities in the repression of evil-doers" (Mill [1861] 2001, 9). They also included a certain degree of development characterized, for example, by a press capable of propagating public opinion and a tax system "sufficient for keeping up the force necessary to compel obedience throughout a large territory" (Mill [1861] 2001, 11). Mill was clearly a strong believer that legislators should take account of "pre-existing habits and feelings" when creating political institutions in a country ([1861] 2001, 11).

It's important, however, not to interpret Mill's statements as if they're arguments that certain cultures are incompatible with political institutions, such as democracy. In fact, Mill was highly critical of those who believe that culture prevents political actors from choosing the institutions they desire. Although he thought that "people are more easily induced to do, and do more easily, what they are already used to," he also believed that "people . . . learn to do things new to them. Familiarity is a great help; but much dwelling on an idea will make it familiar, even when strange at first" (Mill [1861] 2001, 11). Ultimately, Mill did not see particular cultural traits as necessary conditions for democracy. This is because he thought that culture was inherently malleable and that, as a result, people could learn to live with democracy. As you can see, Mill asserted a constructivist cultural argument regarding the prospects for democracy.

The cultural arguments put forth by both Montesquieu and Mill were later incorporated into strands of **cultural modernization theory**. As you'll remember from the previous chapter, modernization theory predicts that "immature" societies (those with large agricultural sectors and authoritarian institutions) will eventually become "mature" societies (those with large industrial and service sectors and democratic institutions) as they develop economically. Cultural modernization theory states that socioeconomic development transforms societies with primitive cultures into societies with civilized cultures—only when this happens are societies ready for democracy. In other words, cultural modernization theory argues that socioeconomic development does not directly cause democracy; instead, economic development produces certain cultural changes, and it is these cultural changes that produce democratic reform. As Inglehart and Welzel (2005, 15) put it, "socioeconomic development brings roughly predictable cultural changes . . . [and] these changes make democracy increasingly likely to emerge where it does not yet exist, and to become stronger and more direct where it already exists."

The claims Montesquieu and Mill made regarding culture and democracy illustrate several potential problems that characterize some cultural arguments to this day (Przeworski, Cheibub, and Limongi 1998). How would you test the claims Mill and Montesquieu made? What exactly would the hypotheses be? Try to state one of them in a way that can be tested. One obvious problem is that neither scholar specifically states exactly what it is about culture that matters for democracy. Both men provide a whole host of cultural things that might affect the emergence and survival of democracy—religion, customs, morals, manners, marital institutions, and so on. Indeed, most of these things are left quite vague. For example, what particular morals are incompatible with democracy? Which customs are problematic? Moreover, both scholars point to numerous noncultural things that also affect democracy such as the climate of a country, the quality of the soil, and the economy. The key point here is that cultural arguments must specify exactly what it is about culture that matters; otherwise it will never be possible to conclude that culture doesn't matter. Put simply, one of the problems with cultural arguments such as those made by Montesquieu and Mill is that they're so vague or nonspecific that they become nonfalsifiable (Przeworski, Cheibub, and Limongi 1998). In effect, they become "nonscientific" in the terms we outlined in Chapter 2.

The second problem relates to the purported causal relationship between cultural, economic, and political factors. Does culture shape our political institutions? Does it also affect our economic development? Or do political institutions and economic development shape culture? In other words, which way does the causal arrow go? In Figure 6.1, we illustrate some of the causal arguments that scholars have made concerning the interaction between culture, economic development, and democracy. Mill and Montesquieu clearly believed that economic development and culture both matter for democracy. From what they wrote, however, it's hard to discern what they thought the exact causal relationship was between these factors.

FIGURE 6.1 ■ Culture, Economic Development, and Democracy: Some Potential Causal Relationships

DOES DEMOCRACY REQUIRE A CIVIC CULTURE?

Gabriel Almond and Sidney Verba reopened the debate about culture and democracy in the 1960s with their book *The Civic Culture*. Although they recognized the importance of economic development for democracy, they believed that only a "civic culture" could provide the "psychological basis of democratization" and that without this, the prospects for democracy were slim (Almond and Verba [1963] 1989, 9). Almond and Verba claimed that there were three basic types of political culture in the world—parochial, subject, and participant/civic. According to them, the civic culture was the only culture compatible with democracy. In contrast, parochial cultures were compatible with the traditional political systems of African tribes, and subject cultures were compatible with the centralized authoritarian institutions seen in Soviet-dominated Eastern Europe (Almond and Verba [1963] 1989, 20, 33).

A political culture, for Almond and Verba, was something that captured how individuals think and feel about the political system. They believed that it was possible to study culture by conducting surveys and asking individuals about their feelings toward political institutions, actors, and processes. The idea was that the distribution of responses to these survey questions would identify a nation's political culture. In this sense, a political culture simply refers to a relatively coherent cluster of attitudes in society. According to Almond and Verba, a civic culture reflects a particular cluster of attitudes that includes (1) the belief on the part of individuals that they can influence political decisions, (2) positive feelings toward the political system, (3) high levels of interpersonal trust, and (4) preferences for gradual societal change. In contrast, parochial and subject political cultures reflect different clusters of attitudes on these same issues. Applying their methodology to the study of Germany, Italy, Mexico, the United States, and the United Kingdom, Almond and Verba found that the United States and the United Kingdom were not only the most stable democracies in their sample but also the countries that most closely resembled their ideal civic culture. As a result, they concluded that a **civic culture** was necessary for democratic stability (see Box 6.1, "Does Good Democratic Performance Require a Civic Culture?").

Inglehart (1990) reached a similar conclusion after studying survey responses from twenty-five industrial nations in the 1980s. Like Almond and Verba ([1963] 1989), he believed that "different societies are characterized to very different degrees by a specific syndrome of political cultural attitudes; that these cultural differences are relatively enduring, but not immutable; and that they can have major political consequences, one being that they are closely linked to the viability of democratic institutions" (Inglehart 1990, 15). According to Inglehart, political culture is determined by, among other things, the levels of overall life satisfaction, the levels of interpersonal trust, and the support for gradual societal change among the individuals of a nation. Clearly, these determinants of political culture are very similar to those Almond and Verba proposed. In his analysis, Inglehart (1990, 43) found that countries in which levels of life satisfaction, interpersonal trust, and support for gradual societal change were high were more likely to be stable democracies. In other words, he too found that some kind of civic culture is required for stable democracy.

There has never been complete agreement on the precise cluster of attitudes thought to compose a civic culture. In their recent work, Inglehart and Welzel (2005) claim that there are two major dimensions of cross-cultural variation in the world today. The first dimension has to do with whether countries exhibit traditional values or secular-rational values. Traditional values emphasize the importance of religion, traditional family roles, and deference to authority. Individuals who hold traditional values typically exhibit national pride and reject things like

BOX 6.1 DOES GOOD DEMOCRATIC PERFORMANCE REQUIRE A CIVIC CULTURE?

In this chapter, we primarily focus on how political culture affects democracy. Several scholars claim that political culture is also important for the overall *performance* of democracy. In *Making Democracy Work: Civic Traditions in Modern Italy*, Robert Putnam (1993) argues that cultural norms produce variation in the economic and political performance of regional governments in Italy. Putnam's starting point was the observation that regional governments in the north of Italy function far more effectively than those in the south. He wanted to know why this was the case.

Putnam argued that institutions couldn't possibly be the explanation for the variation in government performance between the north and south of Italy, as Italian regional governments all shared a similar institutional structure. Instead, he looked at cultural explanations and focused on the presence or absence of a civic culture. For Putnam, the key to a civic culture was **social capital**. Social capital refers to the collective value of social networks and shared norms that promote reciprocity, trust, and social cooperation. In his work on Italy, Putnam (1993, 167) argued that social capital and, in particular, "norms of reciprocity and networks of civic engagement," were the key to good government performance.

In line with his expectations, Putnam found that regions with more social capital had better government performance than regions with less social capital. In effect, Putnam showed that the high-performing regions in the north of Italy were

characterized by a "good" civic culture that encouraged working for the common good and that the low-performing regions in the south were characterized by a "bad" culture of "amoral familism," in which norms of reciprocity and engagement were limited to one's family and in which self-interest was the primary motivating force behind individual actions. According to Putnam, the civic culture in the north could be traced back to the communal relations exhibited by republican towns in this region in Italy's medieval past, whereas the culture of amoral familism in the south could be traced back to this region's monarchic past.

Putnam's work on Italy has energized many in the policymaking community. "From the World Bank to city hall, the creation of social capital [and civic culture] has been embraced as a solution for social problems as diverse as promoting economic development in Africa and stemming urban decay in Los Angeles" (Boix and Posner 1996). Putnam's study of Italy has also been a catalyst for research on political culture in the United States. In *Bowling Alone*, Putnam (2000) argues that the number of people participating in voluntary associations—one place in which social networks can be built—has been falling in the United States and that people have become disconnected from family, friends, and neighbors. Putnam's book created quite a stir, because the decline in social capital that it described was seen to have potentially negative consequences for the state of American democracy.

divorce, euthanasia, suicide, and abortion. Secular-rational values place less emphasis on religion, traditional family roles, and deference to authority. Individuals who hold these values typically find things like divorce, euthanasia, suicide, and abortion more acceptable. The second dimension has to do with whether countries exhibit survival values or self-expression values. Survival values emphasize the importance of physical and economic security. Individuals who hold survival values typically hold an ethnocentric worldview and exhibit low levels of interpersonal trust and tolerance. Self-expression values emphasize the importance of gender, racial, and sexual equality; environmental protection; tolerance of diversity; civic activism; and life satisfaction. Individuals who hold these values often exhibit high levels of interpersonal trust and demand a greater say in how political and economic decisions are made.

Like Almond and Verba, Inglehart and Welzel (2005) use survey responses to determine the extent to which different societies exhibit traditional versus secular-rational values and the extent to which they exhibit survival versus self-expression values. With these survey responses, it's possible to create a "cultural map" of the world. Figure 6.2 shows a cultural map of the world based on data from the 2010–2014 World Values Survey. Moving upward on this map represents a shift from traditional to secular-rational values, while a move to the right represents a shift from survival to self-expression values. Countries that exhibit high levels of traditional and survival values (bottom left) include Jordan, Yemen, and Morocco. Countries that exhibit high levels of traditional and self-expression values (bottom right) include Mexico, Colombia, and Ecuador. Countries that exhibit high levels of secular-rational and survival values (top left) include Russia, Belarus, and Ukraine. Countries that exhibit high levels of secular-rational and self-expression values (top right) include Sweden, Norway, and Denmark. Figure 6.2 identifies nine subjective "cultural zones." The countries within each cultural zone are thought to share similar cultural values and hence exhibit distinct political cultures.

In line with cultural modernization theory, Inglehart and Welzel (2005) argue that socio-economic development generally produces a change in cultural values that sees countries move from the bottom left quadrant in Figure 6.2 where they are poor and authoritarian to the top right quadrant where they are rich and democratic. According to Inglehart and Welzel (2005), the modernization process is not linear; instead, it occurs in two distinct phases. The first phase—the industrialization phase—sees countries move upward in Figure 6.2 away from traditional values to secular-rational values. In the pre-industrial world, most people earn their living from agriculture and rely on God to provide them with good weather and good health. Social interactions with outsiders are limited, reputation rests on kinship ties, tradition is valued, and comfort is sought in religion. The shift to an industrial society changes things. Technology gives people more control over their environment and science provides a rational explanation for the previously inexplicable. The result is a decline in the importance of religion and the rise of secular authorities. The modernization process is, in this sense, a secularization process (Norris and Inglehart 2004; Gaskins, Golder, and Siegel 2013a, b).

The second phase—the post-industrialization phase—sees countries move rightward in Figure 6.2 away from survival values to self-expression values. While industrialization brings certain changes, people generally remain poor, and they continue to be concerned about their physical and economic security. They worry about putting a roof over their head and food on the table. As socioeconomic development continues and societies become wealthier, though, existential security concerns recede and people can begin to focus on expanding their opportunities for self-expression and personal autonomy. In his earlier work, Inglehart (1977) refers to this change as a "silent revolution" in which materialist worries are replaced by post-materialist concerns. A growing sense of human autonomy leads people to question authority, hierarchies, and dogmatism. As self-expression values spread, so do demands for political liberalization, greater emancipation, and a greater say in how political and economic decisions are made. This puts pressure on authoritarian regimes to democratize and for democratic regimes to act more effectively. As you can see, Inglehart and Welzel (2005) see self-expression and secular-rational values as the core components of a civic culture.

Over the years, there's been considerable debate about the exact causal relationship between culture, economic development, and democracy. On one side of the debate are scholars who argue that economic development produces cultural change and that it's cultural change that produces democracy (Inglehart 1990, 1997; Inglehart and Welzel 2003, 2005). This potential causal relationship, which as we've seen forms the basis for cultural modernization theory, is illustrated in Figure 6.1d. According to this story, cultural values act on, shape, and cause

FIGURE 6.2 ■ A Cultural Map of the World

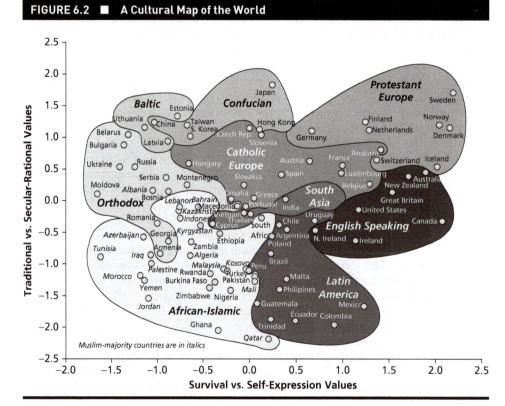

Source: World Values Survey, http://www.worldvaluessurvey.org/WVSContents.jsp.

Note: The cultural map of the world shown in Figure 6.2 is based on data from the sixth wave (2010–2014) of the World Values Survey. The different clusters indicate countries that Inglehart and Welzel identify as sharing similar cultural values—they represent distinct political cultures.

political institutions. We might call this the "values story." On the other side of the debate are scholars who argue that this causal story is backward (Barry 1970; Muller and Seligson 1994; Seligson 2002). These scholars argue that economic development produces democracy and that it's experience with democracy that produces cultural change. This potential causal relationship is illustrated in Figure 6.1f. We might call this the "institutional story." According to the institutional story, cultural values are a *consequence,* not a *cause,* of democracy.

There is, however, no reason to think that both stories can't be true. It seems reasonable to us that societal development might increase the likelihood of democracy through its effects on cultural values as cultural modernization theorists propose—and that it could also increase the likelihood of democracy through other mechanisms such as those examined in Chapter 5. This means that whatever the existing cultural values are in some country, an increasingly modern social structure will increase that country's probability of experiencing democracy. This experience with democracy can, in turn, contribute to cultural change that reinforces democratic practice in the future. Thus, we're not forced to choose between the institutional and values stories. Perhaps these stories work together to create a virtuous cycle tying changes in social structure to increasingly democratic outcomes.

Surveys and Comparative Research

One of the major impacts of Almond and Verba's ([1963] 1989) *Civic Culture* was to encourage the use of surveys to examine the relationship between culture and democracy. One of the most commonly used surveys today is the World Values Survey. This is the survey that provided the data for the cultural map of the world shown in Figure 6.2. Scholars particularly interested in the relationship between culture and democracy are frequently drawn to the following question from the World Values Survey:

> Democracy may have problems, but it's better than any other form of government. Could you please tell me if you strongly agree, agree, neither agree nor disagree, disagree, or strongly disagree?

Many people believe that mass support for a particular system of government, and mass confidence in specific institutions, provides political systems with the legitimacy they need to operate effectively (Newton and Norris 2000). In effect, mass support for democracy is seen by some as essential in delegitimizing dictatorial rule and legitimizing democratic rule. Thus, when a low level of public support is reported in questions like this one from the World Values Survey, it's often seen as a harbinger of democratic instability or collapse.

Surveys such as the World Values Survey are increasingly being used to examine many important questions in comparative politics. Researchers who use surveys often confront certain problems, two of which we briefly discuss here. The first problem arises when surveys address sensitive topics. One of the implicit assumptions in survey research is that respondents are answering the survey questions truthfully (Blair 2015). Unfortunately, respondents often have incentives to lie or conceal their true beliefs. For example, a respondent in a dictatorship may not feel comfortable revealing her true preferences when asked about the value of democracy. This is because democracy is a sensitive topic in most authoritarian regimes. We discuss the issue of "preference falsification" in dictatorships in more detail in the next chapter. Similarly, respondents may feel unwilling to express negative attitudes toward particular ethnic, racial, religious, or sexual groups if these attitudes run counter to social norms. **Social desirability bias**, in which individuals tend to overreport "good behavior" and underreport "bad behavior," helps to explain why surveys often underestimate the support for extremist anti-immigrant parties in Europe or overestimate the degree of support for minority political candidates in the United States. Social pressure, potential legal sanctions, and fear of retaliation can create incentives for respondents to lie on surveys. Indeed, these concerns can even lead to certain types of people not participating in surveys in the first place, with the result that these surveys are no longer "representative." It's easy to see how surveys might produce biased and misleading estimates in these circumstances. For example, if citizens in authoritarian societies underreport their enthusiasm for democracy because they believe they'll be punished for expressing their sincere beliefs, cross-national surveys will overstate the positive association between attitudes toward democracy and democratic persistence.

The second problem, which applies in particular to cross-national surveys, such as the World Values Survey, has to do with the fact that respondents don't always comprehend survey questions in the same way. Consider the following example about self-reported health in India and the United States. Sen (2002, 860–861) writes:

> The state of Kerala has the highest rates of literacy . . . and longevity . . . in India. But it also has, by a very wide margin, the highest rate of reported morbidity among all

Indian states. . . . At the other extreme, states with low longevity, with woeful medical and educational facilities, such as Bihar, have the lowest rates of reported morbidity in India. Indeed, the lowness of reported morbidity runs almost fully in the opposite direction to life expectancy, in interstate comparisons. . . . In disease by disease comparisons, while Kerala has much higher reported morbidity rates than the rest of India, the United States has even higher rates for the same illnesses. If we insist on relying on self-reported morbidity as the measure, we would have to conclude that the United States is the least healthy in this comparison, followed by Kerala, with ill provided Bihar enjoying the highest level of health. In other words, the most common measure of the health of populations is negatively correlated with actual health.

Clearly, the respondents in the different regions of India and in the United States either understood the survey questions differently or evaluated their levels of health on very different scales. This problem is commonly referred to as **differential item functioning (DIF)**. A key point here is that measuring or inferring reality by comparing people's attitudes or perceptions across different regions, countries, or cultures can often be "extremely misleading" (Sen 2002). This particular issue is especially relevant for survey research related to democracy. This is because democracy means different things to different people around the world. For example, democracy may conjure up images of economic and political equality for some, but it may simply mean holding competitive elections for others. It's noteworthy that political scientists often disagree about exactly how to think about democracy in their own research (Collier and Levitsky 1997, Collier and Adcock 1999, Munck and Verkuilen 2002, Cheibub, Gandhi, and Vreeland 2010). If experts can't agree on what they mean by democracy, why would we expect individuals in different countries to have the same concept in mind when answering survey questions about it?

Political scientists are increasingly aware of these problems with surveys and have begun to develop ingenious methods to get around them. Blair (2015) describes four methods for addressing sensitive topics with surveys. The first method focuses on survey administration. The core idea here is to adopt practices that build trust with respondents. Some scholars recommend using interviewers who share similar demographic characteristics, such as age, gender, or ethnicity, with the respondent. Adida and colleagues (2016) find that respondents in Africa give systematically different answers to survey questions if the people who interview them are coethnics as opposed to non-coethnics. Others have highlighted the importance of allowing respondents to report their answers in private rather than aloud to an interviewer (Krysan 1998; Krysan and Couper 2003). In a study of caste-sensitive attitudes in India, Chauchard (2013) provided his respondents with MP3 players so they could self-report their answers in private.

The second method involves the use of randomized response techniques (Gingerich 2010; Blair, Imai, and Zhou 2015). The core feature of these techniques is the introduction of a randomizing device, such as a coin or a die, into the survey response process to guarantee the confidentiality of individual responses. For example, before answering a sensitive survey question that requires a "yes" or "no" answer, a respondent might be asked to roll a die in private. If the die shows a 1, the respondent is told to report "yes." If the die shows a 6, the respondent is told to report "no." If the die shows a 2, 3, 4, or 5, the respondent is told to answer the question truthfully, either "yes" or "no." As you can see, the interviewer never knows whether a given individual response is true or not; hence, the confidentiality of the individual response is guaranteed. The key, though, is that the interviewer knows the probability with which truthful answers are given (if the respondents follow the instructions) and can therefore calculate the overall numbers of respondents who said "yes" and "no" to the sensitive question. Randomized response techniques have been used to study a variety of phenomena, such as corruption within bureaucracies (Gingerich 2013), cheating by undergraduates (Fox and Meijer 2008), sexual attitudes (De Jong, Pieters, and Stremersch 2012), and the prevalence of xenophobia and anti-Semitism (Krumpal 2012).

The third method involves the use of list experiments. The core idea in list experiments is to protect the confidentiality of individual responses by mixing sensitive items into lists that include nonsensitive "control" items. In a list experiment, some survey respondents are presented with a list of nonsensitive control items and are then asked to indicate the number with which they agree. Another set of survey respondents are presented with the same list of control items except that a sensitive item is now also included. These respondents are also asked to indicate the number of items with which they agree. By comparing the number of items that respondents agree with across these two randomly selected groups, it's possible to identify the level of support for the sensitive item. As you may have realized, this method doesn't always guarantee that individual responses are kept confidential. This is because a respondent who answers that she agrees with none or all of the items in the list containing the sensitive item reveals her preferences about the sensitive item. As a result, researchers need to be careful about what items they include in the list of control items. List experiments have been used to study a variety of phenomena such as public support for coalition forces in Afghanistan (Blair, Imai, and Lyall 2014), vote buying in Nicaragua (Gonzalez-Ocantos et al. 2012), and the impact of citizen preferences on policy in China (Meng, Pan, and Yang, 2017).

The fourth method involves the use of endorsement experiments. The core idea in endorsement experiments is to protect the confidentiality of individual responses by mixing attitudes toward a sensitive political actor with attitudes toward one or more policies. In an endorsement experiment, some survey respondents are asked to give their attitudes toward a policy that a "sensitive" political actor has endorsed. The responses to this question mix the preferences of the respondents toward the policy and their preferences toward the sensitive actor. Other survey respondents are asked to give their attitudes toward the same policy but without any mention of the endorsement. The responses to this question isolate the preferences of the respondents toward the policy. By comparing the responses across the two groups, it's possible to identify just the preferences toward the sensitive political actor. Endorsement experiments have been used to study a variety of phenomena such as attitudes toward the Taliban in Afghanistan (Lyall, Blair, and Imai 2013) and militants in Pakistan (Blair et al. 2013).

The fact that respondents don't always comprehend survey questions in the same way, perhaps because they come from different cultures, is problematic. This is particularly the case if one wants to compare survey responses to learn about cultural differences. One way in which political scientists attempt to deal with this issue is through the use of anchoring vignettes (King et al. 2004; King and Wand 2007). Anchoring vignettes are useful for survey questions that use an ordinal scale—say, strongly disagree, disagree, neutral, agree, strongly agree—such as the "democracy" question seen earlier from the World Values Survey. Anchoring vignettes use additional survey questions to create "anchors" that allow for a common scale of measurement across respondents. Respondents are asked to provide a self-assessment of a particular issue. They're then asked to provide an assessment of a vignette (short story) that depicts a particular outcome of that issue. For example, respondents might be asked to judge their own political efficacy, that is, their belief that they can get their representatives to address issues important to them. They're then confronted with a vignette that includes information about some other individual's political efficacy. The vignette provides a common reference point, or "anchor," for the respondents and therefore allows the researcher to place the respondents' self-assessments on a common scale. For example, the researcher could code the respondent self-assessments as "less than," "equal to," or "greater than" the efficacy depicted in the vignette (King and Wand 2007). Anchoring vignettes have been used in numerous settings. For example, the World Health Organization has used them to examine various health indicators, the World Bank has used them to investigate economic welfare, and other scholars have used them to look at things like corruption, political efficacy, and women's autonomy.

The development of these new techniques for overcoming the challenges of using survey responses to measure cultural differences is promising. But their application to the study of political culture is in its infancy, and only time will tell whether the canonical findings of political culture scholars will stand up to this more careful analysis.

ARE SOME RELIGIONS INCOMPATIBLE WITH DEMOCRACY?

Recent arguments linking culture and democracy have increasingly focused on religion. These cultural arguments have strongly influenced public discourse and shaped the direction of public policy. For example, Samuel Huntington's (1996) book *The Clash of Civilizations and the Remaking of World Order,* in which he argues that Islamic and Confucian cultures are incompatible with democracy (see Box 6.2, "The Clash of Civilizations"), was reportedly recommended reading for many of the soldiers heading to Iraq during the second Gulf War in 2003. It's worth noting, however, that contemporary debates concerning the relationship between religion and democracy actually have a long and storied history—a history that should perhaps make us wary of unthinkingly accepting claims that certain religions are incompatible with democracy.

Historically, scholars have argued that Protestantism encourages democracy but that Catholicism, Orthodox Christianity, Islam, and Confucianism inhibit it (Lipset [1960] 1994, 5). Max Weber ([1930] 1992) is commonly thought to have provided the first argument linking Protestantism with democracy in his book *The Protestant Ethic and the Spirit of Capitalism.* The basic claim is that Protestantism encourages economic development, which in turn creates a bourgeoisie, whose existence is a necessary condition for democracy. In effect, the proposed causal relationship mirrors the one shown earlier in Figure 6.1c. The notion that Protestantism promotes democracy was later taken up by other scholars such as Inglehart (1990), for whom the percentage of Protestants in a country is one element of his civic culture.

Rodney Stark (2004a, 2004b) has criticized the Weberian emphasis on Protestantism by pointing out that many of the attributes of modern capitalism were already present in the Italian city-states prior to the Protestant Reformation. Stark's controversial study suggests that it's Christianity in general, not Protestantism per se, that encouraged the growth of capitalism and democracy. He argues that because Christianity focuses on orthodoxy (correct belief) rather than orthopraxy (correct practice, which is the focus of Islam and Judaism) and posits a rational and personal God, a brand of science and philosophy arose in predominantly Christian countries that supported the development of democratic self-rule.

Other scholars have suggested that Protestantism really is favorable to democracy, but not for the reasons suggested by Weber. For example, Woodberry (2004, 2012; Woodberry and Shah 2004) argues that the depth and breadth of Protestant missionary activity during colonial periods helps to explain why certain countries are democracies today and others are not.

BOX 6.2 THE CLASH OF CIVILIZATIONS

In 1992 Francis Fukuyama famously declared the "end of history." With the end of the Cold War, Fukuyama believed that liberal democracy had finally won the battle with other rival ideologies such as fascism and communism. Liberal democracy was the "end point of mankind's ideological evolution" and hence the "end of history." Although Samuel Huntington (1993, 1996) took issue with the claim that we were witnessing the end of history, he agreed with the claim that conflict in the world would no longer be based on ideological divisions. He wrote,

> It is my hypothesis that the fundamental source of conflict in this new world will not be primarily ideological or primarily economic. The great divisions among humankind and the dominating source of conflict will be cultural. Nation states will remain the most powerful actors in world affairs, but the principal conflicts of global politics will occur between nations and groups of different civilizations. The clash of civilizations will dominate global politics. The fault lines between civilizations will be the battle lines of the future. (Huntington 1993, 22)

For Huntington (1993, 24), a civilization is the "highest cultural grouping of people and the broadest level of cultural identity people have short of that which distinguishes humans from other species." Huntington identifies many different civilizations in the world today—Western Christian, Confucian, Japanese, Islamic, Hindu, Slavic-Orthodox, Latin American, African, and others. The exact number is ambiguous because he refers to different civilizations in different studies. On the whole, Huntington uses religion as a way to classify civilizations, although linguistic commonalities and geographic proximity also seem to play a role in some cases.

Huntington argues that the widespread Western belief in the universality of the West's values and its insistence on imposing these values through democratization efforts will only antagonize other civilizations and lead to conflict. He believes that these conflicts will be less amenable to diplomacy and peaceful resolution than previous economic and ideological conflicts because cultural differences are less mutable and less easy to compromise. In effect, Huntington argues that certain cultures are incompatible with democracy. In particular, he claims that Islamic and Confucianist countries can't support democracy; even Catholic countries will find it hard to sustain democratic regimes. He also notes that violent conflict will be "particularly prevalent between Muslims and non-Muslims" because Muslims are prone to violence (Huntington 1996, 256–258).

The reason has to do with the emphasis that Protestants placed on teaching people to read the scripture in their own language. These missionary efforts spearheaded mass education and the introduction of modern printing to colonial regions, which in turn unleashed many modernizing forces that encouraged democracy, such as increased literacy, greater equality, a more independent workforce, and a larger middle class. Whatever the causal process, Protestantism has historically been seen by many as a religion that encourages democracy.

In contrast to Protestantism, Catholicism has traditionally been seen as antithetical to democracy. For example, Lipset ([1960] 1994, 72) argues that Catholicism's emphasis on there being only one church and one truth is incompatible with democracy's need to accept different and competing ideologies as legitimate. The hierarchy in the Catholic Church and the clear distinction between the clergy and laity are also thought to pose particular problems for the acceptance of more egalitarian institutions, such as democracy. Those who believe that democracy is difficult to establish in Catholic countries often point to the support the Catholic Church has given to dictatorships around the world in the past. For example, the Catholic Church was an open supporter of fascist Italy under Benito Mussolini and of authoritarian Spain under Francisco Franco. The Catholic Church has historically also supported several dictatorships in South America and Asia.

Confucianism and Islam have come to be seen as posing even bigger problems for the successful establishment of democracy. Huntington (1993) is perhaps the most vocal proponent of this belief. He argues that we're currently observing a clash of civilizations and that "Western concepts differ fundamentally from those prevalent in other civilizations. Western ideas of individualism, liberalism, constitutionalism, human rights, equality, liberty, the rule of law, democracy, free markets, the separation of church and state, often have little resonance in Islamic, Confucian, Japanese, Hindu, Buddhist or Orthodox cultures" (40). Huntington goes so far as to say that Confucian democracy is a contradiction in terms and that "almost no scholarly disagreement exists regarding the proposition that traditional Confucianism was either undemocratic or anti-democratic" (1993, 24).

Huntington is not alone in claiming that Confucianism is incompatible with democracy. In what became known as the Asian values debate in the 1990s, scholars argued that Confucianism's respect for authority and its emphasis on communalism and consensus rather than individual rights and competition made it incompatible with democracy (Kim 1997; Pye 1985; Scalapino 1989). To a large extent, the catalyst for this debate was the Bangkok Declaration that was signed in April 1993 by the political leaders of China, Indonesia, Malaysia, and Singapore. This declaration stated that Asian values justify a different way of understanding human rights and democracy. Along these lines, Lee Kuan Yew (1994), Singapore's prime minister from 1959 to 1990, suggested that Confucianism's respect for authority and its emphasis on the community are antithetical to Western images of liberalism. Various authoritarian leaders in Asia used this line of reasoning to justify the ongoing existence of their nondemocratic forms of government (Dalton and Ong 2004, 3).

As with Confucianism, numerous reasons have been proposed for why Islam might be incompatible with democracy. One of the earliest arguments dates back to Montesquieu, who claimed that Islam had a violent streak that predisposed Muslim societies to authoritarianism. While comparing Christianity and Islam, Montesquieu ([1752] 1914, 24:3–4) writes that "the Christian religion is a stranger to mere despotic power. The mildness so frequently recommended in the Gospel is incompatible with the despotic rage with which a prince punishes his subjects, and exercises himself in cruelty. . . . The Mahometan [Islam] religion, which speaks only by the sword, acts still upon men with that destructive spirit with which it was founded." Huntington (1996, 256–258) is a modern-day proponent of the same idea. He too argues that one of the reasons democracy is so difficult to establish in Islamic countries is that Muslims are prone to political violence. A second proposed reason for the incompatibility of Islam and democracy concerns the purported inability of Islam to disassociate religious and political spheres. The recognition in Islam that God is sovereign and the primary lawgiver has led some to argue that the Islamic state is in principle a theocracy (Lewis 1993) or, as Huntington (1996, 70) puts it, that "in Islam God is Caesar." A third proposed argument for the incompatibility of Islam and democracy concerns Islam's unequal treatment of women (Fish 2002; Norris and Inglehart 2004). Some believe that the repressiveness and dominance of the father in the family and of men in relation to women more generally in Islamic culture replicate themselves in the larger society, thereby creating a culture suitable for authoritarianism. Others claim that the social marginalization of women in the political sphere leaves society susceptible to dictatorship because men hold attitudes that are more conducive to domination.

Although arguments that particular religions are incompatible with democracy have strong supporters around the world (notably among the authoritarian leaders of certain countries), there's good reason to doubt their veracity. Why might these arguments be flawed? Note that many of the arguments presented so far rest on claims that there's something about the doctrine of each religion that makes them particularly compatible or incompatible with democracy. One problem with this is that virtually all religions have some doctrinal elements that can be seen as compatible with democracy and others that are not (Stepan 2000, 44). This is true even of "pro-democratic" Protestantism. For example, Przeworski and colleagues (1998, 132) argue that Protestantism's legitimization of economic inequality and the ethic of individual self-interest associated with it provide "a poor moral basis for living together and resolving conflicts in a peaceful way."

What about Confucianism and Islam? Well, many people argue that these religions have elements that make them compatible with democracy. For example, some claim that Confucianism's meritocratic system and its emphasis on the importance of education and religious tolerance suggest that it can sustain democracy (Fukuyama 1995a). Indeed, Taiwan's president from 1988 to 2000, Lee Teng-hui, even claims that traditional Confucianism calls for limited government. In addition, the existence of a public sphere in Korea during the Joseon (Chosun or Choson) dynasty from 1392 to 1910 would seem to contradict those who assert that Confucianism has no concept of civil society and cannot therefore sustain democracy (Im 1997). Thus, despite claims to the contrary by some authoritarian leaders in Asian countries, there seems to be nothing explicit in Confucianism itself that would necessitate an authoritarian government. In fact, many of the elements of Confucianism mentioned above seem quite well suited to a democratic form of government. Friedman (2002) even suggests that "Buddhist and Confucian cultures may actually have more democratic elements than Greco-Christian culture."

Many scholars have also taken issue with the claim that Islam is doctrinally incompatible with democracy (Abootalebi 1999; Esposito and Voll 1996; Filali-Ansary 1999; Hefner 2000; Price 1999; Rahman 1979; Sachedina 2000). For example, several scholars find a basis for democracy in the Koran's emphasis on *shura* (consultation). *Shura* requires that even the messenger of Allah should consult with his people in earthly matters and that Muslims should consult with each other in their secular affairs. This process of consultation is in many respects similar to the process of consultation that underpins elections and legislatures in democracies. Indeed, many Islamic scholars "have come to the conclusion that general elections and a parliament properly serve that concept of consultation" (Yazdi 1995, 18). Other scholars have interpreted Islamic concepts such as *ijma* (consensus of the community) and *ijtihad* (reinterpretation), as well as legal principles, such as *maslaha* (public welfare), as providing a basis for Islamic forms of parliamentary governance, representative elections, and religious reform (Esposito 2003).

Still others have suggested that those who portray the rule of law in a democratic state ("law of man") as being inherently in conflict with sharia, or Islamic law ("law of God"), are creating a false dichotomy. It's true that the primary lawgiver in Islam is God and that God's agents such as the Islamic state enjoy only marginal autonomy to implement and enforce God's laws. In other words, it's true that sovereignty lies in different places in democracy (with the people) and Islam (with God). Still, the reason this distinction should not be overemphasized is that, in practice, it's the state, and not God, that actually exercises sovereignty in Islam. Worth noting here is that one of the underlying concerns in both Islam and democracy is the need to limit the power of the state and the people who rule. That this is achieved in Islam by arguing that God is the primary lawgiver and that the state should simply implement God's laws—whereas it's achieved in democracy by holding elections and implementing checks and balances—should not be allowed to hide the fact that both Islam and democracy share the same goal of limited government.

We should also point out that there's nothing inherent in democratic theory that requires a democratic state to be secular anyway (Stepan 2000, 40). It may be true that most contemporary democracies tend to separate church and state (although there's considerable variation even in this), but it's important to recognize that this is a choice and not necessarily part and parcel of democratic theory. Indeed, it's illuminating to remember that until the eighteenth century, many leaders of the Christian church vehemently opposed both democracy and secularism, just like many proponents of Islam today. For decades, there was a great struggle between the church and princely rulers on the one hand and between Christians and secularists on the other. It was only during the nineteenth century that democracy and secularism became broadly acceptable within Western Christian society. Even today, some Christians believe that the strict separation of church and state should be relaxed. In sum, Islamic doctrine, like the doctrines of other religions, contains elements that make it compatible with many traditional aspects of democracy.

Given that almost all religions contain doctrinal elements that can be viewed as harmful to democracy and others that can be seen as helpful, it becomes an empirical question as to whether certain religions pose particular difficulties for democracy (Przeworski, Cheibub, and Limongi 1998). So, what does the empirical evidence say?

The growing evidence that cultures are invented, constructed, and malleable rather than primordial, inherited, and unchanging suggests that it's inappropriate to view particular religions or civilizations as being permanently incompatible with democracy. For example, Eickelman and Piscatori (1996) point out that Islamic doctrine has historically been interpreted in various ways to justify many different types of government. As to Confucianism, the fact that the comments of Singapore's former prime minister, Lee Kuan Yew, concerning the relationship between Confucianism and democracy run directly counter to the comments of Taiwan's former president, Lee Teng-hui, suggests that Confucianism can be interpreted differently by different people and that it can be adapted to suit different purposes.

Considerable evidence supports the claim that the stance of different religions toward political institutions often depends less on the content of religious doctrine and more on the interests of religious leaders. For example, Kalyvas (1996) shows in his study of the rise of European Christian democracy that the relationship between Catholicism and democracy had less to do with the actual content of Catholic faith and more to do with the strategic considerations of elites in the Catholic Church. Balmer (2006) makes a similar point with respect to Protestants in his account of the rise of the "religious right" in the United States. Elsewhere, Kalyvas (1998, 2000) examines why Catholic fundamentalism proved compatible with the successful establishment of democracy in nineteenth-century Belgium but Islamic fundamentalism did not in Algeria during the 1990s. He argues that the reasons for the different outcomes in the two countries had little to do with actual doctrinal issues and more to do with the different organizational structures of the two religions. Numerous other scholars have similarly highlighted the role played by "cultural entrepreneurs" in producing cultural change, thereby suggesting that conflicts over culture tend to be matters of interest and strategy rather than any primordially given cultural content (Laitin 1983, 1986, 1992; Posner 2004, 2005). In other words, a vast amount of empirical evidence undermines the implication made by scholars such as Huntington that the antidemocratic tendencies of certain religions and civilizations are given once and for all.

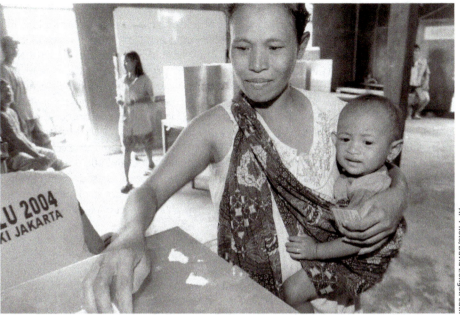

A Jakarta mother carries her child as she votes Monday, July 5, 2004, in the first direct presidential election in the vast archipelago of Indonesia, the world's most populous Muslim-majority country.

The empirical reality is that all religions have historically been compatible with a broad range of political institutions. For example, Fukuyama (1995b, 12) claims that many different types of government are compatible with Confucianism. The fact that it's possible to distinguish between "political" and "everyday" Confucianism helps to explain why the imperial system mandated by traditional political Confucianism could be abolished relatively easily in China in 1911 and replaced with a variety of different political institutions without the loss of Chinese society's essential coherence. According to Fukuyama, the important legacy of traditional Confucianism is not its political teaching but rather the personal ethic that regulates attitudes toward family, work, education, and other elements of everyday life. This helps to explain why Confucian society can exist easily in democracies like Japan, South Korea, and Taiwan, in semi-authoritarian regimes like Singapore, or in more obvious dictatorships like China and North Korea.

Islamic countries also have considerable experience with different forms of political systems. Although it's often asserted that Islam requires an Islamic state, the empirical reality is that, with the exception of Iran since the 1979 revolution and of Afghanistan during the period of Taliban rule in the 1990s, there have been few historical precedents for mullahs, or religious leaders, controlling political power in Islamic countries. On the whole, secular political elites have controlled political power in Islamic countries for the roughly 1,400 years since the Prophet Muhammad died in 632. Despite claims that Islam is incompatible with democracy, it's important to remember that hundreds of millions of Muslims live today in such democratic countries as Canada, France, Germany, India, the Netherlands, the United Kingdom, and the United States (Stepan 2000, 49). Indeed, several countries with majority Muslim populations are today considered democracies—Albania, Indonesia, Mali, Niger, Senegal, and Turkey. Clearly, being Muslim doesn't preclude someone from living a peaceful and constructive life in a democratic society.

Not only can we find evidence for the compatibility of Islam and democracy by looking at the world today, but we can also find evidence of at least quasi-democratic institutions and practices in Islam's past. Perhaps the most notable example is the Constitution of Medina. In 622 the Prophet Muhammad established the first Islamic state when he migrated from Mecca to Medina. Medina was a highly diverse city—45 percent of the residents were non-Muslim Arabs, 40 percent were Jews, and 15 percent were Muslims. Rather than rule by force, Muhammad explicitly sought the consent of the people he would govern by having them agree to a constitution. Interestingly, this means that Jews were constitutional partners in making the first Islamic state (M. Khan 2001). The Constitution of Medina represents a social contract between the ruler and his people, one that occurred almost six centuries earlier than the much more famous Magna Carta in England (A. Khan 2006). Social contract theorists, such as Hobbes and Rousseau, have typically portrayed the social contract as a "fictional" document that helps to explain the emergence of the modern state (see Chapter 4). The Constitution of Medina represents one of the few real-world examples of such a document (A. Khan 2006, 2–3).

In addition to highlighting the importance of having the people's consent and cooperation for governance, the Constitution of Medina is also a symbol of pluralism and religious tolerance in Islam (Shah 2012). The constitution created a pluralistic state with a common citizenship that guaranteed identical rights and duties across the various religious and tribal communities in Medina. Among other things, the constitution guaranteed social, legal, and economic equality; cooperation; freedom of conscience; and other human rights. Importantly, Muslims and non-Muslims were free to practice their own religions and were duty bound to come to each other's defense. As A. M. Khan (2010, 6) notes, the Constitution of Medina "was the first document in history to establish religious freedom as a fundamental constitutional right." In effect, the constitution envisioned a religiously pluralistic Islamic state.

Despite the fact that cultures tend to be malleable and that all religions have been compatible with a variety of political institutions throughout history, one might still wonder whether certain religions are *more* or *less* compatible with democracy than others. In this vein, several empirical studies have suggested that Islam is bad for democracy—Islamic countries typically have lower democracy scores than non-Islamic countries. For example, Karatnycky (2002) finds that there were twenty-eight Islamic dictatorships in 2001 and only one Islamic democracy. In contrast, there were eighty-five non-Islamic democracies in the same year and only twenty-one non-Islamic dictatorships. Fish (2002) argues that the reason Islam is so bad for democracy has to do with its treatment of women. Why? First, he finds that Islamic countries tend to be characterized by a wider literacy gap between men and women, fewer women in government, and lower measures of overall gender empowerment. Second, he finds that all of these measures of women's status are associated with lower democracy scores. This leads him to infer that it's the poor treatment of women in Islamic countries that leads to their low democracy scores.

Despite the evidence presented in these studies, we should not rush to conclude that Islam is bad for democracy. One reason for such caution is that several of the studies mentioned above examine the effect of Islam on democracy at a fixed point in time. For example, Karatnycky (2002) examines the effect of Islam on a country's democracy score in 2001, while Fish examines the effect of Islam on a country's average democracy score in the 1990s. Why might this be problematic? Well, what do you think a researcher would find if she examined the relationship between Catholicism and democracy in, say, 1976? She'd find that there were fourteen Catholic majority democracies and sixteen Catholic majority dictatorships. In contrast, there were eleven Protestant majority democracies and only one Protestant majority dictatorship. This would suggest that Catholicism is bad for democracy, at least in comparison with Protestantism. However, if the same researcher examined the relationship between Catholicism and democracy in 2004, her conclusion would be very different. She'd find that there were forty Catholic majority democracies and only three Catholic majority dictatorships. As you can see, whereas Catholicism seemed to pose some difficulties for democracy from the perspective of 1976, this was no longer the case from the perspective of 2004. Our point here is that it can be dangerous to draw strong inferences about the incompatibility of a religion with democracy from a single point in time.

Note that it would be equally dangerous to draw inferences about the compatibility of a *civilization* with democracy from a single point in time as well. For example, consider Huntington's assertion that Western civilization is obviously compatible with democracy. Such a claim might seem eminently reasonable from our perspective today. However, it would hardly seem this way to someone living in Europe during the 1930s. As Mazower (2000, 5) notes,

> It is hard to see the inter-war experiment with democracy for the novelty that it was: yet we should certainly not *assume* that democracy is suited to Europe. . . . Triumphant in 1918, it was virtually extinct twenty years on. . . . Europe found other, authoritarian, forms of political order no more foreign to its traditions. (italics in original)

It turns out that most of the arguments claiming that particular religions or civilizations are incompatible with democracy are implicitly based on observations of the world at a particular point in time. For example, arguments linking Protestantism to democracy and Catholicism to authoritarianism tended to be made most frequently when Protestant countries around the world were predominantly democratic and when Catholic countries were largely authoritarian. This observed variation encouraged some scholars to look for reasons why Protestantism might promote democracy and why Catholicism might impede it. In other words, theory construction came after observing the world. Because explanation always begins with a puzzling observation, there's nothing inherently wrong with this. But if the explanation doesn't suggest testable implications other than those that led to it, we call this an *ex post,* or ad hoc, explanation. Such explanations violate the norms of science because they don't invite falsification.

Of course, the argument that Catholic countries are inherently antidemocratic has now lost most of its force because Catholic countries today are predominantly democratic. In fact, one might now even argue that Catholicism helps democratization, given the important role that the Catholic Church played in aiding democratic transitions in countries like Chile, Paraguay, the Philippines, and Poland in the 1980s. Despite this, the exact same type of argument that used to be made about Catholicism is now frequently made about Islam: we observe that there are few Islamic democracies at this point in time, and we therefore conclude there must be something about Islam that's antidemocratic. The history of arguments concerning Catholicism (and Confucianism) should make us wary of accepting this type of reasoning.

What about the evidence that Islam is particularly bad for democracy because of its treatment of women (Fish 2002)? Unfortunately, the particular measure of democracy used by the author of this research means that it's hard to know if his evidence is truly compelling. His democracy measure is based on a series of questions regarding the level of political rights and civil liberties in a country. Countries that have more political rights and civil liberties are considered more democratic. The problem is that some of these questions take into account, at least implicitly, the treatment and status of women. In other words, the overall democracy score for each country automatically varies with that country's treatment of women simply because of the way it's constructed. As a result, it's inappropriate to use this measure to test whether the treatment of women affects a country's democracy score—we already know it will by construction. Thus, the question as to whether Islam is bad for democracy because of its treatment of women remains an open question in our eyes.

EXPERIMENTS AND CULTURE

We now examine some results from experiments that suggest culture might be important for democracy. The experiments involve individuals playing what are commonly known as *ultimatum games* and *dictator games*. In an ultimatum game, individuals (known as subjects or players) are paired together. The first player, often called the "proposer," is provisionally allotted a divisible "pie" (usually money). The proposer then offers a portion of the total pie to the second player, called the "responder." The responder, knowing both the offer and the total amount of the pie, can either accept or reject the proposer's offer. If the responder accepts, he receives the amount offered, and the proposer gets the remainder (the pie minus the offer). If the responder rejects the offer, neither player receives any money. In either case, the game ends, and the two subjects receive their winnings and leave. In the experiments, the players are anonymous to each other. An example might help. Imagine the proposer is given $100 and offers $40 to the responder. If the responder accepts the offer, the responder keeps the $40 and the proposer keeps the remaining $60. If the responder rejects the offer, both the responder and the proposer get nothing. The dictator game is similar to the ultimatum game except that responders are not given an opportunity to reject the proposer's offer; they simply get whatever the proposer dictates.

Note that there are two potential reasons for a positive offer in the ultimatum game. First, the proposer might make a positive offer out of a sense of fairness. In other words, the proposer realizes she was randomly chosen to receive the pie and thinks it only fair that she should offer some of it to the responder. Second, the proposer might make a positive offer out of a fear of rejection. In other words, the proposer only makes a positive offer in order to reduce the risk that she would get nothing if the responder rejects it. In the dictator game, there's no fear of rejection, because the responder can't reject the proposer's offer. As a result, any positive offer in the dictator game must be from a sense of fairness. Thus, the dictator game allows the experimenter to distinguish between proposers who make positive offers out of a sense of fairness and those who make positive offers out of a fear of rejection.

What would you expect individuals who care only about their own share of the pie to do if they are the proposer in an ultimatum game? What would you expect them to do if they are the responder? We sometimes refer to individuals who care only about their own share of the pie as *Homo economicus*. It turns out that we'd expect a proposer who cares only about her own share of the pie to offer ε (epsilon) to the responder, where ε is only slightly larger than 0. We'd then expect the responder to accept this offer because receiving ε is clearly better than getting nothing, which is what both players get if the responder refuses. Thus, if we continue our example from above and assume that we're in the world of *Homo economicus*, we'd expect the proposer to get $100 - \varepsilon$ and the responder to get ε. Things look only slightly different in the dictator game. Now we'd expect a proposer who cares only about her own share of the pie not to offer anything to the responder and to simply keep all of the $100 for herself. Remember, these are the theoretical predictions if we were in the world of *Homo economicus*. But what do we actually observe when individuals play this game in an experimental setting?

Both the ultimatum and dictator games have been played in numerous experimental settings in virtually all of the industrialized democracies in the world. Typically, the experiment involves a group of students who are paired up anonymously in a computer lab. One student is randomly chosen to be the proposer and the other becomes the responder. The game then begins. What do you think happens in these games? Somewhat remarkably, there's a great deal of similarity in the results that these experiments produce despite the fact that they're conducted in different countries around the world. It turns out that the modal offer—the most common offer—in student populations playing the ultimatum game is almost always 50 percent, with the mean, or average, offer varying somewhere between 40 percent and 45 percent. Offers of less than 20 percent of the pie are rejected by responders about half the time. In contrast, the modal offer in student populations playing the dictator game is normally 0 percent. The large difference in the modal offers between the two games would suggest that many of the positive offers in the ultimatum game come about because of a fear of rejection, rather than a sense of fairness, on the part of the proposer. Although this is certainly true, the mean offer in the dictator game is still typically in the 20 percent to 30 percent range. In other words, some individuals still make quite large positive offers even when they know their offers can't be rejected. These proposers are clearly acting out of a sense of fairness; they exhibit what some call a prosocial behavior. Overall, the results from these experiments indicate that a substantial portion of the students playing these games do not approximate the theoretical *Homo economicus*.

Several scholars began to wonder whether these deviations from the theoretical predictions for *Homo economicus* were evidence of a universal pattern of human behavior or whether the deviations varied with an individual's economic and cultural setting. Do some cultures exhibit behavior that more closely resembles that of *Homo economicus* than others? Of course, these questions can't be answered with any satisfaction simply by looking at experimental results from student populations around the world. Although there are some cultural differences among students in different countries, these differences are quite small compared with the full range of cultural environments that exist in the world. As a result, a group composed primarily of anthropologists and economists decided to conduct experiments using ultimatum and dictator games in fifteen small-scale societies in twelve countries around the world (Gintis 2003; Henrich et al. 2001, 2005). These societies exhibited a wide range of cultural and economic environments: foraging societies, slash-and-burn horticulture groups, nomadic herding groups, and sedentary, small-scale agriculturalist societies. Information on these societies is shown in Table 6.1.

How did the individuals in these societies act in the ultimatum and dictator games? The mean offers made in the ultimatum game, measured as the average proportion of the pie offered to the responder, are shown in a bubble plot in Figure 6.3. Data from an experiment using students at the University of Pittsburgh are included as a benchmark against which to compare the results from the fifteen small-scale societies. The size of the bubble at each location along each row represents the proportion of the sample that made a particular offer. The right edge of the lightly shaded horizontal gray bar gives the mean offer for that group. For example, if you look at the row associated with the Machiguenga from Peru, you can see that the mode (the most common offer) is 0.15, the secondary mode is 0.25, and the mean is 0.26.

The information in Figure 6.3 illustrates that no society conforms well to the predictions for *Homo economicus*. The second thing to note, though, is that there's much more variation in the offers made in the fifteen small-scale societies than in the student populations of the advanced industrial countries. Remember that the mean offer among students typically varies from about 40 to 45 percent in ultimatum games. In contrast, the range for the mean offers in

TABLE 6.1 ■ Fifteen Small-Scale Societies			
Group	Country	Environment	Economic base
Machiguenga	Peru	Tropical forest	Horticulture
Quichua	Ecuador	Tropical forest	Horticulture
Achuar	Ecuador	Tropical forest	Horticulture
Hadza	Tanzania	Savanna-woodlands	Foraging
Aché	Paraguay	Semi-tropical woodlands	Foraging and horticulture
Tsimané	Bolivia	Tropical forest	Horticulture
Au	Papua New Guinea	Mountainous tropical forest	Foraging and horticulture
Gnau	Papua New Guinea	Mountainous tropical forest	Foraging and horticulture
Mapuche	Chile	Temperate plains	Small-scale farming
Torguud	Mongolia	High-altitude desert, seasonally flooded grassland	Pastoralism
Khazax	Mongolia	High-altitude desert, seasonally flooded grassland	Pastoralism
Sangu (farm/herd)	Tanzania	Savanna-woodlands, seasonally flooded grassland	Agro-pastoralists
Orma	Kenya	Savanna-woodlands	Pastoralism
Lamelara	Indonesia	Tropical island coast	Foraging-trade
Shona	Zimbabwe	Savanna-woodlands	Farming

the fifteen small-scale societies is much larger, varying from 26 percent for the Machiguenga in Peru to 58 percent for the Lamelara in Indonesia. Whereas the modal offer among students is 50 percent, the modal offer among the fifteen small-scale societies ranges from 15 percent to 50 percent.

Although we don't show any evidence here, it turns out that the rejection rates in these fifteen societies also vary quite considerably between the groups. Whereas offers below 20 percent in industrial democracies are rejected with a probability of 0.4 to 0.6, the experimenters found that rejections of very low offers such as this are quite rare in some groups. For example, the Machiguenga rejected only one offer even though 75 percent of the offers made were below 30 percent. In some groups, though, the experimenters found that rejection rates

FIGURE 6.3 ■ Offers from an Ultimatum Game

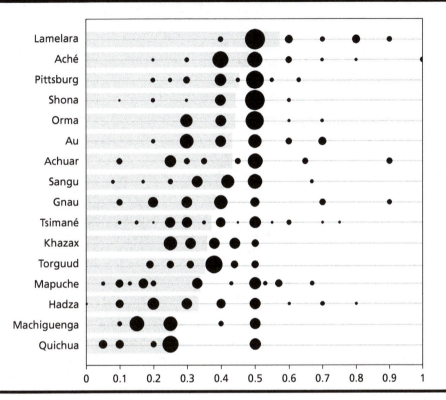

Source: Henrich and colleagues (2005).

Note: The size of the bubble at each location along each row represents the proportion of the sample that made a particular offer. The right edge of the lightly shaded horizontal gray bar gives the mean offer, measured as the average proportion of the pie offered to the responder.

were quite high even when offers were over 50 percent of the pie. For example, the Au and the Gnau in Papua New Guinea were equally likely to reject offers that were below or above 50 percent. The results from the dictator game also showed considerable variation. Among student populations, the distribution of offers has a mode at zero and a secondary mode at 50 percent. In contrast, the Orma had a mode at 50 percent, and the Hadza had a mode at 10 percent. There were no zero offers among the Tsimané; the mean was 32 percent, and the mode was 25 percent.

What explains this large variation in behavior between the different cultural groups? The researchers found that individual level characteristics such as the proposer's (or responder's) sex, age, education, and wealth couldn't explain the variation. Instead, what mattered was how group-specific conditions such as social institutions or cultural fairness norms affected individual preferences or expectations. The researchers rank ordered the fifteen societies along two dimensions: (1) payoffs to cooperation and (2) market integration. Payoffs to cooperation refer to how important it is to cooperate with non-immediate kin in economic production. Market integration refers to how much the groups relied on market exchange in their everyday lives. At the low end of the "payoffs to cooperation" dimension were the Machiguenga and Tsimané, whose members rarely engage in cooperative production with individuals outside of the family. At the high end of this dimension were the Lamelara, whose members hunt whales in large canoes manned by twelve or more people at a time. The researchers expected that groups in which the payoffs to cooperation were high would make high offers in situations like the ultimatum game. At the low end of the "market integration" dimension were the Hadza, whose members rarely engage in market activity. At the high end of this dimension were the Orma, whose members often work for wages and sold livestock. The researchers expected that groups with greater market integration would make high offers in situations like the ultimatum game. This is because the more frequently people experience market transactions, the more they should also experience abstract sharing principles concerning behavior toward strangers. As predicted, the researchers found that higher values on both dimensions were associated with higher mean offers in the ultimatum game. In fact, these two dimensions alone could fully explain 68 percent of the variation in the offers.

How should we interpret these results? One interpretation is that the individuals in these societies looked for similar situations in their everyday lives when they were faced with the novel situations presented by the ultimatum game and the dictator game. Rather than reason through the logic of the game, it seems that they asked themselves the following question: "What familiar situation is this game like?" They then acted in a way appropriate for this analogous situation. Consider the hyperfair offers and the frequent rejections of these offers among the Au and Gnau in Papua New Guinea. This behavior can be explained by the culture of gift giving in these societies. Providing expensive gifts is a signal of prestige and importance in these societies. At the same time, it's recognized that accepting gifts commits one to reciprocate at some future time determined by the gift giver. Moreover, accepting particularly generous gifts put one in a clearly subordinate position. The culture of gift giving not only explains the generous offers the Au and Gnau proposers made, but also explains why the responders so readily rejected large offers; these "excessively" large gifts tended to produce anxiety about the unspoken strings that were attached to them.

Consider now the low offers and high rejection rates of the Hadza. This behavior is entirely compatible with the fact that Hadza hunters often try to avoid sharing their meat. One ethnographer goes so far as to call this reluctance to share "tolerated theft." What about the Lamelara's tendency to divide the pie equally or to offer the respondent slightly more than a fair share? In real life, when a Lamelara whaling crew returns with a large catch, a designated person carefully divides the whale into predesignated parts allocated to the harpooner, crew members, and others participating in the hunt, as well as the sailmaker, members of the hunters' corporate group, and other community members. The Lamelara may well have seen dividing the large pie in the ultimatum game as similar to dividing up a whale. Similar stories to these could be told to explain the behavior of individuals from the other societies in the study.

By now, you're probably wondering what these experiments have to do with culture and democracy. The results from these experiments suggest that culture might be considered a shared way of playing everyday games that has evolved over many years (Bednar and Page 2007). It seems clear that individual choices are shaped by the economic and social interactions of everyday life. It appears that people often search for analogous situations when trying to figure out how to act in new situations. If this is true, then it seems reasonable to think that the shared way of playing games in some societies might be less compatible with the game of democracy than it is in other societies. For example, the game of democracy often requires cooperation, competition, and compromise. Societies that already require this type of behavior in their everyday "games" should find it easier to adopt and support democratic institutions. In contrast, societies in which individuals are engaged in games that don't encourage this type of behavior will find it much harder to democratize.

CONCLUSION

As we noted at the beginning of this chapter, the notion that political institutions, such as democracy and dictatorship, are more suited to some cultures than others is not new. The rather vague claims made by scholars such as Montesquieu and Mill in the eighteenth and nineteenth centuries regarding the compatibility of democracy with particular cultures were later taken up in a more systematic fashion by cultural modernization theory. Cultural modernization theory argues that economic development produces certain cultural changes and that it is these cultural changes that allow for democratization (Inglehart and Welzel 2005). A key cultural change according to this line of reasoning is the emergence of what political scientists call a "civic culture."

For many, the existence of a civic culture is seen as a prerequisite for democracy. In addition to its importance for democracy, a civic culture is also seen by some as crucial for the good performance of government. Although there are strong proponents of the idea that democracy requires a civic culture, others question the direction of causality. Does a civic culture produce democracy, or does experience with democracy produce a civic culture? As we suggested earlier, the answer to both of these questions may well be "yes." Societal development may foster democratization by producing certain cultural changes, but it may also affect democratization through other channels such as those examined in Chapter 5. Similarly, it seems reasonable that experience with democracy can contribute to producing a civic culture that in turn reinforces democratic practice in the future. If we're correct, there may be a virtuous cycle linking social development, cultural change, and democratic outcomes.

More recently, the focus of cultural arguments regarding democracy has shifted to questions of whether certain religions are compatible with democratic institutions. Given the current state of world affairs, it's not surprising that particular attention has been paid to whether Islam is compatible with democracy. As we indicate in this chapter, though, a quick glance at the history of these types of arguments should make one very cautious of unthinkingly accepting that certain religions are incompatible with democracy. For example, some political scientists used to claim as recently as the 1970s that Catholicism was antithetical to democracy, but few do now, given how firmly established democracy has become in many Catholic countries around the world.

Many scholars point to particular religious doctrines to explain why such and such a religion is inimical to democracy. As we've sought to demonstrate, however, virtually all religions, including Islam, have some doctrinal elements that seem incompatible with democracy and others that seem compatible. This hardly seems a firm basis on which to draw such strong conclusions about the incompatibility of certain religions with democracy. Moreover, there's growing empirical evidence that the stance of different religions toward various political institutions often depends less on the content of their doctrine and more on the interests and strategic concerns of religious leaders (Kalyvas 1996, 1998, 2000). When combined with the vast literature showing that culture is constructed and malleable rather than primordial and inherited, this growing evidence helps to explain why all religions have historically been compatible with a broad range of political institutions, including democracy.

Many arguments about the cultural determinants of democracy implicitly assume that democracy is increasingly likely to arise and be sustained as more citizens come to appreciate the benefits of democracy. But "liking democracy" is almost certainly not a sufficient condition for democracy, and it may not even be a necessary one. Indeed, a more cynical view suggests that democracy is at best most people's second favorite form of government. Recall from the comparison of the behavior in the ultimatum and dictator games that most individuals might take most or all of the pie when they're confident they can get away with it. Similarly, individuals might prefer monarchy if they were allowed to be the ruler, but they reluctantly accept democracy when they realize that they, or their chosen one, may not be permitted to rule. Such strategic calculations turn out to be important in the transition process from dictatorship to democracy. We focus on precisely that in the next chapter.

Key Concepts

primordialist arguments—arguments that treat culture as something that's objective and inherited, fixed since "primordial" times

constructivist arguments—arguments that treat culture as something that's constructed or invented rather than inherited

cultural modernization theory—a theory that predicts that socioeconomic development does not directly cause democracy; instead, economic development produces certain cultural changes, such as the emergence of a civic culture, and it is these cultural changes that ultimately produce democratic reform

civic culture—a shared cluster of attitudes that are thought to promote democracy and democratic performance

social capital—the collective value of social networks and shared norms that promote reciprocity, trust, and social cooperation

social desirability bias—the tendency of individuals to overreport "good behavior" and underreport "bad behavior"

differential item functioning (DIF)—different items, such as particular survey questions, may function differently across individuals or groups; exists when individuals or groups understand survey items differently or evaluate survey items using different scales

DEMOCRATIC TRANSITIONS

The most radical revolutionary will become a conservative the
day after the revolution.

Hannah Arendt, quoted in *The New Yorker,* 1970

Those who make peaceful revolution impossible will make
violent revolution inevitable.

John F. Kennedy, in a speech at the White House, 1962

OVERVIEW

1. In this chapter, we examine bottom-up and top-down transitions to democracy. A bottom-up democratic transition is one in which the people rise up to overthrow an authoritarian regime in a popular revolution. A top-down democratic transition is one in which the dictatorial ruling elite introduces liberalizing reforms that ultimately lead to a democratic transition.

2. Collective action theory throws light on why popular revolutions are so rare and why authoritarian regimes frequently appear stable. The prevalence of preference falsification in dictatorships helps to explain why revolutions nearly always come as a surprise yet appear so inevitable in hindsight. Tipping models highlight why even small changes in people's preferences can sometimes rapidly transform previously subservient individuals into revolutionary protesters.

3. Authoritarian elites occasionally introduce liberalization policies. The goal of these policies is the stabilization of dictatorial rule in the form of a broadened dictatorship rather than a full democratic transition. However, these policies can sometimes lead to a democratic transition when actors lack information and make mistakes. Our analysis of top-down transitions highlights the important role that information, beliefs, and uncertainty play in democratic transitions—and politics more generally.

The number of independent countries in the world has grown from 70 in 1946 to over 190 today. This increase in the number of independent countries is largely the result of the decolonization process forced upon European powers in the 1950s and 1960s and the breakup of the Soviet Union in the early 1990s. Figure 7.1 illustrates how the number of independent countries, dictatorships, and democracies in the world has changed since 1946. Despite the consensus that now exists in favor of democracy, it's only since 1992 that the number of democracies has been greater than the number of dictatorships. Of those countries that gained independence in the 1950s and 1960s, the vast majority soon became dictatorships. By 1977 there were 2.7 times as many dictatorships as there were democracies—only 27 percent of the countries in the world were democratic.

The mid-1970s, though, ushered in an era of democratization that Samuel Huntington (1991) has called the **third wave of democratization**. On April 25, 1974, Portuguese military officers, unhappy with the ongoing colonial conflicts in Mozambique and Angola, conducted a coup, triggering events that eventually led to the first democratic multiparty elections in Portugal since 1926. Although it was not foreseen at the time, the movement toward democracy in Portugal was soon to be followed by democratic stirrings elsewhere. For example, Greece returned to the democratic fold in 1974 following conflict with Turkey over the island of Cyprus, and Spain finally threw off four decades of dictatorial rule under General Francisco Franco in 1977. This reemergence of democracy in much of

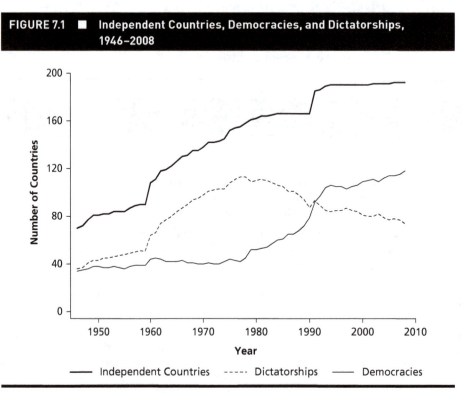

FIGURE 7.1 ■ Independent Countries, Democracies, and Dictatorships, 1946–2008

Source: Data from Cheibub, Gandhi, and Vreeland (2010).

southern Europe in the 1970s was followed by a global wave of democratization over the next twenty or so years in Africa, Asia, Eastern Europe, and Latin America (see Box 7.1, "Three Waves of Democracy").

In the previous two chapters, we examined economic and cultural arguments for democracy. Although those chapters were useful in giving us an aggregate view of democratization, you may be wondering how democratic transitions actually occur. In this chapter, we flesh out two types of democratic transition, drawing on historical evidence from Eastern Europe. A **bottom-up democratic transition** is one in which the people rise up to overthrow an authoritarian regime in a popular revolution. In contrast, a **top-down democratic transition** is one in which the dictatorial ruling elite introduces liberalizing reforms that ultimately lead to a democratic transition. Although most real-world cases are probably characterized by aspects of both types of transition process, it can be illuminating to examine these two transition processes separately.

BOX 7.1 THREE WAVES OF DEMOCRACY

Samuel Huntington (1991, 15) has argued that the spread of democracy around the world has come in waves, where a wave "is a group of transitions from non-democratic to democratic regimes that occur within a specified period of time and that significantly outnumber transitions in the opposite direction during that period of time." Specifically, Huntington argues that there have been three waves of democracy in the modern world. The first "long" wave between 1828 and 1926 had its roots in the American and French Revolutions. Countries that transitioned to democracy during the first wave include Argentina, France, Great Britain, Iceland, Ireland, Italy, Switzerland, and the United States. The second "short" wave between 1943 and 1962 had its origins in World War II. Countries that became democratic during the second wave include Austria, Brazil, Costa Rica, India, Israel, Italy, Japan, Malaysia, Nigeria, Sri Lanka, Turkey, Uruguay, and West Germany. The third wave started with the end of the Portuguese dictatorship in 1974 and, arguably, continues to this day. Numerous authoritarian regimes have been replaced by democratic forms of government in Africa, Asia, Latin America, and southern and Eastern Europe since the mid-1970s.

- First wave of democratization 1828–1926
- First reverse wave 1922–1942
- Second wave of democratization 1943–1962
- Second reverse wave 1958–1975
- Third wave of democratization 1974–

As with real waves, the three waves of democracy have experienced weaker undercurrents flowing in the opposite direction. Thus, between the three waves of democracy have been periods in which some, but not all, of the countries that had previously made the transition to democracy slipped back into dictatorship. For example, the 1920s and 1930s saw the collapse of democracy in much of Europe and a return to traditional forms of authoritarian rule. Transitions to dictatorship also predominated in the 1960s and early 1970s, with military intervention in much of Latin America—Peru (1962), Bolivia (1964), Brazil (1964), Argentina (1966), Ecuador (1972), Chile (1973), and Uruguay (1973). Numerous authoritarian regimes also emerged during the 1960s in Asia and Africa. Thus, Huntington's analysis suggests that the global spread of democracy over the last two centuries has been marked by an ebb and flow, largely characterized by a two-step-forward and one-step-back pattern.

BOTTOM-UP TRANSITIONS TO DEMOCRACY

We begin our examination of bottom-up democratic transitions by looking at the example of East Germany in 1989.

East Germany 1989

Between 1945 and 1947, the temporary wartime alliance that had fought against Nazi Germany collapsed and a period known as the Cold War began. The **Cold War** describes a period of global geopolitical tension in which countries in the Eastern bloc, primarily the Soviet Union and its satellite states, competed economically, socially, and politically with countries in the Western bloc, primarily the United States and its NATO allies. The term "cold" refers to the fact that although the two sides supported significant regional wars around the world, sometimes called "proxy wars," they didn't engage in direct large-scale fighting with each other. The symbolic manifestation of the Cold War in Europe was the "Iron Curtain," which separated the capitalist West from the communist East. The central and east European territories that had been liberated from the Nazis and occupied by the Soviet army in 1945 became satellite states of the Soviet Union. Although formally independent, countries like Albania, Poland, Bulgaria, Romania, Czechoslovakia, Hungary, and East Germany were essentially under the control of the Soviet Union during the Cold War (see Box 7.2, "A Brief History of East Germany, 1945–1990"). The Cold War lasted for over forty years. In 1989, a series of protests and revolutions took place in several East European countries in which the people rose up to overthrow their communist governments and demand a transition to democracy. With the collapse and breakup of the Soviet Union in 1991, the Cold War came to an end.

One of the most dramatic examples of a bottom-up democratic transition occurred in East Germany in November 1989 when protests on the streets of Leipzig and Berlin forced the Communist East German government to open up the Berlin Wall and allow free multiparty elections. The end result was the emergence of a democratic East Germany and the eventual reunification of Germany in 1990. Few alive at the time will forget the scenes of East and West German citizens happily dancing together on top of the Berlin Wall under the watchful eyes of the East German border guards—guards who until recently had been under strict orders to shoot anyone who attempted to cross the border.

Although the collapse of communism in East Germany, and Eastern Europe more generally, seems inevitable from our vantage point, it came as a complete surprise to most observers at the time. Until 1989, Communist regimes had proved to be remarkably stable. Indeed, there had been very few major uprisings or revolts in Eastern Europe during the entire postwar period. With the exception of revolts in East Germany in 1953, in Poland and Hungary in 1956, in Czechoslovakia in 1968, and in Poland in 1981, the Communist regimes of Eastern Europe had been relatively unchallenged for forty years or more. The revolts that did occur were put down by considerable force and direct Soviet military intervention, which only further discouraged Eastern Europeans from publicly opposing their Communist governments. Of all the governments in the Eastern bloc in 1989, the one in East Germany was arguably the most stable, prosperous, and hard-line. The East German secret police—the *Staatssicherheitsdienst,* or *Stasi* for short—were infamous for their ability to monitor and control the lives of ordinary citizens. In 1989 there were 85,000 full-time Stasi officers and

BOX 7.2 ■ A BRIEF HISTORY OF EAST GERMANY, 1945–1990

At the Potsdam Conference in August 1945, the Allied powers divided Germany into four zones, to be occupied by France in the southwest, Britain in the northwest, the United States in the south, and the Soviet Union in the east. Berlin, which was more than 100 miles inside the eastern

MAP 7.1 ■ Divided Germany

Legend:
- United States
- United Kingdom
- France
- Soviet Union

(Continued)

(Continued)

zone controlled by the Soviet Union, was also divided into four occupation zones. As the postwar rivalry between the Western powers and the Soviet Union increased, the Americans, French, and British signed the London Agreements in June 1948, joining their sectors together and introducing a new currency—the deutsche mark. In response to this perceived act of aggression, the Soviets responded by blocking all ground transportation between the western sectors and West Berlin on June 24, 1948. The next day, the Western powers began a massive airlift to supply West Berlin with essentials such as food and fuel. The Berlin Airlift, or the Berlin Blockade as it became known, finally ended ten months later when the Soviets realized that the West would not simply give up West Berlin. By now the division of Germany was almost inevitable. The Federal Republic of Germany (West Germany) was formally established on May 23, 1949, and

the German Democratic Republic (East Germany) was established on October 7, 1949.

Between 1949 and 1961, 2.7 million people reacted to the increasingly dismal economic and political conditions in East Germany by emigrating to the West. It was in response to this that the East German government closed the borders to the West and began construction of the ninety-six-mile-long Berlin Wall during the night of August 12–13, 1961. The Berlin Wall split numerous families and separated many Berliners from their places of employment. Although the whole length of the border between East and West Germany was closed with chain-link fences, walls, minefields, and other installations, it was the Berlin Wall that arguably became the most iconic symbol of the Cold War. Over the years, thousands of attempts were made to breach the wall and reach the West. In all, about 200 people were killed trying

MAP 7.2 ■ The Division of Berlin

East and West Germans stand on the Berlin Wall in front of the Brandenburg Gate the day after the wall opened on November 9, 1989.

to escape, with Chris Gueffroy being the last to be shot dead in February 1989.

During the summer and autumn of 1989, massive changes occurred in East Germany that eventually led to the reunification of Germany. Tens of thousands of East Germans fled to the West, taking advantage of the Hungarian government's decision to open its border to Austria. Increasingly, growing numbers of East Germans began protesting on the streets of Leipzig and Berlin, demanding reform within East Germany itself. Ongoing protests forced the East German government to allow free, multiparty elections in March 1990. These elections produced a victory for the pro-unification forces headed by West German chancellor Helmut Kohl. East Germany entered into an economic and monetary union with West Germany in July 1990. On September 12, 1990, East Germany, West Germany, and the four powers that occupied Germany at the end of World War II signed the Treaty on the Final Settlement with Respect to Germany. This treaty paved the way for German reunification on October 3, 1990.

more than 100,000 informers (Lohmann 1994, 59). With a population of slightly less than 17 million, these figures reveal the shocking fact that there was one Stasi officer or informer for every ninety East German citizens. To most observers, East Germany didn't look on the brink of collapse in 1989.

The eventual collapse of communism in East Germany had much to do with the election of Mikhail Gorbachev to the position of general secretary of the Communist Party in the Soviet Union on March 11, 1985. In many ways, Gorbachev inherited a Soviet Union in crisis. The economy that had seemed to perform so well during much of the postwar period had begun to stagnate by the mid-1980s, and the Soviet invasion of Afghanistan in 1979 to prop up a Communist government against Islamic rebels was increasingly taking up valuable resources. The 1986 Chernobyl disaster, in which a nuclear reactor exploded and spread radioactive fallout across much of Europe, revealed the dysfunctional nature of a deeply sclerotic and secretive Soviet state.

Gorbachev responded to these crises with two reform policies, called *perestroika* and *glasnost*. Perestroika was a policy aimed at liberalizing and regenerating the Soviet economy, whereas glasnost was a policy designed to increase political openness and encourage freedom of expression. We all know what happened to the Soviet Union and Eastern Europe, but it's important to recognize that Gorbachev was an ardent Communist who deeply believed in socialism. It was his hope that the policies of perestroika and glasnost would save the Soviet Union; he didn't intend for them to facilitate its breakup, as they arguably did.

The liberalizing reform policies Gorbachev introduced in the Soviet Union encouraged reformists and opposition groups in other countries throughout Eastern Europe. Following a big wave of strikes, the Polish government convened a conference in August 1988, known as the Roundtable Talks, with the main opposition group, Solidarity, to help reach a compromise on how to deal with the growing economic and political problems. These talks resulted in the legalization of the independent trade union—Solidarity—and nationwide elections in 1989, which produced the first non-Communist prime minister in Eastern Europe in forty years. These changes in Poland served to encourage liberalizers in other Communist countries. For example, talks in Hungary, known as the Triangular Table Talks, which began about three months after those in Poland, resulted in cautious moves toward easing censorship and legalizing an independent trade union. When this brought little response from the Soviet Union, further reforms were introduced—the Communist Party renamed itself the Socialist Party, the country's name was changed from the Hungarian People's Republic to the Republic of Hungary, and multiparty elections were planned for 1990.

Although these changes in Eastern Europe were clearly significant, people at the time didn't see them as signs of the imminent collapse of Communist control. The Chinese Communist Party's use of tanks and soldiers to violently disperse thousands of protesters in Tiananmen Square in June 1989 clearly illustrated that some Communist regimes were willing to use overwhelming force to retain power (see Box 7.3, "Tiananmen Square, Beijing, June 4, 1989").

The situation in East Germany began to change when Hungary decided to open its border with Austria in August 1989, thereby breaching the Iron Curtain for the first time. Although East Germans had always been relatively free to travel to other Communist countries in Eastern Europe, it had been all but impossible to get permission to travel to the West. In September 1989, 13,000 East Germans fled to the West across Hungary's open border. Thousands of other East Germans tried to reach the West by staging sit-ins at West German embassies in other Eastern European capitals, such as Prague. In response to these "refugees," the East German government eventually provided special trains to carry them to the West. Before doing so, East German officials took away their passports and claimed they were expelling "irresponsible antisocial traitors and criminals." In a matter of weeks, thousands of East Germans had left their possessions and relatives behind to make a dash for freedom. The willingness of East Germans to leave so much behind is further evidence that few at the time foresaw the imminent collapse of the Communist system in East Germany.

BOX 7.3 TIANANMEN SQUARE, BEIJING, JUNE 4, 1989

Between April 15 and June 4, 1989, students, intellectuals, and labor activists held mass demonstrations against the Chinese Communist government in Tiananmen Square, Beijing. After the demonstrators refused to disperse, a hard-line faction in the Communist Party decided to use force against them. On May 20 the government declared martial law, and on June 4 army tanks and infantry troops were sent in to crush the protest. Estimates of civilian deaths vary from a low of 23 according to the Chinese Communist Party to a high of 2,600 according to the Chinese Red Cross. The Chinese government then conducted widespread arrests to suppress remaining opposition groups.

Over the years, we've had dozens of Chinese students in our classes. Many have told us they were unaware of the events that took place in Tiananmen Square in 1989. Our students aren't unusual. In one study, only 15 out of 100 students

at Beijing University were able to recognize the "Tank Man" photo shown below (Lim 2015). This is despite the fact that this photo has become the international symbol for the Tiananmen Square protests.

The reason for this lack of awareness has to do with China's massive censorship apparatus. The events of Tiananmen Square are considered a political taboo and inappropriate for public conversation. Individuals in China aren't allowed to make websites related to the events that took place in Tiananmen Square, and Internet searches, if they return anything, return only government mandated versions of the events. The system of censorship in China is massive. It's enforced by the government and by technology companies. "Internet content providers . . . may be fined or shut down if they fail to comply with government censorship guidelines. To comply with the government, each

AP Photo/Jeff Widener

A Chinese man stands alone to block a line of tanks heading east on Beijing's Chang'an Boulevard in Tiananmen Square on June 4, 1989.

(Continued)

[Continued]

individual site privately employs up to 1,000 censors. Additionally, approximately 20,000–50,000 Internet police (*wang jing*) and Internet monitors (*wang guanban*) as well as an estimated 250,000–300,000 '50 cent party members' (*wumao dang*) at all levels of government—central, provincial, and local—participate in this huge effort" (King, Pan, and Roberts 2013, 1). Among other things, it's the job of censors to update the lists of sensitive words to take account of the new references and creative expressions that individuals have adopted to beat the censorship system (Hui and Rajagopalan 2013). *China Digital Times,* a news website based in the United States, has found that at least 262 different Tiananmen-related phrases have been censored since 2011 (Ser 2016).[1] The goal of the censorship system as it relates to the events of Tiananmen Square is to erase it from Chinese history, especially among the younger generation. Our experience with Chinese students suggests that it's been quite effective at achieving its goal.

[1]You can find (more) examples of the censorship patterns at www.pri.org/stories/2016-06-03/how-china-has-censored-words-relating-tiananmen-square-anniversary.

Although tens of thousands of East Germans fled the country, a fledgling opposition group called Neues Forum (New Forum) surfaced in East Germany demanding reform. Opposition protests began to take place on the streets of Leipzig and East Berlin. Initially, the crowds chanted, "Wir wollen raus!" (We want to leave!). Soon, however, they began to defiantly chant, "Wir bleiben hier!" (We're staying here!). It was the emergence of protesters demanding reform and refusing to leave that proved to be the real threat to the government's hold on power. The early protests were small, but they soon began to grow as the failure of the East German government to successfully intimidate the initial demonstrators encouraged more and more people to participate. By October 1989 more than 250,000 people were regularly taking part in pro-democracy demonstrations. In a clear challenge to the Communist Party's claim to represent the East German people, the protesters famously chanted, "Wir sind das Volk!" (We are the People!).

Despite the protests, the East German government went ahead with celebrations on October 7 to mark the fortieth anniversary of the founding of the East German state. These celebrations included extravagant military parades, orchestrated pro-regime demonstrations, and a visit by Mikhail Gorbachev. To the embarrassment of the East German leadership, or politburo, the crowd at the parades began chanting for Gorbachev to help them. In defiance of Gorbachev's advice that "Life will punish latecomers"—a clear reference to the necessity for reform—the hard-line East German leader, Erich Honecker, reacted within days of Gorbachev's departure by signing the *Schiessbefehl* (order to shoot) for a Chinese solution to the protests (Lohmann 1994, 69). East Germany was on the brink of civil war. As troops were being assembled and armed, the rest of the East German politburo rebelled, countermanded the order, and replaced Honecker with the more moderate Egon Krenz.

Despite the introduction of minor reforms, the mass protests continued and were emboldened when Gorbachev announced that the Soviets would no longer intervene militarily in Eastern Europe to prop up Communist governments. On November 4, more than 1 million East Germans took to the streets of East Berlin. In a final attempt to ward off ever larger protests, the East German government agreed on November 9 to remove all restrictions on travel to the West. The announcement of this decision on television led to tens of thousands of East Berliners rushing to the Berlin Wall, where surprised border guards eventually allowed them to pour through. In the following weeks, the whole socialist system in East Germany unravelled. Despite brief attempts to create a nonsocialist East Germany, elections on March 18, 1990 demonstrated that an overwhelming majority of East Germans wanted reunification with West Germany. By now, instead of shouting, "Wir sind das Volk!" (We are the People!), the protesters were shouting, "Wir sind ein Volk!" (We are one People!). Reunification finally took place on October 3, 1990, when the areas of the former German Democratic Republic were incorporated into the Federal Republic of Germany.

The transition to democracy that occurred in East Germany in 1989 represents but one case of a bottom-up transition, in which popular mobilization led to the overthrow of an authoritarian regime. There are many other examples. For instance, a few weeks after the fall of the Berlin Wall, mass protests forced the overthrow of the Communist government in Czechoslovakia in what became known as the Velvet Revolution because of its lack of violence (Garton Ash 1999). A few weeks after this, in December 1989, crowds played an integral role in removing the Communist dictator Nicolae Ceaușescu from power in Romania. Other examples include the EDSA Revolution, or the People Power Revolution, which saw massive demonstrations of up to three million people remove Ferdinand Marcos from power in the Philippines in 1986, or the June Resistance, which saw mass protests force South Korea's General Roh Tae Woo to allow direct presidential elections in mid-1987. The list could go on and on.

As political scientists, we need to ask ourselves how we can explain these types of bottom-up transitions. How can we capture the surprise with which actual participants greeted the events that were unfolding around them? Why did the collapse of communism in Eastern Europe occur in 1989? Why did Eastern Europe, which in retrospect seems to have been filled with extremely fragile Communist regimes, seem so stable before 1989? Why are revolutions like those in Eastern Europe and elsewhere so rare? Why are they so hard to predict? Collective action theory and tipping models provide answers to some of these questions. We begin by examining collective action theory.

Collective Action Theory

Collective action theory focuses on forms of mass action, or "collective action," such as the protests in East Germany in 1989. Other examples of **collective action** are revolutions, interest group activities, strikes, elections, and the like. Typically, collective action concerns the pursuit of public goods by groups of individuals. A public good has two characteristics: (1) **nonexcludability** and (2) **nonrivalry**. A good is nonexcludable if you can't prevent those in the group who didn't contribute to its supply from consuming it, and it's nonrivalrous if its consumption by one individual doesn't reduce the amount available for consumption by other individuals in the group.

Some examples should clarify the idea of a public good. One example of a public good is clean air. Clean air is nonexcludable in that people can't be stopped from breathing it, and it's nonrivalrous in that one person's consumption of it doesn't diminish the amount of clean air others can consume. Another example of a public good is a lighthouse. A lighthouse is nonexcludable in that ships in the sea can't be prevented from seeing the light irrespective of whether they contribute to the building and upkeep of the lighthouse, and it's nonrivalrous in that there's just as much light for everyone to see no matter how many ships are taking advantage of it. Other examples of public goods include public parks, fire stations, public radio, and national defense. We can also think of democracy as a public good—it's non-excludable in that anyone living in a democracy gets to enjoy living under democratic rule irrespective of whether they helped bring democracy about or whether they help to sustain it, and it's nonrivalrous because one person's enjoyment or consumption of democracy doesn't reduce the amount of democracy others can consume.

Most people recognize that the nature of public goods makes them quite desirable. This might lead you to think that individuals who expect to benefit from a public good would be enthusiastic contributors to the provision of that good—at least as long as the benefit from the good outweighed the cost of providing it. Put more starkly, you might expect that groups of individuals with common interests would act collectively to achieve those interests. Although this might seem reasonable, a famous economist, Mancur Olson ([1965] 1971), has shown that there are compelling reasons to doubt whether individuals will actually contribute to the provision of public goods or take collective action to achieve their common interests. The difficulty that groups of individuals have in providing public goods that all members of the group desire is commonly known as the **collective action, or free-rider, problem**. As we'll see, the free-rider problem provides an explanation for why protests were so rare in Eastern Europe prior to 1989 and why the Communist regimes in that part of the world seemed stable for so long; in fact, it provides an explanation for why revolutions and public displays of opposition in dictatorships are so rare in general.

Start by asking yourself whether you would contribute to the provision of a public good that you value. Would you join a pro-democracy protest like those in East Germany in 1989, or would you stay at home? It's important to recognize that your *individual* decision to contribute to the public good or to participate in the pro-democracy protest is unlikely to be the decisive factor in determining whether the public good is provided or whether the protest is successful. What possible difference could one person make to the success of a mass protest? Given that you're individually unlikely to influence the outcome of the protest, why pay the costs that come with participation? The costs of participation include time, possibly expense, and perhaps even loss of life. The potentially high costs associated with joining pro-democracy rallies in Communist Eastern Europe would have been only too clear to would-be participants at the time. All in all, the decision not to participate in a pro-democracy protest (or not to contribute to a public good more generally) is very appealing. If the pro-democracy rally fails, you'll not have paid any costs or run the risk of incurring the dictatorship's wrath. And if the pro-democracy rally succeeds, you can "free ride" on the participation of others because everyone gets to benefit from the establishment of democracy irrespective of whether they participated in the rally or not. This is the basic logic underlying the collective action problem.

To better understand this logic, let's try to be a little more analytical. Imagine a group made up of some number of individuals, N. For example, we could think of the group as being the entire East German population. Now imagine that some number K of those N individuals must contribute or participate for the public good to be provided. We could think of the public good as being democracy and K as being the number of pro-democracy protesters that are necessary to make the Communist government in East Germany (or any other dictatorship) back down and allow democracy to emerge. If democracy is achieved, everyone receives a benefit irrespective of whether everyone participated in the pro-democracy rally. If you participate in the pro-democracy rally, you must pay a cost. To capture the notion that the provision of the public good provides more benefits to you than the individual cost of participating in the protest, let's assume that the value of the benefit to you outweighs its cost. If we didn't make this assumption, no one would ever have an incentive to contribute to the public good. Now ask yourself whether you'd ever contribute to the public good under these circumstances. Would

TABLE 7.1 ■ Pro-Democracy Protest: Do I Participate or Not?			
	Scenario 1	Scenario 2	Scenario 3
	Fewer than $K - 1$ Participate	Exactly $K - 1$ Participate	K or more Participate
Participate	Pay cost; don't receive benefit.	*Pay cost; receive benefit.*	Pay cost; receive benefit.
Don't participate	*Don't pay cost; don't receive benefit.*	*Don't pay cost; don't receive benefit.*	*Don't pay cost; receive benefit.*

Note: K = the number of individuals that must participate for the pro-democracy protest to be successful. Each cell indicates what will happen in each of the three possible scenarios depending on whether the individual chooses to participate in the protest or not. The shaded cells indicate the individual's best choice in each of the three scenarios. It's assumed that the value of the benefit received by the individual when the protest is successful outweighs her cost of participating in the protest.

you participate in a pro-democracy protest? As Table 7.1 illustrates, your decision will depend on your conjecture or expectation about what the other group members will do.

As you can see from Table 7.1, it makes no sense for you to participate in the pro-democracy protest if you expect that fewer than $K - 1$ others will participate (Scenario 1). Your individual participation won't make the protest successful as adding your support to the protest still leaves fewer than K people participating. If you were to join in, you'd pay the cost of participation and receive no benefit. As a result, you'd be better off staying at home. It also makes no sense for you to participate if you conjecture that at least K others will participate (Scenario 3). This time your individual participation is not necessary for a successful protest. Therefore, you might as well stay at home and free ride on the successful participation of others without paying any costs. It only makes sense for you to participate if you expect that exactly $K - 1$ others will participate (Scenario 2). In this scenario, your participation is decisive because it turns an otherwise unsuccessful protest into a successful one. By participating, you pay the cost of participation but you also receive the benefit from a successful protest. By not participating, you condemn the protest to failure and you get nothing. Given that the value of the benefit from a successful protest outweighs the individual cost of participation, it makes sense for you to participate. The outcomes resulting from the individual's best actions in each of the three possible scenarios are shown in the shaded cells in Table 7.1.

Two factors are particularly crucial for determining the likely success of collective action: (1) the difference between K and N and (2) the size of N.[2] Why would the difference between K and N matter? Suppose that the number of people required for a successful pro-democracy protest, K, was equal to the size of the group, N. In this situation, all in the group know that their participation is crucial for the success of the protest and that they each prefer a successful protest to a failed one. As a result, there's no incentive for any group member to free ride by staying at home. Suppose now that only some of the group members are required for a successful pro-democracy protest; that is, $K < N$. In this situation, group members know that a successful rally can take place without everyone's participation. It's this realization that creates the incentive to free ride. It doesn't take much of a leap to realize that the incentive to free ride

---

[2]It seems reasonable to think that the likelihood of successful collective action also depends on (1) the costs of participation and (2) the size of the benefit. As participation becomes more costly (holding N, K, and the value of the benefit fixed), it's likely that group members will be less willing to participate. Similarly, as the value of the benefit to be obtained from successful collective action increases (holding N, K, and the cost of participation fixed), it seems likely that the group members will be more willing to participate.

becomes greater the larger the difference between K and N. For example, if K is only slightly smaller than N, most group members are still going to think that their participation will be crucial to a successful protest. The result is that participation rates and, hence, the likelihood of a successful protest, remain relatively high. If K is much smaller than N, however, then most group members are going to think that they're not critical to the success of the protest and that they can get away with free riding on the participation of others. Given the increased level of free riding, the likelihood of a successful protest is going to decline in this situation.

The bottom line is that forms of collective action, such as protests, strikes, revolutions, lobbying, and the like, are less likely to be successful when the number of group members required for success, K, is significantly smaller than the number of people who will benefit from the success, N. Somewhat counterintuitively, this means that group leaders interested in some form of collective action, such as a demonstration or a letter-writing campaign, will be more successful if they tell their members that success depends on the participation of nearly all of their members rather than just a few of them. The logic of collective action we've just presented helps to explain why political parties try to convince their supporters that all of their votes are crucial to their electoral success or why pledge drives for public television or National Public Radio in the United States continually state that the contributions of all listeners are crucial to the ongoing existence of these institutions even if this is not true—they're trying to persuade voters, listeners, and viewers to participate rather than free ride.

Why would the size of the group matter? The size of N matters because it influences the likelihood that you'll think of yourself as critical to the form of collective action under consideration. Should you run the risks associated with participating in a pro-democracy rally where N is large? Will it make a difference? If hardly anyone else participates, then the pro-democracy protest is unlikely to be successful. And if lots of people participate, it's unlikely that your individual participation will make much of a difference. Given this, why participate? The size of N also matters because it influences the ability of group members to monitor and punish free riders. The larger the group, the harder it is to monitor, identify, and punish those who don't participate in the protest. The result is that larger groups tend to be characterized by higher levels of free riding and a lower likelihood that collective action will be successful.

The relationship between group size and successful collective action has some important and counterintuitive implications. Most important, it suggests that small groups may be more politically and economically effective than large groups because of the small group's increased ability to solve the free rider problem. This challenges the common concern in democratic theory that the majority will tyrannize and exploit the minority. In fact, the opposite may well occur in some circumstances. For example, the positive relationship between small groups and successful collective action helps to explain why business groups (relatively small) seem to have greater lobbying power and influence over policy than, say, consumer groups or workers (relatively large). It also helps to explain why relatively small constituencies such as religious fundamentalists can have a significant influence on political outcomes compared with the much larger constituencies made up of religious moderates and secularists. In sum, the free-rider problem is likely to damage the ability of large groups to conduct forms of collective action much more than that of small groups.

Collective action theory provides an explanation for the apparent stability of communism in postwar East Germany and for why public demonstrations of regime opposition are so rare in dictatorships more generally. Collective action theory reminds us that the fact that many East Germans shared a common interest—in the overthrow of the Communist regime and the establishment of democracy—didn't automatically translate into their taking collective action to bring this about. The public goods nature of democracy created an incentive for East Germans to avoid the potential costs of participating in pro-democracy rallies and to free ride on the participation of others. The incentives to free ride in East Germany were large because the number of people who would benefit from democracy, N—virtually the entire 17 million population—was huge and because the number of protesters necessary to bring democracy about, K—several hundred thousand in the end—was relatively small in comparison. The costs of participating in pro-democracy demonstrations were largely prohibitive as well. The violent and deadly outcome of the Berlin Uprising in 1953 was a stark reminder to potential protesters of the dangers they faced if they publicly opposed the Communist government. It's important to recognize that the lack of public opposition in East Germany for most of the postwar period was not necessarily a sign that the Communist regime enjoyed widespread support; it may simply have been that the collective action problem made it difficult for the opposition to organize itself into a coherent force.

Tipping Models

Although collective action theory helps to explain why revolutions are so rare and why dictatorships often appear stable, it can't explain the mass protests that eventually brought communism to its knees in 1989. Participation now becomes the puzzle to be explained. One explanation for the mass protests that occurred in East Germany can be found in what political scientists call "tipping," or "threshold," models (Ginkel and Smith 1999; Kuran 1991; Lohmann 1994).

We start with an individual who must decide whether to publicly support or oppose a dictatorship. The individual has a private preference and a revealed public preference. Her private preference is her true attitude toward the dictatorship, and her public preference is the attitude toward the dictatorship she reveals to the outside world. The dangers that come from publicly revealing one's opposition to a dictatorship often mean that individuals who oppose the regime falsify their true preferences; instead of opposing the dictatorship in public, they support it. In East Germany, as elsewhere in Eastern Europe, "people routinely applauded speakers whose message they disliked, joined organizations whose mission they opposed, and signed defamatory letters against people they admired" (Kuran 1991, 26). One consequence of **preference falsification** is that individuals don't know the true level of opposition in a dictatorship because they all seem to be publicly supporting it. The perception is that society is publicly behind the dictatorship and that there's no point in opposing it. As the political dissident Aleksandr Solzhenitsyn (1975, 275) wrote about the Soviet Union, "The lie has been incorporated into the state system as the vital link holding everything together."[3] Note that preference falsification provides an alternative, but complementary, explanation to that provided by collective action theory for the relative stability of Eastern Europe in the postwar period. It suggests that even if collective action could be effectively organized, individuals might still choose not to protest because they're unsure of the extent to which others really oppose the regime.

Although many people may be engaged in preference falsification, there's probably some protest size at which they'd be willing to publicly reveal their true preferences. In other words, an opponent of the regime might not wish to participate in a pro-democracy rally that comprises a few hundred people but may be willing to participate in one that comprises tens of thousands or hundreds of thousands of people. We'll refer to the protest size at which an individual is willing to participate as her **revolutionary threshold**. The intuition behind the

---

[3]The state itself, often through the use of state-controlled media, reinforces the "lie" referred to by Solzhenitsyn. State officials can use a combination of propaganda and censorship to provide the public with the version of information, both about contemporary and historical events, that helps the state maintain its authority. The combination of censorship and propaganda make it particularly difficult to know what other citizens believe.

notion of a revolutionary threshold is relatively straightforward. As the size of a protest grows, it becomes harder for the state to identify and punish individuals for participating. In other words, the costs of participation decline in rough proportion to the number of protesters.

Individuals have different revolutionary thresholds. Some people are really brave and are quite happy to oppose dictatorial rule irrespective of whether others do. These people are commonly referred to as *political dissidents* and often include academics, writers, or religious figures. For example, Aleksandr Solzhenitsyn and Andrei Sakharov were both political dissidents who challenged the police state and nuclear weapons policy of the Soviet Union. Other people may be scared and unwilling to publicly show their opposition to a dictatorship unless lots of others also do so. Still others may actually support the regime; these people are unlikely to join in a pro-democracy protest under any circumstances. As you might expect, people's thresholds are likely to depend on many different factors, such as whether they have benefited or suffered under the regime, whether they have much to lose from participating in protests, and whether they believe that the regime is fragile or stable. The point is that revolutionary thresholds vary across individuals.

An example might make this concept clearer.[4] Below is an example of a ten-person society labeled A.

$$A = \{0, 2, 2, 3, 4, 5, 6, 7, 8, 10\}.$$

The numbers in the brackets indicate the revolutionary threshold of each of the ten people in Society A. The first individual in this society has a revolutionary threshold of 0, meaning that she's willing to protest on her own. The second and third individuals in this society have a revolutionary threshold of 2, meaning they need two other people to be protesting before they're willing to join in. In this example, the tenth individual has a revolutionary threshold of 10. Given that there are only ten people in this society, this means that the tenth individual will never participate in a protest, because there can never be ten people already protesting without her participation.

The distribution of revolutionary thresholds in a society is crucial for determining whether a revolution occurs. Consider the example of Society A. In this society, only one person will protest. The individual with a revolutionary threshold of 0 will protest, but no one else will. It's unlikely that a one-person protest will be successful. Now consider a slightly different society, A':

$$A' = \{0, 1, 2, 3, 4, 5, 6, 7, 8, 10\}.$$

The only difference between Society A and Society A' is that the second individual's revolutionary threshold has dropped from 2 to 1. We can think of these two examples as the same society at two different points in time. For example, we can think that the government took some action or introduced some policy that made the second individual more willing to publicly oppose the government. Although this small change in one person's revolutionary threshold might appear inconsequential, it actually has quite a dramatic effect on the size and likely success of a protest. This is because the second individual is now willing to join the first individual who is protesting. Now that there are two people protesting, the third individual with a revolutionary threshold of 2 is willing to join in as well. This, in turn, causes the fourth individual to join in. Before you know it, there's a nine-person protest going on. The fact that fully 90 percent of the people in this society are now protesting is likely to mean that this

---

[4]Several of the examples that follow were provided by a former colleague, Marek Kaminski.

protest is successful. In this example, the slight shift in the revolutionary threshold of one individual has caused what we call a **revolutionary cascade**. This example should make it clear why these types of models are referred to as "tipping," or "threshold," models.

Note that a small shift in the revolutionary threshold like that in the previous example won't always produce a revolution or protest. Consider Society *B*:

$$B = \{0, 2, 3, 3, 4, 5, 6, 7, 8, 10\}.$$

The only difference from Society *A* is that the third individual now has a revolutionary threshold of 3 instead of 2. Notice, though, what happens when the government takes the same action or introduces the same policy as before, causing the second individual to reduce her threshold from 2 to 1.

$$B' = \{0, 1, 3, 3, 4, 5, 6, 7, 8, 10\}.$$

As you can see, the change of threshold produces only a two-person protest this time. In other words, there's a slight decline in the popularity of the regime but no revolution. Thus, a slightly different distribution of a society's revolutionary thresholds can mean the difference between a small, abortive, and ultimately unsuccessful protest (Society *B'*) and a revolutionary cascade (Society *A'*) that produces the overthrow of the dictatorship.

This result has implications for those who argue that revolutions and protests are caused by structural factors such as relative deprivation, grievances, or oppression (Gurr 1970). As the tipping model suggests, things like economic recession or the introduction of a repressive policy may cause private preferences and revolutionary thresholds to move against the regime without actually producing a revolution. For example, economic recession may cause the regime in some Society *C* to become deeply unpopular (as exhibited by the relatively low revolutionary thresholds).

$$C = \{0, 2, 2, 2, 2, 2, 2, 2, 2, 10\}.$$

The low threshold of virtually every individual in this society indicates that it wouldn't take much for a revolutionary cascade to occur. Despite this, though, the distribution of revolutionary thresholds indicates that the regime won't experience a revolution as things stand. Structural factors such as an economic recession aren't sufficient in and of themselves to produce revolutions. All we can say is that structural factors can make revolutions more likely by reducing individual thresholds; they don't make revolutions inevitable. In effect, structural factors may create an environment in which idiosyncratic events, such as Mohamed Bouazizi's ill treatment by local officials in Tunisia and his subsequent self-immolation in December 2010 (see Chapter 1), can turn an act of desperation into the start of a revolution.[5] But similar acts of desperation in situations where structural factors have not lowered the revolutionary thresholds of individuals in society might well be remembered as tragic, largely private, acts that have few consequences beyond those directly affected.

---

[5] In a recent study of Moroccan protesters during the Arab Spring, Lawrence finds that the people who were "first movers" tended to have family members who had previously suffered repression at the hands of the regime. She argues that the friends of these first movers are likely to increase their support for anti-regime activity if new repression occurs, suggesting that if "repression generates support among first movers' friends, all else equal, their probability of mobilizing is likely to increase. Once they join, the movement is one step closer to triggering cascades of participation" (Lawrence 2017).

It's important to remember at this point that preference falsification means that a society's distribution of revolutionary thresholds is never known to the individuals of that society. Each individual knows her own revolutionary threshold, but not that of anyone else. This means that a society can come to the brink of revolution without anyone's ever knowing it. In effect, people may be ready to participate in a full-scale revolt as long as one more person goes out to protest. If that one extra person doesn't protest, however, then no revolution occurs and the dictatorship appears entirely stable. Note that even if people know for sure that preference falsification is occurring (as they surely must), they can't know if they live in a society like *A* or one like *B*. This implies that it's often impossible for observers to distinguish between very stable and very fragile dictatorships. Moreover, our inability to observe both private preferences and thresholds conceals potential revolutionary cascades and makes it impossible to predict when a revolution will occur. In effect, revolutions will always come as a surprise. This is why we talk about the "predictability of unpredictability" when it comes to revolutions (Kuran 1989, 1991). Note, though, that our inability to predict revolutions such as the fall of communism in Eastern Europe in 1989 or the overthrow of various dictators in the Arab Spring of 2011 (see Box 7.4, "Revolutionary Cascades, Social Media, and the Arab Spring") shouldn't lead us to think that revolutions are somehow irrational. As the logic underlying the tipping model indicates, our failure to predict revolutions "is entirely consistent with calculated, purposeful human action" (Kuran 1991, 45).

Preference falsification helps explain why the Communist regimes in Eastern Europe were substantially more vulnerable than their subservient populations had made them seem prior to 1989. During the 1980s, a series of structural changes had the effect of lowering revolutionary thresholds in Eastern Europe to such an extent that they triggered a revolutionary cascade both within countries and between countries. For example, the appointment of Gorbachev to power in the Soviet Union and his introduction of reformist policies, such as perestroika and glasnost, reduced the perceived risk of challenging the political status quo, thereby reducing people's thresholds. Revolutionary thresholds were also lowered by the increasingly poor economic performance of many Eastern European countries from the mid-1980s on and Gorbachev's statement in 1989 that the Soviet Union would not intervene militarily to help sustain Communist rule in Eastern Europe. Once pro-democracy reforms were successfully introduced in one Eastern European country, they started to have demonstration effects in other countries, further reducing revolutionary thresholds. The end result was a democratic cascade with the diffusion of democracy from one country to another (Brinks and Coppedge 2006; O'Loughlin et al. 1998; Starr and Lindborg 2003). The democratic cascade that occurred in Eastern Europe is best summed up by a protest banner seen at a pro-democracy rally in Prague in 1989 stating simply, "Poland—10 years, Hungary—10 months, East Germany—10 weeks, Czechoslovakia—10 days" (Garton Ash 1999). The message of the banner was that a democratic transition had finally taken place roughly 10 years since the rise of Solidarity in Poland, roughly ten months since the introduction of reforms in Hungary, roughly ten weeks since the start of mass protests in East Germany, and roughly ten days since pro-democracy rallies began in Czechoslovakia.

In hindsight, many have come to see the collapse of communism in Eastern Europe as inevitable. Numerous historians, sociologists, and political scientists who interviewed individuals across Eastern Europe reported that there'd been a huge pent-up pool of opposition to Communist rule and that this was bound to break out at some point in time. Almost all of the interviewees reported that they had opposed Communist rule and wanted it to end. These reports certainly make it seem that the collapse of communism was inevitable, but the notion of preference falsification should make us extremely wary of drawing this inference.

BOX 7.4 REVOLUTIONARY CASCADES, SOCIAL MEDIA, AND THE ARAB SPRING

In this chapter, we've focused on the revolutionary cascade that occurred across Eastern Europe in 1989. As we described in more detail in Chapter 1, though, another revolutionary cascade occurred more recently in the Middle East and North Africa. This particular revolutionary cascade began in December 2010 when Mohamed Bouazizi set himself on fire in Tunisia to protest his poor treatment by local officials. In the weeks that followed Mr. Bouazizi's self-immolation, mass protests spread from his hometown to the capital city, Tunis. On January 15, 2011, Tunisian president Zine al-Abidine Ben Ali fled to Saudi Arabia, making him the first Arab leader in generations to leave office in response to public protests. Over the next several months, protests spread beyond the Tunisian border to other countries such as Egypt, Libya, Syria, Yemen, and Bahrain. Protesters in one country after another began to emulate the rebellious actions of protesters in other countries, and belief began to spread that the dictatorial regimes in the region could be toppled. With the diffusion of protests across national borders, the Arab Spring was born.

Information is central to the success of a revolutionary cascade. For example, protesters need to know about events in other countries. They also need to be able to pass on various pieces of information such as where and when to meet so they can coordinate their protests successfully. Some commentators have referred to the Arab Spring as the "Twitter Revolution," suggesting that new developments in information technology, such as Twitter, Facebook, and YouTube, which enable information to be shared quickly with others, are empowering citizens, weakening authoritarian elites, and helping to make revolutionary cascades more likely.

It's certainly true that protesters during the Arab Spring used these new technologies in various capacities. For example, they were used to spread the word about the location of government crackdowns and "flash" protests.

Moreover, opposition leaders, like Nobel Peace Prize winner Mohamed ElBaradei, are known to have used things like Twitter to launch attacks on dictatorial rulers, such as Egyptian president Hosni Mubarak (Hammer 2010). Similarly, YouTube was used on numerous occasions to publicize government massacres, thereby building support among both domestic and foreign audiences for opposition movements. It's unclear, though, exactly how big a role these new technologies played in the Arab Spring. For example, no scholar has so far carefully matched up specific bursts of, say, Twitter communication with data on subsequent protests. Until this is done, we won't know the true magnitude, if any, of the causal effect of these new technologies (Voeten 2010).

It should be pointed out that these new forms of social media don't necessarily weaken the power of authoritarian elites to control their citizens. Indeed, there's growing evidence that dictatorial regimes may well be able to use these new forms of social media to their own advantage. Indeed, the British police demonstrated how this might be done during the August 2011 riots in London when they monitored social networks related to Twitter and BlackBerry Messenger to stay one step ahead of protesters. In the process, they prevented attacks on the Olympic site and the main shopping areas around Oxford Street ("Riots Thwarted" 2011). In 2009, China simply closed Twitter messaging sites and blocked access to websites that were reporting on the ethnic protests in Xinjiang province ("Scores Killed" 2009). Recognizing that people will often find alternative ways to reach the outside world if social network systems are simply shut down, some authoritarian regimes have adopted more ingenious strategies whereby they create state-controlled intranets and Internet providers that give people the "illusion" of access to the outside world. For example, Iran has established a "halal" Internet

(Continued)

(Continued)

that has been described as "a stilted alternative reality of government-approved content on controlled national intranets" (US Department of State 2011). In many ways, traditional off-line surveillance can be difficult and expensive for authoritarian regimes. Emerging new technologies actually make it easier and cheaper for them to monitor their citizens. For instance, the government in China often forces companies to log social network users' Internet protocol (IP) addresses. Similarly, the Egyptian state security apparatus under Mubarak collected records of activists' text messages, e-mail exchanges, and Skype chats (Saletan 2011).

It should also be noted that the new social media are but the latest example of the way communications technologies may play a role in the diffusion and coordination of protest. Historians have pointed to the explosive growth of newspaper circulation during the revolutions of 1848 and the role increased readership played in the dissemination of information about revolutionary protests occurring across Europe. Similarly, some analysts have pointed to the role twenty-four-hour news networks played in the spread of information across Eastern Europe in 1989.[6] The bottom line is that political scientists don't yet have a firm understanding of exactly how new forms of social media will influence the likelihood of protests and other forms of collective action. This is an area in which we expect to see a lot of new research in the coming years.

---

[6]Although the idea of the media influencing protests is intuitively appealing, the empirical evidence is not always strong. One recent study looking at the events of 1989 in East Germany found no evidence to "support the widely accepted 'fact' that West German television served as a coordination device for antiregime protests during the East German revolution" (Crabtree, Darfomal, and Kern 2015, 269).

For example, put yourself in the shoes of a Communist Party supporter. As the revolutionary cascade starts to snowball into an overwhelming majority, it becomes unwise for you to remain a government supporter. You may even feel obliged to join the pro-democracy protests even though you'd have preferred they fail. We might call this a revolutionary *bandwagon* to distinguish it from a revolutionary *cascade*. Just as pro-democracy supporters falsify their preferences under dictatorship to avoid punishment, pro-dictatorship supporters falsify their preferences under democracy for similar reasons. Supporters of the former Communist regime are likely to lie about their true preferences and indicate that they were long-standing opponents of the toppled government. In effect, the evidence from these people will make it seem as if the former dictatorship was much more unstable and unloved than it actually was. As Kuran (1991, 23) puts it, "Having misled everyone into seeing a revolution as highly unlikely, preference falsification now conceals the forces that were working against it. One of the consequences of post-revolutionary preference falsification is thus to make it even less comprehensible why the revolution was unforeseen." In other words, revolution will often seem inevitable in hindsight even though this is, in fact, far from the case at the time.

TOP-DOWN TRANSITIONS TO DEMOCRACY

Some transitions to democracy don't happen through a bottom-up process as occurred in East Germany. Instead, they result primarily from a policy of liberalization on the part of authoritarian elites themselves. This policy of liberalization is often designed to stabilize a dictatorship but sometimes inadvertently leads to democracy. Periods of liberalization have preceded many transitions to democracy throughout history. For example, Generals Ernesto Geisel and João Figueiredo introduced a period of liberalization in Brazil between 1982 and 1985 as they tried to strengthen their position in relation to hard-liners like General Sylvio Frota. This period of liberalization ultimately led to an implicit pact between government soft-liners, the regime party, the military, and the opposition to name the opposition leader, Tancredo Neves, as president in 1985.

A similar period of liberalization preceded the democratic transition in Uruguay between 1983 and 1984. In this case, month-long discussions between soft-liners in the authoritarian regime and representatives of the opposition led to the Naval Club Accord and the reintroduction of presidential elections in 1984 (Colomer 1991, 1295). Chile, similarly, experienced a period of liberalization before its return to the democratic fold in 1988. Chile's transition to democracy began in 1980 with the introduction of a new constitution that contained provisions for the transfer of power from the military government of Augusto Pinochet to a civilian government within eight years. Chile's slow democratization process was tightly orchestrated, culminating in a defeat for Pinochet in a plebiscite on his leadership in October 1988 and the reintroduction of presidential elections later that year. As discussed in more detail a little later in this chapter, Poland's transition to democracy in 1989 was another case in which a period of liberalization introduced by authoritarian elites preceded democracy.

A Strategic Theory of Top-Down Democratic Transitions

While each top-down democratic transition is historically unique, they often follow a similar process. Top-down democratic transitions frequently result from a split between soft-liners and hard-liners in an authoritarian regime. Typically, the dictatorship has come under some sort of pressure, possibly having to do with declining economic conditions, and the soft-liners have come to prominence. Whereas hard-liners are usually satisfied with the political status quo, soft-liners may prefer to liberalize and broaden the social base of the dictatorship in an attempt to gain allies, strengthen their position in relation to the hard-liners, and manage opposition groups.[7] The soft-liners have a choice to make. Should they open up the political regime through a process of liberalization or should they stick with the political status quo?

A **policy of liberalization** entails a controlled opening of the political space and might include the formation of political parties, holding elections, writing a constitution, establishing a judiciary, opening a legislature, and so on. It's important to recognize that the goal of any "opening" for the soft-liners is not to bring about democracy but to incorporate various opposition groups into authoritarian institutions. As we discuss in more detail in Chapter 9, the liberalization process is typically an attempt by dictatorial elites to co-opt opposition groups or, at least, to divide and control them (Gandhi and Przeworski 2006; Przeworski 1991). The intended goal is not a democracy, but what we might call a "broadened dictatorship."[8] As an example, Lust-Okar (2005) uses evidence from Egypt, Jordan, and Morocco to illustrate how authoritarian elites have employed periods of liberalization and institutionalization to divide and control opposition groups. She shows how dictators in these countries

---

[7]The decision to liberalize is rarely taken in a vacuum. Instead, it often occurs after the authoritarian elites have come under some form of pressure from opposition groups in society. In this sense, it's hard to entirely disentangle bottom-up and top-down processes of democratization. As we noted at the beginning of the chapter, we believe that both processes typically interact with each other in the real world.

[8]Political scientists have used different terms to capture the concept of a "broadened dictatorship." For example, scholars have sometimes referred to these regimes as "competitive authoritarianism," "electoral authoritarianism," "soft-authoritarianism," "semi-authoritarianism," "pseudo-democracy," "illiberal democracy," "hybrid regimes," and other terms (Diamond 2002; Karl 1995; Levitsky and Way 2002, 2003; Schedler 2002; Zakaria 1997).

have been able to influence the timing of when political opponents unite and divide, as well as when they emerge and dissolve, by creating rules and institutions that allow some groups to participate in the formal political sphere but not others. In taking these steps, the authoritarian elites in these Middle Eastern countries have been able to lower the opposition's willingness and ability to challenge them. As the events of 2011 clearly demonstrate, however, this doesn't mean that even skilfully strategic authoritarians will always be able to control the actions of opposition groups.

It's worth noting that broadened dictatorships characterized by seemingly democratic institutions such as elections and legislatures are increasingly common in the world today (Diamond 2002; Levitsky and Way 2002, 2003). Many people have championed the introduction of these types of institutions in several dictatorships as signs that these states are gradually moving toward democracy. The implication is that the liberalization process will eventually lead to a transition to full democracy. It's this belief that often encourages some scholars to label these regimes as "mixed," "hybrid," or "partial democracies," as if they were some halfway house between dictatorship and democracy. Strong, and growing, empirical evidence, however, shows that broadened dictatorships are not necessarily undergoing a prolonged democratic transition (Carothers 2002; Herbst 2001). Indeed, it appears that liberalization and institutionalization can, under many circumstances, significantly enhance the stability of dictatorial rule.

Given the potential benefits of liberalization, you might wonder why authoritarian elites don't always liberalize. The basic problem is that the soft-liners can't guarantee that liberalization will successfully produce a broadened dictatorship. As you might expect, the liberalization process is inherently unstable. If the soft-liners do liberalize, then the democratic

AP Photo REPORTAGEBILD

Lech Walesa, head of the striking workers' delegation, stands in the Lenin shipyard in Gdansk, Poland, as he addresses striking workers after negotiations on August 26, 1980, that led to a preliminary contract between the striking workers and the Polish government.

opposition has two options. On the one hand, it can accept the concessions offered by the authoritarian elites and enter the institutions of a broadened dictatorship. In this case, the democratic opposition essentially agrees to maintain the dictatorial rules of the game in return for entrance into the formal political sphere. The soft-liners would obviously see this as a success. On the other hand, however, the democratic opposition can take advantage of its new freedoms to further organize and mobilize against the dictatorship. In many cases around the world, this is precisely what happened. For example, the Polish Communist Party agreed to allow the formation of the independent trade union Solidarity in September 1980. Within just two weeks, Solidarity had 3 million members and was rapidly becoming a direct threat to ongoing Communist rule (Garton Ash 1999, 34). It's easy to see that the soft-liners in an authoritarian regime are playing a dangerous game when they liberalize—they could unleash forces that might escape them.

If the democratic opposition does choose to continue organizing and mobilizing against the regime, then this is evidence that the controlled opening the soft-liners initiated has failed. As a consequence, the position of the soft-liners in the dictatorship is undermined. At this point, two choices are available to the authoritarian elites. The first choice is to use force in an attempt to repress popular mobilization and restore order. If the repression is successful, the result is a "narrow dictatorship" in which the soft-liners pay the consequence for having introduced a failed liberalization policy and are replaced by hard-liners. This particular scenario has played out quite frequently throughout history. For example, the experiment with liberalization King Hussein of Jordan attempted in the 1950s, and King Hassan II of Morocco tried in the 1960s, failed to appease their opponents, who simply demanded more significant reductions in, and even the elimination of, the monarchs' power. The two kings both responded to ongoing mobilization by imposing martial law, removing the men they had assigned to implement liberalization, and excluding all opposition groups from the formal political system (Lust-Okar 2005, 49–60). Periods of liberalization in Eastern Europe prior to 1989, such as the 1968 Prague Spring, also ended in repression and the establishment of narrow dictatorships led by hard-liners (see Box 7.5, "Prague Spring, 1968"). Of course, state repression may prove to be unsuccessful, at which point the dictatorship is likely to have an insurgency on its hands. Clearly, authoritarian elites must weigh the likelihood that repression will be successful before deciding to take this route.

The second choice available to the soft-liners if the democratic opposition continues to organize and mobilize is to accept its demands and allow the emergence of truly democratic institutions. This is essentially what happened in South Korea when pro-democracy rallies through the 1980s finally transformed the regime's soft-liners from liberalizers into democratizers; free elections were allowed in 1987. It's arguably what also happened in the Soviet Union under Gorbachev, and, as we'll see shortly, it's what happened in Poland in 1989. The argument that we've presented basically suggests that failed "liberalizations are either reversed, leading to grim periods euphemistically termed normalization, or continue to democratization" (Przeworski 1991, 60).

Given all of this, under what conditions can we expect authoritarian elites to introduce a period of liberalization? When does liberalization bring about an institutionalized and broadened dictatorship? When do opposition groups agree to enter authoritarian institutions, and when do they choose to continue mobilizing outside of regime institutions? If liberalization fails, when do authoritarian elites respond with repression, and when do they allow a transition to full democracy? Clearly, the authoritarian elite's choice to stick with the political status quo or liberalize depends on how it thinks the democratic opposition will respond to liberalization. Similarly, the democratic opposition's choice to enter a broadened dictatorship

BOX 7.5 PRAGUE SPRING, 1968

By the mid-1960s, the Czechoslovak economy had stalled, and moderate Communists were increasingly calling for economic, social, and political reform. In January 1968 the soft-liner Alexander Dubček replaced the hard-liner Antonín Novotný as leader of the Czechoslovak Communist Party. The period from March to August 1968 is known as the Prague Spring, and was a period in which Dubček tried to open up the political regime and introduce a policy of liberalization. The goal of these reforms was not the end of the socialist state but what Dubček called "socialism with a human face." Dubček wanted to overcome the disillusionment of the people with the previous two decades of Communist rule and breathe new life into socialism. He attempted to do this by increasing the freedom of the press, reducing censorship, and encouraging more participation in politics.

The introduction of these rather limited reforms encouraged further mobilization by the democratic opposition. Within weeks, the people were demanding still more reforms, and Communist control of the country faltered. Anti-Soviet statements appeared in the press, the Social Democrats began to form a separate party, and independent political clubs were created. At this point, the Soviet Union and its leader, Leonid Brezhnev, demanded that Dubček stop the reforms. Although Dubček had not originally intended for his policy of liberalization to go this far, he refused. The Soviets and their Warsaw Pact allies responded by invading Czechoslovakia. Dubček called on the people not to resist, but there were numerous acts of nonviolent resistance anyway. For example, one man, Jan Palach, set himself on fire in Prague's Wenceslas Square to protest the renewed suppression of free speech. Dubček was eventually replaced by the hard-liner Gustáv Husák, who introduced a period of "normalization." Husák reversed Dubček's reforms, purged the Communist Party of its soft-liners, and repressed remaining dissidents with the help of the secret police.

In 1987 Gorbachev acknowledged that his liberalizing policies of glasnost and perestroika owed a great deal to Dubček's vision of "socialism with a human face." When asked what the difference was between the Prague Spring and his own reforms, Gorbachev simply replied, "Nineteen years."

Given the renewed repression that followed the Prague Spring, it's bitterly ironic that observers quickly dubbed the events of early 2011 in the Middle East and North Africa (MENA) region the "Arab Spring." Gorbachev's willingness to link his reforms to those of his predecessor, Dubček, reminds us that the effects of political actions may be felt over decades and that current setbacks in the democracy movements in the MENA region may be masking long-run democratizing effects.

or to continue mobilizing depends on how it thinks the dictatorship will respond to ongoing mobilization. In Figure 7.2, we present a decision tree that captures this strategic situation between authoritarian soft-liners and democratic opposition groups (Przeworski 1991).

Let us consider the case where there's been a split in the authoritarian elite between soft-liners and hard-liners, and for some reason the soft-liners have come to prominence. As the top of the decision tree indicates, the soft-liners must decide whether to do nothing or open up the regime. If the soft-liners do nothing, we're left with the political status quo (O1). If they decide to open up, the democratic opposition groups must choose whether to enter the authoritarian institutions or to continue organizing. If they enter, the result is a broadened dictatorship (O2). If they organize, the soft-liners must decide whether to repress or democratize. If they repress, there are two possible outcomes. If the repression is successful, there'll be a narrow dictatorship in which the hard-liners return to prominence (O3). If the repression

FIGURE 7.2 ■ The Decision Tree for the Authoritarian Soft-Liners and Democratic Opposition

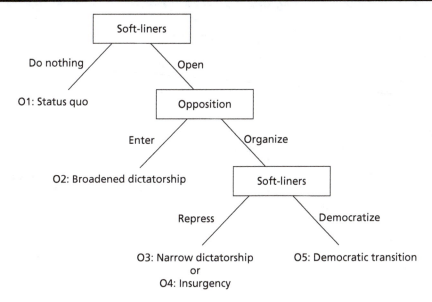

is unsuccessful, there'll be an insurgency (O4). Whether state repression is successful or not is likely to depend on the strength of the opposition groups. In what follows, we assume that state repression is successful and leads to a narrow dictatorship if the democratic opposition is weak but is unsuccessful and produces an insurgency if the democratic opposition is strong. Finally, if the soft-liners choose to democratize, the result is a democratic transition (O5).

Based on the story we've just told, the ideal outcome for the soft-liners is a broadened dictatorship in which opposition groups are co-opted and their position in the dictatorship is strengthened relative to that of the hard-liners. If they can't obtain this outcome, they'd like to keep the political status quo—the dictatorship is maintained, and they're still in a position of power. If this outcome can't be achieved, they'd prefer maintaining the dictatorship by handing power to the hard-liners in the form of a narrow dictatorship over having a democratic transition or an insurgency. If the dictatorship can't be maintained in any form, we'll assume the soft-liners would prefer a democratic transition to a potentially costly insurgency. It turns out that this last assumption is not important for determining what will happen.

The ideal outcome for the democratic opposition is obviously a full transition to democracy. If this outcome isn't possible, however, the opposition would like a broadened dictatorship in which it gets to enjoy some concessions from the soft-liners. The political status quo is better than both an insurgency in which many people are likely to die and a narrow dictatorship in which the democratic opposition is repressed by hard-liners. We'll assume that the opposition prefers an insurgency to a narrow dictatorship. Again, it turns out that this last assumption is not important for determining what will happen.

In Figure 7.3, we show how the authoritarian soft-liners and the democratic opposition are likely to behave in the case where the opposition is weak (on the left) and in the case where the opposition is strong (on the right). In the case where the opposition is weak, the outcome is a broadened dictatorship. Why? Well, the soft-liners know they can successfully repress the

FIGURE 7.3 ■ A Strategic Theory of Top-Down Transitions to Democracy

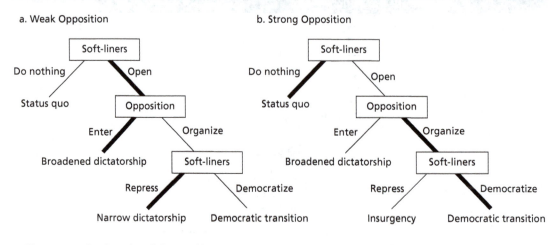

Note: The bold lines indicate the optimal choices of the soft-liners and the opposition at each of the points in the decision tree. The decision tree on the left examines the case where the soft-liners are faced by a weak opposition. The decision tree on the right examines the case where the soft-liners are faced by a strong opposition.

democratic opposition if they need to because the opposition is weak. Knowing that they'll be repressed if they continue to organize, the democratic opposition prefers to enter a broadened dictatorship if the opportunity arises. Since the democratic opposition prefers to enter a broadened dictatorship if the opportunity arises, the soft-liners are willing to liberalize and we end up with a broadened dictatorship.

In the case where the democratic opposition is strong, the outcome is the status quo. Why? This time the soft-liners know that if it came to it they wouldn't be able to successfully repress the opposition. If the soft-liners did try to repress the opposition, they'd end up with an insurgency they don't want. Knowing that the soft-liners won't repress them if they continue to organize, the opposition will want to organize and push for a full democratic transition rather than enter into a broadened dictatorship. Knowing that the opposition will just continue organizing if they liberalize and that in the end they'll be forced to allow a full democratic transition to avoid an unwanted insurgency, the soft-liners will choose to do nothing at the start and simply maintain the status quo.

What have we learned from our analysis so far? The most important insight is that a democratic transition is *not* possible as things stand. The only two possible outcomes are a broadened dictatorship or the political status quo. But we know that top-down democratic transitions do occur. So what's going on? Is there something wrong with our theory of top-down democratic transitions?

To this point, we've assumed that the soft-liners and the democratic opposition know everything there is to know about the strategic situation that they're involved in. What we've seen is that if the soft-liners and democratic opposition know everything, then a top-down democratic transition is not possible. But what happens if we relax the assumption that everyone knows everything? One of the key assumptions underlying our analysis so far is that the soft-liners know whether they're dealing with a strong opposition or a weak opposition. But what if this isn't the case? What if the soft-liners are uncertain about whether the democratic opposition is weak or strong?

Given our earlier discussion of preference falsification, it seems almost certain that authoritarian soft-liners will often be uncertain or misinformed about the true strength of the democratic opposition. Although citizens are likely to support the regime in public, they may well oppose it quite vehemently in private. Opposition groups are likely to take great care to keep their activities hidden from the prying eyes of the dictatorship and its secret police. Despite their best efforts, it's almost impossible for dictatorships to successfully shut down all forms of autonomous organizations that escape their control; there'll nearly always be underground resistance networks of some sort.

It turns out that top-down democratic transitions can occur if authoritarian soft-liners are incorrect about the type of opposition they're facing. Suppose the soft-liners think the democratic opposition is weak and that they're involved in the strategic situation captured by the decision tree on the left side of Figure 7.3. As we saw earlier, the soft-liners will choose to liberalize and open up the political regime in this scenario because they expect the opposition to enter into a broadened dictatorship. But what happens if the soft-liners are mistaken in their beliefs about the strength of the democratic opposition? What happens if the opposition is strong and the soft-liners are actually involved in the strategic situation captured by the decision tree on the right side of Figure 7.3? If this is the case, we've already seen that a strong opposition will continue organizing when the soft-liners open up. As soon as the soft-liners see the opposition organizing, they'll immediately realize they've made a dreadful mistake. This is because they know that only a strong opposition would take such an action; a weak opposition would have entered a broadened dictatorship. Now that the soft-liners know for sure that they're facing a strong opposition, they'll realize that repression won't be successful and that their best option is to allow further democratization. The end result is a top-down democratic transition.

The central point to take away from this is that democratic transitions from above are not possible when everyone knows everything. They can occur only when there is some uncertainty and when someone makes a mistake. In the case we just examined, the mistake was that the soft-liners thought they were dealing with a weak opposition when, in fact, they were dealing with a strong opposition.

Our strategic theory of top-down democratic transitions has two further implications. The first has to do with when we're likely to see institutionalized dictatorships—those with legislatures, political parties, elections, and so on. If we conceive of a broadened dictatorship as an institutionalized one, then the results from our theory indicate that dictatorial institutionalization is likely to occur only when the authoritarian soft-liners believe the democratic opposition has moderate strength. The opposition has to be strong enough for the soft-liners to feel they can benefit from making some liberalizing concessions, but not so strong that they think they won't be able to repress the opposition if it looks like they're about to lose control of the liberalization process. Although our theory has something to say about the conditions under which we expect to see institutionalized dictatorships, it doesn't provide a firm prediction as to whether liberalization and institutionalization actually help dictatorships survive. Dictators may well establish seemingly democratic institutions in the hope that they'll improve their chances of staying in power. Our theory, though, illustrates that the effectiveness of the liberalization process in achieving this objective depends heavily on whether the beliefs of the authoritarian elites about the strength or weakness of the democratic opposition are correct. If a dictatorship establishes institutions such as elections and legislatures under the mistaken belief that the democratic opposition is weak, then these institutions may, in fact, accelerate the dictatorship's collapse.

The second implication is that it's possible to have authoritarian soft-liners who would like to open up the political system by introducing liberalizing reforms but who choose to do nothing because they're not sure that the democratic opposition is sufficiently weak that they could control the liberalization process if they start it. This suggests that some people living in dictatorships are living under more repressive conditions than need be the case. If the democratic opposition could somehow commit to not taking advantage of the liberalization process by organizing and pushing for full democracy, then soft-liners might be willing to introduce some liberalizing reforms. The result wouldn't be full democracy, but it may be a more palatable and less repressive form of broadened dictatorship. The difficulty facing a weak opposition is that they can't simply tell the soft-liners they're weak, as a strong opposition would say the exact same thing in an attempt to trick the soft-liners into introducing a liberalization process that would eventually result in democratization.

Applying the Theory to Poland

We now illustrate the usefulness of our theory by applying it to help explain the democratic transition that occurred in Poland in 1989. In the late 1970s, the Polish economy was in a state of crisis. The Communist government had borrowed money from the West that it then used to subsidize prices on things like food to keep its citizens satisfied. From 1975 to 1981, Poland's foreign debt increased from $700 million to $23 billion (Hitchcock 2004). When the repayment of this huge debt began to come due, the leader of Poland's Communist Party, Edward Gierek, was forced to raise prices. This led to strikes that started in the Gdansk shipyards. The strikers presented twenty-one demands to the government. These demands included things like freedom of expression, a right to strike, access to the media, and better housing, but the most important one was for a trade union independent of Communist Party control. Unsure of whether the Polish army would actually fire on its own people, Gierek backed down, and the independent trade union, Solidarity, was formed in September 1980. Within two weeks of its formation, 3 million Poles had joined Solidarity under the leadership of an electrician by the name of Lech Walesa. By 1981, Solidarity had 10 million members and had come out in direct opposition to the Communist regime. At this point, Solidarity had become much more than just a trade union.

The Soviets were becoming increasingly worried about the situation in Poland, and there were rumors they were drawing up invasion plans. By now, Gierek had been replaced by the hard-liner General Wojciech Jaruzelski. In December 1981, Jaruzelski declared martial law. Overnight, thousands were arrested, the army occupied factories and smashed strikes, Solidarity was banned, and a military dictatorship was established. Martial law remained in place until 1983. This particular episode in Polish history illustrates just how a period of liberalization could get out of control and eventually produce a repressive backlash resulting in the coming to power of hard-liners like Jaruzelski—a "narrow dictatorship" in the terms of our theory.

Despite attempts to solve the economic problems that plagued Poland, the economy didn't significantly improve over the next few years. As a new wave of strikes threatened to get out of control and turn violent in mid-1988, the Polish Communist Party (PUWP) attempted to introduce a new period of liberalization. In December 1988 the government agreed to convene a conference with the banned trade union Solidarity to see if they could hammer out a compromise. These talks, which took place between February and April 1989, became known as the Roundtable Talks. At these talks, it was agreed that Solidarity would be legalized and that nationwide legislative elections would occur in June. The goal of this liberalization process was to defuse social unrest, co-opt the democratic opposition, and get Solidarity to lend its moral authority to the electoral process.

Like most elections in dictatorships, the proposed legislative elections in Poland were not entirely open. All 100 seats in the Polish Senate were to be freely contested, but 65 percent of the seats in the lower house, or Sejm, were reserved for the Communists and their allies. With 65 percent of the seats in the Sejm, the Communists could expect to appoint the prime minister; they were already guaranteed the presidency because there were to be no presidential elections. The Polish Communist Party expected to do quite well in the legislative elections and didn't believe that Solidarity was strong enough to realistically challenge its hold on power. Just after introducing martial law in 1981, General Jaruzelski had established a special Center for Public Opinion Research (CBOS; Kaminski 1999). CBOS was designed to provide information about the level of support enjoyed by the regime among the public and to reduce incentives for bureaucrats and administrators to paint an overly rosy picture of regime stability. Opinion polls since the mid-1980s had consistently shown that the Communist Party enjoyed more confidence than Solidarity.

Given the beliefs that the Communist Party had about the strength of Solidarity, the election results came as a complete surprise. Solidarity won all 35 percent of the Sejm seats it was allowed to contest and 99 of the 100 seats in the Senate. Up until the time the election results were announced, the process surrounding the Roundtable Talks had been understood as one designed to bring about a "big thaw" and not the end of Communist rule. The election results of June 4, 1989, and the overwhelming victory for Solidarity changed this understanding dramatically. That night, a popular Polish actress, Joanna Szczepkowska, announced on official television: "Friends, this is the end of communism in our country!" What happened next, though, also came as a surprise. The 65 percent of the guaranteed seats had "symbolically" been divided between the Communist Party (37.6 percent) and the so-called "deaf and speechless" puppet parties that were allied to it (26.9 percent). After the election, two of these previously loyal parties joined forces with Solidarity to give it more than 50 percent of the Sejm seats. With this legislative majority, Solidarity was able to appoint the first non-Communist prime minister in Eastern Europe in forty years. In contrast to 1981, the Soviets now made it abundantly clear they would not intervene in Polish affairs, which meant that the Communists could not feasibly break the agreement they'd reached with Solidarity and reverse the liberalization process. As we saw earlier in the chapter, the events in Poland had the effect of encouraging the democratic opposition in other East European countries to challenge their own Communist rulers. Within months, Communist control in Eastern Europe had essentially come to an end.

As our theory of top-down democratic transitions predicted, one of the key elements in Poland's democratic transition was the Communist Party's incorrect beliefs about the strength of Solidarity. The opinion surveys CBOS conducted turned out to be poor indicators of the political support enjoyed by Solidarity. Although they were carefully conducted, they were deeply flawed in many ways. For example, roughly 30 percent of respondents refused to complete the surveys. To a large extent, this high refusal rate was the result of Solidarity supporters not wanting to interact with Communist institutions. Many of those who opposed Communist rule but who actually agreed to complete the surveys would have falsified their preferences out of fear anyway. Much of the Solidarity organization remained underground, out of sight of the Communist Party. The considerable strength of this underground Solidarity network is described by a former colleague, Marek Kaminski, who also spent time in a Polish jail as a political prisoner:

In 1985, I was running an underground publishing house, STOP, that employed about twenty full-time workers and up to 100 moonlighters. Between 1982 and 1989, we published about thirty-five titles of more than 100,000 books combined. We were a part of a decentralized network that included about 100 underground publishing houses, hundreds of periodicals, thousands of trade union organizations with a hierarchically organized leadership structure, a few Nobel Prize winners, and even underground theaters, galleries, and video rentals. We called it an "independent society." (2004, 2)

It's worth noting that Kaminski was a twenty-two-year-old student at Warsaw University in 1985—probably not much older than most of you reading this book. It's easy to see from what Kaminski writes why the Polish Communist Party might have seriously overestimated its own strength relative to that of Solidarity. Mistaken beliefs were crucial to the Polish transition to democracy in 1989, and they are, in fact, central to top-down democratic transitions more generally.

CONCLUSION

Democratic transitions tend to result from bottom-up processes, in which the people rise up to overthrow an authoritarian regime in a popular revolution, or from top-down processes, in which dictatorial elites introduce liberalizing reforms that inadvertently lead to democracy. In this chapter, we've examined bottom-up and top-down democratic transitions drawing on historical evidence from Eastern Europe.

Collective action theory throws light on why bottom-up democratic transitions like those that took place in East Germany, Czechoslovakia, and Romania in 1989 are so rare and why authoritarian regimes frequently appear stable. Because democracy is a form of public good, attempts at collective action to bring it about suffer from a free-rider problem. This means that individuals have strong incentives not to participate in mass protests or demonstrations calling for democratic reforms and instead free ride on the actions of others. The end result is that public displays of opposition are extremely rare in dictatorships. A consequence of this is that authoritarian elites usually seem, at least on the surface, to have a strong hold on power.

Because there can be significant dangers associated with publicly opposing dictatorships, individuals who dislike authoritarian regimes tend not to reveal their true preferences—instead of opposing the dictatorship in public, they support it. The prevalence of this type of preference falsification helps to explain the puzzle of why popular revolutions nearly always come as a surprise yet appear so inevitable in hindsight. Revolutions come as a surprise because nobody can be exactly sure about the true level of opposition in a dictatorship—societies can come to the brink of revolution without anyone's realizing it. Revolutions frequently appear inevitable in hindsight because few people will openly claim to have supported the old dictatorial regime, even if they did, once it has been overthrown and replaced by a democracy; the danger now comes from publicly opposing the democracy. The tipping models we examined in this chapter provide further insight into why revolutions are so unpredictable and why even small changes in people's preferences can sometimes rapidly transform previously subservient individuals into revolutionary protesters. Because each society has a different distribution of revolutionary thresholds, policies or actions that lead to a revolutionary cascade in one dictatorship may have little, or at least appear to have little, effect in some other dictatorship.

Our analysis of top-down democratic transitions like the one that occurred in Poland in 1989 suggests that they can happen only when someone makes a mistake. Although authoritarian elites sometimes introduce periods of liberalization, the goal of liberalization policies is typically to strengthen and stabilize the dictatorship rather than produce a democratic transition. In effect, the objective of the dictatorship is to broaden its social base in an attempt to maintain its hold on power. According to the theory we presented in this chapter, top-down democratic transitions won't occur if the relevant actors—the authoritarian elite and democratic opposition groups—know everything there is to know about each other. They *can* occur, however, if a lack of information leads actors to have mistaken beliefs about the types of actors with whom they're interacting. For example, a democratic transition can occur in our theory if the authoritarian elite mistakenly believes that the opposition is weak when, in fact, it's strong. Our analysis of the strategic interaction between an authoritarian elite and a democratic opposition highlights the important role that information, beliefs, and uncertainty can play in democratic transitions—and politics more generally.

We should remind readers that the distinction between top-down and bottom-up transitions we've made in this chapter is, to some extent, an analytical convenience. Bottom-up transitions may *begin* with the largely autonomous actions of mass publics—like many of the demonstrations in the Middle East and North Africa (MENA) region in the spring of 2011—but once they do, opposition groups often become involved in a game of strategic interaction with elites. In some cases, elites may respond to pressures from below with liberalizing reforms, or at least the promise thereof. For example, Egypt's Hosni Mubarak responded to the first wave of protests in January 2011 with promises of a crackdown. But when his military seemed unwilling to engage in widespread repression, he promised to step down in six months after an election to choose his successor. This move—clearly in response to bottom-up pressures—could be thought of as the start of the decision tree associated with our strategic theory of top-down democratic transitions. Not surprisingly, however, since this offer came from a position of weakness relative to the opposition, it didn't lead to a broadened dictatorship. Instead, the opposition organized another wave of protests and demanded that Mubarak step down immediately. A few weeks later Mubarak did, in fact, step down, and new elections were held in 2012. Within a year, though, the newly elected president, Mohammed Morsi, was ousted in a military coup, his supporters were attacked, and the constitution was suspended. Thus, continued mobilization by the opposition has led to repression and a narrow dictatorship in Egypt, at least for now.

The bottom-up pressures for democracy expressed across the MENA region during the spring of 2011 have not, with the exception of Tunisia, led to democratic transitions. In many cases, the Arab Spring has resulted in authoritarian reactions similar to the "return to normalcy" that occurred following the 1968 Prague Spring (see Box 7.5, "Prague Spring, 1968"). In an analysis written shortly after the MENA protests, Way (2011) argued that there were reasons to be pessimistic about the probability of successful democratic transitions in many of the countries that were experiencing pressures for change in the MENA region. He argued that a decade after the fall of communism, structural factors such as the level of economic development and the presence of natural resources turned out to be the best predictors of which Eastern European countries would experience successful democratic consolidations. As we suggested in Chapter 5, these factors don't provide the basis for optimism in most of the MENA countries. In addition, Way argued that external factors encouraging democracy in Eastern Europe, such as the hands-off approach the Soviet Union adopted and the desire of the Eastern European countries to join the democratic club of the European Union, are also largely absent in the MENA region. In fact, concerns about radical Islam and access to oil resources have historically led the United States to support authoritarian regimes in the region. Nearly eight years after the Arab Spring, it's clear that the early optimism felt by many participants was not warranted.

Key Concepts

third wave of democratization—the surge in democratic transitions that has occurred around the world since 1974

bottom-up democratic transition—when the people rise up to overthrow an authoritarian regime in a popular revolution

top-down democratic transition—when the dictatorial ruling elite introduces liberalizing reforms that ultimately lead to a democratic transition

Cold War—a period of global geopolitical tension in which countries in the Eastern bloc, primarily the Soviet Union and its satellite states, competed economically, socially, and politically with countries in the Western bloc, primarily the United States and its NATO allies

collective action—the pursuit of some objective, typically the provision of a public good, by a group of individuals

public good—a good that is nonexcludable and nonrivalrous

nonexcludability—a good is nonexcludable when no one can be excluded from consuming it

nonrivalrous—a good is nonrivalrous when its consumption by one individual does not reduce the amount available for consumption by other individuals.

collective action, or free-rider, problem—the idea that individual members of a group often have little incentive to contribute to the provision of a public good that will benefit all members of the group

preference falsification—not revealing one's true preferences

revolutionary threshold—the size of protest at which an individual is willing to participate

revolutionary cascade—when one person's participation triggers the participation of another, which triggers the participation of another, and so on

policy of liberalization—a controlled opening of the political space; it might include the formation of political parties, holding elections, writing a constitution, establishing a judiciary, opening a legislature, and so on

VARIETIES OF DICTATORSHIP

A monarchy is the best kind of government because the King is the owner of the country. Like the owner of a house, when the wiring is wrong, he fixes it.

Italian peasant, quoted in Banfield and Banfield (1958, 26)

There can be no government without an army. No army without money. No money without prosperity. And no prosperity without justice and good administration.

Ibn Qutayba, ninth-century Muslim scholar

OVERVIEW

1. In this chapter, we examine the wide variety of dictatorships around the world. One common way to distinguish between dictatorships is in terms of their "support coalitions." Such an approach indicates that there are three main types of dictatorship: (1) monarchic dictatorships, (2) military dictatorships, and (3) civilian dictatorships. Civilian dictatorships can be further classified into those that are personalist and those that have a dominant regime party.

2. There are two fundamental problems of authoritarian rule. The *problem of authoritarian power-sharing* recognizes that authoritarian regimes face potential intra-elite conflict and that the dictator must satisfy those with whom he shares power. The *problem of authoritarian control* recognizes that authoritarian regimes face potential elite-mass conflict and that the dictator must deal with threats from below. These two problems of authoritarian rule shape the institutional structure, policies, and survival of authoritarian regimes.

3. Selectorate theory provides an explanation for the variation we observe in the economic performance of dictatorships. Selectorate theory distinguishes governments based on the size of their selectorate—those with a say in selecting the leader—and on the size of their winning coalition—those in the selectorate whose support is essential for the leader to stay in office.

4. Leaders in systems with large winning coalitions (democracies) tend to use public goods to keep their supporters happy, whereas those in systems with small winning coalitions (dictatorships) tend to use private goods.

5. Leaders in systems where the winning coalition is large relative to the selectorate, such as monarchic and military dictatorships, must produce good economic performance to keep their supporters loyal. In contrast, leaders in systems where the winning coalition is small relative to the selectorate, such as personalist and dominant-party dictatorships, don't have to work as hard to keep their supporters loyal.

In this chapter, we examine the wide variety of authoritarian regimes that exist around the world. We begin by discussing one common typology of authoritarian regimes that distinguishes dictatorships based on the identity of their "support coalitions." This typology suggests that there are three basic types of authoritarian regime: (1) monarchic dictatorships, (2) military dictatorships, and (3) civilian dictatorships. Civilian dictatorships can be further classified into those that are personalist and those that have a dominant party.

There are two fundamental problems of authoritarian rule (Svolik 2012). The first problem is the *problem of authoritarian power-sharing*. Dictators never rule alone. Instead, they rely on support from key groups and allies within the authoritarian elite with whom they share power. Dictators must keep this support coalition satisfied in order to prevent them from challenging their rule. The second problem is the *problem of authoritarian control*. This problem focuses on the conflict that exists between the authoritarian elite and the masses over which it rules. These two problems of authoritarian rule indicate that dictatorial politics is fundamentally shaped by intra-elite conflict and elite-mass conflict. These two sources of conflict shape the institutional structure adopted by dictatorships and the prospects for authoritarian survival.

In terms of their economic performance, some dictatorships perform poorly, but others perform at least as well as the average democracy. In the remainder of this chapter, we explore why this might be the case with the help of selectorate theory. According to selectorate theory, the key to a country's material well-being has less to do with whether it's democratic or dictatorial and more to do with the size of its "winning coalition" and "selectorate," two terms we'll define in more detail shortly. Once we start to think in terms of the size of the winning coalition and the selectorate, it becomes a lot easier to explain why some countries produce better economic policies and provide more public goods than others.

A COMMON TYPOLOGY OF AUTHORITARIAN REGIMES

Dictatorships are not all alike. Indeed, there's a wide variety of dictatorships, and many different ways in which they could be classified (Geddes, Wright, and Frantz 2014; Hadenius and Teorell 2007; Levitsky and Way 2002; Schedler 2002). Cheibub, Gandhi, and Vreeland (2010) provide one common typology of authoritarian regimes. They suggest that a useful way to distinguish between dictatorships is in terms of how authoritarian rulers are removed from office. As dictators are nearly always deposed by fellow members of the regime (Ezrow and Frantz 2011; Geddes 1999; Svolik 2009), this means classifying dictatorships based on the characteristics of their "inner sanctums" or "support coalitions."

A Three-Way Classification: Monarchy, Military, Civilian

According to this approach, the three basic types of dictatorship are: (1) monarchic dictatorships, (2) military dictatorships, and (3) civilian dictatorships. A **monarchic dictatorship** is an autocracy in which the executive holds power on the basis of family and kin networks. A **military dictatorship** is an autocracy in which the executive relies on the armed forces to hold power. All other dictatorships are **civilian dictatorships**. In Figure 8.1, we illustrate the coding rules Cheibub, Gandhi, and Vreeland (2010, 87) employ for identifying each type of authoritarian regime.

The first goal is to identify the effective head of the government. Although this is relatively straightforward in democracies (see Chapter 10), it's not always as easy in dictatorships. In most cases, the head of a dictatorial government will be a king, a president, or a prime minister. Occasionally, "an *eminence grise* lurks behind the scenes. . . . For example, Somoza and his sons installed figurehead presidents in Nicaragua to formally comply with term limits" (Cheibub, Gandhi, and Vreeland 2010, 88). The second goal is to identify whether the head of government bears the title of "king" *and* whether he has a hereditary successor or predecessor. If this is the case, we have a monarchic dictatorship. The third goal is to identify whether the head of government is a current or past member of the armed forces. If so, we have a military dictatorship. And if not, we have a civilian dictatorship. Leaders who come to power as part of a guerrilla movement or insurgency, such as Fidel Castro in Cuba (1959–2011), Yoweri Museveni

FIGURE 8.1 ■ Classifying Dictatorships

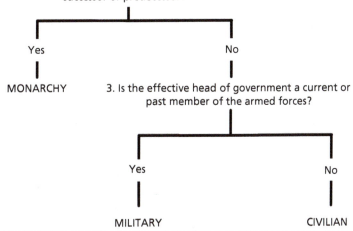

Source: Cheibub, Gandhi, and Vreeland (2010, 87).

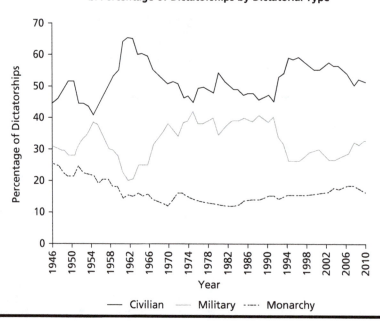

Source: Data from Cheibub, Gandhi, and Vreeland (2010).

in Uganda (1986–), and Paul Kagame in Rwanda (2000–), are considered civilian, rather than military, dictators. Although these leaders often give themselves military titles, they can't rely on the support of the military in the same way that former or current members of the military can. Indeed, the military are often one of the main threats to these types of dictators.

In Figure 8.2 on page 158, we show how the number and percentages of monarchic, military, and civilian dictatorships in the world have changed from 1946 to 2008. The civilian form of dictatorship has always been the most common. The heyday for military dictatorships was in the late 1970s when the military ran almost 40 percent of dictatorships. There's been a significant decline in the number of military dictatorships since the end of the Cold War. While the number of civilian and military dictatorships in the world has changed quite a bit over time, the same is not true of monarchies. This suggests that monarchies have been a particularly stable form of dictatorial regime.

To a large extent, this typology of authoritarian regimes is based on the idea that we can distinguish between different types of dictators in terms of the identity of their support coalitions or what we'll call a little later in the chapter their "winning coalitions." Dictators need to keep their support coalitions happy if they're to stay in power. Although the term *dictator* often conjures up the image of an all-powerful individual, it's important to recognize that all dictators, like their democratic counterparts, rely on the support of a coalition to stay in power.

An implication of this is that when we see a dictator removed from power, we're likely to see him replaced by a defecting member of his own support coalition. As a result, we should frequently see dictators replaced by dictators of a similar type. In fact, there's considerable evidence that this is what happens. Three things can happen when a dictator leaves office (Geddes, Wright, and Frantz 2014). First, democratization may occur with the result that the authoritarian regime is replaced by a democratic regime. Second, the same authoritarian regime may survive but under new leadership. And third, the incumbent authoritarian regime may be replaced by a different type of authoritarian regime. In Table 8.1, we present data showing what happened when 388 authoritarian leaders left office for reasons other than natural death between 1945 and 1996. Dictatorial leaders are replaced by individuals from the same authoritarian regime about 50 percent of the time. Of the 22 monarchs, 11 (50 percent) were replaced by other monarchs. Of the 179 military leaders, 89 (49.7 percent) were replaced by other military leaders. And of the 187 civilian leaders, 103 (55 percent) were replaced by civilian leaders. If we ignore, for the moment, authoritarian leaders who are

TABLE 8.1 ■ Leader Succession in Three Types of Dictatorial Regime, 1946–1996

Type of current dictator	Type of successor				
	Monarchy	Military	Civilian	Democrat	Total
Monarchy	11	6	4	1	22
Military	0	89	38	52	179
Civilian	2	53	103	29	187
Total	13	148	145	82	388

Source: Gandhi and Przeworski (2007, 1289).

Note: Excludes dictators who died of natural causes while in office or who were still in office as of 1996.

succeeded by democratic leaders, then the tendency for authoritarian leaders to be succeeded by leaders of the same type becomes even more pronounced—70 percent of military leaders were followed by a military leader and 65 percent of civilian leaders were followed by civilian leaders. The persistence of an authoritarian leader's type when the particular authoritarian leader is removed is the reason why we often speak not just of individual dictatorial *leaders* but also of dictatorial *regimes*. This point emphasizes the fact that the survival of a dictatorial leader and the survival of a dictatorial regime are not the same thing.

Monarchic Dictatorships

The first type of authoritarian regime comprises monarchies.[1] Dictatorial monarchs rely on their family and kin network to come to power and stay in power. As an example, Gandhi and Przeworski (2007, 1288) note how the emir of Qatar "reshuffled his cabinet in 1992, installing his sons as ministers of defense, finance and petroleum, interior, and economy and trade; his grandson in charge of defense affairs; and his nephews in public health and Islamic affairs." In general, the family and kin members in a monarchy play an important role when it comes to the issue of succession. Although the successor is typically a member of the royal family, she needn't be the monarch's firstborn; that is, the system of succession needn't be based on primogeniture. In fact, Herb (1999, 80) notes that "the most basic rule of the succession [in Kuwait] is that the family 'elects' the ruler by consensus, based on the perception by family leaders of their own best interests." Even if the established procedure for succession is violated in a monarchy, it's typically the case that the new leader must have the support of the royal family elite.

The Kingdom of eSwatini, formerly Swaziland, highlights the important role the royal family can play in choosing the monarch and the lengths that some monarchs go to in order to stabilize their base of societal support (Woods 2012, 2017). Historically, the king (*Ngwenyama,* Lion) and "senior queen" (*Ndlovukati,* She-Elephant) have ruled together. The senior queen is typically the king's mother. When the king's mother is dead, the role of senior queen goes to one of the king's wives. The king and senior queen must come from different families, and they each have separate royal villages that act as their headquarters. No king can appoint his successor to the throne. In fact, the key role in the choice of a successor is played by the Royal Council (*Liqoqo*), a traditional advisory council made up of members of the royal family. The new king must be chosen from the royal family line, the Dlaminis. Although the exact rules of succession are shrouded in secrecy, it's thought that the Royal Council chooses someone who is unmarried and the only child of his mother; the mother, in turn, becomes the new senior queen. The king is expected to consolidate his position over time by choosing wives from every clan. The first two wives are chosen for the king from specific clans—the Matsebula clan and the Motsa clan—by the Royal Council, and their children can't become king. The current king, Makhosetive Dlamini (Mswati III), came to power in 1986 and has fifteen wives and twenty-three children. Other contemporary examples of monarchic dictatorships include Jordan, Bahrain, Kuwait, and Saudi Arabia.

As Figure 8.2 suggests, dictatorial monarchies are a particularly stable form of authoritarian regime. Empirically, monarchic dictatorships suffer from less violence and political instability than other forms of dictatorship, and monarchic leaders survive in office longer than other authoritarian leaders. There's also some evidence that monarchies have more stable property

---

[1]As we'll see in Chapter 10, some democracies—parliamentary democracies—can have a monarch as the head of state. Thus, the presence of a monarch is not necessarily a sign that a country is a dictatorship.

rights and experience faster economic growth than other types of dictatorship (Menaldo 2012). As Table 8.1 indicates, only one monarchic dictatorship (Nepal) has transitioned to democracy in the postwar period. In 1991, the Nepalese king, faced with societal opposition demanding multiparty elections, negotiated a transition to a parliamentary democracy in which he would remain as the head of state. In effect, he agreed to transform Nepal from an authoritarian monarchy to a constitutional monarchy in a parliamentary democracy. Not only are democratic transitions quite rare among monarchic dictatorships, but when a dictatorial monarchy does collapse, it's often followed by periods of violence and the installation of an even more repressive authoritarian regime. As Geddes, Wright, and Frantz (2014, 326) point out, the overthrow of monarchic dictatorships has led to long and bloody civil wars in three countries—Yemen (1962–1970), Ethiopia (1974–1991), and Afghanistan (1978–). Similarly, the Libyan monarchy was replaced by a repressive civilian dictatorship led by Muammar al-Qaddafi (1969–2011), while the Shah of Iran was removed during the 1979 Iranian Revolution and replaced by the Islamist cleric Ayatollah Khomeini (1979–1989).

Why are monarchic dictatorships so stable? Menaldo (2012) argues that monarchic dictatorships have developed a political culture that allows them to solve credible commitment problems with respect to their support coalitions. To motivate his argument, Menaldo starts by contrasting the experience of monarchies in the Middle East and North Africa (MENA) during the Arab Spring of 2011 with the experience of other types of dictatorship in the region. He indicates that monarchies, such as Morocco, Jordan, Saudi Arabia, Bahrain, the United Arab Emirates, and Oman, were largely spared the sort of political violence that plagued dictatorial leaders in the rest of the region. As we noted in Chapter 5, some monarchies, like Saudi Arabia, did feel it necessary to pump billions of dollars into public programs to keep the populace on their side (Ross 2011). Indeed, Bahrain's king Hamad bin Isa al-Khalifa went further than this, imprisoning hundreds of protesters, imposing martial law, and calling in thousands of troops from Saudi Arabia to clamp down on emerging protest movements. Overall, though, the level of political violence and instability in the region's monarchies was considerably less than that in non-monarchic dictatorships, such as those in Tunisia, Egypt, Syria, Yemen, and Libya. Why?

As we noted earlier, monarchs often seek to maintain the loyalty of their support coalition by allowing members of the royal family to colonize government posts that they can then use for their own material benefit. Obviously, other dictatorships distribute rents in a similar way to keep their own support coalitions happy. What's different in monarchies, at least according to Menaldo, is that they've generated a political culture where a leader's promise to distribute rents to his support coalition is more credible than in other types of dictatorship. This "monarchic culture" rests on three things. First, there are clear rules as to who the insiders and outsiders are. In general, monarchies tend to depend on tightly knit family structures that are reinforced through intermarriage. These rules allow insiders to know that their privileged position in the regime is relatively secure. Second, monarchies tend to have rules or norms that indicate exactly how regime rents are to be shared among the various members of the royal family. For example, there is a norm in Kuwait that succession alternates between the two branches of the Sabah family (Herb 1999). This creates a system in which members of the royal family all have a stake in maintaining the regime; in effect, regime collapse threatens access to the political and economic rents they've been promised. Third, monarchies tend to have institutions that allow members of the royal family to monitor the actions of the monarch and enforce the norms regarding the distribution of regime rents. As our earlier example from the Kingdom of eSwatini indicates, most monarchies have royal courts or appointed legislatures that enforce rules relating to the succession of monarchs and that place limits on the actions monarchs can take. These royal courts act as commitment devices, forcing monarchs to follow through on their promises relating to things like the distribution of regime rents. In many ways, these royal courts perform a role similar to the legislatures that were created by monarchs seeking to raise revenue in early modern Europe (see Chapter 5).

Military Dictatorships

The second type of authoritarian regime comprises military dictatorships. In most cases, military leaders rule as part of a "junta," or committee. High-ranking officers who take power on behalf of the military typically have small juntas that comprise the three or four heads of the various armed services. Lower-ranked officers who come to power, perhaps as part of a military coup, often have larger juntas as they seek to build the support necessary to consolidate their hold on power. Military rulers often portray "themselves as 'guardians of the national interest,' saving the nation from the disaster wrought by corrupt and myopic civilian politicians" (Cheibub, Gandhi, and Vreeland 2010, 85). This helps to explain why these juntas frequently adopt titles such as the "Military Council of National Salvation," as occurred in Poland in 1981 when General Jaruzelski imposed martial law, or the "National Council for Peace and Order," as occurred in Thailand following the 2014 military coup.

Of course, it's not clear that military rulers actually have such altruistic motivations. Some scholars have argued, for instance, that military coups are more often than not motivated by class conflict or corporate interests (Finer 1988; Nordlinger 1977; Stepan 1971). For example, many of the military juntas in Latin American countries, such as Argentina (1976), Chile (1973), and Guatemala (1954), resulted from right-wing coups that toppled left-wing democratic governments threatening to redistribute wealth from the rich to the poor (Drake 1996; O'Donnell 1973; Stepan 1985). Similarly, the military junta—the Supreme Council of Armed Forces (SCAF)—that came to power in Egypt after protests forced long-time president Hosni Mubarak to step down in the spring of 2011 was widely perceived to be acting in its own economic interests. The military controlled anywhere from 5 percent to 45 percent of the Egyptian economy (Fadel 2011). It's perhaps not surprising, then, that the military moved against Hosni Mubarak during the Arab Spring protests in 2011; the military saw the people camped out in Tahrir Square as "customers," and it no longer believed that Mubarak could protect its economic interests.

The most pressing threat to the stability of military dictatorships tends to come from within the military itself. Consider the history of military rule in the West African country of Guinea. A military junta, called the Military Committee of National Recovery (CMRN), was established in Guinea in April 1984 following a coup by Lieutenant-Colonel Lansana Conté. The coup had followed the death of independent Guinea's first president, Sékou Touré. The subsequent history of Guinea has seen numerous military protests, coups, and countercoups, some successful and some not. President Conté, for example, had to suppress his first military revolt, led by his deputy Colonel Diarra Traoré, as early as 1985. In 1996 there was another attempted coup when the military mutinied over poor living conditions. The military junta responded by introducing various reforms aimed at appeasing the armed forces. Lansana Conté eventually died on December 23, 2008, after a long illness. According to the constitution, new presidential elections were supposed to be held within sixty days. However, within six hours of the announcement of Conté's death, there was another military coup, this time led by the head of the army, Captain Moussa Dadis Camara ("Military 'Seizes Power'" 2008). In December 2009, President Camara suffered a head wound in an attempted assassination and countercoup led by his aide-de-camp, Lieutenant Aboubacar Sidiki "Toumba" Diakité

(Howden 2009). Camara was forced to leave the country for medical treatment in Morocco and eventually agreed not to return. The military junta then handed power over to Alpha Condé, who won the 2010 presidential elections. After several postponements due to security issues, legislative elections were finally held in 2013 amid ethnic violence and charges of election fraud from opposition groups.

Although we've focused here on military juntas in Guinea, the threat that factions within the military pose to stability is commonplace among all military dictatorships. Indeed, power has changed hands thirteen times between various military factions in Guatemala since 1945 (Gandhi and Przeworski 2007, 1288). Contemporary military dictatorships include Thailand and Chad.

Empirically, military dictatorships tend to have short durations and are more likely to end with negotiations as opposed to violence than other types of authoritarian regime (Geddes 2003). There's also some evidence that military dictatorships are more likely to leave behind competitive and democratic forms of government than other types of dictatorship. As Table 8.1 indicates, 29.1 percent of military dictatorships between 1946 and 1996 ended with democratic transitions; only 15.5 percent of civilian dictatorships and 4.5 percent of monarchic dictatorships ended with democratic transitions. What explains these empirical patterns?

The military tends to value discipline and cohesiveness, autonomy from civilian intervention, and military budgets large enough to attract recruits and buy weapons (Geddes 2003, 54). Officers tend to participate in coups only when a government threatens the interests, or the very existence, of the military (Nordlinger 1977; Stepan 1971). As we've seen, the Egyptian military's decision to end its loyalty to the Mubarak regime following popular protests in 2011 and establish a military junta can be understood in this light. If militaries do come to power, though, they often carry with them "the seeds of their own destruction" (Geddes 2003, 63). Disagreements over, say, economic policy or the distribution of office benefits among senior officers can lead to factionalization. In these circumstances, many officers prefer to return to the barracks and allow elections rather than risk the unity of the military by trying to cling to power. Importantly, the value of the exit option—the value associated with giving up power—is considerably higher for military dictatorships than for other forms of dictatorship. The fact that the military has all the "guns" means that it retains a credible threat to re-intervene in politics in a way that other groups don't necessarily have. In other words, the military can step down from power with a greater sense of assurance that whoever wins the elections will still have to take account of the military's preferences due to the possibility of future coups. In many cases, the military will actually negotiate the handover of power to make sure that its interests are indeed protected.

Marinov and Goemans indicate that the shorter duration of military dictatorships and the propensity of military juntas to leave behind competitive elections are even more pronounced in the post–Cold War period. Some of their empirical evidence is presented graphically in Figure 8.3. There were 167 military coups between 1960 and 1990 in the Cold War period. Only 25 percent of these coups were followed by competitive elections within five years. In contrast, there were 43 military coups between 1991 and 2004 in the post–Cold War period. As we can see, military coups are less common in the post–Cold War period. More significant, though, is the fact that fully 74 percent of these coups were followed by competitive elections within five years.

What explains this dramatic difference between the Cold War and post–Cold War periods? Coup leaders are often very sensitive to how the international community will respond to their actions, particularly if they depend on the outside world for foreign aid. Marinov and Goemans (2014, 805) argue that foreign countries, particularly Western ones, exerted

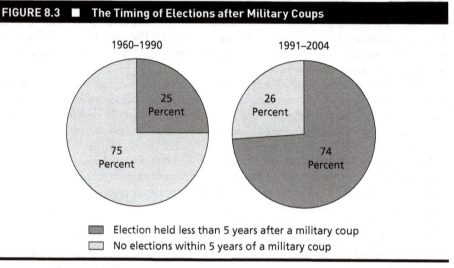

FIGURE 8.3 ■ The Timing of Elections after Military Coups

1960–1990

25 Percent

75 Percent

1991–2004

26 Percent

74 Percent

◼ Election held less than 5 years after a military coup
▢ No elections within 5 years of a military coup

Source: Goemans, Hein, and Nikolay Marinov. 2011. "From Coups to Voting: The International Community and the Coup d'état." Unpublished manuscript.

much less pressure on military dictatorships to hold elections during the Cold War period because they viewed the world as a "chessboard of West vs. East." Essentially, Western countries, like the United States, often preferred to support staunchly anti-Communist military juntas during the Cold War rather than encourage competitive elections that might produce left-leaning governments sympathetic to the Soviet Union.[2] According to Marinov and Goemans, the demise of the Soviet Union has enabled Western countries to push a more pro-democracy agenda. Since 1997, for example, US presidents have been bound by an act of Congress to suspend foreign aid to any recipient country that experiences a coup d'état. In line with their argument, Marinov and Goemans (2014) find that a country's dependence on Western aid increases the likelihood that a postcoup election will take place, but only in the post–Cold War period.

This line of reasoning has led some to wonder whether coups might even be "good" for democracy. Thyne and Powell (2014), for example, suggest that coups, by providing a "shock" to the system, can create opportunities for liberalization that would not otherwise exist. Along similar lines, Collier (2009, n.p.) argues that "coups and the threat of coups can be a significant weapon in fostering democracy" in Africa. As an example of a "good coup," we might consider the February 2010 coup in Niger when the military stepped in to remove the increasingly autocratic president, Mamadou Tandja (Armstrong 2010). Within a year, the military-led Supreme Council for the Restoration of Democracy had allowed free and fair legislative and presidential elections, which brought the former opposition leader Mahamadou Issoufou to power (Freedom House 2012). This optimistic view of military coups, though, is not consistent with the broader empirical evidence. For example, Derpanopoulos and colleagues (2016) find that although military coups in dictatorships are more likely to be followed by democratic transitions in the post–Cold War period than in the Cold War period, the most common outcome is the establishment of a new and more repressive form of authoritarian regime.

---

[2]In some cases, Western countries even helped the military with its coup. For example, it's known that the Nixon administration and the CIA helped in the military overthrow of the left-leaning President Salvador Allende in Chile in 1973.

The apparent break in the behavior of Western countries toward military juntas, and dictatorships more generally, in the post–Cold War world shouldn't be overstated either. It's true that the West is no longer in a global competition with a foe like the Soviet Union and that, therefore, there are fewer countries on which the West must rely to protect its strategic interests. In certain regions of the world, though, Western influence continues to be challenged. In many places, this challenge comes from countries like China or radical Islamist groups like al-Qaida, ISIL, or the Taliban. It's not clear whether Western countries will support elections in these regions with the inherent uncertainties they bring or whether they'll prefer to prop up dictatorships that promise to protect Western interests. To support our concerns here, we point to the reaction of the United States toward the military coup that took place in Egypt in 2013. Following the ouster of the longtime dictator Hosni Mubarak during the Arab Spring, Mohamed Morsi, the candidate for the Islamist Muslim Brotherhood, became in 2012 the first democratically elected president in Egypt's history. The following year, the Egyptian military intervened to remove President Morsi from power. There was a mixed international reaction to these events, with the United States refusing to call them a "military coup" because the 1997 Congressional Act we mentioned earlier would have required it to freeze the substantial economic and military aid it provided to Egypt.

Civilian Dictatorships

The third type of authoritarian regime comprises civilian dictatorships. Unlike monarchic and military dictatorships, which can rely on family and kin networks or the strength of the armed forces to stay in power, civilian dictators don't have an immediate institutional base of support; instead they have to create one. Many civilian dictators do this with the help of regime parties or personality cults. For this reason, some scholars distinguish between two subcategories of civilian dictatorships: (1) dominant-party dictatorships and (2) personalist dictatorships (Geddes 1999).

Dominant-Party Dictatorships

In a **dominant-party dictatorship**, "one party dominates access to political office and control over policy, though other parties may exist and compete as minor players in elections" (Geddes 2003, 51). Just as political parties play an important role in recruiting and socializing the political elite in democracies (see Chapter 12), they can perform a similar function in civilian dictatorships. Consider the role played by the Communist Party in the former Soviet Union (CPSU). For all intents and purposes, membership in the CPSU was a necessary condition for becoming part of the political, economic, and academic ruling class—the *nomenklatura* (Gershenson and Grossman 2001). Describing the Soviet *nomenklatura* in the 1980s, Voslensky (1984, 98) wrote that "while a party card is of course no guarantee of success, lack of it is a guarantee that you will not have a career of any kind." Power and authority increased the higher one rose in the party, as did the monetary and nonmonetary benefits. For example, members of the *nomenklatura* were able to enjoy many of the things denied to the average citizen—they got to shop in well-stocked stores, they had access to foreign goods, and they were allowed to travel abroad. As George Orwell ([1949] 1977, 192) describes in his novel *1984*,

> By the standards of the early twentieth century, even a member of the Inner Party lives an austere, laborious kind of life. Nevertheless, the few luxuries that he does enjoy—his large well-appointed flat, the better texture of his clothes, the better quality of his food and drink and tobacco, his two or three servants, his private motorcar or helicopter—set him in a different world from a member of the Outer Party, and

the members of the Outer Party have a similar advantage in comparison with the submerged masses.

As citizens gained membership into the CPSU and advanced up its ranks, they would be increasingly socialized into following the party line. Demonstrating loyalty to the party was crucial to gaining and retaining the benefits of power associated with membership in the *nomenklatura.*

A further illustration of how political parties can be used to control the masses comes from Gandhi and Przeworski (2006, 25).

> Consider communist Poland. Even though in 1948 communists forced their major rival, the Polish Socialist Party, into a "merger," thus creating the Polish United Workers Party (PUWP), they tolerated a pre-war left-wing United Peasant Party (ZSL), a small private business party (SD), and a Catholic group with direct ties to Moscow. After 1956, two other Catholic groups were allowed to organize. Even though these parties functioned under separate labels in the legislature, they were presented to the voters as a single list, with all candidates approved by the communists. Hence, elections only ratified the distribution of parliamentary seats and the specific appointees of the Communist Party. One way to think of this "multipartism" is that it represented a menu of contracts, allowing people characterized by different political attitudes (and differing degrees of opportunism) to sort themselves out. Membership in each party entailed a different degree of identification with the regime: highest for members of the PUWP, lower for those joining the Peasant Party, the lowest for the Catholic groups. In exchange, these memberships offered varying amounts of perks and privileges, in the same order. Someone not willing to join the Communist Party, with the social opprobrium this membership evoked among Catholic peasants, may have joined the Peasant Party. This choice entailed a less direct commitment and fewer perks, but it did signify identification with the regime, and it did furnish perks and privileges. This separating equilibrium maximized support for the regime and visibly isolated those who were not willing to make any gesture of support.

Hough (1980, 33) makes a similar point, claiming that "the Soviet government has thus far been skillful in the way it has tied the fate of many individuals in the country to the fate of the regime. By admitting such a broad range of the educated public into the party, it has provided full opportunities for upward social mobility for those who avoid dissidence, while giving everyone in the managerial class reason to wonder what the impact of an anti-Communist revolution would be on him or her personally."

The value of a regime party is not restricted to only Communist countries. For example, Magaloni (2006) provides a good description of the types of mobilization techniques that the Institutional Revolutionary Party (PRI) used for many years in Mexico to signal its own strength and highlight the weakness of the opposition. For example, she describes how the PRI regime put in place a series of policies that prevented peasants from rising out of poverty, thereby making them systematically dependent on state patronage through the PRI. Magaloni goes on to talk about the "tragic brilliance" of the regime, in which "citizens' choices are free, yet they are constrained by a series of strategic dilemmas that compel them to remain loyal to the regime" (2006, 19). She also describes how the PRI established various institutions to maintain the loyalty of its party members. For instance, the PRI imposed term limits, which increased the dependence of legislators on the party for future jobs, and at the same time kept ambitious politicians in check as they waited for their turn in power.

After authoritarian monarchies, dominant-party dictatorships are the longest-lived dictatorships (Brownlee 2009; Geddes 2003). Party cadres in a dominant-party dictatorship are similar to politicians in a democracy in that they want to hold office. The best strategy for maintaining access to office is to stay united. Although policy differences and competition for leadership positions are likely to produce factionalism in dominant-party regimes just like they do in other types of dictatorship, everyone is better off if they can stay united and maintain access to power (Geddes 2003, 59). Splits run the risk that an opposition party will come to power. And even if one of the factions is able to stay in office following a split, its grip on power is often significantly weakened. This is why majority factions within regime parties try to co-opt minority factions rather than exclude them from power. When crises do emerge, the dominant faction usually responds by "granting modest increases in political participation, increasing opposition representation in the legislature, and granting some opposition demands for institutional change" (Geddes 2003, 68).

This logic helps to explain why regime parties often engage in widespread electoral fraud even when they know they're going to win elections. Until recently, the traditional view of electoral fraud was that it is most likely to occur when elections are expected to be close, that is, when the incumbent feels she needs to buy some votes to push her over the finish line. However, this view of electoral fraud is not consistent with the empirical record (Simpser 2008, 2013). Incumbents frequently engage in electoral fraud even when there is little chance they'll lose. As an example, consider Georgia's president, Eduard Shevardnadze. As Simpser (2008, 1) points out, Shevardnadze was expected to be reelected in the 2000 presidential elections by a very wide margin. One poll shortly before the election suggested he would win 52 percent of the vote compared with just 19 percent for his closest rival. Nevertheless, Shevardnadze engaged in widespread electoral manipulation and won with close to 80 percent of the vote. One reason for engaging in electoral fraud in this type of situation is that it can help deter regime party defections, discourage opponents in the future, and reduce the likelihood of protests against the dictatorship. In effect, lopsided electoral victories signal the strength of the regime party and the futility of challenging it.

The types of co-optation strategies employed in dominant-party dictatorships obviously require that the dominant faction have sufficient resources to buy off potential rivals and convince minority factions that they're better off sticking with the regime party than siding with the opposition. This suggests that economic downturns can create problems with stability for dominant-party regimes. Stability is also threatened when opposition parties or rival factions do better in elections than expected. Given the tools that dictatorial regimes have at their disposal to guarantee electoral victory, a close-run election can signal weakness in the regime, thereby encouraging opponents. When combined with an economic downturn or widespread protest, a close election result can trigger mass defection from the regime party. As Way (2011) writes, "If a crisis convinces ruling elites that continued loyalty threatens their future access to patronage, it may trigger a bandwagoning effect in which politicians defect en masse to the opposition. As one defecting member of the ruling UNIP party in Zambia that collapsed in 1991 put it, 'only a stupid fly . . . follows a dead body to the grave.'"[3] Arguably, this is the scenario that preceded many of the colored revolutions that occurred in Eastern Europe in the early 2000s.[4]

---

[3]Lucan Way, February 21, 2011 (blog post). "Some Thoughts on Authoritarian Durability in the Middle East." *Monkey Cage* blog (http://themonkeycage.org/blog/2011/02/21/some_thoughts_on_authoritarian/).

[4]The phrase *colored revolutions* refers to revolutions, such as the Bulldozer Revolution in Serbia in 2000, the Rose Revolution in Georgia in 2003, the Orange Revolution in Ukraine in 2004, and the Tulip Revolution in Kyrgyzstan in 2005 (Tucker 2007).

Personalist Dictatorships

In contrast to the leaders in dominant-party dictatorships who use regime parties to maintain their hold on power, some civilian dictators attempt to establish a more personalist form of rule. "Institutionally, what [these **personalist dictatorships**] have in common is that although they are often supported by parties and militaries, these particular organizations have not become sufficiently developed or autonomous to prevent the leader from taking personal control of policy decisions and the selection of regime personnel" (Geddes 2003, 53). Indeed, a personalist dictator often deliberately undermines these institutions so they can't act as a power base for a potential rival. For example, it's typical for regime personnel to be rotated frequently at the whim of the leader to prevent them from building independent bases of support. These dictatorships are also often characterized by a weak or nonexistent press, a strong secret police, and an arbitrary use of state violence that keeps the population living in constant fear.

Many of these dictators cultivate elaborate personality cults in an attempt to maintain the loyalty of their support coalition and the citizenry more generally. These personality cults often seem strange to outsiders. Consider Saparmurat Niyazov, who ruled Turkmenistan from 1985 to 2006. His book, the *Ruhnama* (Book of Souls), which was part spiritual and moral guidance, part revisionist history, and part autobiography, served as the chief textbook for students at all levels of the education system from elementary schools to universities. The *Ruhnama*'s influence extended well beyond the education system, with new government employees tested on the book during interviews and all citizens seeking a driving license required to take a sixteen-hour course on the book ("Turkmenistan Wrestles" 2004). Gurbangly Berdymukhammedov, who replaced Niyazov following his death in 2006, eventually removed the *Ruhnama* as a mandatory subject in Turkmen schools. However, he appears to have simply replaced the *Ruhnama* in the school curriculum with several books of his own (Fitzpatrick 2011).

Kim Jong-il, who ruled North Korea from 1994 until his death in December 2011, inherited a similar personality cult from his father, Kim Il-sung, the "eternal president" ("Toughs at the Top" 2004). Kim Jong-il, who was referred to as the "Supreme Leader," "Dear Leader," "Our Father," and "the General," claimed to be able to control the weather with his mood and to be able to teleport from place to place (Hassig and Oh 2009; Kang and Rigoulot 2005). He was also known to issue various hairstyle guidelines as part of grooming and dress standards. These guidelines have in the past emphasized the negative effects of long hair on human intelligence, noting that long hair consumes a great deal of nutrition and thus robs the brain of energy ("N Korea Wages War on Long Hair" 2005).

Muammar al-Qaddafi is another dictator who also established a cult of personality before his death in 2011. In a similar way to Niyazov in Turkmenistan, al-Qaddafi forced a generation of Libyans to grow up studying his *Green Book* as a great work of social and political theory. Some have described the book as part Chairman Mao, who himself had written the *Red Book*, and part Marx and Engels ("What Now for Colonel Gaddafi's Green Book?" 2011). It appears that tablet-like statues of its three volumes were erected in many Libyan towns. Al-Qaddafi often portrayed himself as a revolutionary against colonial powers who didn't seek power for himself. In keeping with the precepts set out in *The Green Book,* "Colonel [al-Q]addafi eventually gave up any official title in the Libyan government, giving rise to one of the prime examples of Libyan doublespeak. While everyone in Libya regards Colonel [al-Q]addafi as the all-powerful ruler behind every decision of state, he often answers critics calling on him to surrender power by saying it is too late—he already has" (Kirkpatrick 2011).

Al-Qaddafi's outlandish claims perhaps peaked during the Arab Spring in 2011 when he claimed that the people protesting his rule were high on drugs supplied by Osama bin Laden and al-Qaida ("Libya Protests" 2011).

Given how strange these personality cults seem to outsiders (and presumably insiders), it's worth thinking about exactly what role they play in keeping authoritarian leaders in power. Personality cults are often viewed in the media as the creation of narcissistic and megalomaniacal dictators who wish to be flattered and deified. However, this view, while almost certainly true in many respects, probably understates the role that personality cults play in maintaining dictatorial rule. The standard story with respect to personality cults is that they gradually alter the beliefs of the citizenry through a steady process of state indoctrination. By eliminating alternative sources of information, it's thought that personalist dictators are able to use their control of the state media to persuade citizens of their amazing powers and leadership qualities, thereby generating support and loyalty. In effect, the standard story suggests that personality cults are designed to create citizen loyalty by producing false beliefs in the population.

The problem with this story, though, is that the personality cults are often ridiculously unbelievable. Did the North Koreans really believe that Kim Jong-il could control the weather with his mood and teleport from one place to another? Marquez (2011) suggests that although "cults of personality can sometimes 'persuade' people of the superhuman character of leaders . . . or . . . draw on people's gullibility in the absence of alternative sources of information and their need for identification with high status individuals, they are best understood in terms of how dictators can harness the dynamics of 'signaling' for the purposes of social control."[5]

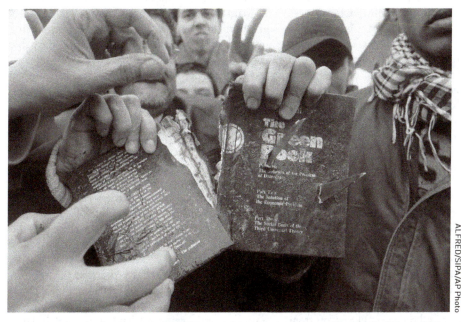

Protesters ripping up Muammar al-Qaddafi's *The Green Book* in the Libyan town of Benghazi in February 2011.

[5]The following discussion of personality cults is based on a very interesting blog post by Xavier Marquez, a political scientist at Victoria University in Wellington, New Zealand, on March 14, 2011 (http://abandoned footnotes.blogspot.com/2011/03/simple-model-of-cults-of-personality.html).

This alternative view of personality cults is premised on something we discussed in Chapter 7, namely, that individuals living in dictatorships often engage in preference falsification. The **dictator's dilemma** is that he relies on repression to stay in power, but this repression creates incentives for everyone to lie so that the dictator never knows his true level of support (Wintrobe 2001). In effect, a dictator is often confronted by two rather unsatisfactory choices. On the one hand, he can limit repression and allow free debate, thereby learning his true level of societal support. This often occurs when the dictator has insufficient resources to establish a reliable spy network to monitor the population (Egorov, Guriev, and Sonin 2009). On the other hand, he can use repression, but run the risk that he'll be surprised by his lack of support at some future point in time.

This is where personality cults can be useful. As Marquez (2011, para. 7) notes, "The dictator wants a *credible* signal of your support; merely staying silent and not saying anything negative won't cut it. In order to be credible, the signal has to be costly: you have to be willing to say that the dictator is not merely OK, but a superhuman being, and you have to be willing to take some concrete actions showing your undying love for the leader." These actions often include things like denouncing others who lack sufficient faith in the leader and ostentatious displays of the dictator's image or ideology. This view of the role of personality cults helps to explain why dictators often make outlandish claims that strain credulity. By slowly raising the degree to which his claims are "over the top," a dictator can better gauge his true level of societal support by finding the point at which the population is no longer willing to publicly accept his "incredible" claims.

In effect, personality cults have three benefits from the perspective of the dictator, in addition to stroking his ego. First, they make it hard for opposition groups to organize and coordinate their actions. Citizens are unwilling to reveal their true preferences for fear of being denounced by others, thereby making it difficult for opposition groups to evaluate their true strength. Second, they help the dictator gain a better handle on his level of societal support. And third, they will, in fact, persuade some segments of society to become "true believers" in the dictator. Marquez (2011, para. 11) writes that personality cults can be difficult to establish in the first place but goes on to note that "once the cult of personality is in full swing, it practically runs itself, turning every person into a sycophant and basically destroying everyone's dignity. It creates an equilibrium of lies that can be hard to disrupt unless people get a credible signal that others basically hate the dictator as much as they do and are willing to do something about that."

To a large extent, we can think of intra-regime politics in a personalist dictatorship as involving the leader's faction and a minority rival faction, with the leader's faction having to decide how much of the spoils of office to share with the rival faction to keep it from defecting (Geddes 2003, 60). Whereas it's common for majority factions in dominant-party dictatorships to try to co-opt or buy off minority factions, this is much less the case in personalist dictatorships, where the leader's faction frequently keeps tight control over the spoils of office. The reason the leader's faction can do this has to do with the huge risk that the minority faction faces if it defects. Recall that in a personalist dictatorship, all spoils from office come from remaining loyal to the leader. If the rival faction defects, it risks everything—life, liberty, and property. The payoff from successfully overthrowing the dictator may well be large, but so are the costs of failure. This, combined with a highly repressive security apparatus that limits the likelihood of a successful overthrow, explains why the leader's faction rarely shares the benefits of office with the rival faction. In effect, the leader's faction gives just enough benefits to the rival faction to prevent it from defecting and keeps the rest for itself.

As with dominant-party systems, the stability of personalist dictatorships rests on them having enough economic resources to keep their support coalitions satisfied. As a result, economic crises can have a destabilizing effect on both types of dictatorship. However, it's generally the case that the depth and duration of the economic crisis has to be greater in a personalist dictatorship than in a dominant-party dictatorship before it becomes unstable. There are at least three related reasons for this. First, the concentration of office benefits in the leader's faction means that a personalist dictator can more easily ride out periods of poor economic performance. Although ordinary citizens may well suffer in an economic downturn, it's often the case that the dictator will retain sufficient resources to keep his support coalition satisfied. Second, the highly repressive nature of the security apparatus in a personalist dictatorship means that the probability of successfully overthrowing the regime is quite low. And third, members of the leader's faction in a personalist dictatorship have less valuable exit options than members of the regime party in a dominant-party dictatorship. Due to the fact that personalist dictators retain personal control of policy decisions and the selection of personnel, members of their support coalition are very closely linked to the incumbent regime. As a result, it's often difficult for them to successfully defect to the opposition, and they typically have to go into exile if the regime is threatened. A consequence of this is that elites in personalist dictatorships often fight to the very end when their access to power is threatened. This helps to explain why personalist dictatorships are more likely to end in violence than other types of dictatorship. On the whole, then, personalist dictatorships tend to become unstable only when there's an economic catastrophe as opposed to a mild downturn, when the security apparatus and military defect, or when the leader dies and the system of patronage based around him collapses.

BOX 8.1 ELECTORAL AUTHORITARIANISM: A NEW TYPE OF DICTATORSHIP?

Elections are increasingly common in dictatorships. Only Brunei, China, Eritrea, Qatar, and Saudi Arabia have failed to hold national-level elections at some point in the postwar period (Golder 2005). The increasing frequency with which elections are taking place in dictatorships has led some scholars to suggest that we're observing the emergence of a new type of dictatorship that goes under the heading of "electoral authoritarianism" (Schedler 2002, 2006). In an **electoral authoritarian regime**, leaders "hold elections and tolerate some pluralism and interparty competition, but at the same time violate minimal democratic norms so severely and systematically that it makes no sense to classify them as democracies" (Schedler 2002, 36). The extent to which competition is allowed in electoral authoritarian regimes varies (Diamond 2002). In some countries, the leader's party routinely wins with overwhelming majorities, and there's no meaningful contestation. These regimes are often called **hegemonic electoral regimes**. In other countries, though, competition is more real and opposition parties are able to win substantial minorities at election time. These latter regimes are often called **competitive authoritarian regimes** (Levitsky and Way 2002). Electoral authoritarian regimes can be contrasted with **politically closed authoritarian regimes** in which no opposition party is granted a legal space in the political arena.

Until recently, there were two rather divergent views about elections in dictatorships. For those who had hegemonic electoral dictatorships in mind, elections were often seen as forms of institutional window dressing with few political consequences. For those who had competitive authoritarian regimes in mind, elections were often seen as a prelude to further shifts toward democratization. Both of these views have been shown to be wrong. The overall consensus is that authoritarian elections have

(Continued)

(Continued)

very significant political consequences, and that dictators use them to help stabilize their rule, not hasten their demise.

Elections can help dictators in at least three ways (Gandhi and Lust-Okar 2009). First, they can help them co-opt elites (Boix and Svolik 2013), party members (Magaloni 2006), or larger societal groups (Gandhi 2008; Gandhi and Przeworski 2006). In effect, elections can be used as an arena for patronage distribution and as a means of recruiting and rewarding local political elites. Second, elections can help dictators co-opt opposition groups, as well as divide and control them. By allowing opposition groups to compete in elections, dictators provide access to political office and some decision-making authority. This provides these groups with a stake in maintaining the existing power structure. And by allowing only some, and not all, opposition groups to compete in elections, dictators sow the seeds of division within the opposition, thereby making it harder for opposition groups to overthrow them (Lust-Okar 2005). Third, elections can provide important information to the dictator. For example, dictators can use

the results from multiparty elections to identify their bases of support and opposition strongholds (Brownlee 2007; Magaloni 2006). In this way, dictators can use election results to identify which regions they should reward and which regions they should punish. Election results can also provide dictators with information about the performance of their local officials (Blaydes 2011). For example, dictatorial elites in China sometimes use low support at the polls in local elections to identify incompetent and poorly performing local officials (Birney 2007).

Although there's a growing literature on electoral authoritarian regimes, we have doubts about whether these regimes truly represent a new "type" of dictatorship. In our opinion, electoral competition is simply a dimension along which *all* dictatorships can be classified. Brownlee (2009) provides evidence in support of this when he maps data on the degree of electoral competition—politically closed, hegemonic electoral, and competitive authoritarian—onto our existing typology of authoritarian regimes. In Table 8.2, we use Brownlee's data to list the number of country-years that have occurred under each

TABLE 8.2 ■ Number of Country-Years by Authoritarian Regime and Degree of Electoral Competition, 1975–2004

		Degree of electoral Competition		
		Electoral authoritarianism		
Regime type	Politically closed	Hegemonic electoral	Competitive authoritarian	Total
Military	178	47	61	286 (14.2 percent)
Personalist	296	86	155	537 (26.7 percent)
Dominant party	586	165	187	938 (46.6 percent)
Monarchy	203	51	0	254 (12.6 percent)
Total	1,263 (62.6 percent)	349 (17.3 percent)	403 (20.0 percent)	2,015

Note: Numbers are based on data from Brownlee (2009).

type of authoritarian regime for each category of electoral competition. The main point to note is that there's considerable variation in the degree of electoral competition across all forms of authoritarian regime. For example, all types of dictatorship come in both "politically closed" and "open" variants. A substantial minority of military, personalist, and dominant-party regimes can be classified as electoral authoritarian regimes, and in all three cases, the nature of electoral authoritarianism is fairly evenly split between hegemonic and competitive authoritarianism. Monarchic dictatorships, in contrast, have a strong tendency toward being politically closed.

Further evidence for our claim that electoral authoritarianism is not a separate category of dictatorship comes from the fact that the degree of electoral competition varies across time *within* authoritarian regimes. Consider, for example, the authoritarian regime of Ferdinand Marcos, which ruled the Philippines from 1972 to 1986. In terms of its support coalition, the Marcos regime is generally considered a personalist dictatorship (Geddes 2003). But what about in terms of its degree of electoral competition? Prior to 1979, the Marcos regime is classified as "politically closed." From 1979 to 1983, though, it's classified as "hegemonic electoral" because Marcos won the 1981 presidential elections in a landslide. One reason for the landslide, and hence the "hegemonic electoral" classification, was that the major opposition parties boycotted these elections. From 1984 to its downfall in 1986,

AP Photo/Alberto Marquez

During the 1986 presidential campaign, presidential candidate Corazon Aquino and running mate Salvador Laurel flash the thumbs down sign under an enormous bust of incumbent president Ferdinand Marcos at a campaign stop in La Union province in northern Philippines.

(Continued)

(Continued)

the Marcos regime is classified as "competitive authoritarian." This is because the major opposition parties decided to compete in the 1986 presidential election and unite behind the candidacy of Corazon Aquino. Corazon Aquino and the opposition parties registered such a strong showing in the 1986 presidential elections that when the National Assembly declared Marcos the winner, it set off the "People's Power Revolution" that ultimately led to Marcos's removal from power.

Although the degree of electoral competition varied significantly during the time that Marcos was in power, few scholars would argue that the Philippines experienced three different authoritarian regimes between 1972 and 1986. From his declaration of martial law in 1972 to his removal from office, there was one Marcos regime. What changed over time were the strategies of the incumbent leader and the opposition. At times the dictator found it helpful to allow elections, and at times the opposition found it useful to participate. While the literature on "electoral authoritarianism" points to an important source of variation across authoritarian regimes, the degree of electoral competition also constitutes an important source of variation *within* authoritarian regimes. The example of the Marcos regime also highlights that the degree of electoral competition at any given point in time is driven in large part by the strategic interaction of dictators and their opposition. For these reasons, we believe that it's best to consider the degree of electoral competition in a dictatorship to be an outcome or policy choice that varies within and across regime types rather than a defining feature of a particular type of authoritarian regime.

To some extent, our concerns with identifying electoral authoritarianism as a "type" of dictatorship also apply to the common typology of authoritarian regimes that we've presented in the main text. To what extent, for example, are military dictatorships really a distinct type of authoritarian regime? One could reasonably argue that civil-military relations represent a continuum and that all authoritarian (and democratic) regimes vary in the extent to which the military is willing and able to intervene in civil affairs. The same is true for personalist dictatorships. All authoritarian (and, again, democratic) regimes vary in the extent to which the leader has personal discretion over policy and personnel choices. We understand that many political scientists like typologies because they seem to simplify the complexity of the world into distinct categories, and students, like yourself, probably value this simplicity as it gives them an accessible way to talk about the diverse forms of authoritarian rule that exist around the world. However, it might be more useful to recognize that authoritarian regimes can be characterized on multiple different (and often continuous) dimensions. Rather than examine the causes and consequences of different discrete types of dictatorship, we could look at why some authoritarian regimes score high on some dimensions but low on others and what this means for their survival and how they behave. In fact, we examine one such approach a little later in the chapter when we discuss selectorate theory.

THE TWO FUNDAMENTAL PROBLEMS OF AUTHORITARIAN RULE

So far we've examined different types of authoritarian regimes separately. Political scientists, though, have identified two fundamental problems of authoritarian rule that exist in all dictatorships—the *problem of authoritarian power-sharing* and the *problem of authoritarian control* (Svolik 2012).[6] These two problems highlight the fact that threats to dictatorial rule

---

[6]In discussing the two fundamental problems of authoritarian rule we follow the theoretical framework outlined by Svolik (2009, 2012) and Boix and Svolik (2013).

can come either from within the authoritarian elite or from the masses. In this section, we take a brief look at each of these problems and examine some of the institutional solutions authoritarian rulers have developed to mitigate them.

The Problem of Authoritarian Power-Sharing

The problem of authoritarian power-sharing focuses on intra-elite conflict. Dictators never come to power on their own, and they rarely control enough resources to govern alone. Instead, dictators rely on a support coalition. As we've seen, this support coalition might include members of the armed forces, key allies in the royal family, economic and religious elites, and so on. If the dictator retains the support of this support coalition, the authoritarian regime stays in power. When the dictator first comes to power, there's an implicit, and possibly explicit, agreement on how to share economic and political rents among the members of the support coalition. The problem is that in a dictatorship there's no independent third-party actor to enforce this "power-sharing" agreement.

The members of the support coalition know that the dictator always has an incentive to alter the power-sharing agreement to his benefit. In effect, the dictator will want to acquire more power at the expense of his allies. The only thing stopping the dictator from grabbing more power is the ability of the support coalition to replace him. When the threat to remove the dictator is credible, we have a contested dictatorship where power is shared between the dictator and his allies. Removing a dictator, perhaps via a coup, can be costly, though. There's a chance the coup will fail, in which case the coup-plotters are likely to be imprisoned or killed. Even if the coup succeeds, it can leave lingering divisions that destabilize the authoritarian regime. Significantly, members of the support coalition have only limited information about exactly what actions the dictator is taking. After all, the dictator is unlikely to publicly announce his intention to usurp power. A consequence of this is that it can be difficult for the support coalition to distinguish between a situation in which the dictator is making a power grab and one in which he's allocating rents in the pre-agreed manner. This can result in "unnecessary" coups where the support coalition attempts to remove a dictator who's following the original power-sharing agreement and "missed opportunities" where the support coalition fails to act against a dictator who is concentrating power in his own hands.

This uncertainty about the dictator's actions and the reluctance of the support coalition to rebel creates incentives for the dictator "to try his luck and attempt to acquire power at their expense" (Svolik 2012, 55). If the dictator is able to make successive power grabs without being stopped, it's possible for him to accumulate sufficient power that the "support" coalition no longer has the ability to credibly threaten to remove him. At this point, the authoritarian regime has shifted from a "contested" dictatorship in which the dictator is constrained by his allies to a "personalist" dictatorship in which the dictator has effectively monopolized power (Svolik 2012). In this account, personalist dictatorships arise when the support coalition repeatedly fails to act in response to a series of power grabs by the dictator. This is essentially the trajectory followed by all personalist dictators, including Mao Zedong in China, "Papa Doc" Duvalier in Haiti, and Joseph Stalin in the Soviet Union. In the case of Stalin, he rose from relative obscurity to become one of the most powerful dictators in the modern era (Suny 1998). He didn't achieve this status immediately, though. Instead, he consolidated power gradually over many years, first eliminating rival factions headed by people like Leon Trotsky and Nikolai Bukharin and then subordinating the power of the Communist Party and the Red Army in what became known as the Great Purges (Svolik 2012, 53–54). The transformation of Stalin into a personalist dictator was possible only because members of his support coalition didn't successfully step in early enough to prevent him from consolidating his hold on power.

AP Photo

General Antonio Kebreau pins a cordon on Dr. François Duvalier, nicknamed "Papa Doc," at Duvalier's presidential inauguration ceremony in Port-au-Prince, Haiti, October 22, 1957. Following an attempted coup in 1958, Duvalier consolidated power, partly by purging military leaders and setting up his own militia (the Tonton Macoute). In 1964, he took the title of President for Life, remaining in office until his death in 1971.

What can the dictator do to solve this power-sharing problem? Dictators and their support coalitions clearly have an incentive to create a power-sharing agreement that allows the dictator to stay in power and the support coalition to benefit from the dictator being in power. However, when the members of the support coalition can't fully monitor the dictator's actions and can't be confident the dictator is following the agreement rather than trying to surreptitiously consolidate power, they might either launch an unnecessary coup or, through inaction, find that they've been marginalized (or worse). For a stable power-sharing agreement to exist, the support coalition and the dictator must find a solution to this "monitoring problem" such that the support coalition receives credible information about the dictator's actions. The dictator can't simply promise to abide by the power-sharing agreement because such a promise isn't credible.

Svolik (2012) suggests that the "monitoring problem" at the heart of intra-regime conflict can be solved, or at least minimized, with appropriate political institutions. In particular, decision-making bodies within legislatures or parties can provide a forum for exchanging information and deliberating about policy. These decision-making bodies, sometimes called *ruling councils* or *politburos*, "typically establish formal rules concerning membership, jurisdiction, protocol, and decision making that both facilitate the exchange of information among the ruling elite and provide for an easy assessment of compliance with those rules" (Svolik 2012, 7). These decision-making bodies are useful because they provide the members of the support coalition with information about the actions of the dictator, making it less likely the dictator can stealthily consolidate power without being called to account for his actions. Having formal rules and protocols makes it easier to see when they've been violated. It's commonly thought that dictators adopt institutions such as legislatures and political parties to reward their allies in the support coalition or to co-opt members of the opposition (Gandhi 2008; Gandhi and Przeworski 2006; see also Chapter 7). The story here, though, is slightly different—dictatorships institutionalize to solve *informational problems* within the authoritarian elite.

Information on its own, though, isn't sufficient to create a stable power-sharing arrangement (Svolik 2012). In addition to being able to detect power grabs, support coalitions must also have the ability to credibly punish the dictator if he reneges on their agreement. This raises the issue of whether support coalitions can overcome the collective action problems that arise when attempting to remove a dictator. Support coalitions will find it easier to overcome collective action problems and punish "rule-breaking" dictators when the distribution of power between the dictator and the support coalition is fairly even. A balance of power in the authoritarian regime means that it's feasible for the support coalition to punish the dictator. If the dictator is particularly powerful, there'll be disagreement among the various factions in the support coalition as to whether they should, or are even able to, move against the dictator. Thus, stable power-sharing agreements in authoritarian regimes require institutionalization *and* a fairly even distribution of power between the dictator and his support coalition.

The argument here has implications both for when we'll see institutionalization in dictatorships and for the effectiveness of authoritarian institutions (Boix and Svolik 2013). If authoritarian leaders have been able to consolidate their hold on power and establish a personalist dictatorship, they have no need to institutionalize. If institutions, like parties or legislatures, exist in these circumstances, they won't have the power to constrain the dictator. If the dictator is relatively weak, he has an incentive to institutionalize so as to establish a stable power-sharing agreement. In these circumstances, institutions will allow the support coalition to monitor the dictator's actions, and the dictator will choose not to violate the agreement because he knows the support coalition can credibly punish him. If the dictator has middling levels of strength relative to his support coalition, things are more complicated. Institutionalization will improve the monitoring capacity of the dictator's support coalition. If there's a sufficient balance of power between the dictator and his support coalition, the dictator will abide by the power-sharing agreement. However, if there's an imbalance in the distribution of power that favors the dictator, we're likely to see the effectiveness of institutional constraints on the dictator gradually erode over time as the dictator successfully consolidates his hold on power.

The Problem of Authoritarian Control

In addition to facing threats from within the authoritarian elite, dictators also face threats from the masses over which they rule. This is referred to as the problem of authoritarian control. What's to stop the masses from rising up and overthrowing the dictator? To a large extent, dictators have two distinct strategies for solving the problem of authoritarian control—they can either repress the masses or co-opt them (Svolik 2012).

From the dictator's point of view, repression is a double-edged sword. On the one hand, repression can keep the masses under control. On the other hand, the dictator must rely on other actors, typically the military, to do the actual repressing, and these actors may or may not share the same preferences as the dictator. By providing the military with the resources necessary to successfully repress the population, the dictator effectively empowers the military to act (if it wishes) against the dictator. If the dictator becomes sufficiently reliant on the military to stay in power, the military can use this leverage to demand policy concessions and other rents from the authoritarian regime. As you can see, dictators face a trade-off. They can keep the military weak but run the risk that they'll be overthrown in a revolution if the masses rise up, or they can maintain a strong military and expose themselves to threats from the military.

How this trade-off is ultimately resolved is likely to depend on the nature of societal opposition (Svolik 2012). When dictators are faced with large-scale, organized, and armed opposition, they'll have little choice but to rely on the military to stay in power. Whereas the internal security forces and secret police may be able to deal with small and irregular protests, only the military has the institutional capacity to put down more widespread and violent unrest. In return for services rendered to the dictator, the military will demand policy concessions, large budgets to buy weapons and attract recruits, and autonomy from authoritarian control (Geddes 2003). Importantly, both the dictator and the military recognize the pivotal role the military play in sustaining the authoritarian regime in this type of situation. As a result, the military won't have to overtly intervene in the day-to-day running of the country. As Svolik (2012, 125) notes, "A politically pivotal military should be an *eminence grise* behind the throne," a situation he refers to as "military tutelage."

If dictators are faced only with small-scale intermittent protests, they're likely to keep the military weak. In these circumstances, dictators will prefer to rely on internal security forces, such as the police, to repress societal opposition. In many cases, the dictator will provide only limited resources to the military writ large but generously reward a small "palace guard" that's loyal to the dictator. This was the general strategy adopted by Tunisian president Zine El Abidene Ben Ali (1987–2011). Historically, there had been few large-scale violent protests in Tunisia. Feeling relatively safe, Ben Ali kept the military small and under-equipped. This came back to haunt him during the Arab Spring in 2010–2011, though, when protests were so large and widespread that they overwhelmed the ability of the police to keep law and order, and the military refused to step in to save his regime. Given that the military is kept weak when the prospects for societal unrest are low, the military doesn't have the ability to openly intervene in the day-to-day running of the country; the civilian government has control over the military in this type of situation.

Svolik (2012) argues that direct military intervention in the political system is likely to occur only when the probability of mass unrest is moderately high. As we've seen, direct military intervention is unlikely to occur when the probability of mass unrest is high. This is because the dictator recognizes the pivotal role the military plays in ensuring his regime's survival and will do whatever the military wants. Direct military intervention is also unlikely to occur when the probability of mass unrest is low. This is because the dictator will keep the military so weak that it's unable to successfully intervene in the political system even if it wants to. Direct military intervention will occur only when the probability of mass unrest is moderately high. This is because the dictator and the military are more likely to hold different beliefs about the probability of mass unrest in these circumstances, and hence, different beliefs about the importance of the military to the survival of the authoritarian regime. Svolik (2012) refers to these types of situations as "military brinksmanship."

In situations of military brinksmanship, the military has incentives to exaggerate or even promote evidence of social unrest in order to highlight its importance to the dictator. The military may also be sufficiently well resourced that it feels tempted to threaten the dictator with military intervention in order to obtain material and policy concessions. In contrast, the dictator may not believe the military is critical to his regime's survival and may also be willing to call the military's bluff on its threat to intervene in the political system. If the military misjudges the resolve of the dictator to stand firm, or the dictator misjudges the military's resolve to intervene, we can end up with a military coup that neither side really wants. In effect, the bargaining that occurs between the dictator and the military in situations of military brinksmanship can easily spiral out of control and lead to direct military intervention.

All of this raises an interesting point about how we judge the power of the military in civil-military relations. You might have thought that military coups or military dictatorships are a sign that the military is strong. In some sense they are. However, the framework we've discussed here suggests that this isn't quite correct. In cases where the military is truly strong, it has no need to conduct coups or directly hold the reins of power. As we noted back in Chapter 3, it's often difficult to identify who has power simply by observing the actions that different actors take. Truly powerful actors rarely need to use their power openly.

Rather than repress the masses, the dictator can try to co-opt them. You'll recall that we discussed this strategy to some extent in Chapter 7 when we discussed top-down transitions to democracy. In that discussion, we suggested that social unrest can produce a split in the authoritarian regime between soft-liners and hard-liners. If the soft-liners gain prominence, they might try to liberalize the regime and broaden the social base of the dictatorship. Liberalization policies typically entail a controlled opening of the political space and are associated with the formation of political parties, holding elections, writing a constitution, establishing a judiciary, opening a legislature, and so on. The goal of this "institutionalization" is to co-opt opposition groups (Blaydes 2011; Gandhi 2008; Gandhi and Przeworski 2006; Lust-Okar 2005; Malesky and Schuler 2010). As we've discussed in this chapter and elsewhere, elections, legislatures, and political parties give regime outsiders access to regime rents they can distribute among their supporters, as well as a formal say in the policymaking process.

But why do dictatorships create institutions to co-opt opposition groups rather than just buy them off directly? Why, for example, don't dictatorships simply use cash transfers, land reform, programmatic redistribution, and other policies to co-opt opposition groups? Well, the answer to some extent is that they do. As Ross (2011, 3–4) notes, Saudi Arabia spent billions of dollars increasing public sector wages, unemployment benefits, and housing subsidies at the height of the Arab Spring protests. One issue with this type of strategy, though, is that dictators tend to make direct transfers when their survival is under threat from mobilized opposition groups but then reverse course once protesters have returned to their homes. If opposition groups recognize this, then direct transfers may not satisfy them and they won't be co-opted. In effect, the dictator's promise to provide direct transfers to opposition groups may not be viewed as credible. As you'll recall from Chapter 5, one solution to credible commitment problems is to create political institutions, such as legislatures, that enable opposition groups to maintain some influence over the dictator into the future, when protesters have left the streets.

Even if direct transfers are considered credible, institutions can provide additional advantages when it comes to co-opting opposition groups. Regime parties are often considered a key institution when it comes to co-opting the masses (Magaloni 2006; Svolik 2012). Members of dominant regime parties gain access to a more rewarding set of benefits as they work their way up the party hierarchy. Initial recruits to the party typically have to engage in costly activity on behalf of the party to prove themselves. The most lucrative benefits of party membership come only after working one's way up the party ranks. After exerting costly effort in the lower echelons of the party, party members develop a stake in seeing the regime survive as this is the only way they can obtain the fruits of their labor. In effect, regime parties not only provide the masses with access to rents, something that can be achieved with direct transfers, but they also incentivize the masses to work on behalf of the regime's survival.

SELECTORATE THEORY

In the remainder of this chapter, we'll examine why there's so much variation in the economic performance of different countries around the world with the help of something called *selectorate theory*. We live in a world that tends to associate good outcomes with democracy and bad ones with dictatorships. In reality, the world is much more complex than this. Although democracies tend to produce relatively high levels of material well-being for their citizens, they don't regularly outperform all dictatorships. Some dictatorships perform quite well even though others perform extremely poorly. Classifying the world into democracies and dictatorship fails to explain this variation in the performance of dictatorships. According to selectorate theory, the key to a country's material well-being has less to do with whether it's democratic or authoritarian and more to do with the size of its "winning coalition" and "selectorate." As we'll see, the typology of dictatorships we presented at the beginning of this chapter fits neatly into the theoretical framework provided by selectorate theory.

The basic assumption underpinning selectorate theory is that all political leaders are motivated by the desire to gain office. Of course, political leaders may have other goals as well, such as implementing particular policies or helping certain groups in society. Although selectorate theory doesn't deny this, it argues that the competitive nature of politics forces leaders in all regimes, democratic and authoritarian, to at least behave "as if" they desire to gain office. Political actors who fail to exert effort in an attempt to win power are likely to be replaced by competitors who do exert such effort. Knowing they can achieve whatever goals motivate them only if they win, all political leaders are, therefore, forced to act as if they care about gaining office even if this isn't their primary motivation.

A key part of this perspective is that there's a challenger willing, at any moment, to replace the incumbent leader. It's important to recognize that leaders always face political competition. It's often easier to identify political challengers in democracies than in dictatorships. Competitors who seek to replace a dictator are likely to face significant threats to their lives, and as a result, they tend to keep a low profile until they deem the moment right to challenge the dictator. The fact that we're not always able to identify who the competitors are in a dictatorship, though, shouldn't lead us to think that there's no political competition or that the dictator's unchallenged. Someone else always wants to be the leader, and incumbent leaders must continually guard against losing power to these competitors.

The puzzle posed by the authors of selectorate theory, Bueno de Mesquita, Smith, Siverson, and Morrow (2003; hereafter referred to as BDM^{2}S^2), is the following: If all political leaders have the same (induced) goals—to gain office—why do we get so much variation in political outcomes? In other words, why do some leaders produce good economic outcomes and some leaders produce bad ones? Why do some leaders provide public goods but others don't? Why do some leaders engage in corruption but others don't?

Given that all political leaders wish to gain power and keep it, you might think that they would all want to produce good economic performance. It turns out, however, that good economic performance doesn't necessarily result in longevity in power. For example, BDM^{2}S^2 (2003, 273–276) provide both a list of the twenty-five "best" leaders in regard to their provision of peace and prosperity from 1955 to 2002 and a list of the top twenty-five longest-ruling leaders in the same period. It turns out that there's *no overlap* between the leaders on the two lists. The high-performing leaders, with an average economic growth rate of 7 percent, last just six years in office on average, whereas the longest-ruling leaders, with an average growth rate of 4.4 percent, last 35.1 years. These data would seem to suggest that producing good performance leads to short terms in office, whereas poor performance produces long stretches of time in office. Why, then, do some political leaders ever produce good performance? What explains the variation in the economic performance of political leaders?

Institutions

Selectorate theory argues that the variation in the performance of political leaders can be explained with regard to the institutional environment in which they operate. Some institutional environments encourage political leaders to behave in ways that benefit society, whereas other environments encourage them to behave in ways that benefit only themselves and a few others. Each country has a fundamental set of institutions or rules that govern interactions between residents within its borders. These include rules that define who is **disenfranchised**, who is part of the **selectorate**, and who is part of the **winning coalition**. The relationship between the disenfranchised, the selectorate, and the winning coalition in a country is shown graphically in Figure 8.4.

The disenfranchised are all those residents who don't have the legal right to participate in choosing the government. The selectorate (*S*), in contrast, is the set of people who have a legitimate say, if they so choose, in the selection of the leader. The term *selectorate* is chosen

FIGURE 8.4 ■ The Institutional Environment in Selectorate Theory

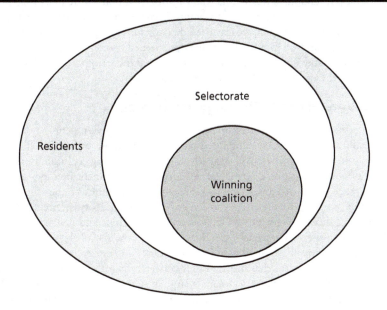

deliberately so as to indicate that the people "selecting" a leader don't necessarily have to do so by voting. In other words, the selectorate isn't always the same as an electorate. In some forms of dictatorship, the selectorate is quite small. For example, the selectorate in a monarchy typically comprises only members of the royal family or, perhaps, the wider nobility and certain religious leaders. Similarly, the selectorate in a military junta usually consists only of members from the armed forces or, perhaps, the heads of each of the military branches. In other forms of dictatorship, though, the selectorate can be quite large. For example, the selectorate arguably consists of all adult citizens with the right to vote in dominant-party dictatorships that hold elections. Although the selectorate can be small or large in dictatorships, it's nearly always large in democracies. In a democracy, the selectorate comprises all those who are eligible to vote. In the past, certain groups such as women, nonwhites, and those without property were ineligible to vote in particular democracies. For example, nonwhites were banned from voting in apartheid South Africa between 1948 and 1994, and women didn't get the right to vote until 1945 in France and until as late as 1971 in Switzerland. In most contemporary democracies, however, the selectorate means all adult citizens.

The winning coalition (*W*) consists of those members of the selectorate whose support is necessary for the leader to remain in power.[7] If the leader is ever unable to keep his winning coalition loyal, he'll lose his position to a challenger. In democracies, the winning coalition is always quite large and comprises those voters who are required to elect the winning candidate or government. If there are only two candidates or parties at election time, the winning coalition is as large as a majority of the electorate. In contrast, the winning coalition in a dictatorship is always quite small. For example, the winning coalition in a military junta might

---

[7]To make meaningful cross-national comparisons, the winning coalition and the selectorate are not conceptualized in terms of the absolute numbers of residents who belong to them; rather, they're conceptualized in terms of the proportion of residents they represent.

be a majority of the officers or a small group of colonels and generals who together control the armed forces. In countries like China, the winning coalition is often just a small subset of the Communist Party. In a monarchy, the winning coalition might consist of a majority of the nobility. Earlier in the chapter, we classified dictatorships in terms of the identity of their "support coalitions," and we indicated that dictators needed to keep these support coalitions satisfied if they're to stay in power. It's now easy to see that these support coalitions are essentially the same as the winning coalitions in selectorate theory.

Mapping *W* and *S* onto a Typology of Regimes

Selectorate theory is able to differentiate various forms of government—monarchic dictatorships, military dictatorships, dominant-party dictatorships, personalist dictatorships, democracies, and so on—by the size of their selectorate and winning coalition. In Figure 8.5a, we plot the *theoretical* location of these various forms of government in a two-dimensional institutional space, where one dimension is the size of the selectorate and the other dimension is the size of the winning coalition. As you can see, selectorate theory differentiates between different types of dictatorships, as well as between dictatorships and democracies. The key factor that distinguishes democracies from dictatorships is the size of the winning coalition. Whereas all dictatorships have small winning coalitions, all democracies have large winning coalitions. And the key factor that distinguishes between the different types of dictatorship is the size of the selectorate. The selectorate is large in dominant-party and personalist dictatorships, particularly those that hold elections. BDM^{2}S^2 refer to these types of systems as "rigged election systems." In contrast, the selectorate tends to be small in military juntas and monarchies.

As you can imagine, measuring the size of a country's winning coalition and selectorate in the real world is extremely difficult. Nonetheless, BDM^{2}S^2 have attempted to do precisely this.[8] In Figure 8.5b, we plot the *actual* location of different forms of government by their average selectorate and winning coalition scores from 1946 to 2000. Even though BDM^{2}S^2 don't use information about the form of government to measure the size of a country's selectorate and winning coalition, Figure 8.5b reveals that the scores for each country situate the different forms of government in the two-dimensional institutional space in a manner that is entirely consistent with the theoretical locations shown in Figure 8.5a. As expected, the average size of the winning coalition in a democracy is much larger than that in any of the various forms of dictatorship. Also as expected, there's considerable variation in the average size of the selectorate among dictatorships. Monarchic and military dictatorships have small selectorates, whereas personalist and dominant-party dictatorships have large selectorates.

Government Performance

How does the institutional environment in which a leader operates influence government performance? According to selectorate theory, political leaders must keep members of their winning coalition happy to stay in power. They can do this by distributing public goods or private goods or both. As you'll recall from Chapter 7, public goods benefit everyone in society regardless of whether they're in the winning coalition or not. This is because they're nonexcludable (once they're provided, anyone can enjoy them) and nonrivalrous (the amount

---

[8]For precise details on how the size of a country's selectorate and winning coalition are measured, see BDM^{2}S^2 (2003, 133–140).

FIGURE 8.5   ■   Selectorate Theory and Regime-Type Locations

a. Theoretical regime-type locations

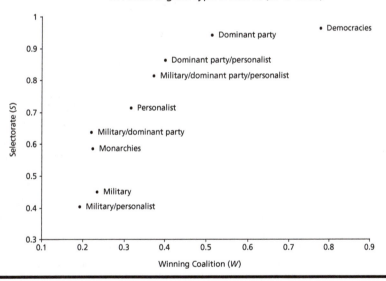

b. Actual regime-type locations (1946–2000)

Source: Data on the size of *W* and *S* are from Bueno de Mesquita and colleagues (2003); data on the different forms of dictatorships are from Geddes (2003).

Note: W and *S* both range from a minimum of 0 to a maximum of 1. Geddes (2003) classifies dictatorships into four types: (1) personalist, (2) military, (3) dominant-party, or (4) hybrid mixtures of these pure types. Countries that are not classified as one of these four types of dictatorships are either monarchies or democracies; we employ data from Polity IV to determine which were monarchies and which were democracies.

of the good available to be consumed isn't diminished by the number of people who consume it). Examples of public goods might be increased spending on education, health care, and infrastructure. In contrast, private goods benefit only some members of society and not others. In effect, private goods, such as business or export licenses, private jets, and villas in the South of France, can be given directly to members of the winning coalition. Those individuals who aren't members of the winning coalition don't receive private goods. It's the job of an incumbent leader to figure out how many public and private goods to distribute in order to keep his winning coalition loyal.

In addition to deciding what mix of public and private goods to hand out to his winning coalition, the leader must pick a tax rate. This tax rate ultimately determines how much money the leader has at his disposal to pay for the provision of public and private goods. Depending on the tax rate chosen, residents decide how to allocate their time between economically productive activities and leisure. At the same time the incumbent is deciding his tax rate and announcing his offer of public and private goods, a challenger also makes an offer to the selectorate (a combination of public goods, private goods, and a tax rate) in an attempt to put together an alternative winning coalition. The bottom line is that the political entrepreneur—the incumbent leader or challenger—who's best able to meet the needs of the winning coalition wins.

Loyalty Norm

Exactly how leaders distribute public and private goods depends on the size of the winning coalition and the size of the selectorate. Recall that the goal of the incumbent leader is to stay in power and that to do this he must keep the winning coalition happy. The key for the leader, then, is to stop members of the current winning coalition from defecting. Given this, let's start by thinking about the conditions under which a member of the current winning coalition might decide to defect and shift her loyalty to a challenger. Clearly, any disgruntled member of the winning coalition must weigh the potential risks and rewards from defecting. Oftentimes, there'll be more than one potential defector in a winning coalition or multiple challengers to whom they can defect or both. Moreover, it's almost always the case that there'll be members of the selectorate who aren't in the winning coalition but who'd like to be. As a result, individuals who defect from the current winning coalition have no guarantee that they'll end up as part of the next leader's coalition. Indeed, any promise by a challenger to make them part of the future winning coalition if they defect and bring down the incumbent leader isn't credible for obvious reasons. Thus, individuals who choose to defect risk losing access to the private goods they presently enjoy as members of the current winning coalition.

The risk that members of the winning coalition face when they think about defecting is embodied in the ratio of the size of the winning coalition to the size of the selectorate (W/S). The ratio W/S essentially represents the probability that a member of the selectorate will be in any winning coalition. This is because S people could be in the winning coalition, but only (some portion) W of them will actually make it into the winning coalition. As you can see, W/S indicates the probability that someone who defects from the current winning coalition will be in the next winning coalition. Members of the selectorate have only a small chance of being in the winning coalition when W/S is small (when few people in the selectorate are needed to form a winning coalition), but they have a large chance when W/S is large (when many people in the selectorate are needed to form a winning coalition). As you can imagine, the size of W/S has important implications for the loyalty of members in the current winning coalition. If W/S is small, members of the winning coalition are likely to be intensely loyal to the incumbent leader, because they realize they're lucky to be part of the winning coalition and that they have a low probability of being in anyone else's winning coalition. As W/S gets larger and the probability of being in the next leader's winning coalition increases, this loyalty to the incumbent leader naturally declines.[9] In effect, W/S represents a sort of **loyalty norm**: there's a strong loyalty norm in small W/S systems and a weak loyalty norm in large W/S systems.

The existence or absence of a strong loyalty norm has important implications for the performance of leaders in power. For example, political leaders in small W/S systems with strong loyalty norms have greater opportunities to engage in **kleptocracy** and **corruption** than leaders in large W/S systems with weak loyalty norms. Why? Consider two societies, A and B. In both societies, the political leader has $1 billion in tax revenue to distribute among the 1,000 members of his winning coalition and himself. The only difference between the two societies is that the selectorate is made up of 100,000 people in Society A and just 10,000 people in Society B. In effect, Society A has a stronger loyalty norm (smaller W/S) than Society B. It's easy to see that the leaders in both societies could pay each member of their winning coalitions up to $1 million in private goods to win over their support, that is, $1 billion divided equally among the 1,000 people in the winning coalition. As we'll see, though, neither leader has to actually pay out this much to ensure the loyalty of his winning coalition. In fact, we'll see that by taking advantage of the strong loyalty norm in his country the leader of Society A doesn't have to pay out as much as the leader of Society B to keep his winning coalition happy. Ultimately, this means that the leader in Society A can keep more of his tax revenue for his own discretionary use. How does this all work exactly?

Let's start with Society A. The probability that a member of the current winning coalition will be a member of the next leader's coalition if she defects is just 1 percent; that is, W/S = 1,000/100,000 = 0.01. It's this low probability of being in the next leader's coalition that generates the strong loyalty norm we mentioned earlier. Anyone who defects from the current winning coalition in Society A has a 1 percent chance of obtaining (at most) $1 million in private goods and a 99 percent chance of obtaining nothing.[10] As a result, the maximum expected value of defecting in terms of private goods is just $10,000.[11] All the incumbent leader, therefore, has to do to stay in power is to offer each member of his winning coalition slightly more than $10,000 in private goods and come close to matching the provision of public goods promised by any challenger. In effect, the incumbent can skim off for himself the difference between the $1 million per supporter he could have distributed and the something over $10,000 per supporter he needs to distribute to stay in power. If the incumbent's challenger offers a particularly attractive set of public goods, the incumbent can give some of this "slush fund" to his supporters to purchase their continued loyalty (Bueno de Mesquita 2006, 421).

What about Society B? Well, the probability that someone in the current winning coalition will be a member of the next leader's coalition if he defects is now 10 percent; that is, W/S = 1,000/10,000 = 0.1. This is somewhat higher than in Society A, and as a result, the loyalty norm in this society is weaker. The maximum expected value of defecting from the current winning coalition in terms of private goods is now $100,000.[12] This means that the incumbent leader in Society B has to pay a little more than $100,000 in private goods

---

[9]In the language of the exit, voice, and loyalty theory examined in Chapters 3 and 5, a large W/S indicates that members of the winning coalition have credible exit threats; that is, they can defect and still have a high probability of being in the next leader's winning coalition.

[10]A million dollars is the most that a defector can receive because that is the most that a challenger can offer to each member of the winning coalition if all tax revenue is spent on private goods.

[11]This is calculated as $1 million × 0.01 + $0 × 0.99 = $10,000.

[12]This is calculated as $1 million × 0.1 + $0 × 0.9 = $100,000.

to each member of his winning coalition and come close to matching whatever provision of public goods a challenger has promised in order to stay in power. In Society B, the incumbent gets to skim off for himself the difference between the $1 million per supporter he could have distributed and the something over $100,000 per supporter he needs to distribute to stay in power. This is still a lot of money, but it's considerably less than the leader in Society A can skim off for himself.

Although we might think that all leaders want to engage in kleptocracy and corruption, the institutional arrangements in a country influence their ability to do so without jeopardizing their hold on power. Specifically, leaders in small *W/S* systems (Society A) have greater opportunities to "steal" from their citizens by skimming off tax revenue into their own pockets than do leaders of large *W/S* systems (Society B). As an example of widespread kleptocracy and corruption, consider the small *W/S* system of Zaire under Mobutu Sese Seko (1965–1997). Mobutu was reportedly able to put as much as a third of the national budget under his personal control and skim off a quarter of all the profits from the country's vast copper mines. As Rose-Ackerman (1999, 116) notes, "Corruption and predation undermined the formal private sector, and grandiose infrastructure projects were used as sources of payoffs" for Mobutu and his supporters. Indeed, in the thirty-two years that Mobutu was in power, he's estimated to have stolen a staggering $4 billion. As another example, consider the small *W/S* system of the Philippines under Ferdinand Marcos (1965–1986). Marcos is thought to have stolen somewhere between $5 billion and $10 billion during the thirty-one years he was in office (BDM²S² 2003, 167).

The strong loyalty norm that encourages leaders in small *W/S* systems, such as dominant-party and personalist dictatorships, to engage in kleptocracy also generates incentives for poor public policy more generally. Note that members of the winning coalition in these systems are loyal because (1) the leader provides them with more private goods than any challenger can and (2) they have to worry about being cut out of the next leader's coalition if they decide to defect. It follows from this that as long as members of the winning coalition are being sufficiently "bribed," they don't really care about the material well-being of the citizenry more generally (Bueno de Mesquita 2006, 423). As a result, leaders in small *W/S* systems have no incentive to produce good public policy—it doesn't help them stay in power. Leaders in small *W/S* systems recognize that they stay in power by keeping their supporters happy with private goods. "Just think of Saddam Hussein's success in holding on to power even after a worldwide trade embargo against Iraqi goods left his nation's economy in shambles. . . . As long as Saddam Hussein continued to pay the military well and keep his clansmen happy, he was unlikely to suffer an internal coup" (Bueno de Mesquita 2006, 424). We should note that not only does good public policy fail to help leaders in small *W/S* systems stay in power but it may actually get the leader ousted as well. This is because allocating resources to things like public goods that benefit the citizenry more widely opens up an opportunity for a challenger to credibly promise to provide more private goods to members of the winning coalition than are currently being provided by the incumbent.

In contrast to these types of systems, large *W/S* systems, such as democracies, don't have strong loyalty norms. For example, voters in a democracy are unlikely to lose access to private goods, such as particular tax policies or redistributive schemes that benefit them if they switch their support from the incumbent leader to the leader of an opposition party. As a result, leaders in large *W/S* systems have to work harder to keep their supporters happy and can't afford to skim off too many resources if they want to stay in power. Moreover, because leaders in large *W/S* systems need more resources to keep their winning coalition loyal, they have a strong incentive to produce good overall economic performance. As a result, they're unlikely to tax or steal from their citizens too much lest this cause the citizens to spend more time relaxing and less time working. Remember that if the citizens don't work, there'll be a smaller economic pie with which the leader can win over the winning coalition. All in all, government performance should be better in large W/S systems than in small W/S systems—kleptocracy should be lower, taxation and state predation should be lower, economic growth should be higher, and so on.

Although large W/S systems encourage leaders to perform well in office, there's no guarantee that their good performance will translate into longevity in office. Due to a weak loyalty norm, leaders in large W/S systems are likely to survive in office for shorter periods of time than leaders in small W/S systems even if they produce better government performance. This helps to explain why democratic leaders rarely last as long in office as even the poorest performing dictators in dominant-party or personalist dictatorships.

The Size of the Winning Coalition

In addition to the strength of the loyalty norm (W/S), selectorate theory indicates that the manner in which leaders distribute public and private goods also depends on the size of the winning coalition (W). Leaders always prefer to use private goods rather than public goods to satisfy their winning coalition. An incumbent leader is always able to defeat a challenger if competition is restricted to the distribution of private goods. This inherent advantage comes from the simple fact that challengers can't credibly guarantee to put would-be defectors in their own winning coalition. Recognizing the uneven playing field, challengers, therefore, attempt to defeat incumbents by emphasizing the provision of public goods. Not only does this help to explain why challengers spend considerable time criticizing incumbents for their poor performance in tackling corruption and providing food, health care, education, and the like, but it also helps to explain why these same challengers frequently maintain the preexisting system of corruption and do little to increase the provision of public goods when they finally come to power. In this regard, we can think of people like Jomo Kenyatta, who railed against corruption in Kenya before coming to power in 1963, but who then did little to stamp it out while in office (BDM²S² 2003, 374–375). Kenya has consistently ranked at the bottom of Transparency International's list of corrupt countries. Selectorate theory suggests that foreign countries that today promote and support seemingly public-minded opposition leaders shouldn't necessarily expect government performance to significantly improve if these opposition leaders ever come to power.

Although incumbent leaders always prefer to use private goods to keep their winning coalition loyal, this isn't always a viable strategy. Much depends on the size of the winning coalition. As the size of the winning coalition increases, the share of private goods that can go to each member of the winning coalition shrinks. In our earlier example, the leaders in both societies A and B had $1 billion in tax revenues to distribute to the winning coalition. Because the winning coalition comprised 1,000 members, the maximum amount of private goods that any one member could receive was $1 million. If the winning coalition in these societies had comprised one million members, then the maximum amount of private goods that any one member could have received would be just $1,000. Clearly, the private goods deal looks a lot better when the winning coalition is small than when it's large. It follows that the advantage the incumbent has over the challenger in regard to the provision of private goods shrinks as the winning coalition gets larger. At some point, the winning coalition is so large that it's no longer efficient or viable for the leader to buy the support of the winning coalition with just the help of private goods. In effect, the value of the private goods going to each member of the winning coalition becomes so small that the members would obtain more value if the leader provided public goods. An implication of this is that leaders in small W systems (dictatorships) will tend to use private goods to stay in power, whereas leaders in large W systems (democracies) will primarily use public goods. The fact that democratic leaders simply don't have sufficient resources to "bribe" all the people they need to win an election with private goods helps to explain why political competition in contemporary democracies is nearly always a contest over public goods—who has the best education policy, who has the best health care plan, and so on.

In Figure 8.6, we summarize how a leader's institutional environment (W and S) affects government performance and the material well-being of citizens. The dotted line indicates those positions where W/S is large; that is, the loyalty norm is low. Note that W/S can be large when both W and S are large, as in democracies, or when both W and S are small, as in monarchic and military dictatorships. As Figure 8.6 illustrates, we can think of three different levels of government performance—good, middling, and poor—depending on the institutional environment in place. Government performance is likely to be good when W and W/S are both large (democracies). This is because leaders are likely to provide public goods rather than private goods (W is large) and because the weak loyalty norm (W/S is large) forces leaders to work hard to stay in office.

In contrast, government performance is likely to be poor when W and W/S are both small (dominant-party and personalist dictatorships). In countries with this type of institutional environment, leaders have little incentive to care about the state of the national economy or the material well-being of the citizenry in general. Instead, they provide small amounts of

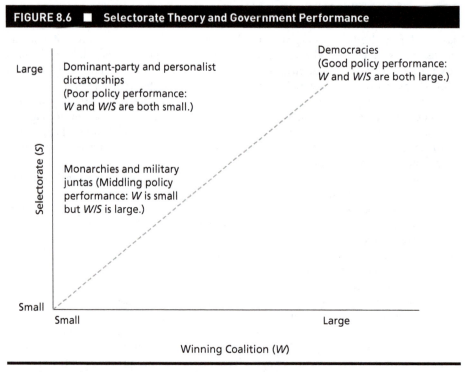

FIGURE 8.6 ■ Selectorate Theory and Government Performance

Note: W/S is large (and the loyalty norm is weak) along the dotted line.

private goods to members of their winning coalition and engage in highly kleptocratic and corrupt activities. The only thing keeping these types of leaders from excessive predation is the refusal of residents to work and therefore the lack of anything to prey on. This constraint is obviously much weaker if the country is rich in natural resources, such as oil and minerals, or if the leaders receive significant amounts of foreign aid.

Government performance is likely to be middling when W is small and W/S is large (monarchies and military juntas). Although leaders in these types of system provide few public goods to the general citizenry, they're forced to care about their overall performance in office because of the weak loyalty norm at work. For example, leaders have an incentive to produce reasonably good economic performance, because this is the only way of generating the necessary resources to pay off their not-so-loyal winning coalition. That these leaders are interested in good economic performance necessarily means they also care, to some extent, about the material well-being of the residents who make up the workforce and thus have an incentive to provide some basic public goods.

Figure 8.6 shows a triangular pattern in the predictions that selectorate theory makes about the likely performance of different types of political systems. While democracies (large W) should perform relatively well, there should be considerable variation in the performance of dictatorships (small W). Some types of dictatorship (large W/S systems) should perform considerably better than other types of dictatorship (small W/S systems). What does the empirical evidence say?

In Figure 8.7, we show how the average level of democracy in eighty-eight countries is associated with six different indicators of material well-being: (1) wealth as measured by GDP per capita, (2) the percentage of births attended by a physician, (3) the percentage of pregnant women receiving prenatal care, (4) the percentage of infants and children receiving vaccinations, (5) infant and child (under five years of age) mortality rates per thousand, and (6) life expectancy as measured in years. Our measure of democracy, which comes from Polity IV, ranges from –10 (most dictatorial) to +10 (most democratic). The key thing to note in each plot is the "triangular" nature of the data. While democracies seldom perform poorly in terms of these indicators of material well-being, dictatorships exhibit much more variation. Although some dictatorships produce outcomes that are substantially worse than most democracies, some seem to perform every bit as well as democracies. This suggests that democracy is *sufficient* for ensuring some degree of success in these various areas of material well-being, but that it's not *necessary* for success. As we've seen, selectorate theory provides an explanation for this pattern of performance across different types of political systems. In particular, it provides an explanation for the varied performance of different authoritarian regimes.

What does all this mean for the *type* of leader necessary to generate good public policy? By now you should realize that implementing good public policy is not as simple as identifying decent human beings who genuinely want to improve their fellow citizens' lives and then ensuring that these people rise to political power. It turns out that having a civic-minded leader is neither necessary nor sufficient for successful public policies. Simply put, what's needed for good public policy is a set of institutions that creates a large W, large W/S system. If the political institutions in a country are such that a large proportion of the residents can participate in choosing their leader and the leader depends on a large proportion of that selectorate to remain in power, then only leaders who provide a sufficiently high level of government performance will be *able* to stay in power. It doesn't matter whether the leader cares about providing good government performance for its own sake or whether he cares about it only because it helps him stay in power; both goals dictate the same course of action. This

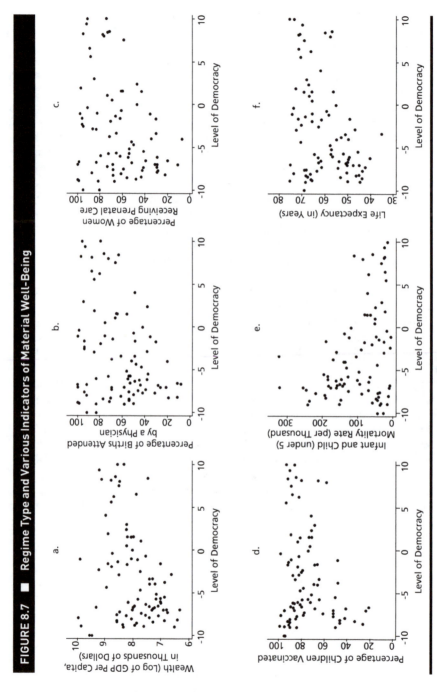

FIGURE 8.7 ■ **Regime Type and Various Indicators of Material Well-Being**

Source: Data from the Polity IV: Regime Authority Characteristics and Transitions Datasets provided courtesy of the Center for Systemic Peace.

Note: The horizontal axes measure a country's average level of democracy from 1960 to 1990 as coded by Polity. The democracy measure ranges from –10 (most dictatorial) to +10 (most democratic). The vertical axes of each graph capture distinct indicators of material well-being (McGuire 2002).

results in competition to provide more, and better, public goods, as well as good economic policies designed to generate higher overall revenue. Under such conditions, residents have incentives to invest, and the economy is expected to grow.

The bottom line is that even if there are two types of leaders in the world—those who are civic minded and those who aren't—all leaders are forced to govern well in large W, large W/S systems and poorly in small W, small W/S systems if they want to stay in power. This point is well illustrated by leaders who had the opportunity to rule over very different systems of government. Consider Leopold II (1835–1909), who was king of Belgium (large W, large W/S) and ruler of the Congo Free State (small W, small W/S). Consider also Chiang Kai-shek (1887–1975), who ruled China (small W, small W/S) for twenty years and then Taiwan (large W, large W/S) for another twenty-five. In both of these cases, the two leaders provided more public goods and better government performance in the large W, large W/S systems that they governed (BDM²S² 2003, 208–213). For more details, see Box 8.2, "The Tale of Two Leopolds."

It follows from this discussion that one's preference for the type of institutions in a country depends on one's position in the society. Leaders prefer to set up institutions that encourage a small winning coalition and a large selectorate, because these institutions help them not only to stay in power but also to enrich themselves at the expense of their citizenry. Members of the winning coalition like institutions in which W is small but W/S is large. This is because a small W means the leader will provide coalition members with private goods, and a large W/S guarantees the leader will have to provide large quantities of these goods to counteract the weak loyalty norm. Members of the selectorate and the disenfranchised classes like institutions in which both W and W/S are large. This is because a large W forces the leader to provide coalition members with public goods and the large W/S provides strong incentives for the leader to perform well in office to counteract the weak loyalty norm. In other words, leaders prefer to rule over dominant-party or personalist dictatorships, members of the winning coalition prefer to live in monarchic or military dictatorships, and everyone else prefers to live in democracies.

BOX 8.2 THE TALE OF TWO LEOPOLDS

Leopold II is remembered as an excellent king of Belgium (1865–1909) who provided his subjects with significant amounts of public goods. He instituted progressive reforms and promoted high levels of economic growth and industrial development. For example, he gave workers the right to strike, expanded the suffrage, set limits on child labor, introduced educational improvements, and supported massive public works projects designed to lower unemployment and enhance the economy.

While Leopold was presiding over this set of progressive policies in Belgium, he was taking a decidedly different approach in the Congo Free State (1885–1908), over which he also ruled. Leopold created a low-paid military force in the Congo, the Force Publique, and offered the soldiers additional wages based on commissions for goods such as rubber and ivory. Without laws to protect Congolese workers, the members of the Force Publique used slave labor, torture, and murder to meet its quotas. The soldiers

(Continued)

(Continued)

The Granger Collection

King Leopold II of Belgium.

were also given rewards for killing "antigovernment rebels," although more often than not these were villagers who simply didn't want to be forced into slave labor. The soldiers would bring hands (or heads) to the Belgian commissioner as proof of the number of "rebels" that had been killed; eyewitness accounts report that some of these hands obviously belonged to women and children and suggested that ordinary Congolese were being killed because doing so meant that soldiers could get higher wages. Leopold and the

Force Publique gained incredible riches from the sale of ivory and rubber on the world market. This revenue was not returned to the Congo Free State in the form of public goods to benefit its residents. The only goods exported to the Congo, in fact, were weapons for the Force Publique to keep the flow of goods (the result of slave labor) headed toward Belgium. Thus, Leopold was allowing—even promoting—slave labor in the Congo at the same time as he was promoting laws protecting workers in Belgium.

What was different about the institutions in the two countries? Belgium was a constitutional monarchy, which means that Leopold's rule relied on the support of a popularly elected government. In effect, the winning coalition size in Belgium was reasonably large. By contrast, the Congo Free State was considered to be Leopold's personal property. Leopold's winning coalition in the Congo consisted of just himself and the members of the Force Publique. As selectorate theory predicts, Leopold worked hard to promote economic growth and provide significant amounts of public goods when his winning coalition was large (Belgium) but provided small amounts of private goods for his supporters and stole the rest of the revenue for himself when the winning coalition was small (Congo).

Which was the real Leopold? BDM²S² (2003, 208–213), who provide the account of the two Leopolds we've drawn on here, conclude that it must have been the "murderous ruler of the Congo" rather than the "civic-minded king of Belgium." Why? Well, Leopold simply inherited his institutions in Belgium and acted accordingly. In contrast, he had free rein to set up any type of government arrangement he wanted in the Congo. Leopold's actions in both countries were entirely consistent with the institutional incentives he faced.

CONCLUSION

In this chapter, we've examined the wide variety of authoritarian regimes that exist around the world. In the first section of the chapter, we examined a common typology of dictatorships. In this typology, dictatorships are classified in terms of the identity of their "support coalitions."

Such an approach indicates that there are three main types of authoritarian regime: (1) monarchic dictatorships, (2) military dictatorships, and (3) civilian dictatorships. Civilian dictatorships are sometimes further classified into those that are personalist and those that have a dominant regime party.

In the second section of the chapter, we focused on the two fundamental problems of authoritarian rule. The problem of authoritarian power-sharing focuses on potential conflict within the regime elite. Many authoritarian regimes create institutions such as legislatures to facilitate power-sharing agreements between the dictator and his support coalition. These institutions help the dictator credibly commit to not violating any power-sharing agreement as they enable the support coalition to better monitor his behavior. As we saw, though, these institutions are effective only if the support coalition can credibly threaten to remove the dictator, which requires power to be evenly distributed between the dictator and his support coalition. The problem of authoritarian control focuses on potential conflict between the dictatorial elite and the masses. Dictators have two strategies for controlling the masses, repression and co-optation. From the dictator's perspective, repression is often a dangerous strategy as the agents of repression, typically the military, may have different preferences from the dictator's and can turn their guns on the dictator rather than the masses. In these circumstances, the dictator can find himself as the figurehead of the regime, with true power lying in the hands of the military. Dictators often use institutions such as regime parties to co-opt the masses. In addition to being a vehicle for transferring regime rents to some opposition groups, these institutions give citizens a stake in promoting regime survival.

In the last part of the chapter, we examined selectorate theory. Selectorate theory provides a potential story both for why democracies produce a relatively high level of material well-being for their citizens and for why some dictatorships perform better than others. Starting from the simple assumption that all political leaders care about winning and retaining power, selectorate theory offers an explanation for the observed variation in the performance of different forms of government that focuses on the institutional structure surrounding political leaders. This "institutional structure" refers primarily to the size of a country's winning coalition and selectorate. Leaders in systems with large winning coalitions and weak loyalty norms like democracies have to provide public goods and a high level of overall government performance if they want to remain in office. In contrast, leaders in systems with small winning coalitions and strong loyalty norms, like dominant-party and personalist dictatorships, are "forced" to provide private goods and produce a poor level of overall government performance, because this is the best way to stay in power in these countries. In between these two ends of the performance spectrum are leaders in systems with small winning coalitions and weak loyalty norms, such as monarchies and military juntas. Although these leaders are more likely to provide private goods than public goods, they do have to care about their overall government performance because of the weak loyalty norm at work.

Selectorate theory provides an answer to an important question raised in Chapter 4. Recall that according to the contractarian view of the state, citizens delegate their right to use violence to the state, which acts as a third-party enforcer and punishes those who take advantage of their fellow citizens. Recall also, that while such a state solves the problem that exists between citizens in the state of nature, it raises the question of "who will guard the guardian?" That is, if the state has a near monopoly on the use of force, what is to stop the state from stealing from its citizens? Like the predatory view of the state discussed in Chapter 4, selectorate theory takes a grim view of the state and emphasizes the degree of competition faced by the incumbent leader. Leaders tend to act in a predatory manner unless they face a realistic chance of being replaced by a rival. Selectorate theory provides insight into the mechanism through which such competition arises. Specifically, leaders will limit their predation when the size of the winning coalition is large relative to the size of the selectorate.

Key Concepts

monarchic dictatorship—a dictatorship in which the executive holds power on the basis of family and kin networks

military dictatorship—a dictatorship in which the executive relies on the armed forces to hold power

civilian dictatorships—all dictatorships other than monarchic or military dictatorships

dominant-party dictatorship—a dictatorship in which a single party dominates access to political office and control over policy, though other parties may exist and compete in elections

personalist dictatorship—a dictatorship in which the leader, although often supported by a party or the military, retains personal control of policy decisions and the selection of regime personnel

dictator's dilemma—the dictator relies on repression to stay in power, but this repression creates incentives for everyone to falsify their preferences so that the dictator never knows her true level of societal support

electoral authoritarian regime—a regime in which leaders hold elections and tolerate some pluralism and interparty competition but violate minimal democratic norms so severely and systematically that it makes no sense to classify them as democracies

hegemonic electoral regime—a regime in which the leader's party routinely wins with overwhelming majorities

competitive authoritarian regime—a regime in which opposition parties win substantial minorities at election time

politically closed authoritarian regimes—a regime in which no opposition party is granted a legal space in the political arena

selectorate theory—a theory that characterizes all governments by their location in a two-dimensional institutional space; one dimension is the size of the selectorate and the second dimension is the size of the winning coalition

disenfranchised—residents who don't have the legal right to participate in choosing the government

selectorate (S)—those people who can play a role in selecting the leader

winning coalition (W)—those people whose support is necessary for the leader to stay in power

loyalty norm—the extent of the winning coalition's loyalty to the leader; its strength is determined by W/S—the probability that a member of the selectorate will be in the winning coalition

kleptocracy—when corruption is organized by political leaders with the goal of personal enrichment

corruption—when public officials take illegal payments (bribes) in exchange for providing benefits for particular individuals

PROBLEMS WITH GROUP DECISION MAKING

Democracy is the recurrent suspicion that more than half of the people are right more than half of the time.

E. B. White, *The New Yorker,* July 3, 1944

OVERVIEW

1. In this chapter, we look at whether the process by which democracies make decisions has appealing features that make it morally or normatively attractive compared with dictatorships.

2. At its very heart, democracy is a system in which the majority is supposed to rule. Still, making decisions that reflect the preferences of a majority can be a lot more complicated and less fair than one might think. Even if all members of a group have rational preferences, Condorcet's paradox shows that it might be impossible to reach a stable group decision using majority rule.

3. The median voter theorem indicates that stable group decisions can be achieved if we're willing to rule certain preferences out of bounds and reduce the policy space to a single issue dimension. Unfortunately, neither of these restrictions is uncontroversial.

4. Arrow's theorem proves that no method of group decision making can guarantee a stable group decision while simultaneously satisfying minimal conditions of fairness. In effect, it proves that there's no perfect set of decision-making institutions; either fairness is compromised or there'll be the potential for unstable group choices.

5. The absence of an ideal decision-making mechanism means that institutional choice is an exercise in the choice of "second bests" and that trade-offs will need to be made. This helps to explain why we observe so many different types of democracy in the world.

What kinds of political institutions should we adopt when we have an opportunity to set up new institutions or change existing ones? One obvious way to begin answering this question is to see which sets of institutions produce good outcomes. For example, do democratic regimes produce better material outcomes, say, than dictatorial ones? If they do, we should recommend adopting some set of democratic institutions. Although it's commonly believed that democracies outperform dictatorships in regard to providing material well-being, some of the data we presented in Chapter 8 suggest that things are not this simple. Citizens living in certain types of dictatorship tend to enjoy a high quality of life that rivals that of citizens in democracies, at least according to various measures of economic development and growth or the provision of government services, such as health care and education. Indeed, several dictatorships regularly outperform many democracies when it comes to the measures of material outcomes we examined.

At this point, the philosophy students among you might point out that we're overlooking some important criteria with which to evaluate sets of political institutions. Political philosophers usually use one of two broad approaches for evaluating the moral or ethical value of adopting a given set of institutions. On the one hand, those inclined toward **consequentialist ethics** ask whether the institutions in question produce good outcomes. This is the approach we adopted in the previous chapter. On the other hand, those favoring **deontological ethics** attempt to evaluate institutions in a way that's independent of the outcomes those institutions produce—they ask whether the institutions are good, fair, or just, in and of themselves. In this chapter, we consider democracy from a deontological perspective. In particular, we examine whether the process by which democratic governments make decisions for the entire country has appealing properties that make it morally or normatively attractive above and beyond any material benefits it might produce. In other words, is the process by which decisions are made in democracies inherently good, fair, or just?

People typically assume that a dictatorial decision-making process is inherently unfair, whereas a democratic decision-making process is inherently fair. We explore this assumption in some detail and lay out several criteria for evaluating how groups of individuals make decisions.[1] Overall, we think the results of our analysis will surprise many of you. As we demonstrate, there are no perfect decision-making processes—all institutional choices, including the decision to adopt democratic institutions, entail a set of significant trade-offs. It's the existence of these trade-offs that helps to explain why there are so many different types of democracies in the world. In effect, different countries choose to make different trade-offs when they decide to adopt democratic institutions.

PROBLEMS WITH GROUP DECISION MAKING

Many people say they like democracy because they believe it to be a fair way to make group decisions. One commonsense notion of fairness is that group decisions should reflect the preferences of the majority of group members. Most people would probably agree, for example,

---

[1]The material in this chapter comes from a part of the political science literature called *social choice theory*. Social choice theory addresses the voting rules that govern and describe how individual preferences are aggregated to form a collective group preference. Much of this literature is highly mathematical. In this chapter, we focus on providing the intuition behind some of the more important ideas in social choice theory. For those interested in examining social choice theory in more depth, we suggest starting with Sen (1970), Riker (1982), Hinich and Munger (1997), and Patty and Penn (2014).

that a fair way to decide between two options is to choose the option that's preferred by the most people. When selecting among just two options, the option most members of a group prefer is necessarily the option a majority of the group prefers. At its very heart, democracy is a system in which the majority rules. In this section of the chapter, we show that there are many situations in which "majority rule" is a lot more complicated and less fair than our commonsense intuition about it would suggest. In effect, we demonstrate that allowing the majority to decide can be deeply problematic in many different ways.

Majority Rule and Condorcet's Paradox

If a group of people needs to choose between just two options, majority rule can be quite straightforward. But what if a group needs to choose between more than two options? For example, imagine a city council deciding on the level of social services it should provide.[2] The proposed options are to increase (*I*), decrease (*D*), or maintain current (*C*) levels of social service provision. Let's assume that the council is made up of three members—a left-wing councillor, a right-wing councillor, and a centrist councillor—who all rank the proposed options differently. Specifically, the left-wing councillor prefers an increase in spending to current levels of spending and prefers current levels of spending to a decrease. The centrist councillor most prefers current levels of spending but would prefer a decrease in spending over any increase if it came to it. The right-wing councillor most prefers a decrease in spending. Because he views current levels of spending as unsustainable, however, the right-wing councillor would prefer to "break the bank" with an increase in spending in order to spur much-needed reforms than maintain the status quo. The preference ordering for each of the council members is summarized in Table 9.1.

Let's assume the council employs majority rule to make its group decisions. In this particular example, this means that any policy alternative that enjoys the support of two or more councillors will be adopted. How should the councillors vote, though? It's not obvious how they should vote given that there are more than two alternatives. One way they might proceed is to hold a **round-robin tournament** that pits each alternative against every other alternative in a set of "pair-wise votes"—*I* versus *D, I* versus *C,* and *C* versus *D*—and designates as the winner whichever alternative wins the most contests. If we assume the councillors all vote for their most preferred alternative in each pair-wise contest (or round), we see that *D* defeats *I, I* defeats *C,* and *C* defeats *D.* The outcomes of these pair-wise contests and the majorities that produce them are summarized in Table 9.2. Notice there's no alternative that wins most often—each alternative wins exactly one pair-wise contest. This multiplicity of "winners" doesn't provide the council with a clear policy direction. In other words, the council fails to reach a decision on whether to increase, decrease, or maintain current levels of social service provision.

TABLE 9.1 ■ City Council Preferences for the Level of Social Service Provision		
Left-wing councillors	**Centrist councillors**	**Right-wing councillors**
I > C > D	*C > D > I*	*D > I > C*

Note: I = increased social service provision; *D* = decreased social service provision; *C* = maintenance of current levels of social service provision; > = "is strictly preferred to."

---

[2]This example comes from Dixit, Skeath, and Reiley (2015).

TABLE 9.2 ■ Outcomes from the Round-Robin Tournament			
Round	Contest	Winner	Majority that produced victory
1	Increase vs. decrease	D	Centrist and right
2	Current vs. increase	I	Left and right
3	Current vs. decrease	C	Left and centrist

This simple example produces several interesting results that we now examine in more detail. The first is that a group of three *rational* actors (the councillors) make up a group (the council) appearing to be incapable of making a rational decision for the group as a whole. What do we mean by "rational"? When political scientists use the word *rational,* they have a very specific meaning in mind. An actor is said to be **rational** if she possesses a complete and transitive preference ordering over a set of outcomes. An actor has a **complete preference ordering** if she can compare each pair of elements (call them *x* and *y*) in a set of outcomes in one of the following ways—either the actor prefers *x* to *y,* she prefers *y* to *x,* or she's indifferent between *x* and *y.* The assumption of completeness essentially states that an individual can always make up her mind as to whether she prefers one option or is indifferent when presented with a pair of options. An actor has a **transitive preference ordering** if for any *x, y,* and *z* in the set of outcomes, it's the case that if *x* is preferred to *y,* and *y* is preferred to *z,* then it must be the case that *x* is preferred to *z.* To put this in context, suppose you're confronted with three ice-cream flavors: vanilla, chocolate, and strawberry. If you prefer vanilla to chocolate, and chocolate to strawberry, then if you have transitive preferences, you'll also prefer vanilla to strawberry. If it turns out that you prefer strawberry to vanilla, then you don't have transitive preferences. Actors whose preference orderings are *not* complete and transitive are said to be irrational.

In the example we've been examining, each of the councillors is rational because each has a complete and transitive preference ordering over the three policy alternatives. For example, the left-wing councillor prefers *I* to *C* and *C* to *D* and also prefers *I* to *D.* The outcome of the round-robin tournament, however, reveals that this set of rational individuals becomes a group that acts like an individual with intransitive preferences. Recall that the group prefers *D* to *I* and *I* to *C.* Transitivity would require that the group also prefers *D* to *C.* Round 3 of the round-robin tournament reveals, however, that the group prefers *C* to *D.* This juxtaposition—of rational individuals forming a group that behaves irrationally—was first described in a paper in 1785 by Marie Jean Antoine Nicolas de Caritat, the Marquis de Condorcet, and is usually referred to as **Condorcet's paradox**.

A second interesting aspect of our example is that a different majority supports the winning alternative or outcome in each round. In Round 1, the majority that votes in favor of a decrease in social service provision is made up of the centrist and right-wing councillors. In Round 2, the majority that votes in favor of an increase in social service provision is a coalition of "odd bedfellows" comprising the left- and right-wing councillors. Finally, in Round 3, the majority that votes in favor of the status quo comprises the left-wing and centrist councillors. Although "letting the majority decide" may sound fair and straightforward, our example here makes it very clear that "a majority" doesn't necessarily exist until the policy debate is framed in a certain way.

Condorcet's paradox points out that individual rationality isn't sufficient to ensure group rationality. A set of actors, each with complete and transitive preference orderings, may behave in a way that reveals group intransitivity. When this occurs, there's no "majority" to speak of; instead, there's a cycle of different majorities. For example, suppose we start with the current level of social service provision as the status quo. A council member who's unhappy with this status quo (say, the left-wing councillor) might propose a vote like that in Round 2 of the round-robin tournament (*C* vs. *I*). In this vote, a majority would support an increase in social service provision over the maintenance of the status quo (see Table 9.2). But as soon as this vote ends, a disgruntled council member (say, the centrist) can propose a vote like that in Round 1 of the round-robin tournament (*I* vs. *D*). In this vote, a majority would support a decrease in social service provision over an increase. But as soon as this vote ends, a different disgruntled council member—in this case, the left-wing councillor—can propose a vote like that in Round 3 of the round-robin tournament (*C* vs. *D*). In this vote, a majority would support maintaining the current level of social service provision rather than decreasing it. Interestingly, the centrist, who just one vote ago proposed decreasing the provision of social services, now votes to maintain current levels of social service provision. Having arrived back where they began (*C*), and absent any institutional mechanism to end the succession of proposals and counterproposals, the scene is set for the cycle to begin anew—with no end in sight. This cycle through the different majorities is illustrated in Figure 9.1.

Some of you may feel that our example of cyclical majorities is unlikely ever to occur in practice. After all, we see deliberative bodies make decisions all the time and, although we may sometimes think they're far from efficient, they don't seem to be caught in the type of endless cycle our example suggests. On the whole, there are two broad reasons for this. One has to do with preference orderings and the other has to do with decision-making rules. Let's start with preference orderings. To some extent, our current example is special in the sense that it depends on the councillors having a particular set of preference orderings. For example, if the right-wing councillor's preferences were the mirror image of those of the left-wing

FIGURE 9.1   ■   An Example of Cyclical Majorities

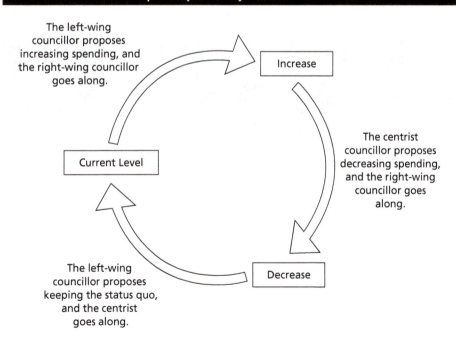

councillor—that is, if the right-wing council member preferred a decrease to the current level but preferred the current level to an increase—then maintaining current levels of social service provision would win both rounds of the round-robin tournament in which it competes. In political science, we call an option like this—that is, one that beats all other options in a series of pair-wise contests—a **Condorcet winner**. Given the decision-making process adopted by the council, and assuming that all councillors vote for their most preferred option, this would mean that maintaining current levels of social service provision is a stable outcome.

To see why, imagine that maintaining current spending on social services is the status quo and ask yourself who would benefit from a change. The answer is that both the left- and right-wing councillors would like to propose a change. The right-wing council member prefers a decrease in social service provision to the status quo. If she proposed a decrease, however, both the centrist and left-wing councillors would vote against the proposal. Similarly, the left-wing council member prefers an increase in social service provision to the status quo. But if she proposed an increase, both the centrist and right-wing councillors would vote against the proposal. In other words, with this new profile of preferences in the group, there's no cycle of majorities, and as a result, current levels of spending constitute a stable outcome. In effect, the group now behaves as if it were an individual with transitive (and complete) preferences—it prefers current levels of social service provision to a decrease and a decrease to an increase.

The point here is that majority rule isn't necessarily incompatible with rational group preferences. All that Condorcet showed was that it's *possible* for a group of individuals with transitive preferences to produce a group that behaves as if it has intransitive preferences. As a result, Condorcet's paradox erodes our confidence in the ability of majority rule to produce stable outcomes only to the extent that we expect actors to hold the types of preferences that cause group intransitivity. So how likely is it that transitive individual preferences will lead to group intransitivity? Modern scholars have analyzed this problem in detail and found, assuming that all preference orderings are equally likely, that the likelihood of group intransitivity increases with both the number of alternatives under consideration and the number of voters. In Table 9.3, we show estimates of the share of all possible strict preference orderings that fail

TABLE 9.3 ■ Proportion of Possible Strict Preference Orderings without a Condorcet Winner						
	Number of voters					
Number of alternatives	**3**	**5**	**7**	**9**	**11 ⟶**	**Limit**
3	0.056	0.069	0.075	0.078	0.080	0.088
4	0.111	0.139	0.150	0.156	0.160	0.176
5	0.160	0.200	0.215			0.251
6	0.202					0.315
↓						↓
Limit	1.000	1.000	1.000	1.000	1.000	1.000

Source: Data based on Riker, William. 1982. *Liberalism Against Populism: A Confrontation between the Theory of Democracy and the Theory of Social Choice.* San Francisco: Freeman. p. 122.

to produce a Condorcet winner (that is, that produce group intransitivity) as the numbers of voters and alternatives increase (Riker 1982, 122).

As Table 9.3 illustrates, the example of the city council we started with, in which a Condorcet winner fails to emerge from a contest among three alternatives and three voters, is indeed a rarity. Nearly all (94.4 percent) of the logically possible strict preference orderings produce a Condorcet winner and, hence, a stable outcome. As the number of voters increases, however, the probability of group intransitivity rises to some limit. When the number of alternatives is relatively small, this limit is still small enough that most of the logically possible preference orderings won't lead to group intransitivity. In contrast, although an increase in the number of alternatives also increases the probability of group intransitivity, this process continues until the point at which group intransitivity is certain to occur. In other words, as the number of alternatives goes to infinity, the probability of group intransitivity converges to one—even when the number of voters is small. This is an extremely important result because many political decisions involve a choice from, essentially, an infinite number of alternatives.

Imagine, for example, what would happen if we introduced a bit more realism into our example about a city council deciding on social welfare spending. Previously, we simplified the situation to one in which the councillors were deciding between three alternatives—increase, decrease, or maintain current spending. In reality, though, the councillors would normally be choosing an exact amount of money to spend on social services. In effect, they'd be choosing a share of the budget to allocate to social service provision from 0 percent to 100 percent. There's an infinite number of choices that could be made in this interval (0–100). As a consequence, if no restrictions are placed on the councillors' preferences, then group intransitivity is all but guaranteed. Significantly, all policy decisions that involve bargaining over some divisible resource—questions relating to things like the distribution of government resources, the allocation of the tax burden, the allocation of ministerial portfolios in the government, the amount of permissible greenhouse gas emissions, and the location of toxic waste—can be seen in a similar light.

To summarize, Condorcet's paradox makes it clear that restricting group decision making to sets of rational individuals is no guarantee that the group as a whole will exhibit rational tendencies. Group intransitivity is unlikely when the set of feasible options is small, but it's almost certain that majority rule applied to a pair-wise competition among alternatives will fail to produce a stable outcome when the set of feasible options gets large. As a result, it's impossible to say that the majority "decides" except in very restricted circumstances.

The analytical insight from Condorcet's paradox suggests that group intransitivity should be common, but, as we've already noted, we observe a surprising amount of stability in group decision making in the real world. Our discussion so far suggests that this must be the result of either of two factors. Either the number of decision makers or issues is kept small *and* the kinds of preferences that produce group intransitivity are rare, or a decision-making mechanism other than a simple pair-wise comparison of alternatives is being used. We've already seen that some of the most common types of political decisions involve a great number of alternatives, so it's likely that any stability we observe in the real world results from the use of alternative decision rules. One such departure from a round-robin tournament based on majority rule is one in which the order and number of alternatives to be evaluated is controlled by an agenda setter.

Majority Rule with an Agenda Setter

A decision-making mechanism that overcomes the potential instability of majority rule in round-robin tournaments requires actors to begin by considering only a subset of the available pair-wise alternatives. For instance, in our original city council example, we might require that both departures from the status quo (that is, increases and decreases in social service spending) first face each other in a pair-wise contest and that the winner then go on to compete in a vote against the status quo. Imposing a voting agenda such as this turns the voting process into a sequential game with three players—each player simultaneously chooses between increasing and decreasing social service provision, and then, each player simultaneously chooses between the winning alternative from the first round and the maintenance of current spending levels in the second round.

Let's assume for a moment that each council member votes for her preferred option when confronted with any two choices. In other words, let's assume that each councillor casts what is known as a sincere vote. In the first round, the councillors choose between increasing social service spending and decreasing it. Given the preferences of the councillors in our example, we know that both the centrist and the right-wing council members prefer a decrease in spending over an increase. As a result, the vote in the first round would be 2–1 in favor of a decrease. This means that the second (and final) round of voting is a choice between decreasing social service spending and maintaining current levels of spending. Because the left-wing and centrist councillors both prefer the current level of social service spending to a decrease, the outcome of this game is the status quo; that is, current spending levels are maintained. (Stop for a moment and ask yourself, which of the councillors is likely to have set this voting agenda.)

But should we expect all of the councillors to vote sincerely in our example? Consider that the councillors know there are only two possible contests in the second round—either D versus C or I versus C. Given the preference orderings in our example, the councillors know that these potential second-round contests will end up with either C defeating D or I defeating C. It follows from this that the councillors know that if D wins in the first round against I, then the final outcome will be the status quo, C. In other words, voting for D in the first round is essentially equivalent to voting for the status quo in the end. As a result, the first round of voting should, in reality, be seen as a contest between I and C (even if the councillors are actually voting between I and D).

Think about how the right-wing councillor might reason through the logic of this voting procedure. Recall that her favorite outcome is a decrease in social service spending, her second-best outcome is an increase in social service spending, and her least preferred outcome is maintaining the current level of social service spending. If she casts her vote in the first round for her most preferred outcome without thinking about the consequences for the rest of the voting agenda, we've already seen that option D will be victorious in the first round but will go on to lose to C in the second and final round. This is, of course, the right-wing councillor's worst possible outcome. As a result, she has a strong incentive to change her vote in the first round from D to I even though this new vote doesn't conform to her sincere preferences. If she does this and votes for an increase in social service spending in the first round, I will win and be pitted against C in the final round. In this final round, I will defeat C. In other words, the final outcome will be an increase in social service provision. Note that by deviating from her sincere preferences in the first round, the right-wing councillor is able to alter the final outcome from her least preferred outcome to her second-best one. In this example, the right-wing councillor casts what political scientists call a **strategic**, or **sophisticated, vote**—a vote in which an individual votes in favor of a less preferred option because she believes doing so will ultimately produce a more preferred outcome than would otherwise be the case. Some analysts find strategic voting lamentable and would prefer decision rules that induce **sincere voting**—voting that constitutes a sincere revelation of an individual's preferences.

The incentives to vote strategically aren't the only thing that scholars find lamentable with voting agendas like the one we just examined. Another thing that many scholars find

TABLE 9.4 ■ Pair-Wise Contests and Different Voting Agendas

Agenda	1st Round	1st-Round winner	2nd Round	2nd-Round winner	Councillor obtaining her most preferred outcome
1	I vs. D	D	D vs. C	C	Centrist councillor
2	C vs. I	I	I vs. D	D	Right-wing councillor
3	C vs. D	C	C vs. I	I	Left-wing councillor

Note: I = an increase in social service provision; D = a decrease in social service provision; C = a maintenance of current levels of social service provision.

disconcerting is that alternative agendas can produce very different outcomes even if we hold all of the actors' preferences constant. In fact, the three alternatives in our city council example can face each other in three different two-round tournaments, all of which produce a different outcome. The three different two-round tournaments and the outcomes they produce are shown in Table 9.4. As you can see, choosing the agenda is essentially equivalent to choosing which outcome will win. For example, if you decide to have a first-round contest between *I* and *D,* you know the eventual outcome will be a victory for *C.* If you decide to have a first-round contest between *C* and *I,* you know the eventual outcome will be *D.* And if you decide to have a first-round contest between *C* and *D,* you know the eventual outcome will be *I.* Consequently, if one of the councillors is given the power to choose the agenda, she is, effectively, given the power to dictate the outcome of the decision-making process. This phenomenon, in which choosing the agenda is tantamount to choosing which alternative will win, is referred to as the "power of the agenda setter," and it exists in many institutional settings. In our example, the agenda setter can obtain her most preferred outcome simply by deciding what the order of pair-wise contests should be. For example, the centrist councillor would choose Agenda 1 in Table 9.4 if she were the agenda setter; the right-wing councillor would choose Agenda 2; and the left-wing councillor would choose Agenda 3.

In sum, it's possible to avoid the potential for group intransitivity that arises in majority rule round-robin tournaments by imposing an agenda—by designating which outcomes will be voted on first and which outcome will, in effect, be granted entry into a second round, in which it will compete against the winner of the first round. Unfortunately, the outcome of such a process is extremely sensitive to the agenda chosen, and consequently, either of two things is likely to happen. Either the instability of group decision making shifts from votes on outcomes to votes on the agendas expected to produce those outcomes, or some subset of actors is given power to control the agenda and therefore given considerable influence over the outcome likely to be produced. Thus, one possible explanation for observed policy stability in democracies is that some subset of the decision makers is controlling the agenda in a manner that prevents its preferred outcome from being defeated as part of a cycle of majorities. While this set of events might introduce desired stability to the policymaking process, it does so by sacrificing the notion that democratic outcomes reflect the will of the majority.

Restrictions on Preferences: The Median Voter Theorem

It appears that institutional factors restricting the agenda may produce stable outcomes, but only at the expense of creating incentives for actors to attempt to manipulate the decision-making process. This obviously raises questions about our ability to design our way around the instability of majority rule in such a way that the cure is not worse than the disease. In the next section of this chapter, we discuss important work that suggests it may be impossible to design a decision-making mechanism that ensures group transitivity while simultaneously meeting minimal criteria for fairness. But before we get there, let's pause briefly to consider the behavior of majority rule in one more special case.

Recall that group intransitivity in our original city council example seemed to stem from the fact that the right-wing councillor has a particular type of preference ordering. Specifically, the right-wing councillor prefers both lower and higher levels of social service provision to the maintenance of current levels of social service provision. The right-wing councillor's most preferred option is to decrease social service spending. But if it came to it, she'd rather increase spending in the hope this would "break the bank" and force the city to adjust to lower levels of spending in the future than maintain current levels of spending (which she thinks are too high) that would slowly bleed the city dry.

It's possible to represent the right-wing councillor's preferences with what political scientists call a **utility function**. A utility function can be thought of as a numerical scale in which higher numbers stand for higher positions in an individual's preference ordering. It essentially indicates how satisfied an individual is with the available alternatives. In Figure 9.2, we display a utility function that is consistent with the preference ordering of the right-wing councillor over the level of social service provision in our example. The utility function is highest over the proposal to decrease social service provision (*D*), it's lowest over the proposal to maintain current levels of social service provision (*C*), and it's between these two extremes over the proposal to increase social service provision (*I*).

Let's now examine the utility function of the centrist councillor. This is shown in Figure 9.3. You'll immediately notice that the centrist councillor's utility function looks very different from that of the right-wing councillor's in Figure 9.2. In particular, the centrist councillor's utility function captures what political scientists call a **single-peaked preference ordering**. In other words, the utility function reaches a "peak" above the centrist councillor's most preferred point. In this particular example, her most preferred point, sometimes called her "ideal point," is *C*. As proposals move away from this "ideal point" in either direction, the centrist councillor experiences a decline in her utility function.[3] The basic intuition behind single peakedness is that individuals prefer outcomes that are closer to their ideal point than those that are farther away. A quick glance at Figure 9.2 again shows that the right-wing councillor's utility function is not single peaked. Although there's a point at which the right-wing councillor's utility function reaches a maximum (around *D*), the utility function doesn't continuously decline as it moves farther away from this point—it starts to go back up to the right of *C*. In other words, the right-wing councillor prefers some outcomes that are farther from her ideal point (say, *I*) than outcomes that are closer (say, *C*).

One of the most important results in all of political science is called the median voter theorem (see Box 9.1, "The Median Voter Theorem and Party Competition"). The **median voter theorem (MVT)** states that no alternative can beat the one preferred by the median voter in pair-wise majority-rule elections if the number of voters is odd, voter preferences are single-peaked over a single policy dimension, and voters vote sincerely. When voters are arrayed along a single issue dimension in terms of their ideal points, the **median voter** is the individual who has at least half of all the voters at her position or to her right and at least half of all the voters at her position or to her left.

---

[3]Note that the decline in utility may occur more rapidly when moving in one direction away from an individual's ideal point than the other.

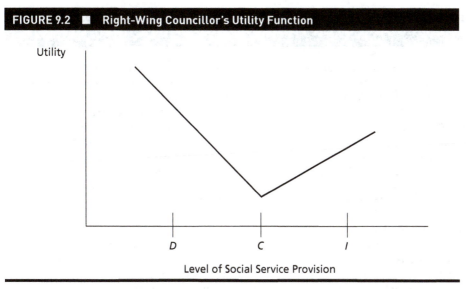

FIGURE 9.2 ■ Right-Wing Councillor's Utility Function

Note: D = decreased social service provision; C = maintenance of current levels of social service provision; I = increased social service provision.

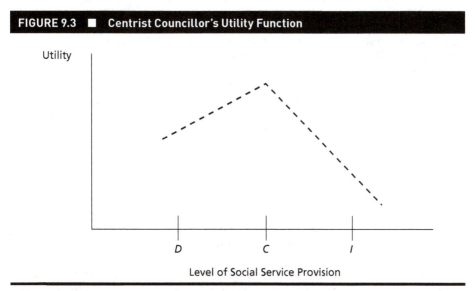

FIGURE 9.3 ■ Centrist Councillor's Utility Function

Note: D = decreased social service provision; C = maintenance of current levels of social service provision; I = increased social service provision.

Suppose that we placed a restriction on the preferences of the councillors in our city council example such that they all had single-peaked preference orderings. For example, we could restrict the preferences of the right-wing councillor such that her most preferred proposal is *D*, her second-best proposal is *C*, and her least preferred proposal is *I*. If we did this, the

BOX 9.1 THE MEDIAN VOTER THEOREM AND PARTY COMPETITION

The median voter theorem (MVT) was originally constructed in the context of committee voting (Black 1948). In his classic book, *An Economic Theory of Democracy*, Anthony Downs (1957) extended the MVT to elections more generally. Building on an earlier model of economic competition presented by Harold Hotelling (1929), Downs shows that if we assume that there's a single issue dimension, an odd number of voters with single-peaked preferences who vote sincerely, and only two parties, then both parties will converge to the ideal point of the median voter. Any other point in the policy space will lose in a pair-wise contest against the policy position preferred by the median voter. Thus, if one party is located at the median voter's ideal point and the competing party is not, the first party will win a majority of the votes. The losing party, therefore, has an incentive to move to the median voter's ideal point as well. The consequence is that both parties will be located at the position of the median voter, resulting in a tied election in which each party wins with equal probability.

The logic of the MVT indicates that political parties have an incentive to converge to the position of the median voter and adopt similar policy positions in two-party systems. The fact that observers of two-party systems frequently criticize the dominant parties in these countries

for being ideologically indistinguishable on the major issues provides some evidence that policy convergence does, indeed, occur. These observers complain that the parties are giving voters an "echo" rather than a "choice" (Monroe 1983; Page 1978). A common expression for the convergence of party platforms in these countries is "Tweedledee-Tweedledum politics" (Goodin and Pettit 1993, 6). For example, while campaigning in the midwestern states in 1968, third-party US presidential candidate George Wallace famously referred to the Democratic and Republican parties in a speech as "Tweedledum and Tweedledee." He argued that both were serving the interests of the "Eastern establishment" and that since around the time of the Civil War, "both parties have looked down their noses and called us rednecks down here in this part of the country. I'm sick and tired of it, and on November 5, they're goin' to find out there are a lot of rednecks in this country" ("Neither Tweedledum Nor Tweedledee," 1968). Similar criticisms are made by smaller parties or outsider candidates in nearly every country that has two large parties that dominate elections. Indeed, political discourse in Britain often refers explicitly to the Tweedledum-Tweedledee phrase. Non-English-speaking countries, of course, have their own expressions for this phenomenon.

preference orderings of all the councillors would be single peaked.[4] In Figure 9.4, we illustrate utility functions that are consistent with the single-peaked preferences of all three councillors. As we saw earlier in the chapter, maintaining current levels of social service provision (*C*) would win a round-robin tournament in which the councillors have preferences consistent with the utility functions shown in Figure 9.4.

Up to this point, we've allowed the city councillors to choose between only three alternatives—increase, decrease, and maintain current levels of social service provision. We're now in a position to consider what might happen if the councillors are free to propose any level of social service spending. In other words, we can now look at the situation in which the councillors can pick any point on the horizontal axis of Figure 9.4 as their proposed level of social service spending.

---

[4]We already showed in Figure 9.3 that the centrist councillor has a single-peaked preference ordering over the level of social service provision. You can check for yourself that the left-wing councillor also has a single-peaked preference ordering.

FIGURE 9.4 ■ When All Three Councillors Have Single-Peaked Preference Orderings

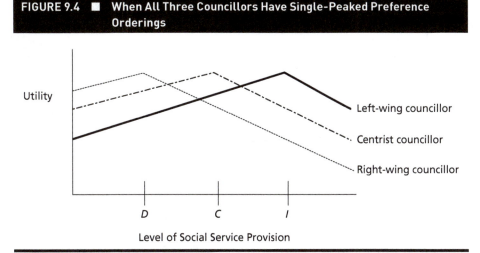

Note: I = the ideal point of the left-wing councillor; C = the ideal point of the centrist councillor; D = the ideal point of the right-wing councillor.

Let's look at what happens if we assume that all the councillors vote sincerely for whichever proposal is closest to their ideal point. We'll look at two kinds of scenarios. First, suppose that the status quo level of social service spending is given by point *C*—the ideal point of the centrist councillor. Clearly, the left-wing councillor would like to move social service spending to the right, toward her own ideal point *I*. Any proposal to do this, however, would be opposed by the centrist and right-wing councillors because any such proposal would be farther from their ideal points than the existing status quo. The right-wing councillor would like to move social spending to the left, toward her own ideal point *D*. Any proposal to do this would now be opposed by the centrist and the left-wing councillors because any such proposal would be farther from their ideal points than the existing status quo. As a result, if the status quo is at the centrist councillor's ideal point, it's stable and can't be beaten.

Second, suppose that the status quo level of social service spending is anywhere other than *C*—let's say somewhere to the left of *C*. This type of scenario is shown in Figure 9.5, with the status quo policy arbitrarily placed at *SQ* (status quo). In this type of situation, both the centrist and left-wing councillors are likely to propose moving social service spending closer to *C*. Let's suppose they propose *A*. Proposal A beats the *SQ* because the left-wing and centrist councillors vote for it and only the right-wing councillor votes against. But is Proposal A stable? The answer is no. The left-wing and centrist councillors would like to move social service provision farther to the right, closer to their ideal points. Let's suppose that they now propose *B*. Proposal B will be adopted because it's closer to the ideal points of both the left-wing and centrist councillors than Proposal A; the right-wing councillor will vote against the new proposal but will lose. Is Proposal B stable? Again, the answer is no. The right-wing and centrist councillors will now want to move social service provision to the left, closer to their ideal points. Any proposal that is closer to *C* than *B* will win with the support of the right-wing and centrist councillors. This process will continue until policy fully converges to the ideal point of the centrist councillor at *C*. Only then will the policy outcome be stable. A similar process of convergence to the position of the centrist councillor would occur if the status quo started off to the right of *C* instead of to the left.

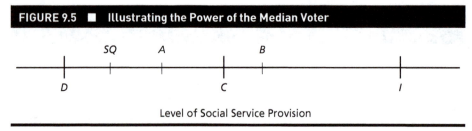

FIGURE 9.5 ▪ Illustrating the Power of the Median Voter

Level of Social Service Provision

Note: D = the ideal point of the right-wing councillor; *C* = the ideal point of the centrist councillor; *I* = the ideal point of the left-wing councillor; *SQ* = status quo level of social service provision; *A* and *B* = proposals for a new level of social service provision.

Even if the centrist councillor is never given the opportunity to propose a policy change, we'd still expect to see alternative offers by the left- and right-wing councillors that slowly converge to the most preferred policy of the centrist councillor. In fact, if making different policy proposals was sufficiently costly, farsighted councillors of the left and right might look to the end of this convergence process and simply propose a policy that matched the policy preferences of the centrist councillor from the very beginning. Whatever the process that produces the convergence to the centrist councillor's ideal point, once policy arrives there, there's no longer any impetus for change in the system. In other words, the policy that the centrist councillor most prefers is the only point on the policy continuum for which there's no policy alternative that's preferred by a majority of the councillors—it's the only stable policy. This is so not because we've labeled the policymaker in the center a "centrist" but because the centrist happens to be the median voter.[5]

The median voter theorem essentially shows that the difficulties we encountered earlier with Condorcet's paradox, such as group intransitivity and cyclical majorities, can be avoided if we're willing to both rule certain preference orderings "out of bounds" and reduce the policy space to a single issue dimension. Unfortunately, neither of these restrictions is uncontroversial. For example, there's nothing intrinsically troubling about individual preferences that aren't single peaked. In fact, there's a whole host of issues for which voters might, like the right-wing councillor in our example, legitimately prefer a lot or a little of something to a moderate amount.[6] As a result, we might have moral objections to a decision-making procedure that prohibits individuals from holding preferences that are not single peaked.

The restriction of politics to a single issue dimension can also be controversial. This is because many political questions are inherently multidimensional. Take, for example, the case of competition between candidates in an election. It's entirely possible that candidates will compete on both domestic policy and foreign policy. Even within domestic policy, candidates might compete in terms of their preferred degree of government involvement in the economy as well as their preferred degree of government involvement in social issues. Or take the case of legislative deliberation. It's possible that a piece of legislation might address the

---

[5]The median voter theorem doesn't assert that the stable policy outcome will be centrist in terms of the underlying issue dimension. All it states is that the stable policy outcome will be the ideal point of the median voter. Whether it's centrist or not will, therefore, depend on the location of the median voter in the issue space.

[6]We suspect that many of you probably have the following non-single-peaked preference ordering over coffee when the single dimension under consideration is the utility you derive from coffee served at different temperatures: you prefer both hot coffee and iced coffee to lukewarm coffee. We see nothing inherently wrong with a preference ordering like this.

size of a spending increase as well as the distribution of the tax burden proposed to pay for it. That multidimensional issue spaces are commonplace is bad news. This is because a famously unsettling theorem called the **chaos theorem** proved that, except in the case of a rare distribution of ideal points, there's no stable outcome if there's more than one issue dimension and three or more voters with preferences in the issue space vote sincerely by majority rule (McKelvey 1976; Plott 1967; Schofield 1978). In such circumstances, whoever controls the order of voting determines the final outcome.

Like Condorcet's paradox, the chaos theorem suggests that unless we're lucky enough to have a set of actors who hold preferences that don't lead to cyclical majorities, either of two things will happen: (1) the decision-making process will be indeterminate and policy outcomes hopelessly unstable; or (2) there'll exist an actor—the agenda setter—with the power to determine the order of votes in such a way that she can produce her most favored outcome. In the absence of institutions that provide an actor with agenda-setting powers, stable outcomes are even less likely to occur in the circumstances covered by the chaos theorem than those covered by Condorcet's paradox. This is because the set of preferences that prevent majority cycling in two or more dimensions is extremely rare and special. The results of the chaos theorem highlight "the importance of investigating the effects of the political institutions within which collective choices are made" (McCarty and Meirowitz 2007, 80), because it's likely that it's these institutions that play a significant role in alleviating the "chaos" that might otherwise reign.

ARROW'S THEOREM

Up to this point, we've seen that thinking about democracy as simply a matter of allowing the majority to make decisions runs into difficulties on several fronts. First, Condorcet's paradox shows that a set of rational individuals can form a group that is incapable of choosing rationally in round-robin tournaments. Specifically, situations might arise in which majorities cycle indefinitely, rendering the group incapable of reaching a decision. Next, we learned that if round-robin tournaments are replaced by "single elimination" tournaments that form a voting agenda, then cyclical majorities may be avoided and a stable outcome achieved. Unfortunately, we also saw that whoever controls the agenda—the order by which alternatives are pitted against each other and submitted to a vote—could dictate the outcome of such procedures.

We saw, though, that the problem of instability could be overcome if the political question to be decided can be thought of as a single issue dimension *and* if each voter has single-peaked preferences over that dimension. When these and other conditions are met, the alternative that's most preferred by the median voter is a stable outcome in the sense that no other alternative exists that can defeat it in a majority-rule pair-wise contest. Unfortunately, the median voter theorem is, at best, cold comfort for a couple of reasons. First, it requires restrictions on the types of preferences that individuals can have. If some voters have non-single-peaked preferences, it's possible for a cycle of majorities to arise—just as in round-robin tournaments. Consequently, the median voter theorem tells us only that we can avoid the potential for decision-making instability if certain preference orderings don't occur, either because we're lucky or because we're willing to rule them out of bounds. This is problematic because it seems reasonable that an individual's preferences should be treated as sacrosanct. A "democratic" decision-making process that works reliably only when we restrict participation to those with the "right kind" of preferences loses much of its ethical appeal. Second, it's likely that many crucial political questions involve more than one dimension. Unfortunately, the stability implied by the median voter theorem occurs only in exceedingly rare circumstances when there are two or more dimensions to a political problem. Worse still, in the absence of such stability, outcomes in two dimensions can vacillate.

Each of these complications with majority rule raises fundamental questions about the ethical appeal of democracy—understood as majority rule—as a mechanism for making group decisions. Specifically, we've seen that it's difficult to guarantee that majority rule will produce a stable group choice without either granting someone agenda-setting power or restricting the kinds of preferences that individuals may hold. In a famous book, Kenneth Arrow (1963) put forth a theorem showing that these problems with majority rule are, in some ways, special cases of a more fundamental problem. Arrow's theorem demonstrates that it's impossible to design any decision-making system—not just majority rule—for aggregating the preferences of a set of individuals that can guarantee producing a rational outcome while simultaneously meeting what he argued was a minimal standard of fairness. When deciding which set of conditions a fair decision-making procedure should meet, Arrow sought a minimal set in the sense that violations of these fairness conditions would lead to a procedure that's unfair in a way that would be evident to all.

Arrow's Fairness Conditions

Arrow presented four fairness conditions he believed all decision-making processes should meet. Each of these four conditions can reasonably be argued to be a part of any conception of democracy that meets minimal ethical standards. We'll discuss each of the four conditions in turn.

Nondictatorship

The **nondictatorship condition** states that there must be no individual who fully determines the outcome of the group decision-making process in disregard of the preferences of the other group members. In fact, this condition is an extremely minimal fairness condition because it only says that there can be no individual who, if she prefers x to y, forces the group choice to be x instead of y, irrespective of the preferences of everyone else. A group decision-making process that pays attention to only one member of the group and disregards the preferences of all the other members is clearly not democratic. Although it's possible that a dictator would be benevolent and choose an outcome that benefits the group, it's clear that a mechanism allowing a single individual to determine group outcomes for everyone else is inherently unfair.

Universal Admissibility

The **universal admissibility condition** states that any fair group decision-making rule must work with any logically possible set of individual preference orderings. This allows actors to adopt any rational preference ordering that they want. This condition is closely related to the philosophical doctrine of individualism. According to this perspective, individuals should be free to formulate their own desires. Although it may be appropriate under some conditions to prohibit individuals from acting on those desires, it's inappropriate to comment on the intrinsic social desirability of another's desires per se. It's on this basis that Arrow believed it inappropriate to exclude individuals from group decision-making processes simply on the basis of the types of preferences they happen to hold. Riker (1982, 117) defends the universal admissibility condition by stating that "if social outcomes are to be based exclusively on individual judgments—as seems implicit in any interpretation of democratic methods—then to restrict individual persons' judgments in any way means that the social outcome is based as much on the restriction as it is on individual judgments." In the context of voting, this condition states that every voter may vote as she pleases.

Unanimity, or Pareto Optimality

The **unanimity**, or **pareto optimality**, **condition** states that if all individuals in a group prefer x to y, the group preference must reflect a preference for x to y as well. A decision-making process that fails to meet this condition is not only unfair, it's perverse. Imagine pressing the Coke button on a vending machine and having a Sprite come out. The unanimity condition is extremely minimal in that it merely states that if everybody in the group is unanimous in sharing a preference for x to y, the group must not choose y when x is available.

Independence from Irrelevant Alternatives

The **independence from irrelevant alternatives condition** states that when groups are choosing between alternatives in a subset, the group choice should be influenced only by the rankings of these alternatives and not by the rankings of any (irrelevant) alternatives that are not in the subset. Suppose that, when confronted with a choice between x, y, and z, a group prefers x to y. The independence from irrelevant alternatives condition states that if one or more individuals alter their ranking of z, the group must still prefer x to y. Or as Varian (1993, 535) puts it, the group's preference "between x and y should depend only on how people rank x versus y, and not on how they rank other alternatives." To put this in context, suppose a group prefers vanilla ice-cream to chocolate ice-cream. If for some reason, one or more members of the group start developing a taste for strawberry ice-cream, the independence of irrelevant alternatives condition requires that the group not suddenly prefer chocolate ice-cream to vanilla ice-cream. A decision rule respects the independence from irrelevant alternatives condition whenever the group's ranking of any two alternatives, x and y, depends only on the relative ranking of these alternatives by every individual in the group (Geanakoplos 2005). Some scholars have, therefore, interpreted this condition to mean that the decision rule should be reliable in the sense that it always returns the same decision if the way individuals rank relevant alternatives remains unchanged (Riker 1982). In this respect, the independence from irrelevant alternatives condition is as much a condition about the reliability of the preference aggregation technology as it is a condition about the fairness of the decision-making mechanism.

In sum, Arrow's four conditions suggest that any fair group decision-making mechanism must prevent dictatorship (nondictatorship), not restrict the type of preferences that individuals can hold (universal admissibility), and link group choice, in at least some rudimentary sense, to individual preferences (unanimity and independence from irrelevant alternatives). We've already seen examples of how particular majority-rule decision-making mechanisms must violate at least one of these requirements if we wish to guarantee that the group's preference ordering will be transitive. As we've seen, group transitivity is necessary in order for the group decision-making process to produce stable outcomes in the absence of manipulation by powerful minorities acting as agenda setters. The real power of **Arrow's theorem**, though, comes from demonstrating that *every* decision-making process we could possibly design that involves ranking outcomes, including any majority-rule one, must sacrifice at least one of Arrow's fairness conditions if it's to guarantee group transitivity and, hence, stable outcomes. Put differently, if we insist that Arrow's four fairness conditions be met, we must accept the possibility of group intransitivity—there's no way around it.

The implications of Arrow's theorem are far-reaching. Suppose we take Arrow's conditions of unanimity and independence from irrelevant alternatives as uncontroversial and given. If we do this, Arrow's theorem tells us that we face an institutional "trilemma" between stable outcomes, universal admissibility, and nondictatorship. In other words, we can design decision-making institutions that have at most two of these three desirable attributes. In Figure 9.6, we illustrate Arrow's institutional trilemma with the help of a triangle.

Basically, Arrow's theorem states that when we design decision-making institutions, we can choose one and only one side of the triangle shown in Figure 9.6. If we want decision-making institutions that guarantee group transitivity and stable outcomes (*A*), we must give up either nondictatorship (*B*) or universal admissibility (*C*). If, on the other hand, we want to avoid dictatorship (*B*), we must give up either transitivity (*A*) or universal admissibility (*C*). Finally, if we hold individual preferences as inviolable (*C*), we must give up either transitivity (*A*) or nondictatorship (*B*). To summarize, Arrow's theorem proves that if the independence from irrelevant alternatives and the unanimity conditions are assumed, then designers of group decision-making institutions will be forced to choose their poison from the following set: restrictions on individual preferences, dictatorship, and the possibility of group intransitivity.

In addition, Arrow's theorem shows that it is, at the very least, difficult to interpret the outcome of any group decision-making process as *necessarily* reflecting the will of the group (Shepsle 1992). When a group comes to a clear decision, it *may* mean that individual preferences lined up in a way that allowed for a clear outcome that represented, in some meaningful way, the desires of a large portion of the group. But it may also mean that individuals with inconvenient preferences were excluded from the process, or that some actor(s) exercised agenda control. In such cases, outcomes may reflect the interest of some powerful subset of the group rather than the preferences of the group as a whole, or even some majority of the individuals in the group. Put differently, when choosing between alternative institutional arrangements that are decisive—that is, they don't display intransitivity—we're essentially engaged in a discussion about *which* minority we'll allow to influence outcomes through the control of the agenda.

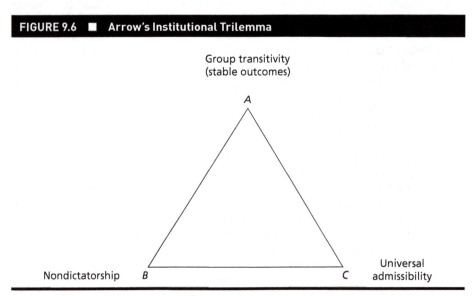

FIGURE 9.6 ■ Arrow's Institutional Trilemma

Group transitivity
(stable outcomes)

A

Nondictatorship   *B*

C   Universal admissibility

Note: Arrow's conditions of unanimity and independence from irrelevant alternatives are assumed as given here.

CONCLUSION

Most people associate democracy with majority rule. In this chapter we've examined various problems with majority-rule decision-making procedures. We've shown, for example, that there's a fundamental tension between the desire to guarantee that a group of individuals will be able to make coherent and stable choices on the one hand and the ability to guarantee the freedom of these individuals to form their own preferences and have those preferences influence group decisions on the other. Arrow's theorem shows that these tensions extend far beyond majority rule to encompass a wide set of minimally fair group decision-making methods. Because most conceptions of democracy would probably be even more ambitious than Arrow's fairness criteria, these results have important and profound implications for democracy.

The most direct implications of Arrow's theorem concern particular mechanisms for group decision making. Arrow's theorem is not in any direct sense about *collections* of decision-making procedures. Consider constitutions. A constitution doesn't typically stipulate *a* decision-making procedure to be used in a country but rather stipulates an entire set of decision-making procedures. For example, a constitution may stipulate how the head of the executive branch will be chosen, how legislators are chosen, how legislators choose laws, how the executive and legislative branches interact, how and if courts decide whether legislation is constitutional, which laws are under the jurisdiction of the national government and which are under local control, and the like. Arrow's theorem applies to each and every one of these decision-making mechanisms, and the way the trilemma that Arrow's theorem poses is resolved may vary from mechanism to mechanism within a particular constitution.[7] Some mechanisms or institutions may privilege group transitivity by reducing the number of alternatives from which people can choose—the two-party system used for electing presidents in the United States can be seen as an example of this. Other mechanisms or institutions may avoid group intransitivity by granting agenda-setting powers to an individual. A large literature on the US Congress argues that committee chairs play this role in the legislative process. Cabinet ministers play a similar role in many parliamentary systems.

The key point is that *every* decision-making mechanism must grapple with the trade-offs posed by Arrow's theorem, and *every* system of government represents a collection of such decision-making mechanisms. Consequently, we can think of a system of government in terms of how its decision-making mechanisms tend to resolve the trade-offs between group transitivity and Arrow's fairness criteria. And to the extent that a set of decision-making mechanisms privileges group transitivity, it's useful to think about *which* of Arrow's fairness criteria tends to be sacrificed. For example, is stability produced because strong agenda setters are present or because restrictions are placed on the preferences that actors hold? If it's the latter, we might ask whether this is achieved because some actors are excluded from deliberations or because strong mechanisms are in place to socialize participants so that they adopt the preferences that are compatible with stable group choice.

It should be clear by now that the most basic implication of Arrow's theorem is this: there's no perfect set of decision-making institutions. Every set of institutions either runs the risk of group intransitivity or compromises a fairness condition. As such, democracy must in some sense be imperfect—either fairness is compromised or there'll be a potential for instability. Perhaps this is what inspired former British prime minister Winston Churchill to

---

[7]Arrow's theorem also applies to decision-making bodies we're involved with on a day-to-day basis—student organizations, faculties, labor unions, religious congregations, corporate boards, families, and groups of friends deciding which movie to see.

say, "Democracy is the worst form of government, except for all those other forms that have been tried from time to time."[8] In the following chapters, we examine the immense variety of democratic forms of government, focusing specifically on different configurations and their consequences.

In the next chapter, we examine the different ways we can choose the head of government and structure the relationship between the head of government and the legislative branch. In Chapter 11 we look at the myriad ways in which legislators are elected around the world. In Chapter 12 we investigate the ways in which group preferences interact with electoral laws to shape party systems. From the perspective of Arrow's theorem, party systems can be thought of as a way of encouraging stability by reducing the number of alternatives to be considered in an election. In Chapter 13 we examine a whole host of other institutional mechanisms, such as the division of powers between national and subnational governments (federalism), the division of powers between different houses of the legislature (bicameralism), and the division of powers between the legislative and judicial branches (constitutional review). From the standpoint of Arrow's theorem, these institutional mechanisms can be thought of as attempts to limit the control of powerful agenda setters by pitting them against each other.

The immense variety of democratic institutions observed in the world is itself implied by Arrow's theorem. Because there's no ideal decision-making mechanism, institutional choice is an exercise in the choice of "second bests," and which institution (or set of institutions) is adopted in any given time or place is going to be dictated by context—some situations make instability sufficiently threatening to make the sacrifice of fairness conditions reasonable, whereas others may permit individuals to accept a certain degree of instability in exchange for protecting the fairness of the decision-making process. Of course, the suggestion that we, as a society, may "choose" optimal institutions is itself in tension with Arrow's theorem. Perhaps the institutions we confront today are the product of choices made by agenda setters in the past, or inherited from times when actors with certain preferences were restricted from participating in the constitutional deliberations.

Key Concepts

consequentialist ethics—when actions, policies, or institutions are evaluated with regard to the outcomes they produce

deontological ethics—when the intrinsic value of actions, policies, or institutions are evaluated in light of the rights, duties, or obligations of the individuals involved

round-robin tournament—a system of selection that pits each competing alternative against every other alternative an equal number of times in a series of pair-wise votes

rational actor—an actor who possesses a complete and transitive preference ordering over a set of outcomes

complete preference ordering—when an actor can compare each pair of elements (call them x and y) in a set of outcomes in one of the following ways—either the actor prefers x to y, or y to x, or she's indifferent between them

transitive preference ordering—if for any x, y, and z in a set of outcomes, it's the case that if x is preferred to y, and y is preferred to z, then it must be the case that x is preferred to z

---

[8]House of Commons speech, November 11, 1947.

Condorcet's paradox—states that individual rationality is insufficient to ensure group rationality

Condorcet winner—an option that beats all other options in a series of pair-wise contests

strategic or sophisticated vote—a vote in which an individual votes in favor of a less preferred option because she believes doing so will ultimately produce a more preferred outcome

sincere voting—a vote for an individual's most preferred option

utility function—a numerical scaling in which higher numbers stand for higher positions in an individual's preference ordering

single-peaked preference ordering—a preference ordering characterized by a utility function that reaches a maximum at some point and slopes away from this maximum on either side, such that a movement away from the maximum never raises the actor's utility

median voter theorem—states that the ideal point of the median voter will win against any alternative in a pair-wise majority-rule election if the number of voters is odd, voter preferences are single-peaked over a single policy dimension, and voters vote sincerely

median voter—the individual who, when voters are arrayed along a single policy dimension in terms of their ideal points, has at least half of all the voters at her position or to her right and at least half of all the voters at her position or to her left

chaos theorem—a theorem that states that if there are two or more issue dimensions and three or more voters with preferences in the issue space who all vote sincerely by majority rule, then except in the case of a rare distribution of ideal points, there'll be no stable outcome

nondictatorship condition—a condition that there must be no individual who fully determines the outcome of a group decision-making process in disregard of the preferences of the other group members

universal admissibility condition—a condition that individuals can adopt any rational preference ordering over a set of available alternatives

unanimity, or pareto optimality, condition—a condition that if all individuals in a group prefer x to y, the group preference must reflect a preference for x to y as well

independence from irrelevant alternatives condition—a condition that group choice should be unperturbed by changes in the rankings of irrelevant alternatives

Arrow's theorem—states that every decision-making process we could possibly design that involves ranking outcomes must sacrifice at least one of Arrow's fairness conditions—nondictatorship, universal admissibility, unanimity, or independence from irrelevant alternatives—if it's to guarantee group transitivity and, hence, stable outcomes

PARLIAMENTARY, PRESIDENTIAL, AND SEMI-PRESIDENTIAL DEMOCRACIES

The essence of pure parliamentarism is mutual dependence. . . . The essence of pure presidentialism is mutual independence.

Alfred Stepan and Cindy Skach, "Constitutional Frameworks and Democratic Consolidation"

A cabinet is a combining committee—a hyphen which joins, a buckle which fastens, the legislative part of the state to the executive part of the state. In its origin it belongs to the one, in its functions it belongs to the other.

Walter Bagehot, *The English Constitution*

OVERVIEW

1. Political scientists often classify democracies as parliamentary, presidential, or semi-presidential. Whether a democracy is parliamentary, presidential, or semi-presidential depends on the relationship between the government, the legislature, and (if there is one) the president.

2. The government formation process in parliamentary democracies can be quite complicated and take a long time. Several different types of government can form: single-party majority governments, minimal winning coalitions, minority governments, surplus majority governments, and so on. The type of government that forms depends on many factors, including whether the political actors in a country are office seeking or policy seeking. Although some governments in parliamentary democracies last several years, others last just a few days.

3. The government formation process in presidential democracies is different from that in parliamentary democracies. Presidential democracies have more minority governments but fewer coalition governments than parliamentary ones. They also have more nonpartisan ministers and a lower proportionality in the allocation of ministerial posts. Governments in presidential democracies look more like those in parliamentary democracies if the president is weak.

4. The government formation process in semi-presidential democracies is relatively understudied. There is evidence, however, that governments in semi-presidential democracies share characteristics from governments in both parliamentary and presidential democracies.

In Chapter 8 we looked at the different types of dictatorships in the world. Our focus now turns to examining the institutional variation among democracies. Democracies can be distinguished in many different ways. Most political scientists, though, tend to classify democracies according to their form of government, that is, according to the rules that define who the government is, how the government comes to power, and how the government remains in power (Cheibub 2007). According to this classification scheme, there are three types of democracy: parliamentary, presidential, and semi-presidential.

In this chapter, we examine how scholars distinguish between these three different types of democracy. We then take a close look at how governments form and survive in each of these systems. First, though, we define what we mean by the government. When people talk about the government in everyday language, they're often referring to a large group of political actors that might include the prime minister, the president, cabinet members, legislators, bureaucrats, and possibly even judges. In political science, though, the **government** refers to a much smaller and more specific group of actors—the political chief executive and the ministers that head the various government departments. Depending on the type of democracy, the political chief executive is either a prime minister or a president. The typical government comprises just thirty to thirty-five individuals.

CLASSIFYING DEMOCRACIES

Whether a democracy is parliamentary, presidential, or semi-presidential depends on the relationship between (1) the government, (2) the legislature, and (3) the president (if there is one). Two questions, shown in Figure 10.1, can be used to classify democracies as parliamentary, presidential, or semi-presidential.

Is the Government Responsible to the Elected Legislature?

The first question is whether the government is responsible to the elected legislature. **Legislative responsibility** refers to a situation in which a legislative majority has the constitutional power to remove the government from office *without cause*. In democracies with legislative responsibility, the legislature can remove the government by calling a **vote of no confidence**. A vote of no confidence is a vote in the legislature initiated by the opposition to determine whether the government should remain in office. The government must resign if a majority of legislators votes against the government. As Figure 10.1 illustrates, presidential democracies are defined by the absence of legislative responsibility. Presidential democracies

FIGURE 10.1 ■ Classifying Parliamentary, Presidential, and Semi-Presidential Democracies

Source: Cheibub, Gandhi, and Vreeland (2010).

are presidential because they don't have votes of no confidence—their legislatures can't remove the government without cause.[1] Democracies that do have legislative responsibility—a vote of no confidence—are either parliamentary or semi-presidential. To help determine which, we must ask a second question.

Is the Head of State Popularly Elected for a Fixed Term?

To determine whether a democracy with legislative responsibility is parliamentary or semi-presidential, we need to know whether it has a popularly elected head of state who serves a fixed term in office. If it does, then it's semi-presidential. And if it doesn't, then it's parliamentary. A head of state is *popularly elected* if she's elected through a process where voters either (1) cast ballots directly for the candidate they wish to elect (as in Benin, Mexico, and the Philippines) or (2) cast ballots to elect an assembly, sometimes called an electoral college, whose sole role it is to elect the head of state (as in the United States). Note that it's possible for a democracy to have an elected head of state who's not "popularly elected." For example, the German head of state is elected by the regional legislatures in Germany and is, therefore, not popularly elected by the voters. To *serve a fixed term* means that the head of state serves for a fixed period of time before she needs to be reappointed and can't be removed from office in the meantime.[2] For example, Irish presidents serve a fixed term of seven years. In a democracy, the head of state is either a monarch or a president. It should be clear by now that the presence of a presidential head of state is neither necessary nor sufficient for distinguishing between the three types of democracy—presidents can exist in parliamentary, presidential, and semi-presidential democracies. In contrast, the presence of a monarchic head of state in a democracy automatically indicates that we're dealing with a parliamentary democracy. This is because monarchs don't serve fixed terms and aren't popularly elected.

As our discussion indicates, we can classify presidential, parliamentary, and semi-presidential democracies in the following way:

---

[1] It's true that legislatures can sometimes remove members of the government in presidential democracies. However, this is only "for cause"—typically incapacitation or criminal behavior.

[2] Some democracies allow for the possibility of removing the head of state before her term is up but only through the extraordinary and costly procedure of impeachment or incapacitation.

- **Presidential democracy**: Democracies in which the government doesn't depend on a legislative majority to exist are presidential.

- **Parliamentary democracy**: Democracies in which the government depends on a legislative majority to exist and in which the head of state isn't popularly elected for a fixed term are parliamentary.

- **Semi-presidential democracy**: Democracies in which the government depends on a legislative majority to exist and in which the head of state is popularly elected for a fixed term are semi-presidential.

An Overview

Of the 165 countries coded by the Polity IV project in 2016, 97 were identified as democracies. Of these democracies, 36 (37.1%) were parliamentary, 29 (29.9%) were presidential, and 32 (33.0%) were semi-presidential. Historically, most democracies have been either parliamentary or presidential, with parliamentary democracies always the most common. According to the Polity IV criteria for identifying democracies, there were only three semi-presidential democracies in the world in 1946—Austria, Finland, and Ireland. Today, though, there are more semi-presidential democracies than presidential ones. Indeed, semi-presidential democracies are now almost as numerous as parliamentary democracies. In Table 10.1, we list all of the parliamentary, presidential, and semi-presidential democracies in the world. In Map 10.1, we show how these different types of democracy are geographically distributed around the world. Presidential democracies are shown in black, semi-presidential democracies in dark gray, parliamentary democracies in medium gray, and nondemocracies in light gray. Presidential democracies tend to predominate in the Americas, particularly in South America. In contrast, presidential democracies are, with the exception of Switzerland, entirely absent in Europe, where there's a mixture of parliamentary and semi-presidential democracies. In Africa, democracies tend to be either presidential or semi-presidential.

TABLE 10.1 ■ Parliamentary, Presidential, and Semi-Presidential Democracies, 2016		
Parliamentary	**Presidential**	**Semi-presidential**
Albania, Australia, Belgium, Botswana, Canada, Denmark, Estonia, Germany, Greece, Guyana, Hungary, India, Iraq, Israel, Italy, Jamaica, Japan, Kosovo, Latvia, Lebanon, Lesotho, Luxembourg, Mauritius, Moldova, Myanmar, Nepal, Netherlands, New Zealand, Norway, Pakistan, Solomon Islands, South Africa, Spain, Sweden, Trinidad and Tobago, United Kingdom	Argentina, Benin, Bolivia, Brazil, Chile, Colombia, Comoros, Costa Rica, Cyprus, Dominican Republic, El Salvador, Ghana, Guatemala, Honduras, Indonesia, Kenya, Liberia, Malawi, Mexico, Nicaragua, Nigeria, Panama, Paraguay, Philippines, Sierra Leone, South Korea, Switzerland, United States, Uruguay	Austria, Bulgaria, Burkina Faso, Cape Verde, Central African Republic, Croatia, Czech Republic, Finland, France, Georgia, Guinea-Bissau, Ireland, Kyrgyzstan, Lithuania, Macedonia, Madagascar, Mongolia, Montenegro, Namibia, Peru, Poland, Portugal, Romania, Senegal, Serbia, Slovakia, Slovenia, Sri Lanka, Taiwan, Timor-Leste, Tunisia, Zambia

Sources: Data come from Robert Elgie (www.semipresidentialism.com/?p=3097) and various country constitutions. Democracies are identified as those receiving a score of 6 or more on the Polity IV scale (Marshall, Gurr, and Jaggers 2017).

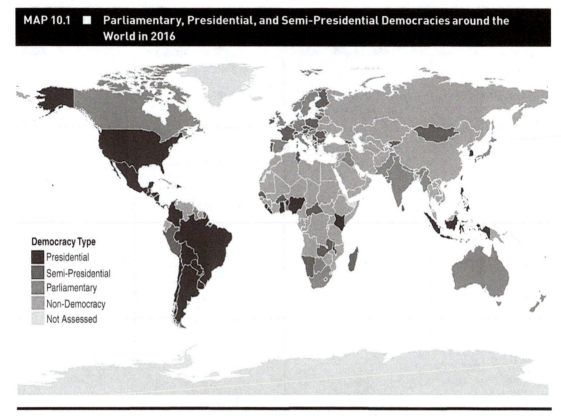

MAP 10.1 ■ Parliamentary, Presidential, and Semi-Presidential Democracies around the World in 2016

Democracy Type
- Presidential
- Semi-Presidential
- Parliamentary
- Non-Democracy
- Not Assessed

Sources: Data come from Robert Elgie (www.semipresidentialism.com/?p=3097) and various country constitutions. Democracies are identified as those receiving a score of 6 or more on the Polity IV scale (Marshall, Gurr, and Jaggers 2017).

GOVERNMENTS IN PARLIAMENTARY DEMOCRACIES

Having addressed the criteria for classifying democracies, we now try to give a more in-depth insight into how these different types of democracy operate in the real world. We do so by examining how their governments form and survive. We start with parliamentary democracies.

The Government

The **government in a parliamentary democracy** comprises a prime minister and a **cabinet**. As an example, Table 10.2 shows the Canadian government in 2018. The prime minister (PM) in a parliamentary democracy is the political chief executive and head of the government. The position of prime minister goes under a number of different titles in various countries—"prime minister" in the United Kingdom, "chancellor" in Germany, and even "president" in the Marshall Islands. We'll follow convention and refer to the political chief executive in a parliamentary system as prime minister.

The cabinet is equivalent in many ways to a "country's board of directors" (Gallagher, Laver, and Mair 2006, 40). The cabinet comprises ministers whose job it is to be in the cabinet and to

TABLE 10.2 ■ Canadian Government in May 2018			
Minister	**Department**	**Minister**	**Department**
Justin Trudeau	Prime Minister	Mélanie Joyly	Canadian Heritage
Navdeep Singh Bains	Innovation, Science, and Economic Development	Dominic LeBlanc	Fisheries, Oceans, and the Canadian Coast Guard
Carolyn Bennett	Crown-Indigenous Relations and Northern Affairs	Diane Lebouthillier	National Revenue
Marie-Claude Bibeau	International Development and La Francophonie	Lawrence MacAulay	Agriculture and Agri-Food
Scott Brison	Treasury Board	Catherine McKenna	Environment and Climate Change
James Gordon Carr	Natural Resources	William Morneau	Finance
Bardish Chagger	Small Business and Tourism	Maryam Monsef	Status of Women
François-Philippe Champagne	International Trade	Seamus O'Regan	Veterans Affair
Jean-Yves Duclos	Minister of Families, Children, and Social Development	Ginette Taylor	Health
Kirsty Duncan	Sport and Persons with Disabilities	Jane Philpott	Indigenous Services
Chrystia Freeland	Foreign Affairs	Carla Qualtrough	Public Services and Procurement
Marc Garneau	Transport	Harjit Sajjan	National Defence
Ralph Goodale	Public Safety and Emergency Preparedness	Amarjeet Sohi	Infrastructure and Communities
Karina Gould	Democratic Institutions	Jody Wilson-Raybould	Justice
Patricia Hajdu	Employment, Workforce Development, and Labour	Ahmed Hussen	Immigration, Refugees, and Citizenship

Source: "Full List of Justin Trudeau's Cabinet" (2015).

head one of the government's various departments, such as Education, Finance, Foreign Affairs, and Social Policy. The department of which the minister is head is often referred to as the minister's portfolio. Each minister is directly responsible to the cabinet for what happens in her department. If a problem arises in a particular department, then the minister is supposed to be held responsible for it. This practice is known as the doctrine of **ministerial responsibility**.

As a member of the cabinet, as well as the head of a government department, a minister is part of a collective entity that is responsible for making the most important decisions about the direction of government policy. Cabinet ministers are typically bound by the doctrine of **collective cabinet responsibility**. This doctrine means that, although ministers may air their disagreements about policy freely in cabinet meetings, once a cabinet decision has been made, each minister must defend the government policy in public. Cabinet ministers who feel they can't do this must resign, as Robin Cook did as foreign minister in the United Kingdom in 2003 when he disagreed with the government's decision to go to war over Iraq. This notion of collective cabinet responsibility stands in stark contrast to the behavior and expectations about cabinet ministers in presidential democracies. This is because cabinet members in presidential democracies are in charge of particular policy areas and are not responsible for, or expected to influence, the overall direction of government policy; that's the domain of the president and her staff.

Government Formation Process

Citizens don't elect the prime minister or the other members of the government in parliamentary democracies; they elect only members of the legislature. So how do governments actually form? Consider the results from the 1987 West German legislative elections shown in Table 10.3. Can you figure out what German government formed after these elections just by looking at the table? It's not obvious, right?

When thinking about the government formation process, it's important to remember that any proposed government must enjoy the "confidence" of the legislature, both to come to power and to stay in power. As we saw earlier, this is a defining characteristic of parliamentary democracies—governments must always enjoy the support of a legislative majority. In some countries, a potential government may have to demonstrate that it has such support before it can take office by holding what's known as an **investiture vote** (Rasch, Martin, and Cheibub 2015). If the proposed government doesn't win a majority in this vote, it can't take office. Even if there's no formal investiture vote, though, a potential government in a parliamentary democracy must still have the *implicit* support of a legislative majority at all times. This is because of the ability of

TABLE 10.3 ■ West German Legislative Elections in 1987		
Party	Seats	Percentage
Christian Democrats (CDU/CSU)	223	44.9
Social Democrats (SPD)	186	37.4
Free Democrats (FDP)	46	9.3
Greens	42	8.5
Total	497	100

Notes: Data from Adam Carr's webpage at http://psephos.adam-carr.net/.

the legislature to call a vote of no confidence in the government at any time. If the government ever loses such a vote because it can't garner the support of a legislative majority, it must resign. Ultimately, a parliamentary government can be removed from office any time a majority of legislators decides that this is what should happen. As a result, governments that come to power in parliamentary systems must always enjoy the implicit support of a legislative majority even if they never have to explicitly demonstrate this in an investiture vote or a vote of no confidence.

If a single party controls a majority of the seats in the legislature, we might expect that party to form a single-party majority government. In fact, this is typically what happens. But what happens when no single party commands a legislative majority, as in our West German example? This is, in fact, the normal situation in most parliamentary democracies. Over 80% of the governments that have formed in Western Europe since 1945 have emerged from situations in which no single party controlled a majority of legislative seats. As we'll see in more detail when we examine electoral rules in the next two chapters, the frequent use of proportional representation electoral systems in Europe helps to explain why so few parties ever win a majority of votes or seats. Only countries like the United Kingdom that employ disproportional electoral rules regularly produce single parties that control a legislative majority.

We know that any potential government must implicitly control a legislative majority before coming to office. There are no rules about who should be in this legislative majority though. As a result, any legislator could conceivably be a part of the government's majority support and, hence, play a role in appointing the government. In practice, however, the tight discipline of political parties in many countries means that the actual business of forming a government tends to be done by a small group of senior politicians in each party (Gallagher, Laver, and Mair 2006, 49). These politicians typically include party leaders and potential cabinet members. After an election or the fall of a previous government, these party leaders bargain with one another, and a government forms as soon as enough party leaders have committed their support (and that of their party) for it to command a legislative majority. But can we say anything more about the government formation process and the type of government that these actors are likely to choose?

Table 10.4 illustrates all of the potential governments that could have formed in West Germany in 1987. It also indicates the number of surplus seats controlled by each potential government that were not required for obtaining a legislative majority. For example, a coalition between the Social Democrats (SPD), the Free Democrats (FDP), and the Greens would have 25 "surplus" seats more than it actually needed to guarantee a legislative majority. In contrast, a coalition between just the SPD and the Greens would be 21 seats shy of a majority. Are all of these potential governments equally plausible? To answer this question, we need to know more about the exact process by which governments form in parliamentary democracies.

The head of state, either a monarch or a president, presides over the government formation process, and it is she who ultimately invests a government with the constitutional authority to take office. The extent to which the head of state actively becomes involved in the actual bargaining varies from country to country. In some countries, the head of state is limited to simply swearing in the government proposed by the party elites. If there's an investiture vote, the proposed government must demonstrate it has a legislative majority. Once this is done, the head of state simply appoints the government. This government stays in power until the next election, until it loses a vote of no confidence, or until it resigns. In other countries, the head of state plays a more active role by choosing a particular politician to initiate the government formation process. This politician is known as a **formateur**. It's her job to construct a government.

In some countries, the constitution explicitly states who the formateur will be. For example, the Greek and Bulgarian constitutions declare that the head of state must appoint the

TABLE 10.4 ■ Potential West German Governments in 1987			
Party	Seats	Percentage	Surplus seats
CDU/CSU + SPD + Greens + FDP	497	100	248
CDU/CSU + SPD + Greens	451	90.7	202
CDU/CSU + SPD + FDP	455	91.5	206
CDU/CSU + FDP + Greens	311	62.6	62
SPD + FDP + Greens	274	55.1	25
CDU/CSU + SPD	409	82.2	160
CDU/CSU + FDP	269	54.1	20
CDU/CSU + Greens	265	53.3	16
SPD + FDP	232	46.7	-17
SPD + Greens	228	45.9	-21
FDP + Greens	88	17.7	-161
SPD	186	37.4	-63
CDU/CSU	223	44.9	-26
Greens	42	8.5	-207
FDP	46	9.3	-203

Note: "Surplus seats" indicate the number of seats controlled by each potential government that were not required for obtaining a legislative majority.

leader of the largest party as the formateur. If this person fails to form a government, the head of state allows the leader of the second largest party to try to build a government by making her the new formateur. This process continues until a formateur successfully forms a government. Obviously, the head of state has little discretion in these countries because the election results determine the order in which parties get to try to form the government.

In other countries, the head of state is less constrained and can actually "choose" the formateur in a more meaningful sense. For example, choosing the formateur has been one of the more important duties belonging to the head of state in countries like the Czech Republic. Following legislative elections in June 2006, the Czech president, Václav Klaus, was able to influence the government formation process in a starkly partisan way because of his power to appoint the formateur. The Czech elections resulted in a dead heat in the 200-seat legislature: a coalition of left-wing parties won 100 seats, and a coalition of right-wing parties won 100 seats. The Czech president, who belonged to a right-wing party, appointed a member of his own party—Mirek Topolánek—to be the first formateur. When his nominated formateur failed to get his proposed government passed in an investiture vote that saw all 100 legislators from the right vote for it and all 100 legislators from the left vote against it, the

Czech president simply renominated the same person to be the next formateur. In somewhat dubious circumstances, Topolánek managed to win a second investiture vote even though he proposed the same government as before—he won the vote 100 to 98 when two left-wing legislators surprisingly decided to abstain rather than vote against the proposed government (S. Golder 2010).

In other countries, the ability of the head of state to engage in partisan politics is seen as inappropriate. This is typically the case when a monarch is the head of state. As a result, such countries have limited the power of the head of state to appointing an **informateur**. An informateur is someone who is supposed to lack personal political ambition and whose job it is to look at politically feasible coalitions and recommend people who would make good formateurs. The existence of an informateur means that the head of state is, at least theoretically, one step removed from the partisan nature of the government formation process. However, this has not always stopped monarchs, such as the Dutch Queen or Belgian King, from intervening more directly in the government formation process in an attempt to influence the final outcome (Andeweg and Irwin 2009; S. Golder 2010).

Despite the discretion some heads of state enjoy, it turns out that the first person appointed formateur is usually the leader of the largest party in the legislature (Bäck and Dumont 2008). In almost all cases, the formateur is also the prime minister designate. All of this is to be expected, given that the leader of the largest party can often credibly threaten to veto any proposal by other possible formateurs. Once the formateur has been chosen, she has to put a cabinet together that is acceptable to a legislative majority.

The ability to nominate cabinet members is one of the most important powers the prime minister (formateur) holds. In single-party majority cabinets, the prime minister has enormous discretion when it comes to making appointments to the cabinet and she is constrained only by the internal politics of her party. Politicians might be rewarded with cabinet appointments because they have demonstrated loyalty to the party or the prime minister, because they represent a particular ideological faction within the party, or because they have useful administrative skills. In some cases, a prime minister might feel that internal party politics require her to appoint internal party opponents to the cabinet. In fact, British Prime Minister Margaret Thatcher, later to be called the "Iron Lady," felt compelled to appoint a cabinet in which her own party supporters were in a distinct minority on first being elected in 1979 (Young 1990, 138). Still, even at this initial moment of relative weakness, Thatcher (1993, 26) later recalled, "I made sure that the key economic ministers would be true believers in our economic strategy."

In coalition cabinets, the discretion that the prime minister has in nominating cabinet members is more constrained. Typically, party leaders in the proposed cabinet will nominate particular ministers to the subset of portfolios that have been allocated to their party during the initial stages of the government formation process. Although possible, it's rare to see the prime minister or party leaders veto another party leader's nomination. On the face of it, this would seem to suggest that the leaders of each government party are free to pick the people they want for "their" portfolios. The fact that we don't see nominations vetoed, though, doesn't necessarily mean that party leaders have full discretion over who they nominate. It might simply be the case that objectionable ministerial choices are not proposed in the first place (Indriðason and Kam 2005). Given the considerable influence that cabinet members have over policy in their respective portfolios, party leaders will bargain hard, first over how many ministerial portfolios they get, and second over who should be appointed to these posts, before deciding whether to support the proposed cabinet.

Once a cabinet has been formed, the support of a legislative majority may or may not have to be demonstrated by a formal investiture vote. If the investiture vote is unsuccessful, the government formation process starts all over again; there may or may not be a new election before this happens. If the investiture vote is successful (or there's no required vote), however, then the head of state simply appoints the cabinet nominated by the formateur to office. At this point, the government is free to rule until it's defeated in a vote of no confidence or until a new election is necessary. If the government is defeated in a vote of no confidence or a new election is called, the incumbent government remains in office to run the country as a **caretaker government**. This caretaker government remains in office until the next round of the government formation process is complete and a new government is ready to take its place. In most countries, there's a strong constitutional convention that caretaker governments won't make any important policy changes to those in place when the outgoing government loses its parliamentary basis (Boston et al. 1998). The fact that caretaker governments generally have no authority to make major policy initiatives can be problematic if the government formation process takes a long time. This is particularly the case if the government has collapsed due to some sort of political, economic, or military crisis.

A Simple Theory of Government Formation

Now that we know more details about the government formation process in parliamentary democracies, we can return to our West German example from 1987. All of the potential governments are listed in Table 10.4. Given what you now know about the government formation process, ask yourself whether all of these governments are equally plausible. Who's likely to be the formateur? Helmut Kohl, the leader of the Christian Democrats (CDU/CSU), was appointed formateur as he controlled the largest party in the Bundestag. Helmut Kohl obviously wouldn't form a government that didn't include his own party. As a result, we can immediately eliminate those potential governments in Table 10.4 that don't include the CDU/CSU.

Now ask yourself whether any of the remaining potential governments are more plausible than others. The fact that a government must have the support of a legislative majority in order to come to power suggests that the government formation process may be easier if the proposed government actually controls a majority of legislative seats. As a result, you might think to eliminate those potential governments that don't have a positive number of surplus seats, that is, those governments that don't control a legislative majority.[3] Table 10.5 lists the remaining potential governments. Which of the seven remaining possibilities do you think is most likely to become the government? To answer this question, we must think about what politicians want.

We might think that there are two types of politicians: (1) those who are "office seeking" and (2) those who are "policy seeking." When forming a government, an office-seeking politician wants to secure as many ministerial portfolios as she can. After the position of prime minister, cabinet positions represent the highest political posts in a parliamentary democracy. Landing a cabinet portfolio is often a signal of a successful political career and is a prize that many politicians seek. Being in the cabinet brings power and fame. An **office-seeking politician** is interested in the "intrinsic" benefits of office. In contrast, a **policy-seeking politician** wants to secure ministerial portfolios in order to influence public policy. This type of politician is not interested in the "intrinsic" benefits of office; she doesn't want to be a minister simply for the sake of being a minister. Instead, a policy-seeking politician wants ministerial portfolios so that she can make a difference in how the country is run.

---

[3]As we'll see shortly, governments that don't explicitly control a legislative majority do sometimes come to power. You should start to think about how and why this might happen.

TABLE 10.5 ■ Potential Majority West German Governments Containing the CSU/CDU in 1987			
Party	Seats	Percentage	Surplus seats
CDU/CSU + SPD + Greens + FDP	497	100	248
CDU/CSU + SPD + Greens	451	90.7	202
CDU/CSU + SPD + FDP	455	91.5	206
CDU/CSU + FDP + Greens	311	62.6	62
CDU/CSU + SPD	409	82.2	160
CDU/CSU + FDP	269	54.1	20
CDU/CSU + Greens	265	53.3	16

A Purely Office-Seeking World

Imagine again that you're Helmut Kohl, the CDU/CSU leader, in West Germany in 1987. If you lived in a purely office-seeking world, what government would you propose? To control a legislative majority, you know you have to get the support of other party leaders because your party controls only a minority of the legislative seats. Because you live in a purely office-seeking world, you can win their support only by giving them office. In effect, you say to them, "I'll give you X ministerial posts in the government in exchange for your legislative support." You'll obviously want to give them as few portfolios as possible, however, so you can keep the rest for yourself. In order to win their support, you'll probably have to give up more cabinet positions to a party leader who controls a large number of legislative seats than to a party leader who controls a small number of seats. In fact, there's strong empirical evidence that a prime minister must give portfolios to other parties in proportion to the number of seats that each party contributes to the government's total number of legislative seats (Laver, de Marchi, and Mutlu 2011; Warwick and Druckman 2001, 2006). This empirical regularity is known as **Gamson's law** (see "Portfolio Allocation and Gamson's Law" in Box 10.1).

One of the implications of the office-seeking logic we've just outlined is that you won't want more parties in government than are strictly necessary to obtain a legislative majority. Thus, you'll want to form a particular type of coalition government called a **minimal winning coalition (MWC)**. A minimal winning coalition is one in which there are just enough parties (and no more) to control a legislative majority. Of the seven remaining potential governments in Table 10.5, there are three MWCs: (CDU/CSU + SPD), (CDU/CSU + FDP), and (CDU/CSU + Greens). In none of these coalitions is it possible to remove a party without, at the same time, giving up your legislative majority. A second implication of the purely office-seeking logic is that you'll choose the smallest MWC, or the **least minimal winning coalition**. The least MWC is the one with the lowest number of surplus seats. You want the least MWC because you don't want to "buy" more legislative seats by giving more cabinet posts to others than you strictly have to. This leads to the hypothesis that if the world is purely office seeking, we should observe the formation of least minimal winning coalitions. In terms of our 1987 West German example, this means we should expect the leader of the CDU/CSU to form a minimal winning coalition with the Greens because this MWC has the fewest surplus seats.

BOX 10.1 PORTFOLIO ALLOCATION AND GAMSON'S LAW

Gamson's law: *Cabinet portfolios will be distributed among government parties in strict proportion to the number of seats that each party contributes to the government's legislative seat total (Gamson 1961).*

Gamson's law predicts that if Party A and Party B form a government together, and Party A has 80 legislative seats, and Party B has 40 legislative seats, then Party A will receive two-thirds of the ministerial portfolios because it provides 80/120 of the government's legislative seats, and Party B will receive one-third of the ministerial portfolios because it provides 40/120 of the government's legislative seats. But what is the empirical evidence in support of Gamson's law?

In Figure 10.2, we plot the share of cabinet portfolios controlled by a government party against its share of the government's legislative seats, using data from fourteen Western

European countries from 1945 to 2000. It should be immediately obvious that there's a strong positive relationship between the share of seats a party contributes to a government's legislative seat total and the share of portfolios it controls. This positive relationship, which is one of the most robust empirical patterns in all of political science, represents strong evidence for Gamson's law. Note, though, that this relationship is not *perfectly* proportional (Golder and Thomas 2014; Indriðason 2015). The solid black line in Figure 10.2 indicates the 1:1 relationship that would exist if portfolios were allocated proportionally. The gray circles tend to be above this line when a government party is small but below it when a government party is large, indicating that smaller parties tend to be slightly overrepresented in parliamentary cabinets and larger parties tend to be slightly underrepresented.

FIGURE 10.2 ■ Portfolio Allocation in Western Europe, 1945–2000

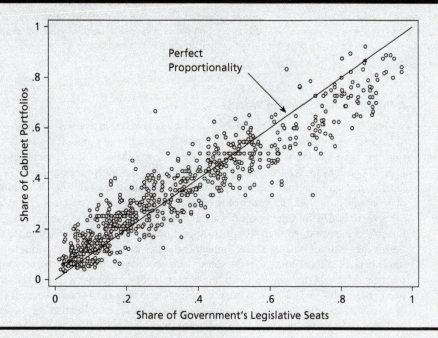

Note: Based on data from Warwick and Druckman (2006).

(*Continued*)

(Continued)

The fact that there's a slight bias in favor of smaller parties when it comes to portfolio allocation turns out to be a puzzle for political scientists. Most bargaining models that have been developed to explain government formation predict that large parties, not small parties, will do better when ministerial portfolios are allocated (Austen-Smith and Banks 1988; Baron and Ferejohn 1989). So, what's going on?

One possible answer is that although larger parties may be receiving slightly fewer ministerial portfolios than their size would predict, they're getting the more powerful ones such as the prime minister, the finance minister, the foreign minister, or the defense minister. In fact, there's some evidence that this is the case (Warwick and Druckman 2001). Another possible answer, though, has to do with the existence of the vote of no confidence in parliamentary democracies (Indriðason 2015). Rather than give their smaller coalition partners just enough portfolios to make them willing to join the government, large formateur parties may well see it in their interests to give them slightly more portfolios so that they'll be less likely to leave the cabinet and trigger a vote of no confidence at a later point in time. By doing this, large for-

mateur parties can expect to receive a slightly smaller share of the overall cabinet pie, but for a longer period of time (Penn 2009).

Evidence for this line of reasoning comes from a study by Golder and Thomas (2014) that began as an undergraduate honors thesis. The study looks at portfolio allocation at the national and subnational level in France. Although the vote of no confidence exists for governments at the national level in France, this isn't the case for governments at the regional level. In line with their predictions, Golder and Thomas find that smaller parties receive a greater share of portfolios at the national level (where the existence of the vote of no confidence leads large formateur parties to worry about government survival) than at the regional level (where the vote of no confidence is absent and formateur parties don't need to worry about government survival). The logic here also suggests that large formateur parties in presidential democracies, where votes of no confidence are absent, should, all else being equal, receive a greater share of portfolios than their counterparts in parliamentary democracies. This is precisely what Ariotti and Golder (2018) find when comparing ministerial portfolio allocation across Africa's presidential and parliamentary democracies.

A Purely Policy-Seeking World

Imagine you're Helmut Kohl again, but that you now live in a purely policy-seeking world. Which of the potential governments in Table 10.5 would you propose? To answer that question, you'll need to know something about the policy positions of the parties along the salient issue dimensions in West Germany in 1987. Figure 10.3 illustrates the policy positions, or "ideal points," of the four German parties with legislative seats on the left-right dimension of economic policy. As the leader of the CDU/CSU, you know you must get the support of other party leaders in order to control a legislative majority. Because you now live in a purely policy-seeking world, you can win their support only by giving them policy concessions. This means that instead of being able to implement policy at your own ideal point, you'll have to implement a coalition policy that lies somewhere between the ideal points of all your coalition partners. It's likely that you'll have to make more policy concessions to win the support of a party leader who controls a large number of legislative seats than you will to win the support of a party leader who controls a small number of legislative seats. In other words, large parties will tend to be able to pull policy more toward their ideal point than small parties.

One of the implications of this logic is that you'll want to form governments with parties that are located close to you in the policy space. Political scientists often refer to this type

FIGURE 10.3 ■ German Party Positions on the Left-Right Economic Dimension, 1987

of coalition as a "connected coalition." A **connected coalition** is one in which all members of the coalition are located next to each other in the policy space. For example, a coalition between the CDU/CSU and the FDP is a connected coalition. A coalition between the CDU/CSU and the Greens, however, is not a connected coalition because a noncoalition party (the SPD) lies between them in the policy space. Of the seven potential governments in Table 10.5, five are connected coalitions: (CDU/CSU + SPD + Greens + FDP), (CDU/CSU + SPD + Greens), (CDU/CSU + SPD + FDP), (CDU/CSU + SPD), and (CDU/CSU + FDP). The parties in each of these coalitions are located next to each other in the policy space. A second implication of the purely policy-seeking logic is that you'll choose the connected least minimal winning coalition. You want the connected least MWC because you don't want to "buy" more legislative seats with policy than you strictly have to. This leads to the hypothesis that if the world is purely policy seeking, we should observe the formation of connected least minimal winning coalitions. In our West German example, this means we should expect the leader of the CDU/CSU to form a coalition government with the FDP.

The Trade-Off between Office and Policy

The actual government Helmut Kohl formed in 1987 was a coalition between the CDU/CSU and the FDP. This was the prediction from the purely policy-seeking logic. Does this mean that policy seeking dominates office seeking in Germany? There's a vast literature in political science that seeks to answer questions like this, but we believe that this sort of question is hard to answer empirically. Consider our example again. It's difficult to know if policy seeking really dominated office seeking in Germany, because the CDU/CSU didn't have to give up too much extra office in order to get a coalition policy closer to its ideal point. In effect, the CDU/CSU preferred to give up slightly more office by forming a government coalition with the FDP (four extra surplus seats) in exchange for a coalition policy that was likely to be much closer to its ideal point than if it had formed a coalition with the Greens. In practice, we believe that politicians probably care about both office and policy and are, therefore, always making trade-offs. They're always asking how much extra office they should give up to get policy closer to their ideal point, or how much policy they should give up to get more office. If this is the case, it probably makes little sense to categorize real-world politicians into purely policy-seeking or purely office-seeking types.

Even if politicians were pure office seekers or pure policy seekers, we believe that the reality of political competition would force them to act *as if* they cared about both policy and office. For example, a politician who wishes to affect policy must win office in order to be in a position to change policy. As a result, a policy-seeking politician will have to care about office, if only as a means to affect policy. Similarly, an office-seeking politician will realize that voters are unlikely to elect her if she cares only about office and being famous. A consequence is that an office-seeking politician will have to care about policy, if only to make sure that she wins election. Ultimately, this suggests that all politicians will act *as if* they care about both office and policy to some extent, which suggests that it probably makes slightly more sense to think that government coalitions are likely to be connected least MWCs rather than just least MWCs.

Different Types of Government

We know that a government in a parliamentary democracy must control an implicit legislative majority in order to come to power and remain in office. Up to this point, we've assumed that governments must contain enough parties that they *explicitly* control a majority of the legislative seats. In fact, the logic presented in the previous section suggests that governments should contain just enough parties to obtain this legislative majority and no more. It's for this reason that we've focused until now on single-party majority governments and various forms of minimal winning coalitions. When we look around the world, though, we sometimes observe other types of government in parliamentary democracies—minority governments and surplus majority governments. In Figure 10.4 we show the proportion of governments of different types that formed in West European parliamentary democracies between 1945 and 1998.

FIGURE 10.4   ■   Government Types in West European Parliamentary Democracies, 1945–1998

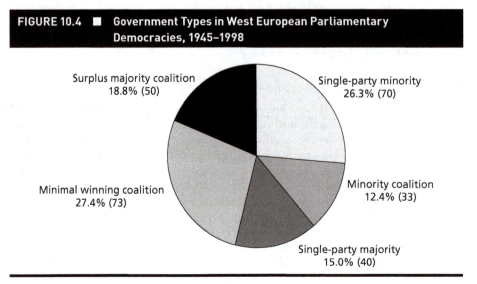

Surplus majority coalition
18.8% (50)

Single-party minority
26.3% (70)

Minimal winning coalition
27.4% (73)

Minority coalition
12.4% (33)

Single-party majority
15.0% (40)

Source: Data from the Comparative Parliamentary Democracy (CPD) project (Müller and Strøm 2000; Strøm, Müller, and Bergman 2003).

Note: Data do not include caretaker or nonpartisan governments. The numbers in parentheses indicate the number of governments of different cabinet types.

Minority Governments

A **minority government** is one in which the party or parties in power do not explicitly command a majority of legislative seats. Minority governments may be single-party minority governments or minority coalition governments. You're probably wondering how a minority government could be in power in a parliamentary democracy. After all, the opposition in parliament controls enough seats that it could remove the government through a vote of no confidence whenever it wants to do so. A minority government can exist only as long as the opposition chooses not to bring it down. This means that whenever we observe a minority government, we know there must be an implicit majority in the legislature that supports it.

In some countries, we know precisely who makes up this implicit majority because some nongovernmental party or parties publicly state that they'll sustain the government against votes to overthrow it but that they don't want to actually be in the cabinet. In exchange, the government usually agrees to consult these "support parties" on various policy matters. This occurred in Britain in 1977 when the Liberals agreed to support the Labour Party when it lost its majority. This also occurred more recently after the 2010 legislative elections in the Netherlands when a populist far right party—the Freedom Party (PVV)—publicly agreed to support a minority coalition government made up of the People's Party for Freedom and Democracy (VVD) and the Christian Democratic Alliance (CDA). In other countries, minority governments don't rely on specific support parties but instead build legislative majorities on an ad hoc basis. In effect, these minority governments build different majorities for each piece of legislation they want to pass. In these countries, it isn't always easy to figure out exactly who in the legislature is keeping a minority government in power; all we know is that at least one of the nongovernmental parties must be helping it at any given point in time. One consequence of this is that it becomes difficult for voters to know who's responsible for policy and to hold them accountable for it.

For a long time, minority governments were seen as undemocratic. They were seen as something that should occur only infrequently and something that, if they did occur, should be short-lived. Strøm (1990) was one of the first political scientists to challenge this accepted wisdom. He argued that minority governments should be seen as a normal and "democratic" outcome of party competition in parliamentary democracies. One thing he illustrated was the high frequency with which minority governments formed in West European democracies and the relative stability that characterized these cabinets. As Figure 10.4 indicates, over a third (38.7 percent) of all governments that formed in West European parliamentary democracies from 1945 to 1998 were minority governments. In countries like Denmark (82 percent), Sweden (81 percent), and Norway (65 percent), minority governments were the norm in this period. In addition to their numerical frequency, minority governments have also been in power for long stretches of time. For example, minority cabinets have ruled in West European parliamentary democracies for more than a quarter of the postwar period.

Several theories have been proposed to explain the apparent puzzle of why minority governments exist. All of these theories point to the importance of policy in the government formation process. If politicians cared only about office, then it's hard to understand why any nongovernmental party would ever choose not to be in the cabinet when it has the power to force its way into it. In other words, why would nongovernmental parties ever allow a minority government to enjoy all the benefits of office without controlling a legislative majority? The simple answer is they wouldn't. If politicians care about policy, however, then we can think of situations in which a party might decide it can better achieve its policy objectives by remaining outside the cabinet.

Minority governments are more likely in countries where nongovernmental (opposition) parties have a strong say over policy. In some countries, the legislative committee system is structured to disperse policymaking influence to many groups, including nongovernmental parties. We would expect minority governments to be more likely when opposition parties can influence policy through legislative committees—because they don't need to be in the government to affect policy (Strøm 1990). A related explanation for the existence of minority governments comes from Luebbert (1984), who argues that the ability of opposition groups to influence policy depends heavily on whether a country provides a formal institutional role for key social and economic actors in making policy. For example, ministries in Norway and Sweden that contemplate legislative or administrative action that might affect a particular interest group are obliged to consult with that interest group before proceeding. Thus, the cabinet is only *one* of the arenas in which fundamental social and economic decisions are made. As a result, we should see more minority governments in such countries because of the lower incentive for parties to enter government in order to influence policy.

You might be wondering why a party would ever choose to influence policy from outside the government rather than from inside it. Why not be in the government and enjoy the benefits of office while making policy? There are several reasons why a party might prefer to shape policy from outside the government. First, parties may be reluctant to take responsibility for the policies that'll be implemented. Governing parties are much more likely to be held responsible for failed policies than opposition parties. By remaining in the opposition, parties can often achieve some of their policy objectives while being held less accountable if things go wrong. These types of concerns are particularly strong during periods of economic crisis when governments may have to introduce unpopular austerity policies. Second, a party may have made an election pledge not to go into government with certain parties. Breaking this promise might be electoral suicide at the next election. Third, opposition parties have more flexibility in choosing their campaign strategies in future elections because they don't have a past record in office to constrain them. These are all possible reasons why parties might choose not to be in government in countries that allow them to influence policy from the opposition benches.

Minority governments are less likely in countries that require an investiture vote (Strøm 1990). This is because potential minority governments face a higher hurdle to taking office than in countries in which no investiture vote is required. If a formal investiture vote is required, opposition parties must choose to openly support a minority government, something that might be difficult to justify to their constituents. Some parties that wouldn't necessarily support a particular minority government in a public vote, though, may find it acceptable to tacitly lend their support to a government if no investiture vote is required.

Policy divisions within the opposition also affect the formation of minority governments (Laver and Shepsle 1996). Minority governments can survive and be relatively stable when opposition parties are ideologically divided and can't reach an agreement on a replacement. For example, the Congress Party was able to dominate Indian politics as a minority government for many years because the opposition parties on each side of it couldn't agree on a suitable replacement. A similar situation occurred with the Social Democrats in Sweden and the Christian Democrats in Italy. These parties were consistently able to form minority governments by being relatively large parties located in the middle of the ideological spectrum with opposition parties on either side.

Surplus Majority Governments

Although governments that appear "too small" (minority) often form, cabinets that appear "too large" (surplus majority) also emerge from time to time. A **surplus majority government** is one in which the cabinet contains more parties than are strictly necessary to control a legislative majority. In effect, the government could lose or remove a party and still control a majority of the seats in the legislature. Like minority governments, it's often thought that surplus majority cabinets are rare. The data don't support this view, however. As Figure 10.4 indicates, a little under a fifth (18.8 percent) of all governments that formed in West European parliamentary democracies from 1945 to 1998 were surplus majority governments.

In fact, surplus majority governments have made up almost half the governments in Italy and the Netherlands. In addition to their numerical frequency, surplus majority governments have also been in power for reasonably long stretches of time. For example, surplus majority cabinets have ruled in Western Europe for about 14 percent of the postwar period.

Several arguments have been proposed to explain the apparent puzzle as to why surplus majority governments form. Just as with minority governments, these arguments emphasize the importance of policy in the government formation process. If politicians were purely office seekers, it's hard to see why surplus majority governments would ever form, because they require political actors to give up office when they don't have to. This implies that the existence of surplus majority governments must be a signal that policy matters.

Surplus majority governments often form in times of political, economic, or military crisis. These crisis governments are sometimes referred to as "national unity" governments. For example, national unity governments formed in Belgium, Germany, Italy, Luxembourg, and the Netherlands immediately after World War II. They also formed in several East European countries following the collapse of communism in 1989. A national unity government also formed in Iraq following the 2006 legislative elections. The belief is that only by bringing together parties from across the ideological spectrum and giving them a reason to be invested in the existing political system is it possible to resolve whatever crisis is afflicting the country. The goal is to put the everyday partisan, ethnic, or religious nature of politics on hold for the sake of the country's immediate future. Although governments of national unity often have strong popular support, this particular type of surplus majority government tends to be short-lived in practice. Political parties that aren't required to sustain a legislative majority are often quickly pushed into opposition. The desire on the part of politicians to enjoy as much office and policy influence as possible essentially overrides the wishes of the electorate that parties work together to rescue a country from whatever ails it.

In some circumstances, the formation of a surplus majority government may actually be necessary to pass particular pieces of legislation. For example, constitutional amendments often require "supermajorities," which are made up of more than a legislative majority. If a government wants to pass a constitutional amendment that requires a supermajority, it might choose to have more parties in the cabinet than are strictly necessary just to remain in power. Of course, the surplus majority government in this case doesn't actually contain more parties than are strictly necessary to pass the constitutional amendment. In fact, you might say that this type of government is "oversized" in name only and that in practice it's no different from a minimal winning coalition given its policy objectives. A country that often produces this type of surplus majority government is Belgium (Gallagher, Laver, and Mair 2006, 392). The Belgian constitution requires that laws affecting the relationship between different language groups in the country receive the support of two-thirds of the legislators and a majority of each language group. This has led to several surplus majority governments in Belgium.

Another explanation for the formation of surplus majority governments focuses on the strategic interaction between coalition partners. If a minimal winning coalition takes office, any party in the cabinet, no matter how small, can bring the government down simply by resigning. This situation allows for the possibility of blackmail by a single dissatisfied party (Luebbert 1984, 254). In particular, it allows a small party to extract significant policy concessions from its coalition partners in vast disproportion to its size simply because its votes are critical to the government's continued existence. To prevent this scenario from occurring, larger parties in the coalition may decide to form surplus majority coalitions so that the government isn't automatically brought down if a single party decides to resign. The fact that parties typically agree on a set of coalition policies prior to forming the government—but ultimately have to implement these policies in some order—also creates incentives for surplus majority governments (Carrubba and Volden 2000). Consider two parties that agree on a set of coalition policies prior to coming to power. As soon as one of the parties has managed to implement the policies it wants, it'll have an incentive to defect from the government and bring it down if it doesn't like any of the policies still to be introduced. This incentive is reduced with a surplus majority coalition, because the defection of one party won't prevent the government from implementing the remaining policies.

Duration of Governments: Formation and Survival

The government formation process in parliamentary democracies can be quite complex. Even if parties agree to go into government together, they still have to haggle over who gets which portfolio and what the government policy should be. This bargaining process can sometimes last a long time. In Table 10.6, we present information about the length of time in days that it typically takes governments to form after an election in eleven West European parliamentary democracies from 1945 to 1998.

As Table 10.6 indicates, there's considerable cross-national variation in the length of time it takes to form a government following an election. If a single party obtains a majority of the legislative seats, it's normally understood that this party will form a cabinet on its own, and the only question is who from this party will get which portfolio. This explains why it takes only about a week on average for a cabinet to form in the United Kingdom, because it usually has a majority party. In countries in which many parties gain legislative representation, it can take much longer to form a cabinet, because it's not always obvious which combination of parties will be able to form the government, how these parties will allocate portfolios among themselves, and what the coalition policy will be. For example, the average length of the government formation process in the Netherlands is about three months. For many years, the Netherlands held the record for the longest delay in government formation in Europe at 208 days. Belgium broke this record in 2010. Although elections took place in Belgium in June 2010, a new government didn't enter office until the beginning of December 2011, more than 500 days later! This particular government formation process in Belgium is clearly an outlier. As Table 10.6 indicates, it takes, on average, about a month for a government to form after an election in Western Europe.

Delays in the government formation process can have important implications for governance. You may recall that caretaker governments, which administer the affairs of state while negotiations are proceeding, don't generally have the authority to make major policy initiatives. This means that delays in the government formation process can be quite problematic, particularly if the previous cabinet has fallen because of some sort of crisis. Until a cabinet is finally formed, the identity of government parties, the allocation of portfolios to particular politicians, and the content of policy compromises among coalition partners have yet to be determined. The uncertainty that surrounds the future direction of government policy can have serious consequences on the behavior of economic and political actors, both domestic and international. For example, consider the seven-month delay in forming a government that followed the June 2006 elections in the Czech Republic (S. Golder 2010). By August, the Czech media were already reporting on the deleterious consequences of the prolonged period under a caretaker government. The *Prague Post Online* (Alda 2006, n.p.) wrote, "Lawmakers are getting nothing done, while legislation and important reforms rest in a state of limbo, including long awaited pension reform, the privatization of many state-owned companies, an overhaul of the country's Criminal Code, and the fate of the controversial flat tax. A non-functioning parliament costs taxpayers as much as 3 million Kč ($136,500) a day." A number

TABLE 10.6 ■ Duration of Government Formation Process after Elections, 1945–1998 (Days)				
Country	Minimum	Maximum	Average	N
Belgium	2	148	59.7	17
Denmark	0	35	9.4	22
Germany	23	73	36.4	14
Greece	3	19	7.5	8
Italy	11	126	47.3	14
Luxembourg	19	52	31.2	12
Netherlands	31	208	85.7	16
Norway	0	16	2.5	14
Spain	2	58	28.6	7
Sweden	0	25	5.7	17
United Kingdom	1	21	8.7	15
All	0	208	29.9	156

Notes: Data come from the Comparative Parliamentary Democracy (CPD) project (Müller and Strom 2000; Strom, Müller, and Bergman 2003) and cover governments that formed after an election between 1945 and 1998. Bargaining duration measures the number of days between the election and the day on which the new government is officially inaugurated.

of empirical studies paint a similar picture, finding that uncertainty over the government formation process affects exchange rate markets (Leblang 2002) and the types of assets that market actors choose to invest in (Bernhard and Leblang 2006). Delays in government formation have real consequences for many people.

Not only is there considerable variation in the length of time it takes governments to form but there are also large differences in the amount of time that governments stay in power. Of the governments that formed in West European parliamentary democracies from 1945 to 1998, less than a quarter actually stayed in office for their maximum permitted term. On average, governments lasted only 60 percent of their permitted time in office. In Figure 10.5, we illustrate the average duration of governments in days by cabinet type. Single-party majority governments last the longest at 910 days on average, closely followed by minimal winning coalitions at 893 days. Both of these types of government last considerably longer (about a year in all) than minority or surplus majority governments. As Figure 10.6 illustrates, there's also considerable cross-national variation in the length of time a government stays in office. Governments last longest in Luxembourg (1,170 days), the United Kingdom (981 days), and Spain (957 days). They last much less time in Italy (354 days) and Belgium (520 days).

Governments end for both "technical" and "discretionary" reasons (Müller and Strøm 2000, 25–27). Technical reasons are things that are beyond the control of the government. For example, a government might end because the prime minister dies or resigns due to ill health or because there's a constitutionally mandated election. Discretionary reasons are political acts on the part of the government or opposition. For instance, a government might

FIGURE 10.5 ■ Average Parliamentary Government Duration by Cabinet Type, 1945–1998 (Days)

Source: Data from the Comparative Parliamentary Democracy (CPD) project (Müller and Strøm 2000; Strøm, Müller, and Bergman 2003).

Note: Data cover eleven Western European parliamentary democracies.

FIGURE 10.6 ■ Minimum and Average Duration of Governments, 1945–1998 (Days)

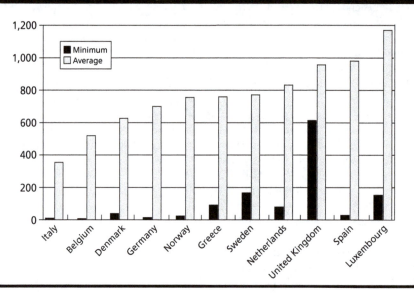

Source: Data from the Comparative Parliamentary Democracy (CPD) project (Müller and Strøm 2000; Strøm, Müller, and Bergman 2003).

end because the government dissolves the parliament and calls early elections (see Box 10.2. "Endogenous Election Timing"), because the opposition defeats the government in a vote of no confidence, or because conflicts between or within the coalition parties force the government to resign.

BOX 10.2 ENDOGENOUS ELECTION TIMING

In some countries, the government gets to choose when it wants to hold elections. For example, governments in Sweden are constrained to hold an election at least once every four years but can choose exactly when to hold the election in this four-year window. This possibility is known as endogenous election timing. Three different stories have been proposed to explain the timing of elections. All three stories assume that politicians want to win elections and that voters hold governments accountable for their past economic performance.

1. *Political surfing:* The government waits until the economic conditions are right before calling an election. The government doesn't actively manipulate the economy but waits until the economy, for whatever reason, is at a high point before announcing the election (Kayser 2005).

2. *Political business cycle:* The government actively manipulates the economy to engineer a short-term economic high and then calls an election. The election is then followed by an economic decline. Thus, the economy goes through cycles of boom and bust that are politically driven (Clark 2003).

3. *Signaling:* The government is better informed about future economic performance than the voters and so can time elections to occur prior to any expected economic decline. In effect, the government calls early elections in order to cash in on its past successes by censoring the public's ability to observe the future decline. The very act of calling an early election, however, sends a signal to voters that the future performance of the economy looks bad. If voters are naive or have short-term memories, or if the opposition is unprepared, the government may prefer to call an early election.

Otherwise, governments might be reluctant to take advantage of good economic times by calling an early election because they want to avoid sending voters a signal that they don't expect the good times to last (A. Smith 2003).

Several different predictions can be derived from these stories. Both the political surfing and political business cycle stories predict that elections are called when the economy is doing well, whereas the signaling story says that current economic conditions should not matter. Both the political business cycle and signaling stories predict that calls for early elections should be followed by economic declines (if for different reasons), but the political surfing story makes no prediction about future economic performance. The signaling story predicts that government support in the opinion polls will fall if it calls early elections because voters learn that the government is about to produce bad economic outcomes; the other stories have nothing to say about the government's electoral support. The signaling story predicts that the earlier an election is called, the greater the economic decline to come—why else risk losing office? The other stories make no such prediction.

Alastair Smith (2004) has tested these predictions on data from the United Kingdom and finds strongest support for the signaling story. He finds that when elections are called early relative to expectations, support for the government in opinion polls declines, stock market indexes fall, and postelection economic performance worsens. When elections are called especially early, he finds that postelection economic performance is particularly bad. There was little evidence that the current performance of the economy affected the probability that a government would call an early election. All of these findings are consistent with the signaling story but not the other stories.

Does it really matter whether a government survives for a long time? It's perhaps a natural reaction to think that cabinet instability is a bad thing, but why exactly might this be the case? You might think that governments that don't survive long result in policy instability and cabinet ministers who lack experience. It's long been known, however, that cabinet instability doesn't automatically imply ministerial instability. For example, Allum (1973, 119) found that a set of politicians had been "in office almost continuously for over twenty years" during the heyday of cabinet instability in Italy. Huber and Martinez-Gallardo (2004) also find that cabinet instability isn't necessarily associated with high levels of turnover in cabinet membership. They measured cabinet duration, portfolio experience (the average amount of experience that ministers have in the specific cabinet portfolio they hold), and political experience (the average amount of experience that ministers have in *any* significant cabinet portfolio) in nineteen democracies from 1945 to 1999. What they find is that cabinet duration isn't necessarily the same thing as political or portfolio experience. For example, cabinets in the United Kingdom, Canada, and the Netherlands last quite a long time but have low levels of portfolio and political experience because of the frequent **cabinet reshuffles** in these countries (Indriðason and Kam 2005). In contrast, while cabinets in Germany, Sweden, and Belgium don't last a long time, they have relatively high levels of portfolio and political experience because the same individuals are often returned to the cabinet and their former ministries. Huber and Martinez-Gallardo's (2004) analysis suggests that we should be less concerned about what affects cabinet duration and more interested in discovering what influences the degree of portfolio and political experience in a country. Political scientists are only now beginning to look at this (Dowding and Dumont 2009).

GOVERNMENTS IN PRESIDENTIAL DEMOCRACIES

The **government in a presidential democracy** comprises the president and her cabinet. The president is the political chief executive and head of the government; she's also the head of state. While the literature on governments in parliamentary democracies is large, relatively little is known about governments in presidential democracies. This situation has recently begun to change, though (Amorim Neto 2006; Chaisty, Cheeseman, and Power 2014; Cheibub, Przeworski, and Saiegh 2004; Escobar-Lemmon and Taylor-Robinson 2016; Martinez-Gallardo 2012). In this section, we summarize some of the principal lines of research that have been followed so far.

Government Formation Process

The government formation process in presidential democracies is different in many important ways from that in parliamentary democracies. First, and most fundamentally, legislative responsibility doesn't exist in presidential democracies. As a result, governments in presidential systems don't have to maintain majority legislative support to stay in power as they do in parliamentary systems. Second, unlike in most parliamentary democracies, there's no uncertainty about the identity of the formateur in presidential democracies. This is because the president is *always* the formateur, irrespective of whether her party does well or poorly in legislative elections. Coupled with the absence of legislative responsibility, this means that the president appoints whomever she wants to the cabinet (and dismisses them as she wishes). Third, the fact that the president is always the formateur means that the president's party must be included in each cabinet regardless of its legislative size. Note that this doesn't necessarily mean that the cabinet will exclude all other parties, just that it must include the president's party.

Finally, the "reversion point" of the government formation process is different in presidential democracies. A "reversion point" refers to what happens when a minority formateur fails to form a coalition. In a parliamentary system, the failure of a minority prime minister to obtain an implicit legislative majority results in—or causes the actors to "revert" to—an early election, a new round of bargaining, or a caretaker government. In a presidential system, though, the failure of a minority president to win the support of opposition parties simply results in the president's party ruling alone. Recall also that elections occur at fixed intervals in presidential democracies; the president can't simply dissolve the legislature when she wishes. As a consequence, members of the legislative delegation of a government party can often vote against cabinet-sponsored bills without the fear of forcing new elections (which they may lose). Consequently, a **portfolio coalition** (government) doesn't imply a **legislative coalition** in presidential democracies to the extent that it does in parliamentary democracies.

These differences create particular incentives and opportunities that help to distinguish presidential governments from parliamentary ones. We'll focus here on differences in the type and composition of presidential governments.

Types of Presidential Cabinets

In a parliamentary system, the prime minister must appoint a cabinet that enjoys an implicit legislative majority. We've seen that this doesn't necessarily imply that she must appoint a cabinet that controls a majority of legislative seats—opposition parties in the legislature may be willing to support minority cabinets on policy grounds. Clearly, presidents will form majority cabinets whenever their party controls a majority of the legislative seats. But what happens when the president's party is not a majority party? Presidents have no constitutional imperative to form majority cabinets—they're free to form minority cabinets whenever they want. Some of these minority governments will rule with the support of an implicit legislative majority, just like minority governments in parliamentary systems; that is, some opposition party or parties in the legislature will support the government without receiving posts in the cabinet. Other minority governments, however, will rule without this kind of support. This second type of minority government is not possible in a parliamentary system because of the existence of legislative responsibility. This difference suggests that, all things being equal, minority governments will be more frequent in presidential systems than in parliamentary ones.

The empirical evidence supports this claim. It's widely recognized that about a third of all parliamentary governments are minority governments (Strøm 1990). As Table 10.7 indicates, 47 percent (6) of the governments in Latin America's presidential democracies from the late 1970s to 2000 were minority governments. This difference in the frequency of minority governments in presidential and parliamentary systems is even more marked if we focus explicitly on minority situations, that is, situations in which the party of the president or prime minister doesn't control a legislative majority. Of the minority situations in the world from 1946 to 1999, 65 percent resulted in minority governments in presidential democracies compared with just 35 percent in parliamentary ones (Cheibub, Przeworski, and Saiegh 2004, 574).

The fact that presidents can appoint whomever they like to the cabinet might lead you to think that they'd rarely form coalition governments. Indeed, Linz (1994, 19) predicts that coalition governments in presidential democracies will be "exceptional." Coalition governments would certainly be unexpected if political actors lived in a purely office-seeking

TABLE 10.7 ■ Government Types in Latin America's Presidential Systems (Late 1970s–2000)					
Country	Single-party majority	Majority coalition	Single-party minority	Minority coalition	Total
Argentina	1	0	3	2	6
Bolivia	0	4	1	3	8
Brazil	0	11	0	4	15
Chile	0	5	0	0	5
Colombia	0	10	1	0	11
Costa Rica	3	0	3	0	6
Ecuador	0	1	4	15	20
Mexico	2	0	0	0	2
Panama	0	3	0	4	7
United States	2	1	2	0	5
Uruguay	0	6	0	0	6
Venezuela	1	1	3	1	6
Total	9	42	17	29	97

Source: Data from Amorim Neto (2006).

world—why would they form a coalition and give up cabinet seats if they didn't have to? As we noted earlier, however, political actors are likely to care to some extent about policy or, at least, to act as if they care about policy. If this is the case, it's easy to see why presidents might have an incentive to form coalition governments. The extent to which this incentive is felt will depend to a large extent on the legislative powers of the president.

All presidents have the ability to issue a **presidential decree**—a presidential order that has the force of law. The scope and strength of these decrees, however, vary from country to country (Shugart and Carey 1992). For example, decrees in the United States, known as executive orders, allow the president only to regulate and interpret statutes already enacted by the legislature and give orders to the public administration; the president can't enact *new* laws. In other countries, though, presidents can issue "decree-laws"—decrees that immediately become law—even when faced with a hostile legislature. Presidents who have relatively weak decree power and whose party doesn't control a majority of legislative seats need support from other parties if they're to achieve any of their policy goals. As a result, these presidents will have an incentive to form coalitions. The bottom line is that coalition governments shouldn't be exceptional in presidential systems for this reason. In fact, the empirical evidence suggests that coalition governments occur quite frequently in presidential democracies. Ariotti and Golder (2018), for example, find that almost half of the governments formed in Africa's presidential democracies between 1990 and 2014 were coalition governments. As Table 10.7 indicates, almost three quarters of the governments that formed in Latin America's presidential democracies have also been coalition governments.

The frequency with which coalition governments form in presidential systems has led some scholars to conclude that "it is not true that incentives for coalition formation are any different in presidential than in parliamentary democracies" (Cheibub and Limongi 2002, 168). This conclusion is probably an exaggeration, however. Why? Much has to do with the "reversion point" we mentioned earlier. If negotiations over the formation of a coalition government break down in a presidential democracy, the result is that the president's party gets to rule on its own. This implies that the president ultimately has the last word over policy in a way that isn't true of a prime minister (Samuels 2007). In a parliamentary system, we've seen that the prime minister may have to concede control over particular ministries to her cabinet partners in order to be able to form a government (Laver and Shepsle 1996). In a presidential system, the president doesn't face the same need to make such policy concessions. This is particularly the case if she can use presidential decrees or vetoes to achieve her policy goals. Even if the president does make policy concessions in order to get opposition parties to join her cabinet, these policy promises lack a certain amount of credibility because the president has the right to dismiss these parties without losing office whenever she wants. The ability of some presidents to use decrees and the inability of opposition parties to bring the government down therefore reduce the expected benefits (in regard to both office and policy) of opposition parties that are thinking about joining the government. The fact that legislators belonging to coalition parties can vote against government-sponsored bills without running the risk of causing the government to fall, however, implies that the costs (in regard to committing support to the government's legislative agenda) of belonging to a coalition may also be lower. Thus, although presidents may want to form coalition governments in some circumstances, it isn't clear that they'll always find willing coalition partners; if they do find coalition partners, they're likely to be less reliable.

Two implications follow from this logic. First, although coalition governments should not be exceptional in presidential democracies, they should be less common than in parliamentary ones. Again, there's some empirical evidence to support this. When examining minority situations in the world between 1946 and 1999, Cheibub, Przeworski, and Saiegh (2004) find that coalitions formed 78 percent of the time in parliamentary democracies but only 54 percent of the time in presidential ones. The second implication is that coalition governments in presidential systems may be more unstable and survive a shorter amount of time than coalition governments in parliamentary countries. Alternatively, coalitions in presidential regimes may survive as long as coalitions in parliamentary regimes, but they may not govern as effectively because it's possible for a portfolio coalition to outlive the legislative coalition implied by its membership. To our knowledge, these last two hypotheses haven't been tested.

The Composition of Presidential Cabinets

We've illustrated that presidential democracies tend to be characterized by more minority governments and fewer coalition governments than parliamentary ones. It turns out that the composition of presidential cabinets also differs systematically from the composition of parliamentary cabinets. There are typically more nonpartisan ministers in presidential cabinets. A nonpartisan minister is someone who doesn't come from the legislature; she might be someone like a technocrat, a crony, or a representative of an interest group. Ministerial portfolios are also allocated in a less proportional way in presidential cabinets than in parliamentary ones (Amorim Neto and Samuels 2006; Ariotti and Golder 2018). Table 10.8 provides empirical evidence in support of these claims from thirty parliamentary and thirteen presidential democracies from 1980 to 2000.

The composition of cabinets in any democracy reflects the extent to which formateurs must negotiate with political parties. Although political parties exert a relatively strong impact over the allocation of cabinet seats in parliamentary systems, this isn't necessarily the case in presidential democracies. Prime ministers almost always appoint partisan ministers—individuals from political parties in the legislature—to the cabinet as a way of building the legislative majority they need to stay in power. It's for precisely the same reason that prime ministers tend to allocate cabinet seats in proportion to the seats each party provides to the government coalition. Recall that this was the basis for Gamson's law. Because presidents don't depend on having a legislative majority to stay in office, they don't have to negotiate with political parties to the same extent as prime ministers. As a result, they're much freer to vary both the partisan nature and the proportionality of their cabinets. The policy positions and types of parties in the legislature also affect the degree of flexibility that presidents have in making cabinet appointments. Kellam (2015) distinguishes between programmatic parties that have strong policy interests and particularistic/clientelistic parties that simply want resources for their supporters. She finds that presidents who need support to pass their legislation tend to form coalition governments when confronted with programmatic parties, but they head minority cabinets and use government transfers when confronted with particularistic parties.

On the whole, presidential democracies have fewer partisan ministers and lower cabinet proportionality than parliamentary ones. Some presidential cabinets, however, look more like parliamentary ones than others. This is because of the variation in the legislative powers of presidents we mentioned earlier. Presidents can choose to achieve their policy goals either through the legislature or through decrees. Those presidents who have relatively weak decree power, whose parties in the legislature are quite small, and whose parties exhibit low levels of party discipline, appoint cabinets that look more like those found in parliamentary democracies—more partisan ministers and a more proportional allocation of cabinet portfolios—because they rely on winning the support of opposition parties to pass their policies. As Table 10.9 illustrates, there's considerable variation in the extent to which presidents appoint partisan and proportional cabinets. Cabinets tend to be very partisan and highly proportional in countries like Costa Rica, Mexico, and the United States but much less so in countries like Brazil and Venezuela. Amorim Neto (2006) has shown that this variation is systematically related to the need of presidents to negotiate with opposition parties to achieve their policy objectives.

TABLE 10.8 ■ Government Composition in Presidential and Parliamentary Democracies		
Democratic system	Average percentage of nonpartisan ministers	Average proportionality of cabinet portfolio allocation
Parliamentary	2.12	0.90
Presidential	29.17	0.65

Notes: Numbers are based on data from Amorim Neto and Samuels (2006). Proportionality is measured from 0 to 1, with 1 being perfect proportionality.

TABLE 10.9 ■ Government Composition in Presidential Systems (Late 1970s–2000)		
Country	Average percentage of nonpartisan ministers	Average proportionality of cabinet portfolio allocation[†]
Argentina	7.2	0.89
Bolivia	20.5	0.73
Brazil	46.9	0.50
Chile	6.7	0.85
Colombia	5.6	0.87
Costa Rica	1.8	0.98
Ecuador	65.3	0.27
Mexico	3.6	0.96
Panama	17.8	0.71
Uruguay	1.5	0.77
United States	0	0.91
Venezuela	43.7	0.56
Total	29.2	0.64

Source: Data from Amorim Neto (2006).

[†]The proportionality of cabinet portfolio allocation refers to the extent to which government parties receive the same percentage of cabinet posts as the percentage of legislative seats they provide to the government's seat total.

GOVERNMENTS IN SEMI-PRESIDENTIAL DEMOCRACIES

A semi-presidential democracy is one in which the government depends on the legislature to stay in power and in which the head of state—a president—is popularly elected for a fixed term. As with presidential democracies, there's been relatively little research that addresses governments in semi-presidential democracies. This is likely to change with the growing number of countries that have become semi-presidential democracies in recent years. In Eastern Europe, Armenia, Bulgaria, Croatia, Georgia, Kyrgyzstan, Lithuania, Macedonia, Poland, Romania, Russia, Serbia, Slovakia, and Ukraine all adopted semi-presidential forms of democracy following their democratic transitions in the late 1980s and early 1990s. Semi-presidential democracies are also common in Africa in countries like Burkina Faso, Cape Verde, Guinea-Bissau, Namibia, Niger, Senegal, Tunisia, and Zambia. As we saw earlier, semi-presidential democracies are now the second most common type of democracy around the world after parliamentary democracies.

The **government in a semi-presidential democracy** comprises the prime minister and her cabinet. The president is not part of the government itself, but is part of the executive. The executive comprises the government (prime minister and cabinet) and the president. In most semi-presidential democracies, the president has the power to remove the government and, as a result, these systems are characterized by both legislative responsibility *and* presidential responsibility.[4] The president can be a powerful actor in semi-presidential systems and the government must take account of her policy preferences. On the whole, both the president and the prime minister are involved in the day-to-day administration of the state. The precise way in which executive power is divided between the president and the prime minister varies from one country to another. It's often the case, however, that the president has more influence over foreign policy, whereas the prime minister is more powerful in domestic politics.

Given that presidents in semi-presidential democracies are popularly elected, there's nothing to guarantee that the president and the prime minister will come from the same political party. Periods in which politicians from different political parties or blocs hold the presidency and prime ministership are often referred to as **cohabitation**. During cohabitation, the president's party is in the legislative opposition rather than the cabinet. Given that the president nearly always gets to appoint the prime minister in semi-presidential democracies, you might wonder why the president would ever appoint a prime minister from an opposing political party. The answer has to do with the fact that the government (prime minister and cabinet) must enjoy the support of a legislative majority to remain in office. A president may need to appoint a prime minister from an opposition party when the president's party or political bloc doesn't control a majority of legislative seats. In effect, the potential for cohabitation results from the duality of the executive—a president who is not elected by the legislature and a prime minister who must enjoy a legislative majority.

At first glance, cohabitation sounds very similar to divided government in the context of presidential democracies. Cohabitation, though, is not the same as divided government. Indeed, cohabitation is effectively impossible in a presidential democracy. The reason for this is that unlike in a semi-presidential democracy, a president in a presidential system is free to appoint whomever she likes to the cabinet (and the legislature is able to appoint whomever it wants as its presiding officers). To make things a little clearer, consider the United States in 2011 after the Republicans had regained control of the House of Representatives from the Democrats. If the United States had allowed for cohabitation, the new Republican speaker of the House, John Boehner, would have been able to remove the cabinet appointed by the Democratic president, Barack Obama, and replace it with a cabinet of his own choosing. This was not possible, though. The United States of 2011 had divided government, not cohabitation.

France has experienced three periods of cohabitation since 1986. Cohabitation could have occurred even earlier, in 1981, when a Socialist president, François Mitterrand, was voted into office (for a seven-year term) by the French electorate. At the time, a right-wing coalition controlled the legislature. On coming to office, though, Mitterrand used his constitutional power to dissolve the legislature and call for new legislative elections. In these elections, Mitterrand's Socialist Party won an absolute majority of seats (for a five-year term), thereby preempting a period of cohabitation. France's first experience with cohabitation came just five years later when a right-wing coalition won a two-seat majority in the constitutionally mandated legislative elections in 1986. Despite the small size of the legislative majority, Mitterrand was forced to appoint Jacques Chirac, the leader of the main right-wing party, as prime minister because a left-wing prime minister would have been unacceptable to the right-wing majority

[4]Semi-presidential democracies in which there is legislative responsibility and presidential responsibility are referred to as president-parliamentary systems. Those semi-presidential systems in which the president can't remove the government are referred to as premier-presidential systems (Elgie 2011; Shugart and Carey 1992).

in the legislature. An uneasy two-year period of cohabitation ensued in which each leader felt constrained by the powers of the other. This initial period of cohabitation came to an end in 1988 when Mitterrand defeated Chirac in presidential elections. Mitterrand immediately dissolved the legislature, and the Socialist Party won a sufficient number of legislative seats for him to be able to appoint a left-wing prime minister.

In 1993 President Mitterrand found himself in a similar position to that in 1986, when a right-wing coalition won 80 percent of the seats in the legislative elections. Mitterrand was again forced to appoint a right-wing politician, Édouard Balladur, to be prime minister. This second period of cohabitation ended when the right-wing candidate Jacques Chirac was elected president in 1995. Because the right already controlled a legislative majority, Chirac was able to appoint a right-wing prime minister. This alignment of a right-wing president and a right-wing legislature should have lasted until the normally scheduled legislative elections in 1998. President Chirac made the ill-fated decision, however, to dissolve the legislature and call early elections in a strategic attempt to build more support for his reform policies. Chirac's plan backfired, and the left won the 1997 legislative elections. As a result, Chirac was forced to appoint the leader of the Socialist Party, Lionel Jospin, as prime minister. Jospin remained prime minister until 2002, when Chirac was reelected president. On winning the presidential elections, Chirac immediately dissolved the legislature. Chirac's right-wing party won an overwhelming majority in the legislative elections that followed, allowing Chirac to appoint a right-wing prime minister and end France's third period of cohabitation after five years.

For much of the history of the French Fifth Republic, it was thought that the president was the dominant political figure in French politics. The constitution provides the president with significant powers, such as the power to appoint the prime minister, the authority to dissolve the legislature (not more than once a year), and the ability to take on emergency powers if the integrity of France's territory is under threat. Until 1986, the president seemed to dominate both domestic and foreign policy in France. The first period of cohabitation, though, quickly revealed that the dominance of the French president prior to 1986 was not automatic but was, in fact, contingent on the president's controlling a majority in the legislature. Without a legislative majority, the president is forced to defer on domestic politics and, to some extent, on foreign policy, to the prime minister. In periods of cohabitation, France functions very much like a parliamentary democracy with executive power in the hands of the prime minister and the cabinet. This has led some to claim that semi-presidentialism is, at least in the case of France, just an alternation between presidential and parliamentary forms of government, depending on whether the president controls a legislative majority or not (Duverger 1980).

Other semi-presidential democracies, such as Ukraine's, have also experienced cohabitation. In 2006 President Viktor Yushchenko was forced to appoint his political rival, Viktor Yanukovych, as prime minister. The rivalry between these two men dates back at least as far as the 2004 presidential elections, when the pro-Western Yushchenko eventually defeated the pro-Russian Yanukovych in rather controversial circumstances. During the bitter and often violent presidential electoral campaign, Yushchenko became extremely ill, and it was later alleged that he had been poisoned with dioxin, possibly by elements associated with the Russian Federal Security Service. Neither candidate won the required majority in the first round of voting to be elected president. The second round of voting, which was marred by significant electoral fraud, saw Yanukovych declared president. Due to electoral irregularities, Yushchenko and his supporters refused to recognize the results. Following thirteen days of protest that became known as the Orange Revolution, the Ukrainian Supreme Court overturned the election results and ordered a rerun of the second-round runoff, which Yushchenko eventually won. A year and a half later, the Party of Regions, led by Yanukovych, won the most seats in the 2006 legislative elections. Despite the obvious personal hostility between the two men, the election results forced Yushchenko and Yanukovych to reach a compromise. Yushchenko eventually appointed Yanukovych to be prime minister in a coalition government that included both men's parties. Relations between the president and the prime minister were not smooth during this period of cohabitation, with both actors involved in an apparent power struggle. In April 2007, President Yushchenko dissolved parliament and called for new elections that he hoped would reduce the power of Yanukovych. This decision plunged Ukraine into a political crisis, with legislators calling it a coup d'état. Eventually, both the president and the prime minister agreed to hold new elections in an attempt to end weeks of political deadlock. Parties aligned with President Yushchenko won these elections, and the period of cohabitation came to an end. Although periods of cohabitation in semi-presidential democracies can often be characterized as an effective system of checks and balances, this example from Ukraine illustrates that cohabitation can also be characterized by bitter and violent conflict when the political actors involved share starkly different ideologies and goals.[5]

AP Photo/RTR Russian Channel

Viktor Yushchenko, a Western-leaning reformer (right), and Prime Minister Viktor Yanukovych, seen as an ally of Russia (left), appear in a television debate in Ukraine's capital, Kiev, on Monday, November 15, 2004, between the first and second rounds of the presidential elections. Due to allegations of voter fraud following the second round, an unprecedented third round was held, and Yushchenko eventually took office in January 2005.

---

[5]The political situation in Ukraine remains tense today. Yanukovych finally became president after winning the 2010 presidential elections. In 2014, large crowds of Ukrainians took to the streets to protest Yanukovych's pro-Russian policies and his decision to renege on an association agreement with the European Union. These protests, known as the Euromaidan protests, turned violent and President Yanukovych was forced to flee the country and seek sanctuary in Russia. Russia, which called the overthrow of Yanukovych a coup d'état, refused to recognize the new Ukrainian government and annexed Ukraine's Crimean Peninsula. The Ukrainian government is currently engaged in armed conflict with pro-Russian forces in the east of the country.

Few studies have examined the composition of governments in semi-presidential democracies. One study, though, argues that it's perhaps appropriate to think that both the president and the prime minister have de facto vetoes over cabinet appointments (Amorim Neto and Strøm 2006). Thus, the president is not as strong as she would be in a presidential democracy and the prime minister is not as strong as she would be in a parliamentary one. Thus, we might expect semi-presidential democracies to possess both parliamentary and presidential characteristics when it comes to the composition of cabinets. An implication of this is that cabinets in semi-presidential democracies should be characterized by fewer partisan ministers and a lower proportionality in the allocation of portfolios than in parliamentary regimes but more partisan ministers and a higher proportionality in the allocation of portfolios than in presidential regimes. This is precisely what we find when we look at Europe's semi-presidential democracies (Amorim Neto and Strøm 2006). As with presidential democracies, we'd expect there to be variation in cabinet partisanship and proportionality across different semi-presidential democracies. For example, when the president's party controls a legislative majority, we'd expect cabinets to look more like those found in presidential democracies. In contrast, when the president faces a legislature dominated by an opposition party, we'd expect cabinets to look more like those found in parliamentary democracies. The historical experience of French governments seems to bear this out.

Scholars are beginning to explore the duration and stability of semi-presidential democracies. The conventional wisdom has held that semi-presidential institutional arrangements are a dangerous choice for new democracies, and the struggles between the president and the prime minister during cohabitation in Ukraine help to explain why this would be the case (Elgie 2011). Some recent work, though, suggests that we don't yet have a complete understanding of how executive-legislative relations in semi-presidential democracies affect government and regime stability. For example, Schleiter and Morgan-Jones (2009) find that if we take account of government attributes and the constitutional rules surrounding the dissolution of the legislature, then governments in semi-presidential democracies are no less stable than governments in parliamentary democracies. Given the recent proliferation of semi-presidential democracies, additional research on the consequences of this set of institutions will be important for scholars and policymakers alike.

CONCLUSION

One way to classify democracies is in terms of whether they are parliamentary, presidential, or semi-presidential. As we've seen, whether a democracy is parliamentary, presidential, or semi-presidential depends on the relationship between three "actors"—the president, the government, and the legislature. In effect, the different institutional forms of democracy examined in this chapter represent three alternative ways to structure the relationship between the executive and legislative branches of government.

The defining feature of presidentialism is the absence of legislative responsibility—the government serves at the pleasure of the president, not the legislature. Consequently, even when members of the president's own party call for the resignation of one of her cabinet appointees, the most the legislature can do when faced with a president who fails to heed its council is to hold a *symbolic* "no confidence vote" to register its disapproval. These forms of symbolic no confidence votes are rare in presidential systems, in part because they're not binding. During President George W. Bush's second term in office, a Democratic-led Senate in the United States scheduled a no confidence vote to register its disapproval of the activities of Attorney General Alberto Gonzales (Johnston and Lewis 2007). Although such a measure might have conveyed the "sense of the Senate," any successful vote would have had no legal status to compel Gonzales's removal from the government. For example, the Senate passed a similar vote in 1950 when it determined that Secretary of State Dean Acheson was not doing enough to combat the spread of communism; despite the vote, Acheson retained his post for the remainder of the Truman administration (Tsai 2007). The ability of a cabinet member to stay in office despite the explicit disapproval of a legislative majority demonstrates a key feature of presidential systems—a separation of powers between the executive and legislative branches.

In stark contrast, the defining feature of parliamentary systems is that the legislature directly controls the composition of the government. In this chapter, we've outlined the negotiations among party elites that result in the appointment of prime ministers and cabinets in parliamentary systems in some detail. The prime minister—typically the head of the largest legislative party—will, de facto, play a central role in the appointment of the heads of the ministries. Nevertheless, the members of the cabinet—including the prime minister herself—ultimately serve at the pleasure of the legislature in parliamentary systems. Consequently, in 1990 when the United Kingdom's Margaret Thatcher—who had been elected prime minister three times, most recently in 1987 with a 102-seat majority for the Conservative Party—lost the support of party members in the cabinet and in the House of Commons, she stepped down, thereby avoiding a vote of no confidence that had been proposed by Neil Kinnock, the leader of the opposition Labour Party. Before a vote of no confidence occurred, Thatcher was subjected to a leadership challenge from within her own party. After Thatcher's longtime supporter Deputy Prime Minister Sir Geoffrey Howe resigned in frustration with her opposition to a single European currency, Michael Heseltine (who had resigned from the cabinet four years earlier) challenged her in a Conservative Party leadership vote. Although Thatcher managed to win more votes than Heseltine, she fell short of the supermajority needed under Conservative Party rules to prevent a second-round election. She agreed to step down before the second ballot, which was eventually won by John Major.

Although the intricacies of party leadership elections vary from country to country and from party to party, this dramatic episode highlights important characteristics of parliamentary systems. Ministers serve at the pleasure of the legislature. Shifts in opinion or circumstances in the legislature can remove the head of government—oftentimes without recourse to the voting public. Margaret Thatcher was elected to the House of Commons as a representative of a London suburb and was elevated to the head of the government by a vote of her fellow Conservative members of Parliament. Eleven years later a similar vote, in which she garnered support from 204 of the 362 valid votes cast by Conservative members of Parliament, led to her removal from the position of prime minister. For students familiar with the workings of the US government, a simple (but fairly accurate) way to think about parliamentary government is to imagine a US government in which the Speaker of the House, rather than the president, is the head of government.

Semi-presidential systems are as they sound. Cabinets require the support of a majority of the legislature, but the head of state is a popularly elected president. In many semi-presidential democracies, the government can be formed and reformed by either presidential or legislative initiative. Earlier in the chapter, we described how France's Socialist president François Mitterrand decided to dismiss the right-wing-dominated cabinet in 1981 by dissolving the legislature to which it was responsible. The ensuing election returned a Socialist majority in the National Assembly, and as a result, Mitterrand was free to appoint a Socialist as prime minister. The 1986 legislative elections, however, produced a slight majority for a coalition of right-wing parties, and, as a consequence, the cabinet was changed to reflect the new parliamentary reality—most visibly in the form of a new right-wing prime minister, Jacques Chirac. In semi-presidential democracies, therefore, governments can be said to have two masters—the president and the legislature. Which one dictates at any given time, though, depends on the electoral fortunes of the political parties involved.

Thus, the relationship between the country's chief executive officer (whatever her title), the cabinet, and the legislature is fundamentally different in presidential and parliamentary democracies. Some political scientists have used these differences to conclude that presidentialism is a system of governance based on the division of executive and legislative powers, whereas parliamentarism is a system based on the fusion of these powers. There is, indeed, a good deal of truth in Stepan and Skach's (1993) assertion that the essence of parliamentarism is "mutual dependence" and that the essence of presidentialism is "mutual independence." In Chapter 14, we'll examine the strategic dynamic between the executive and legislative branches in more detail when we explore how the decision to adopt parliamentary or presidential systems of government affects the survival of democracy.

Key Concepts

government—the political chief executive and the ministers that head the various government departments; depending on the type of democracy, the political chief executive is either a prime minister or a president

legislative responsibility—a situation in which a legislative majority has the constitutional power—a vote of no confidence—to remove a government from office without cause

vote of no confidence—a vote initiated by the legislature; if the government doesn't obtain a legislative majority in this vote, it must resign

presidential democracy—a democracy in which the government doesn't depend on a legislative majority to exist

parliamentary democracy—a democracy in which the government depends on a legislative majority to exist and the head of state is not popularly elected for a fixed term

semi-presidential democracy—a democracy in which the government depends on a legislative majority to exist and the head of state is popularly elected for a fixed term

government in a parliamentary democracy—comprises a prime minister and the cabinet

cabinet—the group of ministers whose job it is to be in the cabinet and head the various government departments

ministerial responsibility—the idea that cabinet ministers should bear ultimate responsibility for what happens in their ministry

collective cabinet responsibility—the doctrine by which cabinet ministers must publicly support collective cabinet decisions or resign

investiture vote—a formal vote in the legislature to determine whether a proposed government can take office

formateur—a person designated to form the government in a parliamentary regime; often the PM designate

informateur—a person who examines politically feasible coalitions and nominates a formateur

caretaker government—a government that occurs when an election is called or when an incumbent government either resigns or is defeated in a vote of no confidence; it rules the country for an interim period until a new government is formed

office-seeking politician—a politician interested in the intrinsic benefits of office

policy-seeking politician—a politician interested in shaping policy

Gamson's law—states that cabinet portfolios will be distributed among government parties in strict proportion to the number of seats that each party contributes to the government's legislative seat total

minimal winning coalition (MWC)—a coalition in which there are no parties that aren't required to control a legislative majority

least minimal winning coalition—the MWC with the lowest number of surplus seats

connected coalition—a coalition in which the member parties are located next to each other in the policy space

minority government—a government in which the governmental parties don't jointly command a majority of legislative seats

surplus majority government—a government in which the cabinet includes more parties than are strictly necessary to control a majority of legislative seats

cabinet reshuffle—when the prime minister rotates or changes the individual ministers in the cabinet, but doesn't change the parties represented in the cabinet

government in a presidential democracy—comprises the president and the cabinet

portfolio coalition—a coalition composed of those legislators belonging to parties in the cabinet

legislative coalition—a voting bloc composed of legislators who support a piece of legislation

presidential decree—an order by a president that has the force of law; the scope and extent of these decrees vary from country to country

government in a semi-presidential democracy—comprises the prime minister and the cabinet

cohabitation—a president from one political bloc and a prime minister from another; occurs when the party of the president doesn't control a majority in the legislature and is not represented in the cabinet

11

ELECTIONS AND ELECTORAL SYSTEMS

It's not the voting that's democracy; it's the counting.

Tom Stoppard, *Jumpers*

The most important choice facing constitution writers is that of a legislative electoral system.

Arend Lijphart, "Constitutional Design for Divided Societies"

OVERVIEW

1. Elections are one of the defining characteristics of democracies and provide the primary mechanism by which democratic governments obtain the authority to rule.

2. Although there's a great deal of variety in the types of electoral systems employed around the world, most political scientists categorize them into two main families based on the electoral formula used to translate votes into seats: majoritarian or proportional.

3. After discussing issues related to electoral integrity, we take a close look at how majoritarian and proportional electoral systems work in practice. We also discuss the effect of these systems on things like proportionality, ethnic accommodation, accountability, minority representation, and the revelation of sincere preferences.

A defining feature of democracies is the use of elections. Many political scientists distinguish between democracies based on the type of electoral system they employ in their elections. An **electoral system** is a set of laws and regulations that govern the electoral competition between candidates and parties (Cox 1997, 38). These laws and regulations relate to a whole host of things such as the **electoral formula** (how votes are translated into seats), the **ballot structure** (whether individuals vote for candidates or parties, and whether they cast a single vote or express a series of preferences), and the **district magnitude** (the number of representatives elected in a district). Despite the different dimensions along which electoral systems can vary, most political scientists categorize electoral systems into two main families based on the electoral formula they use to translate votes into seats: majoritarian or proportional. Indeed, it's partly on this basis that some political scientists talk of majoritarian and proportional democracies (M. Golder and Stramski 2010; Lijphart 1999; Powell 2000).

In this chapter, we explore how various electoral systems work. We also discuss some of the advantages and disadvantages associated with each of these systems. Before we address these issues, though, we provide a brief overview of elections and electoral integrity around the world.

ELECTIONS AND ELECTORAL INTEGRITY

Elections are increasingly being used to fill legislative and executive offices around the world. Indeed, 185 of the world's 193 independent states now use direct elections to elect people to their lower house of parliament (Norris et al. 2016a, 19). In democracies, elections serve both a practical and a symbolic role. In a practical sense, elections provide the primary means by which citizens select their representatives. As such, they provide citizens with an opportunity to influence the government formation process, to reward or punish politicians for their time in power, and to shape the direction of future policy. In a symbolic sense, the legitimacy of a democratic government comes from the fact that it was chosen through an electoral process—citizens have an equal and relatively low-cost opportunity to participate in selecting the people who rule over them and hence the types of policy that should be implemented. Democratic elections provide the primary mechanism by which the people's consent is translated into the authority to rule.

In Figure 11.1, we show how the number of legislative and presidential elections in democracies has increased over the last six decades. There were more legislative and presidential elections in the last decade than at any other point in the postwar period (or, indeed, ever). Between 2001 and 2010, 299 legislative and 133 presidential elections were held in 120 different democracies (Bormann and Golder 2013). Seven countries held democratic elections for the first time: East Timor (2002), Georgia (2004), Kyrgyzstan (2005), Liberia (2005), Mauritania (2006), Bhutan (2008), and the Maldives (2008). The increase in the number of democratic elections since the 1970s is largely a consequence of the third wave of democratization (see Chapter 7) in Eastern Europe, Latin America, Asia, and Africa. Presidential elections now make up a larger share of all democratic elections than they did in the past. To a large extent, this has to do with the increasing proportion of semi-presidential democracies in the world (see Chapter 10), as these regimes have popularly elected presidents.

Elections don't occur only in democracies. As we saw in Chapter 8, elections are also increasingly common in dictatorships. Only Brunei, China, Eritrea, Qatar, and Saudi Arabia have failed to hold national-level elections at some point in the postwar period (M. Golder 2005). Of course, elections are not a defining characteristic of dictatorships in the same way that they are of democracies. More significantly, elections tend to serve very different purposes in dictatorships than in democracies. Among other things, dictatorial elections are often used to co-opt elites and larger societal groups, to gain good favor with foreign aid donors, as a safety valve for public discontent, or to gather information about the strength of the opposition (Gandhi and Lust-Okar 2009). Dictatorial elections are almost never used as a mechanism for translating the people's consent into the authority to govern.

FIGURE 11.1   ■   Legislative and Presidential Elections by Decade in Democracies

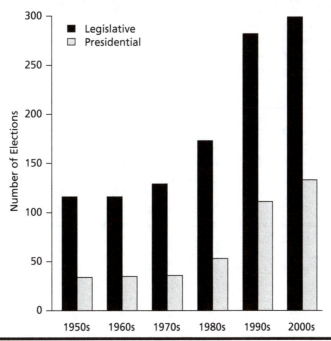

Source: Bormann and Golder (2013, 361).

Electoral Integrity: An Overview

The increasing use of legislative and presidential elections around the world has been accompanied by growing concerns about **electoral integrity**. The concept of electoral integrity is somewhat vague and remains contested in both academic and policy circles. Here we follow the definition provided by the Electoral Integrity Project (EIP, n.d.).[1] According to the EIP, electoral integrity refers to the extent to which the conduct of elections meets international standards and global norms concerning "good" elections as set out in various treaties, conventions, and guidelines issued by organizations such as the UN General Assembly, the Organization for Security and Cooperation in Europe, the Organization of American States, and the African Union (Norris et al. 2016a, 13). Electoral integrity has to do with the conduct of elections at all stages of the electoral cycle, including the preelection period, the campaign, the polling day, and the election aftermath (Norris 2013).

Violations of electoral integrity, which include things like ballot stuffing, electoral violence and voter intimidation, pro-government media bias, and restrictive ballot access are generally referred to as **electoral malpractice**. Although you might think that electoral malpractice is restricted to underdeveloped countries, authoritarian regimes, or new democracies, evidence of electoral malpractice also exists in established democracies like the United States. Electoral malpractice in these settings often has to do with political interference in how district boundaries are drawn, problems with voter registration, technical failures with online or early voting procedures, and unfair campaign finance rules. The authors of *The Year in Elections 2015*

[1]For more information about The Electoral Integrity Project, visit www.electoralintegrityproject.com.

report produced by the EIP stated that 12 percent of the elections that have taken place in the last decade have triggered opposition boycotts, 17 percent have experienced postelection protests, and 18 percent have led to electoral violence in which at least one citizen has died. Electoral integrity matters because flawed elections can reduce trust in the political system, fuel social instability, undermine recent democratic gains, discourage voter participation and other forms of civic activism, and exacerbate ethnic, religious, and other grievances that can in extreme circumstances lead to civil war (Norris 2014).

The Electoral Integrity Project has measured electoral integrity in 285 legislative and presidential elections in 164 countries between 2012 and 2017. To measure electoral integrity, the EIP surveyed more than 3,000 country experts to ask about their perceptions of forty-nine electoral integrity issues, grouped into eleven categories that relate to the whole electoral cycle. In terms of the preelection period, the country experts were asked to evaluate electoral integrity as it relates to (1) the electoral laws, (2) the electoral procedures, (3) district boundaries, (4) voter registration, and (5) party registration. In terms of the election campaign, they were asked to consider (6) the campaign media environment and (7) campaign finance regulations. With respect to the election day itself, they focused on (8) the voting process. And with respect to the postelection period, they considered (9) the vote counting process, (10) the response to the election results, and (11) the role played by the electoral authorities. Based on expert responses to the forty-nine electoral integrity indicators, each election in a country is given an overall Perceptions of Electoral Integrity (PEI) score that runs from 0 to 100, with higher scores indicating higher electoral integrity (Norris, Wynter, and Cameron 2018a).[2]

In Map 11.1, we show how electoral integrity varies across the world in 2017. Darker colors indicate higher levels of electoral integrity. Countries in the lightest gray don't currently have electoral integrity scores, either because they don't hold national-level elections or because their elections have yet to be evaluated. There's considerable variation in the level of electoral integrity across countries. The ten countries with the highest electoral integrity scores are Denmark, Finland, Norway, Iceland, Germany, Costa Rica, Sweden, the Netherlands, Estonia, and Switzerland. The ten countries with the lowest electoral integrity scores are Equatorial Guinea, Ethiopia, Burundi, Syria, the Republic of Congo, Djibouti, Haiti, Chad, Cambodia, and Afghanistan. The highest scores tend to occur in the established democracies of Western Europe, whereas the lowest scores are concentrated in the authoritarian regimes found in Africa and parts of Asia.

Electoral Integrity in Four Countries

We now take a closer look at electoral integrity in four specific countries, the United States, Turkey, Belarus, and Egypt. The "star-plots" in Figure 11.2 show how these countries do on each of the eleven categories of electoral integrity as well as their overall PEI score. The shaded gray area in the star-plot is large when a country scores highly on each of the eleven categories in the PEI measure. To help provide context, we overlay each country's star-plot (filled, gray) with a star-plot (black dashed line) showing the average *global* score on each of the eleven categories in the PEI measure. This allows us to see where the countries are doing better or worse than the global average when it comes to electoral integrity. The star-plots are drawn for the 2014 legislative elections in the United States, the November 2015 legislative elections in Turkey, the 2015 presidential elections in Belarus, and the 2015 legislative elections in Egypt.

---

[2]Additional information about how the PEI scores are calculated, along with the data itself, can be found online (Norris, Wynter and Cameron 2018a). The data used here were from the PEI 6.0 release (Norris, Wynter and Cameron 2018b).

MAP 11.1 ■ Electoral Integrity across the World in 2017

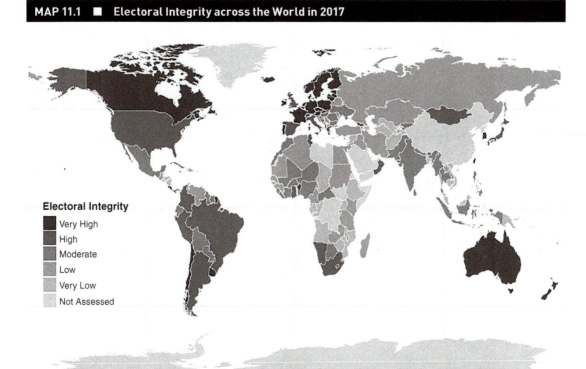

Electoral Integrity

- Very High
- High
- Moderate
- Low
- Very Low
- Not Assessed

Source: Data come from the Perceptions of Electoral Integrity expert survey (PEI 6.0) and are based on national-level elections that have taken place between July 1, 2012, and December 31, 2017 (Norris, Wynter, and Cameron 2018b). Darker colors indicate higher levels of electoral integrity.

Although established democracies tend to have high PEI scores, there's some variation. The 2014 legislative elections in the United States received the lowest overall PEI score among established democracies (62), leaving them ranked 107th out of the 285 elections evaluated by the Electoral Integrity Project. As the top left panel of the star-plot in Figure 11.2 indicates, the low PEI score for the United States in 2014 was primarily driven by concerns about the quality of voter registration, the process of drawing district boundaries, campaign finance regulations, and the electoral rules. Long-standing issues related to voter registration have been politically salient in the United States since the US Supreme Court intervened in the recount of the votes cast in Florida during the 2000 presidential elections. Republicans have repeatedly raised concerns about voter fraud and have sought to pass voter identification laws that critics claim will suppress turnout, particularly among minority voters and the poor. The highly politicized way in which district boundaries are drawn in the United States sees it receive the fourth lowest PEI score on this dimension, with only Nicaragua, the Central African Republic, and Syria doing worse. The 2014 PEI score for the United States is also negatively affected by the partisan and decentralized nature of the electoral administrative bodies that oversee American elections and by the majoritarian electoral system that makes it difficult for small parties to win legislative representation.

The November 2015 legislative elections in Turkey received a PEI score of 47, meaning that they were characterized by low levels of electoral integrity. According to its constitution,

FIGURE 11.2   ■   Electoral Integrity in Four Countries

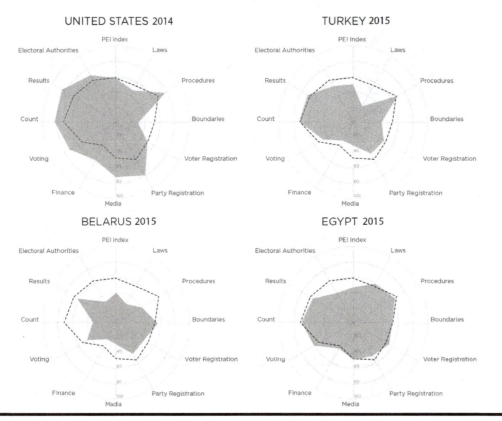

Source: Data for the star-plots come from the Perceptions of Electoral Integrity expert survey (PEI 6.0). The gray star-plots indicate how the four countries score on each of the eleven categories of electoral integrity. They also show each country's overall PEI score. The black dashed line indicates the average global score across the same categories of electoral integrity. The United States plot refers to the 2014 legislative elections, the Turkey plot refers to the November 2015 legislative elections, the Belarus plot refers to the 2015 presidential elections, and the Egypt plot refers to the 2015 legislative elections.

Turkey is a secular democracy. The Turkish military has historically seen itself as the defender of the country's secular democracy and has intervened in politics on several occasions to keep religion out of politics ("Timeline" 2016). Turkey has been ruled by the Justice and Development Party (AKP) since 2002 when it won a legislative majority with just 34.3 percent of the vote. Although the AKP is popular among large segments of the population, critics claim that the AKP is weakening Turkey's secularism and has a hidden agenda to make the country more Islamist. In 2013 a wave of demonstrations known as the Gezi Park protests, in which large numbers of Turks criticized restrictions on the freedom of the press and attacked the perceived authoritarianism of the government, was violently suppressed by the police (Letsch 2013).

There were two legislative elections in Turkey in 2015. In the June elections, the AKP remained the largest party but lost its legislative majority, forcing it to begin coalition negotiations with other legislative parties. When these negotiations failed, the AKP called for new elections in November. In these elections, the AKP regained its legislative majority and was able to form a government without any coalition partners. As the top right panel of the star-plot in Figure 11.2 indicates, several factors drive the low PEI score for Turkey. The Turkish electoral threshold requires that parties must win 10 percent of the vote before they can receive any legislative seats. This is the highest threshold in the world and makes it very difficult for small parties to win legislative representation. The government has significant control of the national media, and journalists critical of the regime have faced considerable intimidation. There were reports during the 2015 elections of the AKP's improper use of state resources for campaigning. Between the two elections, the AKP also ramped up its attacks on the minority Kurdish population, hoping to evoke a nationalist response and a demand for political stability.

The political situation in Turkey has become more polarized since the 2015 legislative elections. Shortly after the elections, the AKP renewed its call to increase the power of the executive relative to the legislature by altering the constitution so that Turkey becomes a presidential democracy. This constitutional change was approved in an April 2017 referendum that was marred by electoral irregularities. In July 2016, a section of the Turkish military conducted a failed coup in which it claimed that the AKP was eroding the tradition of secularism, violating human rights, and becoming more authoritarian. According to some sources, President Erdoğan has used the failure of the coup as an opportunity to conduct a "counter-coup" and purge tens of thousands of his rivals in the military and the civil service, including judges, teachers, and academics ("After the Coup" 2016). These events do not bode well for electoral integrity in future Turkish elections.

Belarus is an authoritarian former Soviet republic in Eastern Europe. It's been referred to as Europe's last dictatorship (Wilson 2012). The 2015 presidential elections in Belarus received a very low PEI score of 40, which ranked them 240th out of the 285 elections coded by the Electoral Integrity Project. Belarus has been ruled by President Alexander Lukashenko since 1994. Lukashenko is the longest-serving leader among post-Soviet heads of state, and he regularly wins presidential elections with massive majorities. The bottom left panel of the star-plot in Figure 11.2 indicates that there are many reasons for Belarus's low PEI score. Over his time in office, Lukashenko has expanded executive control over the legislature, consolidated state control of the media, and built the largest security apparatus in Europe (Crabtree, Fariss, and Schuler, 2016). There were four candidates in the October 2015 presidential elections. At least two of these candidates were considered "shadow" candidates who ran only to create the impression of political competition (Wilson 2015). During the campaign, Lukashenko played on Belarusians' fear that if he were to lose, Russia would intervene in Belarus as it had done in Ukraine. Fear of Russian intervention limited the extent to which the other candidates were willing to attack Lukashenko. Lukashenko easily won reelection with 83.49 percent of the vote, with more voters casting a ballot marked "against all" than for any of the other three candidates (Crabtree, Fariss, and Schuler, 2016). Election observers and human rights organizations have reported evidence of widespread voter coercion, incorrect ballot counting, and election fraud.

Egypt is a dictatorship in North Africa. The October-December 2015 legislative elections received a low PEI score of 46, which ranked them 208th out of the 285 elections coded by the Electoral Integrity Project. Many observers had high hopes for democracy in Egypt following the overthrow of the longtime dictator Hosni Mubarak during the Arab Spring in February 2011. In 2012, Mohamed Morsi, the Muslim Brotherhood candidate, became the first democratically elected president in Egypt's history. After a year of divisive rule, though, the Egyptian military, led by General Abdel Fattah el-Sisi, intervened to remove President Morsi from power in July 2013. There was a mixed international reaction to these events, with the United States refusing to call the events a "military coup" as this would have required freezing the substantial economic and military aid it provided to Egypt. A new Egyptian constitution, which critics claim gives too much power to the military, was passed in a January 2014 referendum. Shortly afterward, General Sisi was elected president in May 2014. The October-December legislative elections in 2015 were supposed to mark the final step in the restoration of democracy. Following the military coup, the Muslim Brotherhood was banned and labeled a terrorist organization, and many of its members were arrested and sentenced to death. Dissidents and journalists critical of the regime have been repressed. Indeed, the regime rejected several political parties who sought to place candidates on the ballot for the 2015 elections. Many of those candidates who were allowed to run were supporters of President Sisi, and a number were closely tied to the ousted dictator, Hosni Mubarak. Secular and leftist parties, many of whom had helped to organize the protests during the Arab Spring, chose to boycott the elections. The boycott and the banning of the Muslim Brotherhood depressed turnout, with some reports putting it as low as 10 percent ("Low Turnout" 2015). The Carter Center, which monitors elections for electoral malpractice, closed its Cairo office ahead of the election and stated "that the political space has narrowed for Egyptian political parties, civil society, and the media. As a result, the upcoming elections are unlikely to advance a genuine democratic transition in Egypt" ("Carter Center Closes Egypt Office" 2014).

The Determinants of Electoral Integrity

Experts tend to perceive democratic elections as displaying more electoral integrity than dictatorial elections. This is not surprising given that elections tend to serve different purposes in democracies and dictatorships. However, this observation doesn't help us explain the variation we see in electoral integrity among democracies or among dictatorships.

Norris (2015) identifies a number of factors that influence electoral integrity. One factor concerns domestic structural constraints such as the level of economic development, a country's dependence on natural resources, a legacy of conflict, or inhospitable geography. Wealthy countries are more likely to be democratic (see Chapter 5), and they have more resources they can devote to the electoral process. A salient issue for many poor countries is the cost of actually holding elections. As we'll see shortly, electoral systems vary in the costs they impose on a political system. The political resource curse suggests that countries dependent on natural resources will exhibit high levels of corruption and that ruling elites will use natural resource revenue to manipulate elections, intimidate opponents, and suppress opposition. This helps to explain the low levels of electoral integrity in countries like Equatorial Guinea, Iraq, and the Democratic Republic of Congo. Countries that have a legacy of conflict, such as Afghanistan, Rwanda, Sri Lanka, and Burundi, typically have deep divisions and high levels of mistrust that can also hinder electoral integrity. The logistical, financial, and technical difficulties of running a well-functioning election are harder in large states with mountainous and other difficult-to-reach areas. For example, the 2014 legislative elections in India took place over nine phases of voting, cost $5 billion, and involved 930,000 polling stations and 814 million eligible voters (Norris 2015, 78).

A second factor concerns the international community. One claim is that countries more integrated into the global system will be more likely to adopt international norms and practices that encourage electoral integrity. Regional intergovernmental organizations can also play a role. For example, those European countries seeking membership in the European Union have strong incentives to respect human rights and produce free and fair elections. In contrast, countries associated with regional organizations where member states tend to be authoritarian are less likely to feel pressure to produce high levels of electoral integrity. It's often claimed that donor countries can use foreign aid to encourage recipient countries to increase human rights protections, strengthen civil society associations, and increase media independence. Elections in developing countries frequently receive considerable financial aid and technical assistance from a variety of international organizations and donor countries.

As we discussed in Chapter 5, though, there are many reasons to doubt the ability and willingness of donor countries to bring about meaningful democratic and electoral reforms in recipient countries.

A particular international factor that has received growing attention in recent years has been the role played by nonpartisan international organizations that monitor elections. Election observer missions have become increasingly common over the last three decades (Hyde 2011). Organizations such as the Carter Center, the Organization for Security and Cooperation in Europe (OSCE), the African Union (AU), the Organization of American States (OAS), and the European Union (EU) have deployed thousands of international and domestic observers in numerous countries in an attempt to deter incumbents from committing electoral fraud. Very few elections these days have no international observers.

The effectiveness of these observer missions remains open to debate, though. Although some studies find that electoral irregularities are lower in polling stations that have observers (Hyde 2007a, b), others suggest that election monitors simply displace irregularities from the places they visit to surrounding areas they don't visit (Ichino and Schündeln 2012). Observer missions aren't always perceived as impartial, and reports can sometimes be politicized and reach contradictory conclusions. For example, the OSCE reported significant irregularities in Azerbaijan's 2013 presidential election, but the delegation of former members of the US House of Representatives declared that the elections had been free, fair, and transparent (Norris 2014, 9). In some cases, observer missions have incentives to understate the degree of electoral malfeasance so that they're invited back to monitor the next elections or because they wish to prevent postelection violence that might result from charges of electoral fraud.

Two other factors influence electoral integrity—institutional design and electoral management bodies. Some scholars argue that countries with power-sharing institutions exhibit higher levels of electoral integrity than countries with institutions that concentrate power in the hands of the majority (Lijphart 2004; Norris 2015). This is because power-sharing institutions create checks and balances that limit the ability of incumbents to abuse their power and encourage minority groups to "buy in" to the political system. Other scholars, though, argue that power-sharing institutions make it harder to hold political actors accountable and that they tend to reify social divisions in the political system. We'll revisit the relative benefits and costs of power-sharing institutions in more detail in Chapters 13 and 14. Electoral management bodies refer to the institutions and authorities that administer elections. Electoral management bodies that are independent of the executive branch and have functional capacity (technical expertise, trained officials, adequate budgets, and so on) are often key to holding high-quality elections. Strengthening these bodies would seem to be an easy step to improve electoral integrity. It's often the case, though, that those actors who have an incentive to strengthen these institutions (opposition and minority groups) are not the actors who have the ability to strengthen them (incumbents and majority groups).

ELECTORAL SYSTEMS

Although elections always involve citizens casting votes for candidates or political parties, there's a great deal of variation in the precise set of rules employed by the world's electoral systems. Some allow citizens to vote for candidates, whereas others allow them to vote only for political parties; some allow citizens to cast only one vote, whereas others allow them to cast multiple votes; some allow for only one round of voting, whereas others allow for two or more; some involve electing only one representative in each district, whereas others involve electing many. The list of differences could go on and on. Despite the many different ways in which one might think to distinguish among the world's electoral systems, most political scientists categorize electoral systems into two main families—majoritarian or proportional—based on the electoral formula they use to translate votes into seats. In what follows, we examine some of the more common majoritarian and proportional electoral systems.

Majoritarian Electoral Systems

A majoritarian electoral system is one in which the candidates or parties that receive the most votes win. The word *majoritarian* is somewhat misleading. Although some majoritarian systems require the winning candidate or party to obtain an absolute majority of the votes, others require only that the winning candidate or party receives more votes than anyone else. In other words, not all majoritarian systems require the winning candidates or parties to obtain a majority of the votes. Probably the main reason why majoritarian systems are referred to as "majoritarian" is that they frequently produce outcomes in which the largest party wins a majority of the legislative seats even if it doesn't win a majority of the votes. In effect, majoritarian systems tend to help the largest party obtain a legislative majority. There are many different types of majoritarian electoral systems.

Single-Member District Plurality System

A single-member district plurality (SMDP) system is the simplest and most commonly used majoritarian system in the world. It's employed primarily in the United Kingdom and in former British colonies, such as Belize, Canada, India, Nigeria, and the United States. In an SMDP system, voters cast a single candidate-centered vote in single-member districts. The candidate with the most votes, even if she doesn't have a majority of the votes, is elected from the district. SMDP systems are sometimes referred to as "first-past-the-post." This name, though, is misleading as it suggests that a candidate is elected once she gets past a certain vote total. In theory, a candidate can win in an SMDP system with as few as two votes if all the other candidates win only one vote each. An example of the operation of an SMDP system in the Bath constituency during the 2015 United Kingdom legislative elections is shown in Table 11.1. Ben Howlett of the Conservative Party won the most votes and was, therefore, elected as the Member of Parliament for this district.

SMDP electoral systems have both strengths and weaknesses. Perhaps the greatest strength of SMDP systems is their simplicity. This means that they're easy for voters to understand. It also means that they're easy and relatively inexpensive to administer. A second strength of SMDP systems has to do with the fact that only one representative is elected in each district. This means that responsibility for what happens in the district lies squarely with one person. In other words, SMDP systems make it easy for voters to identify who is responsible for policies in their district and therefore to hold them accountable in the next election. By making it easier for voters to hold representatives accountable, SMDP systems create incentives for representatives to perform well in office. As a result, SMDP systems tend to produce high levels of constituency service and close bonds between constituents and their representatives.

Despite these strengths, SMDP electoral systems have many critics. Some critics point to the fact that SMDP systems have the potential to produce unrepresentative outcomes. As our example in Table 11.1 illustrates, it's possible for a candidate to win without obtaining a majority of the votes; in fact, 62.2 percent of Bath voters didn't support the winning candidate. Candidates can win in SMDP systems with even lower vote shares than that obtained by the winning candidate in Bath. As an example, the winning candidate in the Kerowagi constituency in Papua New Guinea won with just 7.9 percent of the vote in the 1987 legislative elections (Cox 1997, 85).

TABLE 11.1 ■ Election Results from the Bath Constituency, UK Legislative Elections, 2015			
Candidate	Party	Votes	Percentage
Ben Howlett	Conservative	17,833	37.8
Steve Bradley	Liberal Democrat	14,000	29.7
Ollie Middleton	Labour	6,216	13.2
Dominic Tristram	Green	5,634	11.9
Julian Deverell	UKIP	2,922	6.2
Lorraine Morgan-Brinkhurst	Independent	499	1.1
Jenny Knight	Independent	63	0.1

Not only are SMDP systems criticized for producing unrepresentative outcomes at the district level, but they're frequently criticized for their potential to produce unrepresentative outcomes at the national level as well. Under an SMDP system, it's entirely possible for a party that wins a significant percentage of the national vote to obtain very few legislative seats because it fails to come first in many constituencies. For instance, in the 1983 legislative elections in the United Kingdom the coalition between the Social Democratic Party and the Liberal Party, which was known as the Alliance, won 25.4 percent of the national vote but received just 3.5 percent of the seats. In fact, the Alliance won only 675,985 votes (out of 30,661,309 votes) fewer than the Labour Party but received 186 fewer legislative seats. In stark contrast to the Alliance, the Conservative Party won 61.1 percent of the seats and formed a single-party government even though it had won only 42.4 percent of the votes. As this example demonstrates, SMDP systems can produce a highly disproportionate translation of votes into seats that tends to favor larger parties at the expense of smaller ones.

Some also criticize SMDP systems for encouraging individuals to vote strategically rather than in accordance with their true preferences. Sincere voting means voting for your most preferred candidate or party. In contrast, strategic voting means voting for your most preferred candidate *who has a realistic chance of winning*.[3] To see how the SMDP system creates an incentive to vote strategically, consider the Bath example in Table 11.1 again. Imagine an individual who prefers the Labour candidate to the Liberal Democrat candidate and the Liberal Democrat candidate to the Conservative candidate. If this individual votes for the Labour candidate, she'll be voting sincerely. However, this individual has an incentive to vote strategically because opinion polls are likely to show that the Labour candidate is going to finish in third place and has little to no chance of coming in first. Thus, a vote for the Labour candidate will be "wasted." As a result, the individual may decide to vote strategically for the Liberal Democrat candidate (who has a more realistic chance of winning) in an attempt to stop the Conservative candidate (the least-preferred candidate) from winning. Clearly, we prefer electoral systems that encourage voters to express their sincere preferences. Unfortunately, though, scholars have shown that *all* reasonable electoral systems create incentives for individuals to act strategically; there are no "strategy-proof" systems (Gibbard 1973; Satterthwaite 1975). Nonetheless, some electoral systems, such as SMDP, create stronger incentives to act strategically than others.

[3]For more detailed definitions of sincere and strategic voting, see Chapter 9.

Another criticism of SMDP systems is that they can encourage the creation of ethnic parties in countries in which ethnic groups are regionally concentrated. This can result in regional fiefdoms or party strongholds in which there's little electoral competition, the party of the majority ethnic group is dominant, and minorities have little sway over public policy or the allocation of private goods. This type of situation frequently occurs in African countries like Malawi and Kenya, where ethnic groups are geographically concentrated in particular regions (Barkan 1995; Posner 2005). In effect, the use of SMDP electoral systems in Africa has helped produce countries that are "divided into geographically separate party strongholds, with little incentive for parties to make appeals outside their home region and cultural-political base" (Reynolds, Reilly, and Ellis 2005, 43). Similarly, the use of SMDP probably helped segregationist Democrats maintain single-party dominance in the southern United States for almost a century (Mickey 2015).

Single Nontransferable Vote

The single nontransferable vote (SNTV) is a second type of majoritarian system. SNTV is essentially the same as an SMDP electoral system except that it works in multimember districts instead of single-member districts. Basically, each party competing in a district puts up a list of candidates, and individuals vote for one of the candidates. The candidates that win the most votes are elected. For example, in a three-seat district, the top three vote-getters are elected. In a four-seat district, the top four vote-getters are elected, and so on. One advantage of SNTV systems over SMDP ones is that they tend to produce more proportional outcomes and greater representation for smaller parties and minority ethnic groups. This is because candidates from smaller parties and minority ethnic groups can now get elected even though they don't win the most votes in a district.

Interestingly, candidates in an SNTV system know exactly what percentage of the votes they need to win in order to guarantee their election. For example, if there are n district seats to be filled, then any candidate A can guarantee being elected by receiving one more than $1 / (n + 1)$ of the votes. This is because n other candidates can't all receive more than candidate A. Thus, in a four-seat district, a candidate can guarantee winning one of the seats by winning more than 20 percent of the vote. An SNTV system was employed for legislative elections in Japan until 1994 and in Taiwan until 2005. It's currently employed for legislative elections in Afghanistan and Vanuatu.

SNTV electoral systems are often considered problematic. First, they tend to weaken political parties by creating incentives for intraparty fighting and factionalization. This is because candidates are competing against candidates not only from other parties in their district but also against candidates from their own party. The result is that electoral campaigns are often centered on candidate characteristics rather than policy differences, with candidates going to great lengths to cultivate personal reputations. SNTV systems may even impede the emergence of fully fledged parties. In 2005, for example, Afghan president Hamid Karzai adopted an SNTV electoral system and pronounced that candidates could not show a party affiliation on the ballot (Reynolds 2006).[4] The system has produced a great deal of voter confusion.

---

[4]That the SNTV system can work without fully fledged parties was one of the reasons why it was adopted (Reynolds 2006). As the *New York Times* reported, Afghans "associate parties with both the Communists who brought the Soviet invaders and the ethnic militias that pillaged the country after the Communists' downfall" ("Afghanistan: The Wrong Voting System" 2005). A law introduced in 2009 allows candidates to have their party's symbol on the ballot. However, only thirty-four candidates had their party's name added to the ballot in the 2010 legislative elections (Reynolds and Carey 2012).

Election workers and donkeys carry voting material to remote villages on September 17, 2010 (the day before the election), in the Panjshir province, Afghanistan. More than 2,500 candidates contested 249 seats in the lower house of the Afghan parliament, using the single nontransferable vote electoral system.

Voters in Kabul, for example, were confronted with more than four hundred candidates on the ballot, all vying for the thirty-three seats up for election. Over two-thirds of the votes were cast for losing candidates and therefore wasted. The end result was a highly fragmented legislature containing more than thirty factions with shifting loyalties (Reynolds 2011, 9–10). The 2010 legislative elections produced even higher levels of fragmentation. With weak or nonexistent parties in the legislature, it can be difficult for governments to build legislative coalitions to keep them in power and support their policy objectives.

Second, the fact that candidates can guarantee their own election with a specific percentage of votes encourages clientelistic behavior and the development of patronage systems, in which candidates target electoral bribes at well-defined interest groups. For example, candidates of the Liberal Democratic Party (LDP) in Japan were notorious for engaging in constituency service and targeting subsidy (pork) allocations toward their districts (Hirano 2011). Clientelism is likely to be particularly prevalent when candidates don't need to win many votes to guarantee themselves a seat. This will be the case when the SNTV system is combined with a large multimember district. Recall that a candidate in an SNTV system can guarantee election if they receive one more than $1 / (n + 1)$ of the votes, where n refers to the number of district seats to be filled. It's perhaps worth noting that Japan, which was infamous for its system of political clientelism, employed an SNTV system in relatively small multimember districts comprising three to five seats. In contrast, the SNTV system in Afghanistan is being employed in districts where the magnitude ranges from a low of two to a high of thirty-three. This means that Afghan candidates in some districts can *guarantee* winning seats with less than 3 percent of the vote. Indeed, several candidates in the provinces of Helmand, Kandahar, and Zabul were able to win seats in the 2010 legislative elections with just a few hundred votes. As one would expect, the "cheapness" of an Afghan seat encourages vote buying. As the *New York Times* reported in 2010, political candidates were literally

Paula Bronstein/Getty Images

buying Afghan votes for anywhere from a high of about $18 in Ghazni province to a low of about $1 in Kandahar (Nordlan 2010). This is a small price for Afghan candidates to pay given that legislative seats come with a high monthly salary and the opportunity to exploit the corrupt patron-client political system.

Third, the SNTV system tends to favor both incumbent and well-organized parties. As we've seen, SNTV systems encourage the development of political systems based on patronage and other particularistic connections. Incumbent parties are advantaged in these systems because they have greater access to state resources and can more credibly commit to allocating those resources to their supporters. Well-organized parties are better equipped to make sure that sufficient goods are distributed to their voters, and also better placed to deal with the strategic quandaries that political parties and voters face in an SNTV system. Although all parties in an SNTV system want to win as many seats as they can in each multimember district, they don't want to put up too many candidates in case their party supporters split their vote between these candidates to such an extent that none, or only a few, of the candidates actually finish among the top vote winners. In the extreme, it's possible in an SNTV system for a party whose candidates together obtain a substantial percentage of the votes, even an absolute majority, to win no seats. This suggests that political parties have to be very careful in choosing how many candidates to run in each district. Similarly, supporters of each party must think hard about which candidate from their party most needs their vote to be elected; if they give their vote to a candidate who is already likely to obtain a sufficient number of votes, their vote will be wasted. Well-organized parties are better able to deal with these issues because they can often coordinate their nominations and distribute their supporters' votes in a way that maximizes the number of their candidates elected in each district. For example, the Kuomintang in Taiwan used to assign its candidates to particular geographic zones in a district and send party members a letter telling them which candidate to vote for (Liu 1999; Patterson and Stockton 2010).

Finally, the fact that candidates under an SNTV system can win with only a small fraction of the vote share means that they don't have to moderate their political message and can instead espouse a more extremist rhetoric that appeals to a specific segment of the electorate. As such, some believe that the SNTV system increases the likelihood that extremists will be elected, potentially destabilizing the political system in the process.

Alternative Vote

The alternative vote (AV) is a majoritarian system in which the winning candidate must obtain a majority of the votes. The alternative vote is a candidate-centered preference voting system used in single-member districts where voters rank order the candidates. Voters typically have to place numbers next to the names of the candidates on the ballot to indicate whether each is the voter's first choice, second choice, third choice, and so on. Some AV systems require that voters rank order all of the candidates, whereas others allow voters to rank order only some of the candidates. If a candidate wins an absolute majority of first-preference votes, she's immediately elected. If no candidate wins an absolute majority, the candidate with the fewest first-preference votes is eliminated, and her votes are reallocated among the remaining candidates based on the designated second preferences. This process repeats until one candidate has obtained an absolute majority of the votes. The alternative vote is sometimes referred to as an instant-runoff vote because it's much like holding a series of runoff elections in which the candidate with the fewest votes is eliminated in each round until someone receives an absolute majority of the vote.

Australia uses the AV system for its legislative elections. Australian voters must rank order all of the candidates on the ballot. Table 11.2 shows how the AV system worked in the Richmond constituency of New South Wales in the 1990 elections. When the first-preference votes from all the voters were initially tallied up, Charles Blunt came first with 40.9 percent of the vote. Because no candidate won an absolute majority, the candidate with the lowest number of votes (Gavin Baillie) was eliminated. As Table 11.2 illustrates, Baillie was ranked first on 187 ballots. These 187 ballots were then reallocated to whichever of the remaining candidates the voters ranked second after Gavin Baillie. For example, the fact that Ian Paterson received 445 votes in the first count but 480 votes in the second count indicates that thirty-five of the people who had listed Gavin Baillie as their most preferred candidate had listed Ian Paterson as their second-choice candidate. Because there was still no candidate with an absolute majority after this second count, the new candidate with the lowest number of votes (Dudley Leggett) was eliminated, and his ballots were reallocated among the remaining candidates in the same manner as before. This process continued until the seventh round of counting, when Neville Newell became the first candidate to finally obtain an absolute majority of the votes and hence the elected representative for the Richmond constituency of New South Wales.

It's worth noting that Charles Blunt had won by far the most votes in the first round and had been leading on all of the counts up until the very last one. It was only when the last votes were reallocated according to the preferences of the voters that it became clear that an absolute majority of those who voted in Richmond preferred Neville Newell to Charles Blunt. As this example illustrates, the reallocation of votes from eliminated candidates to remaining candidates can play an important role in determining the outcome of elections in AV systems. It's for this reason that political parties in Australia often give voters "how-to-vote" cards outside polling stations with clear instructions on how to rank candidates so that the flow of preferences will benefit them either directly or, by helping any allied parties, indirectly. An example of a how-to-vote card for the Liberal Party is illustrated in Figure 11.3.

AV systems retain many of the strengths associated with SMDP electoral systems. For example, the fact that there's only one representative elected per constituency means that it's easy for voters to identify who's responsible for district policy and hold them accountable. As a result, we can expect high levels of constituency service and strong bonds between citizens and their representatives. AV systems have several additional strengths, though. One is that voters have a greater opportunity to convey information about their preferences than they have under an SMDP system. This is because they get to rank order the candidates rather than simply vote "yes" and "no" for one of them. A second strength is that there's less of an incentive for voters to engage in strategic voting because they know that their vote won't be wasted if the candidate they most prefer is unpopular and unlikely to win; their vote is simply transferred to the candidate they prefer next. We should note, though, that strategic incentives don't disappear entirely. For example, voters may decide not to rank the candidates according to their sincere preferences because they want to influence the order in which candidates are eliminated and hence who ultimately wins in a district. That this type of strategic concern matters is one explanation for why Australian parties hand out how-to-vote cards at the polling stations.

A third strength is that AV systems encourage candidates and parties to win the votes from not only their base supporters but also the "second preferences" of others. This is because these second preferences may end up being crucial to their election. To attract these votes, candidates are likely to have to make broadly based centrist appeals to all interests rather than focus on narrow sectarian or extremist issues. Some evidence for this comes from Australia, where

TABLE 11.2 ■ Richmond Constituency, New South Wales, Australian Legislative Elections, 1990

Candidate	First count (no.)	First count (%)	Second count (no.)	Second count (%)	Third count (no.)	Third count (%)	Fourth count (no.)	Fourth count (%)	Fifth count (no.)	Fifth count (%)	Sixth count (no.)	Sixth count (%)	Seventh count (no.)	Seventh count (%)
Stan Gibbs	4,346	6.3	4,380	6.3	4,420	6.4	4,504	6.5	4,683	6.8				
Neville Newell	18,423	26.7	18,467	26.7	18,484	26.8	18,544	26.9	18,683	27.1	20,238	29.4	34,664	50.5
Gavin Baillie	187	0.3												
Alan Sims	1,032	1.5	1,053	1.5	1,059	1.5	1,116	1.6						
Ian Paterson	445	0.6	480	0.7	530	0.8								
Dudley Leggett	279	0.4	294	0.4										
Charles Blunt	28,257	40.9	28,274	41.0	28,303	41.0	28,416	41.2	28,978	42	29,778	43.2	33,980	49.5
Helen Caldicott	16,072	23.3	16,091	23.3	16,237	23.5	16,438	23.8	16,658	24.1	18,903	27.4		

Note: Blank cells indicate that a candidate was eliminated.

FIGURE 11.3 ■ Australian "How-to-Vote" Card from the 2001 Legislative Elections

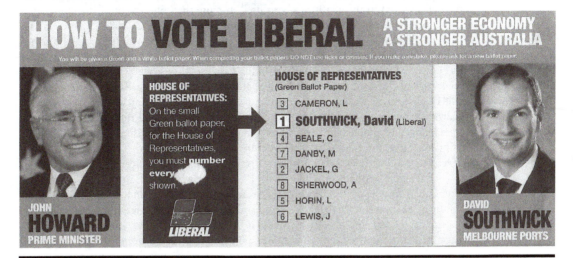

Source: Reproduced by permission of International IDEA from Electoral System Design: The New International IDEA Handbook © International Institute for Democracy and Electoral Assistance 2018.

the major parties frequently attempt to negotiate deals with smaller parties for their second preferences prior to an election in a process known as "preference swapping" (Reilly 2001, 45). The incentive to build broadly based support helps to explain why the AV system is often advocated for elections in deeply divided societies, such as the ethnically fragmented Bosnia and Herzegovina, Fiji, Papua New Guinea, and South Africa (Horowitz 1991; Reilly 2001).

Recall that one of the most common criticisms made of SMDP electoral systems is that they allow candidates to win who don't obtain majority support. AV systems address this problem because candidates are eliminated one at a time until one has an overall majority. Although this would appear to be one of the main strengths of AV systems, some critics claim that the winning candidate doesn't necessarily obtain a "genuine" majority. By this, they mean that it's possible for a majority of the voters in a district to prefer some other candidate to the one who actually wins. The reason why this possibility exists is that a candidate who is preferred to all the other candidates in a series of head-to-head races can be eliminated early on in an AV system because she receives an insufficient number of first-place votes. A clear weakness of the AV system is that it's rather complicated. From the point of view of the voters, it requires a reasonable degree of literacy and numeracy. And from the point of view of the election authorities, the counting process can be costly and drawn out.

Majority-Runoff Two-Round System

Another majoritarian electoral system is the majority-runoff two-round system. A two-round system (TRS) has the potential for two rounds of elections. The majority-runoff TRS is a system in which voters cast a single candidate-centered vote in a single-member district. Any candidate who obtains an absolute majority of the votes in the first round is elected. If no candidate wins an absolute majority, the top two vote winners go on to compete in a runoff election one or two weeks later. Whoever wins the most votes in this runoff election— necessarily an absolute majority as there are only two candidates—is elected.

The majority-runoff TRS is by far the most common method for electing presidents around the world. While the majority-runoff TRS was used in just 6 percent of the presidential elections that occurred in the 1950s, it's been used in more than 65 percent of the presidential elections that have occurred since 2000 (Bormann and Golder 2013, 368). Tables 11.3 and 11.4 show the results from the Burkina Faso presidential elections in 2015 and the Benin presidential elections in 2016. Roch Christian Kaboré won an absolute majority of the votes (53.49 percent) in the first round of the Burkina Faso presidential elections and was therefore elected without the need for a second-round runoff. In the Benin presidential elections, no candidate obtained an absolute majority in the first round. Patrice Talon was eventually elected president after winning 65.4 percent of the vote in the second-round runoff. A few countries such as Haiti and Comoros use the majority-runoff TRS for their legislative elections.

The majority-runoff TRS has a number of strengths, particularly when compared with SMDP systems. The first is that it gives voters more choice than they enjoy in SMDP systems. For example, individuals who vote for a candidate who "loses" in the first round get a second opportunity to influence who gets elected in the second round. The majority-runoff TRS also allows voters to change their mind and switch their votes even if the candidate they supported in the first round actually makes it into the second round. Voters might want to change their mind as a result of new information that emerges between the first and second rounds. Changing one's ranking of candidates in this way isn't possible in a preference voting system, such as the alternative vote.

A second strength is that voters have less incentive to behave strategically than they do in SMDP systems because they have two opportunities to affect the election outcome. Individuals can vote for their most preferred candidate in the first round even if this candidate has little chance of winning in the end and then switch their support to a more well-placed candidate in the second round. Of course, strategic incentives don't disappear entirely, and things can go wrong if individuals vote sincerely in this way. Voters need to think about whether their decision to vote sincerely in the first round positively affects the likelihood that a candidate whom they don't like will win either the first or the second round. For example, the 2002 presidential elections in France produced a second-round runoff between a candidate from

TABLE 11.3 ■ Burkina Faso Presidential Elections 2015		
First round		
Candidate	Party	Vote share (%)
Roch Christian Kaboré	People's Movement for Progress	53.49
Zéphirin Diabré	Union for Progress and Reform	29.65
Tahirou Barry	National Rebirth Party	3.09
Bénéwendé Stanislas Sankara	Union for Rebirth	2.77
Ablassé Ouedraogo	Alternative Faso	1.93
Saran Sérémé	Party for Development and Reform	1.73
Others		7.33

TABLE 11.4 ■ Benin Presidential Elections 2016		
First round		
Candidate	Party	Vote share (%)
Lionel A. L. Zinsou-Derlin	Cowry Forces for an Emerging Benin	28.4
Patrice A. G. Talon		24.8
Sébastien G. M. A. Adjavon		23.0
Abdoulaye B. Bio-Tchane	Alliance for a Triumphant Benin	8.8
Pascal J. I. Koupaki	New Consciousness Rally	5.9
Robert Gbian		1.6
Fernand M. Amoussou		1.2
Salifou Issa		1.0
Others		5.3
Second round		
Patrice A. G. Talon		65.4
Lionel A. L. Zinsou-Derlin	Cowry Forces for an Emerging Benin	34.6

the mainstream right, Jacques Chirac, and a candidate from the extreme right, Jean-Marie Le Pen. One reason why there was no left-wing candidate was that the left-wing electorate split its vote among so many left-wing candidates in the first round that none made it into the second round. As a result, the only choice that left-wing voters had in this second round was between a candidate whom they disliked (Chirac) and a candidate whom they really disliked (Le Pen). It's arguable that France's left-wing voters would have been better off had they voted more strategically in the first round.

A third strength of the majority-runoff TRS is that it creates incentives for candidates who make it into the second round to look beyond their own electoral base and reach compromises with the leaders of parties who are already eliminated in an attempt to win over their supporters. In addition, because voters are not required to rank order candidates with numbers to express their second choice, some have argued that the majority-runoff TRS is more suitable for countries with widespread illiteracy and low levels of education than preference voting systems, such as the alternative vote (Reynolds, Reilly, and Ellis 2005, 53). A final strength of the majority-runoff TRS is that the winning candidate can claim to have won the support of a majority of the voters.

The majority-runoff TRS also has a number of weaknesses. One is that it imposes significant costs on the electoral administration. After all, the electoral administration has to conduct two sets of elections instead of one. The majority-runoff TRS also imposes significant costs on individuals, who potentially have to vote in two elections. Empirical evidence suggests that there's a considerable drop-off in the level of turnout between the two rounds of elections. A second weakness is that, like SMDP electoral systems, the majority-runoff TRS often produces a disproportional translation of votes into seats. Indeed, there's some evidence that it produces the most disproportional results of any electoral system used in Western democracies (Reynolds, Reilly, and Ellis 2005, 53). According to some critics, a third weakness of the majority-runoff TRS is that it hurts minority representation. For example, Guinier (1994) has argued that, on extending the right to vote to African Americans, several southern states in the United States adopted the majority-runoff TRS in an attempt to reduce the ability of African American candidates to win. Evidence that the majority-runoff TRS does, indeed, hurt minority candidates comes from a series of elections conducted in the laboratory by Morton and Rietz (2008).

Proportional Electoral Systems

The rationale behind proportional, or proportional representation (PR), electoral systems is to consciously reduce the disparity between a party's share of the vote and its share of the seats. In other words, the goal of proportional representation systems is to produce proportional outcomes—if a party wins 10 percent of the vote, it should win 10 percent of the seats; if it wins 20 percent of the vote, it should win 20 percent of the seats; and so on. This proportionality should exist both within districts and in the country as a whole.

Many scholars have argued that proportional systems have a number of strengths when compared with majoritarian ones (Lijphart 1999). Perhaps the main strength of PR systems is that they tend to produce a more accurate translation of votes into seats. This means that PR systems avoid the possibility that a party wins a large percentage of the vote but only a few legislative seats. Recall that this was one of the possible anomalies with majoritarian systems. It also means that small parties are able to win representation in proportion to their size. As a result, minorities are likely to be better represented in a PR system than in a majoritarian one. The fact that small parties have a greater chance of winning seats means that individuals face weaker incentives to vote strategically. As a consequence, electoral outcomes in PR systems should be a more accurate reflection of voters' sincere preferences. Arguably, it's also the case that individuals are more likely to turn out and vote in PR systems because they know their votes are less likely to be wasted (Blais and Carty 1990; Blais and Dobrzynska 1998).

Some have argued that PR systems are all but essential for maintaining stability in ethnically and religiously divided societies (Lijphart 1990, 1991; Norris 2008). The claim is that the stakes of the game are often high in a divided society and that the risk of state instability is simply too great for parties to view elections as a winner-take-all contest (Reynolds 2011, 19). PR makes it easy for social groups to organize into ethnic and religious parties that can obtain legislative representation in proportion to their size. This, in turn, produces legislatures that reflect all the significant segments of society and leads to coalition governments based on power-sharing arrangements. The implicit assumption here, of course, is that the different ethnic groups will ultimately choose to work together in the legislature and the government.

The notion that PR systems are essential for stability and democratic rule in divided societies is widely, but not universally, accepted. A few scholars, for example, argue that preference voting systems, such as the alternative vote, are superior (Horowitz 1985, 1991; Reilly 1997, 2001). These scholars note that PR systems may simply replicate bitter societal divisions in the legislature without creating incentives for cooperation and accommodation across the different ethnic parties. In contrast, they argue that preference voting systems encourage political parties to run moderate broad-based campaigns that are appealing beyond their core set of supporters because they know that their electoral success is likely to depend on the transfer of preference votes from other ethnic groups. Of course, this is likely to happen only if ethnic groups aren't geographically concentrated in such a way that parties can win a majority by appealing to a single ethnic or religious group.[5]

In effect, when it comes to dealing with divided societies, one can think of the choice of electoral system as being one between replicating ethnic divisions in the legislature and hoping that political leaders will cooperate after the election, and creating institutional incentives that seek to weaken or even transcend the political salience of ethnicity altogether. We'll return to the discussion of electoral system choice in divided societies in Chapter 14.

Other scholars have offered more general criticisms of proportional electoral systems. One of the most common is that they tend to produce coalition governments. As we noted earlier, it's often difficult to hold political parties accountable in coalition governments because it's hard to identify who's responsible for policy and hence whom to hold accountable at election time. Even if those responsible for policy could be identified, it's still difficult to hold them accountable because parties that lose significant numbers of votes frequently make it back into coalition governments anyway. As the empirical evidence we presented in Chapter 10 indicates, coalition governments are also more unstable than the single-party majority governments that are typically produced by majoritarian electoral systems. A second criticism of PR systems is that they allow small, extremist parties to win representation. This is frequently seen as problematic. For example, some have argued that the existence of extremist parties undermines democracy. A third criticism is that small parties in PR systems frequently have a strong role in the government formation process and receive concessions that are disproportionate to their actual level of support in the electorate. It's rare for parties to obtain a majority of the legislative seats in PR systems, so large parties often rely on the support of some smaller party to get into government. These smaller parties can often use their leverage to wring concessions from the larger party. Some of these concessions may be quite radical and lack the support of an electoral majority. In Israel, for example, small ultrareligious parties have won support for many of their policies by threatening to pull out of the government. A fourth criticism is that PR systems create a weak link between constituents and their representatives, because no single representative is responsible for policy in a given district. Voters might also wonder which of the elected representatives from their districts actually represent them.

List PR Systems

Almost all proportional electoral systems involve parties presenting a list of candidates to voters in each multimember district. Parties then receive legislative seats in proportion to the overall share of votes going to their list. These proportional systems are known as list PR systems. Despite obvious similarities, list PR systems are not all alike.

District Magnitude. The most important factor influencing the proportionality of an electoral system is the district magnitude (Cox 1997). District magnitude refers to the number of representatives elected in a district. Electoral systems are more proportional when the district magnitude is large, as smaller parties are much more likely to win seats in these circum-

---

[5]Fiji introduced the alternative vote in 1997 in the hopes of encouraging political parties to make appeals across ethnic groups. However, things didn't work out entirely as planned because the small size of the electoral districts and the geographic concentration of indigenous and Indo-Fijians meant there were too few constituencies with a sufficient mix of ethnic groups to make a strategy of appealing across ethnic group lines worthwhile. Some have argued that the choice of an AV system in this setting actually precipitated the collapse of Fijian democracy following a coup in 2000 (Reynolds 2011, 27–28).

stances. For example, a party would need to win more than 25 percent of the vote to guarantee winning a seat in a three-seat district, but it would need to win only a little more than 10 percent of the vote to guarantee winning a seat in a nine-seat district.

Although all PR systems use multimember districts, the average size of these districts—the average district magnitude—can vary quite a lot from one country to another. At one extreme is Serbia, which elects all 250 of its legislators in a single national district. In fact, Ukraine had a district magnitude of 450 in its 2006 and 2007 legislative elections. At the other extreme is Chile, which has historically had an average district magnitude of 2. In 2015, though, Chile adopted a new electoral system that saw its average district magnitude increase to 5.5. Other countries have district magnitudes of varying size between these two extremes. In addition to the proportionality of the electoral system, a country's district magnitude also affects the strength of the linkage between elected representatives and their constituents. As district magnitude increases and with it the geographical size of the district, the linkage between representatives and their voters weakens.

Electoral Thresholds. All PR systems have an **electoral threshold** that stipulates the minimum percentage of votes a party must win, either nationally or in a particular district, before it can win any legislative seats. This threshold is either legally imposed (**formal threshold**) or it exists as a mathematical property of the electoral system (**natural threshold**). The size of the electoral threshold has a strong effect on the proportionality of an electoral system.

Natural thresholds are not written into electoral laws; instead, they're a mathematical by-product of certain features of the electoral system, such as the district magnitude. For example, any party in the Netherlands must win more than 0.67 percent of the national vote before they win a seat, not because this is legally stipulated, but simply because there are 150 legislative seats allocated in a single national district; that is, 100 percent / 150 = 0.67 percent. All electoral systems have a natural threshold. In contrast to natural thresholds, formal thresholds are explicitly written into the electoral law. For example, political parties in Israel have to win 3.25 percent of the national vote before they can win seats in the Knesset (the natural threshold in Israel is only 0.83 percent). In Turkey, political parties must win more than 10 percent of the national vote before they can gain representation in parliament. Formal thresholds always increase the disproportionality of an electoral system because the votes for parties that might otherwise have won representation are wasted.

Formal thresholds are often introduced in an attempt to reduce party system fragmentation by preventing very small parties from gaining representation. For example, the adoption of a formal electoral threshold in Germany after World War II was largely a response to the fractious and unstable party system of Weimar Germany in the interwar period. Similarly, many Eastern European countries have imposed high formal thresholds in an attempt to reduce the number of parties and encourage the consolidation of a stable party system.

Formal thresholds can have a significant effect on election outcomes. For example, there were so many parties that didn't surpass the 10 percent threshold in the Turkish legislative elections of 2002 that fully 46 percent of all votes cast in these elections were wasted. Similarly, 34 percent of the votes cast in the Polish legislative elections of 1993 were wasted because of the 5 percent electoral threshold. In the Polish case, these wasted votes were crucial in allowing the former Communists to return to power only a few years after the collapse of communism in that country (Kaminski, Lissowski, and Swistak 1998). These examples from Turkey and Poland force us to think about whether the problems arising from formal thresholds (wasted votes and increased disproportionality) are more or less acceptable than the problems they're designed to solve (fragmented party systems).

Types of Party List. Parties receive legislative seats in proportion to the overall share of votes going to their party list. Thus, a party that receives 20 percent of the vote for their list will win 20 percent of the seats available in the district. But which specific candidates on a party list get the seats allocated to their party? It all depends on whether the party lists are closed, open, or free.

In a **closed party list**, which is the most common type of party list, the order of candidates elected is determined by the party, and voters are not able to express a preference for a particular candidate. The first seat a party wins goes to the candidate listed first on the party's list, the second seat goes to the second candidate on the list, and so on. Thus, if a party wins four seats in a district, the top four candidates on the list obtain seats, and the remaining candidates don't win any. In some cases, the ballot paper in a closed list system will contain the names of the individual candidates and their positions on the list. More frequently, though, ballot papers in closed list systems don't contain the names of individual candidates. Instead, the only information on the list is the party names and symbols, and perhaps a photograph of the party leader. As Figure 11.4 illustrates, this type of ballot paper was used in South Africa's 1994 legislative elections.

One of the potential advantages of closed party lists is that parties can more easily include minority or women candidates who might otherwise have had difficulty getting elected. Of course, some voters may consider this potential advantage a disadvantage in that they're unable to choose the candidates they most desire and may have to elect unpopular and undesirable candidates if they wish to vote for their preferred party.

Leaders of political parties often prefer closed party lists because they provide a useful way of disciplining and rewarding candidates. Candidates that are important in the party hierarchy can be guaranteed relatively safe seats by being placed toward the top of the party list, whereas candidates who fail to toe the party line can be placed toward the bottom of the party list. Political parties tend to be more important than individual candidates in closed list systems for this reason.

In an **open party list**, voters can indicate not just their preferred party but their favored candidate within that party. In most open list systems, it's up to the voter to choose whether to indicate her preferred candidate as well as her preferred party. If individuals simply vote for a party and don't indicate a preferred candidate, the candidate-choice option of the ballot paper will obviously have little effect. If we look at Sweden and its open list system, we find that over 25 percent of Swedish voters regularly choose an individual candidate within a party list; many of these candidates wouldn't have been elected had the party list been closed (Reynolds, Reilly, and Ellis 2005, 84).

Figure 11.5 illustrates an open list ballot from the 1994 legislative elections in Denmark. In Danish elections, voters cast a single vote either for their preferred party (party vote) or for their preferred candidate from among that party's list of candidates (personal vote). The total number of seats a party wins is determined by its total number of votes, which is just the sum of its party votes and its personal votes. Each individual candidate is credited with all of the personal votes given to her plus a share of the votes cast for her party. The order in which the party's seats are allocated among the individual candidates is determined by the number of total votes (personal and party) that are credited to them.

Although voters normally have a choice in open list systems as to whether to vote for a particular candidate, this isn't the case in all open list PR systems. For example, individuals have to vote for a party candidate in countries like Brazil and the Netherlands. The total number of seats each party wins in these countries is determined by the total number of votes given to its candidates, and the order in which each party's candidates receive these seats is determined by the number of individual votes they receive.

FIGURE 11.4 ■ South African Closed List PR Ballot Paper

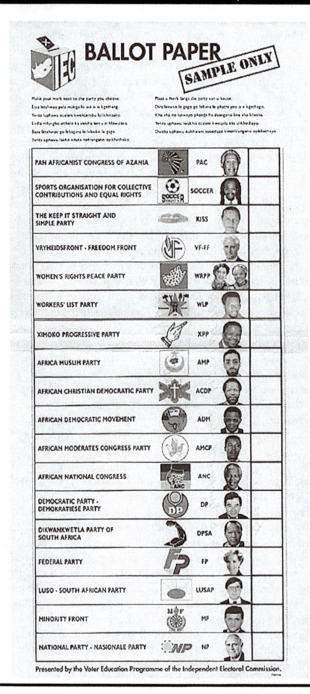

Source: Reproduced by permission of International IDEA from *Electoral System Design: The New International IDEA Handbook* © International Institute for Democracy and Electoral Assistance 2018.

FIGURE 11.5 ■ Danish Open List PR Ballot Paper

Source: Reproduced by permission of International IDEA from Electoral System Design: The New International IDEA Handbook © International Institute for Democracy and Electoral Assistance 2018.

Open list systems clearly give voters greater freedom over their choice of candidates and weaken the control of party leaders over their party's candidates. A frequent consequence of open lists, though, is that they generate internal party fighting, because candidates from the same party are effectively competing with each other for the same votes. A result of this is that political candidates in open list systems have incentives to cultivate a personal vote rather than a party vote (Carey and Shugart 1995). A personal vote occurs when an individual votes based on the characteristics of a particular candidate rather than the characteristics of the party to which the candidate belongs. Building a personal vote is frequently associated in the United States with legislators bringing back pork-barrel projects to their single-member districts. As you can see, though, incentives to build personal votes also exist in multimember districts, where the election of candidates can depend on personal reputations in open list systems. In addition to internal party fighting, some scholars worry that open lists make it less likely that minority candidates will be elected. In Sri Lanka, for instance, majority Sinhalese parties tried to place minority

Tamil candidates in winnable positions on their open party lists. These efforts at improving minority representation were rendered ineffective, however, when many voters deliberately voted for lower-placed Sinhalese candidates instead (Reynolds, Reilly, and Ellis 2005, 90).

Voters have even more flexibility in **free party lists**. This is because voters in free list systems have multiple votes, typically as many as there are seats available in the district, that they can allocate to candidates either within a single party list or across different party lists. The capacity to vote for candidates from different party lists is known as *panachage*. Panachage is attractive if there are particular types of candidates you'd like to support, say women candidates or candidates who share the same position on some policy, that appear across different party lists. Some countries, like Switzerland, allow voters to give more than one vote to the same candidate. The capacity to give more than one vote to a single highly favored candidate is known as cumulation. Some scholars have argued that cumulation can help boost minority representation (Guinier 1994). This is because minority groups can cumulate their votes on a single minority candidate while majority groups spread theirs across multiple candidates.

Single Transferable Vote

The only proportional electoral system that doesn't employ a party list is the single transferable vote (STV). STV is a candidate-centered preference voting system used in multimember districts where voters rank order the candidates. Candidates must obtain a particular number of votes, known as the quota, in order to win a seat. Votes go initially to each voter's most preferred candidate. If an insufficient number of candidates obtain the quota to fill all of the district seats, the candidate with the lowest number of first-choice votes is eliminated. The votes from the eliminated candidate, as well as any surplus votes from candidates that are already elected, are then reallocated to the remaining candidates according to the designated second preferences. This process continues until enough candidates meet the quota to fill all of the district seats. If you think the STV system sounds familiar, you'd be right: it's essentially the same as the alternative vote but applied in multimember districts.

One of the strengths of STV systems is that they provide voters with an opportunity to convey a lot of information about their preferences (Bowler and Grofman 2000). Like other preference voting systems, individuals in STV systems have the opportunity to rank order all of the candidates rather than simply voting "yes" or "no" to one of the candidates as in most majoritarian and list PR systems. Because an individual's preferences end up being reallocated whenever a candidate is elected or eliminated, the STV system minimizes wasted votes. STV systems also allow individuals to vote for candidates from different parties. This means that individuals can vote for candidates who share a similar policy stance even though the candidates may come from different parties. This might be useful in cases in which an issue cuts across traditional party lines such as abortion. With the exception of those systems that allow for panachage, the vast majority of list PR systems don't allow for this type of cross-party voting. It's worth noting that STV is a proportional electoral system that doesn't require the existence of political parties—individuals vote for candidates, not parties. This could be important in countries in which political parties are yet to organize or political elites don't wish to allow the formation of political parties (see Box 11.1, "Strategic Miscalculation: Electoral System Choice in Poland in 1989").

Like other preference voting systems, an additional strength of STV systems is that they create incentives for candidates to appeal to groups outside their core set of supporters and campaign on broad-based centrist platforms. This is because a candidate's election may well depend on the transfer of votes from different social groups. Recall that this is why some scholars advocate the use of preference voting systems in divided societies (Horowitz 1985,

1991; Reilly 1997, 2001). One criticism of the preference voting systems we've examined to this point, such as the alternative vote, is that they're majoritarian and can produce highly disproportional outcomes. An advantage of the STV system is that it works in multimember districts and typically produces more proportional outcomes than majoritarian systems. Thus, the STV holds out the possibility of combining relatively proportional outcomes with incentives for candidates to make cross-cleavage appeals and build electorates that bridge religious and ethnic lines.

Another strength of STV its supporters highlight is that it tends to create a strong link between representatives and their constituents. Since the STV is a candidate-centered rather than a party-centered system, candidates have an incentive to build personal votes and engage in constituency service. For example, there's evidence the STV system in Ireland leads to an emphasis on local campaigning, a focus on district work and local concerns, and a low importance attached to ideology and national issues (Katz 1980). In this respect, STV "involves a notion of the connection between the individual representative and his or her constituency that is much closer to the notion of representation implicit in the [SMDP] system than to the notion of representation of parties underlying list systems" (Sinnott 1992, 68). A further strength of STV systems is that they reduce the incentive for voters to behave strategically because their votes are less likely to be wasted. As with any electoral system, though, strategic concerns are never entirely absent. In an attempt to strategically channel the transfer of votes in an STV system so as to benefit their candidates as much as possible, parties in Ireland hand out "candidate cards" in a similar way to how parties hand out how-to-vote cards in the alternative vote system used in Australia.

Despite these strengths, the STV system has its critics. One criticism is that it tends to weaken the internal unity of parties and make them less cohesive. Because voters are allowed to rank order candidates from the same party, these candidates have incentives to criticize and campaign against one another. As Farrell and McAllister (2000, 18) note, "[T]he problems of intraparty factionalism and excessive attention to localist, particularistic concerns [in Ireland] are attributed to politicians who must compete with each other for votes on ordinally ranked STV ballots." You'll perhaps recall that the single nontransferable vote (SNTV) also creates incentives for intraparty factionalism. It's worth noting, though, that the incentives for factionalism are weaker under the STV system because candidates can expect to receive votes from fellow party members who are eliminated. This means that candidates from the same party in an STV system don't want to harm each other too much.

A second criticism of STV is that it's hard to operate when the district magnitude is large. This is because the ballot paper could contain a large number of candidate names. In fact, the ballot for the Australian Senate elections in New South Wales in 1995 contained the names of ninety-nine candidates and was several feet long (Farrell and McAllister 2000, 29). It's not unknown for Australian electoral officials to order thousands of magnifying glasses just so that voters can read the candidate names on the ballot ("Magnifying Glasses" 2013). It's difficult to believe voters would have sufficient information to rank candidates beyond the first ten or so names on a ballot. For this reason, constituencies in STV systems tend to be relatively small. For example, the largest district magnitude in Ireland and Malta is five. These small district magnitudes limit the proportionality with which votes are translated into seats.

Mixed Electoral Systems

In some countries, voters elect some of their legislative representatives with a majoritarian electoral system and some of them with a proportional electoral system. These countries are said to employ a mixed electoral system. Most mixed systems employ multiple electoral tiers.

An **electoral tier** is a level at which votes are translated into seats. The lowest electoral tier is the district or constituency level. Higher tiers are constituted by grouping together different lower-tier constituencies, typically at the regional or national level. A majoritarian electoral system is used to allocate some of the legislative seats in the lowest tier (district level), and a proportional electoral system is used to allocate the other legislative seats in the upper tier (regional or national level).

Ukraine used a mixed electoral system with two electoral tiers for its 2014 legislative elections. Two hundred and twenty-five legislators were elected using a majoritarian SMDP electoral system in single-member districts at the constituency level, and 225 legislators were elected using an open party list proportional representation system in a single district at the national level. The precise balance between "proportional" and "majoritarian" seats varies from country to country. For example, seventy-one (59%) of the legislators in New Zealand's 2014 elections were elected using majoritarian rules and forty-nine (41%)

FIGURE 11.6 ■ A Sample Ballot Used in New Zealand's Dependent Mixed Electoral System

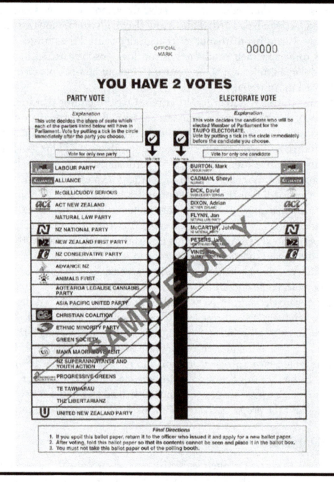

Source: Reproduced by permission of International IDEA from Electoral System Design: The New International IDEA Handbook © International Institute for Democracy and Electoral Assistance 2018.

were elected using proportional rules. In some mixed systems, like the one in South Korea, individuals have only one vote, which is used for both parts of the electoral system. In these mixed systems, an individual's vote for a constituency candidate also counts as a vote for that candidate's party in the higher electoral tier. In most mixed systems, though, individuals have two votes. The first vote is cast for a representative at the constituency level (candidate vote) and the second vote is cast for a party list in a higher electoral tier (party vote). These types of mixed systems allow individuals to give their first vote to a constituency candidate from one party and to give their second vote to a different party if they wish. This is called split-ticket voting. Figure 11.6 shows a sample ballot from New Zealand that has two votes.

In many respects, mixed electoral systems are an attempt to combine the positive attributes of both majoritarian and proportional systems. In particular, mixed electoral systems help produce proportional outcomes at the same time as ensuring that some elected representatives are linked to particular geographic districts. One issue with mixed systems is that they can create two classes of legislators—one that is responsible and accountable to a geographic constituency and one that is more beholden to the party. This can influence the cohesiveness of political parties (Reynolds, Reilly, and Ellis 2005).

LEGISLATIVE ELECTORAL SYSTEM CHOICE

In Map 11.2, we illustrate the global distribution of majoritarian, proportional, and mixed electoral systems around the world in 2018. Some regions are relatively homogeneous in the type of electoral systems they use. The vast majority of countries in Latin America and Western Europe, for example, use a proportional system. In contrast, other regions such as Oceania, North Africa and the Middle East, and sub-Saharan Africa display much more heterogeneity in their choice of electoral system. Of the 178 countries coded by the Inter-Parliamentary Union in Map 11.2, 67 (37.6%) employ a majoritarian system, 76 (42.7%) a proportional system, and 35 (19.7%) a mixed system. There are distinct differences in the type of electoral systems used by democracies and dictatorships. Of those countries coded as democracies by Polity IV, 53.7% use a proportional system, 25.3% use a majoritarian system, and 21.1% use a mixed system. In contrast, of those coded as dictatorships, 81% use a majoritarian system and 19% use a proportional system.[6] In effect, dictatorships are much more likely to use majoritarian systems than democracies.

There's been relatively little work on the choice of electoral systems under dictatorship. However, we can throw out some conjectures for why dictatorships might favor majoritarian systems. First, most proportional systems other than the single transferable vote use party lists and hence require the existence of political parties. As we discussed in Chapter 8, dictatorships vary in the extent to which political parties are allowed to exist. Second, there's some evidence that majoritarian systems may be easier to manipulate than proportional ones. Evidence for this comes from a study of twenty-four Communist countries in which the author finds that elections using the majoritarian SMDP system were much more likely to be the object of manipulation than those using a list PR system (Birch 2007). Third, many dictatorships are poor with low levels of education. The simplicity of majoritarian electoral systems, such as SMDP, may be helpful in these conditions as they impose lower cognitive costs on voters.

---

[6]Recall that democracies are those countries that receive 6 or higher on the Polity IV scale and dictatorships are those countries that receive -6 or lower on the Polity IV scale (Marshall, Gurr, and Jaggers 2017).

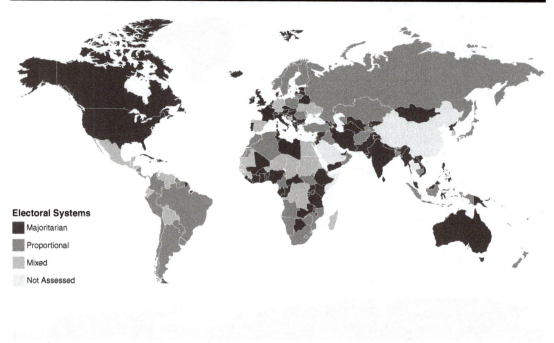

Electoral Systems

■ Majoritarian
■ Proportional
■ Mixed
■ Not Assessed

Note: The data for this map come from the Inter-Parliamentary Union at https://www.ipu.org/.

A final conjecture focuses on the fact that majoritarian systems tend to produce disproportional outcomes that reward large parties and punish small parties. This may well appeal to large incumbent parties in dictatorships. Of course, the disproportionality of majoritarian systems creates incentives for opposition groups to coalesce, whereas proportional systems may help keep the opposition divided. In this respect, dictatorial incumbents face a trade-off between benefiting from disproportional majoritarian systems and hindering opposition coordination with proportional systems (Barberá 2013). Lust-Okar and Jamal (2002) suggest that this trade-off plays out differently depending on dictatorial type. Specifically, they claim that majoritarian systems are more likely to be adopted by dominant-party dictatorships, whereas proportional systems are more likely to be adopted by monarchic dictatorships. The idea is that leaders in these two types of dictatorship have divergent preferences. Monarchs are political arbitrators whose legitimacy typically comes from things like the royal family, religious authorities, or historical tradition rather than popular support. "For the monarch, then, political division and competition in popular politics, not unity, is the basis of stability. Kings have no interest in creating a single contender who could vie with them for power" (Lust-Okar and Jamal 2002, 253). As a result, monarchs prefer proportional systems that allow for the representation of competing political parties while they maintain their role as chief arbiter. In contrast, leaders in states dominated by a regime party are forced to enter politics to maintain their rule. For this reason, they want majoritarian systems that disproportionately favor their (large) political party. Lust-Okar and Jamal support this line of reasoning with empirical evidence from the Middle East.

Studies of electoral system choice in democracies are more common. Various explanations have been proposed for why democracies have the electoral systems they do. These explanations focus on the self-interest of political parties, historical precedent, external pressures, and idiosyncratic occurrences (Benoit 2004, 2007). Self-interest explanations examine the preferences that political parties have for various electoral systems. Because electoral systems are basically distribution mechanisms that reward one party at the expense of another, parties are likely to have conflicting preferences for alternative electoral rules. The adoption of an electoral system is ultimately a struggle between political parties with competing interests. In one study, Boix (1999) sets out to explain the spread of proportional electoral systems at the beginning of the twentieth century. He argues that conservative ruling elites who were historically elected using some kind of majoritarian system began to take an interest in proportional systems when suffrage was being extended to the poor and the level of support for socialist parties was growing.

BOX 11.1 STRATEGIC MISCALCULATION: ELECTORAL SYSTEM CHOICE IN POLAND IN 1989

One explanation for why countries adopt the electoral system they do focuses on the strategic calculations of political parties. In effect, parties in power choose to adopt electoral rules that benefit them at the expense of their rivals. Although the stakes involved in choosing an electoral system can often be extremely high, history has shown us that political parties frequently make strategic miscalculations.

In a 1999 article titled "How Communism Could Have Been Saved," Marek Kaminski describes the bargaining that took place between the opposition movement, Solidarity, and the Communist Party over the electoral law to be used for the 1989 legislative elections in Poland. At the time, these elections were to be the first semi-free elections held in the Soviet bloc. During these negotiations, the Communist Polish United Workers' Party (PUWP) made two strategic miscalculations.

Mistake 1: The first mistake was that the PUWP overestimated its support in the electorate. Following the imposition of martial law in 1981, the PUWP under General Jaruzelski set up a Center for Public Opinion Research (CBOS) to keep better track of public opinion and support for the Communist regime. If you recall from our discussion of democratic transitions in Chapter 7, preference fal-

sification is likely to be rampant in dictatorships because members of opposition groups are unwilling to publicly reveal their opposition for fear of punishment. This was certainly the case in Poland, where roughly 30 percent of respondents simply refused to complete surveys conducted by CBOS. Much of the opposition in Poland essentially remained underground and out of the sight of the PUWP. The result was that the PUWP went into the negotiations over the electoral law with Solidarity in 1989 with an overly optimistic belief about its electoral strength.

Mistake 2: The second mistake was that the PUWP didn't adopt a proportional electoral system. As you may recall from our discussion in Chapter 7, the 1989 legislative elections turned into an electoral disaster for the PUWP with Solidarity winning all 35 percent of the legislative seats for which it was able to compete. The size of Solidarity's victory and the subsequent divisions that appeared between the PUWP and its supporters eventually led to the appointment of the first non-Communist prime minister in Eastern Europe. The reason that Solidarity won all the seats in these elections had a lot to do with the electoral system that was

(Continued)

(Continued)

chosen—a majority-runoff TRS. Because Solidarity turned out to have the largest support in each district, this electoral system translated the 70 percent of the vote won by Solidarity into 100 percent of the seats and the roughly 25 percent of the vote won by the PUWP into zero seats. Had the PUWP adopted a proportional electoral system, though, the outcome of the elections would have been very different.

So why did the PUWP not adopt a proportional system? One reason has to do with the PUWP's belief that it had sufficient support to win seats in a majoritarian system. A second reason, however, has to do with the fact that the PUWP didn't want to legalize any additional political parties. The maximum concession the PUWP was willing to make during the negotiations was to legalize Solidarity as a trade union; Poland was to remain a one-party state. As a result, the PUWP refused to consider adopting any electoral system that required individuals to vote for parties rather than candidates. At the time, the PUWP believed that all proportional systems required the presence of political parties. As you now know from reading this chapter, this isn't true. The STV is a proportional system in which individuals vote for candidates. It appears that the PUWP was simply unaware that the STV system existed. In his article, Kaminski indicates that had the option of the STV come up, it would have been acceptable to both Solidarity and the PUWP. The STV would have guaranteed a significant representation for Solidarity in the legislature and provided a greater margin of safety for the PUWP. It seems likely that with a more proportional allocation of seats, as would have occurred under an STV system, the PUWP may have been able to hold on to power and not had to appoint a prime minister from Solidarity.

This leads to an interesting counterfactual question one might ask. What would have happened to communism in Eastern Europe had the PUWP adopted a proportional STV system in 1989 rather than the majoritarian TRS? What we know is that the collapse of communism in Poland had a snowball effect on the rest of the Eastern bloc. A different course of events in Poland could

perhaps have prevented the breakdown of the Communist system. This leads one to wonder whether communism in Eastern Europe could have been saved if the political leaders in Poland had only been more aware of the information on electoral systems presented in this chapter.

After the Polish version of Kaminski's 1999 article was published, he received several letters from Premier Tadeusz Mazowiecki and other Solidarity leaders. Below, we list some of the responses he received from former Communist dignitaries.

Jerzy Urban (former Communist spokesman, number 4 in Poland in the 1980s):

> You are absolutely right that we did not read the surveys properly ... we were ignorant about various electoral laws ... probably nobody knew STV. ... I distributed copies of your paper among General Jaruzelski, Premier Rakowski, and [the present] President Kwasniewski.

Hieronim Kubiak (former Politburo member, top political adviser):

> The negative heroes of Kaminski's article are the "ignoramus"—we, communist experts. ... [He thinks that the communist regime could have survived] if General Jaruzelski had known the STV electoral law and if he had chosen differently!

Janusz Reykowski (former Politburo member, the designer of the 1989 electoral law):

> [The value of Kaminski's work] is in showing that technical political decisions [that is, the choice of the electoral law] may have fundamental importance for a historical process.

Maria Teresa Kiszczak (the wife of General Czeslaw Kiszczak, Number 2 in Poland in the 1980s):

> You based your story on the bourgeois literature. ... [C]ommunists did not really want to keep power. ... [My husband] resisted a temptation to cancel the 1989 elections and to seize power.

The interest in proportional systems was particularly strong in those countries in which conservative parties on the right were fragmented and the presence of a strong socialist party posed a threat to their continued rule. In effect, Boix claims that conservative parties, faced with the rise of socialism, chose to adopt proportional systems as a preemptive strategy to guarantee their strong representation in the legislature even if they remained divided.

External pressures and historical precedent can also affect the choice of electoral system. The choice of electoral system in many countries has been heavily influenced by their former colonial ruler (Blais and Massicotte 1997). For example, nearly every African country that employs an SMDP system is a former British colony. Similarly, many former French colonies, such as the Central African Republic, Comoros, and Mali, have adopted the same majoritarian two-round system used in France. Other countries seem to have adopted a particular electoral system for the simple reason that they've had some experience with it in the past. For example, there's some evidence that the newly democratic Czechoslovakia chose a proportional system in 1990 because it had used a similar system in the interwar period. Similarly, France's adoption of a two-round system in 1958 can perhaps be traced back to its use in the Second Empire (1852–1870) and much of the Third Republic (1870–1940; Benoit 2004, 370).

It appears that some electoral systems are even chosen by accident. As an example, consider the following description from Benoit (2007, 376–377) of how New Zealand came to adopt a mixed electoral system in 1993.

> In a now famous incident of electoral reform through accident, ruling parties in New Zealand found themselves bound to implement a sweeping electoral reform that traced back in essence to a chance remark, later described as a gaffe, by Prime Minister David Lange during a televised debate. In New Zealand, the use of first-past-the-post [SMDP] had virtually guaranteed a two-party duopoly of the Labor Party and the National Party, producing continuous single-party majority governments since 1914—often cited as the textbook example of the "majoritarian" or Westminster type of democracy (Nagel 2004). Grassroots dissatisfaction with the electoral system began in the 1970s among Maori and minor-party supporters who consistently found it difficult to obtain any representation, and increased with the 1978 and 1981 elections, in which Labor received a plurality of the vote yet National won a majority of the seats. This led Labor to pledge in the 1980s to establish a Royal Commission to reappraise the electoral law. The commission compared many options and finally recommended [a mixed electoral] system combining single-member districts with lists, although the majority of Labor's Members of Parliament opposed this system. Because the commission was politically independent and had very broad terms of reference, its considerations were disconnected from the strategic considerations of any particular party. After the commission's report, "horrified politicians of both parties attempted to put the genie of reform back in the bottle" (Nagel 2004, 534). This succeeded for six years, until the televised leaders' debate in which Labor Prime Minister David Lange inadvertently promised to hold a binding referendum on electoral reform in response to a question from the leader of the Electoral Reform Coalition. Labor initially refused to honor this pledge when elected in 1987, but after the National Party politically exploited the incident as a broken promise, both parties promised a referendum in their 1990s manifestos. The National Party elected in 1990 finally held a referendum on electoral system reform in 1992, in which voters rejected the existing first-past-the-post system . . . . in favor of a [mixed electoral system] ... (Roberts 1997). New Zealand's long-standing first-past-the-post system owes its changeover to [a mixed electoral] system not so much to "a revolution from below [as to] an accident from above." (Rudd and Taichi 1994, p. 11, quoted in Nagel 2004)

A second referendum was held in 2011 when a majority of New Zealanders reaffirmed their support for a mixed electoral system.

CONCLUSION

Elections are increasingly being used by both democracies and dictatorships to fill political offices. The growing use of elections around the world has fostered a concern with electoral integrity. Flawed and contested elections can have significant negative consequences. They can produce social instability, undermine democratic consolidation, reduce trust in the political system, and exacerbate ethnic and religious grievances. As we've seen in this chapter, there's significant variation in electoral integrity across countries, both democracies and dictatorships. How can we promote "good" electoral practice? Unfortunately, many of the factors that influence the level of electoral integrity relate to domestic structural constraints such as a country's level of development or its dependence on natural resources that are difficult to change, at least in the short term. One possibility is to strengthen the electoral management bodies that oversee and administer the elections. The problem here is that the set of actors who have the strongest incentive to strengthen these organizations are often not the same set of actors who have the power to actually do this. Some people are optimistic that international donors can help promote free and fair elections in recipient countries by making their foreign aid conditional on electoral and democratic reform. This optimism must be tempered, though, by the fact that foreign aid donors are not always willing or able to follow through on their threats to withdraw aid if their conditions are not met.

In the second half of this chapter, we examined the different types of electoral system used in elections around the world. Most political scientists classify electoral systems into two main families: majoritarian or proportional. We're often asked whether there's a single electoral system that is better than all the others. As our discussion indicates, though, each electoral system has its strengths and weaknesses. For example, some electoral systems promote proportionality but lower the ability of voters to hold representatives accountable. Others allow voters to more accurately convey their sincere preferences but are complicated for individuals to understand and costly for electoral agencies to administer. In an echo of our comments from Chapter 9, there's no perfect electoral system—there are always trade-offs to be made.

Of course, you may be more willing to make certain trade-offs than others. Perhaps you think proportionality is the key criterion for evaluating different electoral systems and are less concerned with having a close link between the representative and her constituents. When we think about the actual adoption of an electoral system, though, we need to stop and ask what's in the interests of the actors involved in choosing the electoral system. Rather than thinking about which electoral system is best at meeting some objective criteria we might care about, such as proportionality, we now need to think of which electoral systems are politically feasible, given the preferences of the actors involved. We can then try to choose the "best" electoral system from within the set of politically feasible systems.

As we noted earlier, electoral systems are distributive mechanisms that reward one set of actors at the expense of another. This means that no electoral system is a winning situation for everyone involved. This has important consequences for any budding electoral reformers among you. It's nearly always the case that the political actors who won under the existing electoral system are the ones who are in a position to determine whether electoral reform should take place. Given that these actors won under the existing system, they're unlikely to be willing to reform the electoral system except in ways that solidify their ability to win in the future. Only when there's some impending threat to their continued electoral success, as was the case with conservative parties at the beginning of the twentieth century when the right to vote was extended to the working class, are they likely to consider major electoral reform. Although many people in the United States complain about the existing SMDP electoral system and advocate for the adoption of a more proportional one, we suggest that they not hold their breath. Why would either the Democratic or Republican party choose to adopt a more proportional system that would hurt their chances to be reelected and help smaller political parties? Of course, as the New Zealand case we just described illustrates, electoral reform can happen "by accident."

Key Concepts

electoral system—a set of laws that regulates electoral competition between candidates and parties

electoral formula—a formula that determines how votes are translated into seats

ballot structure—the way in which electoral choices are presented on the ballot paper

district magnitude—the number of representatives elected in a district

electoral integrity—the extent to which the conduct of elections meets international standards and global norms concerning "good" elections; these norms and standards are usually set out in treaties, conventions, and guidelines issued by international and regional organizations

electoral malpractice—violations of electoral integrity

electoral threshold—the minimum level of voter support a party needs to obtain legislative representation

natural threshold—the minimum level of voter support a party needs to obtain legislative representation that arises as a mathematical by-product of the electoral system

formal threshold—the minimum level of voter support a party needs to obtain legislative representation explicitly written into the electoral system

closed party list—a party list in which voters can only indicate their preferred party and can't express a preference for a particular candidate

open party list—a party list in which voters can indicate not only their preferred party but also their favored candidate within that party

free party list—a party list in which voters have multiple votes that they can allocate either within a single party list or across different party lists

electoral tier—a level at which votes are translated into seats; the lowest tier is the district or constituency level; higher tiers are constituted by grouping together different lower-tier constituencies, typically at the regional or national level

12

SOCIAL CLEAVAGES AND PARTY SYSTEMS

Party is organized opinion.

Benjamin Disraeli

OVERVIEW

1. Political scientists sometimes categorize democracies in terms of the type of party system they exhibit. When they do this, they typically distinguish between party systems based on the number and size of the parties they contain.

2. A political party is an organization that includes officials who hold office and people who help get and keep them there. Parties help to structure the political world, recruit and socialize the political elite, mobilize the masses, and provide a link between rulers and the ruled.

3. In this chapter, we investigate where parties come from and examine why some countries have few parties and others have many. As we'll see, the general structure of a country's party system results from the complex interplay of both social and institutional forces.

In addition to classifying democracies according to the type of government they have or the type of electoral system they employ, political scientists sometimes categorize democracies by the type of party system they exhibit. Although there are obviously many facets to a party system one might examine, people often focus on the number and size of the parties in a country. As a result, you'll frequently see scholars distinguish between democracies that have a two-party system, like the United States, and democracies that have a multiparty system, like the Netherlands. Although the type of government and electoral system in a country is nearly always enshrined in a constitution or some other legal document, this isn't the case for the type of party system (Stokes 1999, 245). Rather than something that is intentionally designed by particular individuals, the structure of a party system is shaped by the changing nature of political competition in a country. Socioeconomic forces largely drive the structure of a country's party system, but these forces are channelled in powerful and important ways by the kinds of political institutions we've examined in the last two chapters. In effect, the structure of a country's party system results from the complex interplay of both social and institutional forces.

POLITICAL PARTIES: WHAT ARE THEY, AND WHAT DO THEY DO?

A **political party** "is a group of officials or would-be officials who are linked with a sizeable group of citizens into an organization; a chief object of this organization is to ensure that its officials attain power or are maintained in power" (Shively 2001, 234). As this definition suggests, a political party comprises a broad collection of actors that can range from officials who actually attain power to individuals who regularly vote for the party and people who contribute money or time to campaign for a party member. In other words, a party can be thought of as a group of people that includes those who hold office and those who help get and keep them there. One of the primary goals of political parties is to attain power; it's this goal that differentiates them from interest groups. In contrast to political parties, interest groups, such as the National Rifle Association, the American Medical Association, and Greenpeace, are organizations that attempt to influence policy without actually taking power.

One thing to note about the definition we've just given is that political parties aren't restricted to democracies or electoral activity. As we saw in Chapter 8, political parties exist in many dictatorships around the world. Some of these parties, such as the Communist Party in China, control the levers of power without holding national-level elections. That some dictatorships have chosen to have political parties even in the absence of elections should immediately alert you to the fact that political parties can serve important purposes beyond simply helping officials get elected to power. In what follows, we focus on how political parties (1) structure the political world, (2) recruit and socialize the political elite, (3) mobilize the masses, and (4) provide a link between the rulers and the ruled (Shively 2001).

Political Parties and the Structure of the Political World

Political parties help to structure the political world for both political elites and the masses. For the elites, political parties provide some kind of order to the policymaking process. Imagine, for a moment, a world in which there are no political parties. In other words, imagine a world in which every legislator is an independent with no institutionalized link to other legislators. Given that legislators must make policy decisions in numerous issue areas and that there's likely to be disagreement over which policies are most appropriate, the outcome of the policymaking process in this type of environment is probably going to be highly chaotic and unstable. Political parties help to overcome some of these problems by coordinating the actions of individual legislators and simplifying the issue space. In effect, parties help to provide structure to an otherwise unstable policymaking process. Aldrich (1995) argues that the need to coordinate votes on many issues among congressional representatives with similar, but not identical, preferences is precisely the explanation for why political parties were formed in the United States in the eighteenth century.

Just as for elites, political parties also structure the political world for voters. One way in which they do this is by providing "information shortcuts" to voters (Downs 1957;

Fiorina 1981). Voters seldom have the opportunity, time, energy, or even inclination to gather information about particular political issues. For these uninformed voters, party labels and party attachments can be an information shortcut in the sense that these things tell voters how to feel about certain issues. In effect, voters might decide they're against a particular piece of legislation not because they've read up on it and realized that it's not in their interests but simply because the party to which they feel attached dislikes it. In many ways, one's political identity is frequently tied up with one's **party identification** (Campbell et al. 1960). For example, simply admitting to being a Democrat or a Republican in the United States or a Labour or Conservative supporter in the United Kingdom can convey a lot of information about a person's likely stance on a whole host of different issues. All of this helps to explain why so many people seem to view politics in terms of the fortunes of political parties rather than the fate of political issues.

Recruitment and Socialization of the Political Elite

In addition to structuring the political world, parties play an important role in recruiting and socializing the political elite. In many countries, it's extremely difficult to get elected as an independent. In other words, being selected as a party's candidate is often a necessary condition for a successful run for office. Similarly, cabinet positions are frequently restricted to senior members of a political party. In effect, "gaining access to political power requires being accepted by a party, and usually being a leading figure in it. Parties also socialize the political elite; most government ministers have spent a number of years as party members, working with other party members and learning to see the political world from the party's perspective" (Gallagher, Laver, and Mair 2006, 308). To see a more concrete example of this, consider the description Shively (2001, 238) gives of how an ambitious young woman interested in entering politics in Britain might behave:

> [She] might work for a while at lesser tasks for one of the major parties, such as the Conservative Party. Before too long, if she were interested in standing for Parliament, she might be nominated from a district. To get the nomination, she would have to convince the local selection committee of the Conservative Party in that district that she was their best nominee. As a beginner, she would probably be selected in a hopeless district, where no Conservative had much of a chance; but once she had proved she could campaign well in one or two lost causes, she might get the nomination from a decent district, win, and enter the House. In the House, she would continue to be molded and guided by the party. If she were the sort that party leaders like—witty in debate, hard working, and above all a faithful party voter—she might advance into positions of real responsibility, such as party spokesperson on defense or on health. Eventually, she might aim so high as to be prime minister. To be selected for this position, she would have to win an internal election at which all the Conservative members of Parliament vote to choose their leader. Throughout this career, her advancement would have been primarily due to her support from her party organization, and she would have risen to the top only because she was the sort of person her party wanted and because, in each position she held, she had learned from the rest of the party how to behave in ways they preferred. This is essentially the only way to make a political career in Great Britain.

To some extent, the role parties play in recruiting and socializing the political elite is more important in parliamentary democracies than in presidential ones. Although it's true that much of the political elite in presidential democracies will have worked their way into place through the apparatus of one political party or another, parties aren't the monopolistic gatekeepers to power they frequently are in parliamentary systems. For example, our discussion of presidential governments in Chapter 10 indicated that presidents are much more likely to appoint nonpartisan ministers to their cabinets than prime ministers are in parliamentary systems. The reason for this is that the president has less need to negotiate with political parties in the legislature over the composition of the cabinet because the vote of no confidence is absent in presidential systems.

Presidential regimes that allow for primaries, like the United States and, increasingly, many Latin American countries (Carey and Polga-Hecimovich 2006, 2008), further weaken the role that political parties play in recruiting and socializing the political elite. By allowing candidates to appeal directly to the voters rather than rely on party leaders, primaries can allow candidates with little political or party experience to win elections. This was recently illustrated by the success of Donald Trump in winning the Republican Party's nomination in the 2016 US presidential primaries. Indeed, Trump won the nomination, and then the presidency, despite considerable opposition from within the Republican Party itself. The existence of primary elections is a key reason for the organizational weakness of political parties and the dominance of candidate-centered, rather than party-centered, election campaigns in the United States (Aldrich 1995). In presidential democracies, it's even possible for complete political outsiders to win the presidency. This is precisely what happened when the academic and TV presenter Alberto Fujimori surprisingly won the 1990 presidential elections in Peru. The election of such a candidate to a position equivalent to that of prime minister in a parliamentary democracy is almost unthinkable.

That political parties don't exert the same degree of control over the recruitment and socialization of the political elite across different types of democracy suggests that the political direction of leaders in presidential democracies is inclined to be inherently less stable and more unpredictable than that of political leaders in parliamentary democracies (Gallagher, Laver, and Mair 2006, 308).

Mobilization of the Masses

Political parties are also key tools for mobilizing the masses. This is particularly important at election time when ordinary citizens must be encouraged to vote. A large literature suggests that people won't necessarily choose to vote given that turning out to vote is costly—it takes time, they could be doing something else, it might be raining, and so on—and that the likelihood of anyone's individual vote determining the outcome of the election is incredibly small (Aldrich 1993; Gomez, Hansford, and Krause 2007). This suggests that organizations such as political parties have a significant role to play in getting people to the polls (Morton 1991; Uhlaner 1989). Political parties are well placed to carry out this role because they're likely to have membership and organizational structures that extend deeply into each constituency. Moreover, they have a strong incentive to get people (at least particular people) to the polls—they want to win elections.

The ability of political parties to mobilize the masses can be important even when elections are not being held. As an example, French president Charles de Gaulle used his Gaullist Party to mobilize his supporters against student and worker protests in 1968 (Lacouture 1986, 719–720). To many observers at the time, these protests, which had grown in size over several weeks, threatened the very existence of the French Fifth Republic. After initially keeping a low profile as events developed, de Gaulle eventually delivered a radio address that preyed on the French people's fears of a Communist revolution. He said that he would dissolve the

National Assembly, that he would hold new elections, and that the country was "threatened with dictatorship, that of totalitarian communism." He also called on the people to come to the defense of the republic against the "Communist" students and workers. As Hitchcock (2004, 251) notes, "Within an hour of de Gaulle's address, crowds began to form on the Place de la Concorde. . . . Perhaps as many as half a million people poured out of their homes into the streets, and marched up the Champs-Elysées behind the major political leaders of the Gaullist and right-wing parties." In the new elections that took place about a month later, the electorate gave a huge majority to the Gaullist candidates.

Although this particular example from France illustrates how political parties can be used to mobilize the masses in support of a regime, there are numerous other cases in which parties have been used to mobilize the people against the ruling order. For example, the Ukrainian political party known as Our Ukraine played an important role in organizing protests in Kiev that led to the Orange Revolution in 2004. Other examples of political parties mobilizing the masses against the ruling regime include the Congress Party in India and the National Front for Liberation in Algeria. Both of these parties were originally established as a means to mobilize the masses against British and French colonial rule (Shively 2001, 237).

A Link between the Rulers and the Ruled

Political parties also provide a link between the rulers and the ruled. According to most democratic theorists, democratic governments are supposed to reflect the preferences of their citizens (Dahl 1956; Pitkin 1967). As discussed in Chapter 10 in our examination of the government formation process, the political party is the primary vehicle ensuring that citizen preferences are reflected in government policy. In fact, it's probably the central function of a political party in a democracy to represent, articulate, and champion the interests of its membership. Political parties are also the main means by which democracies can be induced to be responsive. In democracies, the people should be able to hold elected leaders accountable for their actions in office. The problem is that government policy is frequently determined by the collective actions of many officeholders. As a collective group, the political party provides the main means by which voters can hold elected officials responsible for what they do collectively. Fiorina (1980, 26) goes so far as to write that "the only way collective responsibility has ever existed, and can exist . . . is through the agency of the political party."

It's important to recognize that the link parties create between officials and citizens runs both ways. We've just described the political party as an organization that citizens can use to control the actions of officials and hold them responsible for what they do in office. However, political parties can also help officials exert control over other political actors and citizens as well. Party leaders have many carrots and sticks at their disposal that they can use to deliberately enforce the obedience of legislators when it comes to voting in the legislature. For example, they can use promotion within the party, promises of campaign resources, threats of expulsion, and the like to induce legislators to vote the "right" way on pieces of legislation. Most political parties have an individual called a **whip**, whose job it is to ensure that members of the party attend legislative sessions and vote as the party leadership desires. Although the power of whips varies from country to country, whips are frequently some of the most important political actors in a country (see Box 12.1, "Party Whips in the United Kingdom"). The importance of whips often goes unrecognized by the public because these actors rarely appear in the media, at least in their capacity as whips.

BOX 12.1 PARTY WHIPS IN THE UNITED KINGDOM

The term *whip* to describe someone who ensures that party members attend legislative sessions and vote as the party leadership desires originated in the English Parliament in the 1880s. The term derives from the "whipper-in" at a fox hunt, whose job it is to keep the pack of hounds together and under control. The role of a whip is particularly important when the voting strengths of the government and the opposition are close. The duties of a whip include (1) keeping legislators informed of forthcoming parliamentary business, (2) maintaining the party's voting strength by ensuring that members attend important debates and vote as the party leadership desires, and (3) passing on the opinions of legislators to the party leadership. Each of the three major parties in the United Kingdom—the Conservatives, Labour, and the Liberals—have a chief whip, a deputy chief whip, and a varying number of junior whips. The government chief whip is directly answerable to the prime minister, attends cabinet meetings, and makes the day-to-day arrangements for the government's program of business.

The term *whip* also applies to a weekly circular sent out by each party's whips to all their Members of Parliament (MPs), notifying them of parliamentary business and the schedule for the days ahead. This circular includes the sentence "Your attendance is absolutely essential" next to each debate in which there'll be a vote. The degree of importance of each debate is indicated by the number of times this sentence is underlined. Sentences that are underlined once are considered routine and attendance is optional. Those that are underlined twice are more important and attendance is required unless a "pair"—a member from the opposing side who also intends to be absent from the debate—has been arranged. Those that are underlined three times are highly important and pairing is not normally allowed. The number of underlines determines whether there is a one-line, two-line, or three-line whip on a vote. Three-line

whips are imposed on important occasions such as for votes of no confidence.

The consequences of defying the party leadership depend on the circumstances surrounding a vote and are usually negotiated with the party whips in advance. Cabinet ministers who defy the whips are immediately dismissed. The consequences for defying the party whip for a backbencher—someone who is not in the cabinet or the "shadow" cabinet of the Opposition—can include being overlooked for future promotions to a cabinet post; being given little support by the party organization when seeking reelection; being deselected by local party activists or moved to a different, and less safe, constituency seat; or being expelled from the party altogether. Failure by MPs to attend a vote with a three-line whip is usually treated as a rebellion against the party and, theoretically, leads to suspension from the party. As an example, nine Conservative MPs were suspended from the party in 1994 when they voted against the position of John Major's government regarding the European Union.

Party whips can be extremely forceful in obtaining the votes of their backbenchers, even engaging in "blackmail, verbal intimidation, sexual harassment and physical aggression" from time to time to force some unpopular votes (Dixon 1996, 160). Occasionally, whips bring in very sick MPs for important votes. A former MP, Joe Ashton, describes such a case from the final days of James Callaghan's Labour government (1976–1979).

I remember the famous case of Leslie Spriggs, the then [Labour] Member for St. Helens. We had a tied vote and he was brought to the House in an ambulance having suffered a severe heart attack. The two Whips went out to look in the ambulance and there was Leslie Spriggs laid there as though he was dead. I believe that John Stradling Thomas

[Conservative whip] said to Joe Harper [Labour whip], "How do we know that he is alive?" So he leaned forward, turned the knob on the heart machine, the green light went around, and he said, "There, you've lost—it's 311." [The vote had been tied 310–310.] That is an absolutely true story. It is the sort of nonsense that used to happen. No one believes it, but it is true. (Hansard 1997, Column 507)

PARTY SYSTEMS

Political scientists sometimes categorize democracies in terms of their party system. When they do this, they typically classify party systems based on the number and size of the parties they contain. In what follows, we identify five different types of party system: **nonpartisan system**, **single-party system**, **one-party dominant system**, **two-party system**, and **multiparty system**. Single-party systems exist only in dictatorships, and nonpartisan and one-party dominant systems are relatively rare in democracies. It's for this reason that political scientists usually distinguish between democracies on the basis of whether they have a two-party system, like the United States, or a multiparty system, like the Netherlands.

The existence of political parties is often seen as a necessary condition for the existence of modern democracy. For example, scholars have claimed that "parties are the core institution of democratic politics" (Lipset 1996), that "democracy is unthinkable save in terms of parties" (Schattschneider 1942), and that "modern democracy is party democracy" (Katz 1980). Despite these claims, though, a small handful of democracies can be considered nonpartisan, that is, ones in which there are no official political parties. The absence of political parties may be because a law prohibits their existence or simply because they have yet to form. Historically, the administration of George Washington and the first few sessions of the US Congress were nonpartisan. Today, the only democracies that can be considered nonpartisan are the small Pacific islands of Kiribati, the Marshall Islands, Micronesia, Nauru, Palau, and Tuvalu (Veenendaal 2016). Although nonpartisan democracies at the national level are extremely rare, a few countries have some nonpartisan governments at the subnational level. For example, the unicameral legislature of Nebraska is nonpartisan, as are some Swiss cantons and some Canadian territories.

In single-party systems, only one political party is legally allowed to hold power. Liberia is generally considered the first single-party state in the world. The True Whig Party ruled Liberia from 1878 to 1980, when it was ousted by a military coup. Current single-party states include such countries as China, Cuba, Laos, North Korea, and Vietnam. Although these party systems are called single-party systems, minor parties are sometimes allowed to exist. These minor parties, however, are always legally required to accept the leadership of the dominant party. For example, consider Communist Poland (1945–1989). The Polish United Workers' Party (PUWP) allowed a prewar left-wing United Peasant Party (ZSL), a small private business party (SD), and a Catholic group with direct ties to Moscow to coexist with it under separate labels in the legislature (Gandhi and Przeworski 2006). During elections, though, these small parties had to present their legislative candidates on a single PUWP party list. In other words, the candidates of these minor parties had to be approved by the PUWP ahead of time. All single-party systems occur in dictatorships.

ADALBERTO ROQUE/AFP/Getty Images

Cuban president Raúl Castro (*left*) and Botswana's president Ian Khama (*right*) attend the welcoming ceremony in Havana for Khama's June 2010 visit to Cuba. Khama's Botswana Democratic Party has ruled Botswana since independence in 1966. Ian Khama's father, Seretse Khama, founded the Botswana Democratic Party in 1961 and was himself president from 1966 to 1980.

In some countries, multiple parties are legally allowed to exist, but only one party has a realistic chance of gaining power. States in which this is the case are said to have one-party dominant systems. Many of these one-party dominant systems occur in dictatorships. In these countries, the dictatorship might allow certain opposition parties to legally operate, but they then use various means to prevent them from actually coming to power (Lust-Okar 2005). Examples of one-party dominant systems in dictatorships include the Patriotic Salvation Movement (MPS) of Idriss Déby in Chad and the Cameroon People's Democratic Movement (CPDM) of Paul Biya in Cameroon. Not all one-party dominant systems are necessarily undemocratic, though. For example, there are several cases of democracies in which a single party is dominant for long periods of time. This dominance is normally attributed to things like long-running popularity, a divided opposition, the efficient use of patronage systems, and, occasionally, electoral fraud. Examples of one-party dominant systems in states that many consider democratic include the African National Congress in South Africa since 1994, the Botswana Democratic Party in Botswana since 1966, the Democratic Party in the southern United States from the 1880s to the 1960s, the Liberal Democratic Party in Japan from 1955 to 1993, and the Congress Party in India from 1947 to 1977. Although a one-party dominant system is similar in many ways to a single-party system, "the availability of other active parties does guarantee that there will be fairly open discussion and debate, and it also provides for possible long-term flexibility and adjustment in the system" (Shively 2001, 249).

A two-party system is one in which only two major political parties have a realistic chance of holding power. In democracies with this type of party system, nearly all elected offices are held by candidates endorsed by one of the two major parties; electoral success under the label of some third party, although not impossible, is extremely difficult. Examples of two-party systems include the systems in Jamaica, the United Kingdom, and the United States. As of

2016, all 435 seats in the US House of Representatives and 98 of the 100 seats in the US Senate were controlled by either the Democratic Party or the Republican Party. The 2016 elections in Jamaica resulted in all 63 legislative seats going to either the Jamaica Labour Party or the People's National Party. Although the United Kingdom has recently seen some electoral success for third parties, the two major parties—the Conservatives and Labour— still managed to win 89 percent of the legislatives seats in the most recent elections in 2017. Despite their name, virtually all two-party systems have many more than two parties competing for office. As of 2016, for instance, there were 432 registered political parties in the United Kingdom (394 in Great Britain and 38 in Northern Ireland) and at least 50 national-level parties in the United States. Both the United Kingdom and the United States, however, are traditionally seen as two-party systems because only the two major parties usually have any expectation of controlling the government.

A multiparty system is one in which more than two political parties have a realistic chance of holding power, either separately or as part of a coalition. Most democracies have multiparty systems. Examples include Brazil, Israel, and the Netherlands. In Table 12.1, we list those parties holding legislative seats in the Israeli Knesset following the 2015 elections. As you can see, the seats in the legislature are split among numerous political parties, with no single party coming close to obtaining a legislative majority. The coalition government formed by Israeli Prime Minister Benjamin Netanyahu after the 2015 elections included his own Likud Party, Kulanu, Shas, United Torah Judaism, and Habayit Hayehudi.

We've just described how political scientists frequently distinguish between democracies based on the number and size of the parties that exist. In general, they tend to distinguish between two-party and multiparty democracies. Rather than lump democracies into just these two categories, however, we might want to know how many parties there are in each country. This requires us to think about how we count political parties. Political scientists typically

TABLE 12.1 ■ Political Parties with Seats in the Israeli Knesset, 2015	
Political party	**Number of seats**
Likud	30
Zionist Union	24
Joint List	13
Yesh Atid	11
Kulanu	10
Habayit Hayehudi	8
Shas	7
United Torah Judaism	6
Yisrael Beiteinu	6
Meretz	5
Total	120

don't count every party that contests national elections. If they did, the number of parties in many countries would be extremely large and include "joke" parties, such as the "The True English (Poetry) Party" and the "Monster Raving Loony Party" in the United Kingdom, the "Guns and Dope Party"—which advocates replacing one-third of Congress with ostriches—in the United States, and the "Beer Drinkers Party" in many countries. The problem is that a party system in which votes are divided evenly among ten parties is quite different from a system in which two parties get 90 percent of the votes with eight parties splitting the rest; this difference would be lost if we simply described both systems as "ten-party" systems.

To take account of this, political scientists frequently use a measure called the **effective number of parties** to count political parties (Laakso and Taagepera 1979). This measure counts each party in a system but first weights them by their size. If we use each party's "vote share" to weight the parties, we're measuring the **effective number of electoral parties**. This gives us a sense of how many parties earned votes and how the electorate's votes are distributed across the parties. If, instead, we use each party's "seat share" to weight the parties, we're measuring the **effective number of legislative parties**. This gives us a sense of how many parties won seats in the legislature and how those seats are distributed across the parties.

The effective number of parties can vary quite a lot from one country to another. For example, the effective number of electoral parties in Belize in 2008 was 2 and the effective number of legislative parties was less than 1.5. The reason why the effective number of parties was so low is that the United Democratic Party won 56.6 percent of the vote and 80.6 percent of the legislative seats in the 2008 elections. In effect, one party dominated the 2008 Belizean elections, at least with respect to obtaining legislative seats. In contrast, there were eleven effective electoral parties and ten effective legislative parties in Brazil at the end of the 2000s. The very high effective number of parties in Brazil reflects the fact that votes and seats were shared fairly evenly among a very large number of parties. Political scientists often classify democracies as having a two-party system if the effective number of parties is less than three and a multiparty system if the effective number of parties is three or more.

WHERE DO PARTIES COME FROM?

Why do democracies have the types of party systems they do? To answer this question, we need to understand where parties come from. Political scientists have two basic views—primordial and instrumental—on this. The primordial view treats parties as the natural representatives of people who share common interests. In effect, this view takes it as given that there are "natural" divisions, or cleavages, in society. As groups of individuals form around these cleavages, political parties emerge and evolve to represent these interests. This is sometimes referred to as the "bottom-up" approach to party formation. In contrast, the instrumental view of party formation treats parties as teams of office seekers and focuses on the role played by political elites and entrepreneurs. According to this "top-down" approach, political parties are created by individuals who, perhaps because of certain informational advantages and additional resources, are able to discern an opportunity to represent a previously unrepresented interest. Indeed, the instrumental approach recognizes that political entrepreneurs may even help citizens become aware that such an interest exists; in other words, they can even "create" divisions or cleavages in society.

These two views of party formation are similar to what economists would call supply and demand factors. The primordial view takes the social demand for the representation of particular interests as given and explains the existence of political parties as a response to those demands. In contrast, the instrumental view holds that "supply creates its own demand." Just as advertising and marketing firms can shape the tastes of consumers, savvy political entrepreneurs might help create the demand for particular policies and ideologies. As in the case with supply and demand, understanding the origins of political parties involves recognizing the interaction of both primordial and instrumental forces. To a large extent, social demands for representation drive the formation of political parties. These demands, however, are channelled in powerful and important ways by political institutions that structure the environment of would-be political entrepreneurs and voters. In what follows, we examine how social (primordial) and institutional (instrumental) forces interact to shape party systems.

TYPES OF POLITICAL PARTIES AND SOCIAL CLEAVAGES

As we noted earlier, perhaps the central function of a political party in a democracy is to represent, articulate, and champion the interests of its membership. These interests are, by their very nature, shared by only a part of the overall population. The Oxford English Dictionary recognizes this when it defines a party as "a division of a whole; a part, portion, or share." By this definition, political parties arise when officials or would-be officials seek office to pursue goals that are shared by a part, but not all, of society. This suggests that the types of parties that exist in a country are closely related to the divisions or social cleavages that exist in that country. Below we discuss some of the more common cleavages that occur in countries around the world and talk about the evolution of their salience over time.

The Urban-Rural Cleavage

The conflict between rural and urban interests is one of the oldest political conflicts in the world. Moreover, it remains salient in many countries to this day. The conflict in early modern Europe between feudal lords on the one hand and town dwellers—freemen, burghers, or the bourgeoisie—on the other had both an economic and a cultural dimension. Economically, rural dwellers were typically associated with agricultural production and city dwellers with trade, crafts, and commerce. The most basic point of conflict between rural and urban interests, therefore, involved the price of food. Town dwellers were consumers, not producers, of food, and as a result, they typically experienced an increase in their living standards when food prices dropped. Rural dwellers were more likely to be producers of food and, so, benefited from increased food prices. In addition, much of rural life took place through a barter system that involved the trading of goods and services. Reputation was an important element in making the complex set of commitments surrounding such trades "credible," and reputation typically rested upon ties of kinship. In contrast, economic exchange in towns tended to be monetized and to take place between relatively anonymous actors. Consequently, urban commitment problems often surrounded the credibility of the money used to buy goods or the weights and measures employed to apportion them. It was because of this that the development of contract law, clearly defined property rights, and financial innovation became more of a priority in towns than in rural areas. Culturally, rural actors tended to value tradition, whereas town dwellers favored change.

The Confessional Cleavage

Another important conflict in many countries centers on confessional, or religious, differences. Conflict over religious differences emerged in European countries during the Protestant Reformation in the early sixteenth century. At this time, the authority of the

Roman Catholic Church was challenged by the rise of Protestantism and men like Martin Luther in Germany and John Calvin in Geneva. For several decades, Europe was thrown into tumult as struggles between Protestants and Catholics, which would later become known as the Wars of Religion, tore apart countries, principalities, and the Holy Roman Empire. Religious conflict also fueled war between various political entities that lasted well into the seventeenth century. When the Peace of Westphalia (1648) ended both the Thirty Years' War and the Eighty Years' War (or Dutch Revolt), it also reinvigorated the norm of *cuius regio, eius religio*. This Latin phrase means "whose region, his religion" and is used to describe the notion that the leader of a country, city-state, or principality is entitled to choose the religion for those who live under his rule. Although the Peace of Westphalia may have led to a reduction in religious conflict between jurisdictions and helped create the modern state by rendering the Holy Roman Empire irrelevant, it did little to resolve religious conflicts within states. In fact, by empowering leaders to declare a state religion, it all but dictated religious intolerance. The result was that individuals who confessed a commitment to a particular brand of Christianity often found themselves in conflict with devotees of other denominations.

The continued salience of the Protestant-Catholic cleavage depends largely on whether or not one or the other side was able to establish its dominance. In some places, the division led to two different countries. For example, the Eighty Years' War split the Low Countries into the Protestant (mostly Calvinist) dominated Dutch Republic (now the Netherlands) and the Catholic-dominated southern Netherlands (today's Belgium). In some places such as Germany, Catholics and Protestants eventually formed an uneasy truce, and in other countries such as Sweden (Lutheran) or France (Catholic), one or the other church became dominant. Finally, it's worth mentioning that in some countries such as Italy and Spain, the Protestant Reformation never made any significant inroads. Whatever the settlement, many European party systems bear the imprint of the now centuries-old conflict between Protestants and Catholics.

Confessional cleavages continue to be salient in many non-European countries as well. For example, conflict between Hindus and Muslims led to the partition of India into a predominantly Hindu India and a Muslim-dominated Pakistan in 1947. Following the creation of Pakistan, millions of Muslims moved from India to Pakistan, and millions of Hindus and Sikhs moved from Pakistan to India. The conflict between Hindus and Muslims continues to be salient in this region today, particularly in the disputed region of Kashmir. Deep divisions between Sunni and Shia Muslims have been central to the politics of many Middle Eastern countries for centuries. The removal of Saddam Hussein by US forces in 2003 exacerbated these divisions in Iraq and beyond. Nigeria and Sudan are two other countries with historically deep confessional divisions, this time between a predominantly Muslim north and a predominantly Christian south. Indeed, the divisions in Sudan played an instrumental role in the establishment of South Sudan as an independent country in July 2011; an internationally recognized referendum in January 2011 saw 98 percent of southerners vote to break away from what is now North Sudan. Finally, nowhere is the confessional cleavage more institutionalized than in Lebanon, where high political offices are explicitly reserved for representatives of different religious groups. For example, the president, prime minister, and speaker of the parliament are constitutionally mandated to be held by a Maronite Christian, Sunni Muslim, and Shia Muslim, respectively.

The Secular-Clerical Cleavage

In the last two centuries, political competition around religious issues in European democracies has taken place primarily along a church-state axis (Lipset and Rokkan 1967). The conflict "between the growing state, which sought to dominate, and the church, which tried to maintain its historic corporate rights," had been growing for some time (Lipset 2001, 6). This conflict was particularly pronounced in France, where close cooperation between the nobility and the Catholic clergy had helped maintain the Bourbon monarchy in power since the sixteenth century. The Roman Catholic Church was the largest landowner in the country and had, since CE. 585, the right to exact a tax of 10 percent (or *la dîme*) on all agricultural products. These church taxes fueled resentment among many French people, in part because these resources, which were originally meant to provide for local parishes, were often siphoned off by the church hierarchy to support remote monasteries and bishops. Consequently, when the French Revolution was launched in 1789 against Louis XVI, the popular uprising was, to a large extent, aimed at the church as much as the monarchy. Legislation that was passed in 1790 abolished the church's authority to levy la dîme, confiscated church property, and canceled special privileges for the clergy. The 1790 Civil Constitution of the Clergy turned clergy into employees of the state, thereby subordinating the Roman Catholic Church to the French government and removing it from the authority of the pope.

In order to solidify his hold on power after a coup d'état in 1799, though, Napoleon Bonaparte reached an agreement with the Roman Catholic Church—the Concordat of 1801—to restore some of the church's power. With the brief restoration of the monarchy in 1814, the Catholic Church regained even more of its former status, and the clergy continued to enjoy privileges into the late nineteenth century. French **anticlericalism**—opposition to religious institutional power and influence in public and political life—once again grew stronger as the nineteenth century drew to a close. In the 1880s, religious figures began to be expelled from public schools, and the Jules Ferry laws mandated that the French state provide a free and lay education for its citizens. Numerous conflicts broke out at this time between supporters of the Catholic Church and supporters of a secular state.

In 1905 France passed a law requiring the complete separation of church and state. The law states, "The Republic neither recognizes, nor salaries, nor subsidizes any religion." In effect, this law established state secularism in France and is the backbone of the current French principle of *laïcité*. **Laïcité** refers to the division between private life, where religion belongs, and public life, where religion doesn't belong. To a large extent, this principle rests on the belief that citizens should be treated equally in the public sphere and that things like religion (and ethnicity), which might distinguish between individuals and lead to unequal treatment by the state, should be ignored. Laïcité is distinct from anticlericalism in that it doesn't necessarily imply any hostility on the part of the state toward religion; it's simply the idea that the state and political issues should be kept separate from religious organizations and religious issues.

Although the secular state is now well established and laïcité is overwhelmingly supported by the French people, religion remains a source of political conflict in contemporary France. In the 1990s, for example, it led to a political conflict that has come to be known as the Headscarf Debate. This debate was primarily about whether Muslim girls wearing headscarves in public schools were violating the principle of laïcité by wearing a religious symbol (the headscarf) in a state-funded institution (public school). After several years without a clear policy, the French National Assembly passed a law against pupils wearing "conspicuous" or "ostentatious" symbols of belonging to a religion in 2005. Although the law doesn't mention any particular religious symbol, the prohibited items are generally recognized to include headscarves for Muslim girls, yarmulkes for Jewish boys, turbans for Sikhs, and large Christian crosses. In April 2011, the French government enacted an even more controversial law banning people from covering their faces in public. It's widely recognized that this law is targeted at Muslim women who wear full-face veils, or the *niqab*. In September 2011, the French government responded to growing public unease about street prayers in Paris by banning them. At that

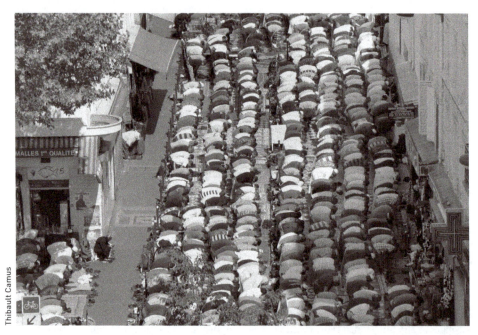

Thibault Camus

Friday prayers in Paris, September 2011. Muslims pray in the Paris streets due to the lack of mosques, while French authorities have sought to find unoccupied state-owned buildings that can be converted into prayer halls.

time, many Muslims in parts of northern Paris had taken to the streets to conduct their daily prayers due to a lack of mosque space in the French capital. Marine Le Pen, the leader of the far-right National Front, sparked outrage when she called these street prayers a "political act of fundamentalists" and likened them to the Nazi occupation of Paris in the Second World War "without the tanks or soldiers" (Samuel 2011, para. 5). Debate is ongoing as to whether these laws and the strict implementation of laïcité is actually encouraging the integration of religious groups, mainly Muslims, into mainstream French society or alienating them.

The specifics of the French case should not distract us from a broader trend toward secularism in Europe from the dawn of the Enlightenment in the eighteenth century into the twenty-first century. Although the degree of secularization in terms of individual piety is the subject of considerable debate (Gaskins, Golder, and Siegel 2013a, b; Norris and Inglehart 2004; Stark and Finke 2000), there's little question that this period saw a persistent retreat by religious institutions from the public square. Modernizing elites around the world argued persuasively that state and church should be separated. Much of the popular appeal of this argument stemmed from the frequent association of the church with the unpopular *ancien régime*—conservative, monarchist forces seeking to protect aristocratic privilege.

Church officials and some believers resisted the separation of church and state, arguing that Christian values of charity for the poor, protection of the family, and the like needed to be protected against what they saw as the corrosive effects of secularism. As a consequence, religious parties formed in many countries. For example, the Tories in Britain originally rallied around the slogan "For Church and King." Separate Protestant and Catholic parties competed in the Netherlands, although by the late nineteenth century, they were typically making common cause against "secular" parties. Indeed, political conflicts between Catholics and Protestants subsided in many countries as the cleavage between confessional and secular groups became increasingly salient. For example, the Christian Democratic Appeal (CDA) in the Netherlands is explicitly nondenominational and seeks to unite Catholics and Protestants. In many countries in Europe and Latin America, Christian Democratic parties combine a conservative position on social issues like abortion and same-sex marriage with an activist position on economic policy. Although staunchly anti-Communist, many Christian Democratic parties take an organic or corporatist view of the economy that emphasizes individuals' obligation to serve their community. This stands in stark contrast to the economic position of Liberal parties in Europe, which derive their identity from the defense of individual, rather than group, rights. European liberals are staunchly secular in their social orientation and champion free-market capitalism in the economic world.

The Class Cleavage

Lipset and Rokkan (1967) refer to the preceding cleavages as "pre-industrial cleavages." This is in marked contrast to the class cleavage, which is said to have become salient during the Industrial Revolution at the end of the eighteenth century. Like the urban-rural cleavage, the class cleavage pits actors against each other over conflicting economic interests. Whereas the urban-rural cleavage involves horizontal conflicts between different sectors in society, however, the class cleavage involves vertical conflicts within sectors between actors who derive their livelihood from the use of their labor and those who derive their livelihood from the use of their property or capital. Class conflict takes place most fundamentally between workers and capitalists in industrial sectors of the economy, but it takes place primarily between peasants (or, later, agricultural workers) and large landowners in the agricultural sectors. Class conflict typically involves attempts to use the state to redistribute wealth from the rich to the poor. Capitalists tend to favor the free market, a small state, and a restricted franchise; in contrast, workers support greater state intervention in the economy and an expansion of the franchise.

The class cleavage became increasingly salient in most European countries during the nineteenth century as demands for franchise expansion, particularly from the working class, grew. At the beginning of the nineteenth century, the right to vote was typically restricted to adult male citizens who owned large amounts of property. Although the Great Reform Act of 1832 expanded the franchise in Great Britain, it still allowed only about one in five male adults to vote. The 1867 Reform Act expanded the suffrage further to include all working-class males. Through this process, and analogous processes in other European states, workers became relevant at the ballot box, and the state was set for full-scale competition between parties claiming to represent the industrial working class and parties that represented economic elites.

For the next hundred years, politics in Europe revolved around the "left-right" divide. The terms *left* and *right* were first used to describe the seating location of competing factions in the French National Assembly in 1791. From the viewpoint of the speaker's chair, monarchists sat to the right and bourgeois reformers sat to the left. This pattern was replicated in other continental parliaments: protectors of aristocratic and clerical interests sat on the right, and middle-class reformers sat on the left. At the time, people sitting on the left—the "left-wingers"—were advocating laissez-faire capitalism and democratization. Through the nineteenth century, though, the political center of gravity shifted further leftward throughout Europe so that by the beginning of the twentieth century, protectors of free markets and democracy were considered "right-wing," and those in favor of workers' rights and socialist revolution were considered "left-wing." Eventually the "Left" came to be represented by Communist, Social Democratic, and Labor parties and the "Right" by Christian Democratic, Conservative, and Liberal parties.

In the nineteenth century, many socialists were in favor of democracy and the socialist transformation of society. Marxist theory predicted the expansion of the industrial working class (proletariat) as capitalism expanded. Under such conditions it was thought that the expansion of the franchise and the natural course of economic development would in short order produce huge Socialist majorities that would then implement the transition to a socialist society by legislative means (Przeworski and Sprague 1988, 22–25). Several factors, however, conspired to inhibit the unfolding of this set of historical developments that many Marxists had once thought inevitable.

First, not all actors voted according to their class interests. In his book *The Poverty of Philosophy*, Karl Marx ([1847] 1995) makes the distinction between a class "in itself" and a class "for itself." Individuals are members of a class "in itself" simply by virtue of their objective "relation to the means of production." In other words, individuals who sell their labor for a wage are workers, and those who earn a profit are capitalists. In contrast, individuals are members of a "class for itself" only if they are actually conscious of their status as a member of that class. Thus, the socialist project can be thought of as a process of class formation. In effect, the goal was to make workers realize they were workers and to transform the proletariat from a "class in itself" into a "class for itself." Marxist orthodoxy held that this process of class formation was a historical inevitability. When the radicalization of workers didn't occur as quickly as many Marxist theorists hoped, scholars put the continued commitment of some workers to bourgeois parties and institutions down to a form of "false consciousness" (Engels [1893] 1968). Whether workers perceived their interests differently from the way that Marxist theorists suggested they should, or whether they were, in fact, suffering from "false consciousness," it's a historical fact across a wide range of countries and time periods that a nontrivial portion of manual laborers voted against left-wing parties and that a substantial share of managers and professionals voted for left-wing parties.

Second, workers "never were and never would become a numerical majority in their respective societies" (Przeworski and Sprague 1988, 31). As a consequence, Socialist parties found it necessary either to broaden their appeals to attract salaried workers and other members of the bourgeoisie or to govern in coalition with bourgeois parties. Przeworski and Sprague (1988) note how these strategies, which were designed to help win elections and gain office, ultimately ended up diluting the salience of class as a basis for individual behavior in some countries.

Finally, even where Socialist parties were electorally successful, there were structural factors at work to limit the extent to which they could bring about a socialist transformation. As we discussed in Chapter 5, part of the reason why Socialist parties didn't institute a socialist transformation had to do with the disciplining effects that investors can play in deterring radical policies. As you'll recall, this disciplining effect is referred to as the "structural dependence of the state on capital." In addition to this pressure from external actors, scholars have identified organizational factors that helped to moderate the policy positions of Socialist parties. With some irony, German sociologist Robert Michels ([1911] 2001, 13) noted that "[i]n theory, the principal aim of social and democratic parties is the struggle against oligarchy in all its forms. The question therefore arises how we are to explain the development in such parties of the very tendencies against which they have declared war." Michels responded to this puzzle by arguing that in all sufficiently complex organizations, including political parties, a division of labor arises between rank-and-file members and professional managers. Because the leaders of the organization develop lifestyles, skills, and interests that are different from those of the rank and file, the organization will inevitably begin to pursue goals that are different from those it was originally formed to pursue. In the case of labor unions and Socialist parties, the leadership exists to represent the "ruled" but is inevitably transformed into part of the ruling class by virtue of its position at the head of the organization. This notion that the leadership of an organization will develop goals that are distinct from those of the organization's rank and file, and that because they are leaders their goals will become dominant, is known as **Michels's iron law of oligarchy**. Michels's iron law of oligarchy has been used to explain organizational dynamics in many different social settings, from trade unions and political parties to religious denominations, corporations, and nonprofit organizations.

The Post-Material Cleavage

Lipset and Rokkan (1967) observed that European party systems were remarkably stable during most of the twentieth century. They observed that the cleavages we've examined so far were all activated during a period when new groups were in the process of being politically mobilized. For example, the urban-rural cleavage and the various religious cleavages became salient at the same time that new elites (the landed gentry and commercial elites in urban areas) were being incorporated into national politics in competition with traditional elites (the nobility and the clergy). The class cleavage became salient during a period when the franchise was expanded to include male workers and eventually women. As these cleavages were activated, new parties could be formed to capture segments of the population that hadn't previously been active in electoral politics. Lipset and Rokkan argued that European party systems became "frozen" with the achievement of universal suffrage during the 1920s. Social structures might change, as they had in the past, but there was no longer any untapped electoral base for new parties to mobilize. According to this argument, the barriers to successful entry for new parties seeking to represent emerging interests became too high after the 1920s. Either political positions associated with new cleavages would go unrepresented or existing parties would alter their positions to capture "unrepresented" voters. Lipset and Rokkan's famous **freezing hypothesis** was used to explain why the ideological dimensions of most European party systems were so similar. Although there was some interesting variety across cases, the modal European party system in the middle of the twentieth century had two parties on the left (Socialist and Communist, with Socialists being more hostile to Soviet influence than the Communists) and a Conservative Party (often Christian Democratic) and a Liberal Party on the right.

European party systems began to "thaw" in the 1960s as societies underwent what Inglehart (1977, 1997) calls a post-materialist value shift. Having been raised in an environment of plenty in which their existential security was taken for granted, new generations of European voters began to prioritize the expansion of human freedom. This new generation of voters was more concerned with issues relating to multiculturalism, gender and racial equality, reproductive choice, and sexual freedom than the standard bread-and-butter issues of the past. In effect, the transition to a postindustrial society was accompanied by a decline in the salience of the economic cleavage and the emergence of a new post-materialist cleavage. When existing parties were slow to adapt to this, a niche emerged that new parties were able to exploit (Rydgren 2005).

The first parties to exploit this opportunity emerged on the left in the 1970s. These parties, which Kitschelt (1988) calls left-libertarian parties, differed from the "Old Left" in that they were less closely tied to the industrial working class and were likely to privilege issues such as environmentalism and immigration that can be perceived to run against working-class interests. According to Kitschelt (1988, 195), left-libertarian parties, such as the Greens, "are critical of the logic of societal development and the institutions that underlie the postwar compromise between capital and labor in industrial societies." They oppose the priority that

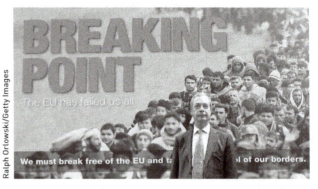

Far right parties in Europe often campaign on anti-immigrant policies. The poster on the left, put up by the Swiss People's Party for the 2007 federal elections, was criticized for its exclusionary message. On the right, UK Independence Party leader Nigel Farage poses in front of a poster in London, urging people to vote to leave the European Union in the June 2016 Brexit referendum. Many condemned the poster, which showed a largely non-white group of migrants crossing the Croatia-Slovenia border in 2015, for stoking anti-immigrant and racist sentiments.

economic growth has on the political agenda, the patterns of policymaking that restrict democratic participation to elite bargaining among centralized interest groups and party leaders, and the bureaucratic welfare state. Their political alternatives conform neither to traditional conservative nor to socialist programs but rather link libertarian commitments to individual autonomy and popular participation with a leftist concern for equality.

The second set of parties to exploit the new post-materialist cleavage appeared on the far right. In many ways, the emergence of these new parties on the far right can be seen as a direct reaction to the post-materialist agenda of the libertarian left (Ignazi 1992). In contrast to the libertarian left, populist parties on the far right emphasize traditional values and highlight how immigration is threatening national identity and culture as well as the jobs and economic welfare of native workers (Bustikova 2014; Dancygier 2010; M. Golder 2016; Ivarsflaten 2008; Mudde 2007). These parties see themselves as the true representatives of "the people" and in conflict with corrupt and immoral elites, a group that typically includes political parties, intellectuals, and the "liberal" media among others (Mudde 2004). The populism they espouse is exclusionary in that certain groups, such as immigrants and homosexuals, are not considered part of "the pure people" (Mudde and Kaltwasser 2013). These parties also espouse nativist policies whereby welfare benefits, public housing, and jobs are to be reserved for the native population. While these parties aren't antidemocratic per se, their radicalism comes in their opposition to liberal democracy and their desire for a fundamental reform of the political and economic system. The combination of radicalism, populism, and nativism has been referred to as the "master frame" of European far-right parties (Rydgren 2004, 2005).

Ethnic and Linguistic Cleavages

In various countries around the world, ethnic or linguistic cleavages are another important source of conflict. Exactly what counts as an "ethnic" cleavage is not obvious because there are many different definitions of what makes a group an "ethnic" group. One common characteristic in definitions of an ethnic group, though, is an emphasis on the role of "descent" (Chandra 2006). In effect, members of ethnic groups share some characteristic more closely with fellow group members than with nongroup members, and this characteristic is inherited in some way from their parents. What scholars tend to differ with one another about is what the particular characteristic or trait is that is shared by the ethnic group members. Thus, an individual's eligibility for membership in an ethnic group is based on the possession of certain attributes that are at least believed to be related to descent. We say "believed to be" because the claims of many ethnic groups to having a common ancestry or common place of origin are simply myths. Chandra (2006, 400) notes that "descent-based attributes" shared by ethnic group members can be "acquired genetically (e.g., skin color, gender, hair type, eye color, height, and physical features), through cultural and historical inheritance (e.g., the names, languages, places of birth and origin of one's parents and ancestors), or in the course of one's lifetime as markers of such an inheritance (e.g., last name or tribal markings)."

Eligibility in an ethnic group doesn't mean the same thing as "membership." As with class, there's a natural tension between ethnic groups "in themselves" and ethnic groups "for themselves." On the one hand, there are circumstances in which individuals can choose the extent to which they identify with an ethnic group. For example, one of the authors of this book (Clark) might embrace his Irish American heritage at a Celtic music performance or poetry reading but shy away from that same heritage when confronted with particularly crass and distasteful "St. Paddy's Day" debauchery. On the other hand, there are circumstances in which individuals might be classified by others (such as in-group "gatekeepers" or government officials) as belonging or not belonging to a particular ethnic group.

As with class, social scientists have differed on the extent to which they see ethnic group membership as based on objective or subjective traits. Scholars who emphasize the objective nature of ethnic identification have been termed "primordialists" and those who emphasize the subjective nature of ethnic identification have been called "constructivists" or "instrumentalists." Briefly, primordialists believe that ethnic attachments are transmitted automatically and that group composition is naturally and externally determined. Constructivists, in contrast, believe that group attachments are socially constructed. In other words, they believe that group identities today are the result of choices made by social actors in the past; social groups don't fall from heaven, nor do they spring from some primordial ooze. "Instrumentalism" might be thought of as a subcategory of constructivism in that instrumentalists believe that group attachments result from the intentional acts of social actors who see group attachments as serving some other purpose, such as aiding their political survival or giving them access to state resources.

Given the salience of various ethnic cleavages around the world, it's little surprise that ethnic parties exist in many countries. An ethnic party "appeals to voters as the champion of the interests of one ethnic category or set of categories to the exclusion of others, and makes such an appeal central to its mobilizing strategy. The key aspect of this definition is exclusion. An ethnic party may champion the interests of more than one ethnic category, but only by identifying the common ethnic enemy to be excluded" (Chandra 2005, 236). Although most people probably think of Africa when they think of ethnic parties, ethnic parties exist and do well in most regions of the world. In fact, probably the first ethnic parties were Jewish parties in the Russian and Austro-Hungarian empires and the Swedish Party in Finland, all founded in the nineteenth century or the first decade of the twentieth century. Relatively successful ethnic parties exist today in countries as far afield as Canada, Fiji, India, Ireland, Israel, Macedonia, New Zealand, Romania, Russia, Spain, Sri Lanka, and Turkey. One continent where there have historically been few ethnic parties is Latin America. This has begun to change, however, with the emergence of various ethnic parties in countries such as Bolivia, Colombia, Ecuador, and Venezuela to represent indigenous populations (Van Cott 2005).

NUMBER OF PARTIES: DUVERGER'S THEORY

Social cleavages help to explain the types of parties that exist in a country. But what explains how many parties there are?

Social Cleavages

Our current understanding of the factors influencing the size of party systems is due, in large part, to the seminal work of a French political scientist, Maurice Duverger ([1954] 1963). Duverger argued that the primary engine behind the formation of political parties can be found in social divisions—the more divisions there are, the greater the demand for political parties to form (Clark and Golder 2006). In effect, he believed that there's some natural tendency for cleavages within society, such as those discussed earlier, to be represented in the party system. It's not just the number of cleavages per se but the way in which membership in society is distributed across those divisions that determines the pressures for distinctive representation.

For example, imagine that two countries, A and B, have the same number of social cleavages as each other. Let's suppose that the cleavages are wealth and religion—citizens are either rich or poor, and they're either Catholic or Protestant. The distribution of people across the cleavages in Country A is shown in Table 12.2. Twenty-five percent of the population are rich Catholics, 25 percent are poor Catholics, 25 percent are rich Protestants, and 25 percent are poor Protestants. As you can see, the two cleavages in Country A are uncorrelated (not associated) with each other. In other words, if we knew whether someone was rich or poor, we wouldn't be able to predict whether they were Catholic or Protestant. Similarly, if we knew whether someone was Catholic or Protestant, we wouldn't be able to predict whether they were rich or poor. A country with uncorrelated cleavages is said to have **cross-cutting cleavages**. The categories rich, poor, Catholic, and Protestant are equally distinctive in Country A and hence equally likely to demand political representation. Indeed, the people in Country A are just as likely to demand political representation as rich Catholics, rich Protestants, poor Catholics, and poor Protestants as they are as Catholics, Protestants, the rich, and the poor. According to Duverger, the "engine" of social forces in Country A is propelling the party system toward a large multiparty system.

The distribution of people across the cleavages in Country B is shown in Table 12.3. Half the population are rich Protestants and half are poor Catholics. Unlike in Country A, the two cleavages in Country B are perfectly correlated. If we knew whether someone was rich or poor, we'd know if they were Catholic or Protestant. Similarly, if we knew whether someone was Catholic or Protestant, we'd know if they were rich or poor. A country with correlated

TABLE 12.2 ■ Cross-Cutting Cleavages in Country A		
	Catholic	**Protestant**
Rich	25	25
Poor	25	25

Note: The numbers indicate the percentage of the population falling into each category.

TABLE 12.3 ■ Reinforcing Cleavages in Country B		
	Catholic	Protestant
Rich	0	50
Poor	50	0

Note: The numbers indicate the percentage of the population falling into each category.

cleavages is said to have **reinforcing cleavages**. Although there are technically two cleavages in Country B (wealth and religion), political competition will be characterized by just one cleavage, the one between poor Catholics and rich Protestants. According to Duverger, the "engine" of social forces in Country B is propelling the party system toward a small two-party system.

The key aspect of a country's social structure influencing the demand for the number of parties, therefore, is not necessarily the total number of cleavages in a country but rather the total number of cross-cutting cleavages. As you might suspect, most cleavages in a country won't be perfectly cross-cutting or reinforcing as in our examples. The same logic as that outlined above, however, suggests that the social pressure for distinctive representation (and a large party system) depends on the number of cleavages in a country and increases with the degree to which these cleavages are cross-cutting rather than reinforcing.

Electoral Institutions

Although Duverger believed that social divisions create the demand for political parties, he argued that electoral institutions play an important role in determining whether this demand for representation actually leads to the existence of new political parties. Recall the earlier claim that European societies have seen the emergence of a new post-materialist cleavage since the 1960s (Inglehart 1977). If social cleavages were the only factor influencing the size of party systems, then all European countries should have experienced an increase in the number of parties competing for office. However, Kitschelt (1988) finds that the share of votes going to "left-libertarian parties" increased only in some countries. The existence and electoral fortunes of populist far-right parties has also varied across European countries (M. Golder 2003). This should make one wonder why an increase in the number of cleavages would have a different effect on the size of party systems in different countries.

Although one explanation for this might be that the shift to post-materialist values was more pronounced in some countries than others, Duverger claims that it's likely to have something to do with the electoral institutions used in each country. In other words, he argues that the same value change can have a significant effect on the party structure of one country but not on that of another due to differences in electoral rules. The reason for this is that nonproportional electoral systems, such as the single-member district plurality (SMDP) system, act as a "brake" on the tendency for social cleavages to be translated into new parties. Put differently, Duverger's theory states that increasing the number of social cleavages in a country has less of an effect on party system size if the electoral system is nonproportional than if it's proportional. There are two reasons, commonly known as the "mechanical" and "strategic" effects of electoral laws, for why nonproportional electoral systems have this moderating effect.

The Mechanical Effect of Electoral Laws

The **mechanical effect of electoral laws** refers to the way that votes are translated into seats. The mechanical effect of all electoral systems systematically punishes small parties and rewards large parties. The extent to which small parties are punished and large parties are rewarded, however, depends on the proportionality of the electoral system. Specifically, small parties will find it harder to win seats and large parties are more likely to be rewarded when the electoral system is highly disproportional, as in an SMDP system. To illustrate how the mechanical effect of electoral laws affects parties of different sizes, consider the following two examples. One is based on a hypothetical country called "Duvergerland" and the other is based on real-world electoral returns from the United Kingdom.

Duvergerland is a country that has historically been divided by a single class cleavage—the electorate has been divided fairly evenly between supporters of a workers' party and supporters of a party that represents the interests of the business class. The one hundred-person legislature in Duvergerland is elected using an SMDP electoral system. Recently, social transformation has led to an increase in the number of voters holding post-materialist values. In recent elections, 20 percent of voters cast ballots for the newly formed Green Party, with the rest split in different ways between the Business and Labor parties in each district. In Figure 12.1, we illustrate the distribution of electoral results across twenty of the one hundred districts using a "doughnut" graph. Although the Green Party wins 20 percent of the vote in each district, at least one of the other parties always wins more votes than this. As a result, the Green Party doesn't win a single legislative seat under the SMDP system.

In Figure 12.2a, we illustrate the distribution of legislative seats if the pattern in the twenty districts shown in Figure 12.1 is reproduced throughout Duvergerland. The Labor

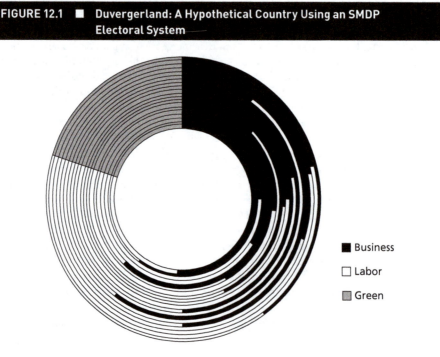

FIGURE 12.1 ■ Duvergerland: A Hypothetical Country Using an SMDP Electoral System

■ Business
□ Labor
▨ Green

FIGURE 12.2 ■ Distribution of Seats in Duvergerland under SMDP and PR Electoral Rules

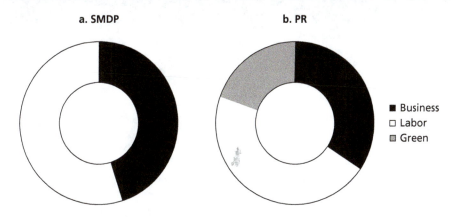

a. SMDP

b. PR

■ Business
□ Labor
▨ Green

and Business parties each get close to 50 percent of the seats in the legislature and the Green Party goes completely unrepresented even though it won 20 percent of the vote. Simply as a result of the way in which votes are translated into seats—the mechanical effect of the SMDP system—a party in Duvergerland that receives 20 percent of the population's support receives 0 percent of the legislative seats being contested. Moreover, although there's clearly support for three parties in the electorate, there are only two parties in the legislature.

Now contrast the way this same distribution of votes would have been translated into seats if Duvergerland had used a proportional representation system in a single national district. Given that the Green Party won 20 percent of the vote, it now obtains twenty legislative seats. This distribution of seats in this new legislature is shown in Figure 12.2b. The fate of the small party—the Green Party—is substantially different under the different electoral systems. The Green Party goes from controlling 20 percent of the legislative seats under PR to being excluded entirely from the legislature under SMDP. This reductive effect in the representation of the small party, as well as the electoral bonus given to the two large parties, is a direct result of the mechanical effect of the majoritarian SMDP electoral system employed in Duvergerland.

The mechanical effect of the SMDP electoral system that reduces the number of parties in the legislature by penalizing parties that win smaller shares of the vote isn't just a matter of theoretical interest. In Table 12.4 (page 312) we report the electoral returns for the St. Ives constituency during the 1992 legislative elections in the United Kingdom. In these elections, the Conservative Party candidate, David Harris, edges out the Liberal Democrat candidate, Andrew George, by fewer than 2,000 votes. Harris, who won just under 43 percent of the vote, becomes the sole representative of the St. Ives constituency. In contrast, Andrew George, who was supported by 40 percent of the voters in his constituency, is awarded nothing.

If the type of situation that occurred in the St. Ives constituency is repeated in a large number of constituencies, the "winner-take-all" logic of SMDP systems can lead to the introduction of a large gap between the share of votes that a party obtains and the share of seats that it ultimately wins. In Table 12.5 (page 312) we show some fairly typical national election results from the United Kingdom. One thing to notice about these results is that both of the two larger parties—the Conservatives and Labour—won about 20 percent more seats than

TABLE 12.4 ■ Legislative Elections Results, St. Ives Constituency, United Kingdom, 1992		
	Votes	% of vote
David Harris (Conservative)	24,528	42.9
Andrew George (Liberal Democrat)	22,883	40.1
Stephen Warr (Labour)	9,144	16.0
Graham Stevens (Liberal)	577	1.0
Harris is elected		

Source: Political Science Resources, http://www.politicsresources.net/area/uk/ge92/i17.htm

their percentage of votes would suggest they should have won. In the case of the Conservative Party, this "electoral bonus," which resulted from the mechanical way in which the SMDP system translates votes into seats, was enough to turn an electoral plurality into a legislative majority. This type of legislative majority is sometimes referred to as a "manufactured" majority. The other thing to notice is that the smaller party—the Liberal Democrats—won only 3.1 percent of the legislative seats even though it won 17.8 percent of the vote. In Figure 12.3 we illustrate graphically how the mechanical effect of the SMDP electoral system used in the 1992 UK legislative elections rewarded the larger parties and punished the smaller ones.

A quick comparison of the hypothetical case of Duvergerland and the real-world example from the 1992 UK legislative elections reveals that the extent to which nonproportional electoral systems, such as SMDP, punish small parties depends on the way that the votes for these parties are distributed across electoral districts. In Duvergerland, we assumed that the support for the Green Party was evenly distributed across all of the electoral districts. This particular distribution of support resulted in the Green Party's failing to win a single seat. Contrast this with the fact that the Liberal Democrats managed to win twenty seats (3.1 percent) in the 1992 UK elections even though they won a smaller share of the national vote than the Greens won in Duvergerland. The reason for this difference is that the size of the support for the Liberal Democrats varied across different districts. Although the support for the Liberal

TABLE 12.5 ■ Legislative Elections Results, National Totals, United Kingdom, 1992 (Percentages)		
	Votes	Seats
Conservative	41.9	51.6
Labour	34.9	41.6
Liberal Democrats	17.8	3.1
Others	5.4	3.7
Total	100	100

FIGURE 12.3 ■ **Distribution of Votes and Seats in Legislative Elections in the United Kingdom, 1992**

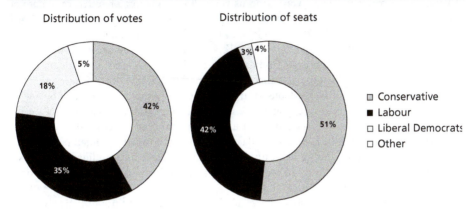

Democrats was not sufficient to produce victory in the St. Ives constituency, it was big enough to win seats in twenty other districts. This indicates that the extent to which the mechanical effect of the SMDP system punishes small parties is directly related to how geographically dispersed their electoral support is.

The Liberal Democratic Party in the United Kingdom has generally been penalized quite heavily by the UK's SMDP electoral system because its support tends to be broadly distributed across many electoral districts. In contrast, small regional parties, such as Plaid Cymru in Wales, the Scottish National Party in Scotland, and Sinn Féin and the Ulster Unionists in Northern Ireland, which garner a much smaller share of the national vote, have experienced very little disadvantage from the way in which the UK's SMDP system translates votes into seats. This is because the support for these parties is heavily concentrated in a small number of districts. In fact, in the 2015 legislative elections in the United Kingdom, the Scottish National Party won 8.6 percent of the legislative seats (56 of the 59 seats available in Scotland) even though it won only 4.7 percent of the national (England, Scotland, Wales, Northern Ireland) vote.

The Strategic Effect of Electoral Laws

As we've just seen, the mechanical way in which votes are translated into seats in nonproportional systems tends to penalize small parties and reward large parties. The benefits that majoritarian systems like SMDP bestow on large parties are further enhanced by a second institutional effect called the **strategic effect of electoral laws**. To this point, we've isolated the mechanical effect of electoral laws by taking the way votes are distributed as given. Now we must ask how voters and party elites are likely to respond to the mechanical effect of electoral systems. The strategic effect of electoral laws refers to how the way in which votes are translated into seats influences the "strategic" behavior of voters and elites. When electoral systems are disproportional, their mechanical effect can be expected to reward large parties and punish small parties. Recognizing that this is going to happen, voters in these systems have an incentive to engage in strategic voting, and political elites have an incentive to engage in strategic entry. Both of these actions—strategic voting and strategic entry—bestow even more benefits on large parties and further penalize small parties.

Strategic Voting

Strategic voting means voting for your most preferred candidate who has a realistic chance of winning. In contrast, sincere voting means voting for your most preferred candidate or party. To help refresh your mind about the logic of strategic voting in nonproportional electoral systems, such as SMDP, take a look again at the election results from the St. Ives constituency in the 1992 UK elections (Table 12.4). Imagine that you preferred the Labour candidate to the Liberal Democrat candidate and the Liberal Democrat candidate to the Conservative candidate. Imagine also that you had reliable polling data indicating that the Labour candidate was trailing the Conservative and Liberal Democrat candidates by a wide margin. If you cast a sincere vote, you'd vote for the Labour candidate. However, a sincere vote is likely to be "wasted" in the sense that it has little chance of affecting the outcome of the election given how far the Labour candidate trails behind the other candidates. As a result, you have an incentive to vote strategically for the Liberal Democrat candidate (who has a more realistic chance of winning) in order to try to stop the Conservative candidate (who is your least-preferred candidate) from winning.

As this example illustrates, supporters of small parties that have little realistic chance of winning seats due to the way that votes are translated into seats have an incentive to vote strategically. In other words, they have an incentive not to vote for their most preferred party—a small party—and, instead, give their support to one of the larger parties they like. This incentive to vote strategically increases as the electoral system becomes more disproportional. As a result, small parties are penalized in nonproportional systems not only because of the way that votes are translated into seats but also because voters in these systems have an incentive not to vote for them in the first place. Similarly, large parties benefit in nonproportional systems not only due to the electoral bonus they receive from the way votes are translated into seats but also because voters who prefer other parties often have an incentive to strategically vote for them.

Strategic Entry

Nonproportional electoral systems create similar incentives for political elites to engage in what is called **strategic entry**. Strategic entry refers to political elites' decisions about whether to enter the political scene under the label of their most preferred party or under the label of their most preferred party that has a realistic chance of winning. Imagine you're an aspiring political entrepreneur in Duvergerland who has an interest in environmental politics. If this is the case, you confront a dilemma. On the one hand, you could run as a candidate for the Green Party. The Green Party is your most preferred party because it shares your attitudes on environmental policy. The problem is that you won't get elected as a candidate for the Green Party given the use of an SMDP electoral system and the way that the party's support is distributed across Duvergerland. On the other hand, you could decide to run in the "lesser of two evils" from among those parties you estimate to have a realistic chance of winning seats. Furthermore, even if the party that reflects your policy preference (Green Party) is able to gain a few seats in the legislature, you must consider whether you can better further your policy agenda by representing that party or by working within a different party that actually stands a chance of commanding a legislative majority.

In contrast to political elites who compete under an SMDP electoral system, political entrepreneurs in proportional systems don't face such a stark trade-off. This is because even a small amount of electoral success in garnering votes can often allow one to win legislative seats. Indeed, if there are many parties in the legislature, leaders of small parties might even find themselves in the enviable position of being a kingmaker in the government formation process and a highly sought-after junior coalition partner. All of this suggests that small parties in SMDP systems will find it more difficult to attract and retain high-quality leaders than small parties in more proportional systems. For similar reasons, small parties in SMDP systems will also find it harder to attract private financial support. The lack of high-quality candidates and other resources in small parties that compete in SMDP systems will, in turn, make it harder for these parties to win votes.

Note that the example we've just presented assumes that the Green Party actually existed in Duvergerland. Now imagine you're the same political entrepreneur as before with a strong interest in environmental politics. The social transformation that's seen an increase in the number of voters holding post-materialist values has just taken place. You must decide whether to form a Green Party to represent this new constituency or try to represent it within one of the established parties. Given that a Green Party is unlikely to win any seats in Duvergerland, you'll have a strong incentive to work within one of the existing parties to achieve your political and policy goals. As this example illustrates, not only do disproportional electoral systems mean that small parties will receive a lower percentage of the vote because they're less likely to attract high-quality candidates and other resources, but they also mean that these small parties are less likely to exist in the first place.

Summarizing Duverger's Theory

To sum up, **Duverger's theory** states that the size of a country's party system depends on the complex interplay of both social and institutional forces. The precise causal story underlying Duverger's theory is illustrated in Figure 12.4. Characteristics of a country's social structure provide the driving force behind the formation of parties. When there are many cross-cutting cleavages, there are many distinct positions that, in some sense, need to be represented. Whether these distinct positions are ultimately translated into distinct parties, however, will depend on the proportionality of the electoral system.

Disproportional electoral systems translate votes into seats in such a way that small parties are penalized and large parties are rewarded. In other words, the "input-output" ratio by which votes are turned into seats in disproportional systems is smaller for small parties than it is for large parties. In contrast, proportional electoral systems translate votes into seats at a relatively constant rate. The way in which the mechanical effect of disproportional systems helps large parties and hurts small parties creates incentives for voters and political elites in these systems to engage in strategic voting and strategic entry. Supporters of small parties are more likely to see a vote for their most preferred party as a "wasted vote" in disproportional systems than in more proportional ones. Consequently, these voters are more likely to transfer their support to a larger party that is lower ranked in their preference ordering but that has a realistic chance of winning. Similarly, political entrepreneurs connected to policy positions that are not represented by existing parties or are associated with small parties have strong incentives to work within existing large parties if the electoral system is disproportional. As a result, disproportional electoral systems discourage the formation and electoral success of new parties in two related ways. First, the mechanical effect of these systems leaves small parties with fewer seats in the legislature than the votes cast for them would have produced in a PR system. Second, the strategic effect of these systems leaves small parties with fewer votes than the latent support for their policies in the electorate would suggest they could attract.

FIGURE 12.4 ■ Duverger's Theory: Social Cleavages and the Modifying Effect of Electoral Institutions

Social cleavages

Strategic effect of electoral laws

Electoral parties

Mechanical effect of electoral laws

Legislative parties

Duverger succinctly summed up the observational implications of his theory in two statements that have become known as **Duverger's law** and **Duverger's hypothesis**:

Duverger's law: Single-member district plurality systems encourage two-party systems.

Duverger's hypothesis: Proportional representation electoral rules favor multiparty systems.

Unfortunately, it turns out that the simple prediction that we should expect to find two-party systems when SMDP electoral laws are employed is a valid inference from Duverger's broader theory only when some auxiliary assumptions are satisfied. As Duverger himself noted, the logic by which the mechanical and strategic effects of SMDP electoral systems produce two-party systems works only at the district, and not the national, level. To see why, recall our example from the St. Ives constituency in the United Kingdom. If voters know that the Labour Party has no chance of winning in this district, then the benefits of strategic voting accrue to the Conservatives and the Liberal Democrats in this district. In other districts—indeed, in most districts in the UK—it's the Liberal Democrats who are the "also ran" party. As a result, it's the Conservative and Labour parties that benefit in most districts from the strategic voting induced by the mechanical effect of the SMDP electoral system.

As you can see, the logic of Duverger's argument leads us to expect a *national* two-party system in SMDP countries only to the extent that the same two parties are favored by strategic voting across the lion's share of the electoral districts. It's possible, for example, for some parties to be favored by SMDP in some regions of the country and other parties to receive an electoral boost from SMDP in other parts of the country. The net effect of these offsetting distortions may leave the country with different two-party systems at the district level and hence a multiparty system at the national level. In short, if the party system is not fully nationalized with the same parties advantaged in each district, SMDP electoral systems could very well have more than two parties nationally. These cautions, however, do little damage to Duverger's broader theory. This is because his theory is more concerned with how changes in social conditions or electoral laws result in changes in the number of parties, and there's considerable evidence consistent with his predictions in this area (Amorim Neto and Cox 1997; Clark and Golder 2006; Ordeshook and Shvetsova 1994).

Duverger used the metaphor of a car to explain why some countries have many parties and other countries have few. Social structure is the "engine" that drives the multiplication of parties, whereas electoral laws serve as the brake pedal. Disproportional electoral systems, such as SMDP, depress the brake pedal and therefore prevent the engine of social division from producing multiparty systems. Another metaphor that describes this process focuses on how social divisions create a storm of policy demands and how the electoral system determines if those demands will be permitted to flow downstream and be translated into distinctive parties. Just as a dam in a river moderates the flow of water, electoral laws moderate the way social divisions get turned into parties (see Figure 12.4). When the dam is closed, it prevents some of the water from flowing downstream; when the dam is open, it permits more of the water to flow downstream. SMDP electoral systems are like a closed dam that, for the reasons described above, prevents some societal demands from being transformed into political parties. Proportional electoral systems are like an open dam in that they permit more of these demands to be translated into parties. It's for this reason that political scientists frequently say that proportional electoral systems are permissive and disproportional ones are nonpermissive.

As we've seen, the effect of social structure on the size of a country's party system depends on the permissiveness of the electoral system. Similarly, the effect of the electoral system on party system size depends on a country's social structure. Consider the four different scenarios shown in Table 12.6. The case in which there are many social divisions—high social heterogeneity—and a permissive electoral system (top right) is like a river filled with storm water meeting an open dam. Because the dam is open, it has little effect on the current of the river, and most, if not all, of the water flows unimpeded downstream. In other words, social heterogeneity is expected to result in the formation of many parties when a PR electoral system permits it to. Contrast this with the case in which there are many social divisions and

TABLE 12.6 ■ The Interplay of Social Heterogeneity and Electoral System Permissiveness on Party System Size			
		Electoral system permissiveness	
		Low (SMDP)	High (PR)
Social heterogeneity	High	Few parties	Many parties
	Low	Few parties	Few parties

a nonpermissive electoral system (top left). This situation is like having a storm-filled river confront a closed dam—some of the water won't get to flow downriver and, instead, will form a reservoir on the upstream side of the dam. In other words, some of the societal demands in a socially heterogeneous country that employs a nonpermissive electoral system won't be translated into political parties.

Now consider the two cases in which there are few social divisions—social heterogeneity is low (bottom left and bottom right). This situation is equivalent to having a dry season that results in an almost entirely dry river. We can imagine that the river is so low that water can't reach the gates or valves in the dam. Clearly, little water will be getting downstream in this situation, irrespective of whether the dam is open or closed. In other words, when social heterogeneity is low, we don't expect much of a demand for political parties. As a result, few parties will be formed whether or not the electoral system is permissive.

A key implication of Duverger's theory, then, is that there are two reasons why a party system may have few parties. Some countries may have few parties, despite the fact that they are socially heterogeneous, because they have a nonpermissive electoral system that prevents this heterogeneity from being reflected in the party system. Alternatively, some countries may have few parties regardless of how permissive their electoral system is because they have few social divisions. In contrast, there's only one way, according to Duverger's theory, to end up with many parties—you need a heterogeneous society and a permissive electoral system.

CONCLUSION

Political scientists sometimes categorize democracies in terms of the type of party system they have. When they do this, they tend to focus on the number and size of the parties in a country. But what explains why some countries have many parties and others have few? As we've seen, party system size is shaped by the interaction between social heterogeneity and the permissiveness of electoral institutions. Social divisions provide the demand for distinctive representation and, hence, the driving force behind the multiplication of political parties. However, electoral laws modify the way that these social divisions are translated into parties that win votes (electoral parties) and parties that win seats (legislative parties). According to Duverger's theory, countries will only have a large multiparty system if they're characterized both by high levels of social heterogeneity and by permissive electoral systems.

When electoral systems are permissive (high district magnitude), social heterogeneity is translated into electoral and legislative parties with very little distortion. In contrast, nonpermissive (low district magnitude) electoral institutions are likely to produce party systems that are much smaller than the number of social cleavages in a country might lead us to imagine. In effect, nonpermissive electoral laws introduce a large amount of distortion in how social heterogeneity is translated into parties at the electoral and legislative levels. It's important to remember, though, that the precise amount of distortion that's introduced by nonpermissive electoral rules depends on the way that social heterogeneity is geographically distributed in a country. For example, if the supporters of small parties are distributed fairly evenly across electoral districts, we should expect nonpermissive electoral laws to produce legislatures with many fewer parties than social cleavages. If the supporters of small parties are geographically concentrated, however, the reductive effect that nonpermissive electoral rules exercise on the number of parties will be greatly curtailed.

Key Concepts

political party—a group of people that includes those who hold office and those who help get and keep them there

party identification—an attachment to a party that helps citizens locate themselves on the political landscape

whip—an individual whose job it is to ensure that members of a party attend legislative sessions and vote as the party leadership desires

nonpartisan system—a system with no official political parties

single-party system—a system in which only one political party is legally allowed to hold power

one-party dominant system—a system in which multiple parties may legally operate but in which only one particular party has a realistic chance of gaining power

two-party system—a system in which only two major political parties have a realistic chance of holding power

multiparty system—a system in which more than two parties have a realistic chance of holding power

effective number of parties—a measure that captures both the number and size of parties in a country

effective number of electoral parties—a measure of the number of parties that win votes

effective number of legislative parties—a measure of the number of parties that win seats

anticlericalism—opposition to religious institutional power and influence in public and political life

laïcité—the notion that there's a division between private life, where religion belongs, and public life, where it doesn't; it doesn't necessarily imply any hostility to religion

Michels's iron law of oligarchy—states that the leadership of organizations such as political parties will never be faithful to the program and constituency that gave rise to the organization in the first place

freezing hypothesis—states that Western European party systems became frozen following the extension of universal suffrage in most countries during the 1920s

cross-cutting cleavages—occur when a country's cleavage structure is uncorrelated

reinforcing cleavages—occur when a country's cleavage structure is correlated

mechanical effect of electoral laws—the impact of electoral laws on how votes are translated into seats; when electoral systems are disproportional, the mechanical effect punishes small parties and rewards large parties

strategic effect of electoral laws—the impact of electoral laws on the "strategic" behavior of voters and political elites

strategic entry—the decision by political elites about whether to enter the political scene under the label of their most preferred party or under the label of their most preferred party that has a realistic chance of winning

Duverger's theory—states that the size of a country's party system depends on both social and institutional factors; social divisions create the "demand" for political parties, and electoral institutions then determine the extent to which this demand is translated into parties that win votes (electoral parties) and parties that win seats (legislative parties)

Duverger's law—states that single-member district plurality systems encourage two-party systems

Duverger's hypothesis—states that proportional representation electoral rules favor multiparty systems

13

INSTITUTIONAL VETO PLAYERS

The accumulation of all powers, legislative, executive, and judiciary, in the same hands, whether of one, a few, or many, and whether hereditary, self appointed, or elective, may justly be pronounced the very definition of tyranny.

James Madison, *The Federalist Papers*, No. 47

It is very dangerous to allow the nation as a whole to decide on matters which concern only a small section, whether that section be geographical or industrial or defined in any other way. The best cure for this evil, so far as can be seen at present, lies in allowing self-government to every important group within a nation in all matters that affect that group much more than they affect the rest of the community.

Bertrand Russell, *Proposed Roads to Freedom*

[In government] the constant aim is to divide and arrange the several offices in such a manner as that each may be a check on the other; that the private interest of every individual may be a sentinel over the public rights.

James Madison, *The Federalist Papers*, No. 51

OVERVIEW

1. In this chapter, we examine the origins and consequences of federalism, bicameralism, and constitutionalism.

2. A federal state is one in which sovereignty is constitutionally split between at least two territorial levels so that independent governmental units at each level have final authority in at least one policy realm. It's important to distinguish between "federalism in structure" and "federalism in practice."

3. A bicameral state is one in which legislative deliberation occurs in two distinct assemblies. Although bicameral legislatures were originally designed to represent different social classes, they're now more closely associated with the representation of different territorial units.

4. Constitutionalism refers to the commitment of governments to be governed by a set of authoritative rules and principles laid out in a constitution. Constitutionalism is associated with a codified constitution, a bill of rights, and constitutional review.

5. Rather than view the world in terms of institutional dichotomies, comparative scholars are increasingly recognizing that institutions such as federalism, bicameralism, and constitutionalism are conceptually similar. All three of these institutions act as checks and balances, thereby influencing how easy it is to change the political status quo. This new approach to understanding political institutions is called veto player theory.

There are many different types of democracy in the world. Political scientists sometimes distinguish between democracies in terms of the type of government they have (Chapter 10), the type of electoral system they employ (Chapter 11), and the type of party system they have (Chapter 12). In this chapter, we focus on other institutional dimensions of democracy. Specifically, we examine federalism, bicameralism, and constitutionalism. All three of these institutions can be thought of as forms of checks and balances on the political system. In effect, they can all be conceptualized as "institutional veto players" that influence the ease with which the political status quo in a country can be changed. As such, their causes and consequences are closely related.

FEDERALISM

Political scientists sometimes distinguish between countries according to whether they're federal or unitary. When it comes to federalism, it can be useful to make a distinction between countries that are "federal in structure" and countries that are "federal in practice" (Bednar 2009). In what follows, we refer to federalism in structure as **federalism** and federalism in practice as decentralization.

Federalism: Federalism in Structure

We can determine whether a country is federal by looking at its constitution. A country is federal if it satisfies three criteria: (1) geopolitical division, (2) independence, and (3) direct governance (Bednar 2009, 18–19).

1. *Geopolitical division* requires that the country be divided into mutually exclusive regional governments that are recognized in the constitution and that can't be unilaterally abolished by the national government.

2. *Independence* requires that the regional and national governments must have independent bases of authority. This is typically ensured by having them elected independently of one another.

3. *Direct governance* requires that authority be shared between the regional governments and the national government such that each citizen is governed by at least two authorities. Each level of government must have the authority to act independently of the other in at least one policy realm, and this authority must be protected by the constitution.

According to these criteria a **federal country** is one in which sovereignty is constitutionally split between at least two territorial levels so that independent governmental units at each level have final authority in at least one policy realm. Countries that aren't federal are known as **unitary countries**.

Federalism is relatively rare in the world. Only about 10 percent of the world's independent countries are federal: Argentina, Australia, Austria, Belgium, Bosnia and Hercegovina, Brazil, Canada, Ethiopia, Germany, Malaysia, Mexico, Micronesia, Nigeria, Pakistan, Russia, South Africa, Switzerland, the United Arab Emirates, the United States, and Venezuela. Federal countries tend to be either large, like Australia, Brazil, Russia, and the United States, or relatively diverse, like Belgium, Ethiopia, Malaysia, and Switzerland.

Brazil is an example of a federal country. Brazil has a long history with federalism dating back to the 1891 constitution of the Old Republic (1889–1930). The existing federal arrangements date to the 1988 constitution, which was written following the reemergence of democracy from military dictatorship in 1985. Most federal countries have two different levels of territorial units. Brazil is unusual in that it has three—federal, state, and municipal. At the federal level, executive power is in the hands of the president. At the state level, there are twenty-six states based on historical borders that have developed over centuries and a "federal district" that comprises Brazil's capital, Brasília. As Map 13.1 illustrates, the federal district is in the state of Goiás. Executive power at the state level is in the hands of governors. At the municipal level, there are 5,570 different municipalities with their own legislative council; executive power is in the hands of mayors. The federal nature of Brazil's government is guaranteed in Article 1 of the constitution, which states that Brazil is formed by "the indissoluble union of the states and municipalities and of the federal district." Political authority is constitutionally shared among all three levels of government. In effect, state governments are allowed to pass legislation in any area that's not explicitly prohibited to them in the constitution (Article 25). Similarly, municipal governments are permitted to pass laws on any matter that doesn't contradict either the state or national constitutions (Article 30).

MAP 13.1   ■   Brazil's States and Federal District

There's a great deal of variation in the precise form that federalism takes in different countries (Lijphart 1999). Federalism can be congruent or incongruent. **Congruent federalism** exists when the territorial units of a federal country share a similar demographic (ethnic, cultural, linguistic, religious, and so on) makeup. In a perfectly congruent federal system, each of the territorial units would be a precise miniature reflection of the country as a whole. Examples of a congruent federal country include the United States and Brazil. In both countries, the demographic composition of the territorial units doesn't vary significantly along ethnic, linguistic, cultural, or religious lines. In contrast, **incongruent federalism** exists when the demographic makeup of the territorial units differs among the units and the country as a whole. Examples of an incongruent federal country include Switzerland and Belgium. In both countries, the territorial units differ from one another along linguistic lines.

One way to think about congruent and incongruent federalism is in regard to whether the political boundaries of the territorial units line up with the geographic boundaries of ethnic, linguistic, cultural, or religious groups in a country. In an incongruent federal system, political boundaries tend to align with the geographic boundaries of these social groups, whereas they tend to cut across them in congruent federal systems (Lijphart 1999, 196). One of the purported advantages of incongruent federalism is that it can transform highly diverse and heterogeneous countries that have geographically concentrated social groups into a federation of relatively homogeneous territorial units. As an example, consider Switzerland. Although Switzerland has four official language groups—German, French, Italian, and Romansch—the way that the territorial boundaries are drawn in the Swiss system of incongruent federalism means that twenty-two of the twenty-six cantons officially have only one language; three cantons—Bern, Fribourg, and Valais—are bilingual; and only one—Graubünden—is trilingual (McRae 1983, 172–179). In effect, Switzerland comprises a collection of homogeneous cantons within a relatively diverse country.

BOX 13.1 DEVOLUTION VERSUS FEDERALISM

Although only twenty countries satisfy all three criteria for federalism, several other countries such as Comoros, India, Italy, Spain, Tanzania, Ukraine, and the United Kingdom satisfy two of them (Bednar 2009). On the whole, the criterion that most of these unitary countries fail to meet is that of geopolitical division. Recall that this criterion requires that a country be divided into mutually exclusive regional governments that are constitutionally recognized and that can't be unilaterally abolished by the national government. Many of the aforementioned countries, like India, Spain, and the United Kingdom, have transferred a considerable amount of power from the central government to regional governments. In all of these countries, however, the central government retains the right to unilaterally recall or reshape the powers given to the regional governments. Ultimately, political power resides in the central government of these countries; regional governments don't have a constitutional right to any of their powers. This type of situation is known as **devolution**, not federalism.

Consider the case of India. India has many characteristics of a federal country. For example, it has two different levels of government—national and state. At present, twenty-nine states have their own local governments. There are also seven union territories, which differ from states in that they don't have their own local governments and are, instead, governed directly by the national government. Map 13.2 shows the states and union territories of India. Article 246 of the Indian constitution divides political author-ity between policy areas that are the exclusive concern of the national government (Union List) and policy areas that are the exclusive concern of the state governments. India clearly satisfies two of the criteria for a federal country: independence and direct governance. However, India is not a federal country because it fails to satisfy the criterion of geopolitical division.

Two articles in the Indian constitution are of particular relevance here. The first is Article 3, which states that the national legislature has the power to change the boundaries of individual states and to create new states by separating territories from existing ones. The newest Indian state was created in June 2014 when the Indian legislature voted to create Telangana by bifurcating the existing state of Andhra Pradesh. This action reversed a 1956 legislative decision that had merged Telangana with Pradesh to form Andhra Pradesh. The second is Article 356, which allows for the imposition of emergency presidential rule in a state that can't be governed "in accordance with the provisions of the Constitution." This article is commonly known as "President's Rule." Article 356 was originally designed to allow the central government to take control of a state in the event of civil unrest. There have been numerous criticisms, though, that its use has been politically motivated—Indian presidents have often invoked Article 356 to dissolve state governments ruled by political opponents. Despite sharing some of the features of a federal country, India remains a unitary country even though significant power has been devolved to the regions.

(Continued)

(Continued)

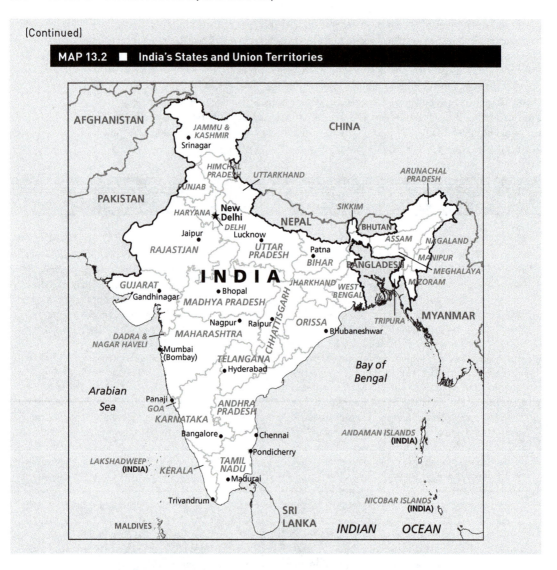

MAP 13.2 ■ India's States and Union Territories

Federalism can also be symmetric or asymmetric. **Symmetric federalism** exists when the territorial units of a federal country possess equal powers relative to the central government. This is the case in the United States—the Constitution gives each state equal standing and power vis-à-vis the central government. In contrast, **asymmetric federalism** exists when some territorial units of a federal state enjoy more extensive powers than others relative to the central government. On the whole, asymmetries in the division of power are designed to satisfy the different needs and demands that arise from ethnic, linguistic, demographic, or cultural differences between the separate subnational units. Examples of asymmetric federal countries include Belgium, Canada, Malaysia, Russia, and Switzerland.[1] In Canada, the

[1]Unitary states can devolve power in an asymmetric manner as well. For example, the Navarra and Basque communities have more extensive tax and spending powers than the other "autonomous communities" in Spain; Galicia and Catalonia enjoy special authority in the areas of education, language, and culture (Congleton 2006). In the United Kingdom the Scottish parliament enjoys more power, particularly in the area of taxation, than the Welsh senate.

French-speaking province of Quebec enjoys significantly more autonomy in relation to the central government than the other nine English-speaking provinces. In addition to having special powers to promote and protect its French-Canadian culture, Quebec has considerable authority over employment and immigration issues within its borders; it's also the only Canadian province to have its own pension plan.

Decentralization: Federalism in Practice

As we noted earlier, it's possible to make a conceptual distinction between federalism in structure (federalism) and federalism in practice (**decentralization**). Whether a country is federal or unitary is ultimately a constitutional issue. It depends on whether a country has certain structural characteristics written into its constitution. Whether a country is federal or unitary, though, says little about exactly *where* policy is made in practice. Knowing that a country is federal doesn't immediately imply that significant policymaking power is in the hands of regional governments. Similarly, knowing that a country is unitary doesn't necessarily mean that all policymaking power is in the hands of the national government. The degree to which actual policymaking power lies with the national or regional governments in both federal and unitary countries determines the extent to which political scientists view these states as centralized or decentralized.

Determining the extent to which a state is centralized or decentralized can be quite difficult. You might think that we need only look at what a country's constitution has to say about the division of power between different levels of government. This, however, can be problematic for several reasons. Consider unitary countries. In almost all unitary countries, policymaking authority constitutionally resides with the central government. Still, as indicated in Box 13.1, "Devolution versus Federalism," significant amounts of policymaking power can be devolved to regional governments in unitary countries. In other words, subnational governments can play an important policymaking role even when they derive no explicit authority to do so from the constitution.

Now consider federal countries. Oftentimes, the constitution of a federal country will delineate the specific policy realms in which the central or regional governments can act. Although this is somewhat informative, having the *authority to act* in a policy realm can be very different from having the practical *ability to act* in that area. Consider, for example, a country in which the regional governments have the authority to make health or education policy. Unless these regional governments also have the ability to raise their own tax revenue, they may find it difficult to actually implement policy in these areas. Put another way, regional governments in a federal country may have a much weaker role in the policymaking process than a reading of the country's constitution might suggest, because they don't have the financial wherewithal to implement their policy choices. The bottom line is that looking at a constitution, whether in a federal or unitary country, can be misleading if one wants to know the extent to which that country is centralized or decentralized in practice.

In recognition of these difficulties, political scientists frequently use the percentage of all tax revenue that's collected by the central government as a measure of state centralization. This is often referred to as "fiscal (de)centralization." The basic assumption underlying this measure is that governments need tax revenue to implement policies. Thus, the scope of policymaking activities at any one level of government will ultimately depend on the share of tax revenues it collects. The higher the share of all tax revenues collected by the central government, the more centralized the country. The lower the share of all tax revenues collected by the central government, the more decentralized the country. In sum, although political scientists tend to see federalism as a constitutional issue, they tend to see decentralization as a budgetary one.

In Figure 13.1, we illustrate the share of tax revenue collected by the central government out of the total tax revenue collected by all levels of government for fifty-three countries in 1997. As we might expect, the average degree of revenue centralization is lower in federal countries (74.6 percent) than in unitary ones (87.95 percent). In other words, federalism and decentralization tend to go together. There is, however, a substantial amount of variation in revenue centralization in both unitary and federal countries (Arzaghi and Henderson 2005). For example, some unitary countries (China, Denmark, Finland, India, Japan, Sweden) are more decentralized than the average federal country. Indeed, China, where the central government collects only 48.6 percent of the country's tax revenue, is the most decentralized state in the whole sample. Similarly, some federal countries (Belgium, Malaysia, South Africa) are much more centralized than the average unitary state. Fully 97.6 percent of the tax revenue collected in federal Malaysia is collected by the central government.

To summarize, federalism can be distinguished along two dimensions: federalism in structure (federal versus unitary) and federalism in practice (decentralized versus centralized). Whereas federalism in structure is a dichotomy—a country is either federal or unitary—decentralization is best thought of as a continuum, with some countries being more decentralized than others. In Figure 13.2, we simplify the world somewhat and show the names of various countries in a two-dimensional plot. Those countries in the top right quadrant, such

FIGURE 13.1 ■ Revenue Centralization: Central Government's Share of Tax Revenue

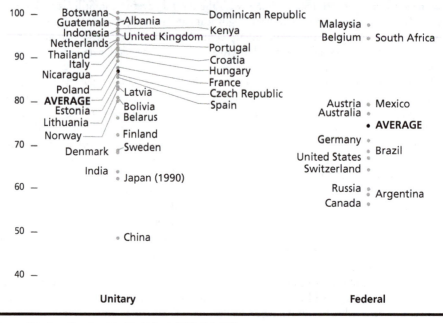

Source: Data from Yusuf and the World Bank (1999, 216–217).

Note: With the exception of Japan, all data points are for 1997; Japan's data point is for 1990. Tax revenue that's legally mandated to be transferred to regional governments through a revenue-sharing scheme is treated as belonging to the regional governments even if it's first collected by the central government. The names of some unitary countries have been omitted for visual clarity.

FIGURE 13.2 ■ Two Dimensions of Federalism

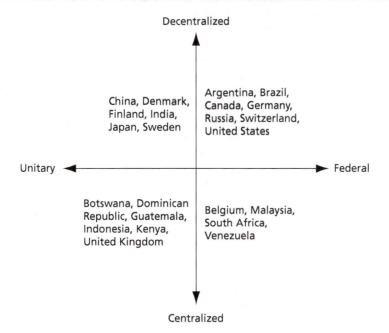

as Brazil, Canada, and Germany, are federal both in structure and in practice. Those countries in the bottom left quadrant, such as Botswana, the Dominican Republic, and Kenya, are unitary both in structure and in practice. Those countries in the top left quadrant, such as China, India, and Sweden, are unitary in structure but federal in practice. Finally, those countries in the bottom right quadrant, such as Belgium, Malaysia, and Venezuela, are federal in structure but unitary in practice.

Why Federalism?

Why do some states adopt federal arrangements?[2] Political scientists often distinguish between "coming-together" federalism and "holding-together" federalism (Stepan 1999, 21–22). **Coming-together federalism** results from a bottom-up bargaining process in which previously sovereign polities come together and voluntarily agree to pool their resources in order to improve their collective security and achieve other, typically economic, goals, such as a common currency and increased trade (Riker 1964). Australia, Switzerland, and the United States are examples of coming-together federalism. Although there's some variation, coming-together federations are typically characterized by a symmetric form of federalism.

In contrast, **holding-together federalism** is the result of a top-down process in which the central government of a polity chooses to decentralize its power to subnational governments. This process typically occurs in multiethnic states in which the central government fears that the continued existence of the country is threatened by one or more territorially-based

[2]In this section, we use the term *federalism* quite broadly to capture both dimensions of federalism—"federalism in structure" and "federalism in practice."

"ethnic" groups that wish to secede. In order to appease these secessionist groups and keep the country together, the central government decentralizes power to those subnational units in which the aggrieved ethnic group is dominant, thereby making the group more content to live within a unified state. For example, Belgium adopted federal arrangements in the 1990s to placate the demands of its different linguistic groups. Although they remain unitary states in their constitutional structure, India, Spain, and the United Kingdom are also examples of countries that have engaged in "holding-together federalism"—they've all devolved significant policymaking power to regional governments in an attempt to defuse secessionist pressures. In general, holding-together federations are characterized by both incongruent and asymmetric federalism. These federations are incongruent because their whole reason for existing is to decentralize power to territorially based ethnic groups; they tend to be asymmetric because they're trying to satisfy the different needs and preferences of the various ethnic groups in the country.

Over the years, supporters of federalism have sought to highlight its advantages over other forms of government. For example, some scholars have argued that decentralized forms of government are best for satisfying popular preferences in democratic countries in which individuals hold heterogeneous preferences (Alesina and Spolaore 1997; Buchanan and Tullock 1962; Tiebout 1956; Tullock 1969). It seems reasonable to expect that fewer citizens will be dissatisfied with public policy in a federal country than in a unitary one. Consider the following example. Suppose that sixty citizens in a unitary country prefer Policy A and forty citizens prefer Policy B. In this situation, Policy A will be adopted and forty citizens will be unhappy. Suppose now that we have a federal country with two regions. Imagine that fifty citizens prefer Policy A and ten prefer Policy B in the first region, whereas thirty citizens prefer Policy B and ten prefer Policy A in the second region. In this scenario, Policy A will be adopted in one region and Policy B will be adopted in another. Only twenty citizens will now be dissatisfied with government policy in our federal country. Obviously, if citizens are free to move from one region to another, even greater citizen satisfaction can be achieved—citizens can simply "sort" themselves by moving to the region that best satisfies their policy preferences. As this example suggests, government policy is more likely to match citizen preferences in a federal country than in a unitary one. This is particularly the case in large countries in which individuals hold diverse policy preferences.

Another purported advantage of federalism is that it brings the "government" closer to the people. Some have claimed that this leads to an increase in the amount of information available to both citizens and governments (Hayek [1939] 1948; Oates 1972). By being closer to the people, subnational governments in federal systems should have better information about exactly what it is that their citizens want. This means that they'll be able to tailor policies to the specific needs of their citizens. By being closer to the government, citizens in federal systems should have better information about exactly what it is that their government is doing. This means that they'll be better placed to hold their government accountable. As a result, federalism is often linked to increased government accountability and responsiveness to citizen preferences (Lijphart 1999). By bringing the government closer to the people, federalism is also thought to encourage political participation and enhance perceived levels of legitimacy in the democratic process.

It's commonly claimed that subnational governments in federal systems have a strong incentive to perform well in office if citizens and investors have the ability to move from one region to another. This is because poor performance is expected to cause citizens and investors to move to better performing regions, taking their tax dollars and other assets with them. This is sometimes referred to as "voting with one's feet" (Tiebout 1956) and is a prime example of the power that comes from having an exit option (see Chapters 3 and 5). The competition between subnational governments for investment and citizens engendered by federalism is often expected to result in smaller, more efficient, and less corrupt government (Buchanan 1995). This competition is also at the heart of arguments suggesting that federalism enhances market economies and produces higher economic growth (Weingast 1995).

Advocates of federalism also point to its ability to encourage policy experimentation and innovation. For example, subnational governments in federal systems have the opportunity to experiment with, and evaluate, different policies for tackling social, economic, and political problems. As US Supreme Court Justice Louis D. Brandeis put it in 1932, subnational governments in federal systems are "laboratories" for democracy and innovative government action. The ability to experiment with different policies is important because it means that policymakers can learn more quickly about which policies work and which ones don't. In effect, federalism allows subnational governments to quickly learn from the experimentation of others without putting the whole country at risk of a single failed policy.

Federalism has also been promoted as a bulwark against tyranny. Many of the Founding Fathers in the United States believed that the interlocking arrangements of federalism reduced the risk of tyranny because the subnational governments could, and would, check each other. As James Madison put it, "A rage for paper money, for an abolition of debts, for an equal division of property, or for any improper or wicked project, will be less likely to pervade the whole body of the Union than a particular member of it" (Madison, 1787–1788, *The Federalist Papers*, No. 10). Alexander Hamilton also believed that the interlocking nature of federalism protected individual rights against abuse by authorities at both the national and the subnational level (Hamilton 1787). Others have argued that federalism also has the ability to protect territorially based groups whose preferences diverge from those of the majority population from being subject to majority decisions that run counter to their preferences (Horowitz 1985). As such, federalism can be thought to minimize citizen coercion.

Although federalism has many supporters, several scholars have questioned its purported benefits (Rose-Ackerman 2000). Rather than leading to a more efficient form of government as proponents of federalism maintain, critics claim that the different layers of federalism can lead to the unnecessary duplication of government and the inefficient overlapping of potentially contradictory policies. Critics also argue that federalism exacerbates collective action problems in the formulation and implementation of economic and other policies, particularly in developing countries. For example, Rodden and Wibbels (2002, 500) argue that "[f]ederalism empowers regional politicians who face incentives to undermine macroeconomic management, market reforms, and other policies that have characteristics of national public goods. Self-interested regional elites do this either through autonomous policies made at the local level or through their [ability to block] the policy-making process at the center." Because provincial politicians ultimately care about their own political success, they face only weak incentives to make economic and other decisions in the interests of the federal system as a whole. For example, regional governments often block attempts at fiscal reform by the central government, particularly if these reforms are expected to be painful for their constituents. Regional governments also have incentives to spend beyond their means if there's an expectation the central government will come to their rescue and bail them out. Evidence in support of this line of reasoning comes from several scholars who've found that federal systems are more prone to economic mismanagement than unitary systems (Rodden 2002, 2006; Treisman 2000; Wibbels 2000).

Although supporters of federalism regularly point to the benefits that accrue from having competition between different subnational governments, critics point to the possible deleterious consequences that such competition can have. For example, in attempting to attract investment and retain their citizens, competition between subnational governments may lead to "downward harmonization" or a "race to the bottom" in which levels of regulation, welfare, taxes, and trade barriers are continuously lowered (Hallerberg 1996). One consequence of downward harmonization is that it becomes difficult to implement local redistributive tax systems because the wealthy simply move to those regions with the lowest tax rates. Another potential consequence is increased poverty, with the poor migrating to those regions that still maintain some form of welfare protection; these regions will, in turn, be forced to lower their welfare protection as a result of the added fiscal strain of dealing with the arrival of poor migrants from other regions.

Competition, particularly in asymmetric federations in which some regions enjoy more power and discretion than others, may also lead to the amplification of preexisting inequalities in population, wealth, and political power (Congleton 2006; Peterson 1995). If favored regional governments can take advantage of their additional authority to attract residents and enlarge their tax base, they'll likely prosper relative to other regional governments. The expectation of greater regional inequality is, in turn, likely to create conflict and political instability, with advantaged communities demanding increased autonomy and disadvantaged communities attempting to reverse asymmetries in the regional distribution of power.

Far from enhancing government accountability, as its supporters claim, critics argue that federalism is just as likely to undermine it. By adding layers of government and expanding areas of shared responsibility, federalism facilitates blame shifting and credit claiming (Rodden 2004, 494). This is because federalism can make it difficult for citizens to know which level of government is responsible for policy successes and which is to blame for policy failures. For example, if the regional economy performs poorly, is this the result of policies adopted by the subnational government or those implemented by the national government? In this type of situation, neither the subnational nor the national government will want to take responsibility for the poor economic performance and will likely try to blame the other. If federalism does lower government accountability, as critics maintain, it may actually increase, rather than reduce, levels of corruption (Rose-Ackerman 1978; Schleifer and Vishny 1993). Indeed, this is precisely what Treisman (2002) finds in a study examining the effect of decentralization on the quality of government. He concludes that countries with higher levels of decentralization have higher levels of corruption and lower levels of public goods provision.

BICAMERALISM

In addition to distinguishing between countries according to whether they're federal or unitary, political scientists sometimes distinguish them according to whether they have a unicameral or bicameral legislature.[3] Whereas a **unicameral legislature** is one in which legislative deliberation occurs in a single assembly, a **bicameral legislature** is one in which legislative deliberation occurs in two distinct assemblies (Tsebelis and Money 1997, 15). About forty percent of the countries in the world have a bicameral legislature (IPU 2016).

Having a second assembly can have a significant effect on a country's legislative process. This is fairly obvious when the upper chamber is powerful. In the United States, the House of Representatives and the Senate are equal partners in the legislative process. Both chambers have the power to veto bills proposed by the other chamber. The equal power of the two

---

[3]Much of the information in this section comes from Tsebelis and Money (1997) and Lijphart (1999).

chambers in the United States opens up a range of strategic possibilities that aren't always available to legislators in unicameral systems (Tsebelis and Money 1997). For example, US legislators in one chamber can often get away with voting for a politically popular but ideologically unpalatable bill if they know that the other chamber is going to reject it. It's much harder for legislators in a unicameral legislature to engage in this type of position taking or credit claiming.

Bicameral systems can also have a significant impact on the legislative process even when the upper chamber is relatively weak, as in the United Kingdom. Ever since the Parliament Acts of 1911 and 1949, the lower house in the United Kingdom, the House of Commons, has had the power to make legislative decisions. The only real power the upper house, the House of Lords, has in the legislative process is the ability to delay the passage of nonfinancial legislation for one calendar year. Although this power might seem relatively inconsequential, it can be very important in the year leading up to an election when delaying a bill may mean killing it. As Tsebelis and Money (1997, 2) point out, the ability to delay legislation in the year prior to an election has enabled the House of Lords to kill several pieces of significant legislation proposed by both Conservative and Labour governments.

Types of Bicameralism

There's a great deal of variation in the precise form that bicameralism takes in different countries. Bicameralism can be congruent or incongruent (Lijphart 1999). Congruence has to do with the political composition of the two legislative chambers. **Congruent bicameralism** occurs when the two chambers have a similar political composition, whereas **incongruent bicameralism** occurs when they have a different political composition. Whether bicameralism is congruent or incongruent depends on how the two chambers are elected and whom they're supposed to represent. If the same methods are used to elect the members of each legislative chamber and both chambers represent the same set of citizens, the political composition of each chamber will be congruent. When this is the case, the policy preferences of the two chambers will be identical or, at least, very similar.

When it comes to electing bicameral legislatures, it's almost always the case that members of the lower chamber are directly elected through systems in which all eligible voters are given equal weight. This isn't necessarily the case with members of the upper chamber, though. Members of the upper chamber usually owe their position to heredity, political appointment, indirect elections, or direct elections (Tsebelis and Money 1997). Historically, it was quite common for monarchs to grant seats in the upper chamber to members of the aristocracy, which would be passed down from generation to generation. Since the 1999 House of Lords Act in the United Kingdom, though, which significantly reduced the number of hereditary positions in the upper chamber, there are no longer any contemporary bicameral systems that use heredity as the predominant means for selecting members of the upper chamber.

Appointment is a common method for selecting members to an upper chamber. A whole host of countries such as Belize, Germany, Ireland, Jordan, Madagascar, Russia, and Thailand have fully or partially appointed upper chambers. Although a monarch appoints the members of the upper chamber in a few countries (Jordan, Malaysia, Thailand), it's much more common for an elected government to make these appointments. Germany is somewhat unusual in that the members of the upper chamber are appointed by regional governments. In almost every other case, it's the national government that appoints individuals to serve in the upper chamber. One of the rationales behind appointing, rather than electing, members of the upper chamber is that it facilitates the selection of individuals who have specific skills, knowledge, or experience that might be useful when debating particular pieces of legislation.

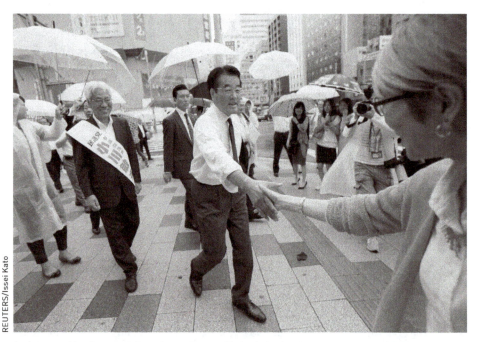

Japan's opposition Democratic Party leader Katsuya Okada shakes hands with a voter on the last day of campaigning for the July 2016 upper house election.

Like hereditary methods, though, appointing individuals to an upper chamber is often perceived as undemocratic. As a result, many countries allow their citizens to *indirectly* or *directly* elect the members of the upper chamber. Austria, France, India, Madagascar, Mauritania, and the Kingdom of eSwatini, for example, all employ indirect elections. In most of these countries, citizens directly elect the members of local or regional governments, and it's these local or regional representatives who elect the members of the upper chamber. Many more countries allow their citizens to directly elect individuals to the upper chamber. This is the case in countries such as Argentina, Australia, Bolivia, Brazil, Chile, Colombia, Japan, Malaysia, Mexico, Norway, Poland, Romania, the United States, and Venezuela.

Whether a bicameral legislature is congruent or not depends not only on whether the members of the two chambers are selected in the same way but also on whether they represent the same set of citizens. In almost all countries, the members of the lower legislative chamber are supposed to represent all citizens equally under the general principle of "one person, one vote." In a few countries such as Italy and Japan this is also the case for members of the upper chamber. In these countries, the political composition of the upper house tends to mimic that of the lower house. On the whole, though, this type of situation is quite rare. In the vast majority of bicameral systems, the upper chamber is not designed to represent the entire population equally. For example, the Irish Senate provides representation for certain professional occupations—most Irish senators are elected by five vocational panels representing culture and education, labor, industry and commerce, agriculture, and administration. In other countries, the upper chamber is supposed to ensure that minorities (Venezuela) or linguistic communities (Belgium) are represented.

By far the most common role for the upper chamber in a bicameral system is to represent the citizens of subnational geographic units. Although this is always the case in federal systems, such as Austria, Germany, Mexico, Switzerland, and the United States, it's also the case in some unitary countries, such as Bolivia, the Netherlands, and Spain. The fact that citizens aren't distributed equally across different subnational geographic units often leads to **malapportionment** in territorially-based upper chambers, with the result that some citizens receive significantly more representation than others (Monroe 1994; Samuels and Snyder 2001). This is easily seen in countries such as Australia, Switzerland, Venezuela, and the United States, where the different geographic units all receive the same level of representation irrespective of how many residents they have. For example, each of the fifty US states is represented by two senators. This means that California, with its 38 million residents, receives the same level of representation in the US Senate as Wyoming, with its approximately 0.6 million residents. Other countries, such as Canada and Germany, don't give equal representation to each of their subnational regions but still tend to overrepresent less populous regions and underrepresent more populous ones. Austria is unusual in that the allocation of upper chamber representatives to each subnational unit is roughly proportional to the size of each unit's population.

To get a better idea of the level of malapportionment found in upper chambers that are designed to represent subnational geographic units, consider Table 13.1. Here we illustrate the percentage of seats in the upper chamber going to the most favorably represented citizens in nine countries in 1996 (Lijphart 1999, 208). To see where these numbers come from, imagine that all of the subnational units in a country are lined up from left to right based on the size of their populations, with smaller units to the left and larger units to the right. Starting with the smallest unit and working our way to the right, we identify those units that together comprise 10 percent, 20 percent, 30 percent, and 50 percent of the country's overall population. We then determine the percentage of upper chamber seats that are allocated to these regions. These are the percentages shown in Table 13.1. As an example, consider the case of the United

TABLE 13.1 ■ Malapportionment in Upper Chambers, 1996				
	Seats held by the percentages of the most favorably represented citizens (percentages)			
	10	20	30	50
United States	39.7	55.0	67.7	83.8
Switzerland	38.4	53.2	64.7	80.6
Venezuela	31.6	47.2	60.0	77.5
Australia	28.7	47.8	58.7	74.0
Canada	33.4	46.3	55.6	71.3
Germany	24.0	41.7	54.3	72.6
India	15.4	26.9	37.4	56.8
Austria	11.9	22.5	32.8	52.9
Belgium	10.8	20.9	31.0	50.9

Source: Data from Lijphart (1999, 208).

States. Table 13.1 indicates that the smallest states that together comprise 10 percent of the national population control 39.7 percent of the seats in the US Senate. In other words, these states receive almost four times the amount of representation in the Senate as their population sizes would imply they should. The smallest states, which together constitute 20 percent of the overall US population, control 55 percent of the Senate seats—an overall majority. The other percentages in Table 13.1 can be interpreted in a similar way. As you can see, there's a great deal of variation in the level of malapportionment seen in upper chambers around the world. Countries like the United States and Switzerland exhibit very high levels of malapportionment, whereas countries like Austria and Belgium exhibit low levels.

Thus, the degree of congruence in a bicameral system depends on whether the two legislative chambers employ similar methods for selecting their members and on whether the two chambers represent the same set of citizens. On the whole, congruent bicameralism is relatively rare (Lijphart 1999).

In addition to being congruent or incongruent, bicameralism can also be symmetric or asymmetric. Symmetry relates to the relative power of the two legislative chambers. **Symmetric bicameralism** occurs when the two legislative chambers have equal or near equal constitutional power (Lijphart 1999, 206). Total symmetry exists when the agreement of both chambers is needed to enact a law. In practice, symmetric bicameralism is rare. Countries in which the upper chamber has formally equal powers with the lower chamber include Colombia, Italy, Switzerland, and the United States. Countries in which the two chambers enjoy similar, but not quite equal, power include Australia, Germany, Japan, and the Netherlands. **Asymmetric bicameralism** is more common and occurs when the two legislative chambers have unequal constitutional power. Total asymmetry exists when one chamber is granted ultimate decision-making power. In all cases of asymmetric bicameralism, it's the lower house that has more power. To a large extent, the degree of symmetry in the powers of the two chambers is related to how the members of the upper chamber are selected. Upper chambers are much more likely to have coequal power with the lower house when citizens play a direct role in electing upper chamber representatives (Mastias and Grangé 1987). This is likely due to the increased democratic legitimacy these upper chambers are perceived to have from being directly (or indirectly) elected as opposed to appointed.

To summarize, it's possible to distinguish bicameral systems based on their level of congruence and symmetry. In Figure 13.3, we simplify the world somewhat and plot the names of various countries along these two dimensions. Countries such as those in the upper right quadrant—Australia, Germany, Switzerland, and the United States—exhibit a strong form of bicameralism. In a strong bicameral system, the upper house is likely to be an important political actor because it enjoys similar constitutional powers to the lower house (symmetric) and because the different political composition of the upper chamber (incongruent) means that it has different policy preferences to the lower chamber. Countries such as those in the lower left quadrant—Austria, the Bahamas, and Jamaica—exhibit what might be thought of as an insignificant form of bicameralism. In an insignificant bicameral system, the upper chamber is unlikely to be an important political actor because its constitutional powers are extremely weak (asymmetric) and because its political composition tends to mirror that of the lower chamber (congruent).

Countries in the upper left and lower right quadrants exhibit a weak form of bicameralism. In weak bicameral systems, the upper chamber is likely to be a weak political actor. Although countries such as those in the upper left quadrant—Italy and Japan—have a powerful upper chamber (symmetric), the upper chamber is not expected to significantly affect the policymaking process given its political makeup, which is similar to that in the lower chamber

---

FIGURE 13.3 ■ Two Dimensions of Bicameralism

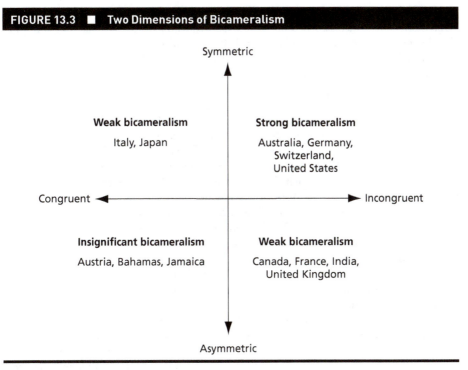

Source: Based on information in Lijphart (1999, 212).

(congruent). Similarly, although countries such as those in the lower right quadrant—Canada, France, India, and the United Kingdom—have an upper chamber that's likely to conflict with the lower chamber as a result of its differing political composition (incongruent), the upper chamber is not expected to play a significant role in the policymaking process because its constitutional powers are weak (asymmetric).

Why Bicameralism?

As Tsebelis and Money (1997, 17) explain, the origins of bicameralism can be traced back to ancient Greece. Rather than a "simple government" in which the interests of only one social class—the one (monarchy), the few (aristocracy), or the many (people)—would be represented, many Greek philosophers, such as Aristotle and Plato, preferred a "mixed government" that would represent all social classes. In practice, mixed governments in ancient Greece saw the aristocracy and the people represented in separate adviser-legislative councils. One of the purported benefits of a mixed government was that it would maintain a balance of power in which no single social class could gain control of the state for itself. By the eighteenth century, most people had come to see the Greek notion of mixed government as entailing a bicameral legislature in which the aristocracy would deliberate in one chamber and the common people in another. A class-based bicameral legislature, along with a monarch as the executive, was seen as an efficient system of checks and balances that helped ensure political stability.

At the end of the eighteenth century, the legitimacy of class-based bicameral legislatures was challenged by the rise of republicanism and the belief that the people should be represented as a whole rather than as a set of competing social classes. In this new environment, bicameralism increasingly came to be associated with federal states that used the upper chamber to guarantee the representation of their constituent territorial units. This new view of bicameralism was first seen in the United States where the "Great Compromise" of 1787 led to the creation of a House of Representatives that was elected on the basis of a state's population and a Senate that granted equal representation to each state. Essentially, the House of Representatives was to represent the popular dimension of the people's will, whereas the Senate was to represent its territorial dimension. This particular form of "incongruent bicameralism" was justified on the grounds that the different territorial units were likely to have distinct needs from the population as a whole. To fully protect the specific needs of the states and federalism as a whole, the Founding Fathers in the United States promoted a symmetric form of bicameralism in which the agreement of both legislative chambers was needed to change the status quo. The distinct interests of constituent territorial units eventually came to replace the differing interests of social classes as the justification for powerful upper chambers (Tsebelis and Money 1997). It's perhaps no surprise then that all of the examples of "strong"—symmetric and incongruent—bicameral systems illustrated in Figure 13.3 are in federal countries.

Strong bicameral systems like the ones that emerged in the United States and Switzerland were harder to justify in unitary countries with no constituent territorial units to represent. Some unitary countries with bicameral systems chose to reduce the power of their upper chambers. For example, the 1911 and 1949 Parliament Acts in the United Kingdom asserted the legislative supremacy of the House of Commons and limited the maximum amount of time the House of Lords could delay legislation to one year. Why keep these weak upper chambers in unitary states rather than just get rid of them? One argument is that members of the upper chamber have characteristics of value—such as wisdom, age, and training—that are often absent among members of the popularly elected lower chamber. Another argument is that the upper chamber's ability to delay legislation can help prevent the production of "bad" laws that are made in haste. In effect, the argument for keeping weak upper chambers in unitary countries rests on the belief that they improve the overall quality of legislation. This line of reasoning obviously requires that the political composition of the upper chamber be different from that of the lower chamber. In many countries, bicameral incongruence is achieved by having an appointed upper chamber in which members are selected on the basis of some special skill, expertise, or experience. This might involve appointing, say, teachers, engineers, scientists, businesspeople, farmers, or religious leaders. An implicit assumption is that individuals such as these may not be elected in sufficient numbers or on a regular enough basis in the popular elections to the lower chamber and must therefore be appointed to the upper chamber.

Whereas some unitary countries, like the United Kingdom, responded to the spread of democratic values by establishing asymmetric, but still incongruent, forms of bicameralism, a few, like Denmark and Sweden, responded by trying to "democratize" the selection procedures used in the upper chamber. This typically involved adopting a similar selection procedure for the upper chamber to the one employed in the popularly elected lower chamber. The result, as one would expect, was that the political composition of the upper chamber in these countries came to increasingly mirror that of the lower chamber. In many places, this congruence between the upper and lower chambers raised questions as to the actual utility of having an upper chamber. As Tsebelis and Money (1997, 35) point out, the general thrust of these questions is best summed up in the famous words of the seventeenth-century philosopher Abbé Sieyès: "If the second chamber agrees with the first, it's useless, and if not, it's bad."

Like several other countries that initially decided to establish congruent upper chambers, Denmark (in 1953) and Sweden (in 1959) eventually resolved the debate over the utility of the upper chamber by abolishing it and establishing a unicameral legislature.

Contemporary debates over bicameralism largely mirror those that have driven the evolution and justification of bicameral systems in the past. In effect, there are two basic arguments in favor of bicameralism. In federal countries, bicameralism is primarily defended as an institutional means for protecting the federal system and promoting the distinct preferences of different territorial units. In unitary countries, bicameralism is primarily defended as an institutional means for improving the quality of legislation.

CONSTITUTIONALISM

Political scientists also distinguish between countries based on the extent to which they accept **constitutionalism**. Constitutionalism refers to a commitment to be governed by a set of overarching rules and principles laid out in a constitution (Stone Sweet 2000, 20). A central part of any commitment to constitutionalism is the establishment of a set of institutions and procedures to protect constitutional rules and principles. These institutions and procedures are known as **systems of constitutional justice** (Stone Sweet 2008). Historically, few countries have had any system of constitutional justice. Until recently, most countries have followed a norm of legislative supremacy. According to this norm, the laws created by the people's elected representatives in the legislature should not be constrained by other authorities, including the constitution. Looking around the world today, though, we see that the norm of legislative supremacy has been replaced by what Shapiro and Stone Sweet (1994) call a "new constitutionalism." This new constitutionalism describes a situation in which virtually all countries now have constitutions containing a charter of human rights that's protected by institutions such as constitutional courts. These institutions can use the power of constitutional review to invalidate legislation that's deemed to violate individual rights and can thereby constrain legislative authority.

Although there's been a general shift toward this new constitutionalism since 1945, there's considerable variation in the extent to which countries have delegated constitutional control over their actions to judges. In this section we briefly describe the historical shift from a norm of legislative supremacy to a situation in which most states now agree to live within the constraints imposed by a constitution. This shift toward a new constitutionalism has increasingly involved judges in the legislative process, leading some to worry about "activist judges" and a possible "government of judges." Following this, we outline some of the distinctive features of the different systems of constitutional justice that have been adopted around the world. As we'll see, there are two basic systems of constitutional justice—the American model and the European model.

The Shift to a New Constitutionalism

A **constitution** provides the formal source of state authority. For example, a constitution establishes governmental institutions, such as legislatures, executives, and courts, and then gives these institutions the power to make, enforce, and interpret laws. Recent constitutions, such as those adopted in the last seventy years or so, also tend to contain a list of guaranteed rights that are protected by some kind of constitutional body. This list of rights, and the constitutional body protecting them, places substantive constraints on what governments can and can't do.

Almost all current constitutions are **codified constitutions** in that they are written in a single document. An **uncodified constitution** is one that has several sources, which may be written or unwritten. Only three countries—Israel, New Zealand, and the United Kingdom—have uncodified constitutions. Some of the United Kingdom's uncodified constitution is written and some of it is not. The written part includes constitutional statutes passed by the legislature, such as the 1998 Scotland Act and the 1998 Human Rights Act, whereas the unwritten part includes things like constitutional conventions, royal prerogatives, customs and traditions, and observations of precedent.

In addition to whether constitutions are codified or not, constitutions also differ in regard to whether they're entrenched or not. An **entrenched constitution** can be modified only through a procedure of constitutional amendment. Constitutional amendments require more than the approval of a legislative majority. Exactly what's required to pass a constitutional amendment varies from country to country. In federal systems, for example, it's often the case that constitutional amendments require the support of a majority of the regional legislatures. Some countries require a popular referendum. Australia and Switzerland both require that a successful amendment win not only a majority of votes nationwide in a popular referendum but also a majority of the votes in every state or canton. Other countries require legislative supermajorities. Successful amendments in Japan must obtain a two-thirds supermajority in both legislative chambers and a majority in a popular referendum. By requiring a special constitutional amendment procedure to be modified, entrenched constitutions recognize that constitutional law has a higher legal status than ordinary statute law. **Unentrenched constitutions** have no special amendment procedures—they can be modified at any point in time by a simple legislative majority just like any other law. As a result, it makes no sense to talk of constitutional amendments in countries like the United Kingdom that have unentrenched constitutions. By their very nature, unentrenched constitutions don't recognize that constitutions have a higher or different legal status from ordinary statutes. Almost all contemporary constitutions are entrenched.

Historically, we can identify two ideal types of constitutions: the **legislative supremacy constitution** and the **higher law constitution**.

Legislative Supremacy Constitution

The core principle behind legislative supremacy constitutions is that "elections legitimize legislative authority, and legislative majorities legitimize statutory authority" (Stone Sweet 2000, 20). According to legislative supremacy constitutions, legislatures can do no legal wrong as they derive their legitimacy from being elected by the people. Legislative supremacy constitutions have three basic features. One is that they're not entrenched and can be revised at the discretion of the legislature. Legislative supremacy constitutions have no special legal status and are the same as ordinary laws in that they can be modified or replaced without recourse to special amendment procedures. The second distinctive feature is that there's no institution with the power to review the constitutional legality of statutes. The authority to make law resides only with the legislature. As a result, statutes can't be challenged once they're promulgated, and they can be replaced or modified only if the legislature passes a new statute. Any perceived conflict between a statute and some constitutional rule or principle must be resolved in favor of the statute. The third distinctive feature of legislative supremacy constitutions is that they don't contain a bill of rights that might constrain legislative authority. The rights that are protected in countries with legislative supremacy constitutions have their source in the ordinary statutes passed by the legislature, not in the constitution. The constitutions of the United Kingdom and New Zealand are examples of legislative supremacy constitutions.

TABLE 13.2 ■ Legislative Supremacy Constitution versus Higher Law Constitution		
Characteristic	**Legislative supremacy**	**Higher law**
Entrenched	No	Yes
Constitutional review	No	Yes
Bill of rights	No	Yes

Higher Law Constitution

According to higher law constitutions, the state *can* do legal wrong and must therefore be constrained in what it can and can't do. The notion of legislative supremacy is rejected. Higher law constitutions typically contain a bill of rights that allows nonstate actors to challenge state actions that violate individual and minority rights. They also establish a mechanism—**constitutional review**—for defending the supremacy of the constitution and the rights it contains. Constitutional review is the authority of an institution to invalidate acts of government, such as legislation, administrative decisions, and judicial rulings that violate constitutional rules (Stone Sweet 2000, 21). Constitutional review can be exercised by judges sitting on special tribunals—constitutional courts—that aren't part of the regular judicial system, as in most European countries, or by ordinary judges in the regular judicial system, as in the United States. When constitutional review is conducted by ordinary judges from the regular judicial system, it's more commonly referred to as **judicial review**. By allowing constitutional review, higher law constitutions signal that constitutional laws are superior to "ordinary" laws passed by the legislature. In recognition of the special status of constitutional law, higher law constitutions are entrenched and stipulate special amendment procedures for modifying constitutional provisions. The differences between legislative supremacy constitutions and higher law constitutions are summarized in Table 13.2.

The New Constitutionalism

Legislative supremacy constitutions were historically quite common but are relatively rare now. Virtually all new constitutions—both democratic and authoritarian—are higher law constitutions that establish constitutional review and include an extensive list of political and social rights. For example, all 106 constitutions that were adopted between 1985 and 2007 contained a bill of rights, and only 5—Iraq (1990), Laos, North Korea, Saudi Arabia, and Vietnam—failed to establish provisions for constitutional review (Stone Sweet 2008, 233–234). As we noted earlier, this convergence around the idea that higher law constitutions are somehow better than legislative supremacy constitutions has been called the **new constitutionalism** (Shapiro and Stone Sweet 1994). But why did this shift to the new constitutionalism happen?

The shift toward this new constitutionalism began in Europe after 1945 with the creation of constitutional courts in Austria (1945), Italy (1948), and West Germany (1949). The adoption of higher law constitutions in these countries was partly a response to the experience with fascism in the interwar period (Stone Sweet 2000, 37). The experience of fascist governments in Italy and Germany illustrated that states could do considerable wrong and that individuals sometimes needed protection from the state. In effect, Europe's experience with fascism undermined much of Europe's faith in a powerful and unconstrained state and highlighted the need to protect individual and minority rights. To a large extent, the subsequent adoption of higher law constitutions in other countries has coincided with democratic transitions. For example, both Portugal (1976) and Spain (1978) adopted constitutional courts following their democratic transitions in the 1970s. Central and eastern European countries, such as the Czech Republic, Hungary, Poland, Romania, Russia, Slovakia, the Baltic states, and the states of the former Yugoslavia, adopted constitutional courts following the collapse of Communist rule in 1989 (Ludwikowski 1996; Schwartz 1999). The strengthening of constitutional courts in Latin America and Asia during the 1980s and 1990s has also been seen as part of a concerted effort to consolidate democracy in these regions of the world (Ginsburg 2003; Helmke 2002; Navia and Ríos-Figueroa 2005). In all of these cases, the adoption of higher law constitutions can be viewed as an attempt to prevent a repetition of the individual abuses inflicted by the state in the recent past (see Box 13.2, "Judicial Power and the Judicialization of Politics," for a discussion of judicial power).

Different Systems of Constitutional Justice

There's a great deal of variation in the precise form that systems of constitutional justice take in different countries (Epstein, Knight, and Shvetsova 2001; Murphy, Pritchett, and Epstein 2001). This is certainly true with respect to constitutional review. Constitutional review, for example, can be abstract or concrete. Abstract review involves the constitutional review of legislation in the absence of a concrete legal case. In contrast, concrete review involves the constitutional review of legislation with respect to a specific case before the court. These two types of constitutional review are not mutually exclusive in that countries can allow both types of review. Constitutional review can also vary in terms of where it takes place. Centralized constitutional review refers to a situation in which only one court is responsible for conducting constitutional review. This single court, called a constitutional court, exists entirely outside of the normal judicial system. It considers only constitutional disputes and doesn't get involved in normal litigation. As such, we might want to think of it more as a special tribunal than a court. Decentralized constitutional review refers to a situation in which more than one court can interpret the constitution and declare laws, decrees, and administrative decisions to be unconstitutional. These courts and the judges that sit on them are part of the regular judicial system. The highest court in a decentralized jurisdiction system, typically called a Supreme Court, has general jurisdiction in that it can settle all legal disputes and not just constitutional ones.

When it comes to classifying systems of constitutional justice, most political scientists focus on the distinction between centralized and decentralized systems. They refer to decentralized systems as the American model of constitutional justice and to centralized systems as the European model of constitutional justice.

The American Model

In the United States, "any judge of any court, in any case, at any time, at the behest of any litigating party, has the power to declare a law unconstitutional" (Shapiro and Stone Sweet 1994, 400). As this quotation makes clear, constitutional review in the United States is decentralized and carried out by ordinary judges in the regular judicial system. Constitutional review in the United States is, as a result, judicial review. The American separation-of-powers system, in which the executive, legislature, and judiciary are separate but equal branches of government, attempts to mark a clear distinction between what we can think of as the "judicial function"—resolving legal cases—and the "political function"—legislating. American courts are supposed to avoid legislating as that's the function of the people's elected

BOX 13.2 JUDICIAL POWER AND THE JUDICIALIZATION OF POLITICS

The spread of constitutional review around the world has raised fears about the possible judicialization of politics. This raises the question of exactly how powerful courts really are in practice. Here we outline what we mean by judicial power and examine the conditions under which courts can effectively influence policy outcomes.

Traditionally, there have been two main approaches to understanding judicial power. One approach looks at the formal powers given to courts. Under this notion of judicial power, a court is powerful whenever it's granted significant legal authority. One obvious problem with this approach is that it doesn't take into account whether courts use their legal authority or whether their decisions are actually implemented. As several political scientists have pointed out, there's ample empirical evidence of courts that appear to be powerful on paper being ignored (Staton 2004). For example, local governments in the United States and Germany have refused to implement various constitutional decisions relating to equal protection and religious establishment (Rosenberg 1991; Vanberg 2005). There's also plenty of evidence to suggest that courts strategically try to avoid conflict by not making decisions they know will be opposed by the other branches of government (Clinton 1994; Epstein and Knight 1998a; Volcansek 1991).

The problem with simply looking at judicial power in terms of the jurisdiction that courts are granted on paper has led most political scientists to focus on the de facto power of courts. In other words, they focus on whether courts have the power to change policy outcomes in practice, not in theory. In this sense, judicial power is defined as the ability of courts to bring about policy outcomes they prefer (Cameron 2002). This definition, along with empirical evidence that courts act strategically, implies that courts aren't always the impartial interpreters of laws that legal scholars and judges frequently claim

them to be. Just like other political actors, judges have their own policy preferences that influence how they make legal decisions.

Judges are constrained in their ability to make legal decisions in line with their own preferences. The central difficulty all courts face is that they're inherently weak institutions that must rely on others to implement and enforce their decisions. This "implementation problem" can be particularly constraining when courts are required to make decisions against the very actors on whom they rely to implement their decisions (Vanberg 2001). It's the existence of this implementation problem that drives the strategic behavior of courts. Given their inability to independently enforce their decisions, it's not surprising that judges sometimes rule that constitutionally suspect policies are constitutional in order to avoid conflict with elected officials (Carrubba 2005; Epstein and Knight 1998b; Helmke 2005; Rogers 2001).

The fundamental insight from the "implementation problem" and strategic models of judicial politics would seem to be that judicial power is inherently constrained. However, we do sometimes see courts acting powerfully. What explains this? Two conditions must be met for courts to exert judicial power (Vanberg 2001, 2005). The first condition is that courts must enjoy public support. If courts enjoy public support and, hence, high levels of legitimacy, elected officials can expect to suffer a negative electoral backlash if they don't comply with court decisions (Gibson and Caldeira 1992; Gibson, Caldeira, and Baird 1998). The fear of such a backlash creates a powerful incentive for legislative majorities to respect judicial decisions (Vanberg 2000). Of course, this "electoral connection" mechanism works only if voters know about court decisions and can identify noncompliance by elected officials. Thus, the second condition needed for a court to exert judicial power is that voters are able to monitor legislative responses to judicial rulings. At a

(Continued)

[Continued]

minimum, this requires that court decisions be transparent and available to the public. Without this information, voters can't hold elected representatives accountable for noncompliance.

These conditions for exercising judicial power create strong incentives for courts to act strategically when publicizing their decisions (Staton 2006, 2010). Courts can expect to gain public support and legitimacy by publicizing their work if their decisions show them to be impartial interpreters of the constitution. We've already seen, however, that judges sometimes act politically and seek to impose their own personal preferences on the legislative process. It's likely that publicizing these types of decisions won't increase public support for the judicial system. As a result, courts will have a strong incentive to publicize only some of their decisions—the impartial-looking ones.

That constitutional judges regularly engage in public relations exercises suggests that they're well aware of the role that public support plays in their ability to assert judicial power. For example, virtually all constitutional courts throughout the world maintain a website on which they provide information on pending and completed cases, descriptions of their jurisdiction, and biographical summaries of their membership. Constitutional judges also give university lectures and media interviews to publicize their decisions and explain their legal reasoning (Staton 2010). Although this type of behavior is to be expected of legislative representatives, who can be held electorally accountable, it's sometimes seen as puzzling as to why unelected and unaccountable constitutional judges would engage in these types of public relations activities. This kind of behavior becomes understandable, though, once we recognize that public support is necessary for courts to exert judicial power.

representatives in the legislature. Still, it's recognized that a constitutional issue in need of resolution might arise in the course of a legal case. It's for this reason that ordinary judges in the United States have the right to conduct concrete constitutional review—they need it to do their prescribed job. Courts in the American model are prohibited, though, from engaging in abstract review or giving advisory opinions on the constitutionality of legislative bills because this isn't part of their job and would be usurping the rightful role of the legislature.

The European Model

The judiciary has traditionally been seen as subordinate to the legislature in Europe. In other words, the judiciary has never been seen as a coequal branch of the government as it is in the United States. Indeed, judicial review has been explicitly prohibited in French and German constitutions since the end of the eighteenth century. This view of the judiciary helps to explain why American-style judicial review has faced so much hostility in much of Europe. From a European perspective, "American-style judicial review, rather than corresponding to a separation of powers, actually establishes a permanent confusion of powers, because it enables the judiciary to participate in the legislative function" (Stone Sweet 2000, 33). To avoid judicial review and a "government of judges" that might ensue, Europeans invented a completely new institution, the constitutional court, to conduct constitutional review.

Constitutional courts have several defining characteristics. First, they have a monopoly on conducting constitutional review. Ordinary courts can't engage in constitutional review and can't appeal any of the decisions made by a constitutional court. Second, constitutional courts are formally detached from the regular judicial system. A constitutional court is, therefore, not a "judicial" institution. These two defining characteristics mean that judicial review remains prohibited in the European model. Third, constitutional courts have jurisdiction

TABLE 13.3 ■ The Geographic Distribution of Different Models of Constitutional Justice, 2010					
Region	American model	European model	Mixed	Other	None
Europe	5	33	3	1	2
Africa	13	28	1	7	2
Middle East	2	5	0	3	0
Asia and Southeast Asia	19	15	2	10	0
North America	2	0	0	0	0
Central America and South America	13	8	8	1	0
Total	54	89	14	22	4

Source: Data from Dr. Arne Mavčič and are available at http://www.concourts.net.

Note: "Mixed" means some combination of the American and European models; "Other" means that the system of constitutional justice is unique or unclassifiable; "None" means that there are no mechanisms for constitutional review. Systems based on France are coded as European.

only over constitutional matters. They can't oversee judicial disputes or litigation as, say, the US Supreme Court can. Fourth, most constitutional courts can engage in abstract constitutional review. In other words, they can evaluate legislative initiatives to see if they're unconstitutional before they actually have the opportunity to harm anyone. Indeed, this is the only type of constitutional review allowed in France. Many constitutional courts can also exercise concrete constitutional review.

Table 13.3 illustrates the geographic distribution of the American and European models of constitutional justice around the world as of 2010. The European model of constitutional justice is more popular than the American one, although there are clear regional differences. For example, the American model is predominant in Asia, North America, and Central and South America, whereas the European model is predominant everywhere else.

VETO PLAYERS

Political scientists sometimes distinguish between democracies by whether they're federal or unitary, bicameral or unicameral, and whether they accept constitutionalism or not. These political scientists see the world in terms of different institutional dichotomies. Recently, though, comparative scholars have begun to move away from this position and to recognize that these institutions are conceptually similar in that they all act as checks and balances on the political system. Put differently, they all affect the ease with which the political status quo in a country can be changed. This new approach to understanding political institutions is called **veto player theory** (Tsebelis 1995, 1999, 2002).

Veto player theory argues that important characteristics of any country's institutional structure are determined by its configuration of veto players. A **veto player** is an individual (such as a president) or collective actor (such as a legislative chamber) whose agreement is necessary for a change of the political status quo.[4] In any given country, there are two types of veto player. First, there are **institutional veto players**. Institutional veto players are those generated by a country's constitution. For example, the US Constitution identifies actors like the president, the Congress, and the Senate as institutional veto players because it gives these actors the right to block legislative changes to the status quo. Second, there are **partisan veto players**. Partisan veto players are those generated by the political game. In other words, partisan veto players aren't specified in a constitution but are determined by the way political competition plays out in a given country. For example, particular parties in a legislature or a coalition government might be considered partisan veto players if they're in a position to block changes to the status quo. Such parties are veto players not because they've been identified as such in some document but rather because of the way that citizens vote, how votes are translated into seats, how governments form, and so on. Whereas the identity of institutional veto players is essentially fixed across time as long as the constitution remains the same, the identity of partisan veto players changes with the vagaries of political competition.

Rather than see federalism, bicameralism, and constitutional review as entirely different institutions that need to be studied separately, veto player theory suggests we might constructively view them as just different types of the same thing—that is, as different types of institutional veto players.[5] All three institutions place hurdles on the ability of political actors to change the status quo. For example, a legislative majority in the lower chamber may require the support of a powerful upper chamber to change some policy status quo. This is the case in the United States, where the agreement of both legislative chambers is required to pass legislation. Courts are not veto players when they interpret ordinary statutes, because their decisions can be overridden by subsequent legislation. They are veto players, however, when they engage in constitutional review (Tsebelis 2002, 226). The French Constitutional Council has the ability to invalidate laws on constitutional grounds before they're applied. This suggests that, in many ways, we can think of constitutional courts like the French Constitutional Council as a third legislative chamber (Stone Sweet 1992). Similarly, the support of a subnational government in a federal system may be necessary for political actors to change the status quo. This is particularly the case for those policy areas that are constitutionally delegated to subnational governments. In this framework, then, adopting federalism, bicameralism, or constitutional review can be thought of as equivalent to increasing the number of institutional veto players in a country.

Veto player theory shows that the number of veto players in a country, as well as the ideological distance between them, has important consequences for policy stability. Remember that a veto player is an actor whose agreement is necessary to change the political status quo. As you can imagine, the more veto players there are in a country (the more actors who can

---

[4]Veto player theory isn't restricted to democracies. In dictatorships, veto players might include the military or particular religious leaders and so on. The key to applying veto player theory in any given setting involves identifying which actors are in a position to block changes to the political status quo. This will vary across countries, across time, and potentially across policy areas.

[5]In previous chapters, we looked at whether countries have single-party or coalition governments and whether they have two-party or multiparty systems. Just as federalism, bicameralism, and constitutional review can be reconceptualized in terms of institutional veto players, the type of government and the size of the party system in a country can be reconceptualized in terms of partisan veto players. If we do this, we can think of countries with coalition governments as having more partisan veto players than countries with single-party majority governments.

say "no" to a new policy), the harder it is to reach an agreement on a new policy to replace the status quo policy. It becomes particularly difficult to reach an agreement on a new policy if the veto players share very different preferences over what the new policy should be. In effect, policy stability will increase with both the number of veto players in a country as well as their ideological divergence. The core result in veto player theory, therefore, is that countries in which there are many veto players with conflicting policy preferences will be characterized by high levels of policy stability. When policy change does happen to occur in these countries, the change from the status quo will be relatively small. Proposals to radically transform the political status quo are unlikely to be successful as they're likely to run afoul of at least one of the veto players. Given that only small policy changes from the status quo are possible in these countries, it doesn't really matter who gets to make policy proposals. In other words, the power of any agenda setter is limited when there are many veto players with conflicting policy preferences. In contrast, countries in which there are few veto players and in which those veto players hold similar policy preferences will be characterized by less policy stability, larger shifts in policy, and stronger agenda-setting powers.

As we noted earlier, federalism, bicameralism, and constitutional review are all institutions that can be reconceptualized as institutional veto players. In regards to policy outcomes, this means we can expect countries with these types of institutions to be characterized by high policy stability, small policy shifts, and weak-agenda setting powers. These characteristics are likely to be particularly prevalent if the institutional veto players have dissimilar policy preferences. For example, we'd expect policy output to be lower and less radical during periods of divided government or cohabitation (Binder 1999, 2003; Erikson, MacKuen, and Stimson 2002; Mayhew 1991) and when coalition governments are ideologically diverse (Tsebelis 2002, 173). We'd also expect greater policy stability when the two legislative chambers in a bicameral system or the central and subnational governments in a federal system are controlled by different political parties.

Consider the United States. Many on the left of the political spectrum were disappointed with the legislative achievements of President Barack Obama after he came to power in January 2009. Obama had run on a platform of "hope" and "change," and many believed he'd push the status quo in a distinctly progressive direction. Obama had proposed radical changes in many areas. For example, he'd supported the introduction of a single-payer health care system, strong regulations on the financial and banking sectors, the closure of Guantanamo Bay, an end to the Bush-era tax cuts for the wealthy, and a large economic stimulus program. In all of these cases, any change, if it occurred at all, didn't lead to dramatic shifts in the status quo. Although many of Obama's supporters felt disappointed, the fact that there's been so little change to the status quo didn't come as a surprise to those political scientists familiar with veto player theory. With its support for constitutionalism, and its bicameral and federal system of government, the US political system is full of veto players. Moreover, the ideological distance between these veto players increased significantly following the 2010 midterm elections when Obama and the Democrats lost control of Congress to the Republicans; the Republicans had a quite different vision for the future of America. Given this situation, changes to the status quo, and in particular radical changes to the status quo, were always going to be extremely unlikely. This lack of radicalism is not something unique to the Obama presidency. American politicians frequently run for office on a platform of "shaking things up" and breaking with the Washington establishment. However, the institutional structure of the United States, with its wide range of institutional veto players, all but guarantees that this isn't going to happen. To a large extent, this is precisely what the Founding Fathers intended when they wrote the constitution—they specifically designed a constitution with a set of institutions that would protect the status quo and, with it, their privileges and power.

The Barack Obama "Hope" poster became synonymous with the 2008 Obama presidential campaign.

AP Photo/Kevork Djansezian

There's nothing inherently good or bad about policy stability. Policy stability is typically viewed as a good thing by those who like the status quo but a bad thing by those who don't. Policy stability, though, can have important consequences for various aspects of a political system, such as government stability, regime stability, and judicial or bureaucratic activism. Consider the effect of policy stability on government and regime stability. Imagine that a government comes to power in a country with the promise to shake up some policy area. Perhaps some crisis requires radical reform. If the configuration of veto players in the country is such that the status quo can't be changed or can be altered only a little, the government will likely appear ineffective and immobilized. If we're in a parliamentary democracy, political and social actors who want to resolve the crisis will likely push for a vote of no confidence in the government. As a result, veto player theory predicts a connection between policy stability and the likelihood of *government* instability in parliamentary democracies. If we're in a presidential democracy, though, there's no institutional mechanism, such as a vote of no confidence, to remove an ineffective government from office. This may lead political and social actors who want to resolve the crisis to look to extraconstitutional means, such as a military coup, to replace the government. As a result, veto player theory predicts that policy stability will increase the likelihood of *regime* instability in presidential democracies.

Now consider the effect of policy stability on judicial and bureaucratic activism. Veto player theory suggests that policy stability leads to high levels of judicial and bureaucratic activism (Tsebelis 2002, 222–247). Why? In many situations, judges have the opportunity to make policy through their ability to interpret statutes. Similarly, bureaucrats get to make policy by virtue of actually implementing policy. Obviously, if the members of the legislature don't like the policies the judges and bureaucrats made, they can write new legislation that will effectively overrule the judiciary or bureaucracy. When policy is stable because there are many legislative veto players with dissimilar policy preferences, however, judges and bureaucrats get to interpret and implement laws close to their own policy preferences, safe in the knowledge that the legislature won't be able to reach an agreement on overriding them. This suggests we should expect to see higher levels of judicial and bureaucratic activism in federal and bicameral countries than in unitary and unicameral ones.

CONCLUSION

As we saw in Chapter 9, constitutional designers necessarily face trade-offs when designing democratic institutions. Arrow's theorem, for example, demonstrates that stable outcomes (group transitivity) can be guaranteed only if the freedom of individuals to form their own preferences (universal admissibility) or the ability of individuals to have their preferences influence group decisions (nondictatorship) is compromised. If we accept universal admissibility as inalienable, then the basic tension that exists in democratic regimes is between instability and dictatorship. As we've noted before, increased stability of outcomes is likely to be the result of someone's having been given agenda power.

In this and the three preceding chapters, we've examined many of the dimensions along which democratic institutions vary. For example, in Chapter 10 we looked at the ways in which the relationship between the executive and legislative branches can be organized. In Chapter 11, we examined the tremendous variety of ways in which elections have been organized. And in Chapter 12, we investigated the structure of party systems. In this chapter, we looked at three more ways in which institutions might vary across democracies—federalism, bicameralism, and constitutionalism. These three institutional forms have a common feature—they create political actors capable of blocking a change in the political status quo. Federalism, for instance, has the potential to create powerful regional actors capable of blocking the implementation of national law. Bicameralism creates a second legislative body capable of blocking legislation. And constitutionalism creates the possibility that judges might overturn laws of which the legislature approves. Each of these institutions, therefore, has the effect of creating an institutional veto player.

Veto player theory can be thought of as a modern-day version of arguments about the effects of mixed government and checks and balances that can be traced back to political theorists such as Aristotle. Countries with many veto players with conflicting preferences are expected to be characterized by high policy stability, small shifts in policy, and weak agenda-setting powers. As a result, systems with many veto players may, in some sense, overcome the instability of democratic institutions without creating a single powerful agenda setter. Unfortunately, the existence of multiple veto players doesn't fully overcome the dilemmas posed by Arrow's theorem, because complex veto structures necessarily mean that current policy decisions are profoundly influenced by the status quo policy. In this sense, they grant something like dictatorial power to the policymakers who chose those policies in the past. As a consequence, circumstances or tastes may change in such a way that a large share of the populace might desire policy change but be unable to achieve it. As Arrow's theorem implies, then, there appears to be some trade-off between policy stability and the responsiveness of decisions to voters' preferences.

Key Concepts

federalism—a government with three structural components: (1) geopolitical division, (2) independence, and (3) direct governance

federal country—a country in which sovereignty is constitutionally split between at least two territorial levels so that independent governmental units at each level have final authority in at least one policy realm

unitary countries—countries that aren't federal

congruent federalism—when the territorial units of a federal country share a similar demographic makeup with one another and the country as a whole

incongruent federalism—when the demographic makeup of territorial units differs among the units and the country as a whole

devolution—when a unitary state grants powers to subnational governments but retains the constitutional right to unilaterally recall or reshape those powers

symmetric federalism—when the territorial units of a federal country possess equal powers relative to the central government

asymmetric federalism—when some territorial units enjoy more extensive powers than others relative to the central government

decentralization—the extent to which actual policymaking power lies with the central or regional governments in a country

coming-together federalism—federalism that results from a bargaining process in which previously sovereign polities voluntarily agree to pool their resources in order to improve their collective security or achieve other economic goals

holding-together federalism—federalism that results from a process in which the central government chooses to decentralize its power to subnational governments in order to diffuse secessionist pressures

unicameral legislature—a legislature in which legislative deliberation occurs in a single assembly

bicameral legislature—a legislature in which legislative deliberation occurs in two distinct assemblies

congruent bicameralism—a bicameral system in which the two legislative chambers have a similar political composition

incongruent bicameralism—a bicameral system in which the two legislative chambers differ in their political composition

malapportionment—when the distribution of political representation across constituencies is not based on the size of each constituency's population; in a malapportioned system, the votes of some citizens weigh more than the votes of others

symmetric bicameralism—a bicameral system in which the two legislative chambers have equal or near equal constitutional power

asymmetric bicameralism—a bicameral system in which the two legislative chambers have unequal constitutional powers

constitutionalism—a commitment to be governed by a set of authoritative rules and principles laid out in a constitution

system of constitutional justice—the set of institutions and procedures that are established to protect constitutional rules and principles

constitution—the formal source of state authority

codified constitution—a constitution that's written in a single document

uncodified constitution—a constitution that has several sources, which may be written or unwritten

entrenched constitution—a constitution that can be modified only through a special procedure of constitutional amendment

unentrenched constitution—a constitution with no special amendment procedure that can be modified at any point in time with the support of a legislative majority

legislative supremacy constitution—a constitution that has no constitutional review, has no bill of rights, and isn't entrenched

higher law constitution—a constitution that has constitutional review, has a bill of rights, and is entrenched

constitutional review—the authority of an institution to invalidate legislation, administrative decisions, judicial rulings, and other acts of government that violate constitutional rules and rights

judicial review—when constitutional review is conducted by ordinary judges from the regular judicial system

new constitutionalism—a situation in which almost all countries now have an entrenched constitution, a bill of rights, and a procedure of constitutional review to protect rights

veto player theory—conceptualizes the institutional structure of a given country in terms of its configuration of veto players

veto player—an individual or collective actor whose agreement is necessary for a change in the political status quo to occur

institutional veto player—a veto player generated by a country's constitution

partisan veto player—a veto player generated by the way the political game is played

CONSEQUENCES OF DEMOCRATIC INSTITUTIONS

Proportional representation will thus create a situation where everyone has his will represented exactly but where no one's will is carried out.

Dankwart A. Rustow, "Some Observations on Proportional Representation"

OVERVIEW

1. Majoritarian and consensus democracies represent two fundamentally different approaches to how democracy should work. What do these two types of democracy mean for political representation?

2. Can the choice of electoral system influence who gets to govern and the types of economic policy they implement?

3. Can federalism and the "right" electoral laws reduce ethnic conflict?

4. When it comes to democratic consolidation, does it matter if we adopt parliamentarism or presidentialism?

As we've seen over the last four chapters, there is what sometimes appears to be a dizzying array of different democratic institutions around the world. The immense variety of democratic institutions should come as no surprise. As our discussion of Arrow's theorem in Chapter 9 illustrates, there's no ideal decision-making mechanism, and institutional choice is ultimately an exercise in the choice of "second bests." This doesn't mean, however, that constitutional designers mix and match institutions with reckless abandon. In practice, constitutional designers choose particular sets of institutions to bring about the political, social, and economic outcomes they desire. This presumes that they have a good idea about how different democratic institutions affect these outcomes. It's to the effects of particular democratic institutions that we now turn.

In this chapter, we introduce you to four different literatures, each of which examines the effect of particular democratic institutions on important political, social, and economic outcomes. We begin by examining the way in which various democratic institutions reflect voter interests. Democracy gets much of its moral authority from being a form of government "of the people, for the people, and by the people." In Chapter 9, we examined the theoretical reasons why such a notion of democracy is complicated. In this chapter, we evaluate the extent to which different institutions facilitate this notion *in practice*. We then examine how political institutions, and in particular, electoral rules, influence who gets to govern and the types of economic policy they're likely to implement. Later, we consider the effects of electoral laws and federalism on the likelihood of ethnic conflict in an attempt to discover whether comparative politics has any advice to offer constitutional designers in ethnically or religiously diverse societies. Finally, we use the knowledge we've learned in the second half of this book about institutions to supplement some of the answers we gave in the first half of the book about the economic and cultural determinants of democracy. In particular, we examine how parliamentarism and presidentialism affect democratic survival.

MAJORITARIAN OR CONSENSUS DEMOCRACY?

As Arrow's theorem makes clear, there's a fundamental tension when designing institutions between the desire to guarantee that a group of individuals will be able to make coherent and stable choices (group transitivity) on the one hand and the ability to guarantee the freedom of these individuals to form their own preferences (universal admissibility) and have those preferences influence group decisions (nondictatorship) on the other. This means that constitutional designers have to make trade-offs when choosing institutions. Although constitutional designers could theoretically make different trade-offs for each individual institution they create, a look at the real world suggests they frequently make a particular trade-off for the system of government as a whole. In practice, constitutional designers have (implicitly) responded to the implications of Arrow's theorem either by creating institutions that disperse power or by creating institutions that concentrate it. Democracies in which power is concentrated are referred to as majoritarian democracies, whereas democracies in which power is dispersed are referred to as consensus democracies. Thus, although there are theoretically many possible combinations of democratic institutions that could occur in the world, political scientists often think in terms of two basic types of democracy: majoritarian or consensus (Lijphart 1999; Powell 2000; Steiner 1971).

Two Visions of Democracy

Majoritarian and consensus democracies differ in how they think about democracy; that is, they pursue different visions of democracy (Powell 2000). According to the **majoritarian vision of democracy**, elections are events in which citizens choose between two alternative teams of politicians. Whichever team wins an electoral majority forms the government and implements the policies it ran on during the election campaign. In the majoritarian vision, citizens know that whichever team forms the government is responsible for the policies that get implemented during its tenure. As a result, citizens can use their evaluations of the policy record when deciding whether to reward or punish the incumbent in the following election.

If citizens wish to reward the government for its performance in office, they vote for the incumbent. And if citizens wish to punish the government, they vote for the opposition team.

One of the central ideas of the majoritarian vision is that policy should be determined by the majority. Citizens who hold minority preferences should have no influence in the policymaking process. To make sure that only the majority rule, policymaking power is to be concentrated in the hands of a majority government. Power isn't to be dispersed among different political actors or institutions as this will require the involvement of minority opposition members in the policymaking process; this is seen as illegitimate. The citizenry's ability to control its elected representatives and, hence, policy decisions through the electoral process is thought to be possible only if there's a clear concentration of power in the hands of a single majority team of politicians.

According to the **consensus vision of democracy**, elections are events in which citizens choose representatives from as wide a range of social groups as possible. These agents are then entrusted to bargain over policy on behalf of the citizens in the legislature. Elections aren't designed to serve as some sort of referendum on the set of policies the government implemented. Instead, elections are there to provide citizens with the opportunity to choose representatives who'll be effective advocates for their interests when bargaining over policy finally begins after the election. The goal of an election is to produce a legislature that's a miniature reflection of society as a whole.

One of the central ideas of the consensus vision is that policy should be determined by as many citizens (and their representatives) as possible. Unlike in the majoritarian vision, citizens with majority preferences aren't to be given any privileged status in the policymaking process; instead, all groups of citizens, including minorities, should have the power to influence policy in direct proportion to their electoral size. One objective of the consensus vision is to prevent the majority from riding roughshod over the preferences of the minority. This is to be achieved by dispersing power in such a way that the minority has some valuable policymaking influence with which to defend its interests. If power becomes too concentrated, there's always the risk the majority will capture it and use it against the minority; this is seen as illegitimate.

Majoritarian and Consensus Institutions

The different institutions we've examined in the last four chapters can be thought of in terms of whether they concentrate or disperse power. In effect, they determine the extent to which a country's constitution is majoritarian or consensual. Table 14.1 illustrates whether a particular "institution" is more majoritarian or more consensual.[1] The decisions to adopt majoritarian or consensus institutions aren't entirely independent of one another. Choosing to adopt certain majoritarian institutions, for example, can virtually guarantee having to live with other majoritarian institutions. This is because many of these institutions are causally related. This causal interdependence among institutions explains why constitutional designers aren't mixing and matching institutions with reckless abandon and why democracies, despite their great institutional variety, tend to come in just two main types—majoritarian and consensus.

[1]Table 14.1 gives the impression that institutions are either majoritarian or consensus. This, however, is somewhat misleading because the extent to which institutions disperse or concentrate power is best thought of as a continuum. For example, some forms of bicameralism disperse power more than others. Similarly, some electoral systems are more proportional than others. The point here is that the extent to which particular institutions disperse power depends crucially on exactly what form they take.

TABLE 14.1 ■ Institutions and the Majoritarian-Consensus Dimension

Institution	Majoritarian	Consensus
Electoral system	Majoritarian	Proportional
Party system	Two parties	Many parties
Government type	Single-party majority	Coalition/minority
Federalism	Unitary	Federal
Bicameralism	Unicameral	Bicameral
Constitutionalism	Legislative supremacy constitution	Higher law constitution

It's easy to see how electoral systems fit onto a majoritarian-consensus dimension. Majoritarian systems concentrate power in that only those candidates or parties with the most votes win. In contrast, proportional systems disperse power among candidates or parties in proportion to the share of electoral support they win. Party systems also fit easily onto a majoritarian-consensus dimension. Power is concentrated in two-party systems as there are two dominant parties in the legislature and only these parties have a realistic chance of holding power. In contrast, power is dispersed in multiparty systems as there are multiple parties in the legislature that have a realistic chance of holding power. The type of government in a country also fits neatly onto a majoritarian-consensus continuum. Power is concentrated in the hands of a single party in single-party majority governments but dispersed more widely among multiple parties in coalition or minority governments.

These three institutions—the electoral system, the party system, and the type of government—are all causally related. As our discussion of Duverger's theory in Chapter 12 illustrates, majoritarian electoral systems are associated with small party systems, whereas proportional electoral systems are associated with large party systems. And as our discussion of governments in Chapter 10 illustrates, the party system, in turn, influences the type of government that forms. Specifically, single-party majority governments are more likely when there are few political parties, because concentrated party systems increase the likelihood a single party will win a legislative majority. In contrast, coalition and minority governments are more likely when there are many political parties, because fractionalized party systems reduce the likelihood a single party will win a legislative majority. As this indicates, the choice of a constitutional designer to adopt a particular type of electoral system tends also to be a choice to have a particular type of party system and a particular type of government.

Federalism, bicameralism, and constitutionalism are three other institutions that easily fit onto a majoritarian-consensus dimension. Federal countries disperse power across different levels of government; in contrast, unitary countries concentrate power in the national government. Bicameral countries disperse power between two legislative chambers; in contrast, unicameral countries concentrate power in a single legislative chamber. Higher law constitutions disperse power by giving constitutional courts the authority to invalidate acts of government. They also contain a bill of rights that protects minority rights. In contrast, legislative supremacy constitutions concentrate power in the hands of legislative majorities and don't allow for constitutional review.

Federalism, bicameralism, and constitutionalism often occur together. Imagine you're a constitutional designer for a country and that you want to set up a decentralized form of government to take account of regional disparities in preferences. A concern you might have is that the central government will try to usurp the power of the regions. To avoid this, you could adopt federalism to constitutionally protect the decentralized system of government. But what's to guarantee that a central government interested in centralizing power will comply with the federal provisions in a constitution? Concerns about compliance might lead you to create a constitutional court with the authority to punish actors who violate the constitution's federal provisions. But what's to stop a legislative majority at the national level from emerging that wishes to amend the constitution to allow a more centralized form of government? At this point, you could adopt a bicameral system in which the upper legislative chamber is territorially based and has a stake in maintaining the federal system. By combining these institutions—federalism, bicameralism, and constitutionalism—it's possible to enhance the stability and credibility of decentralized systems of government (Bednar 2009; Bednar, Eskridge, and Ferejohn 2001).

All institutional choices present trade-offs. We can have a broad representation of social groups, but this may lead to government instability. Or we can have a stable and efficient government, but at the cost of dramatically limiting citizens' choices at the ballot box. Whether you prefer the majoritarian or consensus approach to democracy depends on how you value political representation and meaningful choices versus efficiency and accountability. We now examine in more detail what these two perspectives on democracy mean for political representation.

Political Representation

Political representation can be understood in at least four different ways: formalistic, substantive, descriptive, and symbolic (Pitkin 1967).

Formalistic Representation

Formalistic representation has to do with the formal procedures by which representatives are authorized to act and held accountable for their actions. Authorization and accountability are treated differently in majoritarian and consensus democracies. According to the majoritarian vision of democracy, representatives (legislators, parties, governments) are authorized to wield power whenever they receive majority support. Majoritarian democracies don't always live up to this ideal. For example, the most common majoritarian electoral system, the single-member district plurality system, doesn't require the winning candidate to obtain majority support. In line with the majoritarian vision, most governments in majoritarian democracies are single-party majority governments that dominate the policymaking process. The problem is that many of these single-party majority governments don't actually enjoy majority support in the electorate. In many cases, the party in power has won only a plurality of votes but has seen the mechanical effect of the disproportional electoral system transform its plurality electoral support into a "manufactured" legislative majority.

According to the consensus vision of democracy, representatives don't need to have received majority support for them to wield power. Instead, power is to be distributed among political actors in proportion to their electoral size. As a result, there should be a close connection between the percentage of votes representatives receive and the percentage of policymaking power they enjoy. In practice, consensus democracies approximate this ideal in some respects but not others. On the one hand, the fact that consensus democracies employ proportional electoral systems means there's a close connection between the percentage of votes a party wins and the percentage of legislative seats it obtains. That proportional systems typically produce multiparty systems also means it's rare for a single party to control a legislative majority. Thus, power is almost never concentrated in the hands of a single-party majority government. On the other hand, the complicated nature of the government formation process means there's only a weak connection between the percentage of seats (and votes) a party wins and its share of government power. Some parties can control a significant share of the legislative seats, for example, but not be in the government.

Not only do majoritarian and consensus democracies differ when it comes to authorizing representatives, but they also differ when it comes to holding representatives accountable. **Accountability** refers to the extent to which it's possible for voters to sanction parties for the actions they take while in office. Accountability is often considered desirable, because it provides incentives for politicians to pursue policies that will keep voters—or, at least, a winning coalition of voters—satisfied. Accountability requires that citizens look at how an incumbent party has behaved in the past in order to decide whether to reward or punish it at election time. Such behavior on the part of voters is referred to as **retrospective voting** (Erikson, MacKuen, and Stimson 2002; Fiorina 1981). If citizens decide an incumbent party has performed sufficiently well in office, they'll reward it by voting for it. In contrast, if citizens decide an incumbent party hasn't performed sufficiently well, they'll punish it by voting for another party. If accountability works well, incumbent parties that perform well are reelected into office and incumbent parties that perform poorly are removed from office.

Majoritarian democracies typically have high levels of accountability as it's relatively easy to throw the incumbent out when you have single-party majority governments and two-party systems. If the citizens in a majoritarian democracy are dissatisfied with the performance of the party in power, they simply vote for the opposition party to replace it. Accountability tends to be much lower in consensus democracies. One reason for this is that voters in consensus democracies are rarely in a position to directly choose the government. Elections in consensus democracies almost never determine the identity of the government as it's relatively unusual for a single party to win a legislative majority when there are many parties. Instead, elections usher in periods of negotiations in which party leaders bargain over the identity of the future government. The choices of these party leaders may or may not accurately reflect the preferences of the citizens. A second reason is that citizens may vote against a particular incumbent party at election time yet find that this party is still a member of the next coalition government because the other parties couldn't form a cabinet without it. There are numerous examples of parties losing votes and seats in consensus democracies but nonetheless finding themselves in the next government. Perhaps the most egregious case of this is Switzerland, where the four main parties have agreed since 1959 to form governments together irrespective of how the citizens vote. This arrangement is commonly known as the "magic formula" (Kerr 1987).

A concept closely related to accountability is **clarity of responsibility**. Clarity of responsibility refers to the ability of voters to identify who's responsible for policy outcomes. Clarity of responsibility is a necessary condition for voters to be able to hold their government accountable. If citizens can't identify who's responsible for the policies that get implemented, they won't be able to appropriately sanction those parties for their behavior.

The more that power is concentrated, the greater the clarity of responsibility. Clarity of responsibility is high in those countries in which power is concentrated in the hands of a single-party majority government. In such countries, citizens know exactly whom to reward or blame at election time. Clarity of responsibility is less high in countries in which power is dispersed among multiple parties in a coalition government, because it's not always obvious which coalition party is responsible for the policies that get implemented (Duch, Przepiorka, and Stevenson 2015; Hobolt, Tilley, and Banducci 2013; Powell and Whitten 1993). Clarity of responsibility is even lower in minority governments, as citizens may not know who's keeping the government in power and, hence, who's responsible for the policies that get implemented. Indeed, different parties in the legislature may be keeping the minority government in office at different points in time.

Other institutions that disperse power, such as bicameralism and federalism, also reduce clarity of responsibility. Federalism can make it difficult for citizens to know which level of government is responsible for policy successes and which is to blame for policy failures. For example, is the poor performance of the regional economy the result of policies adopted by the subnational government or of those implemented by the national government? In this type of situation, neither the subnational nor the national government will want to take responsibility for the poor economic performance, and each will likely try to blame the other. In this way, federalism facilitates blame shifting (and credit claiming), thereby making it difficult for citizens to know exactly who's responsible for what. Bicameral systems can have a similar effect, particularly if the two legislative chambers are equally powerful and controlled by opposing political sides.

In sum, by concentrating power, majoritarian democracies produce high levels of both accountability and clarity of responsibility. Not only do majoritarian institutions make it easy for voters to identify which political actors are responsible for the policies that get implemented, they also make it easy for voters to sanction these actors for their performance in office. By dispersing power, consensus democracies produce relatively low levels of accountability and clarity of responsibility. Consensus institutions make it hard for voters to know exactly which political actors are responsible for the policies that a government enacts. And even if voters can figure this out, consensus institutions make it hard for voters to reward or punish these actors for their performance in office.

Substantive Representation

Substantive representation occurs when representatives take actions in line with the substantive and ideological interests of those they represent. For many democratic theorists, substantive representation is the most important form of representation as it focuses on what representatives do in office. Substantive representation is often studied in terms of **ideological congruence** (Golder and Stramski 2010). Substantive representation is high when representatives are ideologically congruent with the preferences of the citizens. In other words, substantive representation is high when representatives hold the same policy positions as the citizens.

The two visions of democracy differ in how they think about ideological congruence. The majoritarian vision demands that representatives be congruent with the preferences of the majority. The ideological position of the median citizen is often taken as indicative of the majority's preferred policy position. Rather than demand ideological congruence with the median citizen, the consensus vision demands that representatives be congruent with as many citizens as possible.

Majoritarian and consensus democracies have very different types of party systems and legislatures. Due to their electoral rules, majoritarian democracies are associated with a small number of large parties that typically adopt similar centrist policy positions. These large parties are "umbrella" parties that represent a broad coalition of diverse voters. Although the parties tend to be congruent with the median voter, the diversity of their bases of support means there's often a large degree of incongruence between a party's policy position and the preferences of many of its voters. For example, many Democratic and Republican voters in the United States hold preferences that are quite distant from their party's policy platform, something that can produce voter dissatisfaction. That parties in majoritarian systems often hold similar policy positions limits the extent to which voters are confronted with meaningful choices at election time.

Party systems and legislatures in consensus systems are different. Due to their electoral rules, proportional democracies are associated with a large number of small parties that disperse throughout the policy space. Parties compete in a permissive environment where they can win legislative seats even if they're not the largest party and even if they don't adopt centrist positions. Parties are able to adopt a wide range of policy positions and carve out niche electorates. This means not only that the diversity of citizen preferences is reflected in the party system but also that the policy platforms of the individual parties are congruent with the preferences of their specific voters. Proportional systems also provide voters with more meaningful choices at election time. Although an individual who holds "green" policy preferences may have little choice but to vote for a center-left party in a majoritarian system, she's likely to have the option of voting for a green party that's more congruent with her preferences in a proportional system. Because proportional systems accurately translate votes into seats, they also produce legislatures that are congruent with the full range of diversity in society.

Governments typically play the dominant role in the policymaking process. As a result, the degree of ideological congruence between citizen preferences and the government's policy position is particularly important. Government congruence is typically thought of as the ideological distance between the government's policy position and the preferences of the median voter, and it's something that's valued in both visions of democracy. Most recent empirical studies find there's no significant difference in the level of government congruence across majoritarian and consensus democracies (Blais and Bodet 2006; Golder and Lloyd 2014; Golder and Stramski 2010).

Descriptive Representation

Descriptive representation has to do with whether representatives resemble and therefore "stand for" their constituents. It calls for representatives who share the same characteristics, such as race, gender, religion, and class, as those they represent. In effect, descriptive representation calls for women representatives to represent women, minority representatives to represent minorities, and so on. It requires that parties, legislatures, and governments accurately reflect the full range of diversity that exists in society. As such, descriptive representation is valued more highly in the consensus vision of democracy.

Democratic theorists generally consider descriptive representation as inferior to substantive representation because it focuses on "who" representatives are as opposed to what representatives "do" (Celis et al. 2008). It seems unreasonable, after all, to hold representatives accountable for their descriptive characteristics, which they can't change, as opposed to what they do, which they can change. Nonetheless, many believe that descriptive representation is important, especially in situations where there are high levels of mistrust between groups or a history of discrimination, or when new issues have emerged on which parties and other representatives have yet to take a clear stance (Mansbridge 1999; Phillips 1998).

Some scholars claim that descriptive representation is important in its own right, either because it signals a policy of recognition and acceptance or because it promotes a sense of fairness and legitimacy. The existence of minority representatives, for example, can challenge social hierarchies and change the social understanding of who gets to rule (Mansbridge 1999). In effect, it can signal, to both the minority group and the larger community, that minorities are accepted as equal members in society and that they can play a legitimate role in determining how the political system is to be run. In doing so, descriptive representation may enhance a sense of fairness and strengthen the attachment that minorities or other groups feel toward the political system. Women and minority representatives can also act as role models, demonstrating to women and minorities that particular careers and positions are not closed off to them.

Other scholars promote descriptive representation not for its own sake but because they see it as a pathway to improving substantive representation. The general idea is that individuals who share similar descriptive characteristics, such as their gender, race, or religion, will have shared experiences and developed a sense of linked fate that generate a common set of perspectives and substantive interests (Dawson 1995; Phillips 1998; Tate 1993; Young 2002). According to these scholars, it's important to have, say, female representatives in the legislature, not because of some reason related to their biology but because they have a common set of experiences that aren't shared by male representatives. These common experiences result from many factors, including the fact that women typically share similar, often subordinate, positions in most societies. These shared experiences are likely to mean there are issues that are particularly salient to women or on which women take distinctive positions. Although men could advocate on behalf of these issue positions, the claim is that women are likely to receive greater substantive representation from a female representative than a male one. One reason for this is that women representatives are likely to have an informational advantage with respect to these issues as a result of their personal experience.

Critics of descriptive representation argue that it can promote group essentialism, the idea that all members of a group share an essential identity that only they can have and understand. Among other things, group essentialism implies that all members of a group share a common interest that overrides any interests that divide them. This is what allows people to talk about "women's issues" or "minority issues." In effect, proponents of descriptive representation have been criticized both for ignoring the diversity that exists within particular groups and for failing to recognize that individuals who aren't members of the group, such as men, can usefully advocate on behalf of group members, such as women (Celis 2009; Childs and Krook 2006).

One response to this criticism has been the increasing focus on "intersectional" identities in which individuals have overlapping or intersecting social identities related to gender, class, religion, ethnicity, and so on (Crenshaw 1989; Hancock 2007; Hughes 2011; Weldon 2006). Rather than treat women as a single group, for example, scholars of intersectionality might distinguish between the representation of black women and white women. Scholars who adopt this approach have demonstrated, among other things, that much of the women's movement in the United States has been driven by middle-class white women and their concerns, whereas little attention has been paid to black women and the representation of their interests (Junn and Brown 2008).

Do majoritarian or consensus institutions produce greater descriptive representation? In what follows, we briefly look at the descriptive representation of women. In Map 14.1, we show the proportion of legislative seats women held in national parliaments around the world in April 2018 using data from the Inter-Parliamentary Union. Darker colors indicate higher levels of women's legislative representation. The average level of women's representation in the world in 2018 is just 21.8 percent. This percentage is lower in dictatorships (19 percent) than in democracies (24.5 percent). The five countries with the highest levels of women's representation are Rwanda (61.3 percent), Cuba (53.2 percent), Bolivia (53.1 percent), Grenada (46.7 percent) and Namibia (46.2 percent). In only three countries—Rwanda, Cuba, and Bolivia—do women make up the majority of legislative representatives. The five countries with the lowest levels of women's legislative representation are Papua New Guinea (0 percent), Yemen (0 percent), Vanuatu (0 percent), Micronesia (0 percent), and Oman (1.2 percent). In 2018, the United States ranked 102nd in the world in terms of women's representation with

MAP 14.1 ▪ Women's Legislative Representation in 2018

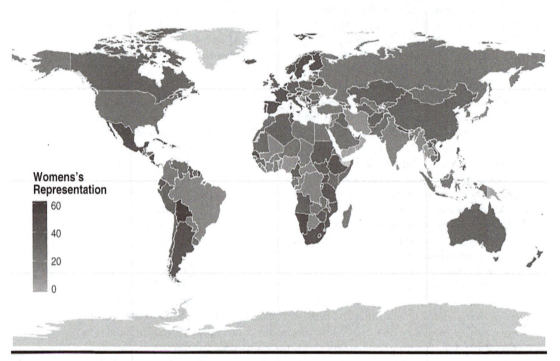

Source: Data from the Inter-Parliamentary Union (http://archive.ipu.org/wmn-e/arc/classif010418.htm).

Note: The map shows the proportion of legislative seats held by women in the lower house of national parliaments in 2018.

just 19.5% of legislative seats held by women. Overall, women representatives hold less than 20 percent of the legislative seats in almost half of the world's countries.

What explains this variation in the level of women's legislative representation? To answer this question, we might begin by considering the steps someone must go through to be elected to the legislature (Krook and Norris 2014). The political recruitment process begins with the set of people who are eligible to run for office. Only a subset of eligible candidates aspire to compete for office, however, and of this group, only some are nominated by a political party to run. Finally, of those candidates who do compete for office, only some are elected. If we assume that women and men place the same value on achieving office and if there are no gender "distortions" at any of these stages, we should see a roughly equal proportion of male and female representatives in the legislature. As the information in Map 14.1 clearly indicates, some distortion is occurring somewhere in the political recruitment process in most countries. In what follows, we focus on the final step in the political recruitment process, and in partic-ular on the role that electoral rules play in the election of female candidates.

Most empirical studies find that proportional electoral systems with large district mag-nitudes are associated with higher levels of women's descriptive representation (Kittilson and Schwindt-Bayer 2012). The precise reason for this, though, isn't entirely clear. At least two explanations have been proposed for this result. One is that majoritarian systems favor

Three members of the Alianza Pais party in Ecuador assumed leadership positions in the legislature during the first session of the new parliament in Quito on May 14, 2013, with Gabriela Rivadeneira (*center*) as president of the National Assembly, Rosana Alvarado (*right*) as first vice president, and Marcela Aguinaga as second vice president. Parties in Ecuador are required to place men and women in alternating positions on the ballot for legislative elections; in the 2013 election, Rivadeneira was placed in the first position on the Alianza Pais party list.

incumbents, and incumbents have traditionally been men (Fréchette, Maniquet, and Morelli 2008). A second has to do with the fact that, as we'll see shortly, left-wing parties tend to perform better under proportional electoral rules than under majoritarian ones. This is important because left-wing parties typically have more women candidates than right-wing parties (Kittilson 2006).

Some scholars have also looked at whether the *type* of proportional system matters. In particular, they've looked at whether open party lists or closed party lists produce higher levels of women's representation. The results, though, are mixed. This isn't entirely surprising. Assuming there are women candidates running for office, the type of party list is unlikely to matter in countries where the demand for women representatives is high. If party lists are open, voters can give their support directly to the women candidates. And if party lists are closed, there's a good chance the parties will respond to voter preferences by placing women candidates toward the top of the list. In either case, the level of women's representation should be high in these countries. It's unclear, however, whether the type of party list will matter in countries where the demand for women representatives is low. If party lists are open, it doesn't matter much whether there are many or only a few women candidates on the party list as voters won't select them. If party lists are closed, parties can "force" voters to elect women candidates by placing them toward the top of the list. This, though, raises the question of why parties would want to increase the number of women representatives when this would run counter to voter preferences. Depending on the demand from voters and party elites for women candidates, the effect of different types of party lists might be either negligible or substantial.

Gender quotas are an increasingly popular tool for parties or countries that want to increase the number of women elected to office (Dahlerup 2006; Krook 2009). There are three general types of gender quotas. First, there are reserved seats where legislative seats are set aside for women candidates only. According to the Global Database of Quotas for Women, twenty-three countries have reserved seats for women, including Burundi, Iraq, Uganda, Kenya, and Tanzania ("Quota Database" 2015). Reserved seats are particularly common in Arab countries, South Asia, and parts of Africa. Second, there are legislated candidate quotas that specify the percentage of women candidates that must appear on party lists. These quotas differ on whether they include placement mandates that indicate where women candidates must be placed on party lists. Fifty-four countries, including Argentina, Bolivia, Ecuador, Nicaragua, and Rwanda, have legislated candidate quotas. The common use of legislated candidate quotas in Latin America helps to explain the relatively high levels of women's legislative representation seen in this region in Map 14.1. Third, there are voluntary political party quotas where individual parties agree to have women candidates make up a certain percentage of all their candidates. These are the most common type of gender quotas in Western Europe. Although not a necessity, gender quotas are often easier to implement in proportional representation systems.

Elections held in post-conflict situations often result in more women being elected than elections held prior to the conflict. This is because post-conflict power-sharing agreements frequently include gender quotas and because incumbents are often killed or exiled during the conflict, leading to more open seats (Tripp and Kang 2008). The particularly high levels of women's legislative representation in Rwanda is partly due to Rwanda's use of gender quotas but also partly due to the fact that the perpetrators of the Rwandan genocide in 1994 targeted men and left the country with a huge gender imbalance. Although Rwanda has the highest level of women's legislative representation in the world (63.8 percent), women are still underrepresented as they compose 70 percent of the population (Bennett 2014).

Does the descriptive representation of women lead to the substantive representation of women? Although there's some evidence linking the descriptive representation of women to the improved substantive representation of women, the strength of the empirical evidence is contested (Wängnerud 2009). For example, Schwindt-Bayer and Mishler (2005) find that increased descriptive representation of women in legislatures does lead to greater responsiveness to women's interests but that the effect is smaller than anticipated. Moreover, there's no compelling evidence for the prediction from critical mass theory (Kanter 1977; Dahlerup 1988) that the substantive representation of women would increase significantly once the level of women's legislative representation passed some threshold, frequently thought to be 30 percent (Childs and Krook 2006). In her study of women's representation in Latin America, Htun (2016) notes that the increased levels of descriptive representation brought about by gender quotas in this region hasn't significantly increased the substantive representation of women. She refers to this as "inclusion without representation." The low substantive representation of women, even in countries with high levels of women's legislative representation, is often attributed to the fact that women legislators have limited legislative experience, that they're rarely given powerful positions, and that they're constrained in what they can do by their party affiliations (Beckwith 2007; Celis et al. 2008; Celis 2009). Many scholars have argued that critical actors, both men and women, who've been "critical" in initiating women-friendly policies are more important to women's substantive representation than high levels of women's descriptive representation (Celis et al. 2008; Childs and Krook 2006; Htun 2016).

Symbolic Representation

Symbolic representation focuses on the symbolic ways representatives "stand for" the citizens. To get a better sense of what this means, it's useful to think about particular symbols we're familiar with in our everyday lives. Two common symbols are flags and company logos. Flags like the Star Spangled Banner in the United States symbolize certain ideals, beliefs, or norms associated with the thing they're representing. Flags evoke meaning, and often emotions; they tell us what it means to be American, British, Chinese, and so on. Similarly, a company's logo, such as the Apple or BMW logos, can evoke images and feelings about the types of products the company sells—high quality, reliable, quirky, stylish, and so on. In both of these cases, the symbol isn't the thing being represented and as such is not a form of descriptive representation. Nor does the symbol—the flag or company logo—take action on behalf of what is being represented; it's not a form of substantive representation. Instead, the symbol "stands for" and symbolizes what's being represented. Political representatives can also perform this function.

The act of giving meaning to something is a constitutive act. Symbolic representation constructs boundaries that allow us to see who and what is being represented. For the Star Spangled Banner to symbolically represent Americans, we first have to construct what it means to be American—we have to create a boundary between what's American and what's un-American. According to symbolic representation, political representatives don't just passively represent some constituency; indeed, constituencies aren't out there waiting to be represented. Instead, representatives must create constituencies for them to represent through the symbolic claims they make about their constituents (Saward 2006, 2009). If constituencies are constructed, symbolic representation is a process by which certain groups or identities are deemed worthy of representation. In addition to identifying who's worthy of representation, the constitutive process of symbolic representation also identifies who can appropriately represent particular groups; that is, it identifies who would be a "good" representative for a particular constituency. The process of constructing constituencies, and hence symbolic representation, isn't unidirectional or fixed in time. The symbolic claims representatives make about the "represented" must be accepted by those being represented for them to have meaning, and they can evolve over time in response to new events and changing values. Thus, symbolic representation is a "dynamic, performative, and constitutive" process that involves a back-and-forth claims-making process between the representative and the represented (Celis et al. 2008, 101–102).

Consider symbolic representation in the context of populist parties. Populism is an ideology that portrays society as divided into two homogeneous and antagonistic groups, "the pure people" and "the corrupt elite" (Mudde 2004, 2007). Many commentators have wondered how a populist candidate like Donald Trump in the 2016 US presidential election could plausibly claim to represent ordinary people given his privileged background. What many of these commentators failed to realize is that Trump was attempting to provide symbolic representation, not descriptive or substantive representation. When Trump referred to America's "forgotten men and women" during his acceptance speech as the Republican nominee for president and said "I am your voice," he wasn't claiming to be one of the forgotten people; instead, he was claiming to symbolically "stand for" them. Other populist leaders have also emphasized their symbolic representation of the people. For example, Venezuelan president Hugo Chávez stated that "I demand absolute loyalty to me. I am not an individual, I am the people" in a clear reference to his perceived role as the embodiment of the Venezuelan people (de la Torre 2016, 43).

Compared with formalistic, descriptive, and substantive representation, symbolic representation is relatively understudied. To our knowledge, there's no research examining the effects of majoritarian or consensus institutions on different forms of symbolic representation. That said, we might expect majoritarian institutions to incentivize political representatives to construct larger, and therefore potentially more diverse, constituencies than proportional institutions. This is because political representatives require greater electoral support to win office in majoritarian systems.

From a normative standpoint with respect to political representation, you probably have your own preferences by now for whether a country should adopt majoritarian or consensus institutions. If you're having trouble deciding which type of democracy you'd recommend to the framers of a new constitution, however, perhaps you need some information about the substantive consequences that are likely to follow from the institutional choices you would make. In the following three sections, we examine the effects of different institutional choices on economic policy, ethnic conflict, and democratic stability.

THE EFFECT OF POLITICAL INSTITUTIONS ON FISCAL POLICY

Economic policy is typically made by elected officials who may have goals other than the provision of "stable growth." Economic policies also have distributional consequences in that they don't affect all citizens in the same way. All of this means that economic policy is fraught with conflicts of interest—between the government and citizens, between citizens themselves, and between members of the government representing different groups of citizens. Although these conflicts of interest arise in all areas of macroeconomic policymaking, we focus in this section on fiscal policy. **Fiscal policy** refers to the set of government policies related to the raising of revenues through taxation and to the set of policies accomplished through government spending. Fiscal policy is of particular interest because it's often used for the purpose of redistribution and because, as we saw in Chapter 4, the raising of revenues is central to what it means to be a state.

In Figure 14.1, we present a "box and whiskers plot" showing how total public fiscal activity—central government revenue and expenditures as a percentage of gross domestic product (GDP)—varies both within and between twenty-one advanced industrialized countries from 1947 to 1997 (Franzese 2002, 16). The black dots indicate the average level of fiscal activity for each country. The "boxes" and "whiskers" display how the level of fiscal activity varied within each country during the postwar period. When the boxes stay close to the country average, as in the United States and Switzerland, it means that fiscal policy varied little during the postwar period. When the boxes are large, as in Belgium, the Netherlands, and Sweden, it means that fiscal activity varied quite a bit in that country. The "whiskers," or vertical black lines, indicate the maximum and minimum levels of fiscal activity in each country during the postwar period. The main thing to note from Figure 14.1 is that there's a tremendous amount of cross-national variation in the level of fiscal activity.

Many economists interpret total public fiscal activity as the "size of government" because it gives an indication of the ratio of total government economic activity to overall economic activity within a country. The traditional explanation for the size of the government is "Wagner's law," which predicts that government size will grow as countries become more industrialized. Wagner's law is often interpreted to mean that the size of government will increase

FIGURE 14.1 ■ Total Public Fiscal Activity in Twenty-One OECD Countries, 1947–1997

Source: Franzese (2002, 16).

Note: AL = Australia; AU = Austria; BE = Belgium; CA = Canada; DE = Denmark; FI = Finland; FR = France; GE = Germany; GR = Greece; IR = Ireland; IT = Italy; JA = Japan; NE = Netherlands; NO = Norway; NZ = New Zealand; PO = Portugal; SP = Spain; SW = Sweden; SZ = Switzerland; UK = United Kingdom; US = United States.

as countries become wealthier. In the broadest sense, Wagner's law seems consistent with the facts—as European countries became richer and more industrialized, the role of the government in the economy did increase as predicted. As Figure 14.2 illustrates, there was an upward trend in fiscal activity among countries in the Organisation for Economic Co-operation and Development (OECD) during the postwar period, a period generally considered a time of economic growth and increased industrialization. This can be seen by looking at how the black dots, which represent the OECD average level of fiscal activity in each year, rise over time. Note, though, that in addition to the black dots rising over time, the "boxes" and "whiskers" also lengthen. This indicates not only that the mean level of government fiscal activity among OECD countries increased during the postwar period but also that the cross-national variation in the level of government fiscal activity increased as well. Wagner's law doesn't provide a straightforward explanation for this continued and increasing variation in the level of fiscal activity across countries that, in regard to wealth and industrialization, were probably becoming increasingly similar over time (Le Pen 2005; Li and Papell 1999).

Political Parties, Electoral Laws, and Fiscal Policy

What explains this cross-national variation in the level of fiscal activity? In what follows, we examine the role played by political parties and electoral rules. In most democracies, voter preferences over policy are aggregated through political parties. Political parties are at the heart of the **partisan model of macroeconomic policy**. According to the partisan model of macroeconomic policy, left-wing parties represent the interests of low-income voters and right-wing parties represent the interests of high-income voters. The main prediction of the

FIGURE 14.2 ■ Total Public Fiscal Activity by Year in Twenty-One OECD Countries, 1947–1997

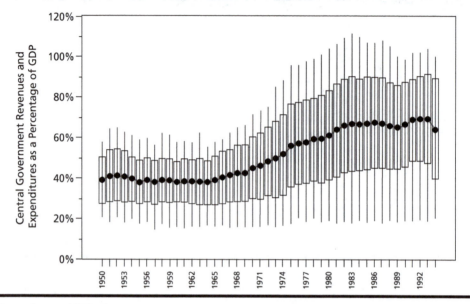

Source: Franzese (2002, 17).

partisan model is that changes in the partisan control of the government produce predictable changes in fiscal policy. Specifically, left-wing governments are expected to engage in more fiscal activity than right wing governments. In particular, left-wing governments are expected to adopt "expansionary" fiscal policies that are thought to favor left-wing voters (Hibbs 1977).

Although this sounds plausible, there's only mixed empirical support for the idea that left- and right-wing governments in the same country adopt different fiscal policies. Some scholars find that left-wing governments adopt more expansionary fiscal policies; some find no relationship between the partisan orientation of the government and fiscal policy; and some find evidence that, if anything, right-wing governments are more expansionary. Of course, the fact that it's difficult to identify a difference in the fiscal policies of left- and right-wing governments in the same country is not evidence in and of itself that these parties—and the voters they represent—don't wish to implement different policies. It may well be the case they'd like to implement different fiscal policies but that incentives to court the median voter or the "structural dependence of the state on capital" prevent them from effectively acting on these desires.

There's also the possibility that the policy preferences of the median voter differ across countries. If the median voter is further to the left in some countries than others, then these countries are likely to have a high frequency of left-wing governments. In such a scenario, we might expect to see evidence for a *cross-national* version of the partisan model. In fact, this is precisely what David Cameron (1978) found in his seminal study of the politics of macro-economic policy. In Figure 14.3, we reproduce a scatterplot from Cameron's article, showing a positive relationship between the percentage of the government's electoral base composed of left-wing parties in a country and the growth of government revenues as a share of GDP.

FIGURE 14.3 ■ The Partisan Composition of Government and the Expansion of the Public Economy, 1960–1975 (Percentages)

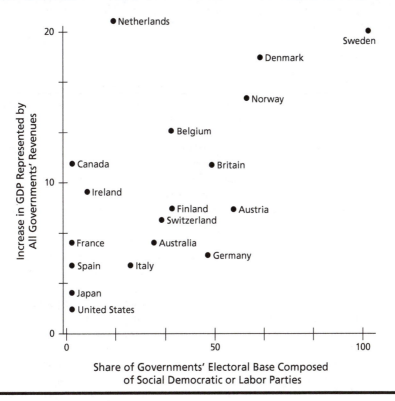

Source: Cameron (1978, 1255, fig. 1).

Overall, there's a fairly close relationship between the percentage of time that a country experiences left-wing rule and increases in the size of government.

Over the last two decades, a steady stream of research has shown that proportional electoral systems are associated with more public goods, larger and more redistributive welfare programs, and a larger overall size of government than majoritarian electoral systems (Iversen and Soskice 2006; Persson and Tabellini 2004). While there's some disagreement as to exactly why this is the case, several studies have argued that it's because proportional systems encourage the election of left-wing governments and majoritarian systems encourage the election of right-wing governments (Iversen and Soskice 2006; Kedar, Harsgor, and Scheinerman 2016; Rodden 2006).

Rodden (2006) argues that electoral institutions influence "who rules" because of the geographic distribution of support for left-wing parties and the way electoral laws overlay this geographic distribution. He points out that left-wing parties have traditionally drawn their electoral support from concentrated pockets of voters in urban industrial and mining areas. This geographic concentration of support for left-wing parties is the product of industrialization in an era when transportation costs were sufficiently high that workers needed to live close to where they worked. Right-wing parties, in contrast, tend to draw their voters from a much broader geographic base. Under majoritarian electoral rules, the geographic concentration of left-wing votes means that left-wing parties win their districts by a large margin, but with a high number of wasted votes. In other words, left-wing support is not efficiently translated into legislative representation in majoritarian systems. The geographic concentration of left-wing voters is less consequential in proportional electoral systems, as votes are more accurately translated into seats. The result is that the bias for right-wing parties in majoritarian electoral systems caused by the geographic concentration of left-wing voters is reduced (or even disappears) in proportional electoral systems.

Empirically, there's a strong association between the type of electoral system in a country and the propensity for left-wing parties to win enough legislative seats to control the government. In Table 14.2, we present data from seventeen advanced industrialized democracies between 1945 and 1998 showing that a left-wing government was in power about three-quarters of the time in countries with proportional electoral systems but only one-quarter of the time in countries with majoritarian systems (Iversen and Soskice 2006). We're not necessarily claiming that proportional systems *cause* left-wing electoral success but merely that the two go together. This is important because several scholars have pointed out that ruling elites in European countries in which left-wing parties were strong replaced their majoritarian systems at the beginning of the twentieth century with proportional ones (Boix 1999). This suggests that the causal relationship between proportional representation and left-wing electoral success may run in both directions—countries in which left-wing parties are strong have tended to adopt PR, and PR, in turn, is likely to reinforce the representation of left-wing parties in government.

Rodden (2006) argues that the electoral system affects not only the probability of left-wing parties gaining power but also the way that left-wing parties behave once in power. Specifically, he claims that left-wing parties in SMDP systems are less aggressive in pressing for redistributive fiscal policies than they are in PR systems. The reason is that, to the extent that parties have incentives to court the median voter, parties have incentives to court the *national* median voter in PR systems but the *marginal constituency* median voter in SMDP systems. Marginal constituencies are basically constituencies in which the electoral support for the two biggest parties is evenly split. In SMDP systems, national parties have incentives to ignore voters in "safe districts"—ones where they're likely to win and ones that are "safe" for their competitors where they're likely to lose. Elections in SMDP systems are won and lost in marginal constituencies because that's where the "swing voters" are. Because of the geographic concentration of support for left parties mentioned earlier, the median voter in marginal constituencies is likely to be far to the right of the average supporter of the left-wing

TABLE 14.2 ■ Electoral Systems and the Number of Years with Left and Right Governments, 1945–1998			
	Government partisanship		
Electoral system	Left	Right	Proportion of left governments
Proportional	342	120	0.74
Majoritarian	86	256	0.25

Source: Iversen and Soskice (2006, fig. 1).

party. As a result, left-wing parties in SMDP systems have an incentive not to be as redistributive in regard to fiscal policy as those same parties would be in PR systems.

Iversen and Soskice (2006) agree that left-wing parties are likely to participate in government more frequently in PR systems than in SMDP systems. They argue, however, that this is because of the difference in coalitional bargaining across the two systems and not because of the geographic distribution of left-wing support. Iversen and Soskice present a theory in which there are three equal-size groups in society based on income level (*low, middle,* and *high*). According to their theory, the low-income voters want to tax the high- and middle-income groups at the highest possible rate and redistribute this wealth to themselves. The middle-income voters want to tax the high-income group and divide this wealth between themselves and low-income voters. Finally, the high-income voters want zero taxes and no redistribution.

Following the logic behind Duverger's theory (see Chapter 12), Iversen and Soskice assume that there'll be only two parties in the legislature of SMDP systems, with the middle-income group splitting its vote between the two other income groups. In effect, some middle-income voters will form a center-left party with low-income voters and some will form a center-right party with high-income voters. Median voter dynamics lead both the center-left and center-right parties to campaign on the policies preferred by middle-income voters. The problem is that neither the center-left party nor the center-right party can credibly commit to implement these policies once the election is over. The problem arises from the fact that if middle-income voters split their support between the center-left and center-right parties, they'll be only a minority faction within each party. The middle-income voters must therefore worry that after the election each party will implement the preferences of its majority faction. If you were a middle-income voter in this situation, how would you vote? If the center-right party comes to power, there's a good chance it'll implement a zero tax, zero subsidy policy—the preferred policy of the high-income group. If the center-left party comes to power, there's a good chance it'll implement a policy that redistributes income from the high- and middle-income groups to the low-income group—the preferred policy of the low-income group. Given these possibilities, middle-income voters are likely to have a greater tendency to vote for center-right parties in SMDP systems than center-left parties.

How do things change in a PR system? According to Duverger's theory, we'd expect a PR system to produce three parties, one for each of the different income groups. In effect, we'd have a left party, a center party, and a right party. As all three income groups have the same size, no single party will control a legislative majority, and so a coalition government will form. Once again, the middle-income voters will be pivotal. The middle-income voters don't have to worry that the center party will deviate to the left or right, as the center party exists to represent the middle-income group. Iversen and Soskice (2006) predict that the center party is likely to form a coalition with the left party in these circumstances. A center-left coalition government will want to redistribute income away from the high-income group. While the left party would like all of this redistribution to go to the low-income group, the fact that the center party is pivotal in the coalition formation process means this won't happen. In effect, the low-income and middle-income groups will both benefit from the redistribution that occurs under a center-left coalition government. A center-right coalition government doesn't offer such benefits to the middle-income group. Although the center party would want to redistribute from the high-income group to the middle-income group, the right party in the coalition will veto this. The fact that the tax and redistribution system is, by assumption, non-regressive (low-income voters can't do worse than middle-income voters, who can't do worse than high-income voters) means that the center-right coalition can't redistribute up the income scale from the poor. As a result, the middle-income group can't benefit from a center-right coalition. According to this argument, center-left coalition governments are more likely to form in PR systems than center-right coalition governments.

We've already seen that a country's electoral system has a strong impact on the partisan orientation of its governments as Iversen and Soskice's theory predicts (see Table 14.2). Their theory also predicts that the electoral system will influence the level of redistribution in society. This is exactly what they find in their empirical analyses. Among other things, they find that right-wing governments are associated with less redistribution than left-wing governments. More important, however, they also show that fiscal policy is more redistributive in countries with PR systems irrespective of the government's partisan orientation. Thus, PR systems don't lead to more redistribution just because they produce more left-wing governments (although they show that this is, in fact, the case). For the reasons outlined above, should a left-wing government come to power in an SMDP system, it's likely to engage in less redistribution than it would if it came to power in a PR system.

Summary

There are good reasons to believe that political institutions have an important influence on macroeconomic policies. PR electoral laws are associated with coalition governments and with left-wing parties entering government more frequently. Both of these factors are associated with more extensive government redistribution and higher levels of spending, larger deficits, and higher debt levels. Although there remains considerable debate about the particular causal mechanisms at work here, there's little question that constitutional choices have important effects on the way governments manage their economies. Macroeconomic outcomes are distributional in nature; that is, they tend to help some citizens and harm others. It isn't, therefore, possible to suggest on the basis of this literature what the best institutions for encouraging good macroeconomic performance would be. Our goal, rather, is to show that there are trade-offs to be made and that a knowledge of comparative politics can be useful in helping citizens and policymakers evaluate some of these trade-offs.

ELECTORAL LAWS, FEDERALISM, AND ETHNIC CONFLICT

Are there constitutional choices that can encourage successful democratic consolidation in ethnically divided countries? The 2011 Arab Spring in the Middle East and North Africa saw the toppling of dictators in Tunisia, Egypt, and Libya. All three of these countries have adopted new constitutions and political institutions in the last few years. Will these institutions solidify moves toward democracy and encourage democratic consolidation? Or will they simply lead to a new dictatorship and possible civil war? Before we examine whether there's an "institutional fix" for ethnic conflict, we start by asking whether there's a connection between ethnic diversity and conflict.

Ethnic Diversity and Conflict

Although large-scale ethnic or religious conflict can be devastating, such conflict is the exception and interethnic peace is the rule. This may be surprising because when such conflict occurs, the memory of its horror tends to stay with us. Indeed, when asked, it may be easy for people to provide a list of tragically violent interactions between ethnic or religious groups.

For example, you might think of the conflicts during the 1990s between Hutus and Tutsis in Rwanda or between Serbs, Croats, and Bosnians in the former Yugoslavia. Or you might think of the more recent conflicts between Africans and Arabs in Sudan; between Shias, Sunnis, and Kurds in Iraq; between Uighurs and the Han-dominated Chinese government in China's Xinjiang province; or between various ethnic groups in post-Communist states, such as Azerbaijan, Georgia, Moldova, and Russia. One problem with simply enumerating ethnic conflicts in this way is that we tend to ignore the even larger list of "nonevents"—incidents in which groups of people with ethnic or religious differences live in peaceful coexistence. Once we take account of these non-events, it quickly becomes clear that ethnic conflict is a relatively rare event.

In Table 14.3, we report data on ethnic violence from thirty-six countries in sub-Saharan Africa, an area of the world often thought to be particularly prone to ethnic conflict. The data are summarized in such a way that we can compare the number of actual incidents of ethnic violence with an estimate of the number of potential incidents of ethnic violence, yielding a ratio of actual incidents of violence to all potential incidents of violence. The first column indicates that there were 20 incidents of ethnic violence in our sub-Saharan countries. Although we'd never seek to minimize the human suffering caused by such violence, it's important to keep these incidents in perspective. Because our sample includes thirty-six countries observed over nineteen years, there are roughly 680 country-years in the data set.[2] One way to estimate the frequency of ethnic conflict is to take the ratio of the number of conflicts to the number of country-years in the data set. The third column shows that this figure is 0.03. This means that there have been 3 incidents of ethnic violence for every 100 country-years in our sub-Saharan countries. This is, however, still an overestimate of the frequency of ethnic violence because it assumes that each country-year represents just one potential incident of ethnic group conflict. In reality, because the typical country in sub-Saharan Africa has more than two dozen ethnic groups, the potential is there for far more than one ethnic conflict per country-year. Once we estimate the number of potential incidents of ethnic conflict based on the number of ethnic groups in a country, we find that the ratio of actual incidents of ethnic violence to potential incidents of ethnic violence is 0.0005 (last column). In other words, there were just 5 incidents of ethnic conflict for every 10,000 potential incidents. Overall, the information presented in Table 14.3 shows that even in very

TABLE 14.3 ■ Actual and Potential Ethnic Violence in Thirty-Six Sub-Saharan African Countries, 1960–1979					
	Number of incidents for all countries and years	Country mean of incidents per year	Number of potential incidents for all countries and years	Country mean of potential incidents per year	Ratio of all actual incidents to all potential incidents
Ethnic violence	20	0.03	38,383	59	0.0005

Source: Fearon and Laitin (1996, 717), based on data from Morrison, Mitchell, and Paden (1989).

---

[2]There are actually somewhat fewer observations because some countries didn't become independent until after 1960.

poor countries where the state has little capacity to rule effectively and society is reeling from decades of colonialism that left a legacy of externally imposed borders, such as in sub-Saharan Africa, ethnic diversity doesn't lead inexorably to ethnic violence.

While ethnic violence is rare, we might still wonder whether ethnic diversity is associated with other forms of conflict. For example, does ethnic diversity in a country—having lots of ethnic groups—increase the likelihood of civil war? In one study, Fearon and Laitin (2003) find that ethnic and religious diversity is not associated with civil wars. They find that what matters most for civil wars are factors that favor insurgency, such as poverty, oil-dependent export sectors, political instability, and rough terrain. Poverty, which lowers tax revenue, and political instability weaken the state, thereby making it easier for rebel groups to mount a successful challenge. Rough terrain, like mountainous regions, gives rebel groups hiding places and strongholds that hinder attempts by the state to crush them. Thus, poverty, political instability, and rough terrain increase the likelihood of civil war by increasing the probability that a challenge to the state will be successful. In contrast, the presence of oil increases the likelihood of civil war by increasing the value of gaining control of the state. All of these factors together increase the expected value of civil war on the part of rebel groups.

Although the study by Fearon and Laitin challenges the popular belief that having more ethnic groups in a country increases the probability of civil war, it's possible that ethnic diversity does increase the risk of civil war—but through an indirect effect that goes undetected in their study. Several economists, for example, have argued that ethnic diversity has a negative effect on economic growth (Easterly and Levine 1997). If this is true, ethnic diversity might contribute to the risk of civil war by helping to keep countries poor. There's some disagreement about the exact process by which ethnic diversity inhibits economic growth. In one study, Easterly and Levine (1997) find that ethnically heterogeneous countries in Africa experience lower economic growth rates than more ethnically homogeneous countries. They argue that this result is because governments in ethnically diverse countries are often politically unstable and tend to choose policies that lead to low levels of schooling, underdeveloped financial systems, distorted financial exchange markets, and insufficient infrastructure. Easterly and Levine suggest that when various ethnic groups in a country have different preferences, they may derive less satisfaction from providing public goods than would be the case in a more homogeneous society. For instance, a public good like a school might lead to lower satisfaction in an ethnically diverse setting if the groups can't agree on the main language of instruction, location, or general curriculum. The result is that the ethnically diverse society is less likely to end up building the school. Part of the problem is also that members of one ethnic group may not be willing to spend resources on providing public goods that members of other ethnic groups get to consume. Whatever the reason behind the low level of investment in public goods, economic growth is likely to be inhibited. Evidence supporting this argument linking ethnic heterogeneity with lower levels of public goods provision can be found in a variety of settings. For example, Alesina, Baqir, and Easterly (1999) compare US cities and find that governments in ethnically diverse cities tend to provide fewer public goods than governments in more ethnically homogeneous cities.

The arguments we've examined so far focus on the claim that it's the number of ethnic groups in a country that affects the risk of conflict and violence. Some scholars, though, argue that it's not the number of ethnic groups per se that matters for conflict but rather the distribution of ethnic group memberships. For example, some studies suggest that it's *ethnic polarization* and not ethnic diversity that increases the likelihood of civil wars (Esteban and Ray 1999, 2008; Esteban and Schneider 2008; Montalvo and Reynal-Querol 2005; Reynal-Querol 2002). According to these studies, civil wars are more likely when there are a few large ethnic groups with opposing interests than when there are many small ethnic groups. Along similar lines, Chandra and Boulet (2012) argue that democratic stability is put at risk not by ethnic diversity but by the existence of a permanently excluded ethnic minority. The idea here is that an ethnic minority that sees no democratic means by which it can ever come to power is more likely to break with democracy than one that foresees coming to power from time to time through the electoral process. Far from hurting democratic stability, this particular line of reasoning suggests that having a large number of evenly sized ethnic groups can help stabilize democracy by making a variety of shifting ruling coalitions possible, something that lowers the likelihood that particular ethnic groups will be permanently excluded from power.

As we'll see, arguments about the effect of electoral laws on ethnic conflict are closely tied to arguments about the existence of permanent ethnic minorities. The main dispute is whether these minorities should receive a guarantee of permanent representation or whether they should be encouraged to form coalitions with other groups and, thereby, avoid being placed in the position of permanent opposition. But before we examine the effect of electoral laws on ethnic conflict in detail, it's important to recognize that other factors influence how responsive voters are to ethnic-based appeals from politicians and, hence, how likely it is that there'll be group-based conflict in the first place.

Varshney (2001, 2002), for example, claims that the pattern of social ties between citizens is an important factor influencing group-based conflict. Specifically, he argues that peace is promoted when citizens form interethnic social ties. Interethnic civic engagement, he finds, promotes peace, and its "absence or weakness opens up space for ethnic violence" (Varshney 2001, 363). As he notes, though, not all forms of interethnic civic engagement are equally effective at promoting peace. For instance, he argues that joining formal associations, such as interethnic business associations, sports teams, reading or film clubs, and labor unions, is more effective at promoting ethnic peace than more everyday forms of interethnic contact, such as regularly eating together or allowing children to play together. Although both forms of interethnic civic engagement promote peace, Varshney finds that the associational form is sturdier than everyday engagement, especially when politicians attempt to polarize people along ethnic lines. This evidence suggests that vigorous associational life, if it has an interethnic aspect, acts as a constraint on the ability of politicians to mobilize voters along ethnic lines, even when ethnic polarization is in their political interest. The more the associational networks cut across ethnic boundaries, the harder it is for politicians to achieve such polarization (Varshney 2001, 363).

Most of the studies on ethnic politics we've examined so far take ethnic identities and how these identities are manifested in associational life as given. However, institutions, such as electoral laws, are likely to influence the type of ethnic identities that become politicized in the first place (Chandra 2004; Chandra and Boulet 2012; Posner 2004, 2005). Chandra (2005) argues that one reason why so many studies find a tension between ethnic diversity and democratic stability is that they treat ethnic identity as given rather than as something that's socially constructed. To demonstrate this point, Chandra presents a theory of electoral competition under an SMDP electoral system in which party leaders are free to define ethnic groups strategically. The results of the theory show that there are conditions in which party leaders will choose to redefine group identity in order to attract voters across ethnic lines. In other words, it's not always the case that party leaders will choose to mobilize voters along ethnic lines. This is an important result because it suggests that the conflict and extremism predicted by traditional models of **ethnic outbidding**, in which the politicization of ethnic divisions inevitably gives rise to competing ethnic parties (Horowitz 1985; Rabushka and Shepsle 1972), are the result of assuming that ethnic identities are fixed.

According to models of ethnic outbidding, once a single ethnic party emerges, it "infects" the political system because it results in a new and more extreme ethnic party emerging to oppose the first one. This, in turn, leads the first ethnic party to become more extreme, and so on, producing a downward spiral in which nonethnically based competitive politics is destroyed altogether. Essentially what Chandra (2005) shows is that this ethnic outbidding process need not occur if ethnic identities aren't fixed. Interestingly, Chandra's study suggests that far from being a cause of concern, ethnic diversity may actually help ensure democratic stability by increasing the number of dimensions along which interethnic alliances can form. In effect, majorities constructed along one dimension are unlikely to be permanent and, hence, dangerous when there's ethnic diversity, because politicians from groups that comprise a minority on that dimension can try to mobilize voters along a different dimension, one in which they'll be part of a majority.

Electoral Laws and Ethnic Conflict

Can institutions help to prevent ethnic conflict? Electoral laws influence how social cleavages are reflected in a country's party system. Proportional representation (PR) electoral laws with a high district magnitude allow social cleavages to be translated directly into the party system. In contrast, less permissive electoral systems, such as SMDP rule, create incentives for political entrepreneurs and voters to put aside some of their differences in an attempt to capture a difficult-to-obtain electoral prize. Anticipating the effect of electoral rules, members of ethnic groups are likely to engage in what Chandra (2004) refers to as an "ethnic head count"—they'll look around to see if there are enough members of their ethnic group, given the electoral rules in place, to make a plausible ethnic-specific bid for a legislative seat. If there are, they'll be encouraged to support a party that appeals mainly to their specific ethnic group. But if the perceived electoral threshold exceeds their subjective assessment of the size of their ethnic group, they'll likely support a more broadly based party—either a nonethnic party or an ethnic party that defines the ethnic group in a more inclusive manner. Thus, the propensity for elites to make ethnic-specific appeals or make interethnic alliances, and the likelihood that voters will respond to such appeals or eschew them and support more broadly based parties, will be a function of the interaction between group size and electoral laws.

Scholars wishing to influence the design of constitutions in ethnically diverse societies don't disagree about the role electoral institutions play. They all recognize that the choice of electoral laws will play an important part in determining whether many ethnically homogeneous parties or a smaller number of broadly based parties, each drawing support from multiple ethnic groups, will form. Rather, the debate is whether democratic stability is best ensured by taking ethnic groups as given and ensuring that minorities are guaranteed adequate representation, or by assuming that group identities are malleable and can be successfully channeled into promoting behavior that supports, rather than challenges, democracy.

Arend Lijphart is the most recognized champion of the view that we should take ethnic groups as given and ensure that minorities receive adequate representation. His approach to dealing with ethnic diversity is known as **consociationalism**. According to Lijphart (2004), ethnic minorities pose an acute danger to democratic stability when they're excluded from participation in formal political institutions. But if ethnic minorities are able to gain access to formal institutions and those institutions are designed to reflect the interests of as broad a set of the population as possible, then these minorities will have a stake in the continued survival of the democratic system. According to Lijphart, it's important there also be multiple checks on governmental power so as to minimize the likelihood the state can be used to systematically abuse minority rights. Consociationalism closely relates to the consensus vision of democracy, which calls for adopting institutional mechanisms that divide power and make it necessary for the government to seek input from as wide a range of citizens as possible. In effect, consociationalism is a particular strategy for implementing the consensus vision of democracy that involves the adoption of institutions guaranteeing the representation of minority groups.

Consociationalism has its roots in the religious and social conflicts experienced by the Netherlands in the late nineteenth and early twentieth centuries. These conflicts eventually resulted in the division of Dutch society into four "pillars," representing Calvinist, Catholic, Socialist, and liberal citizens. Each pillar had its own schools, hospitals, universities, newspapers, political parties, and institutional guarantees of representation. Another famous example of consociationalism is Lebanon. In 1943, Lebanon adopted an unwritten agreement—the National Pact—that guaranteed political representation to Maronite Christians, Sunni Muslims, and Shia Muslims. The National Pact stipulated the president was to be a Maronite Christian, the prime minister a Sunni Muslim, and the speaker of parliament a Shia Muslim. In addition, the Christian and Muslim communities were each to be allotted a specific number of legislative seats. Ministerial portfolios, as well as many government positions in the executive, legislative, and judicial branches, were also allocated along religious lines. Even positions such as those of judges and teachers were divided up, with some attention paid toward sectarian quotas (Bannerman 2002). Due to its application to religious groups, consociationalism in Lebanon is more commonly referred to as **confessionalism**.

Consociationalism is often associated with the adoption of proportional representation (PR) electoral rules. Lijphart (2004, 99) states that "for divided societies, ensuring the

Pool/Dalati and Nohra/Anadolu Agency/Getty Image

The Lebanese parliament elected Michel Aoun (*center*) as president of Lebanon, breaking the deadlock caused by political infighting that had left Lebanon without a head of state for two years. On November 3, 2016, the new president met Lebanese Parliament Speaker Nabih Berri (*left*) and newly appointed Prime Minister Saad Hariri (*right*) at Baabda Presidential Palace in Beirut. Under Lebanon's confessional system, the president is a Maronite Christian, the prime minister is a Sunni Muslim, and the Speaker of parliament is a Shiite Muslim.

election of a broadly representative legislature should be the crucial consideration" and that PR is "undoubtedly the optimal way of doing so" (100). He also claims that the use of majoritarian electoral laws in deeply divided societies is problematic because they can lead to the permanent exclusion of significant societal groups. Some countries such as Bolivia, Colombia, Croatia, India, and Pakistan seek to deal with ethnic diversity by providing reserved legislative seats for specified minorities. For Lijphart, however, guaranteed minority representation is inferior to simply using PR electoral rules because it requires governments to address the difficult and politically incendiary question of which minorities require special representation guarantees and which don't. PR, in contrast, treats all groups the same and, if done correctly, produces the desired minority representation.

The two basic assumptions behind Lijphart's argument are (1) that ethnic and other deep-seated conflicts can be mitigated so long as all the relevant parties to a dispute receive adequate legislative representation and (2) that proportional electoral rules are the best way to achieve this representation. As we saw in Chapter 13, though, scholars have pointed to several drawbacks to proportional electoral systems. For example, some point to how proportional electoral rules sometimes facilitate the election of small antisystem parties that become locked in cycles of legislative conflict, which can then spill over into violent social conflict. The most dramatic and troubling example of this occurred in Weimar Germany, whose highly proportional electoral system helped Hitler's Nazi Party come to power. Others point to how PR systems frequently wind up giving small parties a disproportionate influence in the government formation process. Because it's rare for parties to obtain a legislative majority in PR systems, large parties often rely on the support of smaller parties to get into government. These smaller parties can frequently use their leverage to wring concessions from the larger party. Some of these concessions can be quite radical and lack the support of an electoral majority. In Israel, for example, small ultrareligious parties have won support for many of their policies by threatening to pull out of the government. Recently, some scholars have argued that these particular issues can be mitigated by employing a proportional system with a relatively small district magnitude (about six seats per district). Carey and Hix (2011), for example, find that low-magnitude PR systems produce similar levels of proportionality as large-magnitude systems but without high levels of legislative fragmentation. They refer to these low-magnitude PR systems as the "electoral sweet spot."

The assumption that the representation of distinct groups is either necessary or sufficient to bring about intergroup peace is not held by everyone (Barry 1975). Some scholars wonder, for example, why using PR systems to essentially replicate societal divisions in the legislature will be of any help in reducing conflict if there are no incentives for cross-party cooperation and accommodation. What's missing with PR, according to these critics, is an institutional mechanism that encourages compromise and moderation.

The most widely recognized alternative to PR for deeply divided societies is the alternative vote (Horowitz 1985, 1991). The alternative vote (AV) is a majoritarian electoral system in which one legislator is elected from each district and voters have the opportunity to rank order the candidates. The candidate who wins an absolute majority of the first-preference votes is elected. If no candidate wins an absolute majority, the candidate with the lowest number of first-preference votes is eliminated, and her ballots are reallocated among the remaining candidates according to the indicated second preferences. This process continues until a candidate receives an absolute majority.

Unlike with SMDP systems, voters in an AV system have little incentive to vote strategically because they know their vote won't be wasted if their most preferred candidate is unlikely to win; their vote is simply transferred to the next candidate. This means that voters motivated by ethnic identity are likely to indicate a coethnic as their first preference and the least unsavory candidate from an alternative ethnic group as their second preference. In highly diverse districts, candidates realize their electoral success will depend on the transfer of second preferences from other ethnic groups. Consequently, successful candidates will be those who are effective at making broad-based centrist appeals that cross ethnic lines. This is why many scholars think the alternative vote encourages moderation and compromise across ethnic groups (Horowitz 1985, 1991; Reilly 2001). Empirical evidence to support this belief comes from Australia, where the major parties frequently attempt to negotiate deals with smaller parties for their second preferences prior to an election (Reilly 2001, 55–56). Additional evidence that the alternative vote encourages the building of coalitions across ethnic groups comes from Papua New Guinea and, to some extent, Fiji (Horowitz 2004, 513–514).

The potential benefits of the AV system are realized only if electoral districts are sufficiently diverse that no single ethnic group is large enough to win based on first preference votes alone. If ethnic groups are geographically concentrated in distinct parts of a country, it's unlikely that an AV system will promote cross-ethnic appeals, because each party knows it can win simply by appealing to its own ethnic group. As a result, the success of the AV system in reducing ethnic conflict depends on the geographic distribution of ethnic groups and the ethnic makeup of individual districts.

You can think of the choice between PR and AV as being a choice between replicating ethnic divisions in the legislature hoping that political leaders will cooperate after the election (PR) and creating institutional incentives that seek to weaken or even transcend the political salience of ethnicity altogether (AV). Systematic evidence of the purported benefits of PR or the AV system for divided societies is relatively rare. Some studies find that PR systems are associated with less violence (Cohen 1997; Reynal-Querol 2002; Saideman et al. 2002). However, there are at least two reasons to be cautious about these results. First, although these studies look at the association between PR systems and conflict, none examine whether PR systems *modify* the way that ethnic diversity influences the probability of conflict. As such, they don't really test the claim that ethnic diversity leads to conflict in majoritarian democracies but less so or not at all in proportional democracies. One study that does test this claim finds that, if anything, PR systems exacerbate political violence in ethnically diverse societies (Selway and Templeman 2012). Second, none of the existing studies distinguishes among the different types of majoritarian electoral systems that exist. As a result, they don't test the claim that the alternative vote moderates the effect of ethnic diversity on conflict. One reason why so few studies have focused specifically on the impact of the alternative vote is that only a small handful of countries actually use this electoral system. This makes conducting statistical analyses problematic.

Federalism and Ethnic Conflict

Traditionally, comparative political scientists have found federalism to be a particularly appealing form of government for those countries in which policy preferences differ in significant ways across geographically concentrated ethnic groups (Lijphart 1977, 1996, 1999; Lustik, Miodownik, and Eidelson 2004; Riker 1964; Stepan 1999; Tsebelis 1990). Scholars sometimes refer to **ethnofederalism** when the component territorial governing units are intentionally associated with specific ethnic groups (Hale 2008). By bringing the government closer to the people, increasing opportunities to participate in government, and giving groups discretion over their political, social, and economic affairs, federalism is thought to reduce ethnic conflict and dampen secessionist demands, thereby stabilizing democracy. In effect, federalism helps ethnic groups to protect their interests and concerns—such as language, education, culture, security, and economic development—at the regional level. By providing increased autonomy to regional governments in which national minorities might constitute majorities, federalism effectively shifts power to minorities, thereby making them more content to live within a unified state despite being permanent minorities in the national electorate. Federalism is widely thought to have played an important role in stabilizing democracies in diverse countries, such as Belgium, Canada, India, Spain, and Switzerland.

Several recent studies, though, have argued that federalism may actually intensify, rather than dampen, the flames of ethnic conflict and secessionism. There are at least two reasons for this. First, federalism can reinforce and reify ethnic identity (Hardgrave 1994; Kymlicka 1998). Rather than encouraging the construction of political coalitions across ethnic lines, federalism creates incentives for the politicization of ethnic identities by officially recognizing particular ethnic groups and giving them a sense of legitimacy. In this way, federalism leads to the strengthening of ethnic divisions. Second, federalism provides ethnic elites with access to political and economic resources they can use to bring pressure against the state. Decentralizing power to the regional level may have the unfortunate consequence of supplying groups with the necessary resources—regional legislatures, regional police forces, and regional forms of media—to more effectively engage in ethnic conflict and secessionism (Bunce 1999; Hechter 2000; Kymlicka 1998; Leff 1999; Roeder 1991; Snyder 2000). Indeed, leaders of ethnically diverse states like Sri Lanka and Indonesia have historically opposed federalism on precisely these grounds, seeing political decentralization as a slippery slope that's only likely to strengthen secessionist groups and generate demands for additional autonomy. Several scholars have blamed federalism for the separatist conflicts that occurred in the Soviet Union and Yugoslavia in the 1990s (Bunce 1999, Cornell 2002; Hale 2008).

Most political scientists would probably accept that political decentralization has helped curb ethnic conflict and secessionism in some countries, such as Belgium and India, but exacerbated ethnic conflict and secession in other countries, such as Nigeria and the former Yugoslavia. But what explains this variation? According to Dawn Brancati (2006), the answer has to do with the strength of regional parties. Political decentralization can help reduce ethnic conflict by bringing the government closer to the people; by increasing opportunities to participate in government; and by giving groups discretion over their political, social, and economic affairs. By strengthening regional parties, though, political decentralization can also exacerbate ethnic conflict.

There are several reasons for this. First, regional parties, by their very nature, tend to reinforce regional and ethnic identities by making people who share certain attributes think of themselves as a group with shared needs and goals. For example, the Northern League, a regional party in Italy, has gone to great lengths to make the people of northern Italy think of themselves as Northern Italians rather than simply as Italians. Second, regional parties often try to pass laws that discriminate against regional minorities. As an example, regional parties in Moldova exacerbated ethnic tensions with minority Romanians in Transnistria in 2004 when they passed a law closing schools that didn't use the Cyrillic alphabet, thereby preventing Romanians in this region from being educated in their own language. Third, regional parties sometimes help violent insurgent groups in their activities against the state. For instance, regional parties in Northern Ireland and Spain, such as Sinn Féin and Herri Batasuna, have helped organizations such as the Irish Republican Army (IRA) and the Basque Euskadi Ta Askatasuna (ETA) in their secessionist campaigns against the state.

In sum, Brancati (2006) argues that whether federalism helps reduce ethnic conflict depends on the extent to which decentralization strengthens regional parties. If she's correct, the key for policymakers interested in reducing ethnic conflict and stabilizing democracy is to combine federalism with other institutional features that lower the likelihood that regional parties will be strong. Electoral laws, for example, can be written to discourage the success of regional identity-based parties. One strategy to penalize regional parties would be to impose cross-regional vote requirements that force parties to compete in a certain number of regions and to win a certain percentage of the vote in these regions before they can win seats in the national legislature. Russia, Indonesia, and Nigeria have explicitly adopted these types of cross-regional voting laws in an attempt to prevent identity-based parties from forming (Brancati 2004). An alternative strategy might be to adopt a preference voting system such as the single transferable vote. This is because preference voting systems encourage political parties to make broad-based centrist appeals beyond their core set of supporters in order to obtain the valuable second preference votes of other groups. In effect, preference voting systems weaken the political salience of regional as well as ethnic identities.

Combining federalism with presidentialism may also be helpful. The presidency is nearly always the most important electoral prize in a presidential democracy. Typically, there's only a small number of viable presidential candidates (M. Golder 2006; Hicken and Stoll 2013). Given the importance of the presidency, parties that don't have a viable presidential candidate, even if they're electorally strong in particular regions, are likely to find themselves abandoned by both voters and political entrepreneurs at election time. Parties that have a national base and, hence, a viable presidential candidate will naturally benefit from this strategic behavior. The end result should be a nationalized party system in which regionally based parties struggle to compete.

Overall, it appears that federalism can help reduce ethnic conflict and stabilize democracy in countries with geographically concentrated ethnic groups. But this might be the case only if it's combined with institutional mechanisms designed to prevent regionally based identity parties from dominating the subnational governments.

PRESIDENTIALISM AND DEMOCRATIC SURVIVAL

In Chapters 5 and 6, we examined economic and cultural explanations for democracy. We now turn to institutional explanations for democracy. Are there institutional choices that make the survival of democracy more likely? Although many institutional choices affect the prospects of democratic survival, one that's generated an enormous literature in comparative politics is the choice of whether to adopt presidentialism or parliamentarism (Cheibub 2002, 2007; Linz 1990, 1994; Mainwaring 1993; Mainwaring and Shugart 1997; Shugart and Carey 1992; Stepan and Skach 1993; Valenzuela 2004).

Historically, democracy has been more stable in parliamentary regimes than in presidential ones. On average, parliamentary democracies live three times longer than presidential democracies (Przeworski et al. 2000, 129). This has led some to talk of the "perils of presidentialism" (Linz 1990). For many years, scholars have debated whether the fragility of presidential democracies is really due to something inherent in the structure of presidentialism itself, and, if so, what this might be. Answers to these questions are important because many new democracies have adopted presidential constitutions. If the survival of democracy is inherently problematic in presidential regimes, this doesn't bode well for some of these newly democratic countries. In what follows, we suggest that some presidential democracies, specifically those with multiparty systems, are more unstable than others. As we go on to note, though, ongoing economic development around the world is making all presidential democracies more stable than they were in the past.

The Perils of Presidentialism

Presidentialism can be problematic on a number of different dimensions. For example, presidentialism can make it difficult for citizens to identify who's responsible for the policies that are implemented. The separation of powers between the executive and legislative branches in presidential democracies allows each to blame the other when outcomes are bad and each to engage in credit claiming when outcomes are good. This low clarity of responsibility makes it difficult for voters to hold the government accountable. In addition, the policymaking process in presidential democracies can be slow. New legislation must work its way through the legislature and be accepted by the president before it can be enacted. Such negotiations are often protracted because, unlike in parliamentary democracies where governments must have the support of a legislative majority, a presidential government can face a legislature controlled by parties that don't support the president's legislative goals. Divided government is possible in presidential democracies but not in parliamentary ones.

The pattern of executive recruitment in presidential democracies can also be problematic. In most parliamentary democracies, prime ministers are selected from the leadership of a party's legislative delegation. Membership in that leadership is typically restricted to parliamentarians who've worked their way up from lowly "backbench" positions by gaining policy expertise, honing their debating skills, and demonstrating their loyalty to the party. In contrast, presidential candidates are often drawn from outsiders who are seen to be free from commitments to the party elite. Significantly, this means that presidential candidates are also frequently free of legislative experience and policymaking expertise. As an example, Alberto Fujimori, an academic and TV presenter, won the 1990 presidential elections in Peru. In 2016, political outsider Donald Trump became the president of the United States. The election of such candidates to the "equivalent" position of prime minister in a parliamentary democracy is almost unthinkable.

It turns out that many of these "perils of presidentialism" actually occur in some parliamentary democracies as well. Parliamentary democracies that have coalition governments, for example, also experience difficulty in making policy quickly and voters can find it hard to identify who's responsible for the policies that are implemented. Indeed, some scholars make the case that presidentialism, far from being a cause for concern, is, in fact, the solution to these problems in parliamentary democracies. Rather than talk about the "perils of presidentialism," these scholars choose to focus on the "problems of parliamentarism."

The problems of parliamentarism are, perhaps, best illustrated by the French Fourth Republic (1946–1958). The French Fourth Republic was characterized by high levels of **immobilism** and government instability (Rioux 1989). In the twelve years of its existence, the French Fourth Republic witnessed twenty-four different governments under sixteen different prime ministers (Huber and Martinez-Gallardo 2004). A consequence of this instability was that French governments were unable to deal with the main issues of the day, particularly those having to do with its colonies in Indochina and Algeria. Much of the problem lay with the Fourth Republic's proportional electoral system that helped to produce a highly fragmented and polarized legislature. Roughly 30 percent of the seats in the National Assembly regularly went to parties on the extreme right (Gaullists and Poujadists) and extreme left (Communists) that were not viewed as viable government coalition partners. This meant that the five or six moderate parties that existed in the center of the policy space were forced to try to build legislative majorities from the remaining 70 percent of seats, something that proved extremely difficult. Governments typically had to choose between immobility—doing nothing and remaining in power—and attempting to push forward with their legislative program, which normally resulted in their quick removal from office. In May 1958, a majority of legislators in the National Assembly eventually voted themselves and the constitution out of existence and delegated power to General Charles de Gaulle to write a new constitution. One of the goals of de Gaulle's new constitution was to concentrate power in the hands of a president so that he could override the stalemates that dogged the Fourth Republic. For de Gaulle, a stronger president was the solution to the problems of parliamentarism.

Are the "problems of parliamentarism" greater than the "perils of presidentialism"? Although the example of immobilism in the parliamentary French Fourth Republic is somewhat illustrative, ransacking history for supportive cases in favor of one's favorite or most hated institution is not good scientific practice. As a result, we'll now turn our attention to a more systematic analysis of how presidentialism and parliamentarism affect democratic survival.

Stepan and Skach (1993) claim that the prospects for the survival of democracy are worse under presidentialism than under parliamentarism. They argue that the reason for this can be traced to the fact that the essence of parliamentarism is *mutual dependence,* whereas the essence of presidentialism is *mutual independence.* In a parliamentary democracy, the legislative and executive branches are mutually dependent. On the one hand, the government needs the support of a legislative majority to stay in power. On the other hand, the government can dissolve the legislature by calling new elections. In other words, the government and the legislature can't continue to exist without the support of the other in a parliamentary democracy. In a presidential democracy, in contrast, the executive and legislative branches are mutually independent. Both the legislature and the president have their own independent sources of legitimacy and their own fixed electoral mandates. The legislature can't remove the president from office, and the president can't remove the legislature.

Stepan and Skach (1993) argue that the mutual dependence of parliamentarism encourages *reconciliation* between the executive and legislative branches, whereas the mutual independence of presidentialism encourages *antagonism* between them. In presidential democracies, this antagonism, which can arise when the president is faced by a legislature dominated by opposition parties, can lead to legislative deadlock. With no constitutional mechanism to resolve the deadlock, politicians and citizens in presidential democracies may look to the military to break the stalemate. In contrast, if deadlock occurs between the executive and legislative branches in a parliamentary democracy, there are constitutional means for resolving the crisis. Either the legislature can pass a vote of no confidence and remove the government, or the prime minister can dissolve the parliament and call for new elections. It's the existence of these constitutional means in parliamentary democracies for resolving deadlock situations that's thought to be at the heart of why democratic stability is greater in parliamentary democracies.

Stepan and Skach (1993) present an impressive array of facts to support their claim that parliamentary democracies last longer than presidential ones. They begin by asking how many of the countries that became independent democracies between 1945 and 1979 were able to sustain democracy throughout the 1980s. In Table 14.4, we list the names of all eighty countries that became independent democracies between 1945 and 1979. We also list whether they adopted a parliamentary, presidential, or semi-presidential form of democracy. Countries

TABLE 14.4 ■ Democratic Survival in Newly Independent States after World War II				
a. Form of Democracy Adopted				
Parliamentary N = 41		**Presidential N = 36**		**Semi-Presidential N = 3**
Bahamas	Mauritius	Algeria	Madagascar	Lebanon
Bangladesh	Nauru	Angola	Malawi	Senegal
Barbados	Nigeria	Benin	Mali	Zaire
Botswana	Pakistan	Burkina Faso	Mauritania	
Burma	Papua New Guinea	Cameroon	Mozambique	
Chad	St. Lucia	Cape Verde	Niger	
Dominica	St. Vincent	Central African	Philippines	
Fiji	Sierra Leone	Republic Comoros	Rwanda	
The Gambia	Singapore	Congo	São Tomé	
Ghana	Solomon Islands	Cyprus	Seychelles	
Grenada	Somalia	Djibouti	Syria	
Guyana	Sri Lanka	Equatorial Guinea	Taiwan	
India	Sudan	Gabon	Togo	
Indonesia	Suriname	Guinea	Tunisia	
Israel	Swaziland	Guinea Bissau	Vietnam (N)	
Jamaica	Tanzania	Ivory Coast	Vietnam (S)	
Kenya	Trinidad and Tobago	Korea (N)	Yemen (S)	
Kiribati	Tuvalu	Korea (S)	Zambia	
Laos	Uganda			
Malaysia	Western Samoa			
Malta				
b. Continuously Democratic Countries, 1979–1989				
Parliamentary N = 15/41		**Presidential N = 0**		**Semi-Presidential N = 0**
Bahamas	Nauru			
Barbados	Papua New Guinea			
Botswana	St. Lucia			
Dominica	St. Vincent			
India	Solomon Islands			
Israel	Trinidad and Tobago			
Jamaica	Tuvalu			
Kiribati				

Source: Data from Stepan and Skach (1993, 8–9).

that became independent in the postwar period were about as likely to adopt parliamentarism as they were to adopt presidentialism. In Table 14.4b, we list the names of those countries that were continuously democratic from 1979 to 1989 and the form of democracy they had. Of the eighty countries that became independent democracies in the postwar period, only fifteen were continuously democratic through the 1980s. Incredibly, all fifteen of these countries had adopted parliamentarism. None of the thirty-six countries that adopted presidentialism managed to sustain democracy during the 1980s.

Lest a focus on newly independent countries be a source of bias, Stepan and Skach next present evidence from all countries that experienced democracy between 1973 and 1989 but that were not members of the Organisation for Economic Co-operation and Development (OECD).[3] They wanted to know how many non-OECD countries that experienced democracy for at least a year between 1973 and 1989 were able to sustain it for a continuous ten-year period. Their data are shown in Table 14.5. Countries that experienced democracy for at least a year between 1973 and 1989 were about as likely to adopt parliamentarism as they were to adopt presidentialism. Of those countries that managed to sustain democracy for a continuous ten-year period, though, almost none had a presidential form of democracy. By comparing "democratic experimenters" with "democratic survivors," we can calculate a "democratic survival rate." As Table 14.5 indicates, the democratic survival rate for parliamentary regimes is three times that for presidential regimes.

Although these simple comparisons suggest there's something to the notion that presidentialism imperils democratic survival, they say almost nothing about why this might be the case. In other words, they say very little about the causal link between regime type and democratic survival. Recall, though, that Stepan and Skach do provide a potential causal story for the results in Tables 14.4 and 14.5. Specifically, they argue that presidentialism is more likely to lead to the kind of deadlock between the executive and legislative branches that invites extraconstitutional behavior. Thus, an observable implication of their theory is that military coups should be more common in presidential democracies than in parliamentary ones. In Table 14.6, we present data on the frequency of military coups in the same fifty-three non-OECD countries as before. Military coups are more than twice as likely in presidential democracies as they are in parliamentary ones. Whereas 40 percent of the non-OECD countries that adopted presidentialism experienced a military coup between 1973 and 1989, just 18 percent of the countries that adopted parliamentarism did. This higher coup rate in presidential regimes is exactly as Stepan and Skach (1993) predict.

TABLE 14.5 ■ Democratic Survival in Fifty-Three Non-OECD Countries, 1973–1989		
	Parliamentary	Presidential
Democratic for at least one year	28	25
Democratic for ten consecutive years	17	5
Democratic survival rate	61%	20%

Source: Data from Stepan and Skach (1993, 11).

---

[3]The OECD is essentially a club of rich democracies set up by the Allied powers after World War II. Stepan and Skach focus on non-OECD countries because it's in poor countries that democracy is most unstable.

TABLE 14.6   ■   Military Coups in Fifty-Three Non-OECD Countries, 1973–1989

	Parliamentary	Presidential
Democratic for at least one year	28	25
Number that experienced a coup	5	10
Coup susceptibility rate	18%	40%

Source: Data from Stepan and Skach (1993, 12).

Although these simple statistics are quite illustrative, it's probably the case that some factors causing democracies to fail are also associated with the choice to adopt parliamentarism or presidentialism in the first place. This raises the concern that it may be these other factors, and not presidentialism per se, that lead to the collapse of democracy. The failure to take account of these other factors might lead us to overestimate the true effect of regime type on democratic survival. Recognizing this, Stepan and Skach attempt to deal with it by leaning on the work of a Finnish political scientist named Tatu Vanhanen.

Recall from Chapter 5 that modernization theory predicts a strong association between democracy and societal development. In an attempt to evaluate modernization theory, Vanhanen (1991) constructed an index of democratization—a measure capturing a country's level of democracy—and what he calls an index of power resources—a measure capturing a country's level of societal development. If modernization theory is accurate, countries with a high score on the power resource index should also have a high score on the democratization index. Indeed, this is exactly what Vanhanen finds. Although Vanhanen finds a strong association between his power resource index and the democratization index, the fit is certainly not perfect. Some countries, for example, score significantly higher on the democratization index than their level of modernization would predict. Similarly, some countries score significantly lower on the democratization index than their level of modernization would predict. Stepan and Skach label those countries that score surprisingly high on the democratization index as "democratic overachievers." And they label those countries that score surprisingly low on the democratization index as "democratic underachievers." Table 14.7 presents data showing whether the democratic overachievers and underachievers are presidential or parliamentary democracies.

TABLE 14.7   ■   Democratic Underachievers and Overachievers by Regime Type

	Parliamentary	Presidential
Overachievers	31	10
Underachievers	6	12
Ratio of overachievers to underachievers	5.17	0.83

Source: Data from Stepan and Skach (1993, 10).

Stepan and Skach interpret the comparison of democratic overachievers and underachievers in Table 14.7 to mean that, after taking account of a set of modernization variables thought to influence democratic survival, parliamentary systems are five times more likely to be democratic overachievers than they are to be democratic underachievers. In contrast, presidential systems are slightly more likely to be democratic underachievers than they are to be democratic overachievers. A different way to look at the data is that democratic overachievers are about three times more likely to be parliamentary regimes than they are to be presidential ones. In contrast, democratic underachievers are about twice as likely to be presidential regimes as they are to be parliamentary ones. Overall, the evidence in Table 14.7 provides strong support for the claim that the prospects of democratic survival are lower in presidential systems even after controlling for other factors that affect the survival of democracy.

The Difficult Combination: Presidentialism and Multipartism

So far, the empirical evidence suggests that the prospects for democratic survival are greater in parliamentary democracies than in presidential ones. But recall our earlier discussion of immobilism in the French Fourth Republic. De Gaulle argued that concentrating power in the hands of a president was the key to solving the problems of highly fragmented legislatures, government instability, and immobilism in the French Fourth Republic. De Gaulle's belief that we should call upon a "strong man," such as a president, who can bring the country together in moments of crisis is quite widespread. This has important implications for any causal connection between presidentialism and democratic survival. Specifically, if presidentialism is adopted in moments of crisis, presidential regimes may fail at a higher rate than parliamentary regimes, not because there's something inherently problematic about presidentialism, but simply because presidentialism tends to be adopted in difficult circumstances. One way to think about this is that presidentialism is like a hospital for ailing polities. We wouldn't want to say that "hospitals kill people" just because large numbers of people die in hospitals. If people who go to the hospital are in poorer health than those who don't, the explanation for high mortality rates in hospitals is likely to have more to do with the fact that people in a hospital are very sick than it does with the fact that they're in a hospital. Maybe the same is true for presidentialism. Until we can convince ourselves that countries that adopt presidentialism are the same as countries that adopt parliamentarism, studies such as Stepan and Skach's run the risk of overstating the negative effects of presidentialism.

The standard way to address this issue is, to continue our metaphor, to find a measure of "poor health" and include it as a control variable in an analysis of the relationship between mortality and being in a hospital. With one exception, we know of no empirical analysis that's adopted this approach when examining the relationship between presidentialism and democratic survival.[4] This may, in part, be because the analytical problem before us is probably

---

[4]The exception is Cheibub's (2007) analysis of presidentialism and democracy. He argues that what's made presidential regimes more fragile than parliamentary ones is that presidential regimes are more likely to emerge in countries in which the military has traditionally had a strong political role. As Cheibub demonstrates, any democratic regime, parliamentary or presidential, is more likely to fail in countries with a strong military tradition. This leads him to conclude that presidential democracies are more likely to fail not because they're presidential but because they're more likely to be adopted in difficult circumstances—when the military has a strong political presence. Przeworski and colleagues (2000, 136) argue, however, that "parliamentary democracies . . . are still more stable regardless of their origins. . . . Thus, again, the stability of democracies seems to be an effect of their institutional frameworks, not only of their origins."

more complicated than the one suggested by our hospital metaphor. For example, the factors that cause death in humans—cardiovascular diseases, parasitic diseases, respiratory diseases, and so on—affect those in a hospital and those not in a hospital the same way. But it may be the case that some factors "dangerous" for democracy are dangerous only in parliamentary regimes or only in presidential ones. If this is true, and presidential and parliamentary regimes are different sorts of organisms that process factors such as legislative fragmentation in fundamentally different ways, it may prove extremely difficult to measure the underlying health of a regime independently of its status as a presidential or parliamentary system.

The work of one political scientist, Scott Mainwaring, suggests that presidential and parliamentary democracies *do* process political factors differently. In particular, it suggests they process legislative fragmentation differently. Whereas legislative fragmentation always increases the likelihood of instability, the instability produced in parliamentary democracies is different from that produced in presidential ones. Specifically, legislative fragmentation increases the likelihood of *cabinet instability* in parliamentary systems, whereas it increases the likelihood of *democratic instability* in presidential systems. The work by Mainwaring (1993) ultimately suggests that if legislative fragmentation is viewed as a political ailment in parliamentary democracies, as critics of the French Fourth Republic like de Gaulle and others claim, then presidentialism could well be a form of medicine that's worse than the disease.

Why is legislative fragmentation likely to lead to such different outcomes in parliamentary and presidential democracies? One reason is that legislative fragmentation is more likely to lead to legislative deadlock in a presidential regime than in a parliamentary one. Deadlock in a presidential democracy occurs when a legislative majority opposed to the president is large enough to pass bills in the legislature but not large enough to override a presidential veto. Legislative fragmentation increases the chances the president's party won't command a legislative majority and, hence, the chances that legislative deadlock will occur. But why is legislative fragmentation more likely to lead to legislative deadlock in presidential systems? In a parliamentary democracy, the prime minister serves at the pleasure of the legislature and is, therefore, obliged to form a cabinet made up of a coalition of parties that *does* command a legislative majority. Presidents sometimes form coalitions (Amorim Neto 2006; Cheibub 2007; Cheibub, Przeworski, and Saiegh 2004). The key difference, though, is that when legislators vote against a president's legislation in sufficient numbers, the legislation is blocked, but when legislators vote against a prime minister's legislation, there's a good chance the government will fall. In other words, a coalition government in a parliamentary democracy implies a legislative coalition, whereas this presumption is not the case in presidential democracies. A consequence of this is that legislative fragmentation is more likely to produce deadlock in a presidential democracy than it is to produce immobilism in a parliamentary democracy.

The problem of legislative deadlock in presidential democracies is exacerbated by the way presidents are recruited to office. Presidential candidates are often political outsiders who have relatively little policymaking expertise or experience dealing with the legislature. One of the main reasons for this is that presidents tend to be directly elected by the people and, therefore, have less need to build links with legislative actors than prime ministers do. A consequence of this, though, is that presidents tend to lack the necessary skills or experience to build legislative coalitions to resolve deadlock situations when they arise. Even when they do manage to build a coalition, coalition partners in presidential regimes have acute incentives to distance themselves from the president's policy goals. One reason for this is that they expect to run against the president in a winner-take-all contest in the next election and they want to be able to criticize her policies (Coppedge 1994, 168). In contrast, prime ministers tend to be individuals who've worked in the legislature for many years, who've gained enormous amounts of policy expertise, and who've been schooled in the art of coalition building. A result of this is that prime ministers are often better placed than presidents to build legislative coalitions to resolve deadlock situations. Thus, according to Mainwaring (1993), not only are presidential democracies more apt than parliamentary democracies to have executives whose policy programs will be consistently blocked by the legislature but they're also more apt to have executives who are less capable of dealing with problems when they arise.

When legislative deadlock does occur, it's much more likely to lead to democratic instability in presidential democracies than in parliamentary ones. If legislative deadlock occurs between the executive and legislative branches in a parliamentary regime, there are constitutional means for resolving the crisis. Either the legislature can pass a vote of no confidence and remove the government, or the prime minister can dissolve the parliament and call new elections. As Mainwaring (1993, 208) notes, though, in presidential democracies "there are no neat means of replacing a president who is enormously unpopular in the society at large and has lost most of his/her support in the legislature." Thus, the absence of a vote of no confidence may ensure the stability of the head of government in presidential regimes, but it introduces a rigidity that can threaten democratic stability by encouraging frustrated elites or masses to call for the removal of the president, or the dissolution of legislature, as a way to break the deadlock (Linz 1994). Although there are some circumstances under which political actors can accomplish this within the bounds of some presidential constitutions, the solution to deadlock is more likely to be extraconstitutional in presidential regimes than in parliamentary ones. To be clear, the claim is not that deadlock situations will always lead to democratic collapse in presidential systems, just that deadlock situations are more likely to produce a democratic collapse in a presidential system than a parliamentary one. To sum up, legislative deadlock is likely to be associated with *democratic* instability in presidential democracies. If and when immobilism occurs in parliamentary democracies, it's more likely to be associated with *cabinet* instability.

Earlier, we presented evidence that presidential democracies were more fragile than parliamentary democracies. An important implication of Mainwaring's argument, though, is that democracy should be more fragile in some presidential regimes than in others. Specifically, his argument implies that democracy should be more fragile in presidential democracies characterized by high levels of legislative fragmentation, because legislative fragmentation increases the likelihood of deadlock, which, in turn, increases the likelihood of democratic instability. When legislative fragmentation is low, the likelihood of deadlock and, hence, democratic instability will also be low.

To evaluate his claim that presidential democracies will be unstable particularly when legislative fragmentation is high, Mainwaring (1993) examines all countries that experienced uninterrupted democracy for the twenty-five-year period between 1967 and 1992. Although twenty-four parliamentary regimes were able to sustain democracy during this period, just four presidential regimes were able to do so: Colombia, Costa Rica, the United States, and Venezuela. Mainwaring wanted to know what made these presidential regimes different from other presidential regimes. His answer was that they all effectively had two-party systems, as illustrated in Table 14.8; none of them had multiparty systems. At the time of his writing in 1993, Mainwaring argued that only one multiparty presidential regime had historically managed to sustain democracy for a twenty-five-year period. And this exception was Chile, a democracy, begun in 1932, that experienced a dramatic "death" in 1973 when a military coup overthrew the Socialist president Salvador Allende and replaced him with the dictator General Augusto Pinochet. Allende had been elected in 1970 with a slim plurality of the

TABLE 14.8 ■ Presidential Regimes That Sustained Democracy from 1967 to 1992 and Their Party System Size	
Country (Year)	Effective number of legislative parties
Colombia (1986)	2.45
Costa Rica (1986)	2.21
United States (1984)	1.95
Venezuela (1983)	2.42

Source: Amorim Neto and Cox (1997, 169–170).

vote (35.3 percent) and was immediately beset with problems from every side in the country's highly fragmented and deeply polarized legislature.

In Table 14.9, we use data from Mainwaring (1993, 205–207) to calculate the democratic success rate for parliamentary regimes, multiparty presidential regimes, and two-party presidential regimes. Democratic success is defined here as a sustaining of democracy for an uninterrupted twenty-five-year period at any time between 1945 and 1992. The information in Table 14.9 suggests that democratic consolidation is possible in two-party presidential

AP Photo

La Moneda, the Chilean presidential residence, under ground and air attack by Chilean armed forces during the September 11, 1973, coup d'état that led to the ruthless dictatorship of General Augusto Pinochet. The democratically elected Socialist president Salvador Allende is thought to have committed suicide during the palace siege.

TABLE 14.9 ■ Regime Type, Party System Size, and Democratic Consolidation, 1945–1992

Regime type	Democratic success rate
Multiparty presidentialism	1/15, or 0.07
Two-party presidentialism	5/10, or 0.5
Parliamentarism	25/44, or 0.57

Source: Data from Mainwaring (1993, 205–207).

Note: The democratic success rate refers to the proportion of countries that were able to sustain democracy for an uninterrupted twenty-five-year period at any time between 1945 and 1992.

regimes but not in multiparty presidential regimes. Interestingly, the democratic success rate for two-party presidential regimes (0.50) is almost as high as the democratic success rate for parliamentary regimes (0.57). These results provide strong evidence that it's the combination of presidentialism and multipartism rather than just presidentialism that's inimical to democracy. Indeed, Mainwaring refers to the combination of presidentialism and multipartism as "the difficult combination" for precisely this reason.

It's worth noting that Stepan and Skach (1993) also provide evidence in support of Mainwaring's conjecture in their own analysis. Although they don't make too much of it, they provide data on the size of party systems in those countries that became independent after 1945 and that managed to sustain democracy during the 1980s. These data are shown in Table 14.10. As you can see, long-lived multiparty parliamentary regimes aren't particularly rare, but long-lived multiparty presidential regimes are.

Summary

In this section, we examined an argument that says that presidential constitutions make successful democratic consolidation more difficult than parliamentary constitutions, particularly when the legislature is highly fragmented. The key weakness of presidentialism appears

TABLE 14.10 ■ Consolidated Democracies by Regime Type and Party System Size

Constitution	Effective number of legislative parties	
	Fewer than three	Three or more
Parliamentary	23	11
Semi-presidential	0	2
Presidential	5	0

Source: Data from Stepan and Skach (1993, 8–9).

Note: The numbers in the table refer to those countries that became independent after 1945 and sustained democracy for a continuous ten-year period from 1979 to 1989.

to be its inability to find legal ways out of executive-legislative deadlock, something that's more likely to occur when the legislature is highly fragmented.

It's possible to put this finding in a broader perspective by situating it in the context of veto player theory (see Chapter 13). Recall that an increase in the number of veto players is expected to make it more difficult to change the status quo policy, especially if the veto players hold diverse policy preferences. The policy stability induced by veto players is equivalent in many ways to what we've referred to here as deadlock or immobilism. The father of modern veto player theory, George Tsebelis, has conjectured that although large numbers of veto players with diverse preferences may encourage policy stability, they may also encourage political instability (Tsebelis 1995, 322). The Mainwaring claim that multipartism and presidentialism form a "difficult combination" for democratic consolidation can be interpreted in light of veto player theory. If Tsebelis is correct that an increased number of veto players leads to policy stability, which in its extreme form manifests itself as "deadlock," we should expect presidentialism and parliamentarism to affect the type of political instability that ensues. In other words, multiple veto players lead to policy stability (deadlock), but the form of political instability that results depends on a country's constitution. If the constitution is presidential, policy stability or deadlock is likely to encourage a coup or some other form of democratic instability. If, however, the constitution is parliamentary, the policy stability or immobilism is likely to lead to a vote of no confidence, a cabinet reshuffle, or elections leading to the formation of a new cabinet—that is, cabinet instability. This causal argument is presented in Figure 14.4.

We'd like to point out one last subtlety that involves our discussion of democratic survival in this section and our discussion of the effects of wealth on democratic survival from Chapter 5. Recall that wealth promotes democratic survival. Indeed, Przeworski and colleagues (2000) argue that democracy is invulnerable once countries reach a certain level of wealth. The claim that wealth is sufficient to ensure democratic consolidation leads to a surprising result—the choice of political institutions, say, the combination of multipartism and presidentialism, is likely to have a bigger effect on the chances that democracy will survive in poor countries than in rich ones. This is because democracy is likely to survive in rich countries whether they've chosen felicitous institutions or not. In other words, institutional choice

FIGURE 14.4   ■   Veto Players, Policy Stability, and Different Types of Political Instability

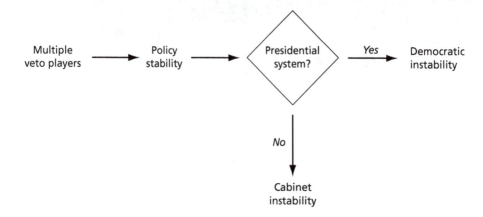

matters much more in poor countries than in rich ones, at least when it comes to democratic consolidation.[5]

Whereas the choice between presidentialism and parliamentarism is typically addressed explicitly by constitution writers, the size of the party system isn't entirely under their direct control. According to Duverger's theory, though, we can expect a country with high levels of social heterogeneity to produce a highly fragmented legislature unless specific electoral institutions (majoritarian ones) are adopted with the goal of reducing the number of parties. Consequently, the analysis in this section suggests that if a presidential constitution is chosen for some reason, then adopting permissive electoral laws, such as PR, with a high district magnitude has the potential to cause problems. In the presence of social heterogeneity, permissive electoral laws can be expected to produce multipartism, which, combined with presidentialism, is likely to inhibit democratic consolidation. Of course, the finding of Przeworski and colleagues (2000) on the apparent sufficiency of wealth may suggest that relatively rich countries have a greater margin of error in choosing their institutions than poor countries. This may explain why some multiparty presidential regimes in Latin America have managed to stay democratic since the wave of transitions to democracy that began there in the mid-1980s. For some time now, many of these countries have exceeded Przeworski and colleagues' "magical" threshold of wealth at which democracy is immune to breakdown.

CONCLUSION

We have, perhaps, gone on long enough. We hope, however, that this chapter has convinced you that comparative politics has a great deal to say that's of vital interest to citizens and policymakers who'd like to know how the institutions they choose are likely to affect the political, social, and economic outcomes they'll experience. Let's briefly summarize the basic results we've presented in this chapter. First, we've shown patterned differences in the way that majoritarian and consensus democracies represent the interests of voters. Second, we've demonstrated that electoral laws influence both who's chosen to rule and how they're likely to wield that power—at least with respect to redistributive fiscal policy. Third, we've highlighted the ways in which constitutional elements, such as electoral laws and federalism, are likely to affect the probability of ethnic conflict. And finally, we've reported results suggesting that the choice of electoral laws and the decision about whether to adopt presidentialism or parliamentarism are likely to strongly influence the survival of new democracies—especially if the country's level of wealth isn't sufficiently high, by itself, to make democratic survival likely.

Many questions remain about how these results interact with each other. We invite you to speculate about such matters. Comparative politics raises and attempts to answer questions with life-and-death implications. We hope that as you finish this book, your development as a student of comparative politics is just beginning.

---

[5]Evidence consistent with this line of reasoning comes from Boix (2003, 153–154). In a study of democratic survival from 1850 to 1990, he finds that presidential democracies are more likely to fail than parliamentary democracies only in underdeveloped countries; he finds no difference in the democratic survival rates of parliamentary and presidential regimes in developed countries.

Key Concepts

majoritarian vision of democracy—is based on the idea that power should be concentrated in the hands of the majority

consensus vision of democracy—is based on the idea that power should be dispersed among as many political actors as possible

formalistic representation—how representatives are authorized and held accountable

accountability—the extent to which voters are able to sanction parties for their behavior in office

retrospective voting—when voters look at the past performance of incumbents to decide how to vote in the current election

clarity of responsibility—the extent to which voters can identify exactly who's responsible for the policies that are implemented

substantive representation—how representatives "act for" the people and promote their interests

ideological congruence—the extent to which the actions of representatives are in line with the interests of the people

descriptive representation—the extent to which representatives resemble and "stand for" their constituents

symbolic representation—the symbolic ways that representatives "stand for" the citizens

fiscal policy—the manipulation of tax and spending decisions to accomplish governmental goals

partisan model of macroeconomic policy—the argument that left-wing parties represent the interests of low-income voters and that right-wing parties represent the interests of high-income voters; changes in the partisan control of the government produce predictable changes in fiscal policy

ethnic outbidding—a process in which ethnic divisions are politicized and lead to the formation of increasingly polarized ethnic parties

consociationalism—a political system that emphasizes power sharing through guaranteed group representation

confessionalism—a political system that emphasizes power sharing by different religious communities through guaranteed group representation

ethnofederalism—when the component territorial governing units in a federal system are intentionally associated with specific ethnic groups

immobilism—a situation in parliamentary democracies in which government coalitions are so weak and unstable that they're incapable of reaching an agreement on new policy

REFERENCES

Abootalebi, Ali. 1999. "Islam, Islamists, and Democracy." *Middle East Review of International Affairs* 3:14–24.

Acemoglu, Daron, and James A. Robinson. 2000. "Why Did the West Extend the Franchise? Democracy, Inequality, and Growth in Historical Perspective." *Quarterly Journal of Economics* 115:1167–1199.

———. 2001. "A Theory of Political Transitions." *American Economic Review* 91:938–963.

———. 2006. *Economic Origins of Dictatorship and Democracy.* New York: Cambridge University Press.

Adida, Claire L., Karen E. Ferree, Daniel N. Posner, and Amanda Lea Robinson. 2016. "Who's Asking? Interviewer Coethnicity Effects in African Survey Data." *Comparative Political Studies* 40: 1630–1660.

"Afghanistan: The Wrong Voting System." 2005. *The New York Times,* March 16. http://www.nytimes.com/2005/03/16/opinion/afghanistan-the-wrong-voting-system.html.

"After the Coup, the Counter-Coup." 2016. *The Economist,* July 23. http://www.economist.com/news/briefing/21702511-failed-putsch-was-bloodiest-turkey-has-seen-backlash-worrying-after-coup.

Ahmed, Faisal Z. 2012. "The Perils of Unearned Foreign Income: Aid, Remittances, and Government Survival." *American Political Science Review* 106:146–165.

Alda, K. 2006. "Legislative Limbo." *The Prague Post,* August 24. http://www.theprague post.com/articles/2006/0/23/legislative-limbo.php.

Aldrich, John H. 1993. "Rational Choice and Turnout." *American Journal of Political Science* 37:246–278.

———. 1995. *Why Parties? The Origin and Transformation of Political Parties in America.* Chicago: University of Chicago Press.

Alesina, Alberto, Reza Baqir, and William Easterly. 1999. "Public Goods and Ethnic Divisions." *Quarterly Journal of Economics* 114:1243–1284.

Alesina, Alberto, and Roberto Perotti. 1994. "The Political Economy of Growth: A Critical Survey of the Recent Literature." *The World Bank Economic Review* 8:351–371.

Alesina, Alberto, and Enrico Spolaore. 1997. "On the Number and Size of Nations." *Quarterly Journal of Economics* 112:1027–1056.

Allum, P. A. 1973. *Italy—Republic without Government?* New York: Norton.

Almond, Gabriel A., and Sydney Verba. [1963] 1989. *The Civic Culture: Political Attitudes and Democracy in Five Nations.* London: Sage.

Althusser, Louis. 1969. *For Marx.* London: Penguin Books.

Altincekic, Ceren, and David H. Bearce. 2014. "Why There Should Be No Political Foreign Aid Curse." *World Development* 64:18–32.

Al-Ubaydli, Omar. 2012. "Natural Resources and the Tradeoff between Authoritarianism and Development." *Journal of Economic Behavior & Organization* 81:137–152.

Amorim Neto, Octavio. 2006. "The Presidential Calculus: Executive Policy Making and Cabinet Formation in the Americas." *Comparative Political Studies* 39:415–440.

Amorim Neto, Octavio, and Gary Cox. 1997. "Electoral Institutions, Cleavage Structures, and the Number of Parties." *American Journal of Political Science* 41:149–174.

Amorim Neto, Octavio, and David Samuels. 2006. "Democratic Regimes and Cabinet Politics: A Global Perspective." Paper presented at the Annual Meeting of the Midwest Political Science Association, Chicago, April 20–23.

Amorim Neto, Octavio, and Kaare Strøm. 2006. "Breaking the Parliamentary Chain of Delegation: Presidents and Non-partisan Cabinet Members in European Democracies." *British Journal of Political Science* 36:619–643.

Andeweg, Rudy B., and Galen A. Irwin. 2009. *Governance and Politics of the Netherlands,* 3rd ed. New York: Palgrave Macmillan.

Ansell, Ben W., and David J. Samuels. 2014. *Inequality and Democratization: An Elite-Competition Approach.* New York: Cambridge University Press.

Ariotti, Margaret H. and Sona N. Golder. 2018. "Partisan Portfolio Allocation in African Democracies." *Comparative Political Studies* 51(3): 341–379.

Aristotle. [350 BCE] 1996. *The Politics and the Constitution of Athens,* edited by Stephen Everson. New York: Cambridge University Press.

Armstrong, Hannah. 2010. "Niger Coup: Can Africa Use Military Power for Good?" *The Christian Science Monitor,* March 25. http://www.csmonitor.com/World/Africa/2010/0325/Niger-coup-Can-Africa-use-military-power-for-good.

Arrow, Kenneth. 1963. *Social Choices and Individual Values.* New Haven, CT: Yale University Press.

Arzaghi, Mohammad, and J. Vernon Henderson. 2005. "Why Countries Are Fiscally Decentralizing." *Journal of Public Economics* 89:1157–1189.

Austen-Smith, David, and Jeffrey Banks. 1988. "Elections, Coalitions, and Legislative Outcomes." *American Political Science Review* 82:405–422.

Bäck, Hanna, and Patrick Dumont. 2008. "Making the First Move: A Two-Stage Analysis of the Role of Formateurs in Parliamentary Government Formation." *Public Choice* 135:353–373.

Bagehot, Walter. 1867. *The English Constitution.* Available from http://www.gutenberg.org/ebooks/4351.

Balmer, Randall. 2006. *Thy Kingdom Come: An Evangelical's Lament.* New York: Basic Books.

Banfield, Edward C., and Laura Fasano Banfield. 1958. *The Moral Basis of a Backward Society.* Glencoe, IL: Free Press.

Bannerman, M. Graeme. 2002. "Republic of Lebanon." In *Government and Politics in the Middle East and North Africa,* 4th ed., ed. David E. Long and Bernard Reich. Boulder, CO: Westview Press.

Baradat, Leon P. 2006. *Political Ideologies: Their Origins and Impact.* Englewood Cliffs, NJ: Prentice Hall.

Barbera, Pablo. 2013. "When Duverger becomes auocratic: Electoral systems and opposition fragmentation in non-democratic regimes." Unpublished manuscript, New York University.

Barkan, Joel D. 1995. "Elections in Agrarian Societies." *Journal of Democracy* 6:106–116.

Baron, David, and John Ferejohn. 1989. "Bargaining in Legislatures." *American Political Science Review* 83:1181–1206.

Barro, Robert J. 1997. *Determinants of Economic Growth.* Cambridge, MA: MIT Press.

———. 1999. "Determinants of Democracy." *Journal of Political Economy* 107:158–183.

Barry, Brian. 1970. *Sociology, Economists, and Democracy.* Chicago: University of Chicago Press.

———. 1975. "Political Accommodation and Consociational Democracy." *British Journal of Political Science* 5:477–505.

Bartlett, Robert. 1993. *The Making of Europe: Conquest, Colonization and Cultural Change 950–1350.* London: Penguin Books.

Bates, Robert H., and Da-Hsiang Donald Lien. 1985. "A Note on Taxation, Development, and Representative Government." *Politics and Society* 14:53–70.

Bearce, David H., and Daniel C. Tirone. 2010. "Foreign Aid Effectiveness and the Strategic Goals of Donor Governments." *Journal of Politics* 72:837–851.

Beblawi, Hazem. 1987. "The Rentier State in the Arab World." In *The Rentier State: Nation, State, and the Integration of the Arab World,* ed. Hazem Beblawi and Giacomo Luciani. London: Croom Helm.

Beckwith, Karen. 2007. "Numbers and Newness: The Descriptive and Substantive Representation of Women." *Canadian Journal of Political Science* 40:27–49.

Bednar, Jenna. 2009. *The Robust Federation.* New York: Cambridge University Press.

Bednar, Jenna, William N. Eskridge, Jr., and John Ferejohn. 2001. "A Political Theory of Federalism." In *Constitutional Culture and Democratic Rule,* ed. John Ferejohn, John Riley, and Jack N. Rakove. New York: Cambridge University Press.

Bednar, Jenna, and Scott Page. 2007. "Can Game(s) Theory Explain Culture? The Emergence of Cultural Behavior within Multiple Games." *Rationality and Society* 19:65–97.

Bennett, Elizabeth. 2014. "Rwanda Strives towards Gender Equality in Government." *Kennedy School Review,* August 15. http://harvardkennedyschoolreview.com/rwanda-strides-towards-gender-equality-in-government/.

Benoit, Kenneth. 2004. "Models of Electoral System Change." *Electoral Studies* 23:363–389.

_____. 2007. "Electoral Laws as Political Consequences: Explaining the Origins and Change of Electoral Institutions." *Annual Review of Political Science* 10:363–390.

Bermeo, Sarah Blodgett. 2016. "Aid Is Not Oil: Donor Utility, Heterogeneous Aid, and the Aid-Democratization Relationship." *International Organization* 70:1–32.

Bernhard, William, and David Leblang. 2006. *Pricing Politics: Democratic Processes and Financial Markets.* New York: Cambridge University Press.

Binder, Sarah. 1999. "The Dynamics of Legislative Gridlock, 1947–1996." *American Political Science Review* 93:519–533.

_____. 2003. *Stalemate: Causes and Consequences of Legislative Gridlock.* Washington, DC: Brookings Institution Press.

Birch, Sarah. 2007. "Electoral Systems and Electoral Misconduct." *Comparative Political Studies* 40:1533–1556.

Birney, Mayling. 2007. "Can Local Elections Contribute to Democratic Progress in Authoritarian Regimes? Exploring the Political Ramifications of China's Village Elections." PhD thesis, Department of Political Science, Yale University.

Black, Duncan. 1948. "On the Rationale of Group Decision-Making." *Journal of Political Economy* 56:23–34.

Blair, Graeme. 2015. "Survey Methods for Sensitive Topics." In Symposium: Studying Sensitive Political Phenomena, eds. Matt Golder and Sona N. Golder. *CP: Newsletter of the Comparative Politics Organized Section of the American Political Science Association,* 25(1):12–16.

Blair, Graeme, Christine Fair, Neil Malhotra, and Jacob N. Shapiro. 2013. "Poverty and Support for Militant Politics: Evidence from Pakistan." *American Journal of Political Science* 57:30–48.

Blair, Graeme, Kosuke Imai, and Jason Lyall. 2014. "Comparing and Combining List and Endorsement Experiments: Evidence from Afghanistan." *American Journal of Political Science* 58(4):1043–1063.

Blair, Graeme, Kosuke Imai, and Yang-Yang Zhou. 2015. "Design and Analysis of the Randomized Response Technique." *Journal of the American Statistical Association* 110(511):1304–1319.

Blais, André, and Marc André Bodet. 2006. "Does Proportional Representation Foster Closer Congruence between Citizens and Policymakers?" *Comparative Political Studies* 39:1243–1262.

Blais, André, and R. K. Carty. 1990. "Does Proportional Representation Foster Voter Turnout?" *European Journal of Political Research* 18:167–181.

Blais, André, and Agnieszka Dobrzynska. 1998. "Turnout in Electoral Democracies." *European Journal of Political Research* 33:239–261.

Blais, André, and Louis Massicotte. 1997. "Electoral Formulas: A Macroscopic Perspective." *European Journal of Political Research* 32:107–129.

Blaydes, Lisa. 2011. *Elections and Distributive Politics in Mubarak's Egypt.* New York: Cambridge University Press.

Boix, Carles. 1999. "Setting the Rules of the Game: The Choice of Electoral Systems in Advanced Democracies." *American Political Science Review* 93:609–624.

_____. 2003. *Democracy and Redistribution.* New York: Cambridge University Press.

_____. 2011. "Democracy, Development, and the International System." *American Political Science Review* 105:809–828.

Boix, Carles, and Daniel N. Posner. 1996. "Making Social Capital Work: A Review of Robert Putnam's *Making Democracy Work: Civic Traditions in Modern Italy.*" Working Paper 96–4, Harvard University, Cambridge, MA.

Boix, Carles, and Susan Carol Stokes. 2003. "Endogenous Democratization." *World Politics* 55:517–549.

Boix, Carles, and Milan Svolik. 2013. "The Foundations of Limited Authoritarian Government: Institutions, Commitment, and Power-Sharing in Dictatorships." *Journal of Politics* 75:300–316.

Bollen, Kenneth A., and Robert W. Jackman. 1985. "Political Democracy and the Size Distribution of Income." *American Sociological Review* 50:438–457.

_____. 1995. "Income Inequality and Democratization Revisited: A Comment on Muller." *American Sociological Review* 60:983–989.

Bormann, Nils-Christian, and Matt Golder. 2013. "Democratic Elections around the World, 1946–2011." *Electoral Studies* 32:360–369.

Boston, Jonathan, Stephen Levine, Elizabeth McLeay, Nigel S. Roberts, and Hannah Schmidt. 1998. "Caretaker Government and the Evolution of Caretaker Conventions in New Zealand." *Victoria University of Wellington Law Review* 28:629–648.

Bowler, Shaun, and Bernard Grofman, eds. 2000. *Elections in Australia, Ireland, and Malta under the Single Transferable Vote: Reflections on an Embedded Institution.* Ann Arbor: University of Michigan Press.

Brambor, Thomas, William Roberts Clark, and Matt Golder. 2006. "Understanding Interaction Models: Improving Empirical Analyses." *Political Analysis* 14:63–82.

⸺. 2007. "Are African Party Systems Different?" *Electoral Studies* 26:315–323.

Brancati, Dawn. 2004. "Can Federalism Stabilize Iraq?" *Washington Quarterly* 27:7–21.

⸺. 2006. "Decentralization: Fueling the Fire or Dampening the Flames of Ethnic Conflict and Secessionism?" *International Organization* 60:651–685.

Bräutigam, Deborah A., and Stephen Knack. 2004. "Foreign Aid, Institutions, and Governance in Sub-Saharan Africa." *Economic Development and Cultural Change* 52:255–285.

Breunig, Charles. 1971. "Part IV: The Age of Revolution and Reaction, 1789–1850." In *The Norton History of Modern Europe,* ed. Felix Gilbert. New York: Norton.

Brinks, Daniel, and Michael Coppedge. 2006. "Diffusion Is No Illusion: Neighbor Emulation in the Third Wave of Democracy." *Comparative Political Studies* 39:463–489.

Brownlee, Jason. 2007. *Authoritarianism in the Age of Democratization.* New York: Cambridge University Press.

⸺. 2009. "Portents of Pluralism: How Hybrid Regimes Affect Democratic Transitions." *American Journal of Political Science* 53:515–532.

Brownlee, Jason, Tarek Masoud, and Andrew Reynolds. 2015. *The Arab Spring: Pathways of Repression and Reform.* Oxford: Oxford University Press.

Buchanan, James. 1995. "Federalism as an Ideal Political Order and an Objective for Constitutional Reform." *Publius: The Journal of Federalism* 25:19–28.

Buchanan, James, and Gordon Tullock. 1962. *The Calculus of Consent: Logical Foundations of Constitutional Democracy.* Ann Arbor: University of Michigan Press.

Bueno de Mesquita, Bruce. 2006. *Principles of International Politics: People's Power, Preferences, and Perceptions.* Washington, DC: CQ Press.

Bueno de Mesquita, Bruce, and Alastair Smith. 2009. "Political Survival and Endogenous Institutional Change." *Comparative Political Studies* 42:167–197.

Bueno de Mesquita, Bruce, Alastair Smith, Randolph M. Siverson, and James D. Morrow (BDM²S²). 2003. *The Logic of Political Survival.* Cambridge, MA: MIT Press.

Bunce, Valerie. 1999. *Subversive Institutions: The Design and the Destruction of Socialism and the State.* New York: Cambridge University Press.

Bustikova, Lenka. 2014. "Revenge of the Radical Right." *Comparative Political Studies* 47:1738–1765.

Cameron, Charles M. 2000. *Veto Bargaining: Presidents and the Politics of Negative Power.* New York: Cambridge University Press.

⸺. 2002. "Judicial Independence: How Can You Tell It When You See It?" In *Judicial Independence at the Crossroads: An Interdisciplinary Approach,* eds. Stephen B. Burbank and Barry Friedman. Thousand Oaks, CA: Sage.

Cameron, David R. 1978. "The Expansion of the Public Economy: A Comparative Analysis." *American Political Science Review* 72:1243–1261.

Campbell, Angus, Philip E. Converse, Warren Miller, and Donald Stokes. 1960. *The American Voter.* New York: Wiley.

Carey, John M., and Simon Hix. 2011. "The Electoral Sweet Spot: Low-Magnitude Proportional Electoral Systems." *American Journal of Political Science* 55:383–397.

Carey, John M., and John Polga-Hecimovich. 2006. "Primary Elections and Candidate Strength in Latin America." *Journal of Politics* 68:530–543.

⸺. 2008. "The Primary Elections 'Bonus' in Latin America." *Designing Democratic Government,* 227–247.

Carey, John M., and Matthew Soberg Shugart. 1995. "Incentives to Cultivate a Personal Vote: A Rank Ordering of Electoral Formulas." *Electoral Studies* 14:417–439.

Carothers, Thomas. 2002. "The End of the Transition Paradigm." *Journal of Democracy* 13:5–21.

Carroll, Susan J. and Linda M. G. Zerilli. 1993. "Feminist Challenges to Political Science." In *Political Science: The State of the Discipline II,* ed. Ada W. Finifter, 55–76. Washington, DC: American Political Science Association.

Carrubba, Clifford J., 2005. "Courts and Compliance in International Regulatory Regimes." *Journal of Politics* 67:669–689.

Carrubba, Clifford J., and Craig Volden. 2000. "Coalitional Politics and Logrolling in Legislative Institutions." *American Journal of Political Science* 44:521–537.

"Carter Center Closes Egypt Office." 2014. Carter Center. October 14. https://www.cartercenter.org/news/pr/egypt-101514 .html.

Celis, Karen. 2009. "Substantive Representation of Women (and Improving It): What It Is and Should Be About." *Comparative European Politics* 7:95–113.

Celis, Karen, Sarah Childs, Johanna Kantola, and Mona Lena Krook. 2008. "Rethinking Women's Substantive Representation." *Representation* 44:99–110.

Chaisty, Paul, Nic Cheeseman, and Timothy Power. 2014. "Rethinking the 'Presidentialism Debate': Conceptualizing Coalitional Politics in Cross-Regional Perspective." *Democratization* 21(1):72–94.

Chandra, Kanchan. 2004. *Why Ethnic Parties Succeed.* London: Cambridge University Press.

———. 2005. "Ethnic Parties and Democratic Stability." *Perspectives on Politics* 3:235–252.

———. 2006. "What Is Ethnic Identity and Does It Matter?" *Annual Review of Political Science* 9:397–424.

Chandra, Kanchan, and Cillane Boulet. 2012. "A Language for Thinking about Ethnic Identity Change." In *Constructivist Theories of Ethnic Politics,* ed. Kanchan Chandra. New York: Oxford University Press.

Chauchard, Simon. 2013. "Using MP3 Players in Surveys: The Impact of a Low-Tech Self-Administration Mode on Reporting of Sensitive Attitudes." *Public Opinion Quarterly* 77:220–231.

Cheibub, José Antonio. 2002. "Minority Governments, Deadlock Situations, and the Survival of Presidential Democracies." *Comparative Political Studies* 35:284–312.

———. 2007. *Presidentialism, Parliamentarism, and Democracy.* New York: Cambridge University Press.

Cheibub, José Antonio, Jennifer Gandhi, and James Raymond Vreeland. 2010. "Democracy and Dictatorship Revisited." *Public Choice* 143:67–101.

Cheibub, José Antonio, and Fernando Limongi. 2002. "Modes of Government Formation and the Survival of Democratic Regimes: Presidentialism and Parliamentarism Reconsidered." *Annual Review of Political Science* 5:151–179.

Cheibub, José Antonio, Adam Przeworski, and Sebastian Saiegh. 2004. "Government Coalitions and Legislative Success under Presidentialism and Parliamentarism." *British Journal of Political Science* 34:565–587.

Childs, Sarah, and Mona Lena Krook. 2006. "Should Feminists Give Up on Critical Mass? A Contingent 'Yes.'" *Politics and Gender* 2:522–530.

Clark, William Roberts. 2003. *Capitalism, Not Globalism: Capital Mobility, Central Bank Independence, and the Political Control of the Economy.* Ann Arbor: University of Michigan Press.

Clark, William Roberts, and Matt Golder. 2006. "Rehabilitating Duverger's Theory: Testing the Mechanical and Strategic Modifying Effects of Electoral Laws." *Comparative Political Studies* 39:679–708.

Clark, William Roberts, Matt Golder, and Sona N. Golder. 2017. "An Exit, Voice, and Loyalty Model of Politics." *British Journal of Political Science* 47: 719-748.

Clark, William Roberts, and Usha Nair Reichert (with Sandra Lynn Lomas and Kevin L. Parker). 1998. "International and Domestic Constraints on Political Business Cycle Behavior in OECD Economies." *International Organization* 52:87–120.

Clinton, Robert Lowry. 1994. "Game Theory, Legal History, and the Origins of Judicial Review: A Revisionist Analysis of *Marbury v. Madison.*" *American Journal of Political Science* 38:285–302.

Cohen, Frank. 1997. "Proportional versus Majoritarian Ethnic Conflict Management in Democracies." *Comparative Political Studies* 30:607–630.

Collier, David, and Robert Adcock. 1999. "Democracy and Dichotomies: A Pragmatic Approach to Choices about Concepts." *Annual Review of Political Science* 2:537–565.

Collier, David, and Steven Levitsky. 1997. "Democracy with Adjectives: Conceptual Innovation in Comparative Research." *World Politics* 49:430–451.

Collier, Paul. 2009. "In Praise of the Coup: Military Takeovers Can Be a Good Thing for African Democracy." *New Humanist,* March 4. https://newhumanist.org.uk/articles/1997/in-praise-of-the-coup.

Collier, Paul, and Anke Hoeffler. 2002. "On the Incidence of Civil War in Africa." *Journal of Conflict Resolution* 46:13–28.

———. 2005. "Resource Rents, Governance, and Conflict." *Journal of Conflict Resolution* 49:625–633.

Collins, Patricia Hill. 1986. "Learning from the Outsider Within: The Sociological Significance of Black Feminist Thought." *Social Problems* 33(6):S14–S32.

———. 1989. "The Social Construction of Black Feminist Thought." *Signs* 14(4):745–773.

Colomer, Josep M. 1991. "Transitions by Agreement: Modeling the Spanish Way." *American Political Science Review* 85:1283–1302.

Congleton, Roger D. 2006. "Asymmetric Federalism and the Political Economy of Decentralization." In *Handbook of Fiscal Federalism,* eds. Ehtisham Ahmad and Giorgio Brosio. Northampton, MA: Edward Elgar.

Coppedge, Michael. 1994. *Strong Parties and Lame Ducks: Presidential Partyarchy and Factionalism in Venezuela.* Stanford, CA: Stanford University Press.

Cornell, Svante E. 2002. "Autonomy as a Source of Conflict: Caucasian Conflicts in Theoretical Perspective." *World Politics* 54(2):245–276.

Cox, Gary W. 1997. *Making Votes Count: Strategic Coordination in the World's Electoral Systems.* New York: Cambridge University Press.

Crabtree, Charles, David Darfomal, and Holger L. Kern. 2015. "A Spatial Analysis of the Impact of West German Television on Protest Mobilization during the East German Revolution." *Journal of Peace Research* 52(3):269–284.

Crabtree, Charles, Christopher J. Fariss, and Paul Schuler. 2016. "The Presidential Election in Belarus, October 2015." *Electoral Studies* 42: 304–307.

Crenshaw, Kimberlé. 1989. "Demarginalizing the Inter-section of Race and Sex: A Black Feminist Critique of Antidiscrimination Doctrine, Feminist Theory and Antiracist Politics," *University of Chicago Legal Forum 1989:* 139–167.

Dahl, Robert A. 1956. *A Preface to Democratic Theory.* Chicago: University of Chicago Press.

———. 1971. *Polyarchy: Participation and Opposition.* New Haven, CT: Yale University Press.

Dahlerup, Drude. 1988. "From a Small to a Large Minority: Women in Scandinavian Politics." *Scandinavian Political Studies* 4:275–298.

Dahlerup, Drude, ed. 2006. *Women, Quotas and Politics.* New York: Routledge.

Dalton, Russell J., and Nhu-Ngoc T. Ong. "Authority Orientations and Democratic Attitudes: A Test of the 'Asian Values' Hypothesis." Unpublished manuscript, University of California, Irvine, 2004.

Dancygier, Rafaela M. 2010. *Immigration and Conflict in Europe.* New York: Cambridge University Press.

Dawson, Michael C. 1995. *Behind the Mule: Race and Class in African-American Politics.* Princeton, NJ: Princeton University Press.

De la Torre, Carlos. 2016. "What Went Wrong? Leftwing Populist Democratic Promises and Autocratic Practices." In Symposium: Populism in Comparative Perspective, eds. Matt Golder and Sona N. Golder. *CP: Newsletter of the Comparative Politics Organized Section of the American Political Science Association* 26(2):40–45.

Derry, Gregory. 1999. *What Science Is and How It Works.* Princeton, NJ: Princeton University Press.

De Jong, Martijn G., Rik Pieters, and Stefan Stremersch. 2012. "Analysis of Sensitive Questions across Cultures: An Application of Multigroup Item Randomized Response Theory to Sexual Attitudes and Behavior." *Journal of Personality and Social Psychology* 103:543.

Diamond, Larry. 2002. "Thinking about Hybrid Regimes." *Journal of Democracy* 13:21–35.

Dietrich, Simone, and Joseph Wright. 2014. "Foreign Aid Allocation Tactics and Democratic Change in Africa." *Journal of Politics* 77:216–234.

Dixit, Avinash K., Susan Skeath, and David Reiley. 2015. *Games of Strategy,* 4th ed. rev. New York: Norton.

Dixon, Patrick. 1996. *The Truth about Westminster.* London: Hodder.

Djankov, Simeon, Jose G. Montalvo, and Marta Reynal-Querol. 2008. "The Curse of Aid." *Journal of Economic Growth* 13:169–194.

Dowding, Keith, and Patrick Dumont, eds. 2009. *The Selection of Ministers in Europe: Hiring and Firing.* New York: Routledge.

Downs, Anthony. 1957. *An Economic Theory of Democracy.* New York: Harper and Row.

Drake, Paul W. 1996. *Labor Movements and Dictatorships: The Southern Cone in Comparative Perspective.* Baltimore: Johns Hopkins University Press.

Duch, Raymond M., Wojtek Przepiorka, and Randolph T. Stevenson. 2015. "Responsibility Attribution for Collective Decision Makers." *American Journal of Political Science* 59:372–389.

Dunning, Thad. 2005. "Resource Dependence, Economic Performance, and Political Stability." *Journal of Conflict Resolution* 49:451–482.

———. 2008. *Crude Democracy: Natural Resource Wealth and Political Regimes.* New York: Cambridge University Press.

Duverger, Maurice. [1954] 1963. *Political Parties.* London: Methuen.

———. 1980. "A New Political System Model: Semi-Presidential Government." *European Journal of Political Research* 8:165–187.

Easterly, William, and Ross Levine. 1997. "Africa's Growth Tragedy: Policies and Ethnic Divisions." *Quarterly Journal of Economics* 112:1201–1250.

Egorov, Georgy, Sergei Guriev, and Konstantin Sonin. 2009. "Why Resource-Poor Dictators Allow Freer Media: A Theory and Evidence from Panel Data." *American Political Science Review* 103:645–668.

Eickelman, Dale F., and James P. Piscatori. 1996. *Muslim Politics.* Princeton, NJ: Princeton University Press.

Electoral Integrity Project, The (EIP). n.d. https://sites.google.com/site/electoralintegrityproject4/home.

Elgie, Robert. 2011. *Semi-Presidentialism: Sub-types and Democratic Performance.* Oxford: Oxford University Press.

Engels, Friedrich. [1893] 1968. "Letter to Mehring." In *Marx-Engels Correspondence.* Geneva, Switzerland: International Publishers.

Emmerson, Donald K. 1995. "Singapore and the 'Asian Values' Debate." *Journal of Democracy* 6: 95–105.

Epstein, David L., Robert Bates, Jack Goldstone, Ida Kristensen, and Sharyn O'Halloran. 2006. "Democratic Transitions." *American Journal of Political Science* 50:551–569.

Epstein, Lee, and Jack Knight. 1998a. *The Choices Justices Make.* Washington, DC: CQ Press.

———. 1998b. "On the Struggle for Judicial Supremacy." *Law and Society Review* 30:87–120.

Epstein, Lee, Jack Knight, and Olga Shvetsova. 2001. "The Role of Constitutional Courts in the Establishment of Democratic Systems of Government." *Law and Society Review* 35:117–167.

Erikson, Robert S., Michael B. MacKuen, and James A. Stimson. 2002. *The Macro Polity.* New York: Cambridge University Press.

Escobar-Lemmon, Maria C., and Michelle M. Taylor-Robinson. 2016. *Women in Presidential Cabinets: Power Players or Abundant Tokens?* New York: Oxford University Press.

Esposito, John L. 2003. "Practice and Theory: A Response to 'Islam and the Challenge of Democracy.'" *Boston Review,* April–May.

Esposito, John L., and John O. Voll. 1996. *Islam and Democracy.* New York: Oxford University Press.

Esteban, Joan, and Debraj Ray. 1999. "Conflict and Distribution." *Journal of Economic Theory* 87:379–415.

———. 2008. "Polarization, Fractionalization, and Conflict." *Journal of Peace Research* 45:163–182.

Esteban, Joan, and Gerald Schneider. 2008. "Polarization and Conflict: Theoretical and Empirical Issues." *Journal of Peace Research* 45:131–141.

Ezrow, Natasha M., and Erica Frantz. 2011. *Dictators and Dictatorships: Understanding Authoritarian Regimes and Their Leaders.* New York: Continuum.

Fadel, Laila. 2011. "Egypt's Military Guards Its Own Power." *The Washington Post,* November 12. http://www.washington-post.com/world/middle_east/egypts-military-guards-its-own-power/2011/11/10/gIQA7QVVFN_story.html.

Fahim, Kareem, and Hwaida Saad. 2013. "A Faceless Teenage Refugee Who Helped Ignite Syria's War." *The New York Times,* February 8. http://www.nytimes.com/2013/02/09/world/middleeast/a-faceless-teenage-refugee-who-helped-ignite-syrias-war.html?_r=1.

Fantz, Ashley, and Ben Brumfield. 2015. "More Than Half the Nation's Governors Say Syrian Refugees Not Welcome." CNN, November 19. http://www.cnn.com/2015/11/16/world/paris-attacks-syrian-refugees-backlash/index.html.

Farrell, David M., and Ian McAllister. 2000. "Through a Glass Darkly: Understanding the World of STV." In *Elections in Australia, Ireland, and Malta under the Single Transferable Vote: Reflections on an Embedded Institution,* eds. Shaun Bowler and Bernard Grofman. Ann Arbor: University of Michigan Press.

Fearon, James D. 2005. "Primary Commodity Exports and Civil War." *Journal of Conflict Resolution* 49:483–507.

Fearon, James D., and David D. Laitin. 1996. "Explaining Interethnic Cooperation." *American Political Science Review* 90:715–735.

Feynman, Richard. 1967. *The Character of Physical Law: The 1964 Messenger Lectures.* Cambridge, MA: MIT Press.

Filali-Ansary, Abdou. 1999. "Muslims and Democracy." *Journal of Democracy* 10:18–32.

Finer, S. E. 1988. *The Man on Horseback: The Role of the Military in Politics.* Boulder, CO: Westview Press.

Fitzpatrick, Catherine A. 2011. "Turkmen Government Removes Ruhnama as Required Subject." Eurasianet, April 26. http://www.eurasianet.org/node/63365.

Fiorina, Morris. 1980. "The Decline of Collective Responsibility in American Politics." *Daedalus* 109:25–45.

———. 1981. *Retrospective Voting in American National Elections.* New Haven, CT: Yale University Press.

Fish, M. Steven. 2002. "Islam and Authoritarianism." *World Politics* 55:4–37.

Fogel, Robert. 2004. *The Escape from Hunger and Premature Death, 1700–2100: Europe, America and the Third World.* New York: Cambridge University Press.

Fox, Jean-Paul, and Rob R. Meijer. 2008. "Using Item Response Theory to Obtain Individual Information from Randomized Response Data: An Application Using Cheating Data." *Applied Psychological Measurement* 32:595–610.

Franzese, Robert J., Jr. 2002. *Macroeconomic Policies of Developed Democracies.* New York: Cambridge University Press.

Fréchette, Guillaume R., François Maniquet, and Massimo Morelli. 2008. "Incumbents' Interests and Gender Quotas." *American Journal of Political Science* 52:891–909.

———. 2012. *Freedom in the World: Niger.* https://freedom-house.org/report/freedom-world/2012/niger.

Freeman, John R., and Dennis P. Quinn. 2010. "The Economic Origins of Democracy Reconsidered." *American Political Science Review* 106:58–80.

Friedman, Edward. 2002. "On Alien Western Democracy." In *Globalization and Democratization in Asia,* eds. Catarina Kinnvall and Kristina Jonsson. New York: Routledge.

Fukuyama, Francis. 1992. *The End of History and the Last Man.* New York: Penguin.

———. 1995a. "Confucianism and Democracy." *Journal of Democracy* 6:20–33.

———. 1995b. "The Primacy of Culture." *Journal of Democracy* 6:7–14.

Gallagher, Michael, Michael Laver, and Peter Mair. 2006. *Representative Government in Modern Europe: Institutions, Parties, and Government.* New York: McGraw-Hill.

Gamson, William A. 1961. "A Theory of Coalition Formation." *American Sociological Review* 26:373–382.

Gandhi, Jennifer. 2008. *Political Institutions under Dictatorship.* New York: Cambridge University Press.

Gandhi, Jennifer, and Ellen Lust-Okar. 2009. "Elections under Authoritarianism." *Annual Review of Political Science* 12:403–422.

Gandhi, Jennifer, and Adam Przeworski. 2006. "Cooperation, Cooptation, and Rebellion under Dictatorships." *Economics and Politics* 18:1–26.

———. 2007. "Authoritarian Institutions and the Survival of Autocrats." *Comparative Political Studies* 40:1279–1301.

Garton Ash, Timothy. 1999. *The Magic Lantern: The Revolution of '89 Witnessed in Warsaw, Budapest, Berlin and Prague.* New York: Vintage Books.

Gaskins, Ben, Matt Golder, and David Siegel. 2013a. "Religious Participation and Economic Conservatism." *American Journal of Political Science* 57:823–840.

Gaskins, Ben, Matt Golder, and David Siegel. 2013b. "Religious Participation, Social Conservatism, and Human Development." *Journal of Politics* 75:1125–1141.

Gat, Azar. 2006. *War in Human Civilization.* Oxford: Oxford University Press.

Geanakoplos, John. 2005. "Three Brief Proofs of Arrow's Impossibility Theorem." *Economic Theory* 26:211–215.

Geddes, Barbara. 1999. "Authoritarian Breakdown: Empirical Test of a Game Theoretic Argument." Paper presented at the Annual Meeting of American Political Science Association Atlanta, September.

———. 2003. *Paradigms and Sand Castles: Theory Building and Research Design in Comparative Politics.* Ann Arbor: University of Michigan Press.

Geddes, Barbara, Joseph Wright, and Erica Frantz. 2014. "Autocratic Breakdown and Regime Transitions: A New Data Set." *Perspectives on Politics* 12(2):331–313.

Gerges, Fawaz. 2013. "Saudi Arabia and Iran Must End Their Proxy War in Syria." *The Guardian,* December 15. http://www.theguardian.com/commentisfree/2013/dec/15/saudia-arabia-iran-proxy-war-syria.

Gerschenkron, Alexander. 1962. *Economic Backwardness in Historical Perspective: A Book of Essays.* Cambridge, MA: Harvard University Press.

Gershenson, Dmitriy, and Hershel I. Grossman. 2001. "Cooption and Repression in the Soviet Union." *Economics and Politics* 13:31–47.

Gibbard, Allan. 1973. "Manipulation of Voting Schemes: A General Result." *Econometrica* 41:587–601.

Gibson, James, and Gregory Caldeira. 1992. "The Etiology of Public Support for the Supreme Court." *American Journal of Political Science* 36:459–489.

Gibson, James, Gregory Caldeira, and Vanessa Baird. 1998. "On the Legitimacy of National High Courts." *American Political Science Review* 92:343–358.

Gingerich, Daniel W. 2010. "Understanding off-the-Books Politics: Conducting Inference on the Determinants of Sensitive Behavior with Randomized Response Surveys." *Political Analysis* 18:349–380.

———. 2013. *Political Institutions and Party-Directed Corruption in South America: Stealing from the Team.* New York: Cambridge University Press.

Ginkel, John, and Alastair Smith. 1999. "So You Say You Want a Revolution? A Game Theoretic Explanation of Revolution in Repressive Regimes." *Journal of Conflict Resolution* 43:291–316.

Ginsburg, Tom. 2003. *Judicial Review in New Democracies: Constitutional Courts in Asian Cases.* New York: Cambridge University Press.

Gintis, Herbert. 2003. "Towards a Unity of the Human Behavioral Sciences." Working Paper 03–02–015, Santa Fe Institute.

Global Database of Quotas for Women. 2015. "Quota Database." http://www.quotaproject.org/.

Golder, Matt. 2003. "Explaining Variation in the Electoral Success of Extreme Right Parties in Western Europe." *Comparative Political Studies* 36:432–466.

———. 2005. "Democratic Electoral Systems around the World, 1946–2000." *Electoral Studies* 24:103–121.

———. 2006. "Presidential Coattails and Legislative Fragmentation." *American Journal of Political Science* 50:34–48.

———. 2016. "Far Right Parties in Europe." *Annual Review of Political Science* 19:477–497.

Golder, Matt, and Gabriella Lloyd. 2014. "Re-evaluating the Relationship between Electoral Rules and Ideological Congruence." *European Journal of Political Research* 53:200–212.

Golder, Matt, and Jacek Stramski. 2010. "Ideological Congruence and Electoral Institutions." *American Journal of Political Science* 54:90–106.

Golder, Sona N. 2010. "Bargaining Delays in the Government Formation Process." *Comparative Political Studies* 43:3–32.

Golder, Sona N., and Jacquelyn A. Thomas. 2014. "Portfolio Allocation and the Vote of No Confidence." *British Journal of Political Science* 44(1):29–39.

Gomez, Brad T., Thomas G. Hansford, and George A. Krause. 2007. "The Republicans Should Pray for Rain: Weather, Turnout, and Voting in U.S. Presidential Elections." *Journal of Politics* 69:649–663.

Gonzalez-Ocantos, Ezequiel, Chad Kiewiet De Jonge, Carlos Meléndez, Javier Osorio, and David W. Nickerson. 2012. "Vote Buying and Social Desirability Bias: Experimental Evidence from Nicaragua." *American Journal of Political Science* 56:202–217.

Goodin, Robert E., and Philip Pettit, eds. 1993. *A Companion to Contemporary Political Philosophy.* Oxford: Blackwell.

Guinier, Lani. 1994. *The Tyranny of the Majority.* New York: Free Press.

Gurr, Ted Robert. 1970. *Why Men Rebel.* Princeton, NJ: Princeton University Press.

Hadenius, Axel, and Jan Teorell. 2007. "Pathways from Authoritarianism." *Journal of Democracy* 18:143–157.

Hale, Henry E. 2008. *The Foundations of Ethnic Politics: Separatism of States and Nations in Eurasia and the World.* New York: Cambridge University Press.

Haggard, Stephen, and Robert K. Kaufman. 2012. "Inequality and Regime Transition: Democratic Transitions and the Stability of Democratic Rule." *American Political Science Review* 106:495–516.

Hallerberg, Mark. 1996. "Tax Competition in Wilhelmine Germany and Its Implications for the European Union." *World Politics* 48:324–357.

Hamilton, Alexander. 1787. "The Union as a Safeguard against Domestic Faction and Insurrection for the Independent Journal." *The Federalist Papers: No. 9.* http://avalon.law.yale.edu/18th_century/fed09.asp.

Hammer, Joshua. 2010. "The Contenders: Is Egypt's Presidential Race Becoming a Real Contest." *The New Yorker,* April 5. http://www.newyorker.com/reporting/2010/04/05/100405fa_fact_hammer.

Hancock, Ange-Marie. 2007. "Intersectionality as a Normative and Empirical Paradigm." *Politics and Gender* 3:248–254.

Hansard. 1997. "Modernisation of the House of Commons" (House of Commons Debate). Vol. 295 Column 507 (4 June 1997). http://hansard.millbanksystems.com/commons/1997/jun/04/modernisation-of-the-house-of-commons#column_506.

Hanson, Russell L. 1989. "Democracy." In *Political Innovation and Conceptual Change,* eds. Terence Ball, James Farr, and Russell L. Hanson. New York: Cambridge University Press.

Haraway, Donna. 1988. "Situated Knowledges: The Science Question in Feminism and the Privilege of Partial Perspective." *Feminist Studies* 14(3):575–599.

Hardgrave, Robert, Jr. 1994. "India: The Dilemma of Diversity." In *Nationalism, Ethnic Conflict, and Democracy,* eds. Larry Diamond and Marc F. Plattner. Baltimore: Johns Hopkins University Press.

Hardin, Garrett. 1968. "The Tragedy of the Commons." *Science* 162:1243–1248.

Hassig, Ralph, and Kongdan Oh. 2009. *The Hidden People of North Korea: Everyday Life in the Hermit Kingdom.* New York: Rowman and Littlefield.

Hayek, Friedrich von. [1939] 1948. "The Economic Conditions of Interstate Federalism." Repr. in *Individualism and the Economic Order.* Chicago: University of Chicago Press.

Hechter, Michael. 2000. *Containing Nationalism.* New York: Oxford University Press.

Hefner, Robert W. 2000. *Civil Islam: Muslims and Democratization in India.* Princeton, NJ: Princeton University Press.

Helmke, Gretchen. 2002. "The Logic of Strategic Defection: Court-Executive Relations in Argentina under Dictatorship and Democracy." *American Political Science Review* 96:305–320.

———. 2005. *Courts under Constraints: Judges, Generals, and Presidents in Argentina.* New York: Cambridge University Press.

Henrich, Joseph, Robert Boyd, Samuel Bowles, Colin Camerer, Ernst Fehr, Herbert Gintis, and Richard McElreath. 2001. "In Search of Homo Economicus: Behavioral Experiments in 15 Small-Scale Societies." *American Economic Review* 91:73–78.

Henrich, Joseph, Robert Boyd, Samuel Bowles, Colin Camerer, Ernst Fehr, Herbert Gintis, Richard McElreath et al. 2005. "Economic Man in Cross-Cultural Perspective: Behavioral Experiments in 15 Small-Scale Societies." *Behavior and Brain Sciences* 28:795–815.

Herb, Michael. 1999. *All in the Family: Absolutism, Revolution and Democracy in the Middle East.* Albany: State University of New York Press.

Herbst, Jeffrey. 2000. *States and Power in Africa: Comparative Lessons in Authority and Control.* Princeton, NJ: Princeton University Press.

———. 2001. "Political Liberalization in Africa after Ten Years." *Comparative Politics* 33:357–375.

Hibbs, Douglas A., Jr. 1977. "Political Parties and Macroeconomic Policy." *American Political Science Review* 71:1467–1487.

———. 2013. "Are All Presidents Created Equal? Presidential Powers and the Shadow of Presidential Elections." *Comparative Political Studies* 46(3):291–319.

Hinich, Melvin J., and Michael C. Munger. 1997. *Analytical Politics.* New York: Cambridge University Press.

Hirano, Shigeo. 2011. "Electoral Institutions, Hometowns, and Favored Minorities: Evidence from Japanese Electoral Reforms." *World Politics* 59:51–82.

Hirschman, Albert. 1970. *Exit, Voice, and Loyalty: Responses to Decline in Firms, Organizations, and States.* Cambridge, MA: Harvard University Press.

Hitchcock, William I. 2004. *The Struggle for Europe: The Turbulent History of a Divided Continent, 1945 to the Present.* New York: Anchor Books.

Hobbes, Thomas. [1651] 1994. *Leviathan,* ed. Edwin Curley. Indianapolis, IN: Hackett.

Hobolt, Sarah B., James Tilley, and Susan Banducci. 2013. "Clarity of Responsibility: How Government Cohesion Conditions Performance Voting." *European Journal of Political Research* 52:164–187.

Horowitz, Donald L. 1985. *Ethnic Groups in Conflict.* Berkeley: University of California Press.

———. 1991. *A Democratic South Africa? Constitutional Engineering in a Divided Society.* Berkeley: University of California Press.

———. 2004. "The Alternative Vote and Interethnic Moderation: A Reply to Fraenkel and Grofman." *Public Choice* 121:507–516.

Hotelling, Harold. 1929. "Stability in Competition." *Economic Journal* 39:41–57.

Houle, Christian. 2009. "Inequality and Democracy: Why Inequality Harms Consolidation but Does Not Affect Democratization." *World Politics* 61:589–622.

Howden, Daniel. 2009. "From Coup to Counter-Coup? Guinea Plunged into Chaos." *Independent,* December 4. http://www.independent.co.uk/news/world/africa/from-coup-to-countercoup-guinea-plunged-into-chaos-1834644.html.

Htun, Mala. 2016. *Inclusion without Representation in Latin America: Gender Quotas and Ethnic Reservations.* New York: Cambridge University Press.

Huber, John D., and Cecilia Martínez-Gallardo. 2004. "Cabinet Instability and the Accumulation of Experience in the Cabinet: The French Fourth and Fifth Republics in Comparative Perspective." *British Journal of Political Science* 34:27–48.

Hughes, Melanie. 2011. "Intersectionality, Quotas, and Minority Women's Political Representation Worldwide." *American Political Science Review* 105:604–620.

Hui, Li, and Magha Rajagopalan. 2013. "At Sina Weibo's Censorship Hub, China's Little Brothers Cleanse Online Chatter." Reuters, September 11. http://www.reuters.com/article/us-china-internet-idUSBRE98A18Z20130912.

Humphreys, Macartan. 2005. "Natural Resources, Conflict, and Conflict Resolution: Uncovering the Mechanisms." *Journal of Conflict Resolution* 49:508–537.

Huntington, Samuel P. 1968. *Political Order in Changing Societies.* New Haven, CT: Yale University Press.

———. 1991. *The Third Wave: Democratization in the Late Twentieth Century.* Norman: University of Oklahoma Press.

———. 1993. "The Clash of Civilizations?" *Foreign Affairs* 72:22–49.

———. 1996. *The Clash of Civilizations and the Remaking of World Order.* New York: Simon and Schuster.

Hyde, Susan. 2007a. "Experimenting in Democracy Promotion: International Observers and the 2004 Presidential Elections in Indonesia." *Perspectives on Politics* 8:511–527.

———. 2007b. "The Observer Effect in International Politics: Evidence from a Natural Experiment." *World Politics* 60:37–63.

———. 2011. *The Pseudo-Democrat's Dilemma: Why Election Observation Became an International Norm.* Ithaca, NY: Cornell University Press.

Ignazi, Piero. 1992. "The Silent Counter-Revolution: Hypotheses on the Emergence of Extreme Right-Wing Parties in Europe." *European Journal of Political Research* 22:3–34.

Im, H. B. 1997. *The Compatibility of Confucianism and Democratic Civil Society in Korea.* Paper presented at the International Political Science Association Seventeenth World Congress, Seoul, Republic of Korea, August 17–21.

Indriðason, Indriði. 2015. "Live for Today, Hope for Tomorrow? Rethinking Gamson's Law." Working Paper, University of California, Riverside.

Indriðason, Indriði, and Christopher Kam. 2005. "The Timing of Cabinet Reshuffles in Five Westminster Parliamentary Systems." *Legislative Studies Quarterly,* 327–363.

Inglehart, Ronald. 1977. *The Silent Revolution: Changing Values and Political Styles among Western Publics.* Princeton, NJ: Princeton University Press.

———. 1990. *Culture Shift in Advanced Industrial Society.* Princeton, NJ: Princeton University Press.

———. 1997. *Modernization and Postmodernization: Cultural, Economic and Political Change in 43 Societies.* Princeton, NJ: Princeton University Press.

Inglehart, Ronald, and Christian Welzel. 2003. "Political Culture and Democracy: Analyzing Cross-Level Linkages." *Comparative Politics* 36:61–79.

———. 2005. *Modernization, Cultural Change, and Democracy: The Human Development Sequence.* New York: Cambridge University Press.

Inter-Parliamentary Union (IPU). 2016. "Home." http://www.ipu.org/english/home.htm.

Ivarsflaten, Elisabeth. 2008. "What Unites Right-Wing Populists in Western Europe? Re-examining Grievance Mobilization Models in Seven Successful Cases." *Comparative Political Studies* 41:3–23.

Iversen, Torben, and David Soskice. 2006. "Electoral Institutions and the Politics of Coalitions: Why Some Democracies Redistribute More than Others." *American Political Science Review* 100:165–181.

Jensen, Nathan, and Leonard Wantchekon. 2004. "Resource Wealth and Political Regimes in Africa." *Comparative Political Studies* 37:816–841.

Johnston, David, and Neil A. Lewis. 2007. "Senate Democrats Plan a Resolution on Gonzales." *The New York Times,* May 18. http://www.nytimes.com/2007/05/18/washington/18gonzales.html.

Junn, Jane, and Nadia Brown. 2008. "What Revolution? Incorporating Intersectionality in Women and Politics." In *Political Women and American Democracy,* eds. Christina Wolbrecht, Karen Beckwith, and Lisa Baldez, 64–78. New York: Cambridge University Press.

Kalyvas, Stathis. 1996. *The Rise of Christian Democracy in Europe.* Ithaca, NY: Cornell University Press.

———. 1998. "Democracy and Religious Politics: Evidence from Belgium." *Comparative Political Studies* 31:291–319.

———. 2000. "Commitment Problems in Emerging Democracies: The Case of Religious Parties." *Comparative Politics* 32:379–399.

Kaminski, Marek M. 1999. "How Communism Could Have Been Saved: Formal Analysis of Electoral Bargaining in Poland in 1989." *Public Choice* 98:83–109.

———. 2004. *Games Prisoners Play.* Princeton, NJ: Princeton University Press.

Kaminski, Marek M., Grzegorz Lissowski, and Piotr Swistak. 1998. "The 'Revival of Communism' or the Effect of Institutions? The 1993 Polish Parliamentary Elections." *Public Choice* 3:429–449.

Kang, Chol-hwan, and Pierre Rigoulot. 2005. *The Aquariums of Pyongyang: Ten Years in the North Korean Gulag.* New York: Basic Books.

Kanter, Rosabeth Moss. 1977. "Some Effects of Proportions on Group Life." *American Journal of Sociology* 82:965–990.

Karatnycky, Adrian. 2002. "Muslim Countries and the Democracy Gap." *Journal of Democracy* 13:99–112.

Karl, Terry Lynn. 1995. "The Hybrid Regimes of Central America." *Journal of Democracy* 6:72–87.

———. 1997. *The Paradox of Plenty: Oil Booms and Petro-States.* Berkeley: University of California Press.

Katz, Richard S. 1980. *A Theory of Parties and Electoral Systems.* Baltimore: Johns Hopkins University Press.

Kayser, Mark Andreas. 2005. "Who Surfs, Who Manipulates? The Determinants of Opportunistic Election Timing and Electorally Motivated Economic Intervention." *American Political Science Review* 99:17–28.

Kedar, Orit, Liran Harsgor, and Raz A. Scheinerman. 2016. "Are Voters Equal under Proportional Representation?" *American Journal of Political Science* 60:676–691.

Kellam, Marisa. 2015. "Parties for Hire: How Particularistic Parties Influence Presidents' Governing Strategies." *Party Politics* 21(4):511–526.

Kerr, Henry H. 1987. "The Swiss Party System: Steadfast and Changing." In *Party Systems in Denmark, Austria, Switzerland, the Netherlands, and Belgium,* ed. Hans Daalder. New York: St. Martin's Press.

Khan, Ali. 2006. "The Medina Constitution." Unpublished manuscript, Washburn University, Topeka, KS.

Khan, Amjad Mahmood. 2010. "Religious Freedom in America." Paper presented at the 62nd Annual Jalsa Salana USA, Los Angeles, California.

Khan, Muqtedar. 2001. "The Compact of Medina: A Constitutional Theory of the Islamic State." May 30. http://www.ijtihad.org/compact.htm.

Kim, Yung-Myung. 1997. "Asian-Style Democracy: A Critique from East Asia." *Asian Survey* 37: 1119–1134.

King, Gary, Christopher J. L. Murray, Joshua A. Salomon, and Ajay Tandon. 2004. "Enhancing the Validity and Cross-Cultural Comparability of Measurement in Survey Research." *American Political Science Review* 98:191–207.

King, Gary, Jennifer Pan, and Margaret Roberts. 2013. "How Censorship in China Allows Government Criticism but Silences Collective Expression." *American Political Science Review* 107:1–18.

King, Gary, and Jonathan Wand. 2007. "Comparing Incomparable Survey Responses: Evaluating and Selecting Anchoring Vignettes." *Political Analysis* 15:46–66.

King, Gary, and Langche Zeng. 2001. "Improving Forecasts of State Failure." *World Politics* 53:623–658.

Kirkpatrick, David D. 2011. "A Libyan Leader at War with Rebels, and Reality." *The New York Times,* March 6. http://www.nytimes.com/2011/03/07/world/middleeast/07qaddafi.html?_r=1&pagewanted=all.

Kitschelt, Herbert P. 1988. "Left-Libertarian Parties: Explaining Innovation in Competitive Party Systems." *World Politics* 40:194–234.

Kittilson, Miki Caul. 2006. *Challenging Parties, Changing Parliaments: Women and Elected Office in Contemporary Western Europe.* Columbus: Ohio State University Press.

Kittilson, Miki Caul, and Leslie Schwindt-Bayer. 2012. *The Gendered Effects of Electoral Institutions: Political Engagement and Participation.* New York: Oxford University Press.

Knack, Stephen. 2004. "Does Foreign Aid Promote Democracy?" *International Studies Quarterly* 48:251–266.

Kono, Daniel Yuichi, and Gabriella R. Montinola. 2009. "Does Foreign Aid Support Autocrats, Democrats or Both?" *Journal of Politics* 71(2):704–718.

Krook, Mona Lena. 2009. *Quotas for Women in Politics: Gender and Candidate Selection Reform Worldwide.* New York: Oxford University Press.

Krook, Mona Lena, and Pippa Norris. 2014. "Beyond Quotas: Strategies to Promote Gender Equality in Elected Office." *Political Studies* 62:2–20.

Krumpal, Ivar. 2012. "Estimating the Prevalence of Xenophobia and Anti-Semitism in Germany: A Comparison of Randomized Response and Direct Questioning." *Social Science Research* 41:1387–1403.

Krysan, Maria. 1998. "Privacy and the Expression of White Racial Attitudes." *Public Opinion Quarterly* 62:506–544.

Krysan, Maria, and Mick Couper. 2003. "Race in Live and Virtual Interviews: Racial Deference, Social Desirability, and Activation Effects in Attitude Surveys." *Social Psychology Quarterly* 66:364–383.

Kuran, Timur. 1989. "Sparks and Prairie Fires: A Theory of Unanticipated Political Revolution." *Public Choice* 61:41–74.

———. 1991. "Now Out of Never: The Element of Surprise in the East European Revolution of 1989." *World Politics* 44:7–48.

Kymlicka, Will. 1998. "Is Federalism a Viable Alternative to Secessionism?" In *Theories of Secessionism,* ed. Percy B. Lehning. New York: Routledge Press.

Laakso, Markku, and Rein Taagepera. 1979. "'Effective' Number of Parties: A Measure with Application to West Europe." *Comparative Political Studies* 12:3–27.

Lacouture, Jean. 1986. *De Gaulle: Le Souverain, 1959–1970.* Paris: Seuil.

Laitin, David D. 1983. "Rational Choice and Culture: A Thick Description of Abner Cohen's Hausa Migrants." In *Constitutional Democracy: Essays in Comparative Politics: A Festschrift for Henry W. Ehrmann,* ed. Fred Eidlin. Boulder, CO: Westview Press.

———. 1986. *Hegemony and Culture: Politics and Religious Change among the Yoruba.* Chicago: University of Chicago Press.

———. 1992. *Language Repertoires and State Construction in Africa.* New York: Cambridge University Press.

Lane, Frederick C. 1958. "Economic Consequences of Organized Violence." *Journal of Economic History* 18:401–410.

LaPalombara, Joseph. 1974. *Politics within Nations.* Englewood Cliffs, NJ: Prentice Hall.

Lasser, William. 1988. *The Limits of Judicial Power: The Supreme Court in American Politics.* Chapel Hill: University of North Carolina Press.

Lave, Charles, and James March. 1975. *An Introduction to Models in the Social Sciences.* New York: Harper and Row.

Laver, Michael, Scott de Marchi, and Hande Mutlu. 2011. "Negotiation in Legislatures over Government Formation." *Public Choice* 147:285–304.

Laver, Michael, and Kenneth A. Shepsle. 1996. *Making and Breaking Governments: Cabinets and Legislatures in Parliamentary Democracies.* New York: Cambridge University Press.

Lawrence, Adria K. 2017. "Repression and Activism among the Arab Spring's First Movers: Evidence from Morocco's February 20th Movement." *British Journal of Political Science* 47: 699-718.

Leblang, David A. 2002. "Political Uncertainty and Speculative Attacks." In *Coping with Globalization: Cross-National Patterns in Domestic Governance and Policy Performance,* eds. Steve Chan and James Scarritt. London: Frank Cass.

Lee, Kuan Yew. 1994. "Culture Is Destiny." An interview with Fareed Zakaria. *Foreign Affairs* 73:109–126.

Leff, Carol Skalnick. 1999. "Democratization and Disintegration in Multi-national States: The Breakup of the Communist Federations." *World Politics* 51:205–235.

Le Pen, Yannick. 2005. "Convergence among Five Industrial Countries (1870–1994): Results from a Time Varying Cointegration Approach." *Empirical Economics* 30:23–35.

Letsch, Constanze. 2013. "Turkey Protests Spread after Violence in Istanbul over Park Demolition." *The Guardian,* May 31. https://www.theguardian.com/world/2013/may/31/istanbul-protesters-violent-clashes-police.

Levi, Margaret. 1988. *Of Rule and Revenue.* Berkeley: University of California Press.

Levitsky, Steven, and Lucan A. Way. 2002. "The Rise of Competitive Authoritarianism." *Journal of Democracy* 13:51–65.

————. 2003. "Autocracy by Democratic Rules: The Dynamics of Competitive Authoritarianism in the Post–Cold War Era." Paper presented at the Conference on Mapping the Great Zone: Clientelism and the Boundary between Democratic and Democratizing, Columbia University, New York, April 4–5.

Lewis, Bernard. 1993. "Islam and Liberal Democracy." *Atlantic Monthly.*

"Libya Protests: Gaddafi Says 'All My People Love Me.'" 2011. BBC News, February 28. http://www.bbc.co.uk/news/world-africa-12603259.

Li, Qing, and David Papell. 1999. "Convergence of International Output: Time Series Evidence for 16 OECD Countries." *International Review of Economics and Finance* 8:267–280.

Lijphart, Arend. 1977. *Democracy in Plural Societies.* New Haven, CT: Yale University Press.

————. 1990. "Electoral Systems, Party Systems, and Conflict Management in Segmented Societies." In *Critical Choices for South Africa: An Agenda for the 1990s,* ed. Robert A. Schreirer. Cape Town, South Africa: Oxford University Press.

————. 1991. "The Power-Sharing Approach." In *Conflict and Peacemaking in Multi-ethnic Societies,* ed. J. V. Montville. New York: Lexington Books.

————. 1996. "Puzzle of Indian Democracy." *American Political Science Review* 90:258–268.

————. 1999. *Patterns of Democracy: Government Forms and Performance in Thirty-Six Countries.* New Haven, CT: Yale University Press.

————. 2004. "Constitutional Design for Divided Societies." *Journal of Democracy* 15(2):96–109.

Lim, Louisa. 2015. *The People's Republic of Amnesia: Tiananmen Revisited.* New York: Oxford University Press.

Linz, Juan J. 1990. "Virtues of Parliamentarism." *Journal of Democracy* 4:84–91.

————. 1994. "Democracy: Presidential or Parliamentary: Does It Make a Difference?" In *The Failure of Presidential Democracy?* eds. J. J. Linz and A. Valenzuela. Baltimore: Johns Hopkins University Press.

Lipset, Seymour Martin. 1959. "Some Social Requisites of Democracy: Economic Development and Political Legitimacy." *American Political Science Review* 53:69–105.

————. [1960] 1994. *Political Man: The Social Bases of Politics.* Baltimore: Johns Hopkins University Press.

————. 1996. "What Are Parties For?" *Journal of Democracy* 7:169–175.

————. 2001. "Cleavages, Parties, and Democracy." In *Party Systems and Voter Alignments Revisited,* eds. Lauri Karvonen and Stein Kuhnle, 3–10. London: Routledge.

Lipset, Seymour Martin, and Stein Rokkan. 1967. "Cleavage Structures, Party Systems, and Voter Alignments: An Introduction." In *Party Systems and Voter Alignments: Cross-National Perspectives,* eds. Seymour M. Lipset and Stein Rokkan. New York: Free Press.

Liu, I-Chou. 1999. "Campaigning in an SNTV System: The Case of the Kuomintang in Taiwan." In *Elections in Japan, Korea, and Taiwan under the Single Non-transferable Vote: The Comparative Study of an Embedded Institution,* eds. Bernard Grofman, Sung-Chull Lee, Edwin Winckler, and Brian Woodall. Ann Arbor: University of Michigan Press.

Locke, John. [1690] 1980. *Second Treatise of Government,* ed. C. B. Macpherson. Indianapolis, IN: Hackett.

Lohmann, Susanne. 1994. "The Dynamics of Informational Cascades: The Monday Demonstrations in Leipzig, East Germany, 1989–91." *World Politics* 47:42–101.

Londregan, John B., and Keith T. Poole. 1996. "Does High Income Promote Democracy?" *World Politics* 49:1–30.

Longino, Helen E. 1987. "Can There Be a Feminist Science?" *Hypatia* 2(3):51–64.

"Low Turnout as Egyptians Shun Elections Designed to Shore up Sisi." 2015. *The Guardian,* October 18. https://www.theguardian.com/world/2015/oct/18/egypt-parliamentary-elections-shore-up-sisi.

Ludwikowski, Rett R. 1996. *Constitution-Making in the Region of Former Soviet Dominance.* Durham, NC: Duke University Press.

Luebbert, Gregory M. 1984. "A Theory of Government Formation." *Comparative Political Studies* 17:229–264.

Lust-Okar, Ellen. 2005. *Structuring Conflict in the Arab World: Incumbents, Opponents, and Institutions.* New York: Cambridge University Press.

Lust-Okar, Ellen, and Amaney Ahmad Jamal. 2002. "Rulers and Rules: Reassessing the Influence of Regime Type on Electoral Law Formation." *Comparative Political Studies* 35:337–366.

Lustik, Ian S., Dan Miodownik, and Roy J. Eidelson. 2004. "Secessionism in Multicultural States: Does Sharing Power Prevent or Encourage It?" *American Political Science Review* 98:209–229.

Lyall, Jason, Graeme Blair, and Kosuke Imai. 2013. "Explaining Support for Combatants during Wartime: A Survey Experiment in Afghanistan." *American Political Science Review* 107:679–705.

Madison, James. 1787–1788. *The Federalist Papers Authored by James Madison* (nos. 10–63). Founding Fathers Info. http://www.foundingfathers.info/federalistpapers/madison.htm.

Madison, James. 1788. "The Structure of the Government Must Furnish the Proper Checks and Balances between the Different Departments." *The Federalist Papers No. 51.* https://en.wikipedia.org/wiki/Federalist_No._51.

Magaloni, Beatriz. 2006. *Voting for Autocracy: The Politics of Party Hegemony and Its Demise.* New York: Cambridge University.

"Magnifying Glasses on Order for Victoria's Metre-Long Senate Ballot Paper." 2014. ABC news, July 8. http://www.abc.net.au/news/2013-07-09/magnifying-glasses-on-order-for-vic-senate-ballot-paper/4807956.

Mahdavy, Hussein. 1970. "The Patterns and Problems of Economic Development in Rentier States: The Case of Iran." In *Studies in the Economic History of the Middle East,* ed. M. A. Cook. London: Oxford University Press.

Mainwaring, Scott. 1993. "Presidentialism, Multipartism, and Democracy: The Difficult Combination." *Comparative Political Studies* 26:198–228.

Mainwaring, Scott, and Matthew Sobert Shugart, eds. 1997. *Presidentialism and Democracy in Latin America.* New York: Cambridge University Press.

Malesky, Edmund, and Paul Schuler. 2010. "Nodding or Needling: Analyzing Delegate Responsiveness in an Authoritarian Parliament." *American Political Science Review* 104:482–502.

Mansbridge, Jane. 1999. "Should Blacks Represent Blacks and Women Represent Women? A Contingent 'Yes.'" *Journal of Politics* 61:628–657.

Marinov, Nikolay, and Hein Goemans. 2014. "Coups and Democracy." *British Journal of Political Science* 44:799–825.

Marquez, Xavier. 2011. "A Simple Model of Cults of Personality." In *Abandoned Footnotes* [blog], March 14. http://abandonedfootnotes.blogspot.com/2011/03/simple-model-of-cults-of-personality.html.

Marshall, Monty G., Ted Robert Gurr, and Keith Jaggers. 2017. *Polity IV Project: Political Regime Characteristics and Transitions, 1800–2016 Dataset.* Center for Systematic Peace. http://www.systemicpeace.org/inscr/p4manualv2015.pdf.

Martínez-Gallardo, Cecilia. 2012. "Out of the Cabinet: What Drives Defections from the Government in Presidential Systems?" *Comparative Political Studies* 45(1):62–90.

Marx, Karl. [1850] 1952. *The Class Struggle in France, 1848 to 1850.* Moscow: Progress.

———. [1847] 1995. *The Poverty of Philosophy.* Amherst, NY: Prometheus Books.

Mastias, Jean, and Jean Grangé. 1987. *Les secondes chambres du parlement en europe occidentale.* Paris: Economica.

Mayhew, David R. 1991. *Divided We Govern: Party Control, Lawmaking, and Investigations, 1946–1990.* New Haven, CT: Yale University Press.

Mazower, Mark. 2000. *Dark Continent: Europe's Twentieth Century.* New York: Vintage Books.

McCarty, Nolan, and Adam Meirowitz. 2007. *Political Game Theory: An Introduction.* New York: Cambridge University Press.

McGuire, James. 2002. "Democracy, Social Provisioning, and Child Mortality in Developing Countries." Wesleyan University.

McKelvey, Richard D. 1976. "Intransitivities in Multidimensional Voting Models and Some Implications for Agenda Control." *Journal of Economic Theory* 12:472.

McRae, Kenneth D. 1983. *Conflict and Compromise in Multilingual Societies: Switzerland.* Waterloo, Ontario: Wilfrid Laurier University Press.

Menaldo, Victor. 2012. "The Middle East and North Africa's Resilient Monarchs." *Journal of Politics* 74:707–722.

Meng, Tianguang, Jennifer Pan, and Ping Yang. 2017. "Conditional Receptivity to Citizen Participation: Evidence from a Survey Experiment in China." *Comparative Political Studies* 50(4): 399–433.

Michels, Robert. [1911] 2001. *Political Parties: A Sociological Study of the Oligarchical Tendencies of Modern Democracy.* Kitchener, Ontario: Batoche Books.

Mickey, Robert W. 2015. *Paths Out of Dixie: The Democratization of Authoritarian Enclaves in America's Deep South, 1944–1972.* Princeton, NJ: Princeton University Press.

"Migrant Crisis: Migration to Europe Explained in Seven Charts." 2016. BBC News, March 4. http://www.bbc.com/news/world-europe-34131911.

"Military 'Seizes Power' in Guinea." 2008. BBC News, December 23. http://news.bbc.co.uk/2/hi/africa/7796902.stm.

Mill, John Stuart. [1861] 2001. *Representative Government.* Ontario: Bartoche Books. Available from http://socserv2.socsci.mcmaster.ca/~econ/ugcm/3113/mill/repgovt.pdf.

Milliken, Jennifer, ed. 2003. *State Failure, Collapse and Reconstruction.* Oxford: Blackwell.

Monroe, Alan. 1983. "American Party Platforms and Public Opinion." *American Journal of Political Science* 27:27–42.

Monroe, Burt L. 1994. "Disproportionality and Malapportionment: Measuring Electoral Inequity." *Electoral Studies* 13:132–149.

Montalvo, José G., and Marta Reynal-Querol. 2005. "Ethnic Polarization, Potential Conflict, and Civil Wars." *American Economic Review* 95:796–816.

Montesquieu. [1721] 1899. *The Persian Letters.* London: Gibbings. Available from http://fsweb.wm.edu/plp/.

————. [1752] 1914. *The Spirit of the Laws.* London: Bell & Sons. Available from http://www.constitution.org/cm/sol.htm.

Moore, Barrington, Jr. [1966] 1999. *Social Origins of Dictatorship and Democracy: Lord and Peasant in the Making of the Modern World.* Boston: Beacon Press.

Morgenthau, Hans. 1948. *Politics among Nations.* New York: Knopf.

Morrison, Donald, Robert Mitchell, and John Paden. 1989. *Black Africa: A Comparative Handbook.* New York: Paragon House.

Morrison, Kevin M. 2007. "Natural Resources, Aid, and Democratization: A Best-Case Scenario." *Public Choice* 131:365–386.

————. 2009. "Oil, Nontax Revenue, and the Redistributional Foundations of Regime Stability." *International Organization* 63:107–138.

————. 2012. "What Can We Learn about the 'Resource Curse' from Foreign Aid?" *The World Bank Research Observer* 27:52–73.

Morton, Rebecca B. 1991. "Groups in Rational Turnout Models." *American Journal of Political Science* 35:758–776.

Morton, Rebecca B., and Thomas A. Rietz. 2008. "Majority Requirements and Minority Representation." *New York University Law Review* 63:691–726.

Moyo, Dambisa. 2009. *Dead Aid: Why Aid Is Not Working and How There Is Another Way for Africa.* New York: Farrar, Straus, and Giroux.

Mudde, Cas. 2004. "The Populist Zeitgeist." *Government and Opposition* 39:541–563.

————. 2007. *Populist Radical Right Parties in Europe.* New York: Cambridge University Press.

Mudde, Cas, and Cristóbal Rovira Kaltwasser. 2013. "Exclusionary versus Inclusionary Populism: Comparing Contemporary Europe and Latin America." *Government and Opposition* 48:147–174.

Müller, Wolfgang C., and Kaare Strøm, eds. 2000. *Coalition Governments in Western Europe.* Oxford: Oxford University Press.

Muller, Edward N., and Mitchell A. Seligson. 1994. "Civic Culture and Democracy: The Question of Causal Relationships." *American Political Science Review* 88:635–652.

Munck, Gerardo L., and Jay Verkuilen. 2002. "Conceptualizing and Measuring Democracy: Evaluating Alternative Indices." *Comparative Political Studies* 35:5–34.

Murphy, Walter F., C. Hermann Pritchett, and Lee Epstein. 2001. *Courts, Judges, and Politics: An Introduction to the Judicial Process.* New York: McGraw-Hill.

Nagel, Jack H. 2004. "New Zealand: Reform by (Nearly) Immaculate Design." In *Handbook of Electoral System Design,* ed. Josep Colomer, 530–543. London: Palgrave.

Navia, Patricio, and Julio Ríos-Figueroa. 2005. "The Constitutional Adjudication Mosaic of Latin America." *Comparative Political Studies* 38:189–217.

"Neither Tweedledum Nor Tweedledee." 1968. *Time,* September 20, Vol. 92, Issue 12, p. 41.

Newton, Kenneth, and Pippa Norris. 2000. "Confidence in Political Institutions: Faith, Culture, or Performance?" In *Disaffected Democracies: What's Troubling the Trilateral Countries?* eds. Susan Pharr and Robert Putnam, 52–73. Princeton, NJ: Princeton University Press.

"N Korea Wages War on Long Hair." 2005. BBC News, January 8. http://news.bbc.co.uk/2/hi/asia-pacific/4157121.stm.

Nordlan, Rod. 2010. "Afghan Votes Come Cheap, and Often in Bulk." *The New York Times,* September 17. http://www.nytimes.com/2010/09/18/world/asia/18vote.html.

Nordlinger, Eric. 1977. *Soldiers in Politics: Military Coups and Governments.* Englewood Cliffs, NJ: Prentice Hall.

Norris, Pippa. 2008. *Driving Democracy: Do Power-Sharing Institutions Work?* New York: Cambridge University Press.

———. 2013. "The New Research Agenda Studying Electoral Integrity." *Electoral Studies* 32:563–575.

———. 2014. *Why Do We Care about Electoral Integrity?* New York: Cambridge University Press.

———. 2015. *Why Elections Fail.* New York: Cambridge University Press.

Norris, Pippa, and Ronald Inglehart. 2004. *Sacred and Secular: Religion and Politics Worldwide.* New York: Cambridge University Press.

Norris, Pippa, Ferran Martínez i Coma, Allesandro Nai, and Max Grömping. 2016a. "The Year in Elections 2015: The Expert Survey on Perceptions of Electoral Integrity (PEI-4.0)." www.electoralintegrityproject.com.

Norris, Pippa, Thomas Wynter and Sarah Cameron. 2018a. *Corruption and Coercion: The Year in Elections 2017.* The Electoral Integrity Project. https://www.electoralintegrityproject.com/the-year-in-elections-2017/

———. 2018b. *The expert survey of Perceptions of Electoral Integrity, Release 6.0, (PEI_6.0), March 2018.* The Electoral Integrity Project www.electoralintegrityproject.com.

North, Douglass C. 1981. *Structure and Change in Economic History.* New York: Norton.

North, Douglass C., and Robert Paul Thomas. 1971. "The Rise and Fall of the Manorial System: A Theoretical Model." *Journal of Economic History* 31(4):777–803.

North, Douglass C., and Barry R. Weingast. 1989. "Constitutions and Commitment: The Evolution of Institutions Governing Public Choice in Seventeenth Century England." *Journal of Economic History* 49:803–832.

Oates, Wallace. 1972. *Fiscal Federalism.* New York: Harcourt Brace Jovanovich.

O'Donnell, Guillermo. 1973. *Modernization and Bureaucratic Authoritarianism: Studies in South American Politics.* Berkeley: University of California, Institute for International Studies.

Offe, Claus. 1983. "Competitive Party Democracy and the Keynesian Welfare State: Factors of Stability and Disorganization." *Policy Sciences* 15:225–246.

O'Loughlin, John, Michael D. Ward, Corey L. Lofdahl, Jordin S. Cohen, David S. Brown, David Reilly, Kristian S. Gleditsch, and Michael Shin. 1998. "The Diffusion of Democracy, 1946–1994." *Annals of the Association of American Geographers* 88:545–574.

Olson, Mancur C. [1965] 1971. *The Logic of Collective Action: Public Goods and the Theory of Groups,* revised ed. Harvard University Press.

Ordeshook, Peter, and Olga Shvetsova. 1994. "Ethnic Heterogeneity, District Magnitude, and the Number of Parties." *American Journal of Political Science* 38:100–123.

Orwell, George. [1949] 1977. *1984: A Novel.* New York: Harcourt, Brace and World.

Page, Benjamin I. 1978. *Choices and Echoes in Presidential Elections: Rational Man and Electoral Democracy.* Chicago: University of Chicago Press.

Paler, Laura. 2013. "Keeping the Public Purse: An Experiment in Windfalls, Taxes, and the Incentives to Restrain Government." *American Political Science Review* 104:706–725.

Patterson, Dennis, and Hans Stockton. 2010. "Strategies, Institutions, and Outcomes under SNTV in Taiwan, 1992–2004." *Journal of East Asian Studies* 10:31–59.

Patty, John W., and Elizabeth Maggie Penn. 2014. *Social Choice and Legitimacy: The Possibilities of Impossibility.* New York: Cambridge University Press.

Peçanha, Sergio, Sarah Almukhtar, and K. K. Rebecca Lai. 2015. "Untangling the Overlapping Conflicts in the Syrian War." *The New York Times,* October 18. http://www .nytimes.com/interactive/2015/10/16/world/middleeast/ untangling-the-overlapping-conflicts-in-the-syrian-war. html?hp&action=click&pgtype=Homepage&module=pho- to-spot-region&region=top-news&WT.nav=top-news&_r=0.

Penn, Elizabeth Maggie. 2009. "A Model of Farsighted Voting." *American Journal of Political Science* 53:36–54.

Persson, Torsten, Gerard Roland, and Guido Tabellini. 2004. "Constitutional Rules and Fiscal Policy Outcomes." *American Economic Review* 94:24–45.

Peterson, Paul. 1995. *The Price of Federalism.* Washington, DC: Brookings Institution.

Phillips, Anne. 1998. *The Politics of Presence: The Political Representation of Gender, Ethnicity, and Race.* New York: Oxford University Press.

Pitkin, Hanna Fenichel. 1967. *The Concept of Representation.* Berkeley: University of California Press.

Plato. [360 BCE] 1991. *The Republic of Plato,* trans. Allan Bloom. New York: Basic Books.

————. 1871. "Apology." In *The Dialogues of Plato, Volume 1,* trans. Benjamin Jowett, 319–356. Oxford University: Clarendon. https://books.google.com/books?id=hbUNAAAAQ AAJ&source= gbs_navlinks_s.

Plott, Charles. 1967. "A Notion of Equilibrium and Its Possibility under Majoritarian Rule." *American Economic Review* 57:787–806.

Popper, Sir Karl. [1959] 2003. *The Logic of Scientific Discovery.* New York: Routledge.

————. 1962. *Conjectures and Refutations: The Growth of Scientific Knowledge.* New York: Basic Books.

Posner, Daniel N. 2004. "The Political Salience of Cultural Difference: Why Chewas and Tumbukas Are Allies in Zambia and Adversaries in Malawi." *American Political Science Review* 98:529–545.

————. 2005. *Institutions and Ethnic Politics in Africa.* New York: Cambridge University Press.

Poulantzas, Nicos. 1975. *Political Power and Social Class.* London: Verso.

————. 1980. *State, Power and Socialism.* London: Verso.

Powell, G. Bingham. 2000. *Elections as Instruments of Democracy: Majoritarian and Proportional Visions.* New Haven, CT: Yale University Press.

Powell, G. Bingham, and Guy D. Whitten. 1993. "A Cross-National Analysis of Economic Voting: Taking Account of the Political Context." *American Journal of Political Science* 37:391–414.

Price, Daniel E. 1999. *Islamic Political Culture, Democracy, and Human Rights: A Comparative Study.* New York: Praeger.

Przeworski, Adam. 1985. *Capitalism and Social Democracy.* New York: Cambridge University Press.

————. 1991. *Democracy and the Market: Political and Economic Reforms in Eastern Europe and Latin America.* New York: Cambridge University Press.

————. 2001. "Why Democracy Survives in Affluent Societies." Unpublished manuscript, New York University.

————. 2006. "Self-Enforcing Democracy." In *The Oxford Handbook of Political Economy,* ed. Donald Wittman and Barry Weingast. New York: Oxford University Press.

Przeworski, Adam, Michael E. Alvarez, José Antonio Cheibub, and Fernando Limongi. 2000. *Democracy and Development: Political Institutions and Well-Being in the World, 1950–1990.* New York: Cambridge University Press.

Przeworski, Adam, José Antonio Cheibub, and Fernando Limongi. 1998. "Culture and Democracy." In *Culture and Development.* Paris: UNESCO.

Przeworski, Adam, and John Sprague. 1988. *Paper Stones: A History of Electoral Socialism.* Chicago: University of Chicago Press.

Przeworski, Adam, and Michael Wallerstein. 1988. "Structural Dependence of the State on Capital." *American Political Science Review* 82:11–19.

Putnam, Robert D. 1993. *Making Democracy Work: Civic Traditions in Modern Italy.* Princeton, NJ: Princeton University Press.

———. 2000. *Bowling Alone: The Collapse and Revival of American Community.* New York: Simon and Schuster.

Pye, Lucian W. 1985. *Asian Power and Politics.* Cambridge, MA: Harvard University Press.

Rabushka, Alvin, and Kenneth A. Shepsle. 1972. *Politics in Plural Societies.* Columbus, OH: Merrill.

Rahman, Fazlur. 1979. *Islam.* Chicago: University of Chicago Press.

Rasch, Bjørn Erik, Shane Martin, and José Antonio Cheibub, eds. 2015. *Unpacking Parliamentarism: How Investiture Rules Shape Government Formation.* New York: Oxford University Press.

Rauch, Jonathan. 1993. *Kindly Inquisitors: The New Attacks on Free Thought.* Chicago: University of Chicago Press.

Reenock, Christopher, Michael Bernhard, and David Sobek. 2007. "Regressive Socioeconomic Distribution and Democratic Survival." *International Studies Quarterly* 51:677–699.

Reilly, Ben. 1997. "Preferential Voting and Political Engineering: A Comparative Study." *Journal of Commonwealth and Comparative Politics* 35:1–19.

———. 2001. *Democracy in Divided Societies: Electoral Engineering for Conflict Management.* New York: Cambridge University Press.

Remmer, Karen. 2004. "Does Foreign Aid Promote the Expansion of Government?" *American Journal of Political Science* 48:77–92.

Reynal-Querol, Marta. 2002. "Ethnicity, Political Systems, and Civil Wars." *Journal of Conflict Resolution* 46:29–54.

Reynolds, Andrew. 2006. "The Curious Case of Afghanistan." *Journal of Democracy* 17:104–117.

———. 2011. *Designing Democracy in a Dangerous World.* Oxford: Oxford University Press.

Reynolds, Andrew, and John Carey. 2012. "Fixing Afghanistan's Electoral System: Arguments and Options for Reform." Afghanistan Research and Evaluation Unit, July . http://www.areu.org.af/EditionDetails.aspx?EditionId=593& ContentId=7&ParentId=7#x0026;.

Reynolds, Andrew, Ben Reilly, and Andrew Ellis. 2005. *Electoral System Design: The New International IDEA Handbook.* Stockholm, Sweden: International Institute for Democracy and Electoral Assistance.

Rhodes, P. J. 2003. *Ancient Democracy and Modern Ideology.* London: Duckworth.

Riker, William. 1964. *Federalism: Origin, Operation, Significance.* Boston: Little, Brown.

———. 1982. *Liberalism against Populism: A Confrontation between the Theory of Democracy and the Theory of Social Choice.* San Francisco: Freeman.

"Riots Thwarted by Blackberry and Twitter Chat—Police." 2011. BBC News, August 16. http://www.bbc.co.uk/news/uk-politics-14542588.

Rioux, Jean-Pierre. 1989. *The Fourth Republic, 1944–1958.* New York: Cambridge University Press.

Roberts, N. S. 1997. "A Period of Enhanced Surprise, Disappointment, and Frustration? The Introduction of a New Electoral System in New Zealand." In *Electoral Systems for Emerging Democracies: Experiences and Suggestions,* ed. Jørgen Elklit. Copenhagen, Denmark: Danida.

Rodden, Jonathan. 2002. "The Dilemma of Fiscal Federalism: Grants and Fiscal Performance around the World." *American Journal of Political Science* 46:670–687.

———. 2004. "Comparative Federalism and Decentralization: On Meaning and Measurement." *Comparative Politics* 36:481–500.

———. 2006. *Hamilton's Paradox: The Promise and Peril of Fiscal Federalism.* New York: Cambridge University Press.

Rodden, Jonathan, and Erik Wibbels. 2002. "Beyond the Fiction of Federalism: Macroeconomic Management in Multitiered Systems." *World Politics* 54:494–531.

Roeder, Philip. 1991. "Soviet Federalism and Ethnic Mobilization." *World Politics* 43:196–232.

Roemer, John E. 1998. "Why the Poor Do Not Expropriate the Rich: An Old Argument in New Garb." *Journal of Public Economics* 70:399–424.

Rogers, James R. 2001. "Information and Judicial Review: A Signaling Game of Legislative-Judicial Interaction." *American Journal of Political Science* 45:84–99.

Rosanvallon, Pierre. 1995. "The History of the Word 'Democracy' in France." *Journal of Democracy* 6:140–154.

Rose-Ackerman, Susan. 1978. *Corruption: A Study in Political Economy.* New York: Academic Press.

_____. 1999. *Corruption and Government: Causes, Consequences, and Reform.* New York: Cambridge University Press.

_____. 2000. "The Economics and Politics of Federalism: Tensions and Complementarities." *APSA-CP Newsletter* 11:17–19.

Rosenberg, Gerald. 1991. *The Hollow Hope: Can Courts Bring About Social Change?* Chicago: University of Chicago Press.

Ross, Michael Lewin. 1999. "The Political Economy of the Resource Curse." *World Politics* 51:297–322.

_____. 2001. "Does Oil Hinder Democracy?" *World Politics* 53:325–361.

_____. 2004. "Does Taxation Lead to Representation?" *British Journal of Political Science* 34:229–249.

_____. 2011. "Will Oil Drown the Arab Spring?" *Foreign Affairs* 90(5):2–7.

_____. 2012. *The Oil Curse.* Princeton, NJ: Princeton University Press.

Rostow, W. W. 1960. *The Stages of Economic Growth: A Non-communist Manifesto.* Cambridge: Cambridge University Press.

Rotberg, Robert I. 2002. "Failed States in a World of Terror." *Foreign Affairs* 81:127–140.

Rousseau, Jean-Jacques. [1762] 1987. *The Social Contract,* trans. Maurice Cranston. New York: Penguin Books.

Rudd, C., and I. Taichi. 1994. *Electoral Reform in New Zealand and Japan: A Shared Experience?* Palmerston North, New Zealand: Massey University Press.

Russell, Bertrand. [1919] 2004. *The Proposed Roads to Freedom.* New York: Cosimo.

Rustow, Dankwart A. 1950. "Some Observations on Proportional Representation." *Journal of Politics* 12:107–127.

Rydgren, Jens. 2004. *The Populist Challenge: Political Protest and Ethno-Nationalist Mobilization in France.* New York: Berghahn Books.

_____. 2005. "Is Extreme Right-Wing Populism Contagious? Explaining the Emergence of a New Party Family." *European Journal of Political Research* 44:413–437.

Sachedina, Abdulaziz. 2000. *The Islamic Roots of Democratic Pluralism.* New York: Oxford University Press.

Saideman, Stephen M., David J. Lanoue, Michael Campenni, and Samuel Stanon. 2002. "Democratization, Political Institutions, and Ethnic Conflict: A Pooled Time-Series Analysis, 1985–1998." *Comparative Political Studies* 35:103–129.

Saletan, William. 2011. "Springtime for Twitter: Is the Internet Driving the Revolutions of the Arab Spring." *Slate,* July 18. http://www.slate.com/articles/technology/future_tense/2011/07/springtime_for_twitter.html.

Samuel, Henry. 2011. "Praying in Paris Streets Outlawed." *The Telegraph,* September 15. http://www.telegraph.co.uk/news/worldnews/europe/france/8766169/Praying-in-Paris-streets-outlawed.html.

Samuels, David. 2007. "Separation of Powers." In *The Oxford Handbook of Comparative Politics,* eds. Carles Boix and Susan C. Stokes. New York: Oxford University Press.

Samuels, David, and Richard Snyder. 2001. "The Value of a Vote: Malapportionment in Comparative Perspective." *British Journal of Political Science* 31:651–671.

Satterthwaite, Mark A. 1975. "Strategy-Proofness and Arrow's Conditions: Existence and Correspondence Theorems for Voting Procedures and Social Welfare Functions." *Journal of Economic Theory* 10:187–217.

Saward, Michael. 2006. "The Representative Claim." *Contemporary Political Theory* 5:297–318.

———. 2009. "Authorisation and Authenticity: Representation and the Unelected." *Journal of Political Philosophy* 17:1–22.

Scalapino, Robert. 1989. *The Politics of Development: Perspectives on Twentieth Century Asia.* Cambridge, MA: Harvard University Press.

Schattschneider, Elmer E. 1942. *Party Government.* New York: Rinehart.

Schedler, Andreas. 2002. "Elections without Democracy: The Menu of Manipulation." *Journal of Democracy* 13(2):36–50.

———, ed. 2006. *Electoral Authoritarianism: The Dynamics of Unfree Competition.* Boulder, CO: Lynne Rienner.

Scheve, Kenneth, and David Stasavage. 2009. "Institutions, Partisanship, and Inequality in the Long Run." *World Politics* 61:215–253.

Schleifer, Andrei, and Robert Vishny. 1993. "Corruption." *Quarterly Journal of Economics* 108:599–617.

Schleiter, Petra, and Edward Morgan-Jones. 2009. "Constitutional Power and Competing Risks: Monarchs, Presidents, Prime Ministers, and the Termination of East and West European Cabinets." *American Political Science Review* 103:496–512.

Schofield, Norman J. 1978. "Instability of Simple Dynamic Games." *Review of Economic Studies* 45:575–594.

Schumpeter, Joseph. [1942] 1962. *Capitalism, Socialism, and Democracy.* New York: Harper Perennial.

Schwartz, Hermann. 1999. "Surprising Success: The New Eastern European Constitutional Courts." In *The Self-Restraining State,* eds. Andreas Schedler, Larry Diamand, and Marc Plattner. Boulder, CO: Lynne Rienner.

Schwindt-Bayer, Leslie A., and William Mishler. 2005. "An Integrated Model of Women's Representation." *Journal of Politics* 67:407–428.

"Scores Killed in China Protests." 2009. BBC News, July 6. http://news.bbc.co.uk/2/hi/asia-pacific/8135203.stm.

Seligson, Mitchell A. 2002. "The Renaissance of Political Culture or the Renaissance of the Ecological Fallacy?" *Comparative Politics* 34:273–292.

Selway, Joel, and Kharis Templeman. 2012. "The Myth of Consociationalism? Conflict Reduction in Divided Societies." *Comparative Political Studies* 45(12):1542–1571.

Sen, Amartya K. 1970. *Collective Choice and Social Welfare.* San Francisco: Holden-Day.

———. 2002. "Health: Perception versus Observation." *British Medical Journal* 324:860–861.

Ser, Kuang Keng Kuek. 2016. "How China Has Censored Words Relating to the Tiananmen Square Anniversary." PRI's *The World,* June 4. http://www.pri.org/stories/2016–06–03/how-china-has-censored-words-relating-tiananmen-square-anniversary.

Shafer, D. Michael. 1994. *Winners and Losers: How Sectors Shape the Developmental Prospects of States.* Ithaca, NY: Cornell University Press.

Shah, Zia H. 2012. "The Constitution of Medina: A Symbol of Pluralism in Islam." *The Muslim Times,* November 9. https://themuslimtimes.info/2012/11/09/the-constitution-of-medina-a-symbol-of-pluralism-in-islam/.

Shapiro, Martin, and Alec Stone Sweet. 1994. "Introduction: The New Constitutional Politics." *Comparative Political Studies* 26:397–420.

Shelton, Cameron A. 2007. "The Size and Composition of Government Expenditure." *Journal of Public Economics* 91:2230–2260.

Shepsle, Kenneth A. 1992. "Congress Is a 'They' Not an 'It': Legislative Intent as Oxymoron." *International Review of Law and Economics* 12:239–257.

Shively, W. Phillips. 2001. *Power and Choice: An Introduction to Political Science.* New York: McGraw-Hill.

Shugart, Matthew Soberg, and John M. Carey. 1992. *Presidents and Assemblies: Constitutional Design and Electoral Dynamics.* New York: Cambridge University Press.

Simpser, Alberto. 2008. "Cheating Big: On the Logic of Electoral Corruption in Developing Countries." Unpublished manuscript, University of Chicago.

————. 2013. *Why Governments and Parties Manipulate Elections: Theory, Practice, and Implications.* New York: Cambridge University Press.

Sinnott, Richard. 1992. "The Electoral System." In *Politics in the Republic of Ireland,* eds. John Coakley and Michael Gallagher. Dublin: Folens and PSAI.

Smith, Alastair. 2003. "Election Timing in Majoritarian Parliamentary Systems." *British Journal of Political Science* 33:397–418.

————. 2004. *Election Timing.* New York: Cambridge University Press.

————. 2008. "The Perils of Unearned Income." *Journal of Politics* 70(3):780–793.

Smith, Benjamin. 2006. "The Wrong Kind of Crisis: Why Oil Booms and Busts Rarely Lead to Authoritarian Breakdown." *Studies in Comparative International Development* 40:55–76.

Smith, Dorothy E. 1974. "Women's Perspective as a Radical Critique of Sociology." *Sociological Inquiry* 44(1):7–13.

Snyder, Jack. 2000. *From Voting to Violence: Democratization and Nationalist Conflict.* New York: Norton.

Solzhenitsyn, Aleksandr Isaevich. 1975. "The Smatterers." In *From under the Rubble,* eds. Aleksandr Isaevich Solzhenitsyn, Mikhail Agursky, and Evgeny Barabanov, 275. Boston: Little, Brown.

Stark, Rodney. 2004a. "SSRC Presidential Address: Putting an End to Ancestor Worship." *Journal for the Scientific Study of Religion* 43:465–475.

————. 2004b. *The Victory of Reason: How Christianity Led to Freedom, Capitalism, and Western Success.* New York: Random House.

Stark, Rodney, and Roger Finke. 2000. *Acts of Faith: Exploring the Human Side of Religion.* Berkeley: University of California Press.

Starr, Harvey, and Christina Lindborg. 2003. "Democratic Dominoes Revisited: The Hazards of Governmental Transitions, 1974–1996." *Journal of Conflict Resolution* 47:490–519.

Stasavage, David. 2002. "Credible Commitment in Early Modern Europe: North and Weingast Revisited." *Journal of Law, Economics, and Organization* 18:155–186.

Staton, Jeffrey K. 2004. "Judicial Policy Implementation in Mexico City and Mérida." *Comparative Politics* 37:41–60.

————. 2006. "Constitutional Review and the Selective Promotion of Case Results." *American Journal of Political Science* 50:98–112.

————. 2010. *Judicial Power and Strategic Communication in Mexico.* New York: Cambridge University Press.

Steiner, Jürg. 1971. "The Principles of Majority and Proportionality." *British Journal of Political Science* 1:63–70.

Stepan, Alfred. 1971. *The Military in Politics: Changing Patterns in Brazil.* Princeton, NJ: Princeton University Press.

————. 1985. "State Power and the Strength of Civil Society in the Southern Cone of Latin America." In *Bringing the State Back In,* eds. Peter B. Evans, Dietrich Rueschemeyer, and Theda Skocpol. New York: Cambridge University Press.

————. 1999. "Federalism and Democracy: Beyond the U.S. Model." *Journal of Democracy* 10:19–34.

————. 2000. "Religion, Democracy, and the 'Twin Tolerations.'" *Journal of Democracy* 11:37–57.

Stepan, Alfred, and Cindy Skach. 1993. "Constitutional Frameworks and Democratic Consolidation: Parliamentarism versus Presidentialism." World Politics 46:1–22.

Stokes, Susan C. 1999. "Political Parties and Democracy." *Annual Review of Political Science* 2:243–267.

Stone Sweet, Alec. 1992. *The Birth of Judicial Politics in France: The Constitutional Council in Comparative Perspective.* Oxford: Oxford University Press.

————. 2000. *Governing with Judges: Constitutional Politics in Europe.* New York: Oxford University Press.

————. 2008. "Constitutions and Judicial Power." In *Comparative Politics,* ed. Daniele Caramani. New York: Oxford University Press.

Strøm, Kaare. 1990. *Minority Government and Majority Rule.* Cambridge: Cambridge University Press.

Strøm, Kaare, Wolfgang C. Müller, and Torbjörn Bergman, eds. 2003. "Parliamentary Democracy and Delegation." In *Delegation and Accountability in Parliamentary Democracies,* eds. Kaare Strøm, Wolfgang C. Müller, and Torbjörn Bergman, 55–106. Oxford: Oxford University Press.

Suny, Ronald Grigor. 1998. *The Soviet Experiment: Russia, the USSR, and the Successor States.* New York: Oxford University Press.

Svensson, Jakob. 2003. "Why Conditional Aid Does Not Work and What Can Be Done about It." *Journal of Development Economics* 70:381–402.

Svolik, Milan W. 2009. "Power Sharing and Leadership Dynamics in Authoritarian Regimes." *American Journal of Political Science* 53:477–494.

———. 2012. *The Politics of Authoritarian Rule*. New York: Cambridge University Press.

"Syria's civil war explained from the beginning." 2017. Al Jazeera, October 1. http://www.aljazeera.com/news/2016/05/syria-civil-war-explained-160505084119966.html

Tate, Katherine. 1993. *From Protest to Politics: The New Black Voters in American Politics*. Cambridge, MA: Harvard University Press.

Thatcher, Margaret. 1993. *Margaret Thatcher: The Downing Street Years*. London: HarperCollins.

Theil, Henri. 1971. *Principles of Econometrics*. New York: Wiley.

Thyne, Clayton L., and Jonathan M. Powell. 2014. "Coup d'état or Coup d'autocracy? How Coups Impact Democratization, 1950–2008." *Foreign Policy Analysis* 12:192–213.

Tiebout, Charles M. 1956. "A Pure Theory of Local Expenditures." *Journal of Political Economy* 64: 416–424.

Tilly, Charles. 1985. "War Making and State Making as Organized Crime." In *Bringing the State Back In*, eds. Peter Evans, Dietrich Rueschmeyer, and Theda Skocpol, 169–191. New York: Cambridge University Press.

"Timeline: A History of Turkish Coups." 2016. *Al Jazeera*, July 15. http://www.aljazeera.com/news/europe/2012/04/20124472814687973.html.

Tocqueville, Alexis de. [1835] 1988. *Democracy in America*. New York: HarperCollins.

"Toughs at the Top." 2004. *The Economist*, December 16. http://www.economist.com/node/3445136.

Treisman, Daniel. 2000. "Decentralization and Inflation: Commitment, Collective Action, or Continuity?" *American Political Science Review* 94:837–857.

———. 2002. "Decentralization and the Quality of Government." University of California, Los Angeles.

Tripp, Aili Mari, and Alice Kang. 2008. "The Global Impact of Quotas: On the Fast Track to Increased Female Legislative Representation." *Comparative Political Studies* 41:338–361.

Tsai, Michelle. "Vote of No Consequence." 2007. *Slate,* May 21. http://www.slate.com/articles/news_and_politics/explainer/2007/05/vote_of_no_consequence.html.

Tsebelis, George. 1990. "Elite Interaction and Constitution Building in Consociational Societies." *Journal of Theoretical Politics* 2:5–29.

———. 1995. "Decision Making in Political Systems: Veto Players in Presidentialism, Multicameralism, and Multipartyism." *British Journal of Political Science* 25:289–326.

———. 1999. "Veto Players and Law Production in Parliamentary Democracies: An Empirical Analysis." *American Political Science Review* 93:591–608.

———. 2002. *Veto Players: How Political Institutions Work.* Princeton, NJ: Princeton University Press.

Tsebelis, George, and Jeannette Money. 1997. *Bicameralism.* New York: Cambridge University Press.

Tullock, Gordon. 1969. "Federalism: Problems of Scale." *Public Choice* 6:19–29.

"Turkmenistan Wrestles with Child Labor Issue as Cotton Harvest Approaches." 2004. Eurasianet, August 31. http://www.eurasianet.org/departments/rights/articles/eav090104.shtml/.

Uhlaner, Carole. 1989. "Rational Turnout: The Neglected Role of Groups." *American Journal of Political Science* 33:390–422.

Uhlfelder, Jay. 2007. "Natural-Resource Wealth and the Survival of Autocracy." *Comparative Political Studies* 40:995–1018.

United Nations High Commissioner for Human Rights. 2013. "Periodic Update." December 20. http://www.ohchr.org/Documents/Countries/SY/ColSyriaDecember2012.pdf.

United Nations High Commissioner for Human Rights. 2017. http://data.unhcr.org/syrianrefugees/regional.php.

United Nations High Commissioner for Human Rights. 2018. "Syria Regional Refugee Response." March 22. https://data2.unhcr.org/en/situations/syria.

US Department of State. 2011. "Internet Freedom and Human Rights: The Obama Administration's Perspective." July 13. http://www.state.gov/j/drl/rls/rm/2011/168475.htm.

Uzonyi, Gary J., Mark Souva, and Sona N. Golder. 2012. "Domestic Institutions and Credible Signals." *International Studies Quarterly* 56(4):765–776.

Valenzuela, Arturo. 2004. "Latin America Presidencies Interrupted." *Journal of Democracy* 15:5–19.

Van Cott, Donna Lee. 2005. *From Movements to Parties in Latin America: The Evolution of Ethnic Politics.* New York: Cambridge University Press.

Vanberg, Georg. 2000. "Establishing Judicial Independence in Germany: The Impact of Opinion Leadership and the Separation of Powers." *Comparative Politics* 32:333–353.

———. 2001. "Legislative-Judicial Relations: A Game-Theoretic Approach to Constitutional Review." *American Journal of Political Science* 45:346–361.

———. 2005. *The Politics of Constitutional Review in Germany.* New York: Cambridge University Press.

Vanhanen, Tatu. 1991. *The Process of Democratization: A Comparative Study of 147 States, 1980–1988.* New York: Crane Russak.

Varian, Hal R. 1993. *Intermediate Economics: A Modern Approach.* New York: Norton.

Varshney, Ashutosh. 2001. "Ethnic Conflict and Civil Society: India and Beyond." *World Politics* 53:362–398.

———. 2002. *Ethnic Conflict and Civic Life: Hindus and Muslims in India.* New Haven, CT: Yale University Press.

Veenendaal, Wouter P. 2016. "How Democracy Functions without Parties: The Republic of Palau." *Party Politics* 22(1):27–36.

Vlasic, Bill, and David M. Herszenshorn. 2008. "Detroit Chiefs Plead for Aid." *The New York Times,* November 19. http://www.nytimes.com/2008/11/19/business/19auto.html?pagewanted=print.

Voeten, Erik. 2010. "A New Twittered Revolution." April 7. http://themonkeycage.org/blog/2010/04/07/a_new_twittered_revolution/.

Volcansek, Mary L. 1991. "Judicial Activism in Italy." In *Judicial Activism in Comparative Perspective,* ed. Kenneth Holland. New York: St. Martin's Press.

Voslensky, Michael. 1984. *Nomenklatura: The Soviet Ruling Class.* Garden City, NY: Doubleday.

Waltz, Kenneth N. 1979. *Theory of International Politics.* New York: McGraw-Hill.

Wängnerud, Lena. 2009. "Women in Parliaments: Descriptive and Substantive Representation." *Annual Review of Sociology* 12:51–69.

Wantchekon, Leonard. 2001. "Why Do Resource Abundant Countries Have Authoritarian Governments?" *Journal of African Finance and Development* 5:57–77.

Warwick, Paul V., and Jamie Druckman. 2001. "Portfolio Salience and the Proportionality of Payoffs in Coalition Governments." *British Journal of Political Science* 31:627–649.

———. 2006. "The Paradox of Portfolio Allocation: An Investigation into the Nature of a Very Strong but Puzzling Relationship." *European Journal of Political Research* 45:635–665.

Way, Lucan. 2011. "Comparing the Arab Revolts: The Lessons of 1989." *Journal of Democracy* 232(4):17–27.

Weber, Max. [1918] 1958. "Politics as a Vocation." In *From Max Weber: Essays in Sociology,* eds. H. H. Gerth and C. Wright Mills, Chapt. IV: 77–128. New York: Oxford University Press.

———. [1930] 1992. *The Protestant Ethic and the Spirit of Capitalism.* New York: Routledge.

Weingast, Barry R. 1995. "The Economic Role of Political Institutions: Market-Preserving Federalism and Economic Development." *Journal of Law, Economics, and Organization* 11:1–31.

Weldon, S. Laurel. 2006. "The Structure of Intersectionality: A Comparative Politics of Gender." *Politics and Gender* 2:235–248.

"What Now for Colonel Gaddafi's Green Book?" 2011. BBC News, April 29. http://www.bbc.com/news/world-africa-13235981.

Wibbels, Erik. 2000. "Federalism and the Politics of Macroeconomic Policy and Performance." *American Journal of Political Science* 44:687–702.

Wiens, David, Paul Poast, and William Roberts Clark. 2014. "The Political Resource Curse: An Empirical Re-Evaluation." *Political Research Quarterly* 67:783–794.

Wilson, Andrew. 2012. *Belarus: The Last European Dictatorship.* New Haven, CT: Yale University Press.

———. 2015. "Belarus Votes—And This Time It Matters." European Council on Foreign Relations, October 9. http://www.ecfr.eu/article/commentary_belarus_votes_and_this_time_it_matters4068.

Wintrobe, Ronald. 2001. "How to Understand, and Deal with Dictatorship: An Economist's View." *Economics of Governance* 2:35–58.

Wood, Elisabeth J. 2000. *Forging Democracy from Below: Contested Transitions in Oligarchic Societies.* New York: Cambridge University Press.

Woodberry, Robert D. 2004. "The Shadow of Empire: Christian Missions, Colonial Policy, and Democracy in Postcolonial Societies." PhD dissertation, Department of Sociology, University of North Carolina.

———. 2012. "The Missionary Roots of Liberal Democracy." *American Political Science Review* 106(2):244–274.

Woodberry, Robert D., and Timothy S. Shah. 2004. "The Pioneering Protestants." *Journal of Democracy* 15:47–60.

Woods, Dwayne. 2012. "Patrimonialism (neo) and the Kingdom of Swaziland: Employing a Case-Study to Rescale a Concept." *Journal of Commonwealth and Comparative Politics* 50:344–366.

———. 2017. "Monarchical Rule in Swaziland: Power Is Absolute but Patronage Is (for) Relative(s)." *Journal of African and Asian Studies* 52: 497–513.

Wright, Joseph. 2009. "How Foreign Aid Can Foster Democratization in Authoritarian Regimes." *American Journal of Political Science* 53:552–571.

Wright, Joseph, and Matthew Winters. 2010. "The Politics of Effective Foreign Aid." *Annual Review of Political Science* 13:61–80.

Yazdi, Ibrahim. 1995. "A Seminar with Ibrahim Yazdi." *Middle East Policy* 3:15–28.

Young, Hugo. 1990. *One of Us: Life of Margaret Thatcher.* London: Pan.

Young, Iris Marion. 2002. *Inclusion and Democracy.* New York: Oxford University Press.

Yusuf, Shahid, and World Bank. 1999. *Entering the 21st Century: World Development Report, 1999/2000.* New York: World Bank.

Zakaria, Fareed. 1997. "The Rise of Illiberal Democracy." *Foreign Affairs* 76:22–41.

Zong, Jie and Jeanne Batalova. 2017. "Syrian Refugees in the United States." 12 January. https://www.migrationpolicy.org/article/syrian-refugees-united-states.

INDEX

NOTE: Page references to boxes, figures, photos, and tables are marked (box), (fig.), (photo), and (table), respectively.

Printed in the USA
CPSIA information can be obtained
at www.ICGtesting.com
JSHW051433300923
49026JS00003B/4